VOLUME

2

The

AMERICAN
HERITAGE
Pictorial History of the
PRESIDENTS
of the United States

*Front endsheet: Washington and Harrison on a cen-
tennial poster of 1889; New-York Historical Society*

*Back endsheet: President Truman addressing the 1948
Democratic convention; United Press International*

VOLUME

2

JAMES A. GARFIELD *through* LYNDON B. JOHNSON

The

AMERICAN
HERITAGE

Pictorial History of the

PRESIDENTS

of the United States

by the Editors of
AMERICAN HERITAGE
The Magazine of History

Published by
AMERICAN HERITAGE PUBLISHING CO., INC.

Book Trade Distribution by
SIMON AND SCHUSTER

CONTENTS
OF VOLUME TWO

ADDITIONAL
BIOGRAPHIES

JAMES ABRAM GARFIELD

A s a rule the American voter has preferred candidates of seeming straightforwardness and homely virtue to men of eloquence and elegance. The exceptions who did achieve high elective office, while they seasoned the nation's history with memorable oratory and their own personal color, did not often become President. Some tried futilely, among them Daniel Webster and silver-tongued William Jennings Bryan, but James A. Garfield, who did not try, succeeded.

Garfield's reputation as a debater and showman is not so great as those of Webster and Bryan. Yet he had been a preacher, an evangelist in fact, and his start in politics had been stimulated by an incident remarkably similar to the far more celebrated one—the Scopes trial of 1925—that closed Bryan's career.

In 1858 debate was probably America's most popular spectator sport. Although it was a year before publication of Darwin's *Origin of Species*, the ideas of evolution were in the air. A well-educated, thirty-seven-year-old Englishman named John Denton was touring the United States, proposing to debate all comers on the proposition: "Man, animals and vegetables came into existence by the operation of the laws of spontaneous generation and progressive development, and there is no evidence that there was ever any exercise of direct creative power on this planet." As Denton approached Ohio, it was reasonable that James A. Garfield, Disciple of Christ, should rise to the challenge.

Born in Cuyahoga County on November 19, 1831, Garfield had grown up in poverty on a farm. His father had died in 1833, and the children—James was the youngest of four—had to help their mother do a man's work. In 1848 the seventeen-year-old Garfield decided to go to sea: the best he could do was get a job on an Ohio canal, and the farthest he sailed was to Pittsburgh. Returning home later that year, he recuperated from an illness and the following

James Garfield, by C. Adele Fassett

The Union setback at the Battle of Chickamauga (above) on September 19, 1863, resulted in the discrediting of General William Rosecrans. But Major James Garfield distinguished himself as a quick-thinking leader.

spring began his formal education at a local denominational secondary school. In 1852 the Western Reserve Eclectic Institute (later Hiram College), where he had been a student for a term, gave him a job as a teacher; and by July, 1854, he had saved enough money to go to New England for a college education and was admitted to Williams College as a junior. At age twenty-four he returned to Ohio. His degree from an Eastern college made him a person of consequence, and in 1857 he became president of Hiram with its faculty of five. He was also an accomplished preacher whose sermons, delivered in a melodic, clear voice under the branches of Ohio trees, made the faithful feel—according to a friend's account—"as if they had been transplanted away from earth to some tranquil, beautiful region of heaven." His personal affairs were going as well as his professional ones: on November 11, 1858, he married Lucretia Rudolph, whom he had been courting since their childhood.

Thus equipped, the preacher-teacher and recent bridegroom prepared for John Denton. And prepare he did: unlike the debater's forty previous opponents, Garfield did not simply rehearse and solidify his own orthodox religious position; instead he read Denton's essays and book, studied biology, geology, and anthropology, and sent friends to take notes on Denton's debating technique.

Unfortunately, although Garfield's preparatory notes have been preserved, a record of the debate has not. It is known, however, that the Chagrin Falls hall, with its capacity of one thousand people, was filled for most of the five days of the debates and that John Denton, at the conclusion, acknowledged that Garfield was his strongest opponent to date. Garfield then made a well-received lecture tour of the state, speaking on "Geology and Religion." And in the spring of 1859, he turned his persuasiveness to different use and ran successfully for the Ohio senate.

Garfield was rapidly becoming Republican leader in the senate when the Civil War broke out and he became colonel of an Ohio regiment. As an officer, Garfield forged success from the same elements that had shaped his political career: he was part evangelist, part scholar. Having filled his regiment with enlistees stimulated by his florid oratory and stirring patriotism, he then had to learn what to do with his soldiers. After thoroughly studying the training manuals, he began to read accounts of famous battles and the tactics of Wellington and Napoleon. He constructed models and plotted his battles, using wooden blocks for men. In January, 1862, he led his men against a Confederate force, led by a West Pointer, at Middle Creek, Kentucky; his victory there was one of the few the Union could count at this stage of the war. Afterward he was promoted to brigadier general.

In September, 1862, the Ohio Republicans met in Garrettsville to select a candidate for the United States House of Representatives. Garfield, the only one of five hopefuls who was absent, was chosen, and for good reason: he was well educated, religious, well-known. Broad-shouldered, about six feet tall, and ruggedly handsome, he had the manners and personality to match his good looks, and he had demonstrated on the battlefield his ability to lead men and impress his colleagues. Garfield promised to return to the war even if elected to Congress, which he was.

In early 1863, Congressman-elect Garfield reported as chief of staff to General W. S. Rosecrans, commander of the Army of the Cumberland. The two officers promptly established an affectionate rapport. In August, Rosecrans, against the advice of most of his officers, but with Garfield's approval, risked his strong position at Murfreesboro, Tennessee, by attempting to drive the Confederate forces under General Bragg from the state. During the engagement at Chickamauga in September, Rosecrans erred in reorganizing his lines, weakening the flanks and forcing his army to fight defensively. Garfield helped prevent a rout by riding along the front and acting as Rosecrans' eyes, but a Union victory was by this time out of the question. After the battle, both armies remained more or less as they had been. Rosecrans, however, was discredited.

The relative responsibility of Garfield and Rosecrans for the wasteful encounter has never been fully explained. When Garfield retired from the battlefield in December, 1863, and took his seat in Congress, he defended his former commander, but in later years was less willing to exonerate General Rosecrans. The general, too, vacillated between praise for and resentment toward his former staff officer. Many years later, when Garfield was being mentioned as a possible candidate for the Presidency, Rosecrans wrote: "When he [Garfield] came to my headquarters I must confess I had a prejudice against him, as I understood that he was a preacher who had gone into politics. . . . The more I saw of him the better I liked him. . . . His views were large and he was possessed of a thoroughly comprehensive mind." But when Garfield actually was the candidate, Rosecrans campaigned against him, claiming that "seventeen years is a long time, and many a splendid young man in less time has descended from honor to infamy."

Garfield, immediately placed on the Committee on Military Affairs, and later on the committees on Appropriations and on Ways and Means, rapidly orated his way to prominence in the House. An advocate of stern Reconstruction and conservative financial policies, he was not always in agreement with Lincoln; but although he was all but certain that General George McClellan, a Democrat, would win the presidential election of 1864, Garfield did not oppose Lincoln's renomination. Garfield was in the Exchange Building on New York's Wall Street when news of Lincoln's assassination reached the city. Outside the building an angry crowd assembled, ready to seek vengeance on the neighboring headquarters of the Democratic New York *World*. After a number of speakers tried without success to quiet the crowd, Garfield stepped out on a balcony. With scarcely fifty words, which rang out across the street, the former evangelist turned an ugly mob into a prayer meeting: "Fellow-citizens: Clouds and darkness are around about Him! His pavilion is dark waters and thick clouds of the skies! Justice and judgment are the establishment of his throne! Mercy and truth shall go before his face! Fellow-citizens: God reigns, and the Government at Washington still lives!"

The grandiloquent rhetoric of Garfield and the political expertise of Maine's James G. Blaine provided ideal support for House Republican leader Thaddeus Stevens. When Stevens retired in 1868, the two representatives became their party's congressional leaders. Temperamental opposites and not without their disagreements, Garfield and Blaine nevertheless made an effective team,

521

providing leadership when President Grant provided none, working well enough together to maintain significant Republican strength even as the barren and stormy years of the Grant administration stimulated the resurrection of the Democratic party. The scandals of the General's Presidency touched both men, but as the administration approached its conclusion, both congressmen seemed to be emerging relatively unstained, and both began to feel the urge to move on to the Senate.

In 1876 Blaine sought and won Maine's senatorial seat. When the presidential election that year was thrown into the House, Garfield led the fight and framed the legislation that resulted in the election of Rutherford B. Hayes. The victory gave Garfield the opportunity to follow his old colleague, Blaine, into the Senate, for Hayes's appointment of Senator John Sherman of Ohio as Secretary of the Treasury vacated the seat that Garfield coveted. At this time, state legislatures still elected United States senators, and the Ohio legislature was dominated by a Republican majority. Garfield's record and his popularity—he had never been de-

feated in an election, even in recent years when Democrats had swept most offices in western Ohio—made him by far the strongest candidate. The new President, however, requested that he remain in the House, with its somewhat more frantic politics, where Garfield's legislative skills would do the administration the most good. The congressman agreed.

In January, 1880, the Ohio legislature convened to elect a senator for the term beginning March 4 of the following year. Garfield, as House Minority Leader, had served the Hayes administration and his party faithfully, and now he wanted that Senate seat. With the support of Secretary Sherman, a candidate for his party's presidential nomination, the congressman was elected with ease. But Garfield's persistent desire to sit in the United States Senate was destined to be frustrated forever. A peculiar accident kept him from that chamber.

Garfield had in his eighteen congressional years earned a nationwide reputation. His election to the Senate was noted with approval throughout the nation: a Milwaukee newspaper commented that he "is exceptionally clean for a man who has been engaged for twenty years in active politics." As a national figure, he was naturally mentioned as a presidential candidate, but he apparently never took the possibility very seriously; besides, he firmly believed that no avowed candidate could win a nomination. Although he refused to seek the office and frequently alluded to his lack of qualifications for it, Garfield was not impervious to the reality that deadlocked conventions frequently turned to men of his mold when seeking a compromise candidate. He was aware that he might become President—but only accidentally. And the Republican party, fast losing the power it had held for two decades, was eminently accident-prone.

The party was divided into two factions: the "Stalwarts" and the "Half-Breeds." In truth there was but a shade of difference be-

FARMER GARFIELD
Cutting a Swath to the White House.

This pro-Garfield print shows him cutting down weeds of corruption surrounding the White House.

tween them, although the former professed to be conservative and the latter, moderate. Led by Senator Roscoe Conkling of New York, the Stalwarts favored the nomination of former President Ulysses S. Grant, recently returned from a triumphant world tour. But the Half-Breeds favored the candidacy of their leader, James G. Blaine. Squeezing between the barely perceptible gap that separated the factions were several candidates, John Sherman being the strongest. Nominating Grant, Conkling announced that the election would determine whether the United States would be "republican or Cossack," and painted the General as the foe of "communism, lawlessness and disorder . . . charlatans, jayhawkers, tramps, and guerillas. . . ."

After a long and spirited demonstration that threatened to carry all the delegates in its swell, the former evangelist stepped forward to nominate Sherman. He remembered his old trade well: the convention quieted and was again transported—this time silently—by the musical voice that so eloquently called for "party harmony." Garfield could not secure Sherman's nomination, but he had stemmed the Grant tide, and after his speech the anti-Grant forces grew harmonious enough to make certain their actions would work against the General as well as for their candidates.

Grant consistently led the balloting with slightly over three hundred votes. But another Garfield coup—political, not verbal— had prevented the ex-President's nomination on the first ballot. The Stalwarts had placed a unit rule before the convention; if it had passed, each state would have had to cast all its votes for the candidate with the majority support. Only because of the successful efforts of the opposition, led by Garfield, was there any contest at all.

On the second day of balloting, Sherman telegraphed the convention, asking his supporters to vote for Garfield. When, on the thirty-fourth ballot, seventeen votes were cast for him, Garfield protested: "I rise to a point of order. No man has a right, without the consent of the person voted for, to an-

At the Republican convention of 1880 Stalwart Roscoe Conkling of New York, above, fought in vain to have ex-President Grant nominated a third time.

nounce that person's name and vote for him in this convention. Such consent I have not given." He was interrupted by the chairman; two ballots later he was the Republican presidential candidate. To appease the Stalwarts, the vice presidential nomination went to Conkling's associate, Chester A. Arthur of New York.

In the almost issueless campaign between Garfield and Winfield S. Hancock, the Democratic party was called "a party of famine . . . a good friend of early frost . . ." and the Republican candidate was accused of having an unpaid tailor's bill in Troy, New York. The Democrats did have one good charge to use against Garfield, but they failed to make the most of it.

One of the major scandals of the Grant administration had involved the government-subsidized Union Pacific Railroad, whose directors also controlled the Crédit Mobilier Company of America, which charged excessively high fees to the Union Pacific for rail-

523

road construction. Congressman Oakes Ames, one of the Crédit Mobilier directors, had a brilliant system for winning the support of his legislative colleagues in a way that did not on the surface appear corrupt. Garfield's involvement in the scheme was typical. In 1868 Ames told Garfield of a fine opportunity to buy some Crédit Mobilier stock; he need not decide then, Ames told him, for the stock would be put aside, on option. Thus Garfield neither bought the stock nor accepted it as a gift. Nevertheless, in June, 1868, he received a dividend check for $329. So during the election campaign of 1880, "three twenty-nine" became a Democratic war cry, and there was little Garfield could do about it.

During that same campaign, however, a letter was forged in Garfield's handwriting. In it, the Republican candidate stated that he favored unlimited importation of Chinese laborers. Calculated to lose him the labor vote, the letter contained two spelling errors, but since his spelling prowess was well-known, the forgery was exposed. The incident more than offset the Democrats' gains from the Crédit Mobilier affair.

Garfield won the presidential election by the comfortable electoral vote of 214 to 155, although he received fewer than ten thousand more votes than General Hancock in an election in which over nine million Americans voted.

No sooner had Garfield been inaugurated than the breach between the Stalwarts and the Half-Breeds reopened. The President's appointment of Blaine as Secretary of State infuriated the Stalwarts; and when William H. Robertson, a long-time antagonist of Conkling, was appointed collector for the Port of New York, thus challenging Conkling's control of patronage, the senator tried to block the appointment. Two days before Congress finally confirmed Robertson's position, Conkling and Thomas Platt, New York's junior senator, resigned. The state legislature failed to re-elect them when they asked Albany for vindication.

When Thomas L. James of New York was appointed Postmaster General, *The New York Times* was crusading for an investigation of what it called the Star Route Frauds. The Post Office Department had for years had huge deficits, and Congress, in passing the necessary appropriations, had assumed that the loss was due to the high cost of delivering mail in the rural West. The *Times* investigation revealed that thousands of dollars were being spent for deliveries to some places that received mail no more than three times a year. With President Garfield's approval and the help of Attorney General Wayne MacVeagh, James began a thorough and public investigation. It was found that under previous Republican administrations, contracts had been awarded to certain carriers closely associated with department administrators and Republican leaders. Although a number of high-ranking Republicans were implicated, Garfield, to his credit, instructed the Postmaster General to continue to release his findings. The scandal, which outlived Garfield, was a catalyst in the establishment of civil service reform.

On July 2, 1881, President Garfield left the White House for a trip to New England, where he intended to introduce his two sons to his alma mater, Williams College. In the Washington train station, a lawyer and disappointed office seeker named Charles J. Guiteau approached the President from behind, and while shouting, "I am a Stalwart and now Arthur is President!" fired two shots from a pistol. One bullet grazed Garfield's arm, but the other lodged in his back. He lay in the White House for two months while doctors weakened his condition by their futile and unsanitary attempts to locate and remove the bullet. Then he asked to be taken to the seaside, hoping that the ocean air would cure him.

The President remained conscious and reasonably alert during his illness. Once— but only once—he asked about Guiteau. "He must be insane," he judged. "Why should he want to kill me?" At Elberon, New Jersey, on September 19, 1881, James A. Garfield died.

—DAVID JACOBS

James A. Garfield.

A PICTURE PORTFOLIO

LAWNFIELD, MENTOR, OHIO

This china pitcher commemorates the death of President James A. Garfield, who was shot by an assassin only four months after his inauguration in 1881.

MAN OF DESTINY

One does not seek office; the office must seek the man. To appear to conform with this mythical tradition was long considered requisite to success in American politics, and for many years most office seekers dutifully played the game of "hide-and-be-found." For James Abram Garfield, however, it was more than a game: because he had gained eminence through nonpolitical achievements, it was absolutely essential that he appear to be bound by destiny for high office. When he decided at the age of twenty-eight to enter politics, he was already well-known throughout Ohio as a former schoolteacher and college president and, especially, as the evangelist with the enchanting voice who had toured the state defending God and good against the heretical assault of an evolutionist. His mother cried when he confided his political ambitions; some friends thought it sacrilegious to turn his prestige as a preacher into a political tool. Clearly, the public could not be allowed to share this opinion. He could not enter politics; he would have to be transported in. So, as Garfield reclined beneath his halo, his good friend Harmon Austin did the work. At first skeptical of Garfield's decision, Austin nevertheless became his friend's lifetime political manager. He helped him win a seat in the state legislature in 1859 and three years later, with Garfield off fighting the Civil War, engineered Garfield's nomination to the House of Representatives. The illusion was perfectly drawn: the candidate was not present when nominated, hardly campaigned, and said that he would continue to serve in the Army if elected. But he won. And thus did office "seek" James A. Garfield.

James Garfield and Lucretia Rudolph (above) were married in 1858. Twenty-two years later, when Garfield was a presidential candidate, the biographical comic strip opposite was published. Number 1 alludes to his role in the Crédit Mobilier scandal of 1873 and number 10 to another scandal of the Grant administration. But 4, 6, 7, and 9 are completely fictional: by the age of fourteen he had memorized several books; his father had died when James was not yet two years old; people were drawn to, not driven from, his preaching; and he did not leave the Army to campaign for Congress. (In fact he stayed in for almost a year after his election.)

1. He was a bright child; his face always wore a Mobile-leer.

2. He never stoned cats—always hung his.

3. Even when a boy he showed a great love of Liberty.

4. When sixteen he could not read or write, which made it very inconvenient when he went—skating.

5. His piety was such that he would say his prayers wherever he happened to be.

6. He was of great assistance to his father on the farm.

7. As a preacher he fairly lifted his hearers from their pews, with his powerful sermons.

8. The General was a man of peace, even in war times.

9. He left the army and ran for Congress.

10. But it was not until he went to Washington as a Representative that he found his proper walk in life.

11. If elected, he may possibly make a few religious changes in the architecture of the White House.

DE GOLYER PAVEMENT

DANGER

PUCK'S LIFE OF GARFIELD.

WINFIELD SCOTT HANCOCK

General Winfield Scott Hancock, the Democrats' colorless presidential candidate in 1880, was described as "a good man, weighing 250 lbs. . . . with a record as stainless as his sword." Named for Winfield Scott, the famous general of the War of 1812, Hancock entered West Point at sixteen. Graduating in 1844, he served in the Mexican War, the Seminole War, and the Kansas Border War. As a major general in the Civil War, he commanded divisions in the battles of Fredericksburg and Chancellorsville and won particular distinction at Gettysburg, selecting the field of battle and repulsing repeated attacks by Lee. In 1868 his war record first brought him consideration for the Democratic nomination. When the party convened in Cincinnati twelve years later, Hancock—the man least likely to offend any of the various factions—was nominated for President. The campaign of 1880 was without major political issues, and both parties indulged in personal invective. Hancock was denounced as one who did "nothing but eat, drink, and enjoy himself sensually," but even his enemies could find little to exploit in his spotless past. Narrowly defeated by James Garfield, whose plurality was fewer than ten thousand votes, General Hancock resumed his military duties as commander of the Division of the Atlantic and of the Department of the East. Hancock died in 1886 on Governor's Island, New York.

A DEADLOCK BROKEN

The Republican convention of 1880 was a drawn-out, stormy affair in which several candidates tried independently to stop the nomination of ex-President Ulysses Grant. Although strong enough to do so, they were unable to agree on another nominee, and the convention was deadlocked for thirty-four ballots. Then Senator-elect James Garfield's name was presented, and on the thirty-sixth ballot he won the nomination. His first job was to heal the rift between the factions—a formidable task. The Half-Breeds (moderates) had managed to secure the adoption of a platform plank pledging civil service reform. Since political power at that time meant control of patronage, the machine-dominated Stalwarts (conservatives) opposed the plank. To pacify both sides Garfield pledged reform, but promised to make appointments in consultation with those "whose knowledge of the communities in which the duties are to be performed best qualifies them to aid in making the wisest choice." Then he embarked on a speaking tour, which turned out to be as successful as his earlier appearances as an evangelist. After an issueless campaign, he defeated Democrat General W. S. Hancock by an electoral vote of 214 to 155. But the election revealed a growing dissatisfaction with both major parties: Peter Cooper, the Greenback party candidate, had received only 80,000 votes in 1876, but this time well over three hundred thousand farmers and laborers cast their votes for the Greenback-Labor nominee, James B. Weaver.

A hand and a cock formed the rather trite campaign symbol of General Winfield
Hancock, Garfield's opponent in the election of 1880. The card above was printed
by a Republican newspaper, which probably distributed campaign souvenirs to
subscribers in both parties. In the Puck cartoon below, titled "Rutherford's
Legacy," outgoing President Hayes leaves his neglected child with Garfield.

A NEEDLESS DEATH

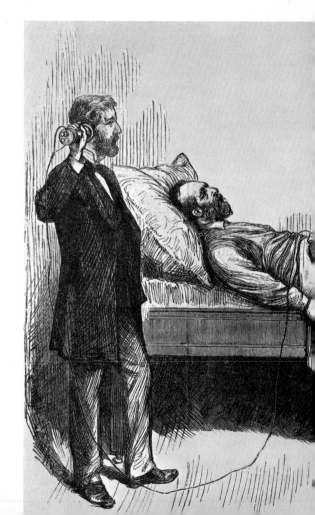

As he was completing his fourth month in the Presidency, Garfield was being surreptitiously stalked by a pistol-bearing maniac named Charles J. Guiteau, a disappointed office seeker. The would-be assassin had his chance on an evening late in June when he found Garfield walking with James G. Blaine, but he lost his nerve. He recovered it, though, on July 2 in the Washington train station. Crying, "I am a Stalwart and now Arthur is President!" Guiteau fired twice, and one of the bullets penetrated the President's body. For two and a half months physicians tried to locate it. Actually—although the doctors could not have known it then—Garfield should have been up and around the whole time, regaining his strength. The bullet had lodged in his back muscles, just a few inches from the entry point, and his body had manufactured a protective cyst around it, rendering it harmless. But Garfield weakened and died, and Charles Guiteau was hanged for murder.

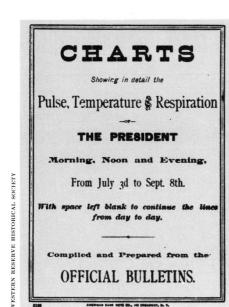

CHARTS

Showing in detail the

Pulse, Temperature & Respiration

—OF—

THE PRESIDENT

Morning, Noon and Evening,

From July 3d to Sept. 8th.

*With space left blank to continue the lines
from day to day.*

Compiled and Prepared from the

OFFICIAL BULLETINS.

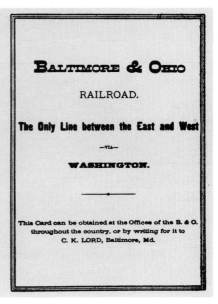

BALTIMORE & OHIO

RAILROAD.

The Only Line between the East and West

—VIA—

WASHINGTON.

This Card can be obtained at the Offices of the B. & O.
throughout the country, or by writing for it to
C. K. LORD, Baltimore, Md.

"People must be tired of hearing of my symptoms," President Garfield said during the seventy-nine days he lay ill, alternately gaining and failing. Actually the public read every bulletin, eagerly seized every scrap of information; the Baltimore and Ohio Railroad even issued, free of charge, the progress chart above. On September 18, 1881, the exhausted President said with finality, "My work is done." He died the next night.

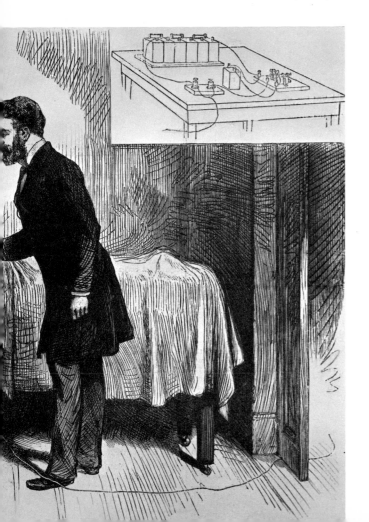

The President's doctors were baffled: Had the assassin's bullet lodged in Garfield's lung or liver or abdomen? They poked and probed and even asked Alexander Graham Bell to locate it with his electrical listening device (left) but without success. So they continued to probe, their unsterile instruments spreading infection throughout their patient's body, weakening him and causing his death. Ironically, the bullet need never have been removed.

531

FACTS IN SUMMARY: JAMES A. GARFIELD

CHRONOLOGY

UNITED STATES		GARFIELD		UNITED STATES		GARFIELD
	1831	*Born November 19*	John Brown's raid at Harpers Ferry	1859	*Elected to Ohio senate*
Van Buren elected President	1836		Lincoln elected President	1860	
Panic of 1837	1837		South Carolina secedes		
Harrison elected President	1840		Fort Sumter fired upon	1861	*Commissioned lieutenant colonel in Ohio Volunteers*
Tyler becomes President	1841		First Battle of Bull Run		*Promoted to colonel*
Polk elected President	1844		Battle of Shiloh	1862	*Defeats Confederates at Middle Creek, Kentucky*
Annexation of Texas	1845		Monitor v. Merrimac		*Promoted to brigadier general*
War with Mexico	1846		Battle of Fredericksburg		*Commands brigade at Shiloh*
Taylor inaugurated as President	1849	*Attends Geauga Academy*			*Elected to U.S. House of Representatives*
Fillmore becomes President	1850	*Joins Disciples of Christ*	Emancipation Proclamation	1863	*Fights at Chickamauga*
Compromise of 1850					*Begins term in Congress*
Clayton-Bulwer Treaty			Battle of Chancellors-ville		
	1851	*Enters Western Reserve Eclectic Institute*	Vicksburg Campaign		
Pierce elected President	1852		Battle of Gettysburg		
Kansas-Nebraska Act	1854	*Enters Williams College*	Lincoln re-elected President	1864	
Republican party formed			Sherman's march to the sea		
Civil war in Kansas	1856	*Graduates from Williams*	Lee surrenders at Appomattox	1865	
Buchanan inaugurated as President	1857	*Appointed president of Hiram College*	Lincoln assassinated		
Dred Scott decision			Johnson becomes President		
Lincoln-Douglas debates	1858	*Marries Lucretia Rudolph*			

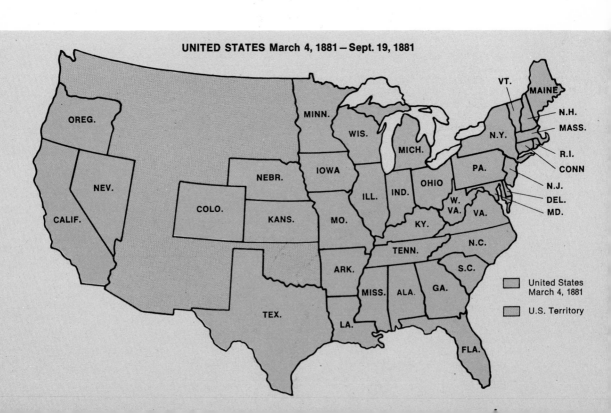

UNITED STATES March 4, 1881 — Sept. 19, 1881

United States March 4, 1881

U.S. Territory

Civil Rights Act	1866	*Introduces bill to create a department of education*
Johnson impeached	1868	
Fourteenth Amendment ratified		
Grant elected President		
	1871	*Appointed chairman of House Committee on Appropriations*
Crédit Mobilier scandal	1872	
	1876	*Becomes Minority Leader in House*
Hayes elected President	1877	
Bland-Allison Act	1878	
	1880	*Elected to U.S. Senate*
		Elected President
Arthur becomes President	1881	*Approves investigation of Star Route Frauds*
		Shot by Charles Guiteau
		Dies of gunshot wound on September 19

LAWNFIELD, MENTOR, OHIO

This stained-glass memorial to Garfield is kept in a standing frame in the study of his home in Ohio.

BIOGRAPHICAL FACTS

BIRTH: Orange Township, Ohio, Nov. 19, 1831

ANCESTRY: English and French

FATHER: Abram Garfield; b. Worcester, N.Y., 1799; d. Orange Township, Ohio, 1833

FATHER'S OCCUPATION: Farmer

MOTHER: Eliza Ballou Garfield; b. Richmond, N.H., 1801; d. Mentor, Ohio, 1888

BROTHERS: Thomas (1822–?); James Ballou (1826–1829)

SISTERS: Mehitabel (1821–?); Mary (1824–1884)

WIFE: Lucretia Rudolph; b. Hiram, Ohio, April 19, 1832; d. Pasadena, Calif., March 14, 1918

MARRIAGE: Hiram, Ohio, Nov. 11, 1858

CHILDREN: Eliza Arabella (1860–1863); Harry Augustus (1863–1942); James Rudolph (1865–1950); Mary (1867–1947); Irvin McDowell (1870–1951); Abram (1872–1958); Edward (1874–1876)

EDUCATION: Attended Geauga Academy and Western Reserve Eclectic Institute; graduated (1856) from Williams College

HOME: Lawnfield, Mentor, Ohio

RELIGIOUS AFFILIATION: Disciples of Christ

OCCUPATIONS BEFORE PRESIDENCY: Schoolteacher; soldier; president of Hiram College

MILITARY SERVICE: Commissioned lt. col. of 42nd Ohio Volunteers in Aug., 1861; rose to brig. gen. of Volunteers (1862) and maj. gen. of Volunteers (1863)

PRE-PRESIDENTIAL OFFICES: Member of Ohio Senate; Member of U.S. House of Representatives; Chairman of House Committee on Appropriations; Minority Leader in U.S. House of Representatives

POLITICAL PARTY: Republican

AGE AT INAUGURATION: 49

DEATH: Elberon, N.J., Sept. 19, 1881

PLACE OF BURIAL: Lake View Cemetery, Cleveland, Ohio

ELECTION OF 1880

CANDIDATES	ELECTORAL VOTE	POPULAR VOTE
James A. Garfield Republican	214	4,453,295
Winfield S. Hancock Democratic	155	4,444,082
James B. Weaver Greenback–Labor	—	308,578
Neal Dow Prohibition	—	10,305

THE GARFIELD ADMINISTRATION

INAUGURATION: March 4, 1881; the Capitol, Washington, D.C.

VICE PRESIDENT: Chester A. Arthur

SECRETARY OF STATE: James G. Blaine

SECRETARY OF THE TREASURY: William Windom

SECRETARY OF WAR: Robert T. Lincoln

ATTORNEY GENERAL: Wayne MacVeagh

POSTMASTER GENERAL: Thomas L. James

SECRETARY OF THE NAVY: William H. Hunt

SECRETARY OF THE INTERIOR: Samuel J. Kirkwood

SUPREME COURT APPOINTMENT: Stanley Matthews (1881)

47th CONGRESS (March 4, 1881–March 4, 1883): Senate: 37 Republicans; 37 Democrats; 1 Other House: 147 Republicans; 135 Democrats; 11 Others

END OF PRESIDENTIAL TERM: September 19, 1881

CHESTER ALAN ARTHUR

T he Gentleman Boss," Chester Alan Arthur, followed an unlikely road to the White House. But he certainly looked like a President—tall, stout, handsome, always nattily attired, "usually wearing," a contemporary Washingtonian observed, "a Prince Albert coat, buttoned closely in front, with a flower in the upper button-hole and the corner of a colored silk handkerchief visible from a side pocket."

Arthur's mother, Malvina Stone, was a frontier Vermonter; his father, William, born in Ireland, was a literate but feisty and foot-loose teacher who became a Baptist preacher, presiding over a succession of parishes in northern Vermont and upstate New York. Chester was born in 1830, but his birthplace is not definitely known. Some said that it was Fairfield, Vermont; others claimed that he came into the world in a log cabin at nearby Waterville; and during his Presidency some opponents stated, without proof, that he had actually been born in Canada and was therefore constitutionally ineligible to be President of the United States.

During the first nine years of his life, Arthur moved with his family five times, settling at last in Union Village, New York, where he attended the local school. Five years later, the Arthurs moved to Schenectady, and after an additional year of preparatory studies, Chester entered Union College there. He helped to pay his way through by teaching school and graduated, a member of Phi Beta Kappa, in 1848. He continued as a schoolmaster while studying law until 1853, when he moved to New York City for a year's polishing in the law office of a family friend. He was then admitted to the state bar. Though handsome, genteel, and well-read, Arthur was just another struggling young lawyer in the big city. In 1855 he argued one case of some importance, in which he represented a Negro woman who, because of her color, had been

President Arthur, as portrayed by Daniel Huntington

ejected from a streetcar in Brooklyn. He won $500 for his client and thereby earned for all Negroes better treatment on New York's public transportation. But, except for this case, Arthur's record was in no way distinguished.

Four years later he married a Virginia girl, Ellen Lewis Herndon, the daughter of a Navy hero. (She bore him three children—two of whom survived to adulthood—before she died of pneumonia in 1880.) Arthur joined the state militia, and he also entered politics. Because he helped return Edwin D. Morgan to a second term as governor of New York in 1860, Morgan made him a member of what was intended to be a purely ceremonial military staff. But when the Civil War began, Engineer in Chief Arthur was given additional duties as assistant quartermaster general and put in charge of feeding, housing, and equipping the thousands of war-bound soldiers pouring into New York City from all over the Northeast. The honesty and ingenuity he displayed in this job led to promotion to quartermaster general of the state; in December, 1863, a year after he retired (along with the outgoing Governor Morgan), his successor, a Democrat, noted admiringly that Arthur had saved the government much money and time by creating "a well-organized system of labor and accountability . . . at a period when everything was in confusion. . . ."

For Arthur the prestige of the position and the many new acquaintances it provided were pivotal; before the war was over he had become a prominent lawyer and was growing wealthy through his handling of war-claims cases. He knew that if he desired, he could rise in politics as well. But in the two and a half decades that followed the Civil War the major political parties were mercenary armies whose major functions were winning elections, getting jobs, and doing favors (for a consideration). One of the qualities that had set Chester Arthur apart was his complete honesty. He reconciled his standards with those that governed the political machine by approaching politics in the gentlemanly guise of a professional dilettante.

If he was going to play it as a game, he was at least in the big leagues: the American political machine had been invented, elaborated, and codified in New York State, which had produced the first boss—Alexander Hamilton—and some remarkably talented successors, such as Martin Van Buren and Thurlow Weed. A machine had to be thoroughly organized, from the local district on up, and had to be led by a strong man who derived his power from control over federal job appointments. At the time, there was no civil service as such; federal appointees were usually picked by and from the "in" party for services rendered at election time; often that was their only qualification for employment. In return, these party workers were expected to pay a percentage of their salaries into the party treasury and perform regular party duties. This method of hiring and firing was not productive of disinterested public service: federal jobholders put themselves and the party ahead of all other responsibilities. Bribery, graft, and thievery were common.

Into this world of high politics Chester Arthur now moved. He did so at a critical moment, for leadership of the state Republican party was in doubt. The old "conservative" leaders—Weed, William Seward, and former Governor Morgan—had remained loyal to Andrew Johnson, and the Radical landslide of 1866 had reduced their influence. But the Radicals were not yet well organized. In this intramural warfare, the newly elected United States senator, Roscoe Conkling, a flamboyant personality and an unforgettable orator, sought strength by wooing the conservative Republicans. This brought to his support Chester Arthur, who was by 1868 chairman of the state Republican executive committee and of the Central Grant Club of New York. The election of 1868 raised Grant to the Presidency, and the Conklingites became his favorites in New York: the New York machine became a Grant machine, nurtured by Grant patronage and controlled by Senator Conkling. For a while Arthur had only the kind of role he preferred—quiet organizer of party affairs.

But in 1871 Grant needed a man with a good reputation to take over the New York Custom House; his earlier appointee, Thomas Murphy, had been exposed as corrupt. So at the end of November, 1871, Chester Arthur reluctantly became collector of customs for the Port of New York.

The custom house was the cornerstone of the machine. It employed over one thousand people, and the turnover when the White House changed hands was enormous: one party's hacks would trail out as another's trailed in. Arthur's supervision of this army and its nominal responsibilities for collecting customs duties was probably better than that of most of his predecessors. Certainly he remained above the sordidness himself. However, at the time he became collector, there was a growing movement for reform of the bureaucracy; the machines and the patronage concept were under fire.

As part of a national reaction to the Grant scandals, a Democratic administration was voted into power in New York State in 1874. Once the Conkling organization failed to hold the state for the Republican party, it was in danger. Reverse followed reverse, and by 1876 the tide was running heavily against the machine. The reformers now felt strong enough to strike at its roots—the custom house. Soon after Hayes came into office in 1877, an investigation was begun. At the time it was not aimed at Arthur; there was general agreement that he had done a good job, although he had clearly allowed the custom house payroll to grow too long. But as the investigation progressed, the politicians who saw the situation as an opportunity to ruin Conkling built a case for removing Arthur and one of his deputies, Alonzo Cornell. The custom house was shown (to no one's surprise) to be tarnished by fraud and inefficiency. Hayes issued an order forbidding government employees to engage actively in partisan politics, and when Arthur and Cornell did not comply with the demand, the administration, in September of 1877, revealed plans for changes of leadership at the Port of New York. For a while the Senate sustained Conkling in his opposition, but by the

Hayes fired Arthur and Cornell from the New York Custom House partly to weaken Senator Conkling's machine. When Conkling won a third term in 1879, Puck saw it as a renewal of the reformers' burdens.

following July, Arthur and Cornell were forced to step down.

The machine, however, was not wrecked yet. Helped by a national issue—Southern exclusion of Negroes from voting—it pulled the state Republicans together to nominate and elect Cornell as governor in 1879. Roscoe Conkling was re-elected to the Senate. And as 1880 approached, the machine began to work for the nomination of Ulysses S. Grant for a third term.

But the Conklingites and the rest of the old-line "Stalwart" allies fell about ninety votes short of success at the convention. Their opponents managed on the thirty-sixth ballot to unite on reformer James A. Garfield of Ohio. The natural inclination of the delegates was to pull the party together for the campaign by choosing a Stalwart from New York as the vice presidential candidate. Levi P. Morton was asked to accept second place, but refused on the advice of Conkling, furious that Grant had not been chosen, and Massachusetts boss George Boutwell. Then the New York delegation took matters into its own hands, informing the Ohio delegation that Chester Arthur would be the state's choice. Ohio, in turn, approached Arthur, who hastened to discuss the matter with Conkling. During a stormy interview, Conkling urged Arthur to drop the offer "as you would a red-hot shoe from the forge." But now Arthur realized that he wanted the nomination. "This trickster of Mentor [Garfield]" might well be "defeated before the country," as Conkling was angrily predicting. Nevertheless, Arthur told him, "The office of Vice President is a greater honor than I ever dreamed of attaining. [Indeed, it would be the first time Arthur stood for election to any public office.] A barren nomination would be a great honor. In a calmer moment you will look at this differently." Conkling thought not and warned him to "contemptuously decline it."

"Senator Conkling," said Arthur evenly, "I shall accept . . . and I shall carry with me the majority of the delegation." Conkling stormed out of the room. Arthur was nominated on the first ballot.

Politically defensible, the nomination nonetheless sent a shudder through liberal Republican ranks. The Republican platform included a reform plank. Arthur had been fired recently by a Republican President under circumstances that associated him with corruption, and he was a henchman of Conk-

The elegant Arthur was appalled at the style of the furnishings that had been gathered in the White House over the years. He refused to move in until twenty-four wagonloads of decorations and furniture, some of it priceless, had been auctioned off and the Mansion completely redone in late-Victorian style (above).

ling's, the man who sneered at a reformed bureaucracy as the "snivel service." What else could be said about him? He was a party committeeman, a back-room operator. He was pleasant and well-mannered enough, and he was known as a first-class fisherman; he could quote from Burns in an amazingly perfect Scottish accent, and he knew how to live graciously. But he had no national reputation save what stemmed from his contretemps with the reformers. To some it seemed that Conkling must have engineered the nomination to wreck the ticket. Readers of the *Nation* who wanted to vote for Garfield wrote to ask if they could do so without also voting for Arthur. Editor E. L. Godkin replied that they could not, but that it did not really matter. "There is no place in which his powers of mischief will be so small as in the Vice Presidency. . ." Godkin wrote. "It is true General Garfield . . . may die during his term of office, but this is too unlikely a contingency to be worth making extraordinary provision for."

In the early months of the campaign Arthur surprised the voters by endorsing in his Letter of Acceptance civil service reform. Even some of his critics felt his letter was better than Garfield's. On the other hand, Garfield would have to assure the Conkling machine of fair treatment in return for dedicated campaigning: New York was a key state. Republican strategists figured on a solidly Democratic South, and if New York and Indiana fell into the Democratic column too, Garfield would be beaten. It was therefore crucial that the New York organization put its whole heart and soul into the canvass. Arthur and Conkling played a waiting game and went off fishing. Finally, in August, Garfield was compelled to come east to deal with the Stalwarts; when he left they felt they had won all the concessions they wanted: the right to name the Secretary of the Treasury in Garfield's Cabinet and control over New York patronage. Garfield, however, believed he had involved himself in "no trades, no shackles"—promising only to discuss the New York appointments with Senator Conkling and the Stalwarts.

The wide divergency in their understanding began to be evident soon after Garfield was elected, with New York going Republican by 21,000 votes. The Stalwarts wanted Levi Morton for the Treasury post; Garfield denied he had ever made a promise about it. He offered to make Morton Secretary of the Navy, but Conkling would not budge. In the end the Cabinet did contain a man from New York, but it was Thomas L. James as Postmaster General.

Even before the inauguration Arthur dissipated the improvement in his public image that he had earned by his Letter of Acceptance: he was seen in Albany vigorously lobbying for the election of a candidate for the United States Senate, an activity that was considered unbecoming to a Vice President-elect. Then, at a testimonial dinner for Stephen Dorsey—who had managed the Republican victory in Indiana—Arthur was, to say the least, tactless and indiscreet. While praising Dorsey he spoke slyly of "the secrets of the campaign." Indiana, he noted, was normally Democratic, but "had been put down on the books" as a state the Republicans might carry "by close and perfect organization and a great deal of—." Here he paused, while knowing laughter burst from his audience along with cries of "Soap! Soap!"—the code word the Republicans had used in telegrams during the campaign when they meant "money." The implication was that the Indiana election had been bought. That kind of inside joke was fine for the drawing room, where Chester Arthur was at his best, but in these circumstances, with reporters listening to his speech, it did him a great deal of harm.

As Vice President, Arthur still demonstrated a lack of respect for his new position. Garfield, trying to keep the Stalwarts, the independents, and the "Half-Breeds" of James G. Blaine all happy, allowed himself to be guided on certain New York appointments by Conkling. But under pressure from Blaine and others to avoid the appearance of domination by "Lord Roscoe," Garfield suddenly named Conkling's leading reform antagonist, William H. Robertson, collec-

The bearded Charles Guiteau (on the witness stand in court, at right) joined with local and federal authorities to turn his trial for the murder of President Garfield into a farce. The police guard of the prisoner was lax; at far right, one of several unsuccessful attempts on his life is depicted. Reported Harper's Weekly: "*A reckless man, mounted on a fleet horse, was allowed to follow the prison van for more than half a mile, approach it, locate his victim, and then fire at him. . . . That the national government, in its own capital . . . should be unable to reserve to its own agencies the punishment of the murderer of the Chief Executive is something intolerable." Guiteau, convicted of murder, was executed on June 30, 1882.*

tor for the Port of New York. The fat was in the fire. At stake was not just the collectorship, but control of the state party, with Robertson building political strength at Conkling's expense. Conkling fought the nomination in the Senate, where the other members were inclined to support him; the old policy of senatorial courtesy, or control over local jobs, was on the line. Conkling, junior Senator Thomas C. Platt, Postmaster General James, and Vice President Arthur sent a letter of protest to Garfield. Arthur tried in private conversations to change the President's mind and in public made no secret of his opposition. Garfield was unmoved. He forced the Senate (which would have preferred to wait awhile in hopes that the crisis would go away) to choose between his wishes and those of Conkling. Conkling, who knew he would be defeated, resigned from the Senate, followed by Platt; they planned to return to Albany, expecting vindication through re-election. Robertson's appointment was quickly confirmed by the Upper House.

Vice President Arthur then hurried to the New York capital to labor in the cause of Conkling and Platt. If his politicking before the inauguration had raised some eyebrows, at this point it occasioned disgust. In Albany the ex-senators and the Vice President found that there would be no vindication; the machine had fallen apart under the stresses of individual ambitions and Conkling's loss of control in Washington. First to fall was Thomas Platt, who was careless enough to be caught *flagrante delicto* with a woman not his wife by a gang of political enemies. As the story was snickered through Albany, Platt decided he had best withdraw from the race. On July 1, 1881, Arthur thus lost one of his candidates, under the most humiliating of circumstances. The next day's events would make defeat of Roscoe Conkling inevitable.

On July 2, Garfield was shot by Charles Guiteau, a Stalwart, who declared he had shot Garfield to make Arthur President and end the quarrels over spoils. Under the darkest of clouds, Arthur left Conkling in New York and hurried to Washington; it was thought at first that the President would die within hours or days. When Garfield was said to be out of danger, Arthur returned to his New York City home for many weeks of seclusion. Government ground to a virtual halt, crippled by the incapacity of its Executive. Talk began to circulate that Arthur might have to step in as substitute, but the constitutional problem caused by Tyler's precedent—could a Vice President merely substitute for an ill President and then hand back the powers and duties when the President recovered, or was he required to *become* President?—was too great a stumbling block. Queried on the matter, Arthur flatly refused to take over. The weeks dragged on. Arthur's anxiety depleted his strength and his sense

of self-possession, so much so that confidants were seriously worried about his health. But the calmness and dignity with which he comported himself in public impressed everyone. When Garfield finally died, an acquaintance said, "Chet Arthur, President of the United States! Good God!" But by that time, the country as a whole was ready to accept Arthur as President, at least on a trial basis.

After taking the oath of office in New York on September 19, 1881, he tried to cope with a frightening situation he had helped create: because of a Democratic majority in the Senate (due to the resignations of Conkling and Platt), he had refused to step down as presiding officer to allow the election of a Senate president pro tempore before adjournment. So there was no one in the line of succession behind him. Supposing he were assassinated or died in a train wreck on his way to the Capital? He sent a letter, addressed to "The President," calling the Congress into emergency session; someone would open it if the tragedy occurred. Then he left for Washington.

As he assumed the Presidency, Arthur was confronted by a number of serious problems. First, he had to assure the country that he would not make Conkling, as some feared, "the power behind the throne." At the same time he had to create his own administration with men he got along with. He had a narrow line to walk. He also had to prosecute the

trial of Guiteau. The Star Route mail frauds, uncovered while Garfield was in office, had to be dealt with. The cries for civil service reform, all the louder now because of Garfield's death, had to be listened to. There was a large and troublesome surplus in the Treasury, which was connected with a demand for reform of tariff schedules.

All told, Arthur did an acceptable job. Gradually the administration developed a definite Stalwart tinge, but at the same time Arthur tried to satisfy the other factions within the party in order to unify it. Conkling was kept at arm's length and so, increasingly, was the old Stalwart figurehead, U. S. Grant. Guiteau was brought to trial—albeit a sensational, ludicrous trial—found guilty, and hanged. And although it caused a great deal of embarrassment to the party in general and to the Stalwarts in particular, Arthur pressed the case against those responsible for the Post Office frauds. Among them were Stephen Dorsey and Thomas J. Brady, another party leader whom Grant had appointed second assistant postmaster general. Arthur was apparently sincere in his desire for convictions in the case, for he assigned two Democrats to handle much of the work and encouraged the Attorney General to prosecute the case "with the utmost vigor of the law." But there were many legal setbacks for the government, and eventually the two accused officials were adjudged legally innocent.

541

In civil service reform the President was more successful, even though it seemed that the Republican machine politicians would be able to block him. Arthur demanded reform in his first annual message; when Congress ignored his request, the voters seconded him by overturning the Republican control of the House in the mid-term elections. In his second annual message Arthur again called on the Congress to act, and the Pendleton bill was passed and was signed into law in January, 1883. The Civil Service Commission, created by the law, gradually brought one-tenth of government jobs under its supervision. Examinations were made prerequisites for employment, and penalties were set up for officials who demanded salary kickbacks. The commission praised the President for his support.

One notable temptation to bad government was provided by the Treasury surplus, which amounted to some eighty to one hundred million dollars a year. Resulting from high tariff revenues and taxes, the surplus money was, in effect, being taken out of circulation, and government spending was the only way of getting it back into the economy. Thus the politicians could justify legislation that had as its main purpose the gratification of their constituents: bills for pensions, bills for local public works. The Forty-seventh Congress requested, for instance, Arthur's signature on an appropriation of more than $18,700,000 to be spent on rivers and harbors; Arthur wanted to cut the surplus, but not by rash spending, and he vetoed the bill. (It was quickly passed over his veto.) He thought there were several better ways of dealing with the extra money: taxes and tariffs could be lowered and money could be spent on defense and reduction of the national debt. While on the one hand espousing a stringent economy in government, Arthur tried to put these alternatives into effective operation.

A tax relief act sponsored by Arthur achieved little. His tariff commission proposed downward revision of import duties, but Congress, goaded on by lobbies for various interests, tore the bill to pieces. A program of reciprocal trade treaties with other nations, which would have eliminated certain tariffs, did not win sufficient support. Arthur also tried to improve the military establishment, particularly the outdated Navy, but a combination of hurried planning by the administration and foot-dragging by the Democratic House limited the results. It was in reducing the public debt—by more than $400,000,000—that Arthur most effectively coped with the surplus, although he eliminated neither it nor its causes.

Perhaps, in the light of how Arthur achieved the Presidency, the most important characteristic of his administration was its tone. ". . . He acted from the start with remarkable tact and grace," commented Matthew Josephson, historian of the Age of Spoils. "In some ways he impressed . . . important businessmen especially as the most effective President since Lincoln"— even though he fell short of attaining many of his goals. And he impressed liberals as well as conservatives. "I can hardly imagine how he could have done better," said Henry Ward Beecher.

But his administration was far from a political success. He was unable to pacify the feuding factions in the party. And he refused to reconstruct the shattered Conkling machine in New York through the judicious use of patronage; he would not even remove Robertson from the New York collectorship. He made Conkling so angry that in the spring of 1883 his former mentor declared, "I have but one annoyance with the Administration of President Arthur, and that is, that, in contrast with it, the Administration of Hayes becomes respectable, if not heroic."

Without a strong party faction behind him, Arthur was unable to win a nomination for a presidential term in his own right in 1884, and the following year he even failed to receive a nomination from New York Republicans for a seat in the United States Senate. Exhausted by the strain of office, Chester Arthur died only twenty months after leaving the White House.

—MICHAEL HARWOOD

A PICTURE PORTFOLIO

Chester Arthur (depicted in a Puck cartoon, above) had to deal with serious schisms in the Republican party during his forty-one and a half months as the President of the United States.

For much of 1881 the nation suffered from the flaws of its system for presidential succession. Garfield (shown with Arthur on the flag at right) lay desperately ill for most of the summer, and because of the Constitution's uncertain phraseology on the matter, the Vice President was unable to take over the reins of government until the Chief Executive died. And for the first three weeks of Arthur's Presidency (he was sworn in by Justice John Brady in New York, below), there was no one behind him in the line of succession, since he and the Republicans in the Upper House had successfully prevented the Democrat-controlled Senate from electing a president pro tempore in its previous session.

The cartoon at right, drawn by Joseph Keppler after Arthur became President, refers to the ending of King Henry IV, Part Two, in which Falstaff assumes that the ascension of Prince Hal to the throne will not change their relationship. His royal friend responds, "I know thee not, old man . . . I have turned away from my former self; So will I those that kept me company." In most respects Keppler's wish came true. Arthur kept Roscoe Conkling out of White House councils, and when he offered a seat on the Supreme Court to the former senator from New York, Conkling, hurt, rejected it.

J. Keppler

A FEARFUL NATION

We learned of the shooting [of Garfield]," wrote a friend to former Secretary of the Treasury John Sherman, ". . . by a special telegram received on the train; and the first remark I heard was from a one-legged soldier, a major, who said: 'I fear that is done to make Arthur President and Conkling Premier Primate of the whole country. . . .' Then we had not even seen the telegram, and of course not the *printed* dispatches giving the words of the assassin at the time ['I am a Stalwart and now Arthur is President!']. . . . How fatal a mistake was made at Chicago in the nomination for the second place. The prayer for poor Garfield is *universal*. There is not popular confidence in the possible succession. . . ." The nation had good reason for its apprehension: Arthur had long been a tool of boss Roscoe Conkling and was apparently nothing but a spoilsman. But the Stalwarts, who must have secretly rejoiced when President Garfield died at last, and the rest of their countrymen were in for a surprise. Chester Alan Arthur filled his new role with dignity, honesty, and ability.

A GRAND SHAKESPERIAN REVIVAL.
(Which We Have But Little Hope of Seeing on the Stage of the National Capital.)

WESTWARD HO!

As have many Presidents, Chester Arthur found his labors and responsibilities exhausting. When he could, he took time off for trips—the most notable of which occurred in the summer of 1883. Accompanied by a few cronies, plus Lieutenant General Philip Sheridan, other high-ranking officers, seventy-five cavalry troopers, Indian guides, a photographer, and 175 pack animals, the President rode through western Wyoming to Yellowstone National Park. No reporters were included in the party, a fact that did not improve Arthur's relations with the fourth estate. He fished, watched Indian ceremonies, and accepted a pinto pony for his daughter, Nell, from the old Shoshoni chief Washakie. The vacation, which proved a tonic for the weary Chief Executive, is commemorated by a Wyoming mountain named Arthur Peak.

Arthur was considered to be one of the finest fishermen in the country, adept at hooking large trout, salmon, and striped bass. One day off the coast of Rhode Island he hauled in an eighty-pound bass, said to be the biggest seen in those parts for many seasons. Above, the President poses for a camera before pushing off for a few hours of fresh-water bass fishing at Alexandria Bay, on the boundary between New York and Canada.

Frontier photographer F. Jay Haynes recorded Arthur's trip to Wyoming. At left are the Arapahoe Indians who welcomed the presidential party to Fort Washakie. The umbrellas that some of them carry are symbols of leadership.

Looking like characters out of a Gilbert and Sullivan operetta, Arthur and a few of his fellow campers (below) lounge around a midday repast on the trail. Arthur is seated in a camp chair at the center of the photograph. Among the other identifiable lunchers is General Philip Sheridan, resting second from left in the foreground. The gentleman between Sheridan and Arthur is probably Secretary of War Robert T. Lincoln, son of the late President.

AN HONEST LOSER

Although he proved to be an honest President (standing for reform of the civil service and against pork-barrel appropriation bills), Chester Arthur failed at that part of the political game that he might have been expected to master: he was unable to weld the Republican party together under his leadership. On the one hand, he attempted to steer a middle course between the opposing factions, being conciliatory toward each of them. This infuriated his friends the Stalwarts. On the other hand, in New York State he forced the party to nominate his Secretary of the Treasury, Charles J. Folger, for governor in 1882 rather than the incumbent Republican, Alonzo B. Cornell. The New York Republicans were so disrupted that many stayed away from the polls that fall, and an obscure Democratic mayor of Buffalo named Grover Cleveland won the governorship. The lack of a firm footing either in New York or within a particular faction of the party, plus the general Republican losses in the mid-term elections around the country, boded ill for Arthur's hopes of being elected to a presidential term of his own. But although he had little support within his party, he was a popular Chief Executive, perhaps because the voters were relieved to have their early fears of his honesty dispelled. Said Mark Twain, "I am but one in 55,000,000; still, in the opinion of this one-fifty-five-millionth of the country's population, it would be hard to better President Arthur's Administration. But don't decide until you hear from the rest." The rest got no chance to express their opinion of Arthur; at the 1884 convention the Republicans chose James G. Blaine to oppose Cleveland and thereby lost control of the White House.

The Democrats had long been crying that it was time to throw the rascals out; government needed a good house cleaning. In the Puck *cartoon (right) they look particularly dejected as they see their entry to the Capital city blocked by Arthur's support of the merit system in civil service employment.*

FACTS IN SUMMARY: CHESTER A. ARTHUR

CHRONOLOGY

UNITED STATES		ARTHUR			
	1830	*Born October 5*	Dred Scott decision	1857	
Jackson re-elected President	1832		Lincoln-Douglas debates	1858	
Van Buren elected President	1836		John Brown's raid at Harpers Ferry	1859	*Marries Ellen Lewis Herndon*
Harrison elected President	1840		Lincoln elected President	1860	
Tyler becomes President	1841		South Carolina secedes		
Polk elected President	1844	*Enters Lyceum School in Schenectady*	Fort Sumter fired upon	1861	*Appointed engineer in chief of New York State*
Annexation of Texas	1845	*Enters Union College as sophomore*	First Battle of Bull Run		
War with Mexico	1846		Battle of Shiloh	1862	*Commissioned inspector general of New York troops*
Taylor elected President	1848	*Elected to Phi Beta Kappa*	Monitor v. Merrimac		
			Battle of Antietam		*Commissioned quartermaster general of New York State*
		Graduates from Union College	Confederate victory at Fredericksburg		
Fillmore becomes President	1850		Emancipation Proclamation	1863	
Compromise of 1850					
	1851	*Teaches school in Vermont*	Battle of Chancellorsville		
Pierce elected President	1852	*Becomes school principal in Cohoes, N.Y.*	Vicksburg Campaign		
			Gettysburg Campaign		
Gadsden Purchase	1853	*Studies law in New York*	Battle of the Wilderness	1864	
		Admitted to the bar			
Republican party formed	1854		Lincoln re-elected President		
Buchanan elected President	1856		Sherman's march to the sea		

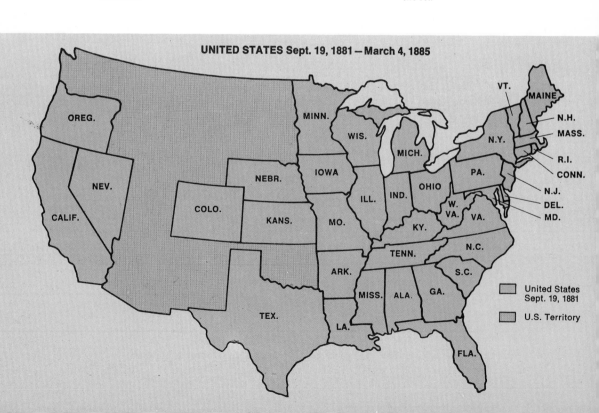

UNITED STATES Sept. 19, 1881 — March 4, 1885

OREG.
NEV.
CALIF.
MINN.
WIS.
MICH.
IOWA
NEBR.
COLO.
KANS.
MO.
ILL.
IND.
OHIO
KY.
TENN.
ARK.
MISS.
ALA.
GA.
TEX.
LA.
FLA.
VT.
MAINE
N.H.
MASS.
N.Y.
R.I.
CONN.
PA.
N.J.
DEL.
MD.
W. VA.
VA.
N.C.
S.C.

United States Sept. 19, 1881

U.S. Territory

Lee surrenders at Appomattox	1865	
Lincoln assassinated		
Johnson becomes President		
Thirteenth Amendment ratified		
Johnson impeached	1868	
Fourteenth Amendment ratified		
Grant inaugurated as President	1869	*Appointed counsel to the New York City Tax Commission*
	1871	*Named collector of customs for the Port of New York*
Grant re-elected President	1872	
Panic of 1873	1873	
	1875	*Reappointed collector of customs*
Hayes named President after disputed election	1877	
	1878	*Suspended as collector*
Garfield elected President	1880	*Ellen Arthur dies*
		Elected Vice President
Garfield assassinated	1881	*Becomes President*
	1882	*Loses control of Congress*
Pendleton Act	1883	*Signs Pendleton Act*
Cleveland elected President	1884	*Loses presidential nomination to James G. Blaine*
Dedication of the Washington Monument	1885	*Retires to New York City*
	1886	*Dies November 18*

BIOGRAPHICAL FACTS

BIRTH: Fairfield, Vt. (?), Oct. 5, 1830
ANCESTRY: Scotch-Irish and English
FATHER: William Arthur; b. County Antrim, Ireland, 1796; d. Newtonville, N.Y., Oct. 27, 1875
FATHER'S OCCUPATION: Baptist minister
MOTHER: Malvina Stone Arthur; b. Berkshire, Vt., April 24, 1802; d. Newtonville, N.Y., Jan. 16, 1869
BROTHERS: William (1834–1915); George (1836–1838)
SISTERS: Regina (1822–1910); Jane (1824–1842); Almeda (1826–1899); Ann Eliza (1828–1915); Malvina (1832–1920); Mary (1841–1917)
WIFE: Ellen Lewis Herndon; b. Fredericksburg, Va., Aug. 30, 1837; d. New York, N.Y., Jan. 12, 1880
MARRIAGE: New York, N.Y., Oct. 25, 1859
CHILDREN: William Lewis Herndon (1860–1863); Chester Alan, Jr. (1864–1937); Ellen (1871–1915)
EDUCATION: Attended public schools and Lyceum School; graduated with honors from Union College (1848)
RELIGIOUS AFFILIATION: Episcopalian
OCCUPATIONS BEFORE PRESIDENCY: Teacher; school principal; lawyer
PRE-PRESIDENTIAL OFFICES: Quartermaster General of New York State; New York Collector of Customs; Vice President

Virginia-born Ellen Lewis Herndon Arthur, above, died at forty-two, before her husband became President.

POLITICAL PARTY: Republican
AGE AT INAUGURATION: 50
OCCUPATION AFTER PRESIDENCY: Retired
DEATH: New York, N.Y., Nov. 18, 1886
PLACE OF BURIAL: Rural Cemetery, Albany, N.Y.

THE ARTHUR ADMINISTRATION

INAUGURATION: Sept. 20, 1881; New York, N.Y.
SECRETARY OF STATE: James G. Blaine; Frederick T. Frelinghuysen (from Dec. 19, 1881)
SECRETARY OF THE TREASURY: William Windom; Charles J. Folger (from Nov. 14, 1881); Walter Q. Gresham (from Sept. 24, 1884); Hugh McCulloch (from Oct. 31, 1884)
SECRETARY OF WAR: Robert T. Lincoln
ATTORNEY GENERAL: Wayne MacVeagh; Benjamin H. Brewster (from Jan. 3, 1882)
POSTMASTER GENERAL: Thomas L. James; Timothy O. Howe (from Jan. 5, 1882); Walter Q. Gresham (from April 11, 1883); Frank Hatton (from Oct. 14, 1884)
SECRETARY OF THE NAVY: William H. Hunt; William E. Chandler (from April 17, 1882)
SECRETARY OF THE INTERIOR: Samuel J. Kirkwood; Henry M. Teller (from April 17, 1882)
SUPREME COURT APPOINTMENTS: Horace Gray (1881); Samuel Blatchford (1882)
47th CONGRESS (March 4, 1881–March 4, 1883):
Senate: 37 Republicans; 37 Democrats; 1 Other
House: 147 Republicans; 135 Democrats; 11 Others
48th CONGRESS (March 4, 1883–March 4, 1885):
Senate: 38 Republicans; 36 Democrats; 2 Others
House: 197 Democrats; 118 Republicans; 10 Others
END OF PRESIDENTIAL TERM: March 4, 1885

THE TWENTY-SECOND PRESIDENT (1885–1889)
THE TWENTY-FOURTH PRESIDENT (1893–1897)

GROVER CLEVELAND

O n March 4, 1885, when Grover Cleveland stood up in the sparkling sun on the east portico of the Capitol to take his presidential oath, he presented an imposing figure. At a burly two hundred and fifty pounds, he was the heftiest Chief Executive the United States had yet had—only the rotund William Howard Taft, at three hundred and forty, would eclipse that record. He was a handsome, beer-drinking, cigar-smoking hunter and fisherman, an indefatigable worker with an inexhaustible store of energy. In a day when government was for sale on the bargain counters of Tammany Hall, when, as Henry Demarest Lloyd put it,"the Standard [Oil Company] has done everything with the Pennsylvania legislature except refine it," Cleveland had the reputation for being "ugly-honest." During his presidential election campaign, when he was attacked over the embarrassing matter of his having sired an illegitimate child, Cleveland gave his aides a directive considered unique in the history of politics: "Tell the truth."

The only Democratic President between 1861 and 1913, Cleveland was also the first and only Chief Executive to serve two nonconsecutive terms. He had entered national politics rather suddenly, as Everyman's hero, a politician of uncompromising independence and integrity. To the surprise and dismay of mentors and opponents alike, he remained incorruptible; by the time he completed his second term, he was despised and had been repudiated by his own party. His stubbornness, in fact, had earned him the title "His Obstinacy."

Born March 18, 1837, in a parsonage in Caldwell, New Jersey, Stephen Grover Cleveland was the fifth of nine children of Ann Neal and Richard Falley Cleveland, the local Presbyterian minister. When the latter secured the job of district secretary for the American Home Mission Society, he moved his family to central New York State, settling eventually in the town of Holland

Grover Cleveland as he appeared in 1892

Patent. From his father the youthful Cleveland learned all of the solid—and some of the stolid—Protestant virtues stressed in provincial America at the time. He memorized the Westminster Confession and *Pilgrim's Progress*. Family worship, as Allan Nevins recorded in his biography of Cleveland, "was held every evening."

The death of his father sent the sixteen-year-old Grover Cleveland out to earn a living. For a while he tried working at a school for the blind in New York City, but at the end of a year he returned to Holland Patent, borrowed twenty-five dollars from an elder of the Presbyterian church, and headed west with another boy from the town. Cleveland got as far as Buffalo; there an uncle, Lewis F. Allen, helped him find a job in a law firm. Seldom venturing far until he was elected governor, he spent the next twenty-six years in Buffalo, a growing brawny town of iron foundries, breweries, furniture factories, and docks busy with Great Lakes traffic.

Sometimes laboring through the night without sleep, Grover Cleveland worked doggedly at learning the law. After he was admitted to the bar in 1859, he worked just as hard, and by the middle of the 1870's he was a moderately well-to-do Buffalo lawyer. A stubborn man, he guarded his independence fiercely and was given to irritability and even wrathfulness when he felt it threatened. Equally fierce was his determination, and his corporation clientele found it more than worthwhile to tolerate his independence. Cleveland avoided ties that might make his time less than his own, remaining unmarried and refusing, for example, a lucrative job with the New York Central Railroad because he did not want to travel when it might be inconvenient. For many years he spent his leisure time in boisterous male company at the better local saloons, but in 1877 he helped found the City Club and took to wearing very correct clothes and a top hat.

From outward appearances Cleveland was a dull, unimaginative, even passionless man—a plodder. Yet, outward appearances do not tell the whole story. Cautious, preserving a proper façade, Cleveland charted

Cleveland was a promising young Buffalo, New York, lawyer when this photograph was taken about 1864.

a course of political advancement for himself. If his comrades did not believe him an ambitious man, it was only because they could not comprehend a man who wished to pursue political goals without the customary wheeling and dealing.

As early as 1858, Cleveland had worked for the local Democratic organization as a volunteer helping to get out the vote. In 1862 he was a delegate to the city convention. That same year, at the age of twenty-five, he was elected a ward supervisor; he was soon after appointed assistant district attorney. He served in this capacity for three years, learning a good deal about crime and corruption, and through his experiences he undoubtedly arrived at conclusions about how government ought to be run. As Nevins put it, "He was completely lacking in martial spirit" and so avoided fighting in the Civil War by furnishing a substitute—not at all an uncommon procedure at the time.

In 1865 Cleveland ran for district attorney, lost, and spent the next few years building up his law practice. In 1870 he ran for sheriff of Erie County—an office that no other reputable, or disreputable, lawyer would have considered worth the trouble—and won by a mere 303 votes. After serving as sheriff for three years, Cleveland joined Lyman K. Bass and Wilson S. Bissell in a law firm that soon became one of the most prominent in Buffalo. Cleveland himself rarely appeared in court, took modest fees and very brief vacations, and saved his money. He gained considerable weight drinking beer and eating sausages at Schenkelberger's Restaurant, played pinochle and poker, owned one of the best bird dogs in town, and had at least one fist fight—with a Mike Falvey, over Democratic politics. Then, in 1881, as Horace Samuel Merrill wrote, "Public indignation placed Grover Cleveland on the road to fame."

If the 1880's were years of "robber barons" and burgeoning trusts, of railroad empires and fights for the regulation of railroads, of rampant discontent among farmers, of industrial warfare and the birth of unions, they were at least in equal measure years of the dirtiest government America had ever seen. It was a time when politicians were bought and sold a dozen times over. *Harper's Weekly* proclaimed the United States Senate "a club of rich men . . . not sensitive to the charge of voting upon questions in which they have a pecuniary interest," a Senate corrupt and indifferent to public opinion.

But there were, of course, reformers, and in 1881 a Buffalo reform group decided to try for city hall. They approached a number of honest men with political experience, but none wanted the thankless job of mayor of Buffalo. So Grover Cleveland became their candidate. He campaigned hard for the office and won without spending a penny for drinks-all-around in the saloons and without making a single political deal.

Within a year of taking office, Cleveland saved Buffalo one million dollars simply by vetoing fraudulent sewage and street-cleaning contracts. He was given to pointing out, with indignant anger, those portions of bills that were nakedly graft grabbing. Crookedness was genuinely offensive to him. Surpris-

The Puck *cartoon at right shows the de-clawed Tammany tiger "made harmless at last" by Cleveland and his young ally, Assemblyman Teddy Roosevelt.*

ingly enough, he was equally candid about his own mistakes, reversing one of his decisions with the statement: "I desire to acknowledge that my action in the matter was hasty and inconsiderate. A little examination and reflection would have prevented it." It was remarkably impolitic of him—with the result that the Buffalo *Sunday Times* editorially proposed that he would make an excellent governor.

Cleveland did not solicit partisans in his bid for the governorship—in fact, he positively avoided any political alliances—but support flocked to him. He was nominated to oppose Republican Charles J. Folger, a good man who had the bad luck to appear a mere puppet of Chester A. Arthur and the everpopular villain, Jay Gould. Cleveland captured thousands of Republican votes. Having incurred no political debts of significance, he was elected, as biographer Robert McElroy wrote, as the "unowned candidate."

Early in Cleveland's term as governor, the legislature passed a bill intended to reduce the fare on the rich, Jay Gould-controlled New York City elevated railway to five cents at all times. The "el" could well afford a nickel fare, but charged ten cents during off-hours. The bill was designed to be a slap on the wrist to Gould. Cleveland, who was no friend of Gould's, nevertheless vetoed the bill, pointing out that to reduce the fare

without a careful examination of the company's finances was a violation of the right of contract protected by the First Amendment. His veto message, though unexpected and eminently impolitic, was so logical, so legally and morally correct, that he received surprisingly little criticism.

Cleveland managed, too—by thwarting Tammany moves to appoint incompetents to public office—to utterly alienate John Kelly of Tammany Hall. Kelly was a dangerous enemy. Without New York State, a presidential candidate stood little chance, and without Tammany, it was generally agreed, New York could not be carried. Yet it was Cleveland's stubborn opposition to Tammany that captured the imagination of the voters and made him a national figure.

In June of 1884 the Republicans convened in Chicago to nominate their candidate for President. A small but distinguished group of reformers—soon known as Mugwumps—was present, headed by Carl Schurz, New York legislator Theodore Roosevelt, President Charles Eliot of Harvard, Henry Ward Beecher, Charles Francis Adams, Jr., Leverett Saltonstall, and Henry Cabot Lodge. The machine Republicans treated them with contempt—noting that they "had their hair parted in the middle" and were "neither male nor female" but some aberration. The convention nominated James G. Blaine, who as Speaker of the House had allegedly sold railroad stocks and bonds under the shadiest of circumstances. The reformers bolted their party, and the Democrats, meeting in Chicago in July, responded by nominating Cleveland on the second ballot.

There followed one of the most memorable mud-slinging campaigns in American politics. Blaine's correspondence with the Boston firm that had handled his stock transactions was published in a local newspaper by the Mugwumps. On the back of one note, written in 1876, Blaine had scrawled, "Burn this letter!" And so the Democrats had their campaign song:

Blaine, Blaine, James G. Blaine,
The continental liar from the State of Maine,
Burn this letter!

In Cleveland's past, the Republicans discovered a Mrs. Maria Halpin, who claimed that the candidate was the father of her illegitimate son. It was not certain who the boy's father was, but Cleveland could have been, and he accepted the responsibility. It was on this occasion that Cleveland made his famous reply to a friend who asked how to respond to the charge: "Tell the truth." The Republicans then sang:

Ma! Ma! Where's my pa?
Gone to the White House.
Ha! Ha! Ha!

But the balance swung against Blaine. A Chicagoan suggested: "We are told that Mr. Blaine has been delinquent in office but blameless in private life, while Mr. Cleveland has been a model of official integrity, but culpable in his personal relations. We should therefore elect Mr. Cleveland to the public office which he is so well qualified to fill, and remand Mr. Blaine to the private station which he is admirably fitted to adorn." And most of the country adopted that position. The Mugwumps drew to Cleveland's support most, if not all, the reformists of the country; Beecher and Schurz led the contingent from New York. Nearly the entire Eastern press fell behind Cleveland.

Blaine made two crucial blunders. He was present at a speech by the Reverend Dr. Samuel Burchard in New York. Burchard said: "We are Republicans and don't propose to leave our party and identify ourselves with the party whose antecedents have been *rum, Romanism and rebellion.*" Blaine, no doubt tired from campaigning, missed the obvious slur against the Catholics and did not dissociate himself from it. Overnight he lost the loyalty of 500,000 Irish voters in the all-important state of New York, not to mention the Catholics in the rest of the nation. On the very same day —six days before the election—he was present at a dinner in his honor, offered by Jay Gould and Russell Sage, at Delmonico's in New York. The next day Joseph Pulitzer's newspaper, the New York *World*, reported in banner headlines: "THE ROYAL FEAST OF

Campaign gadgets, such as this splendid Cleveland noisemaker, were loud in support of their candidate.

BELSHAZZAR BLAINE AND THE MONEY KINGS . . . AN OCCASION FOR THE COLLECTION OF A REPUBLICAN CORRUPTION FUND."

Blaine was finished. Politicians had been deserting him all along. Boss Roscoe Conkling, asked why he had not campaigned for Blaine, had said: "I do not engage in criminal practice." The voters turned to Cleveland, who won the election with a plurality of almost 30,000 votes.

The campaign had hardly dealt with issues, but Cleveland knew precisely what he wanted done. At first he did not consider his role that of a leader of Congress, but believed his job to be one of executing laws and administering the business of the Executive. He waited, therefore, until Congress presented him with problems. In the meantime, he unearthed abuses that came under his jurisdiction. He recovered from the railroads thousands of acres of land that they had held under an exaggeratedly broad interpre-

tation of their land grants and opened them to homesteaders. He reversed a decision of President Arthur's opening up 494,778 acres of Indian land to settlers and land speculators and returned the land to the Indian reservation. He vetoed a bill calling for payments to all Civil War veterans who could claim *any* disability—including old age. He began to reform the civil service. He took great pains to assure that his appointees to the new Interstate Commerce Commission (created by the precedent-breaking Interstate Commerce Act of 1887) would be fair-minded, effective men. But his first three years in office were spent primarily in battling with the endless stream of office seekers who bedeviled him, cajoled him, pressured him—and angered him. "The d——d everlasting clatter for offices continues . . ." Cleveland wrote to a friend, "and makes me feel like resigning and hell is to pay generally." He was threatened with blackmail by at least one New York politician. Joseph Pulitzer's *World* accused him of ingratitude to the loyal workers who put him in office. When Cleveland relented somewhat, Carl Schurz wrote him: "Your attempt to please both reformers and spoilsmen has failed. I warned you more than once that your principal danger was to sit down between two chairs." Schurz should have known better; no one ever warned Cleveland. Cleveland broke off his alliance with Schurz and the Mugwumps.

Even Cleveland's civil service record was, according to the usually sympathetic Nevins, "fumbling and uneven." The President finally replaced 80,000 of 120,000 federal bureaucrats during his first term. Nonetheless, by the end of his second term, he managed to double the number of jobs not subject to patronage. For all the limitedness of the change, it was significant—and it was to alter the very nature of party control. It sharply curtailed the leverage the President was able to use to gain congressional support by promising jobs for votes. For Cleveland personally, it crystallized the hostility of Tammany Hall (one of the factors that cost him the Presidency in 1888), and it set the tone of wrangling with congressmen that was to prevail throughout his career.

Until his election to the Presidency, Cleveland's political record presented a one-dimensional picture of an honest man fighting corruption with little initiative or bold leadership. The character of his career changed, interestingly enough, just after he was married, on June 2, 1886, to the pretty, dark-eyed, twenty-one-year-old Frances Folsom, daughter of one of his Buffalo law partners. He had considered himself her virtual guardian from the time her father died in 1875 and had entertained her and her mother at the White House for ten days in 1885. He proposed to her shortly after her graduation from Wells College. They were married in the White House to the strains of the wedding march played by John Phillip Sousa. Mrs. Cleveland brightened Washington society and her husband's life. He became far more sociable, took more vacations, was generally less irritable, and displayed a more positive, bold leadership with legislators.

As Congress opened its session in the autumn of 1886, Cleveland moved immediately on the two most prominent issues of the eighties other than civil service reform: preservation of the gold standard and the lowering of the tariff. He made little headway in trying to prevent the coinage of silver (the real battle lay ahead, with William Jennings Bryan, in Cleveland's second term). But he mustered all his strength on the tariff question, and in December of 1887, he broke all precedents and devoted his entire annual message to Congress to it. He attacked all tariffs on necessities—those tariffs which were an undoubted hardship on farmers and laborers. He declined to compromise in any way with the powerful business interests that mobilized against him.

Some reduction in the tariff had been recognized as essential. A growing Treasury surplus was keeping excessive amounts of money out of circulation, and most politicians proposed a reduction in internal revenue taxation. Cleveland attacked head on. He observed that on the one hand Ameri-

cans were boasting with a series of centennial celebrations of the strength and accomplishment of American industry and that on the other hand—when the tariff question was raised—"it suits the purposes of advocacy to call our manufacturers infant industries still needing the highest and greatest degree of favor and fostering care that can be wrung from Federal legislation." He castigated trusts and called the tariff laws "vicious."

Before his tariff message, Cleveland had been considered a shoo-in for re-election. But he had said to a friend: "What is the use of being elected or re-elected unless you stand for something?" He was through playing safe. The House passed a tariff measure of which Cleveland could approve with some reservation. Before the Senate could act, however, the election campaign was in full swing and the issue of the tariff was obscured by the tumult.

Although the voters endorsed him with a plurality of nearly 100,000 votes, Cleveland lost to Republican Benjamin Harrison by 223 electoral votes to 168. Tammany Hall, in an alliance with the Republicans, took New York from him; the tariff cost him several other key states. Cleveland left office having accomplished little indeed. His first term was important principally in that he acquired a more certain sense of leadership.

In his last annual message to Congress, Cleveland decried cities where "wealth and luxury" existed callously beside "poverty and wretchedness and unremunerative toil." "The gulf between employers and the employed," he said, "is constantly widening, and classes are rapidly forming. . . ." Corporations, he warned, were "fast becoming the people's masters" while the farmers were struggling against "impoverishment." Perhaps his greatest limitation was that he believed that lowering the tariff would solve most of these difficulties.

Out of office, Cleveland watched with growing uneasiness as the "Billion-Dollar Congress" handed out liberal Civil War pensions, passed the high McKinley Tariff, and placed a severe strain on the gold standard by passing the Sherman Silver-Purchase Act. But he enjoyed private life and spent some of the most pleasurable weeks of his life vacationing and fishing at Buzzards Bay on Cape Cod. He wrote to a friend that "the inclination is growing on me, daily, to permit things other than politics to claim the greatest share of my attention."

Cleveland's most important public act during his four years out of office was to write his famous "silver letter" in 1891, in which he condemned "the dangerous and reckless experiment of free, unlimited, and independent silver coinage." Once again, all the Democrats were horrified by what they considered an impolitic maneuver, and it is not clear, in judging this one action of Cleveland's, whether or not he was for once trying to throw away his political career—so completely had he taken to private life. Nonetheless, in the following year he was nominated by the Democrats on the first ballot, and in the election he routed Harrison, winning a plurality of 400,000 popular votes.

Cleveland took office in his second term at a time when the country was far more restless than it had been in several decades. The Populist candidate for President had won more than a million votes in the 1892 election. William Jennings Bryan had been elected to Congress a year earlier. Eugene V. Debs had just organized the American Railway Union, which, by 1893, had 150,000 members. The General Managers' Association—which employed 221,000 workers—formed to combat the unions. Beneath the glitter of the new skyscrapers and electric lights, a class war was brewing in America. Ten days before Cleveland took office, the Philadelphia and Reading Railroad, with debts of over $125,000,000, went bankrupt. Immediately after his inauguration the great National Cordage Company collapsed, setting off a panic on Wall Street. The Atchison, Topeka and Santa Fe was exposed for defrauding the public of $7,000,000. The Treasury gold reserve dropped below the $100,000,000 mark—considered the balance necessary to guarantee solid money. Some five hundred banks failed before the end of

LIBRARY OF CONGRESS

THOMAS A. HENDRICKS

Thomas A. Hendricks, Cleveland's running mate in 1884, was Indiana's favorite son, an old guard Democrat, and the "soft-money" candidate of the West. Raised on a farm in Shelby County, Indiana, Hendricks took up the study of law, was admitted to the bar, and became a successful attorney. In 1848 the twenty-nine-year-old Hoosier entered the state legislature and later served as a delegate to the state constitutional convention. In 1851 he became a United States representative and in 1855 was appointed commissioner of the General Land Office. Elected to the Senate in 1863, he served for one term as an outspoken critic of the Republican administration. Attacking the draft and heavy taxation, he also opposed general emancipation on the grounds that it was a local matter and that the Negro was indeed inferior. Rising to prominence in the Democratic party, he was a contender for the presidential nomination in 1868, and in 1872 he was elected governor of Indiana. Four years later he became the Democratic candidate for Vice President and was narrowly defeated with Samuel J. Tilden in the contested election. When reformer Grover Cleveland was nominated for the Presidency in 1884, Hendricks was chosen for the second spot to appease the party machine and to strengthen the ticket in the Middle West. His term as Vice President was cut short when he died in November, 1885.

ADLAI E. STEVENSON

Less prominent than his famous namesake grandson, Adlai Ewing Stevenson nonetheless attained a higher office. Elected to the Vice Presidency in 1892, he served under Cleveland for four years as second in command. A country lawyer from Illinois, Stevenson was almost forty when he won a Democratic seat in the House of Representatives in 1874. During two nonconsecutive terms in Congress, he represented the soft-money, low-tariff views of the Midwestern farmer and laborer. As first assistant postmaster general during Cleveland's first term, it was his unpleasant task to remove some forty thousand Republican postmasters to provide jobs for Democratic supporters. Not surprisingly, his subsequent nomination as supreme court justice of the District of Columbia was rejected by a hostile Republican majority in the Senate. When Cleveland, a "hard-money" man, was renominated by the Democrats in 1892, Stevenson was placed on the ticket to please the inflationist forces. Presiding over the Senate with tact and diplomacy, he remained loyal to the administration in spite of his opposite economic views. In 1900 Stevenson ran for Vice President on the Democratic ticket headed by William Jennings Bryan. Eight years later he was narrowly defeated for the governorship of Illinois. Retiring from public life, Stevenson published his memoirs in 1909 and died at the age of eighty in June, 1914.

1893. Mortgages were foreclosed. Within a year, an estimated two to three million American workers were unemployed.

Cleveland's response to the financial panic was to call for the repeal of the Sherman Silver-Purchase Act in an attempt to restore confidence in the American dollar. Westerners and Southerners clamored for silver coinage, believing that if more money were put in circulation the plight of the farmers and laborers would be alleviated. Cleveland firmly believed in Gresham's Law (that bad money drives out good) and insisted on maintaining the gold standard.

As Chief Executive, this was Cleveland's finest hour. He called for a special session of Congress to repeal the Sherman Act. Then, in the very midst of preparation for the battle, Cleveland noticed a rough spot on the roof of his mouth. His doctor advised immediate removal of the cancerous growth, and in order to avoid plunging the country into further panic, Cleveland boarded a yacht in New York and sailed to Buzzards Bay, having the whole of his upper left jaw removed on the way. He debarked at Buzzards Bay and set to work immediately on his message for the special session. (The operation left its mark; Cleveland, though still strong, never again was able to work the long hours he had for so many years. He tired easily, and irritability burst to the surface more frequently.)

Cleveland's leadership of Congress was strong and purposeful. Daniel W. Voorhees of Indiana, the chairman of the powerful Senate Finance Committee, had opposed Cleveland's renomination in 1892 and had been a champion of silver coinage for two decades. His arguments in the Senate would be crucial. He utterly surprised his colleagues by leading the fight for repeal on Cleveland's behalf. The reason for the dramatic switch emerges from Cleveland's correspondence: he had promised all Indiana patronage to Voorhees.

After two months of fights, filibusters, and the sight of grown men reduced to tears in the Senate, the legislators came up with a compromise plan and presented it to Cleveland. The President reportedly erupted in anger, banged his fist on a table, and announced that he would not yield. A moderate statement was issued to the press: "The President adheres to the position that the purchasing clause of the Sherman silver law should be unconditionally repealed. . . ." His refusal to admit defeat heartened his followers, and ten days later, on October 30, 1893, the Sherman Silver-Purchase Act was repealed.

After repeal, Secretary of the Treasury John Carlisle, in an effort to shore up the federal gold reserve, twice issued $50,000,000 worth of bonds in 1894. When the public did not respond to the offering, he was compelled to issue the bonds to Wall Street bankers, who simply cashed in their old notes at the New York Sub-Treasury to obtain the gold to buy the new bonds. Nothing was gained; by January, 1895, the Treasury was losing gold at a rate of $3,000,000 a day. Then J. P. Morgan offered to raise $62,000,000 in gold for the government—half of it to come from abroad—and to ensure that it would not be immediately withdrawn. At 3.75 per cent the interest rate was high, but the main provision was that the government not make a public bond issue again and deal with Morgan alone.

The terms seemed too stiff to Cleveland, and he made preparations for another public issue. A bill was introduced in Congress, where it was defeated on February 7, 1895. At the very moment when Congress was voting, Morgan was on the train from New York. He was greeted in Washington by one of Cleveland's aides and told that the President could not see him that evening. Furious, Morgan said he would get back on the train and let the country go bankrupt. He was persuaded to stay, however, and sat up all night in his hotel room playing solitaire.

The next morning Morgan and Cleveland met at the White House; neither would yield. Then the phone rang; a Treasury official informed the President that there was less than $9,000,000 in gold at the New York Sub-Treasury. Morgan knew of an outstanding note for $12,000,000. "Mr. President,"

he said, ". . . if that [note] is presented today; it is all over." The stubborn, independent Cleveland, the man who responded to coercion with contrariness, gave in.

That Cleveland did acquiesce indicated just how critical the situation was. To most of the country it indicated something far more frightening as well: the unrestricted power of J. P. Morgan. Imprecations fell upon Cleveland with a vengeance. The silverites rose up to condemn him, and Cleveland, in saving the gold standard, had lost the Democratic party to the Populists.

Cleveland, however, had two significant foreign policy achievements in his second term. During Harrison's tenure a treaty to annex Hawaii had been negotiated and sent to the Senate for ratification. Five days after taking office, Cleveland recalled the treaty and quashed it. Some Hawaiians, to be sure, wanted to join America. Most, however, did not. "If national honesty is to be disregarded," Cleveland said in a message to Congress, "and a desire for territorial expansion or dissatisfaction with a form of government not our own ought to regulate our conduct, I have entirely misapprehended the . . . character of our government. . . ."

A drawn-out dispute with Great Britain, dating from 1887, finally exhausted Cleveland's patience in 1895. The crux of the disagreement was over the boundary between British Guiana and Venezuela. Cleveland, invoking the ever-handy Monroe Doctrine, maintained that Britain was attempting to expand its interests in the Americas. He has been criticized for the vehemence with which he finally attacked Great Britain over the matter. Yet, however bellicose his words, he labored to stem any jingoism that might have followed his message, and he brought the issue to arbitration quickly. As Nevins has noted, Cleveland's move had an important side effect in "clearing the atmosphere between Great Britain and the United States" and initiating "a virtual *entente* that within a generation was to prove of the profoundest importance in world history."

Despite such accomplishments, the conflicting forces of the nineties ultimately overwhelmed Cleveland. His fight for a reduction in the tariff, swamped by the strong economic interests that effectively controlled Congress, resulted in the passage of the Wilson-Gorman Tariff, which maintained high tariffs.

The period from July of 1894 to July of 1895, Nevins wrote, "might well be called the *année terrible* of American history between Reconstruction and the World War." It was the year in which Morgan engineered his loan to the government, the year of the Chicago Pullman strike and Coxey's march on Washington, a year in which 750,000 laborers went out on strikes. Cleveland, wrangling with Congress, striking out bitterly at legislators after the passage of the tariff, earned in that year the title "His Obstinacy," and he made repeated mistakes in the handling of labor disputes.

Cleveland's first mistake had been the selection of the hot-tempered, pugnacious Richard Olney of Massachusetts as his Attorney General. Olney—with Cleveland's endorsement, to be sure—applied inexcusably harsh measures in putting down the unemployed citizens, led by Populist Jacob S. Coxey, who marched on Washington to petition for relief. "Coxey's Army" had originally contained more than 25,000 protesters from various parts of the nation, but only about 400 actually reached the Capitol; they were dispersed by police, and many were beaten.

Later in 1894, Cleveland and Olney permitted themselves to be panicked once again when workmen of the Pullman Palace Car Company in Chicago, locked out of their jobs after striking against a wage reduction and the injustices of company-owned stores and homes, allied themselves with Eugene V. Debs's American Railway Union. By the end of the month, a boycott of Pullman cars on all Midwestern railroads had been established, and after Olney swore in 3,400 special deputies, violence erupted. Then Olney (who had been one of the founders of the General Managers' Association, which was backing Pullman) overrode the objections of Illinois's courageous governor, John

Altgeld, and—with Cleveland's approval—sent federal troops to restore order in Chicago. The strike was broken by an injunction, and Debs was sent to jail, where he first read the writings of Karl Marx.

The famous Pullman strike, and its aftermath, pointed up Grover Cleveland's most serious limitation as President. Although Cleveland had foreseen the increasing discontent among American workers and had spoken of it in his message to Congress in 1887, although he was the first President to address a message to Congress concerning labor (calling for a permanent labor-management mediation panel in 1886), he had never really acquainted himself with laborers and their problems. It was in fact a parochialism of the middle class that limited his vision and motivated many of his intemperate and sometimes frightened reactions to both the rich and the poor.

On December 3, 1895, Cleveland delivered his annual State of the Union message to Congress. Only four persons applauded it. The silverites, headed by William Jennings Bryan, had the loyalty of the Democrats. When the Democrats met in 1896, "Pitchfork" Ben Tillman addressed the convention: "We denounce the Administration of President Cleveland as undemocratic and tyrannical. . . ." William Jennings Bryan, his moment having come, made his famous "Cross of Gold" speech and was nominated; in the election that followed, Cleveland was all but forgotten.

Cleveland's reputation did not revive until many years after he left office. But, by the time he died on June 24, 1908, he was a much-respected elder statesman—admired for the stand he took in the Venezuelan border dispute, for the principles he enunciated in the controversy over Hawaii, for his defiance of machine politics, for his dauntless fight for the gold standard. He has finally been accounted a "near-great" President, and he does remain the archetype of a President who stood against political expediency, a man who, right or wrong, said, "Tell the truth."

—CHARLES L. MEE, JR.

A PICTURE PORTFOLIO

*Grover Cleveland's stern visage adorns
the Democratic campaign medal above.*

JAMES G. BLAINE

In James G. Blaine, the magnetic and eloquent "Plumed Knight" of the Republican party, Grover Cleveland had a formidable opponent for the Presidency. Born in Pennsylvania in 1830, Blaine settled in Augusta, Maine, entered the state legislature, and became the acknowledged leader of the Maine Republicans. Elected to Congress in 1862, he served for almost two decades as representative, Speaker of the House, and senator. As leader of the liberal element of the party, Blaine was an attractive presidential prospect. But charges of graft in his dealings with the railroads cost him the nomination in 1876, and he was thwarted again in 1880. In 1884 he finally became the Republican candidate; but the railroad scandal continued to hurt him, and a supporter's reference to the opposition as the party of "rum, Romanism and rebellion" alienated the Irish Catholics in the key state of New York. Defeated by Cleveland, Blaine returned to foreign affairs. In 1881 he had been Secretary of State under Garfield. Supporting Harrison in 1888, he again became Secretary and resumed his fight for a more constructive Latin-American policy. A statesman of vision, he was instrumental in organizing the first Pan-American Conference, in formulating policy for a United States-controlled Isthmian canal, and in increasing trade with Latin America. Blaine died in Washington in January, 1893.

The penny-bank figure (top) shows the Greenback candidate, Benjamin Butler, in the unflattering form of a frog. A Civil War general and a former governor of Massachusetts, Butler ran on both the Greenback and Anti-Monopoly tickets in 1884.

Mrs. Belva Ann Bennett Lockwood was the presidential candidate of the National Equal Rights party in 1884 and 1888. A prominent Washington lawyer (the first woman to plead before the Supreme Court), she often rode through the capital on her three-wheeled cycle, snug in her red stockings.

REFORM CANDIDATE

Fire and smoke burst from the nostrils of Tammany," reported the New York *Sun* when the Brooklyn delegation to the 1884 Democratic convention declared its votes for Cleveland. The former mayor of Buffalo and governor of New York, Grover Cleveland, had alienated New York's powerful Tammany Hall bosses with his reforms, and they were out to block his nomination at all costs. "Cleveland cannot carry the State of New York," proclaimed Tammany henchman Thomas Grady. Tired of Tammany's greed and interference, Edward Bragg of Wisconsin spoke for those who favored the reform candidate. "They love Cleveland for his character," he said, "but they love him also for the enemies he has made." Furiously, Tammany boss John Kelly shouted in response, "In behalf of his enemies, I accept your statement." When the uproar subsided, Cleveland led the first ballot by 224 votes. A last-ditch effort by the marplots to effect a coalition failed, and Cleveland was nominated on the second ballot. The ensuing campaign was a low-level affair. Republicans spread the story of Cleveland's illegitimate son, and Democrats dug up an old railroad scandal involving the Republican candidate, James G. Blaine. But despite the muckraking, a feeling prevailed that Cleveland would restore "good government"; that his election would prove, as one hopeful put it, that "in the end . . . there *is* a public conscience. . . ."

The cartoon above, which appeared in the Republican weekly Judge, *was captioned "Another Voice for Cleveland." Having acknowledged an illegitimate son, "Grover the Good" is plagued by an embarrassing squall.*

A NEW FIRST LADY

Frances Folsom Cleveland (photographed above in her ivory-satin wedding dress) was only twenty-one when she married the forty-nine-year-old bachelor President in 1886. A "tall, very pretty and direct person," she was "the most popular of First Ladies" and made things lively at the White House.

"The White House under its young mistress will now be the scene of charming festivities," predicted *Harper's Weekly* after Cleveland's marriage to the lovely Frances Folsom on June 2, 1886. The ceremony—attended only by the Cabinet, a few close friends, and members of the families—"called a momentary truce to partisan hostility" and generated great public interest. No incident relating to the union was too trivial to be newsworthy, and the couple was beleaguered by an overzealous press. Not even on their honeymoon were they accorded privacy. Reporters followed them to their Maryland retreat, camped near their cottage, and spied on them with field glasses. Enraged by such "colossal impertinence," the President issued a public statement condemning the "professional gossips" for "doing their utmost to make American journalism contemptible. . . ." On another occasion, when reporters continued to hound his wife, he interrupted a speech, and with tears of indignation, rebuked "those ghouls" who would "desecrate every sacred relation of private life."

But if the public hungered for gossip of the First Lady it was out of love, not malice; and Washington was delighted with its new hostess. Standing at a White House reception—a grace of violets at her waist— she would sometimes receive as many as eight thousand callers and had a warm smile of welcome for each. Lively, bright, and unaffected, she softened the edges of her husband's abrasive personality and won the admiration even of his political enemies. The remark of one who managed to resist the First Lady's charms is perhaps the greatest tribute to her universal appeal: "I detest him so much," exclaimed one of President Cleveland's detractors, "that I don't even think his wife is beautiful."

A drawing of Frances Cleveland as the queen of hearts (left) adorned the cover of Judge magazine in October of 1887. The winsome First Lady is portrayed as the President's greatest drawing card, with the caustic commentary: "What a pity it is for Grover that Hearts are not Trumps in politics."

The wedding of President Cleveland and his former ward, Frances Folsom (below), was an unprecedented event in the White House. The bride's fifteen-foot train was a sensation with society writers, but as one observer noted, "It was the woman at whom the women looked rather than the dress."

"LET OUT"—BRIEFLY

The first Democratic victory in twenty-four years was lampooned by Judge magazine in the 1884 cartoon above, entitled "Democracy's Debut." Emblazoned with such mottoes as "Reform" and "Free trade," the ungainly debutante is being presented at Grover Cleveland's inaugural ball, while Democratic party spoilsmen look on from an antechamber.

In 1888 the opposition returned to power committed to a high protective tariff. In the Republican campaign poster at right, Harrison promises protection to everything but polygamy, while Cleveland is presented as the foe of American industry.

M y God," lamented President Cleveland, "what is there in this office that any man should ever want to get into it!" In spite of some first-term accomplishments (he had approved the Interstate Commerce Act, vetoed fraudulent pension bills, repealed the hobbling Tenure of Office Act, and instituted civil service reforms), his administration had not been happy. Party members wrangled for patronage, businessmen fought his tariff reduction proposal, and Civil War veterans resented his pension vetoes. Another political mark against him was his ill-timed gesture of conciliation toward the South. In the summer of 1887 the War Department decided it might be "a graceful act" to return to their former owners "a number of Confederate flags which the fortunes of war placed in our hands during the late Civil War." The recommendation, approved by President Cleveland, created a furor among Republicans and the already hostile veterans of the Grand Army of the Republic. Republican Foraker of Ohio declared, "No rebel flags will be surrendered while I am Governor." The commander of the G.A.R. was more virulent: "May God palsy the hand that wrote the order! May God palsy the tongue that dictated it!" The uproar forced President Cleveland to revoke the order. A shrewder politician might have anticipated the criticisms, and by tactful diplomacy, paved the way for acceptance. But Cleveland, in his straightforward manner, had again bared his breast to the enemy. Small wonder that he confided to a friend, in viewing the coming election, "I should personally like better than anything else to be let alone and let out. . . ." The voters were to grant him only a temporary reprieve. "Four years from now," said an ally after Cleveland lost to Harrison, "we mean to put you back in the White House."

THE WHOLE STORY IN A NUTSHELL!

Harrison's Ideas!

Republican Platform of 1888.

PROTECTION TO AMERICAN BEEF PORK AND MUTTON

ADMIT DAKOTA TO THE SISTERHOOD OF STATES! Population 600,000

PROTECTION TO LUMBER

COPPER

PROTECTIVE DUTIES UPON CANADIAN IMPORTS

SALT AND WOOL INDUSTRIES

IRON

MINERS AND MANUFACTURERS

NO TRIBUTE TO ENGLAND FOR AMERICAN FISH

ENCOURAGEMENT TO AMERICAN COMMERCE

NO MORE COOLIE NOR CONTRACT LABOR

DEATH TO POLYGAMY

PROTECTION TO WOOL GROWERS

DEATH TO WHISKY TRUST AND ALL OTHER TRUSTS

PROTECTION TO TOBACCO GROWERS

PROTECTION TO AMERICAN LABOR

PUBLIC DOMAIN FOR ACTUAL THRIFTY SETTLERS

PROTECTION TO AMERICAN RICE

CORN HEMP AND FRUITS!

INCREASED COMMERCIAL INTERCOURSE WITH FRIENDLY NEIGHBORING STATES AND CONSTRUCTION OF NICARAGUAN CANAL

Honest Enforcement of Civil-Service Reform!

Reduction of Letter Postage To One Cent per Ounce!

Appropriations for Navy and Coast Defenses!

A Free Ballot and an Honest Count!

Reduction of Treasury Surplus by reduction of Direct (Internal-Revenue) Taxation!

Pensions for Union Soldiers!

COPYRIGHT (1888) BY
—ALE PUBLISHING Co.
126 William Street, New York.

PRICES:
10c. per Copy;
$6 per Hundred; $50 per Thousand.

"We must never permit this country to become the dumping ground of the pauperism and indolence and crime of Europe. I believe that we should both protest and legislate against the labor abroad, against contract labor, and against Chinese labor. Our protective system is a barrier against the flood of foreign importations and the competition of underpaid labor in Europe. Do they invite the flood or do they believe in the dyke? We would have more confidence in the profession of these alleged reformers could we hear one of them occasionally say that he was a Protectionist. This is not a question of a seven-per-cent. reduction in tariff schedules; but it is a question of wide-apart principles. But let us turn from these things that are scheduled that have their places in our Census returns to those things which belong to the higher man—his spiritual and moral nature. I congratulate you not so much upon the rich lands of our country as upon your virtuous and happy homes. It is in the home that we first learn obedience and respect for law. Parental authority is the type of beneficent government. It is in the home that we learn to love, in the mother that bore us, that which is virtuous, consecrated and pure. I take more pride in the fact that the Republican party has always been the friend and protector of the American home than in aught else. By the beneficent Homestead Law it created more than a half million of homes, and by the Emancipation Proclamation it converted a million cattle pens into homes. And it is still true to those principles that will preserve contentment and prosperity and purity in our homes.—BENJAMIN HARRISON."

Cleveland's Ideas!

Fruits of "Free-Wool Message," "Mills' Bill" and General Democratic Policy.

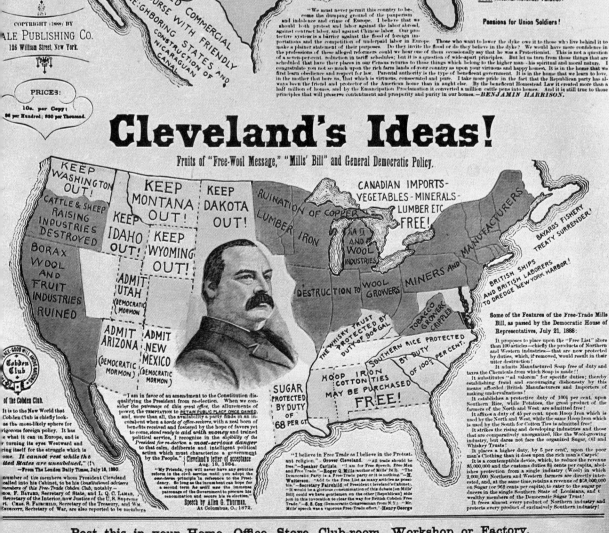

KEEP WASHINGTON OUT!

CATTLE & SHEEP RAISING INDUSTRIES DESTROYED

KEEP MONTANA OUT!

KEEP DAKOTA OUT!

RUINATION OF COPPER

CANADIAN IMPORTS—VEGETABLES—MINERALS—LUMBER ETC. FREE!

MANUFACTURERS

KEEP IDAHO OUT!

KEEP WYOMING OUT!

LUMBER IRON

SALT AND WOOL INDUSTRIES

BAYARDS FISHERY TREATY SURRENDER!

BORAX WOOL AND FRUIT INDUSTRIES RUINED

ADMIT UTAH (DEMOCRATIC MORMON)

DESTRUCTION TO WOOL GROWERS

MINERS AND

BRITISH SAILORS AND BRITISH LABORERS TO DREDGE NEW YORK HARBOR!

Cobden Club

ADMIT ARIZONA (DEMOCRATIC MORMON)

ADMIT NEW MEXICO (DEMOCRATIC MORMON)

THE WHISKY TRUST PROTECTED BY DUTY OF 90c GAL.

TOBACCO GROWERS CRIPPLED

SUGAR PROTECTED BY DUTY OF 68 PER CT.

HOOP IRON COTTON TIES MAY BE PURCHASED FREE!

SOUTHERN RICE PROTECTED BY DUTY OF 100% PER CENT.

—EE GOOD WILL —
—Cobden Club—

of the Cobden Club.

It is to the New World that the Cobden Club is chiefly looking as the most likely sphere for vigorous foreign policy. It has ... what it can in Europe, and is turning its eyes Westward and ... ing itself for the struggle which is ... ome. It cannot rest while the ... ited States are unsubdued." (!)
—From The London Daily Times, July 18, 1880.

... number of the members whom President Cleveland called into his Cabinet, to be his Constitutional advisers ... members of this Free-Trade Cobden Club, notably ... ace, F. Bayard, Secretary of State, and L. Q. C. Lamar, Secretary of the Interior, now Justice of the U. S. Supreme ... rt. Chas. S. Fairchild, Secretary of the Treasury, and Wm. ... dicott, Secretary of War, are also reported to be members

"I am in favor of an amendment to the Constitution disqualifying the President from re-election. When we consider the patronage of this great office, the allurements of power, the temptation to betray public place once gained, and, more than all, the availability a party finds in an incumbent when a horde of office-seekers, with a zeal born of benefits received and fostered by the hope of favors yet to come, stand ready to aid with money and trained political service, I recognize in the eligibility of the President for re-election a most-serious danger to that calm, deliberate and intelligent political action which must characterize a government by the People." | Cleveland's letter of acceptance Aug. 18, 1884.

"My Friends, you will never have any genuine reform in the civil service until you adopt the one-term principle in reference to the Presidency. So long as the incumbent can hope for a second term he will use the immense patronage of the Government to procure his renomination and secure his re-election." Speech by Allen G. Thurman At Columbus, O., 1872.

"I believe in Free Trade as I believe in the Protestant religion."—Grover Cleveland. "All trade should be free."—Speaker Carlisle. "I am for Free Speech, Free Men and Free Trade"—Roger Q. Mills (author of Mills' Bill). "The Democratic Party is a Free-Trade party or it is nothing."—H. Watterson. "Add to the Free List as many articles as possible."—Secretary Fairchild of President Cleveland's Cabinet. "It would be a glorious consummation of this debate [on Mills' Bill] could we have gentlemen on the other [Republican] side ... this invocation to clear the way for British Cobden Free Trade."—S. S. Cox (Democratic Congressman from N.Y.)."Mr. Mills' speech was a vigorous Free-Trade effort."—Henry George.

Some of the Features of the Free-Trade Mills Bill, as passed by the Democratic House of Representatives, July 21, 1888:

It proposes to place upon the "Free List" more than 100 articles—chiefly the products of Northern and Western industries—that are now protected by duties, which, if removed, would result in their utter destruction!

It admits Manufactured Soap free of duty and taxes the Chemicals from which Soap is made!!

It substitutes "ad valorem" for specific duties; thereby establishing fraud and encouraging dishonesty by this means afforded British Manufacturers and Importers of making undervaluations!

It establishes a protective duty of 100½ per cent. upon Southern Rice, while Potatoes, the great product of the farmers of the North and West, are admitted free!

It affixes a duty of 45 per cent. upon Hoop Iron which is used by the North and West, while the same Hoop Iron which is used by the South for Cotton Ties is admitted free!

It strikes the rising and developing industries and those that are comparatively unorganized, like the Wool-growing industry, but dares not face the organized Sugar, Oil and Whiskey Trusts!

It places a higher duty, by 5 per cent., upon the poor man's Clothing than it does upon the rich man's Carpet!

It is a contemptible device, which, to reduce the revenue $5,000,000 and the customs duties 83 cents per capita, abolishes protection from a single industry (Wool) in which 2,000,000 Northern and Western farmers are directly interested, and, at the same time, retains a revenue of $58,000,000 on Sugar (or 96 cents per capita), to cater to the sugar producers in the single Southern State of Louisiana, and t wealthy members of the Democratic Sugar Trust!

It frees almost every product of Northern industry and protects every product of exclusively Southern industry!

Post this in your Home, Office, Store, Club-room, Workshop or Factory.

1889

U.S. TREASURY.

SURPLUS 100,000,000 DOLLARS

LOOTED

U.S.

The Puck cartoon above illustrates the fate of the United States Treasury during the four years of Benjamin Harrison's administration. When Cleveland left office in 1889, the Treasury was swollen with a large surplus; when he returned in 1893, the surplus was depleted and the gold reserve had dropped below the danger point. In the interval the "Billion-Dollar Congress," as the fifty-first was dubbed, had managed to expend—for the first time in peacetime history—over a billion dollars in a single session. "God help the

surplus," *cried Harrison's Commissioner of Pensions "Corporal" James Tanner, whose policy was to give a grant to "every old comrade that needs it." The nation's reaction to such extravagance was manifested in the next presidential election. The cartoon shows Cleveland returning to a looted Treasury, which Harrison, in new spats and top hat, bequeaths with the comment, "The People Wanted A Change, And They Got It." To this* Puck *responds, "But The Change Was Made in 1889, And We Are Still Suffering From It."*

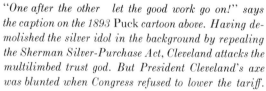

Puck

"One after the other   let the good work go on!" says
the caption on the 1893 Puck cartoon above. Having de-
molished the silver idol in the background by repealing
the Sherman Silver-Purchase Act, Cleveland attacks the
multilimbed trust god. But President Cleveland's axe
was blunted when Congress refused to lower the tariff.

The 1894 photograph at top right shows "Coxey's
Army" on the march to Washington to petition for
relief from mass unemployment. The marchers were
met by Attorney General Richard Olney's police forces,
who dispersed the protesters by force and violence.

A Harper's Weekly artist made the rendition at lower
right of National Guardsmen firing into an angry mob
of demonstrators during the Chicago Pullman strike
of 1894. Cleveland was highly criticized for sending
in the troops against the wishes of Governor Altgeld.

Harper's Weekly

"A MAN OF COURAGE"

Cleveland's second administration was not, to him personally, a greater satisfaction than his first. His achievements in foreign relations—the arbitration of Venezuela's border dispute and his anti-imperialist stand on Hawaii—were largely obscured by the domestic problems following the financial panic of 1893. His heroic fight to preserve the gold standard was not fully appreciated during his administration. What was most obvious during those years was the President's mismanagement of the labor problem, particularly his severe treatment of the Chicago Pullman strikers and the unemployed protesters of "Coxey's Army." In 1897 Cleveland left office in a storm of criticism, gratefully retiring to the quiet college town of Princeton, New Jersey. The Clevelands were welcomed into the social and intellectual life of the community, and in 1901 the ex-President was elected to the university's board of trustees. He formed a lasting friendship with Andrew West, dean of the graduate school, and he was on intimate terms with the university's president, Woodrow Wilson, although his innate conservatism often clashed with the latter's progressive approach to education. He was in great demand as a speaker and in 1904 published a collection of his lectures under the title *Presidential Problems*. Before his death in 1908 he had completely regained the country's veneration. Describing the tumultuous ovation that Cleveland received on a 1903 trip to St. Louis, biographer Allan Nevins remarked, "It was the apology of the West to a man of courage." Many analysts have been disappointed in Cleveland's leadership, complaining that he was most steadfast in his protection of businessmen and that he had little sympathy for the problems of the farmer and the laborer. His friend Woodrow Wilson offered perhaps the most astute observation: "You may think Cleveland's administration was Democratic. It was not. Cleveland was a conservative Republican."

FACTS IN SUMMARY: GROVER CLEVELAND

CHRONOLOGY

UNITED STATES		CLEVELAND		UNITED STATES		CLEVELAND
			1884			*Elected President*
Bank panic	1837	*Born March 18*	Treasury surplus grows	1886		*Suggests reduction in tariff*
Repeal of Independent Treasury Act	1841	*Moves to Fayetteville, N.Y.*				*Marries Frances Folsom*
War with Mexico	1846		Electoral Count Act	1887		*Vetoes dependent pension bill*
Gadsden Purchase	1853	*Teaches school*	Interstate Commerce Act			*Institutes repeal of Tenure of Office Act*
Buchanan elected President	1856		Hatch Act			*Urges tariff reform*
John Brown's raid at Harpers Ferry	1859	*Admitted to the bar*	Harrison elected President	1888		*Loses bid for re-election*
Lincoln elected President	1860		Sherman Antitrust Act	1890		
Civil War begins	1861		Sherman Silver-Purchase Act			
Battle of Shiloh	1862	*Elected ward supervisor*	McKinley Tariff			
Emancipation Proclamation	1863	*Appointed assistant district attorney of Erie County*		1891		*Writes "silver letter"*
Battle of Gettysburg				1892		*Re-elected President*
Lee surrenders to Grant	1865	*Loses election for district attorney*	Bank panic	1893		*Asks repeal of Sherman Silver-Purchase Act*
Lincoln assassinated						*Quashes treaty for Hawaiian annexation*
Johnson impeached	1868		"Coxey's Army"	1894		*Sends troops to restore order during Pullman strike*
Grant elected President						
	1870	*Elected sheriff of Erie County*	Gold reserve depleted	1895		*Makes deal with Morgan to solve Treasury crisis*
Hayes elected President	1877		McKinley elected President	1896		
Arthur becomes President	1881	*Elected mayor of Buffalo*	War with Spain	1898		
	1882	*Elected governor of New York*	Theodore Roosevelt becomes President	1901		*Becomes Princeton University trustee*
				1908		*Dies June 24*

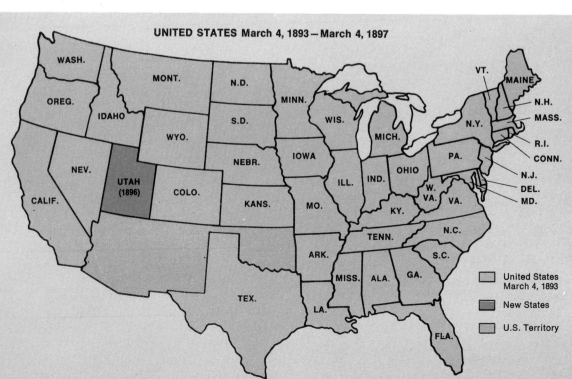

UNITED STATES March 4, 1893 — March 4, 1897

United States March 4, 1893

New States

U.S. Territory

BIOGRAPHICAL FACTS

BIRTH: Caldwell, N.J., March 18, 1837
ANCESTRY: Irish-English
FATHER: Richard Falley Cleveland; b. Norwich, Conn., June 19, 1804; d. Holland Patent, N.Y., Oct. 1, 1853
FATHER'S OCCUPATION: Minister
MOTHER: Ann Neal Cleveland; b. Baltimore, Md., Feb. 4, 1806; d. Holland Patent, N.Y., July 19, 1882
BROTHERS: William Neal (1832–1906); Richard Cecil (1835–1872); Lewis Frederick (1841–1872)
SISTERS: Anna Neal (1830–1909); Mary Allen (1833–1914); Margaret Louise (1838–1932); Susan Sophia (1843–?); Rose (1846–1918)
WIFE: Frances Folsom; b. Buffalo, N.Y., July 21, 1864; d. Oct. 29, 1947
MARRIAGE: Washington, D.C., June 2, 1886
CHILDREN: Ruth (1891–1904); Esther (1893–   ); Marion (1895–   ); Richard Folsom (1897–   ); Francis Grover (1903–   )
EDUCATION: Public schools
RELIGIOUS AFFILIATION: Presbyterian
OCCUPATION BEFORE PRESIDENCY: Lawyer
PRE-PRESIDENTIAL OFFICES: Erie County Assistant District Attorney; Sheriff of Erie County; Mayor of Buffalo; Governor of New York
AGE AT INAUGURATION: 47
OCCUPATION AFTER PRESIDENCY: Princeton University trustee
DEATH: Princeton, N.J., June 24, 1908
PLACE OF BURIAL: Princeton, N.J.

ELECTION OF 1884

CANDIDATES	ELECTORAL VOTE	POPULAR VOTE
Grover Cleveland Democratic	219	4,879,507
James G. Blaine Republican	182	4,850,293
Benjamin F. Butler Greenback-Labor	—	175,370
John P. St. John Prohibition	—	150,369

FIRST ADMINISTRATION

INAUGURATION: March 4, 1885; the Capitol, Washington, D.C.
VICE PRESIDENT: Thomas A. Hendricks
SECRETARY OF STATE: Thomas F. Bayard
SECRETARY OF THE TREASURY: Daniel Manning; Charles S. Fairchild (from April 1, 1887)
SECRETARY OF WAR: William C. Endicott
ATTORNEY GENERAL: Augustus H. Garland
POSTMASTER GENERAL: William F. Vilas; Don M. Dickinson (from Jan. 16, 1888)

SECRETARY OF THE NAVY: William C. Whitney
SECRETARY OF THE INTERIOR: Lucius Q. C. Lamar; William F. Vilas (from Jan. 16, 1888)
SECRETARY OF AGRICULTURE: Norman J. Colman
SUPREME COURT APPOINTMENTS: Lucius Q. C. Lamar (1888); Melville W. Fuller, Chief Justice (1888)
49th CONGRESS (March 4, 1885–March 4, 1887):
Senate: 43 Republicans; 34 Democrats
House: 183 Democrats; 140 Republicans; 2 Others
50th CONGRESS (March 4, 1887–March 4, 1889):
Senate: 39 Republicans; 37 Democrats
House: 169 Democrats; 152 Republicans; 4 Others
END OF PRESIDENTIAL TERM: March 4, 1889

ELECTION OF 1892

CANDIDATES	ELECTORAL VOTE	POPULAR VOTE
Grover Cleveland Democratic	277	5,555,426
Benjamin Harrison Republican	145	5,182,690
James B. Weaver People's	22	1,029,846
John Bidwell Prohibition	—	264,133
Simon Wing Socialist Labor	—	21,164

SECOND ADMINISTRATION

INAUGURATION: March 4, 1893; the Capitol, Washington, D.C.
VICE PRESIDENT: Adlai E. Stevenson
SECRETARY OF STATE: Walter Q. Gresham; Richard Olney (from June 10, 1895)
SECRETARY OF THE TREASURY: John G. Carlisle
SECRETARY OF WAR: Daniel S. Lamont
ATTORNEY GENERAL: Richard Olney; Judson Harmon (from June 11, 1895)
POSTMASTER GENERAL: Wilson S. Bissell; William L. Wilson (from April 4, 1895)
SECRETARY OF THE NAVY: Hilary A. Herbert
SECRETARY OF THE INTERIOR: Hoke Smith; David R. Francis (from Sept. 4, 1896)
SECRETARY OF AGRICULTURE: Julius Sterling Morton
SUPREME COURT APPOINTMENTS: Edward D. White (1894); Rufus W. Peckham (1895)
53rd CONGRESS (March 4, 1893–March 4, 1895):
Senate: 44 Democrats; 38 Republicans; 3 Others
House: 218 Democrats; 127 Republicans; 11 Others
54th CONGRESS (March 4, 1895–March 4, 1897):
Senate: 43 Republicans; 39 Democrats; 6 Others
House: 244 Republicans; 105 Democrats; 7 Others
STATE ADMITTED: Utah (1896)
END OF PRESIDENTIAL TERM: March 4, 1897

BENJAMIN HARRISON

A month after the national election of 1888, Republican National Committee Chairman Matt Quay journeyed to Indianapolis to discuss Cabinet choices with President-elect Benjamin Harrison. Although Harrison had received nearly one hundred thousand fewer votes than his opponent, incumbent Grover Cleveland, he had managed to capture an electoral majority, and he was grateful. "Providence," he said as he greeted Quay, "has given us the victory." For the moment the chairman held his tongue, but later, as he repeated the conversation to a colleague, he remarked, "Think of the man! He ought to know that Providence hadn't a damn thing to do with it."

What had given the Republicans the victory was a combination of good organization and corruption. They bought the votes they needed to win in one of the key states, Harrison's own Indiana. In another crucial state, Cleveland's New York, they dealt and bribed their way into an affiliation with Tammany Hall, which was only too glad to devote its machinery to the defeat of the hated reformer from Buffalo. Such dealings were not too difficult, for this was the era some historians have called "The Period of No Decision" in the United States. It was a time when the nation was converting with incredible speed from an agrarian to an urban-industrial culture, when neither party faced up to the growing labor problems of the expanding cities or to the increasing discontent of the farmer. It was a time when the American people and their leaders enjoyed little or no rapport, when many citizens—not through apathy, but with considerable justice—simply did not care which party was in power; some joined splinter parties; the more cynical put their votes up for sale, cheap. Coldly dignified, honest, but absolutely colorless, Benjamin Harrison was proud of his country's industrial growth but un-

This portrait of Benjamin Harrison hangs near one of his grandfather, William Henry, in the Harrison Memorial Home in Indiana.

This lithograph of Harrison's birthplace at North Bend, Ohio, was made from an oil painting done in 1840.

responsive to the social problems it created. He was above all else a party man, and in those days Republicans regarded party loyalty as tantamount to patriotism. Once he found himself in the office that Providence (and/or Matt Quay) had given him, however, he sincerely tried to do the job. He willingly sacrificed his own popularity and the trust of his party, but he was just the wrong man in the wrong place at the wrong time. As Acting Attorney General William Howard Taft put it in 1890: "The President is not popular with the members of either house. His manner of treating them is not at all fortunate, and when they have an interview with him they generally come away mad. . . . I think this is exceedingly unfortunate, because I am sure we have never had a man in the White House who was more conscientiously seeking to do his duty."

Benjamin Harrison had had a political apprenticeship the equal of which few men could boast. Service to the nation was in his genes: his great-grandfather, also named Benjamin Harrison, had been a signer of the Declaration of Independence; his grandfather, William Henry Harrison, had been a military hero, congressman, senator, diplomat, and, briefly, President of the United States; his father, John S. Harrison, had been a member of the House of Representatives. (Indeed, the Harrison family's record of participation in government is equaled by few in the United States; a twentieth-century William Henry Harrison, grandson of the twenty-third President, has served as a congressman from Wyoming several times since 1951.)

Benjamin Harrison was born on August 20, 1833, on his grandfather's estate at North Bend, Ohio, not far from Cincinnati. He was the second son born to John Scott and Elizabeth Irwin Harrison, but he grew up with two older half sisters, children of his father's earlier marriage. Both scholarly and athletic, young Harrison had a private tutor but attended the country school as well.

Although Scott Harrison was hard hit by recurring bad times in the forties, he sent Benjamin and another son to Farmers' College in Cincinnati in 1847. After three years, Benjamin transferred to Ohio's Miami University, the "Yale of the West." He graduated with distinction in 1852 and the next year married a girl he had met there, Caroline Scott. After two years of law studies with a firm in Cincinnati, Harrison moved with his wife to the growing city of Indianapolis.

Of his early days in the Hoosier capital Harrison later recalled, "They were close times. . . . A $5 bill was an event." Steadily, however, the young lawyer began to make a name for himself. A neighbor, Dr. John M. Kitchen, remembered Harrison as "kindly, agreeable and studious, reserved even then, but attracting persons to him by his intellectual qualities. He was a man of notably clear character and made a success of everything he undertook. . . . I do not think he ever had an acquaintance with anyone that ripened into the hottest kind of friendship."

In early 1855, William Wallace, a young attorney with political ambitions, approached Harrison and proposed that they become partners. For Wallace it meant freedom to campaign for the office of clerk of Marion County without neglecting his growing practice, and for Harrison it meant the clientele he had lacked. Wallace lost the election, but the partnership endured, and after one year the firm was among the most prominent and prosperous in Indianapolis.

Back in Ohio, John Scott Harrison had been twice elected (in 1852 and 1854) to the United States House of Representatives. Although he was a dedicated and hard-working Whig congressman, the elder Harrison had little good to say about the political profession, admonishing his son to stay away from it, from its many "temptations" and "many inducements to stray from the proper path." Nevertheless, Benjamin Harrison was attracted to politics, and to the distress of his father, joined the newly formed Republican party. In 1857 he ran successfully for the office of Indianapolis city attorney and in 1860 became state supreme court reporter.

In July, 1862, when enthusiasm for the Civil War had ebbed, Governor Oliver P. Morton asked Harrison to recruit men for the 70th Indiana Volunteers. Harrison did so and was made colonel of the regiment, which was dispatched to Kentucky to guard the Louisville and Nashville Railroad. He soon realized that his men were soldiers in name only and began to prepare them for battle. There are some men who can apply discipline sternly and retain the respect and even the affection of their men; Harrison was not one of them. His icy coldness and abruptness made him one of the less popular brigade commanders. Still, his record was good, and the performance of his men during the Atlanta Campaign proved his abilities. By the war's end he was a brigadier general.

After the war Harrison returned to his practice and almost immediately became one of the most sought-after lawyers in Indiana. He had a superb memory, the ability to analyze and make sense of a mass of facts and figures at a glance, and a knack for making eloquent, expressive presentations in court. If he was aloof in public, he was affectionate and good-natured at home, devoted to his wife and two children. In appearance he was short—about five feet seven inches—red-bearded, blue-eyed, and fair; his stocky frame moved quickly and was generally attired fashionably.

Although the retired general did not immediately re-enter politics, he remained interested in public affairs and was particularly active in philanthropic activities. He was a religious man: an elder in the Presbyterian church, he taught a Bible class for men and

The photograph above, taken when Harrison was in college, indicates his early fondness for beards.

was superintendent of a Sunday school. Then, in 1872, Harrison received some support for the Republican nomination for governor of Indiana, but Governor Oliver Morton blocked him. Morton, it seemed, was afraid that Harrison's candidacy "would lift him into dangerous prominence." Four years later, however, when the regular Republican candidate was exposed by the Democrats as having a corrupt record, the Republicans replaced him on their ticket with the highly regarded Harrison. In a hard-fought campaign, Harrison lost to James Douglas Williams, although he ran ahead of the ticket throughout the state.

In 1880, Harrison, who was the chairman of the Indiana delegation to the Republican National Convention, was instrumental in securing the presidential nomination for James A. Garfield. Garfield offered him a Cabinet post, but Harrison had been elected that same year to the United States Senate, where he preferred to serve.

Until this point in his career, Benjamin Harrison was notable for his independence, professional competence, and intelligence. He had been, from the start, a good, steady, dependable Republican, but he had not been predictable. A radical in the matter of Reconstruction during Andrew Johnson's ill-fated administration, he had at the same time been a conservative in economic matters. Governor Morton had objected to Harrison's resistance to being "handled." But Hoosier Republicans were disunited, and Harrison, committed to no one faction, seemed just the man to unite the party. When he announced that he would like a Senate seat (legislatures at that time elected senators), the Republican Indiana legislature responded favorably, for Harrison had earned its support.

Having taken his Senate seat, Harrison retained his independence. While generally aligning himself with the moderate wing of his party (the "Half-Breeds"), he remained a fiscal conservative. He favored the programs Republicans favored but favored them only to what he thought was a "reasonable" extent: he was for a protective tariff, so long as it was reasonable; he supported reasonable labor legislation, reasonable railroad regulation, reasonable pensions for veterans. If he departed from the norm at all, it was, to his credit, usually a humanitarian departure. He was, for example, sympathetic to the problems of the Indians and the homesteaders and defied his big-money-dominated party by supporting legislation protecting them from the railroads; and he voted against the Chinese exclusion bill (apparently on constitutional grounds).

During the first Cleveland administration, the Democrats, who had finally pulled

BENJAMIN HARRISON HOME

"Harrison, by God, I'll make you a Brigadier for this fight," said Joe Hooker during the Atlanta Campaign; and in 1865 Harrison was promoted.

alongside the Republicans in national strength, gained control of the Indiana legislature, gerrymandered the state, and defeated Harrison's effort to retain his Senate seat in 1886.

Early in 1888 James G. Blaine announced from Europe that he would not be a candidate for the Presidency again, despite the fact that Cleveland's unpopular tariff made him an eminently beatable opponent. Many of Blaine's supporters rallied behind Harrison, but they had a difficult time convincing him that he was responsible for publicizing his own candidacy. Finally, on Washington's Birthday, he traveled to Detroit, where he more or less officially declared himself available. Before the Michigan Club, he said: "I am a dead statesman ["*No! No!*" protested the audience], but I am a living and a rejuvenated Republican. . . ." The speech was given national press coverage, was called "one of his greatest" orations, and made the expression "rejuvenated Republicanism" the catch phrase of the Harrison drive for the nomination. In a Chicago speech four weeks later, he recalled his Civil War experiences and reminded the nation that the Republican party had taken "the ship of state when there was treachery at the helm, when there was mutiny on the deck, when the ship was among the rocks, and we put loyalty at the helm. . . ." From then on he was General Harrison to the nation—the war-hero grandson of Old Tippecanoe.

At the Chicago convention the presence of James G. Blaine, who was in Scotland, was nevertheless felt. Through the first several ballots, favorite-son candidates were not withdrawn, for the delegates were waiting to hear from Blaine. Then word came from Scotland: Blaine wanted Harrison. He was nominated on the eighth ballot. His running mate was Levi P. Morton of New York.

The American people spoke, but the electoral college spoke louder, and Benjamin Harrison, who received some 90,000 fewer votes than Cleveland, was elected President of the United States. On their way to victory the Republicans contracted so many debts that the possibility of clean-slate ad-

This campaign kerchief shows how determinedly the Republicans meant to protect "infant industries."

ministration was all but destroyed. Harrison had made civil service reform a major campaign issue, but once installed in the White House, he could not follow through on his pledges. The bulk of the Republican party's four-million-dollar campaign fund had been supplied through the influence and intervention of John Wanamaker, the "merchant prince" of Philadelphia. Wanamaker was rewarded with the Postmaster Generalship, and although Harrison had said that "only the interest of the public service should suggest removals from office," Wanamaker permitted the removal of all the Democrats in his department—thirty thousand in the first year. The President even suspended civil service guidelines established by Cleveland, replaced Democratic officeholders with Republicans, and then reinstated the rules. And yet Harrison's meager efforts to reform the service were enough to earn the animosity of Quay and many other Republican regulars, though not nearly enough to win friends among the reformers.

Part of the Republican strategy during the campaign had been to concentrate in the doubtful states on Civil War veterans, who were numerous enough to swing the vote to Harrison. The strategy had worked principally because the Republicans had pledged liberal pensions. Harrison made good the pledge by appointing James Tanner pension commissioner. Interpreting existing legislation in the most liberal manner, Tanner doled out millions more Treasury dollars than had Cleveland's commissioner, and as though that were not enough, Congress passed in 1890 a pension act that awarded still more liberal benefits to veterans (anyone who had served in the Union army ninety days or more qualified) unable to do manual labor—regardless of the cause of disability. Therefore, almost any veteran suffering from old age was eligible. Widows, orphans, and dependent parents of veterans were also given pensions.

In some respects President Harrison was sensitively tuned to his times; in others he was impervious to them. The Industrial Revolution had given way to the Industrial Age; Harrison knew that business—from the gathering of raw materials to manufacturing, distribution, financing, and international trade—was now responsible for the health and wealth of the country. He understood that business was leading the United States—and the other great powers of the world—toward an age of imperialism, and he was proud of the big new Navy and merchant marine fleets being built under Secretary of the Navy Benjamin F. Tracy. But there were social problems that Harrison did not—or could not—appreciate.

First there was the farmer, trying to hold on to his disappearing way of life. The railroads had opened up the width of the continent; by the end of the Civil War, homesteaders farmed the soil from ocean to ocean. But from that point onward, American economics had become industry- and urban-oriented. In 1887, when the land-speculation boom was halted by drought, insects, an early frost, and dollar deflation, the *Progressive Farmer*, a North Carolina journal, noted that there was "a screw loose" in America's new industrial economy: "The railroads have never been so prosperous, and yet agriculture languishes. . . . Towns and cities flourish and 'boom' . . . and yet agriculture languishes. Salaries and fees were never so temptingly high and desirable, and yet agriculture languishes."

Then there was the laborer, who represented the wave of the future. Harrison's administration was part of that incredible period (1880–1910) during which eighteen million immigrants entered the United States. These people not only helped form the great labor class in the United States; their continuing arrival created a gigantic labor issue, for many American workers feared their competition.

It was this great mass of Americans—farmers and laborers—that the administration (indeed, both political parties) ignored.

Hawaii's Queen Liliuokalani (left) opposed American annexation of her kingdom in the early 1890's.

And it was the realization among the people that they were being ignored that created "The Period of No Decision." There was simply nothing for the voters to choose from, nothing in government on which to decide. Harrison did not create this era or its problems, but he did typify the government mentality that avoided the problems and allowed them to smolder for years to come.

And yet the politicians knew that the farmers and workers existed. During the election campaign of 1888 both parties had pledged to do something about the control of trusts and monopolies. In 1890 Congress passed (almost unanimously) the Sherman Antitrust Act, which gave the federal courts power to prevent "conspiracy, in restraint of trade or commerce" and made the forming of a monopoly or "attempt to monopolize" a crime. The trouble with this bill was that "trust" and "monopoly" were never really defined. Ironically, the act was employed most effectively against labor unions.

Even if the Sherman Antitrust Act had actually been intended as corporation-control legislation—which it had not—the administration more than offset its passage by supporting the McKinley Tariff. Drafted by Representative William McKinley of Ohio, the tariff raised duties on dry goods and foodstuffs but removed the rates on sugar (to the benefit of the Sugar Trust). Moreover, it maintained a low tariff on the raw-material imports needed by the iron and steel industries. Prices were raised throughout the country; the consumer outcry was frantic but futile.

The Farmers' Alliances, a union of farm groups that was the forerunner of the Populist party, had long held that the deflation that had cost the farmer so much could be reversed by the free and unlimited coinage of silver. (It was argued, probably correctly, that free silver—regulated by the government, not banks—would stabilize the price of silver and keep much more money in circulation, thus inflating the dollar.) The Bland-Allison Act of 1878 had provided for some silver coinage, but for the most part, American bank notes were based on a gold standard. When, in 1889, the omnibus bill admitted Montana, Washington, and the Dakotas to the Union, the Farmers' Alliances' strength was increased in Congress; and in June, 1890, the Senate passed a free silver coinage bill, but the House blocked its passage. The Westerners then threatened to vote against the McKinley Tariff, which was pending at the same time, and finally negotiated a compromise with the Eastern conservatives: the tariff and the Sherman Silver-Purchase Act were both passed. While not providing for unlimited silver coinage, the silver act did require the Treasury to purchase 4,500,000 ounces of silver monthly and made bank notes payable in gold or silver at the discretion of the Treasury. But, because financiers were afraid of the effects of the act and would not loosen money, deflation was unchecked and nothing was proved.

If Benjamin Harrison's role in these affairs seems understated, it is because his role was in fact small. He had filled his Cabinet with businessmen, and the Republican National Committee seemed to run the government. Though he was not successful at civil service reform, his attempts annoyed Matt Quay and Thomas Brackett Reed of Maine (the "Czar" of the House of Representatives), both of whom helped form an anti-Harrison wing in the party. Reed, despite occasional opposition from the President, continued to encourage lavish spending; Harrison's administration saw the first peacetime "Billion-Dollar Congress."

"A statesman," Reed is supposed to have said, "is a successful politician who is dead." Nevertheless, it was in the field of foreign affairs that the almost politically dead Harrison established his most statesmanly record. James G. Blaine, his Secretary of State, concentrated on bettering Pan-American relations. His most notable achievement was the formation of the International Bureau of American Republics—later renamed the Pan-American Union. Harrison not only supported Blaine in all his policies but often had to implement them himself, for the Secretary of State was ill during much of his term.

Harrison also coped wisely with two international incidents. In 1890 eleven suspected Mafia members were held, acquitted, and then lynched for the murder of the New Orleans police chief who had been investigating the Black Hand. Italy protested (three of the victims were Italian nationals) and could not understand the State Department's explanation that the affair was the province of the state of Louisiana, not of the federal government. The Italians removed their minister from the United States; the American ambassador left Italy; but Harrison concluded the incident with the payment of $25,000 to the Italian government.

During the Chilean civil war of 1891, the United States temporarily held a rebel vessel in San Diego, where it had picked up an arms shipment. Although the vessel was soon released, Chilean resentment toward the United States was high. In October a group of American sailors was attacked by a mob in Valparaiso, and two were killed. A series of indignant notes were exchanged, each demanding an apology for the last. On January 25, 1892, Harrison ended the matter by asking Congress, in so many words, for a declaration of war. Chile promptly apologized and paid an indemnity of $75,000.

The manifest destiny theory of American expansion was briefly, and unsuccessfully, reborn in the Harrison administration. When Queen Liliuokalani of Hawaii ascended to the throne in 1891, she renounced the pro-American constitution of 1887 and assumed autocratic power. American planter Sanford Dole and United States Minister John L. Stevens ordered Marines to be landed to "protect" American property. Without authorization from the State Department, Stevens recognized the "revolutionary" administration of Dole, took over the government buildings, and declared the islands an American protectorate. Harrison acknowledged the treaty of annexation, but the Senate did nothing about it. President Cleveland later withdrew it.

The Democrats had gained overwhelming control of the House of Representatives in the election of 1890. Yet, two years later, the prospect of winning re-election seemed not impossible to Harrison. The Democrats had nominated Cleveland again, but the outcome of the election was unpredictable because of the new Populist party. With some help from city labor groups, the farmers were finally in open revolt. They created a platform demanding free coinage of silver, a government-controlled flexible currency system, a graduated income tax, immigration restriction, prohibition of land ownership by aliens, public ownership of telegraphs, telephones, and railroads, an eight-hour workday for laborers, and the direct election of senators. The Populist candidate, James B. Weaver, had little chance of winning; yet it was obvious that the Populists were strong and that their votes, added to the total of either major party candidate, would probably produce victory.

After a quiet, unexciting campaign, Cleveland won by almost four hundred thousand votes and by an electoral count of 277 to 145. The Populists received over a million votes and were soon absorbed into the Democratic party.

Benjamin Harrison returned to his Indianapolis law practice, wrote a great deal, and remained a moderate voice in his party's affairs. In 1899 he accepted a commission from Venezuela and became its chief counsel in a boundary dispute with Great Britain. He worked on the case for two years, and while he was delivering his twenty-five-hour-long closing argument before the arbitration tribunal in Paris, the English representative is said to have sent a message preparing his superiors for a judgment favorable to Venezuela.

In his last years, Harrison spoke out often on the subject of the obligations of the wealthy and became more dubious about the wisdom of imperialism. In 1896 he had married a niece of his wife's (who had died in 1892). He was still healthy and vigorous and enjoyed once again the pleasures of fatherhood; his daughter was born in 1897. Then, in 1901, he contracted pneumonia and died at Indianapolis on March 13.

—DAVID JACOBS

Benj Harrison

A PICTURE PORTFOLIO

Thomas Nast introduced the elephant and the donkey in the 1870's, but both parties still experimented with symbols. In 1888 the old Democratic rooster was crowing for the G.O.P.

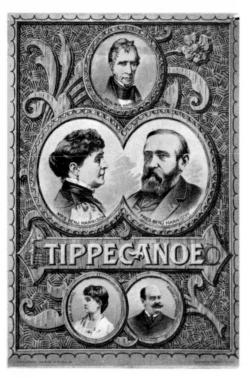

*During the presidential campaign of 1888 a voter could re-
flect the candidates' current relative popularity or predict the
outcome of the race by tipping the above scale in favor of
Harrison (the figurine at left) or Cleveland. A majority chose
Cleveland, but Harrison won the electoral vote, nevertheless.*

*Harrison was not above using family associations to make political hay. Covers of writing tablets, such as the one at
left from the 1892 campaign, gave top billing to William H. Harrison, hero of Tippecanoe; beneath the President
and Mrs. Harrison are their children, Russell and Mary Harrison McKee. William Henry had been a successful
"log cabin" candidate, so in 1888 his grandson used mock log cabins (below) as his campaign headquarters.*

"THE ELECTION EXPENSES"

LEVI P. MORTON

Parties are not built up by deportment, or by ladies' magazines, or gush!" said Roscoe Conkling. Parties were organized—and maintained—by machines whose wheels were oiled by a constant flow of cash; if Benjamin Harrison ever doubted that fact he became aware of its veracity when he assumed the Presidency. He was nominated by the Republicans because he was an inoffensive lawyer from a crucial state—Indiana—with a solid military and political background. But when the machine began to move, Harrison was the passenger, not the driver. Big business, faced with tariff reductions should Cleveland be re-elected, was a natural ally, so the Republicans were able to "put the manufacturers . . . under the fire and fry all the fat out of them." The campaign fund manager was W. W. Dudley, who, it was said, had no peer "in the effective use of money for the purchase of purchasable votes. . . ." Matt Quay bargained for the support of the Knights of Labor; some manufacturers threatened their workers with unemployment should Harrison lose. In critical New York Democratic leaders were wooed and won. "Migrations" of voters to Indiana were facilitated by Pennsylvania Railroad freight trains. When the British minister foolishly told an inquirer who claimed to be an English-born naturalized American to vote for Cleveland, the advice was published and the Irish vote went solidly for Harrison. (The diplomat had been duped, but it was too late for the Democrats to do anything about it.) "When I came into power," Harrison was to reflect, "I found that the party managers had taken it all to themselves. . . . They had sold out every place to pay the election expenses."

Levi P. Morton was a Wall Street banker with a scant six years' experience in politics when he received the Republican vice presidential nomination in 1888. The son of a Vermont pastor, he had entered business as a storekeeper in New Hampshire, became head of a New York wholesale house in 1855, and established his own banking firm eight years later. An eminently successful businessman, he was soon an international figure in the world of finance. In 1879, at the age of fifty-five, he entered politics as a United States representative from New York. After one term he was offered the Republican nomination for the Vice Presidency but declined on the advice of Senator Roscoe Conkling. Upon Garfield's election, however, he was appointed minister to France, where his diplomatic duties during four years included the acceptance of Bartholdi's Statue of Liberty. Defeated for the Senate in 1885 and 1887, he accepted the party's second offer of the Vice Presidency in 1888. Elected to office with Harrison, he presided over the Senate for four years with scrupulous fairness and nonpartisan objectivity. In 1895 he became governor of New York. An advocate of civil service reform, he governed ably and independently, resisting all efforts of domination by Thomas C. Platt and New York's other party bosses. Resigning from office in 1897, he returned to business and established the Morton Trust Company.

"GOD HELP
THE SURPLUS!"

The ideal, or even my own ideal," said President Benjamin Harrison at his inaugural, "I shall probably not attain." His candid remark proved to be an understatement. During Grover Cleveland's administration the Republicans had been the "outs" for the first time since 1861, and the party's leaders were famished for the spoils denied them. "God help the Surplus!" cried Pension Commissioner James Tanner, and soon Congress passed a sixty-million-dollar-a-year disability act benefiting—as one jubilant ex-soldier put it —all veterans "whose conditions of health are not practically perfect." New lords meant new thanes, and heads rolled in all departments overseen by members of Harrison's "Businessmen's Cabinet." Theodore Roosevelt of New York was appointed to the Civil Service Commission, but his efforts at reform were continually frustrated, and he referred to the President as "the little grey man." J. P. Morgan blithely organized his gentlemen's agreement among the railroad barons, although, as historian Matthew Josephson has written, "the ink had scarcely dried on the Interstate Commerce Act." Despite sweeping off-year election gains by the Democrats, the Speaker of the House, "Czar" Thomas Reed of Maine, maintained an iron-fisted rule. When Democratic congressmen, trying to prevent a quorum, would not answer roll calls, Reed had their names recorded as "present and refusing to vote." Reed also killed a sorely needed White House renovation and rebuilding bill advocated by Mrs. Harrison because the President had failed to appoint a Reed man to a collectorship in Portland, Maine.

At top right is a photograph of the First Lady, Caroline Scott Harrison, who died in the White House in 1892. Below her is a steer-horn chair that was presented to Harrison as a gift. His name is spelled out on its back in small diamonds.

BENJAMIN HARRISON HOME

Far from the problems of the White House, Harrison poses (above) with the bag from a day's duckhunting. The stogie in his hand was not atypic; an Indianapolis tobacconist kept the President supplied with cigars.

INNOVATORS

CULVER PICTURES

LIBRARY OF CONGRESS

TERENCE V. POWDERLY

Terence V. Powderly led the Knights of Labor from 1879 to 1893, when the group rose and fell as the nation's mightiest labor organization. A reformer fired by liberal concepts instilled by prior union activity in his native Pennsylvania, Powderly advocated government control of monopolies and trusts and government ownership of public utilities. He urged currency reform and felt the wage system should be supplanted by workers' cooperatives that would "own and operate mines, factories, and railroads." Although the Knights officially shunned strikes and violence (preferring arbitration), membership in the mid-eighties grew to 729,000 on the strength of successful railroad strikes. Other strikes were failures, however, and the collapse of an eight-hour-day movement in Chicago and public disapproval of the Haymarket Massacre led to the decline of the Knights' influence. Powderly, who had been called a Communist by the conservative press, served three terms as mayor of Scranton on the Greenback-Labor ticket, but by 1894 he supported the Republican party and in 1897 became commissioner general of immigration under McKinley. From 1907 until 1921, three years before he died, he headed the Division of Information of the Immigration Bureau. Powderly wrote *Thirty Years of Labor, 1859–1889* and the autobiographical *The Path I Trod*.

SUSAN B. ANTHONY

Devoted to social reform in general and woman suffrage in particular, Susan B. Anthony once said that she "would ignore all law to help the slave" and "ignore it all to protect an enslaved woman." Susan was a strong-willed, precocious child of Quaker background, who learned to read and write at the age of three. Like many women reformers of her day, she began her career as a teacher. At her home in Rochester, New York, she came in contact with such notable reformers as William Lloyd Garrison and William Ellery Channing and formed a lasting alliance with feminist Elizabeth Cady Stanton. Taking up the temperance movement, she helped to organize the first women's temperance society in 1852; she was also among the first to advocate Negro suffrage and unsuccessfully attempted to extend the franchise to women through the Fourteenth Amendment. Concentrating on women's rights, she helped to found the National Woman Suffrage Association in 1869 and served as president of its successor organization from 1892 to 1900. Opposition to the movement was widespread: in 1872 she was arrested and fined for voting in an election, and her lecture tours were often met with taunts, jeers, and flying objects. Undaunted, she continued her campaign, and before her death in 1906 she had won the battle for equal rights for women in four states.

BOOKER T. WASHINGTON

When Booker T. Washington dined with Teddy Roosevelt at the White House in 1910, a Southern newspaper called it "a crime equal to treason." Washington, typically modest, said, "Mr. Roosevelt simply found he could spare the time best during and after the dinner hour. . . ." Twenty years earlier, the ex-slave had helped found a Negro normal school at Tuskegee, Alabama, beginning, as he recalled it, with "a dilapidated shanty" and forty pupils. The institute had grown and would continue to grow; when Washington died in 1915 his teaching and public relations efforts had developed a community of over a hundred buildings (many student-built) on nearly thirty thousand acres with an endowment of almost two million dollars. Washington had toiled in salt furnaces and coal mines as a boy in West Virginia; eventually he worked his way through Hampton Institute, graduating in 1875. By the mid-1890's he was the leader of the American Negro community, always stressing pacific paths—industrial education and self-improvement—to gaining the franchise. Denounced as an "Uncle Tom" by radical Negroes, he realistically held that, at the time, "agitation of questions of social equality is the extremist folly." The most famous of his many books are *Up From Slavery* and *My Larger Education*, and a biography of Frederick Douglass.

SAMUEL GOMPERS

In 1877, after seeing fellow New York City cigar makers fail in a disjointed strike to improve their lot, Samuel Gompers began to weld his trade's many unions into a single organization. An official hierarchy was established; increased dues resulted in a permanent union fund; fringe benefits were planned. The union was a prototype: by 1886 other skilled-worker groups had united internally and joined the cigar makers. Gompers would be president of this American Federation of Labor continuously, except for 1895, until his death in 1924. Born in a London tenement, Gompers was a pragmatist: he sought higher wages and shorter hours "to increase the workingman's welfare year by year." Solidarity was the keystone. Gompers felt that there should be only one union for each American trade—and with no "dual unionism" there could be no pool of strikebreakers to thwart A.F. of L. demands for concessions. Gompers did not agree with those who thought labor could eventually take over management, and this attitude enabled him to negotiate successfully with capitalists. During World War I, Gompers organized the War Committee on Labor, having already been a member of President Wilson's Council of National Defense. Gompers' two-volume *Seventy Years of Life and Labor* remains a significant account of the American labor movement.

591

THE WHEELS STOP

When Benjamin Harrison finally began to assert his executive authority, he contributed inevitably to a party schism. He saw to Quay's ouster from the Republican National Committee, and when J. S. Clarkson, "headsman" of the Postal Department, retired, Harrison sharply increased the number of civil servants under the merit system. His resurgent probity—and his cold, pious manner—were branded "Sunday-school politics" by Quay, who, with boss Thomas Platt, formed an anti-Harrison wing. As H. L. Stoddard, a journalist, noted: "No threats are made, no open opposition shown, but the President suddenly discovers that the wheels are not turning. . . . Nominees are not confirmed . . . departments don't function. . . . There is an inertia that . . . creeps over everything like an incoming tide." Capitalists, souring on Harrison, turned to the Democrats as "the party of business." Although the President was renominated in 1892, it was certain that he would be opposing Cleveland without the machine's power and money. As a droll observer of that campaign wryly noted, "each side would have been glad to defeat the other if it could do so without electing its own candidate." But Harrison had had enough. Approached in 1896 to run again, he echoed many a predecessor: "Why should a man seek that which to him would be a calamity?"

Harrison's term saw over five million acres in Oklahoma opened to settlers, and the rushes were usually chaotic. One protested eviction in 1889 (above) forced a local claims arbitration board to resign. In the 1892 cartoon at right Harrison is depicted as too small to wear his grandfather's hat. Boss James Blaine, Harrison's Secretary of State, perched atop a bust of William Henry, croaks "Nevermore," scuttling Harrison's re-election hopes.

FACTS IN SUMMARY: BENJAMIN HARRISON

CHRONOLOGY

UNITED STATES		HARRISON
	1833	*Born August 20*
Rise of Whig party	1834	
Van Buren elected President	1836	
William Henry Harrison elected President	1840	
Tyler becomes President	1841	
Polk elected President	1844	
Annexation of Texas	1845	
War with Mexico begins	1846	
Battle of Buena Vista	1847	*Enters Farmers' College*
Treaty of Guadalupe Hidalgo	1848	
Taylor elected President		
Fillmore becomes President	1850	*Enters Miami University in Ohio*
Compromise of 1850		
Pierce elected President	1852	*Graduates from Miami University*
Gadsden Purchase	1853	*Marries Caroline Scott*
Kansas-Nebraska Act	1854	*Admitted to the bar*
		Moves to Indianapolis
	1855	*Becomes law partner of William Wallace*
		Becomes notary public
		Appointed commissioner for the court of claims
Buchanan elected President	1856	*Joins Republican party*
Dred Scott decision	1857	*Elected city attorney*
Lincoln-Douglas debates	1858	
John Brown's raid at Harpers Ferry	1859	
Lincoln elected President	1860	*Elected state supreme court reporter*
South Carolina secedes		
Fort Sumter fired upon	1861	*Forms law firm with William Fishback*
First Battle of Bull Run		*Appointed elder of Presbyterian Church*
Battle of Shiloh	1862	*Commissioned second lieutenant*
Battle of Antietam		*Promoted to captain*
Battle of Fredericksburg		*Commissioned a colonel*
Emancipation Proclamation	1863	
Battle of Chancellorsville		
Gettysburg Campaign		
Sherman's march to the sea	1864	*Fights at Nashville*
Battle of Nashville		
Lee surrenders	1865	*Promoted to brigadier general*
Lincoln assassinated		
Thirteenth Amendment ratified		
	1867	*Returns to law practice*

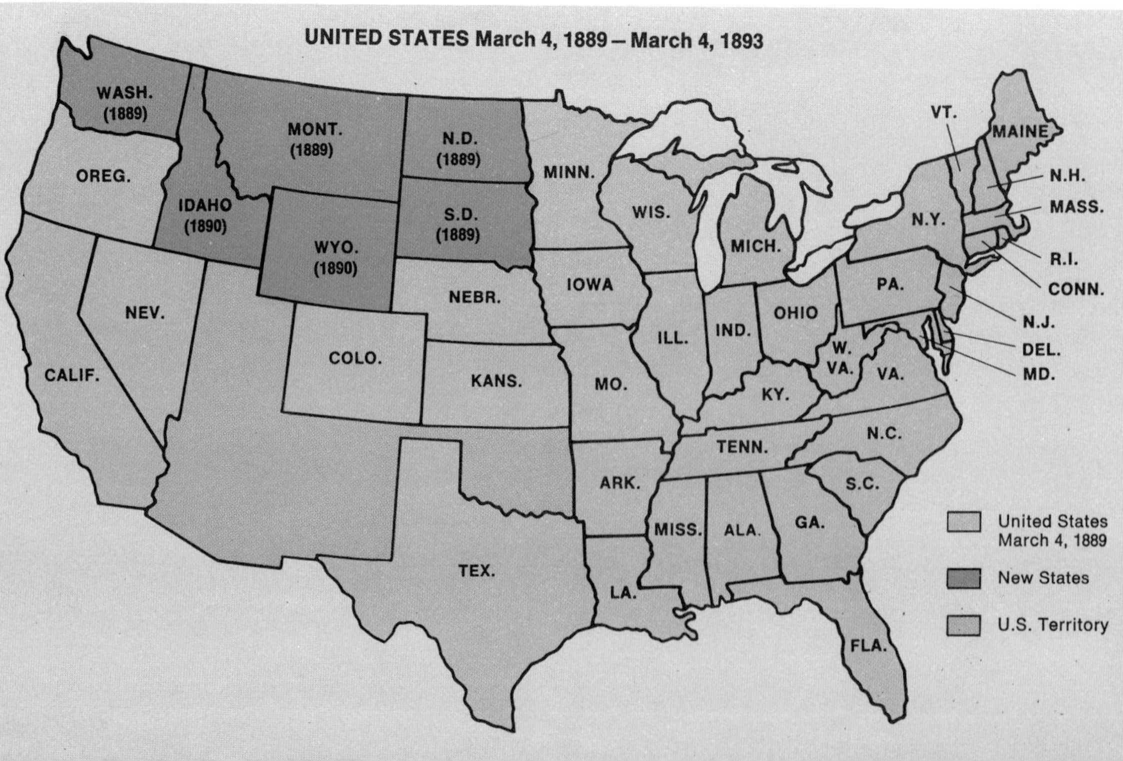
UNITED STATES March 4, 1889 – March 4, 1893
WASH. (1889)
OREG.
IDAHO (1890)
MONT. (1889)
WYO. (1890)
N.D. (1889)
S.D. (1889)
NEV.
CALIF.
COLO.
NEBR.
KANS.
TEX.
MINN.
IOWA
MO.
ARK.
LA.
WIS.
ILL.
MICH.
IND.
OHIO
KY.
TENN.
MISS.
ALA.
GA.
FLA.
S.C.
N.C.
VA.
W. VA.
PA.
N.Y.
VT.
MAINE
N.H.
MASS.
R.I.
CONN.
N.J.
DEL.
MD.
United States March 4, 1889
New States
U.S. Territory

Johnson impeached	1868	
Grant elected President		
Grant re-elected	1872	
	1876	*Loses gubernatorial race*
Hayes elected President	1877	
Bland-Allison Act	1878	
Garfield elected President	1880	
Arthur becomes President	1881	*Elected U.S. senator*
Pendleton Act	1883	
Cleveland elected President	1884	
	1886	*Defeated in bid for re-election*
	1888	*Elected President*
Omnibus bill	1889	
Dependent Pension Act	1890	
Sherman Antitrust Act		
Sherman Silver-Purchase Act		
Cleveland elected President	1892	*Asks Congress to declare war on Chile*
		Caroline Harrison dies
		Defeated in bid for re-election
Cleveland withdraws Hawaii annexation treaty	1893	*Sends Senate treaty annexing Hawaii*
		Returns to Indianapolis
McKinley elected President	1896	*Marries Mary Dimmick*
	1901	*Dies March 13*

BIOGRAPHICAL FACTS

BIRTH: North Bend, Ohio, Aug. 20, 1833

ANCESTRY: English-Scotch

FATHER: John Scott Harrison; b. Vincennes, Ind., Oct. 4, 1804; d. North Bend, Ohio, May 25, 1878

FATHER'S OCCUPATIONS: Farmer; U.S. congressman

MOTHER: Elizabeth Irwin Harrison; b. Mercersburg, Pa., July 18, 1810; d. Aug. 15, 1850

BROTHERS: Archibald Irwin (1832–1870); Carter Bassett (1840–1905); John Scott, Jr. (1844–1926); James Friedlay (1847–1848); James Irwin (1849–1850)

SISTERS: Mary Jane Irwin (1835–1867); Anna Symmes (1842–1926)

HALF SISTERS: Elizabeth Short (1825–1904); Sarah Lucretia (1829–?)

FIRST WIFE: Caroline ("Carrie") Scott; b. Oxford, Ohio, Oct. 1, 1832; d. Washington, D.C., Oct. 25, 1892

FIRST MARRIAGE: Oxford, Ohio, Oct. 20, 1853

SECOND WIFE: Mary Scott Lord Dimmick; b. Honesdale, Pa., April 30, 1858; d. New York, N.Y., Jan. 5, 1948

SECOND MARRIAGE: New York, N.Y., April 6, 1896

CHILDREN: Russell Benjamin (1854–1936); Mary Scott (1858–1930); Elizabeth (1898–1955)

EDUCATION: Private tutoring; attended Farmers' College; graduated (B.A. 1852) from Miami University

HOME: Indianapolis, Indiana

RELIGIOUS AFFILIATION: Presbyterian

OCCUPATIONS BEFORE PRESIDENCY: Lawyer; notary public; soldier

MILITARY SERVICE: Appointed col. in 70th Indiana Volunteers (1862); resigned as brevet brig. gen. in 1865

PRE-PRESIDENTIAL OFFICES: Commissioner for the Court of Claims; City Attorney; Secretary of Indiana Republican Central Committee; State Supreme Court Reporter; Member of U.S. Senate

POLITICAL PARTY: Republican

AGE AT INAUGURATION: 55

OCCUPATION AFTER PRESIDENCY: Lawyer

DEATH: Indianapolis, Ind., March 13, 1901

PLACE OF BURIAL: Crown Hill Cemetery, Indianapolis, Indiana

ELECTION OF 1888

CANDIDATES	ELECTORAL VOTE	POPULAR VOTE
Benjamin Harrison Republican	233	5,447,129
Grover Cleveland Democratic	168	5,537,857
Clinton B. Fisk Prohibition	—	249,506

THE HARRISON ADMINISTRATION

INAUGURATION: March 4, 1889; the Capitol, Washington, D.C.

VICE PRESIDENT: Levi P. Morton

SECRETARY OF STATE: James G. Blaine; John W. Foster (from June 29, 1892)

SECRETARY OF THE TREASURY: William Windom; Charles Foster (from Feb. 24, 1891)

SECRETARY OF WAR: Redfield Proctor; Stephen B. Elkins (from Dec. 24, 1901)

ATTORNEY GENERAL: William H. H. Miller

POSTMASTER GENERAL: John Wanamaker

SECRETARY OF THE NAVY: Benjamin F. Tracy

SECRETARY OF THE INTERIOR: John W. Noble

SECRETARY OF AGRICULTURE: Jeremiah M. Rusk

SUPREME COURT APPOINTMENTS: David J. Brewer (1889); Henry B. Brown (1890); George Shiras, Jr. (1892); Howell E. Jackson (1893)

51st CONGRESS (March 4, 1889–March 4, 1891):
Senate: 39 Republicans; 37 Democrats
House: 166 Republicans; 159 Democrats

52nd CONGRESS (March 4, 1891–March 4, 1893):
Senate: 47 Republicans; 39 Democrats; 2 Others
House: 235 Democrats; 88 Republicans; 9 Others

STATES ADMITTED: North Dakota, South Dakota, Montana, Washington (all 1889); Idaho, Wyoming (both 1890)

WILLIAM McKINLEY

Silent crowds watched the coffin pass through the streets of Buffalo, of Washington, and of Canton, Ohio. It was September, 1901, and the more perceptive mourners may have realized that the casket contained not only the body of an assassinated President, but the remains of an era as well. The last Civil War veteran to be elected to the White House, William McKinley had administered a war of his own, and when it was won, the American flag flew halfway around a shrinking globe. At home McKinley had seen the passing of the frontier and had bequeathed to his successor a restless people whose progress could now be measured by smoking steel mills, rising cities, and the growth of giant trusts.

But while the United States under McKinley broke with its past, it had not yet learned to read the signposts pointing to its future. On the day before he was shot, the President told visitors at the Pan-American Exposition at Buffalo: "Isolation is no longer possible or desirable. . . . The period of exclusiveness is past." And yet, despite his vision of international affairs, he did not seem to recognize the implications of the exhibition itself. He looked at the wonderful and mysterious gadgets with a childlike curiosity but without any true understanding of their portents. For the amiable McKinley was a man of the 1800's, not of the turbulent new century of which he saw so little.

William McKinley, Jr., the seventh of nine children of William and Nancy Allison McKinley, was born on January 29, 1843, in Niles, Ohio. A delicate child, he liked school and developed into a keenly observant and taciturn young man. He was religious, intelligent, and diligent, and his mother hoped that he would become a Methodist minister. At seventeen he entered Allegheny College, but had to withdraw after one term because of illness. By the time he recuperated, the family's finances were depleted and he was unable

President McKinley, by Harry T. See

to return to college. Until the outbreak of the Civil War, he taught school and clerked in a post office.

Stirred by his family's abolitionist sympathies and attracted by the excitement and glamour that war seemed to offer, McKinley enlisted in the Twenty-third Ohio Volunteer Infantry Regiment. He performed credibly through some of the bloodiest battles of the war, and his commanding officer, Rutherford B. Hayes, called him "one of the bravest and finest officers in the army."

After the war McKinley studied law for a term, was admitted to the Ohio bar, and then sought a practice in Canton, a county seat. An elderly judge accepted him as a partner and left him his practice. Friendly, handsome, self-assured, and devoid of pomposity or conceit, McKinley moved confidently in Canton's social and professional circles. A Republican, he worked on behalf of his friend Hayes when the latter ran for the Ohio governorship in 1867. McKinley established a reputation as an effective speaker and vigorous campaigner. Two years

McKinley was a handsome lad of eighteen when he enlisted in the Union army as an Ohio volunteer.

later he was nominated for prosecuting attorney of Stark County and won the post.

Clearly an up-and-coming figure in Canton, Major McKinley was the object of many a local girl's attentions. The prosecutor's own affections were centered on the socially prominent Ida Saxton, a fragile but attractive young woman who returned his love. They were married in January, 1871, and their first child, Katherine, was born on Christmas Day of that year. They were a handsome family, captivated by one another, reasonably prosperous and prominent, with a bright future before them. But just before their second child was due in the spring of 1873, Ida's mother died. The new infant, another girl, lived only a few months, and Ida sank into a mental and physical depression from which she never fully rallied. She began to have convulsions, which were accompanied by a loss of consciousness; she remained an epileptic for life and, in addition, suffered from phlebitis. Her love for Katherine might have stimulated a determination to recover, but in 1875 the four-year-old girl died. Ida was unable to reverse the decline of her mind and body. She clung possessively to her husband and insisted that he cater to her every whim. For the rest of his life McKinley bore his painful burden privately and uncomplainingly.

Politics provided the relief he needed. Elected to Congress in 1876 after a vigorous campaign, McKinley moved with his wife to a Washington hotel and struggled to pay her doctors and the bills run up by her expensive tastes. Rutherford B. Hayes was President at the time, and he introduced McKinley to the political elite. The young congressman enjoyed the masculine political world, where his cordial, graceful manner endeared him to his colleagues.

Representative McKinley was regarded as a moderate, even liberal, legislator. He favored civil service reform, Negro suffrage, the interests of the workingman; he opposed the excesses of big business. His consuming interest, however, was the tariff, and he set out to master its many intricacies. He championed protection, convinced that barriers

*Republican capitalist Mark Hanna sits at the head of the table at a dinner party at his home (above).
The Ohio millionaire used every means at his disposal to secure the 1896 presidential nomination for his
friend McKinley (right), whose epileptic wife, Ida (center), always accompanied him to social events.*

to cheap foreign goods would protect the wage scale of the American laborer and the struggling domestic industries. He considered the McKinley Tariff Act of 1890 a great achievement. Its high rates on agricultural products and manufactured goods reflected the protectionist view, although raw sugar was not taxed at all as a favor to the Sugar Trust. The act included a reciprocity arrangement that permitted the President to place duties on certain articles if he felt that nations exporting these items were imposing excessive duties on American goods.

Like most tariff legislation, the McKinley Tariff Act was controversial, but it made its author a well-known figure across the country. At the 1888 presidential nominating convention, where he endorsed the candidacy of Senator John Sherman of Ohio, McKinley refused to allow his name to be placed in nomination as a compromise candidate. But it was at this convention that Marcus A. Hanna resolved that some day McKinley would become President.

Hanna, a millionaire industrialist, was tough, shrewd, and powerful. He was called a kingmaker, but he and McKinley actually needed each other. By this time Congressman McKinley was beginning to have presidential aspirations. Hanna supplied the money and the organization while McKinley maintained his role as an idealistic statesman.

In 1890 a slump in Republican fortunes and a Democratic gerrymander in Ohio cost McKinley his seat in Congress. The next year, financed by Hanna, he ran for the Ohio governorship and was elected by a comfortable margin. The job was a routine one—the state constitution gave the governor little power—and not particularly demanding. Because he left the operation of the party machinery to Hanna, he had free time to spend with Ida, and she demanded all of it. Every day at exactly three o'clock, McKinley stepped to his office window and waved a handkerchief at his wife, who watched from their nearby home. Ida, who spent her time crocheting bedroom slippers (she reportedly made thousands of them), insisted on accompanying her husband to social affairs. He sat beside her at all functions and became adept at acting swiftly at the first sign of an epileptic attack. Quickly he would place a napkin or handkerchief over her convulsed face and retreat with her to another room. The painful scene was enacted countless times in front of embarrassed friends.

As governor, McKinley reformed the Ohio tax structure, which collected disproportionately high taxes on real estate and low taxes on corporations. He dealt with a violent coal miners' strike in 1894 by calling out the National Guard to prevent the min-

599

ers from doing further damage. For the most part, however, he remained a paternalistic champion of the workingman, winning legislative approval of a board to arbitrate labor disputes and raising funds and food for strikers facing starvation.

McKinley's election to the governorship made him a front-runner for the Republican presidential nomination in 1896. But in 1893 his ability to govern the nation suddenly became questionable. An old friend, Robert Walker, had fallen victim to the financial depression and had asked McKinley to sign a seventeen-thousand-dollar note. McKinley agreed, and he continued to sign notes, thinking that the slips Walker was placing before him were renewals of the first pledge; they were, in fact, notes for additional sums. Finally Walker declared bankruptcy, and McKinley found that he had endorsed pledges totaling one hundred and thirty thousand dollars. Mark Hanna came to the rescue. He set up a trust fund and collected money from industrialists, who were reminded how much McKinley had done for business. (The donors received no favors in return for their help.) In addition, thousands of small contributions poured in from Army comrades, workingmen, and storekeepers, who regarded McKinley as an honest victim of hard times.

Later that year, McKinley was re-elected governor by a landslide. Early in 1896, he and Hanna began to prepare for his presidential quest. The depression during the Democratic administration made Republican chances seem bright, but the monetary issue so disrupted the political scene that nothing was completely predictable. McKinley tried to avoid taking a firm stand on this question, speaking out on some occasions in behalf of sound money and espousing bimetallism at other times.

Hanna, meanwhile, was more concerned about the price of delegates than the price of silver. He did not buy votes, but he awed Republican leaders with the most expensive, best-organized campaign seen up to that time. McKinley was assured of the nomination before the delegates had even convened.

Principal interest at the convention centered on what stand the party—and McKinley—would take on the money issue. The country was bitterly divided: some were for free and unlimited coinage of silver whereas others favored a gold standard exclusively. Western Republicans opposed the latter and said that espousal of it would force them out of the party. Nevertheless, McKinley and Hanna decided to declare forthrightly for gold. Their platform stated that the party was "opposed to the free coinage of silver" and that "the existing gold standard must be maintained." McKinley believed that the plank would clinch the East and give him a chance in the Midwest, where industrial workers could be told that a shift to silver would jeopardize business and their jobs. Garret A. Hobart, a New Jersey lawyer, was chosen to be McKinley's running mate.

The silverites dominated the Democratic convention in July, the high point of which was the speech by former Congressman William Jennings Bryan of Nebraska. Beginning quietly, the masterful orator built toward a peroration that thundered defiance: "Having behind us the producing masses of this nation and the world, supported by the commercial interests, the laboring interests and the toilers everywhere, we will answer their demand for a gold standard by saying to them: You shall not press down upon the brow of labor this crown of thorns, you shall not crucify mankind upon a cross of gold." The Democrats chose Bryan as their nominee, as did the prosilver Populist party.

Bryan traveled far, but had very little money to work with. McKinley, on the other hand, ran a heavily financed front-porch campaign. Hanna raised millions of dollars; he spent money lavishly on pamphlets, posters, and buttons, and gave many state delegations train fare to go and see McKinley in Canton. The railroads cooperated by offering reduced rates so that citizens from many states could journey to the home of the Republican candidate. On one day alone, McKinley spoke to some thirty thousand visitors. He won the Presidency in November by an electoral vote of 271 to 176.

One of President McKinley's first orders of business was, predictably, to restore a Republican tariff. In 1894 the Democrats had replaced the McKinley Tariff with the Wilson-Gorman Act. Having called for higher tariffs in his Inaugural Address, McKinley approved the Dingley bill of 1897, which raised rates to new highs, but empowered the President to negotiate tariff concessions with other nations.

But the tariff and other domestic issues were overshadowed during McKinley's Presidency by the prelude to, and the waging and aftermath of, the Spanish-American War. Partially because of the Wilson-Gorman Act, the Cuban sugar market collapsed in 1895, and the Cubans revolted against their Spanish overlords. Rebel leaders resolved to render the island useless to Spain: plantations and ranches were devastated under a scorched-earth policy. The Spanish governor, Valeriano Weyler, brutally herded rural families into garrisoned towns. By the end of 1897 loss of American property in Cuba amounted to sixteen million dollars.

In his Inaugural Address, McKinley had said that he wanted "no wars of conquest; we must avoid the temptation of territorial aggression." And although he was horrified by events in Cuba, he assured Carl Schurz that there would be "no jingo nonsense under my administration." The new rebellion and the destruction of United States property—along with sensational newspaper coverage that inflamed public opinion—worsened the situation, but McKinley, besieged by advice from many quarters, still preferred being called too cautious to being too rash. He gave the Spanish every opportunity to settle their differences with Cuba. The islanders, however, now wanted what Spain would not grant: full independence.

For more than a year McKinley sought a diplomatic solution. Spain refused his offers to mediate, but Governor Weyler was replaced, his policies were modified, and the Spanish ministry promised a degree of autonomy for Cuba. After the Queen Regent extended to the Antilles all rights enjoyed by Spaniards, the President told Congress

GARRET A. HOBART

Rarely had an American Vice President brought to the office ability as great as that of Garret A. Hobart. In the first two years of the McKinley administration, Senator Lodge of Massachusetts noted, Hobart "restored the Vice-Presidency to its proper position." His administrative and organizational skills were those of a brilliant lawyer, politician, and businessman. Having established a law practice in Paterson, New Jersey, in 1866, Hobart entered the state legislature in 1872, became director of several banks and corporations, and by 1895 was one of the leading Republicans in the state. Ironically, his nomination for the second spot in 1896 was due less to his superior qualities of leadership than to the Republicans' desire to carry the traditionally Democratic state of New Jersey. Elected to the Vice Presidency, Hobart presided over the Senate with intelligence and authority, working constantly to improve communications between the Upper House and the Executive. "He keeps tab on everything," remarked the Washington *Post* in admiration. An intimate of President McKinley, Vice President Hobart was, as his biographer David Magie points out, "consulted in all questions of general policy"; his prestige was so great that newspapers sometimes referred to him as the "Assistant President." Hobart died in office in November, 1899, and was mourned by President McKinley and a genuinely grieved Capital city.

that Spain should have a chance to make good its promises.

The Spanish ambassador to the United States, Dupuy de Lôme, was a very able negotiator, but his moderating influence was lost in February, 1898, when the New York *Journal* secured and published a copy of a letter that he had written to a friend in Havana. De Lôme described McKinley as "weak and a bidder for the admiration of the crowd, besides being a would-be politician who tries to leave a door open behind himself while keeping on good terms with the jingoes of his party."

A few days later disaster struck in Havana Harbor. In late January the battleship *Maine* had come to Cuba on a courtesy call. On February 15 an explosion ripped the ship, killing some two hundred and sixty men. A naval court of inquiry reported in March that the *Maine* had been destroyed "by a submarine mine which caused the partial explosion of two or more of the forward magazines." A Spanish commission attributed the disaster to an internal explosion. Of all parties concerned, the Spanish government had the least to gain from the explosion because in the event of war Spanish defeat was almost certain. Cuban rebels, hoping for United States intervention, may have blown up the *Maine*, or it could have been an accident. In any case the American public cast aside all restraint. Trumpeted the Hearst press: "Remember the *Maine* and to hell with Spain!"

In March the President obtained from Congress a defense appropriation of fifty million dollars to use at his discretion. He told Spain that the United States wanted peace brought to Cuba immediately; implicit was a demand that the island be freed. Although Spanish leaders knew Cuba was lost, they regarded defeat in war as more honorable than surrender without a fight.

On April 9 Spain announced that the military governor of Cuba had been directed to suspend hostilities on the island. But since Spain still refused to guarantee ultimate freedom for Cuba, McKinley sent a war message to Congress. The President had no more time to negotiate; it seemed likely that Congress might declare war without waiting for him to request it. He told Congress, "The only hope of relief and repose

The Dingley Tariff of 1897 created a rigid "protection gate" for American industry, but annoyed the English. In this Judge *cartoon, President McKinley listens as John Bull threatens to "build a gate just like yours."*

from a condition which can no longer be endured is the enforced pacification of Cuba. In the name of humanity, in the name of civilization, in behalf of endangered American interests which give us the right and the duty to speak and to act, the war in Cuba must stop." McKinley deeply regretted this final step, but he believed that he had made every reasonable effort to avert war. Congress approved the declaration on April 25, 1898. The New York *Sun* proclaimed, "We are all jingoes now; and the head jingo is the Hon. William McKinley."

The United States Navy was prepared, modernization having proceeded steadily for about fifteen years. In the fall of 1897 McKinley had approved Navy Department plans to station Commodore George Dewey's Pacific fleet in Hong Kong, from where it could strike at the Spanish-held Philippine Islands. With the declaration of war, Dewey's chance came, and on May 1 he sent most of the Spanish fleet to the bottom of Manila Bay. Before the battle, few Americans knew anything about the Philippines; indeed, McKinley himself had to hunt for them on the White House globe. But the nation went wild at the news of victory.

The American assault on Cuba was carried out jointly by the Army and Navy, which was unfortunate in view of the Army's traditional state of unreadiness. Wheezing, potbellied senior officers faltered in the tropical heat. Ill-trained volunteers were rushed into action because the standing army was too small. Troops massing at Tampa, Florida, suffered from shortages of food, water, and medicine while sweltering in winter uniforms. The Army finally landed east of Santiago de Cuba in late June, and after a series of generally uninspired battles (reports to the contrary notwithstanding), pushed the Spanish back toward the city. Meanwhile, Rear Admiral William T. Sampson trapped a Spanish fleet in Santiago Bay. When the fleet attempted to escape on July 3, it was destroyed by American ships. Two weeks later the city surrendered.

On July 25 an American force landed on Puerto Rico. Late that month Spain conceded the futility of continuing the struggle. McKinley stated his terms: independence for Cuba and transfer of Puerto Rico to the United States as a war indemnity; the fate of the Philippines would be decided at a peace conference. Spain accepted these terms on August 12.

Meanwhile, events of lasting importance occurred in the Pacific. In 1897 McKinley had failed to win approval by two-thirds of the Senate of a treaty annexing the Hawaiian Islands. A year later he accomplished the same end by a joint resolution of Congress, which required only a simple majority; Hawaii was formally annexed on August 12. That same summer American forces bound for the Philippines occupied Wake Island and the Spanish island of Guam, which was later ceded to the United States.

The future of the Philippines was clearly the foremost problem at the peace conference. Judge William R. Day, who had served briefly as Secretary of State, headed the United States delegation. He favored annexing one of the islands, which would be used as a naval base. But the decision was up to McKinley, who later said, "I walked the floor of the White House night after night until midnight, and I am not ashamed to tell you . . . that I went down on my knees and prayed Almighty God for light and guidance more than one night. And one night late it came to me . . . that there was nothing left for us to do but to take them all, and to educate the Filipinos, and uplift them and civilize and Christianize them. . . ."

Spain yielded the islands after the United States agreed to a payment of twenty million dollars, but approval of the treaty by the United States Senate was not so easy. Some senators doubted that the United States had the legal right to annex the islands, and intellectuals, businessmen, and labor leaders fought the treaty. McKinley was denounced as both a tyrant and a weakling by the antiexpansionists, who were horrified that the United States, founded on the principle of democracy, would choose to govern a people without their consent. On the other hand, Indiana Senator Albert J.

Beveridge proclaimed that God "has made us the master organizers of the world to establish system where chaos reigns," and many senators sincerely felt it was time for the United States to assume international responsibilities.

Then, on February 5, the Filipinos rebelled against their American "liberators." Their action probably changed the votes of some previously antitreaty senators who were outraged by the insurrection. The treaty was ratified on February 6 by only one vote more than the two-thirds required.

The rebellion lasted three years. The United States committed 120,000 men, 1,000 of whom were killed. The insurgents, losing battle after battle, reverted to guerrilla warfare in 1900. Not until 1902 was the last rebel leader captured.

Stability and progress eventually replaced chaos in the Philippines, Puerto Rico, and Cuba. McKinley named William Howard Taft to head a commission to establish civil government in the Philippines; Taft's service was a credit to colonial government. Under the Foraker Act the United States instituted civil government in Puerto Rico. The able Major General Leonard Wood was appointed military governor of Cuba and guided the island toward self-government.

The inevitable postwar investigation of the War Department did nothing to enhance the reputation of the waspish, ineffective Secretary of War, Russell A. Alger, and McKinley eventually replaced him with Elihu Root. John Hay, an experienced, international-minded statesman, had become Secretary of State in September, 1898. A potentially dangerous scramble among several major powers for markets in China prompted Hay to win their acceptance of an Open Door policy, guaranteeing equality of commercial opportunity. A group of chauvinistic Chinese, called Boxers, bitterly resented the influence of Western culture in China. When they killed several hundred foreigners and attacked others who had sought refuge in the British legation in Peking, President McKinley attached five thousand United States soldiers to an international expeditionary force, which raised the Boxer siege.

The monetary debate was revived in 1900 with the adoption of the Gold Standard Act, supported by McKinley. This act declared the gold dollar the sole standard of currency. The gold reserve limit was raised to one hundred and fifty million dollars, and safeguards were provided to prevent the gold supply from dropping too low.

McKinley stood for re-election in 1900, though he professed that he had "had enough" of the job. Theodore Roosevelt was picked by party leaders for the Vice Presidency. Bryan, once again the Democratic nominee, spoke out for free silver and against expansionism, but McKinley had the only issue that counted—prosperity.

Prosperity continued into his second term, and social and economic problems were hidden by the glossy façade of wealth. A popular President at election time, McKinley's popularity grew even greater. He continued to study public opinion, to guide it when he could, and to appear to lead it when it formed on its own. (Representative Joseph Cannon once remarked that McKinley's ear was so close to the ground that it was full of grasshoppers.)

His wife's health remained his gravest personal problem. Although she was having fewer and fewer "good days," Ida McKinley would not be shunted aside as White House hostess. Her frequent seizures startled guests at receptions and state dinners. Her stubborn "courage" added immeasurably to her husband's burdens.

On September 5, 1901, McKinley spoke at the Pan-American Exposition. The following day he held a public reception in the Temple of Music on the exhibition grounds. Among those who attended was an anarchist, Leon Czolgosz, who carried a gun in a bandaged hand. He stepped in front of McKinley and shot him twice. His victim suffered terribly, rallied briefly, and finally succumbed to gangrene on September 14. McKinley adhered to his faith until the end. His last words to Ida were those of a favorite hymn, "Nearer, my God to Thee, Nearer to Thee."

—DONALD YOUNG

William McKinley

A PICTURE PORTFOLIO

DO YOU SMOKE?

YES—SINCE 1896!

THAT'S WHAT McKINLEY PROMISED.

The question posed by this political button of 1900 did not refer to tobacco but to the smokestacks of industry; McKinley promised another four years of prosperity.

FROM THE
FRONT PORCH

While the Democratic candidate stumped the country taking his message to the multitudes, William McKinley stayed at home in Canton, Ohio, and let the multitudes come to him. From June to November of 1896 trainloads of delegations, financed by Mark Hanna's abundant campaign coffers, arrived in steady succession. Visitors were met by the Canton Home Guards, a picturesque mounted brigade, and escorted to the McKinley residence to hear the Republican candidate's views. There were two distinct advantages of such a campaign. First, it allowed the major, a Civil War veteran and two-term governor of Ohio, to maintain the proper decorum and dignity from his own front porch. As the president of a New England women's club remarked approvingly, "He does not talk wildly, and his appearance is that of a President." A second and more important advantage of the McKinley campaign was the control it gave the candidate over his audience. To avoid the embarrassment of being caught off guard, each delegation was canvassed well in advance. McKinley would request a copy of the group leader's remarks, return his carefully edited version, and prepare his response accordingly. When the delegation arrived, a member of the Home Guards would gallop ahead to alert the candidate. The ensuing confrontation held no surprises and McKinley made no slips. Yet, facing his audience "like a child looking at Santa Claus," he managed to give the whole charade a look of candid spontaneity.

Defeating William Jennings Bryan and his silver platform by a comfortable margin, the new President prepared to do battle for his high-tariff, sound-money program. With the passage of the Dingley Tariff in 1897, maintaining high protection for industry, and the Gold Standard Act of 1900, McKinley could boast fulfillment of his pledge: "Good work, good wages, and good money."

Advocates of McKinley's gold-standard platform of 1896 often sported handsome goldbug pins like the one above.

"The Republican Two Step and March," on the song sheet below, was one of several 1896 Republican compositions. Others included "The Honest Little Dollar's Come to Stay" and the prosaic "We Want Yer, McKinley, Yes, We Do."

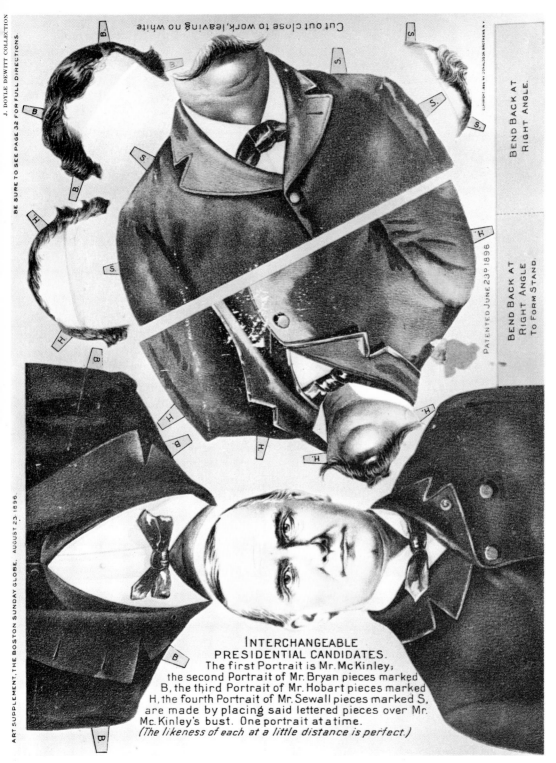

The campaign cutouts above, printed in a supplement to the Boston Sunday Globe, represent the presidential and vice presidential candidates in the election of 1896. By switching the various toupees and torsos, one could create recognizable likenesses of any of the candidates: McKinley, Bryan, Hobart, or Sewall.

POWERS OF THE PRESS

EDWIN L. GODKIN

"To my generation," wrote William James of Edwin L. Godkin, "his was certainly the towering influence in all thought concerning public affairs." Godkin was only twenty-five when he came to America in 1856, but in England he had already established himself as a notable newspaper correspondent and man of letters. In 1865 he helped found the *Nation*, which under his editorship became the country's most powerful journal of opinion despite its small circulation. Dealing with subjects ranging from literature and the arts to politics, but especially with the problems of Negro rights and sound government, the journal was generally liberal in viewpoint. In 1883 Godkin became editor in chief of the New York *Evening Post*, a position he held until 1900, when he resigned because of failing health. A nominal Republican, Godkin displayed a strong independence and believed that national interests transcended those of party. He scored Johnson's Reconstruction programs and condemned the scandals of the Grant years. His commitment to civil reform led him to side with Tilden in the disputed election of 1876 and to lead the Mugwump faction eight years later. He favored Cleveland's fiscal ideas, but flayed his Venezuelan policy. Godkin was praised by educator Charles Eliot Norton as the nation's "soundest and best trained writer on social and economical questions."

WILLIAM RANDOLPH HEARST

William Randolph Hearst built a newspaper empire by refining the ore that others had mined. Noting the success of New York's yellow press, he bought the *Journal* in 1896 and soon was outsensationalizing Joseph Pulitzer's *World*. Born to wealth, Hearst began his career by taking over his father's unprofitable San Francisco *Examiner* in 1887; he turned it into a profit-making enterprise and then headed for New York. Competing against Pulitzer, Hearst successfully raided the *World* staff and used colored comic strips and supplements along with trumpeting headlines and bold, full-page editorials. The paper was frankly chauvinistic, and Hearst called the conflict with Spain "the *Journal*'s war." Hearst served two congressional terms as a Democrat, but his editorial politics fluctuated. He supported Woodrow Wilson, but scored America's entry into World War I and was firmly against the League of Nations. He backed Herbert Hoover in 1928, but came out for Franklin Roosevelt four years later—only to turn on F. D. R.'s New Deal programs. At its peak Hearst's empire included some twenty-five newspapers and numerous magazines and radio stations. His estimated gross worth in 1935 was more than two hundred million dollars, and he lived his last years in eccentric splendor at his extravagant castle, San Simeon, in California. He died in 1951.

ALL.: CULVER PICTURES

ADOLPH S. OCHS

"It is the price of the paper, not its character, that will change," said Adolph S. Ochs, publisher of *The New York Times*, in 1898. Ochs had taken over the impoverished paper two years before; because of its inability to cover the war with Spain as fully as its rich competition, its popularity had not increased. So Ochs gambled. Strongly advised to the contrary and ridiculed by rival sheets, he lowered the price of the *Times* from three cents to a penny. Circulation and advertising shot up, and Ochs proved that there was a market for a "clean, dignified and trustworthy" newspaper even in the heyday of yellow journalism. *The New York Times* was not the first paper the Cincinnati-born Ochs had resuscitated. In 1878, at twenty, he had bought controlling interest in the Chattanooga *Times* for $250. He won a large readership by refusing questionable advertising and by subordinating editorial content to thorough, accurate news copy. In New York Ochs's slogan was "All the news that's fit to print." Throughout his life he maintained his standards of scrupulous, unsensational, in-depth reporting and took great pride in *The New York Times*'s status as a "newspaper of record." He favored sound money, tariff reform, and low taxes, but was not a mouthpiece for any political party or faction. Adolph Ochs was seventy-seven years old when he died in Chattanooga in 1935.

JOSEPH PULITZER

"THE ROYAL FEAST OF BELSHAZZAR BLAINE AND THE MONEY KINGS," screamed the New York *World* during the presidential campaign of 1884. It was a typical *World* headline, reflecting the political and journalistic philosophies of the paper's publisher, Joseph Pulitzer. He had bought the *World* from Jay Gould the year before, and through blaring banners, numerous features and cartoons, and heavy emphasis on crime, scandal, and catastrophe, had become, wrote one historian, "the first publisher to reach a truly massive audience." While the *World*'s news columns appealed to the common man, its editorial pages were aimed at the liberal intelligentsia. After the collapse of the Liberal Republican movement Pulitzer became a staunch Democrat, advocating civil reform and sound money. Hungarian-born, he had emigrated in 1864 and had served in the Union army. He began his newspaper career in St. Louis, where he arranged the merger that produced the successful St. Louis *Post-Dispatch*. In the 1890's the fierce rivalry between the papers run by Hearst and Pulitzer helped generate public desire for war with Spain, but the *World* eventually dropped its sensational format and became the nation's leading Democratic organ. In his will Pulitzer established a journalism school at New York's Columbia University and provided for the annual awarding of Pulitzer Prizes.

NEW YORK JOURNAL
AND ADVERTISER.

The Journal will give $50,000 for information, furnished to it exclusively, that will convict the person or persons who sank the Maine.

The Journal will give $50,000 for information, furnished to it exclusively, that will convict the person or persons who sank the Maine.

NO. 5,572.   Copyright, 1898, by W. R. Hearst.—NEW YORK, THURSDAY, FEBRUARY 17, 1898.—16 PAGES.   PRICE ONE CENT In Greater New York | Elsewhere and Jersey City.   TWO CENTS.

DESTRUCTION OF THE WAR SHIP MAINE WAS THE WORK OF AN ENEMY.

$50,000!

$50,000 REWARD!
For the Detection of the
Perpetrator of
the Maine Outrage!

The New York Journal hereby offers a reward of **$50,000 CASH** for information. **FURNISHED TO IT EXCLUSIVELY,** which shall lead to the detection and conviction of the person, persons or government criminally responsible for the explosion which resulted in the destruction, at Havana, of the United States war ship Maine and the loss of 258 lives of American sailors.

The **$50,000 CASH** offered for the above information is on deposit with Wells, Fargo & Co.

No one is barred, be he the humble, but misguided seaman eking out a few miserable dollars by acting as a spy, or the attache of a government secret service, plotting, by any devilish means, to revenge fancied insults or cripple menacing countries.

This offer has been cabled to Europe and will be made public in every capital of the Continent and in London this morning.

The Journal believes that any man who can be bought to commit murder can also be bought to betray his comrades. **FOR THE PERPETRATOR OF THIS OUTRAGE HAD ACCOMPLICES.**

W. R. HEARST.

Assistant Secretary Roosevelt Convinced the Explosion of the War Ship Was Not an Accident.

The Journal Offers $50,000 Reward for the Conviction of the Criminals Who Sent 258 American Sailors to Their Death. Naval Officers Unanimous That the Ship Was Destroyed on Purpose.

$50,000!

$50,000 REWARD!
For the Detection of the
Perpetrator of
the Maine Outrage!

The New York Journal hereby offers a reward of **$50,000 CASH** for information. **FURNISHED TO IT EXCLUSIVELY,** which shall lead to the detection and conviction of the person, persons or government criminally responsible for the explosion which resulted in the destruction, at Havana, of the United States war ship Maine and the loss of 258 lives of American sailors.

The **$50,000 CASH** offered for the above information is on deposit with Wells, Fargo & Co.

No one is barred, be he the humble, but misguided woman, eking out a few miserable dollars by acting as a spy, or the attache of a government secret service, plotting by any devilish means, to revenge fancied insults or cripple menacing countries.

This offer has been cabled to Europe and will be made public in every capital of the Continent and in London this morning.

The Journal believes that any man who can be bought to commit murder can also be bought to betray his comrades. **FOR THE PERPETRATOR OF THIS OUTRAGE HAD ACCOMPLICES.**

W. R. HEARST.

POWDER MAGAZINE

MAINE

MINE

NAVAL OFFICERS THINK THE MAINE WAS DESTROYED BY A SPANISH MINE.

George Eugene Bryson, the Journal's special correspondent at Havana, cables that it is the secret opinion of many Spaniards in the Cuban capital that the Maine was destroyed and 258 of her men killed by means of a submarine mine, or fixed torpedo. This is the opinion of several American naval authorities. The Spaniards, it is believed, arranged to have the Maine anchored over one of the harbor mines. Wires connected the mine with a powder magazine, and it is thought the explosion was caused by sending an electric current through the wire. If this can be proven, the brutal nature of the Spaniards will be shown by the fact that they waited to spring the mine until after all the men had retired for the night. The Maltese cross in the picture shows where the mine may have been fired.

Hidden Mine or a Sunken Torpedo Believed to Have Been the Weapon Used Against the American Man-of-War---Officers and Men Tell Thrilling Stories of Being Blown Into the Air Amid a Mass of Shattered Steel and Exploding Shells---Survivors Brought to Key West Scout the Idea of Accident---Spanish Officials Protest Too Much---Our Cabinet Orders a Searching Inquiry---Journal Sends Divers to Havana to Report Upon the Condition of the Wreck. Was the Vessel Anchored Over a Mine?

BY CAPTAIN E. L. ZALINSKI, U. S. A.

(Captain Zalinski is the inventor of the famous dynamite gun, which would be the principal factor in our coast defence in case of war.)

Assistant Secretary of the Navy Theodore Roosevelt says he is convinced that the destruction of the Maine in Havana Harbor was not an accident. The Journal offers a reward of $50,000 for exclusive evidence that will convict the person, persons or Government criminally responsible for the destruction of the American battle ship and the death of 258 of its crew.

The suspicion that the Maine was deliberately blown up grows stronger every hour. Not a single fact to the contrary has been produced.

Captain Sigsbee, of the Maine, and Consul-General Lee both urge that public opinion be suspended until they have completed their investigation. They are taking the course of tactful men who are convinced that there has been treachery.

Washington reports very late that Captain Sigsbee had feared some such event as a hidden mine. The English cipher code was used all day yesterday by the naval officers in cabling instead of the usual American code.

The question of who sank the Maine was purely academic in the face of press sensationalism and public clamor for war with Spain. As McKinley vacillated, New York Republican Teddy Roosevelt charged that he "had no more backbone than a chocolate eclair." Public sentiment prevailed and the President declared war.

WAR WITH SPAIN

Thirteen months after McKinley's inauguration, America was at war with Spain. Indignation—fanned by immoderate newspapers—over Spanish oppression in Cuba had long been simmering, but the sinking of the U.S.S. *Maine* in Havana Harbor was the event that prompted the declaration of war in April, 1898. That May, Commodore Dewey eliminated Spanish power in the Philippines, and in June a joint Army-Navy expedition set out to liberate Cuba. While Admiral William T. Sampson held the Spanish fleet in Santiago Bay, General William R. Shafter's land force pushed in to take the port through a series of battles in the surrounding heights. On July 1, some 7,000 United States troops defeated an enemy force of about 600 at the village of El Caney, losing 441 men as against 235 Spanish casualties. One lieutenant described the confusion in American lines: "The bullets . . . are raining into our very faces. A soldier comes running up, and cries out, 'Lieutenant, we're shooting into our own men!'" Meanwhile other American troops—including Teddy Roosevelt's Rough Riders—were charging up San Juan Hill in an assault that increased American casualties to almost 1,600. From their newly won vantage point Shafter's men trained their guns on Santiago Bay. On July 3 the Spanish fleet tried to escape, but was pursued and destroyed by Admiral Sampson's superior naval force. The "war of liberation" was over.

The Kurz & Allison lithograph above depicts in vivid detail the American siege of El Caney and the Spanish fortifications in the heights above Santiago. In the distance lies the Spanish fleet, bottled up in the bay by an American naval blockade. The destruction of the fleet brought the Spanish-American War to a quick end.

AN AMERICAN EMPIRE

The taste of Empire is in the mouth of the people even as the taste of blood in the jungle," proclaimed the Washington *Post* before the outbreak of the Spanish-American War. Whetting the public appetite, President McKinley announced that "when the war is over, we must keep what we want." In the peace that followed, Cuba was granted independence and the United States took over Guam, Puerto Rico, and the Philippines. Expansion was not confined to the spoils of war. Hawaii was annexed in 1898, and Wake Island was also formally occupied. When the islands of Samoa were divided between the United States and Germany in 1899, the press announced proudly, "We have emerged in undisputed possession of the best of that group of islands." American influence in China was reflected in the Open Door trade policy and its unfortunate aftermath, the Boxer Rebellion of 1900, during which American troops joined an expedition sent to rescue besieged foreigners in Peking. In the presidential election of that year the issue of imperialism dominated the Republican platform. McKinley—and imperialism—won the nation's mandate. But as his friend Charles Dawes noted, "The President seems more impressed with his responsibilities than his triumph."

The Battle of Manila Bay in 1898 inspired the handsome Japanese print above. On May 1, Commodore George Dewey entered the bay, delivered a scathing broadside, and destroyed the Spanish squadron. With the fall of Manila in August, the United States proclaimed military occupation of the Philippines.

Filipino insurrectionist Emilio Aguinaldo was against trading Spanish domination for American control. When the United States failed to grant independence, he led the islanders in armed revolt. In the photograph at left, American soldiers dig in for a bloody three-year guerrilla war against the elusive natives.

MEN AROUND McKINLEY

THE PHILLIPS GALLERY

ELIHU ROOT

"Thank the President for me," replied Elihu Root when offered the position of Secretary of War, "but say that it is quite absurd. I know nothing about war. . . ." Informed, however, that McKinley was looking for "a lawyer to direct the government of these Spanish islands," Root, a New York corporation lawyer, agreed to accept the Cabinet post. Taking office in 1899, he formulated policies for the administration of Cuba, the Philippines, and other new colonial possessions. Stressing rehabilitation, the guarantee of individual liberties, development of local institutions, and protection of United States interests, he laid the foundations of American imperialism. Before he resigned in 1904 he reorganized the Army and created the Army War College. As Secretary of State under Roosevelt from 1905 to 1909, Root worked to develop friendly relations with Latin America and Japan; his efforts won him the Nobel Peace Prize in 1912. From 1909 to 1915 he served in the United States Senate. Critical of American neutrality at the beginning of World War I, he favored— with reservations—United States membership in the League of Nations. He also advocated membership in the Permanent Court of International Peace. President of the Carnegie Endowment for International Peace, Root was a respected elder statesman until his death at ninety-one in 1937.

BROWN BROTHERS

MARCUS A. HANNA

"I love McKinley!" declared Republican party leader Marcus A. Hanna. "He is the best man I ever knew." A hardheaded realist with few political scruples, Hanna was attracted by McKinley's idealism. An Ohio capitalist whose interests included the Cleveland *Herald*, the Cleveland Opera House, and control of Cleveland's street railway system, Hanna saw political power chiefly as a means to promote big business. McKinley, he felt, lent the proper touch of ideology to his cause. In 1891 he supported McKinley for governor, worked for his re-election in 1893, and began grooming him for the Presidency in 1896. Advertising him as the "advance agent of prosperity," Hanna secured the nomination for his candidate on the first ballot. Hanna became chairman of the Republican National Committee and raised several million dollars to assure McKinley's election. Appointed to the Senate in 1896, Hanna served as the President's most intimate adviser. Although still a champion of large corporate enterprise, he also defended labor's right to organize. Upon Theodore Roosevelt's succession to the Presidency in 1901, Hanna continued in the role of adviser and helped to settle labor disputes in the anthracite coal industry. Hanna might have become a presidential candidate himself had not his death in 1904 terminated a growing Mark Hanna-for-President movement.

GEORGE DEWEY

When Admiral George Dewey returned from the Spanish-American War in 1899, he was welcomed as a national hero. An Annapolis graduate who had served under David Farragut in the Civil War, Dewey became chief of the Navy Department's Bureau of Equipment in 1889 and president of the Board of Inspection six years later. Promoted to commodore, he assumed command of the Asiatic squadron in 1897. His cool heroics during the ensuing conflict with Spain are legendary. Approaching the enemy guns in Manila Bay, the commander gave the laconic order, "You may fire when ready, Gridley." Dewey went on to victory, annihilating the Spanish squadron, taking the Philippines, and eliminating Spanish naval power in the Far East. A grateful Congress created the rank of admiral of the Navy for him. Returning home a year after his spectacular victory, he was greeted hysterically by the nation. There were Dewey songs, Dewey banners, Dewey neckties, Dewey hatpins, Dewey rattles, and a gum called Dewey chewies. The American public launched a brief Dewey-for-President boom that failed to mature sufficiently, however, to bring him a nomination. In 1900 Admiral Dewey was appointed president of the General Board of the Navy Department and served in that position until his death at the age of seventy-nine on January 16, 1917.

JOHN M. HAY

John M. Hay's record as a statesman was, President McKinley said, "one of the most important and interesting pages of our diplomatic history." Trained as a lawyer, Hay left Springfield, Illinois, in his early twenties to act as assistant private secretary to President-elect Abraham Lincoln, whom he served until 1865. After traveling abroad as a diplomat, he returned to the United States in 1870 and became a writer on the New York *Tribune.* Hay served as assistant secretary of state from 1879 to 1881, and in 1897 he was appointed ambassador to Great Britain by McKinley. Named Secretary of State after the outbreak of the Spanish-American War in 1898, he supported President McKinley's policy of American rule in the Philippines. In 1899 he backed the Open Door policy in China and was largely responsible for the preservation of China's territorial integrity during the Boxer Rebellion of 1900. Retaining his post under Theodore Roosevelt, Hay settled the Alaskan boundary dispute in 1903 and concluded the important Hay-Pauncefote Treaty with Britain, which cleared the way for construction of the Panama Canal. Hay was a poet, novelist, and historian as well as a diplomat. Among his published works are *Pike County Ballads, Castilian Days, The Bread-Winners,* and the ten-volume *Abraham Lincoln: A History,* which he wrote with John Nicolay in 1890.

The Issue — 1900
·LIBERTY·
·JUSTICE·
·HUMANITY·

W.J. BRYAN

1776 LIBERTY
1900 NO IMPERIALISM.

NO CROWN OF THORNS
NO CROSS OF GOLD

E PLURIBUS UNUM
DECLARATION OF INDEPENDENCE

DOLLAR OF THE DADDIES
16
TRUSTS

"GIVE US LIBERTY OR GIVE US DEATH"

EQUAL RIGHTS TO ALL   SPECIAL PRIVILEGES TO NONE.

COPYRIGHT 1900 BY NEVILLE WILLIAMS

TRUTH AND
ELOQUENCE

In 1900 William Jennings Bryan campaigned against McKinley for a second time. Four years had not changed the silver Democrat's views. Except for the new issue of expansion, Bryan might have used his campaign notes from 1896. To the gold-standard adherents in that year he had hurled his famous protest: "You shall not crucify mankind upon a cross of gold." Despite evidence that the gold standard had bolstered the American economy, he continued to call for free coinage of silver as a panacea for the ills of the masses. Bryan saw the campaign as more than a contest of politics and economics. "Every political . . . [and] economic question," he asserted, "is in reality a great moral question." To Bryan it was a contest between good and evil; a class struggle between the "toiling masses" and the big money interests supported by President McKinley.

Bryan's political convictions were rooted in the heritage of his native Middle West. Born in Salem, Illinois, in 1860, he was reared in an agrarian society that stressed Protestant morality, the dignity of the laborer, and government by majority rule. With these ideals the young lawyer moved to Nebraska, where he slipped easily and naturally into local politics, soon establishing a reputation as "the silver-tongued orator from Nebraska." Elected to Congress in 1890, he spoke against the protective tariff and repeal of the silver-purchase law. The Democratic candidate in 1896 and 1900, he campaigned against McKinley as the representative of the common man. One admirer commented that Bryan spoke with an "entire lack of artfulness [that] makes him invincible." But he was not invincible; he lost the first election on the silver issue and the second on the question of expansion. However admirable his anti-imperialist convic-

tions may have been, they were out of harmony with a nation eager to claim the spoils of the Spanish-American War. In 1908 Bryan ran against William Howard Taft—his third and last try for the Presidency. Continuing as a leader of the Democratic party, he kept his ideas before the people through lecture tours and editorials in the *Commoner*, a weekly newspaper that he published from 1901 to 1913. In 1912 he supported Woodrow Wilson, who appointed him Secretary of State. Unable to reconcile his pacifist convictions with United States involvement in World War I, Bryan resigned in 1915.

A pathetic incident marked the end of his career. Shortly before his death in 1925 he became involved in the prosecution of John T. Scopes, indicted for teaching the theory of evolution, which was banned by law from the Tennessee public schools. Bryan, a fundamentalist who had helped to draft such legislation, was subjected to a withering cross-examination by Clarence Darrow that revealed the narrowness of his religious dogma and the limitations of his scientific thought. But Bryan was then a man of sixty-five. At the height of his powers he had expressed unbounded faith in the progress of mankind. "He believes the world is getting better all the time," observed the editor of a Western daily, "and it is impossible to be around him a great deal without sharing his hopeful view of things." To some, William Jennings Bryan appeared to be the "incarnation of demagogy, the apotheosis of riot [and] destruction," and his editorials in the *Commoner* were denounced as an attempt to create dissension between the poor and the rich. But to thousands of others he represented the twin virtues "Truth" and "Eloquence"; to the "plain people" of America he was, as one Nebraskan put it, "the brightest and purest advocate of our cause. . . ."

William Jennings Bryan (left), on a 1900 campaign poster

The 1900 campaign button above shows McKinley and his new running mate, Teddy Roosevelt, who soon succeeded him.

The President delivered his last speech (right) the day before his assassination.

A group of silent mourners thronged the streets of McKinley's home town, Canton, Ohio, as the President's

ASSASSINATION

On September 6, 1901, during a public reception at the Pan-American Exposition in Buffalo, New York, President William McKinley was shot by a vacant-eyed, twenty-eight-year-old anarchist named Leon Czolgosz. Three years earlier, the assassin had suffered a breakdown, left his factory job in Cleveland, and retired to the bleak Ohio farm on which his family lived. Restless and despondent, he moved to Buffalo in the summer of 1901. Hearing of the President's visit, he bought a revolver, walked into the reception, and fired two shots into McKinley's chest and stomach. A nondescript, antisocial outcast, Czolgosz was the complete opposite of the public idol who had stood but a few feet in front of him, unaware of his existence. "I didn't believe one man should have so much service," the assassin said later, "and another man should have none." The President was rushed to an emergency hospital on the exposition grounds, but the second bullet, which had ripped the stomach walls, was never located by the doctors. The lighting in the operating room was inadequate, and the wound was sewn up, without proper drainage, with the aid of the setting sun and a reflecting mirror. McKinley rallied briefly, and on September 7 a medical bulletin assured the worried public that "no serious symptoms have developed." Within a few days, however, a gangrenous infection set in. On the evening of September 14, the physician attending William McKinley announced the tragic news to the nation: "The President is dead."

remains were removed from the church. It was the end of a tragic procession that had begun in Buffalo.

FACTS IN SUMMARY: WILLIAM McKINLEY

CHRONOLOGY

UNITED STATES		McKINLEY
	1843	*Born January 29*
Texas annexed	1845	
Mexican War begins	1846	
Taylor elected President		
Fillmore becomes President	1850	
Compromise of 1850		
Pierce elected President	1852	
Kansas-Nebraska Act	1854	
Buchanan inaugurated as President	1857	
Dred Scott decision		
Lincoln elected President	1860	*Enters Allegheny College*
South Carolina secedes		
Fort Sumter fired upon	1861	*Enlists in Army*
Battle of Antietam	1862	*Fights at Antietam*
		Promoted to first lieutenant
Emancipation Proclamation	1863	
Battle of Gettysburg		
Lee surrenders at Appomattox	1865	*Promoted to brevet major*
Lincoln assassinated		
	1866	*Enters Albany Law School*

	1867	*Graduates from law school*
		Moves to Canton, Ohio
Fourteenth Amendment ratified	1868	*Elected president of Canton Y.M.C.A.*
	1869	*Elected county prosecuting attorney*
	1871	*Marries Ida Saxton*
	1876	*Elected to U.S. House of Representatives*
Hayes elected President	1877	
	1878	*Votes for Bland-Allison bill*
Garfield elected President	1880	*Re-elected to Congress*
		Made temporary chairman of Ohio Republican convention
Cleveland elected President	1884	*Made permanent chairman of Ohio convention*
Hatch Act	1887	
Benjamin Harrison elected President	1888	
	1889	*Becomes chairman of House Ways and Means Committee*
Sherman Antitrust Act	1890	*Sponsors McKinley tariff bill*
	1891	*Elected governor of Ohio*
	1893	*Re-elected governor*
	1896	*Elected President*

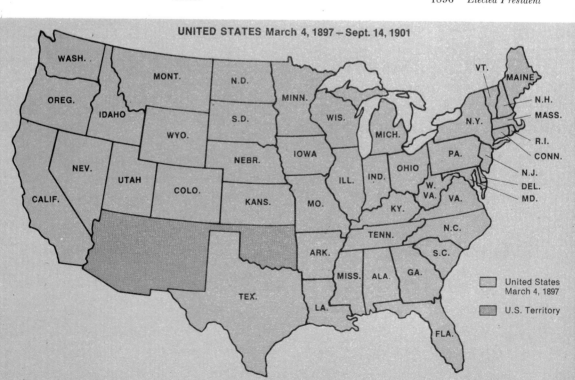

UNITED STATES March 4, 1897 – Sept. 14, 1901

United States March 4, 1897

U.S. Territory

Dingley Tariff	1897	
Sinking of the *Maine*	1898	*Declares war with Spain*
Spanish-American War		*Demands cession of*
Annexation of Hawaii		*Philippines*
Treaty of Paris		
Open Door policy	1899	
First Hague Conference		
Partition of Samoa		
Currency Act	1900	*Re-elected President*
Boxer Rebellion		
	1901	*Appoints Taft civil*
		governor of Philippines
		Shot September 6
		Dies September 14

BIOGRAPHICAL FACTS

BIRTH: Niles, Ohio, Jan. 29, 1843

ANCESTRY: Scotch-Irish and English

FATHER: William McKinley; b. Pine Township, Pa., Nov. 15, 1807; d. Canton, Ohio, Nov. 24, 1892

FATHER'S OCCUPATION: Iron-founder

MOTHER: Nancy Allison McKinley; b. New Lisbon, Ohio, April 22, 1809; d. Canton, Ohio, Dec. 12, 1897

BROTHERS: David Allison (1829–1892); James (?–1889); Abner (1849–1904)

SISTERS: Anna (1832–1890); Mary; Helen; Sarah Elizabeth

WIFE: Ida Saxton; b. Canton, Ohio, June 8, 1847; d. Canton, Ohio, May 26, 1907

MARRIAGE: Canton, Ohio, Jan. 25, 1871

CHILDREN: Katherine (1871–1875); Ida (1873–1873)

EDUCATION: Attended Poland Academy, Ohio, and Allegheny College

RELIGIOUS AFFILIATION: Methodist

OCCUPATIONS BEFORE PRESIDENCY: Teacher; soldier; lawyer

MILITARY SERVICE: Joined Ohio 23rd Volunteers in 1861; rose to rank of major before leaving Army in 1865

PRE-PRESIDENTIAL OFFICES: Member of U.S. House of Representatives; Governor of Ohio

AGE AT INAUGURATION: 54

DEATH: Buffalo, N.Y., Sept. 14, 1901

PLACE OF BURIAL: Canton, Ohio

ELECTION OF 1896

CANDIDATES	ELECTORAL VOTE	POPULAR VOTE
William McKinley Republican	271	7,102,246
William J. Bryan Democratic	176	6,492,559
John M. Palmer National Democratic	—	133,148
Joshua Levering Prohibition	—	132,007

FIRST ADMINISTRATION

INAUGURATION: March 4, 1897; the Capitol, Washington, D.C.

VICE PRESIDENT: Garret A. Hobart

SECRETARY OF STATE: John Sherman; William R. Day (from April 28, 1898); John Hay (from Sept. 30, 1898)

SECRETARY OF THE TREASURY: Lyman J. Gage

SECRETARY OF WAR: Russell A. Alger; Elihu Root (from Aug. 1, 1899)

ATTORNEY GENERAL: Joseph McKenna; John W. Griggs (from Feb. 1, 1898)

POSTMASTER GENERAL: James A. Gary; Charles Emory Smith (from April 21, 1898)

SECRETARY OF THE NAVY: John D. Long

SECRETARY OF THE INTERIOR: Cornelius N. Bliss; Ethan A. Hitchcock (from Feb. 20, 1899)

SECRETARY OF AGRICULTURE: James Wilson

SUPREME COURT APPOINTMENT: Joseph McKenna (1898)

55th CONGRESS (March 4, 1897–March 4, 1899):
Senate: 47 Republicans; 34 Democrats; 7 Others
House: 204 Republicans; 113 Democrats; 40 Others

56th CONGRESS (March 4, 1899–March 4, 1901):
Senate: 53 Republicans; 26 Democrats; 8 Others
House: 185 Republicans; 163 Democrats; 9 Others

ELECTION OF 1900

CANDIDATES	ELECTORAL VOTE	POPULAR VOTE
William McKinley Republican	292	7,218,491
William J. Bryan Democratic	155	6,356,734
John C. Wooley Prohibition	—	208,914
Eugene V. Debs Socialist	—	87,814

SECOND ADMINISTRATION

INAUGURATION: March 4, 1901; the Capitol, Washington, D.C.

VICE PRESIDENT: Theodore Roosevelt

SECRETARY OF STATE: John Hay

SECRETARY OF THE TREASURY: Lyman J. Gage

SECRETARY OF WAR: Elihu Root

ATTORNEY GENERAL: John W. Griggs; Philander C. Knox (from April 10, 1901)

POSTMASTER GENERAL: Charles Emory Smith

SECRETARY OF THE NAVY: John D. Long

SECRETARY OF THE INTERIOR: Ethan A. Hitchcock

SECRETARY OF AGRICULTURE: James Wilson

57th CONGRESS (March 4, 1901–March 4, 1903):
Senate: 55 Republicans; 31 Democrats; 4 Others
House: 197 Republicans; 151 Democrats; 9 Others

THEODORE ROOSEVELT

Theodore Roosevelt of New York could not have been less like his predecessor in the White House. If McKinley had been the archetype of standpat conservatism, Teddy Roosevelt epitomized a brash new breed of political activists. Never sit still, Roosevelt declared. "Get action, do things . . . take a place wherever you are and be somebody. . . ." Hunter and scholar, rancher and soldier, black-tie patrician and reformer, he was a man of volcanic energy. Heedless of precedent, responsive to the new needs and conflicts of a nation expanding industrially and asserting its rank in the world, he was a prime mover in shaping the Presidency as we know it today: a mediating, countervailing force in American affairs; the embodiment of national unity above section, interest, and class; the ultimate custodian of the general good.

"Teedie" Roosevelt was born on October 27, 1858, at 28 East 20th Street in New York City. His grandfather, Cornelius Van Schaack Roosevelt, was an entrepreneur and investor who ranked with Cornelius Vanderbilt and William B. Astor among New York tycoons. Teedie's father, Theodore, Sr.— whom his son considered "the best man I ever knew"—was a prospering glass importer who had substantial banking interests; he was an active Lincoln Republican and a philanthropic Presbyterian. "Take care of your morals first, your health next," he advised Teedie, "and finally your studies." Teedie's mother was Martha Bulloch, an aristocratic Georgian who, despite her husband's friendship with Lincoln, remained loyal to the South during the Civil War. It was a lively family, including three children besides Theodore.

"Nothing in this world is worth having or worth doing," an older T. R. declared, "unless it means effort, pain, difficulty. . . ." Roosevelt's childhood, despite the comforts of wealth and status, gave the future President great

Theodore Roosevelt, painted in 1903 by John Singer Sargent

Roosevelt's birthplace in New York, shown as it was during his youth, is now a museum open to the public.

pain indeed. Frail, nearsighted, wracked by asthma, the boy was confined to a life of private tutors and close supervision. He could remember his father "carrying me in my distress, in my battles for breath, up and down a room all night. . . . I could breathe, I could sleep, when he had me in his arms." Teedie turned inward, read widely and voraciously, and cultivated an abiding interest in natural science, turning his bedroom into a museum of insects and stuffed birds.

En route to Maine's Moosehead Lake after an asthma attack at the age of thirteen, T. R. was taunted by two bullies for his city manners. The bespectacled lad flew into a rage and, fists flying, went at his tormentors—to no avail. Humiliated, Roosevelt vowed to build his strength. In a home gymnasium he took to bar bell and punching bag, building up his muscles. "There were all kinds of things of which I was afraid at first," he later confessed, ". . . but by acting as if I was not afraid I gradually ceased to be afraid." It was a triumph of will over trauma, confirming in Roosevelt a chip-on-the-shoulder truculence that would both ennoble and beset him throughout life. "Don't hit at all if it is honorably possible to avoid

hitting," he would say, "but *never* hit soft."

Preparation for college required intense study after Roosevelt's spotty succession of tutors. But at eighteen he was ready for Harvard, where, he said loftily, his aim was to become a naturalist like Audubon. In Cambridge he lamented that few of his classmates had come there "with the idea of getting an education." Roosevelt himself was a serious scholar, graduating twenty-first in a class of 177. In his senior year he began work on his book *The Naval War of 1812*, a study he preferred to more classical disciplines. But his interest in naval history and natural science did not preclude other activities. He boxed—and boxed hard—in the college gym. Sideburned and dressed to the nines, he hobnobbed with Boston's Brahmins, from whose ranks he picked a bride, Alice Hathaway Lee. Married in 1880, the year of T. R.'s graduation, they moved in with the elder Theodore, who would soon leave his son an inheritance of two hundred thousand dollars.

At Columbia Law School T. R. discovered a distaste for the law. But he remained in school, seeking diversion by joining the National Guard, riding horseback through

Central Park, attending all the big parties, and, while on vacation, scaling the Matterhorn. Itching for action in 1881, he joined New York City's Twenty-first District Republican Club, an organization staffed by ward heelers. Assured by his friends that politics was a muddying business run by society's lowest elements, T. R. replied: "If this were so, it merely meant that the people I knew did not belong to the governing class . . . and that I intended to be one of the governing class."

Thus turning his back on his peers, Roosevelt, at twenty-three, entered the lists of state politics and won the Twenty-first District's seat in the New York assembly. He already looked as he is now remembered: thick-necked and clamp-jawed; with large teeth and piercing blue eyes framed by pince-nez; agile, wiry, and nervous. Roosevelt's boyish, high-pitched voice was promptly heard in the chambers of Albany as the fledgling solon arose to accuse financier Jay Gould of attempting to corrupt a New York State supreme court judge. Urging that the judge be impeached, T. R. thundered his classic charge that Gould was "part of that most dangerous of all dangerous classes, the wealthy criminal class." They were bitter words for the Albany old guard to swallow, and Teddy was contemptuously christened a Harvard "goo-goo," or one committed to good government.

T. R.'s reform record in Albany, however, was equivocal. It is true that after inspecting the sweatshops of New York's cigar industry he voted to abolish them and that he voted to limit the factory workday of women and children. But it is also true that he refused to support prison reform and opposed attempts to tighten enforcement of New York's eight-hour law and to limit to twelve hours the workday of street railway drivers.

Tragedy hit the Roosevelt family in February, 1884, when T. R.'s mother died of typhoid fever and his young wife died of Bright's disease two days after giving birth to a child. Inconsolable, Roosevelt left his infant daughter, Alice, and headed west to the wild Dakota Territory, seeking a conquest of sorrow through "the strenuous life . . . of labor and strife." In the Badlands, branding steers and breaking stampedes at the Elkhorn Ranch, in which he had invested in 1883, T. R. gained strength and confidence. There is no doubt that he won the respect of his ranch hands, despite their initial derision of him as a "four-eyed tenderfoot." Although given to patrician commands, such as "Hasten forward quickly," he could ride herd with the best of them.

Returning to the East, T. R. placed third in an 1886 bid for the New York mayoralty. His disappointment was assuaged in December by his marriage to Edith Kermit Carow, who was to bear him five children.

Political service to Benjamin Harrison won Roosevelt a seat on the United States Civil Service Commission in 1889—a post of scant intrinsic consequence through which T. R., nevertheless, gained national attention. While commissioner, T. R. said with one eye on the press, he would uphold the merit system and "let the chips fall where they will." He spotted blackmail in the New York Custom House and fought campaign assessments of federal workers. Reappointed by Democrat Grover Cleveland, he removed thousands of federal jobs from political patronage before his retirement in 1895.

Appointed New York City police commissioner by reform Mayor William L. Strong that same year, T. R. again courted headlines. Fighting both Democrats and Republicans, he established a merit system of police appointment and promotion. He helped condemn tenements, fought graft, supported social work, and pounded the precincts until dawn to keep police on their toes. But his handling of strikes did not endear him to the oppressed: "The mob takes its own chance," he declared. "Order will be kept at whatever cost."

A reluctant President McKinley yielded to pressure and appointed Roosevelt assistant secretary of the Navy in 1897. Under permissive Secretary John Long, Roosevelt again seized every chance to thrust himself forward. An overt imperialist and a disciple of Alfred Thayer Mahan's theory of naval supremacy as a key to power, he favored the direct annexation of Hawaii as a foil to Japanese expansion and hailed territorial conquest as a hallmark of racial superiority over the "weak and craven." He thought a direct assault upon Spanish-held Cuba would be "a bully war."

On February 25, 1898, during Secretary Long's absence of a day, T. R. boldly cabled Admiral Dewey in the Pacific, ordering the fleet to Hong Kong. "In the event of declaration of war [against] Spain," he ordered, "your duty will be to see that the Spanish squadron does not leave the Asiatic coast, and then offensive operations in Philippine Islands." T. R.'s act, however insubordinate, helped assure American victory in Manila Bay.

Angered by the sinking of the *Maine*, Roosevelt resigned on May 6, 1898, to do battle on the field. With his friend Leonard Wood he rounded up an improbable band of sportsmen, Texas Rangers, and other cronies and whipped them into shape as the First U.S. Volunteer Cavalry Regiment, the renowned "Rough Riders." How much they contributed to the American expeditionary effort in Cuba remains open to question, but there is no doubt of T. R.'s personal courage in leading his men in the teeth of Spanish fire. He emerged from the war a hero.

Roosevelt's great political potential was quickly exploited by New York's Republican bosses, who badly needed a winning candidate for governor. Senator Thomas Platt, high priest of the party and staunch friend of big business, did not like Roosevelt, branding him an "altruist," using the word, said T. R., "as a term of reproach, as if it was Communistic. . . ." Adroit at political arithmetic, however, and persuaded that T. R. could be controlled, Platt permitted Roosevelt's nomination for governor. In a strenuous whistle-stop tour of the state, a Rough Rider escort noisily at his elbow, Roosevelt won the governorship for the G.O.P. by a shaky margin of 18,000 votes. He was now "Teddy" to the public—a name he disliked—and one of the most talked-about politicians in the United States.

Taking office in January, 1899, Governor Roosevelt quickly put Platt in his place. While avoiding an open break, he told Platt that he was the boss, that he would make his own appointments and pursue his own policies of reform. Opposed not only by big-business Republicans but by those he dismissed as "conservative Democrats of the Wall Street type," T. R. appealed directly to the people. Scarcely a radical, he derided reformers "who bathed every day, and didn't steal, but whose only good point was 'respectability'. . . ." His motto was a West African hunting proverb: "Speak softly and carry a big stick; you will go far."

T. R.'s voice, however, could be heard all over Albany. Infuriating Platt, Roosevelt tightened laws regulating sweatshops, pushed for closer supervision of utilities and insurance companies, forced reform in the handling of food and drugs, and sponsored regulations of the workday for women and children. And when labor riots threatened the public safety at the Croton dam, he ordered the state militia to stand by.

T. R.'s greatest victory as governor came with the legislature's passage of a state tax on corporation franchises. The conversion of New York streetcars from horsepower to electricity had afforded venal businessmen and politicians a field day for what Roosevelt condemned as "down-right bribery." Franchises were awarded on the basis of favoritism and kickbacks. But Governor Roosevelt insisted, as "a matter of plain decency and honesty," that corporation franchises be taxed. Platt was furious, and a dutiful legislature dallied, refusing even to introduce, let alone vote on, T. R.'s franchise bill. Only when the governor threatened to march to the assembly and read the bill out himself did the lawmakers, conscious of the public storm Roosevelt had kicked up, put the bill through.

T. R.'s Albany victory won national attention. But if the people hailed a dramatic new advocate in Theodore Roosevelt, Platt and his coadjutors in the G.O.P. most surely did not. "I want to get rid of the bastard," Platt thundered. "I don't want him raising

This cartoon of 1900 shows the regional maidens enticing Roosevelt into vice presidential waters.

hell in my state any longer." So the bosses schemed, torn between a desire to get T. R. out of their hair and a wish to exploit his vote-getting vigor. Their solution: bury the troublemaker in the Vice Presidency.

President McKinley was cool to the idea of Roosevelt as a running mate, and Roosevelt himself opposed the suggestion: "I will not accept under any circumstances and that is all there is about it." Platt, however, engineered a draft movement to nominate the rough-riding Colonel for the second spot. Mark Hanna, the G.O.P. national chairman, erupted: "Don't any of you realize there's only one life between this madman and the White House?" For his own part, Roosevelt said with apparent remorse: "I do not expect to go any further in politics." But he waged a colorful campaign, and his vast popularity greatly increased McKinley's margin of victory.

The Vice Presidency, with its built-in aura of "second best," depressed the mercurial Roosevelt. But his tedium was shattered on

September 13, 1901. While hunting in the Adirondacks, he received word that McKinley, shot by a fanatic a week earlier, was close to death. After a heroic nighttime descent down tortuous, pitch-black mountain roads, Roosevelt arrived in Buffalo, where, on September 14, 1901, he took the oath of office as the twenty-sixth President of the United States. The man who had condemned McKinley's victory in 1896 as a triumph of America's "gold-ridden, capitalist-bestridden, usurer-mastered future" had succeeded him in the White House. "Now look," cried Hanna, "that damned cowboy is President of the United States!"

Assuring Hanna that he would go slowly, the forty-two-year-old Roosevelt announced that he would "continue, absolutely unbroken" the policies of McKinley. The youngest man ever to accede to the Presidency (although John F. Kennedy would be the youngest to be elected to it), Roosevelt wrote: "It is a dreadful thing to come into the Presidency this way; but it would be a far worse thing to be morbid about it. Here is the task, and I have got to do it to the best of my ability. . . ."

Teddy Roosevelt rose to presidential power at a moment of unprecedented social and economic ferment in the nation, which was being rocked by a surging progressive movement that demanded an end to the abuses of an incredibly heartless industrial capitalism, if not to capitalism itself. The progressive cause was espoused by Populists, labor unions, farmers, and workers who cried out for correction of foul working conditions, recurrent depressions, management coercion, and the declining value of real wages. They protested the affluent reign of a big-business aristocracy and of uncontrolled trusts. The oppressed found eloquent champions in Upton Sinclair, Ida Tarbell, Frank Norris, Lincoln Steffens, and Brand Whitlock, who wrote, in fiction and nonfiction, a classic literature of exposure and protest. Progressives such as Robert M. La Follette and William Jennings Bryan and less moderate Socialists such as Eugene V. Debs led the formal political fight for economic reform:

an eight-hour day, a graduated income tax to counter inequities, public ownership of utilities, and varying degrees of government supervision of industry.

All now looked to the popular young President to see what he would do. He did not disappoint the majority of Americans. If Roosevelt could accept "the inevitableness of combinations in business" and dismiss as "rural toryism" progressive attempts to restore the less complicated milieu of mid-nineteenth-century capitalism, he was no less aware than the progressives of the industrial abuses that threatened to precipitate revolt against the very foundations of American society. And though himself a scion of patrician wealth, Roosevelt became a major voice in the progressive movement, lending it the immense prestige of the Presidency.

The new President struck out against the "criminal rich," declaring that "of all forms of tyranny, the least attractive and the most vulgar is the tyranny of mere wealth, the tyranny of plutocracy." He was careful to couch his orations in terms of loyalty to the free enterprise system, assuring big business that his primary aim was to protect capitalism against both socialism and itself.

Roosevelt was not paying mere lip service to reform, as he proved by two decisive confrontations with big business in his first term. Barely six months after his accession to the Presidency, Roosevelt moved against the trusts—illegal combinations of big-business corporations, organized to stifle competition and control prices and rates through collusion. Acting under the neglected Sherman Antitrust Act of 1890, the President filed suit against the powerful Northern Securities Company, a holding company organized by J. Pierpont Morgan and his associates to monopolize transportation in the Northwest by merging three railroad systems. The Supreme Court had declared in 1895 that Congress had no power to prohibit a holding company's operations. But T. R. pressed the fight, filing similar suits against trusts in the beef, coal, and sugar industries. And in

T. R. and John Burroughs posed at Yellowstone Park in 1903. A lifelong outdoorsman, Roosevelt called a national conservation conference in 1908, after which many states formed their own conservation commissions.

1904 the Supreme Court concurred in a decree by the United States circuit court at St. Paul that Northern Securities should be dissolved. An angry J. P. Morgan rushed to the White House, assuring Roosevelt: "We can easily compromise the matter." The President's reply: "There can be no compromise in the enforcement of the law."

In May, 1902, T. R. faced what was perhaps the greatest challenge to his presidential leadership during his entire tenure in the White House. When the United Mine Workers called a strike of 150,000 men for better wages and working conditions, the mine owners, led by Morgan interests and typified by George F. Baer, president of the Philadelphia and Reading Railroad, refused to compromise. Said Baer: "The rights and interests of the laboring man will be protected and cared for—not by the labor agitators, but by the Christian men to whom God in his infinite wisdom has given the control of the property interests of this country." In an attempt to bring pressure on both strikers and management, as well as to win support for his trust-busting policies, Roosevelt embarked on a speaking tour that took him to the Midwest and to New England. Injuries sustained in Pittsfield, Massachusetts, where an electric trolley slammed into his carriage, ended the tour and confined the President to a wheel chair for weeks.

Concerned about the danger of a coal famine as fall approached, Roosevelt asserted the President's right and duty to protect the public interest against assaults by either labor or management. He urged both sides to accept arbitration of the strike. The mine workers agreed but management refused, charging the President with illegal interference in the affairs of business.

Despite a new burst of public anger, industry remained adamant, refusing, at a White House conference on October 3, to accept the union's demands or arbitration and declining to offer terms of its own. An enraged Roosevelt again warned of the revolutionary potential of a coal famine, predicting "the most terrible riots that this country has ever seen." Then the President acted on

his own, making plans, he later revealed, to instruct the Army to seize and operate the coal mines. "I did not intend," he said later, "to sit supinely when such a state of things was impending." Through J. P. Morgan the administration issued its ultimatum to the coal operators, who agreed to support an impartial commission's investigation of the dispute. The workers returned to the mines pending the inquiry. "The whole country breathed freer," said the President, "and felt as if a nightmare had been lifted. . . ."

It was a landmark in presidential initiative and leadership, casting Teddy Roosevelt irrevocably in the image of a popular crusader. Undeterred by the disapproval of his own class, T. R. remained convinced that he had acted correctly. ". . . The Buchanan principle of striving to find some constitutional reason for inaction" was not for him, he declared. Nor did he care for "the little, feeble, snarling men who yell about executive usurpation" whenever a President acts with strength. "My business," he wrote in 1903, "is to see fair play among all men, capitalists or wageworkers," and to face great national crises with "immediate and vigorous executive action." All he wanted, he said, was "to see to it that every man has a square deal, no more and no less."

In 1903 T. R. pursued the Square Deal in an astonishing series of domestic reforms. He established the Department of Commerce and Labor, committing it to increasing industrial growth and improving working conditions; its Bureau of Corporations, one historian wrote, was to be "the eye of the government in matters of business." The Expedition Act gave the United States power to obtain prompter trials of those being prosecuted under the interstate commerce or antitrust laws. The Elkins Act strengthened the Interstate Commerce Commission by forbidding railroads to deviate from published rate schedules. And Roosevelt personally urged states to prohibit the employment of women or children in industries afflicted by unsafe or unsanitary conditions.

In his first term Roosevelt also initiated a vigorous and farsighted program of conservation, beginning with the Reclamation Act of 1902 and the enlargement of the Bureau of Forestry. Defying the landed interests, the President moved to redeem and irrigate neglected or despoiled land in the West. A commission was named in 1903 to study national resources and recommend optimum uses of land. Interstate cooperation was encouraged at regional conferences held through federal incentive. T. R. considered conservation second only to trust-busting as "the most vital internal question of the United States." And he carried the gospel throughout the land: "I recognize the right and duty of this generation to develop and use the natural resources of our land; but I do not recognize the right to waste them, or to rob, by wasteful use, the generations that come after us." Roosevelt went well beyond rhetoric. He set aside some 150,000,000 acres of timberland for national use, established fifty game preserves, doubled the number of national parks, and founded sixteen national monuments.

In foreign policy, too, Roosevelt demonstrated extraordinary executive vigor. An unabashed expansionist, he was committed to a policy of power through naval supremacy, imperial control of the Pacific, and hemispheric dominion. America, he said, was no longer insulated by protective oceans; sea power and modern technology were dissolving old barriers. "We have no choice as to whether or not we shall play a great part in the world," he declared. ". . . All that we can decide is whether we shall play it well or ill." To play the game well, he said, a big stick—ever ready for swinging—was essential.

On December 16, 1901, Roosevelt secured Senate ratification of the second Hay-Pauncefote Treaty, which enabled the United States to emerge as a major military and commercial power. In the treaty, which abrogated earlier agreements, Britain acquiesced to the United States desire to construct a Central American canal in a neutral canal zone. On June 28, 1902, Congress authorized T. R. to build a canal across Panama (then a part of Colombia) on the condition that the President could buy rights from the New Panama Canal Company, the French group that had failed in its attempt to build a canal, and acquire from Colombia permanent control of a canal zone.

The Hay-Hernan Convention, signed with Colombia on January 22, 1903, met United States terms. In less than two months the United States Senate ratified the treaty, but Colombia's legislature rejected it in August, demanding more money and objecting to what it considered an assault on Colombia's sovereignty. An angry Roosevelt assured Mark Hanna that he would "warn these cat-rabbits that great though our patience has been, it can be exhausted." Conveniently, however, Panama declared its independence in a bloodless coup on November 3, 1903, after an uprising spearheaded by Philippe Bunau-Varilla, former chief engineer of the French canal company, and an American attorney named William Cromwell, both of whom would gain financially from the sale of rights to the United States. Troops dispatched by Colombia to quell the revolt were bribed either to join it or to ignore it while the United States Navy stood by at the Isthmus of Panama. Within three days, the United States had recognized the infant republic and on November 18 negotiated—with Bunau-Varilla—a treaty whereby the United States acquired a canal zone ten miles wide and paid forty million dollars directly to the French canal company. Only ten million dollars and a two-hundred-and-fifty-thousand-dollar annuity were paid to Panama. The United States guaranteed the neutrality of the Canal in return for the right to fortify it.

It was an arrogant, flagrantly illegal display of American power and pressure that would plague Washington's relations with Latin America for decades. (President Wilson would urge America to offer a formal apology to Colombia, and financial restitution would one day be made.) But Roosevelt was triumphant. When Congress delayed its decision on the Canal, Roosevelt boasted: "I took the Canal Zone, and let Congress debate, and while the debate goes on, the canal does so also." International propriety aside, there could be no question of the Canal's immense strategic and commercial importance. It made America a major Pacific sea power, a check, as Roosevelt intended, on Japanese and Russian expansion.

As Chief Executive, T. R. also sustained the United States hegemony in Central and South America. When Great Britain, Germany, and Italy blockaded Venezuelan ports in 1902, insisting that Venezuela pay its debts, Roosevelt dispatched Dewey's fleet to Caribbean waters, warning Kaiser Wilhelm II that invasion would be met with naval force. The dispute was submitted to arbitration, and the blockade was lifted in 1903. Similarly, when European powers sought to compel the Dominican Republic to pay its debts in 1904, T. R. proclaimed the celebrated Roosevelt Corollary to the Monroe Doctrine. Continued foreign intervention or wrongdoing in the Western Hemisphere, Roosevelt warned, might force the United States, "however reluctantly . . . to the exercise of an international police power" to repel invaders. T. R. did not content himself with preaching. He persuaded the Dominican Republic to establish a financial receivership whereby an American comptroller would collect and disburse its revenues. Without waiting for congressional approval, Roosevelt dispatched his comptroller to the Caribbean nation. "I put the agreement into effect . . ." Roosevelt declared, "and I would have continued it until the end of my term, if necessary, without any action by Congress."

In another important success T. R. secured Britain's support in settling with Canada the thorny issue of the Alaskan boundary. In 1903 a commission of three Americans, two Canadians, and one Briton voted in favor of the United States, providing new cement for the emerging Anglo-American entente.

Roosevelt's concept of the Presidency was no less explicit in words than in deeds. A prolific writer, he unequivocally expressed his belief in a strong Presidency. "I believe," he wrote in 1908, "that the efficiency of this Government depends upon its possessing a strong central executive, and wherever I

BROWN BROTHERS

At twenty, "Princess" Alice Roosevelt had begun a lifetime of participation in Capital social life.

could establish a precedent for strength in the executive . . . I have felt . . . [that] I was establishing a precedent of value." The President's power, he argued, is "limited only by specific restrictions and prohibitions appearing in the Constitution or imposed by the Congress under its Constitutional powers."

The White House during the Roosevelt years rang with the joy of life: Alice Roosevelt, with her runabout and cigarettes, embodiment of the Emancipated Woman; the irrepressible Theodore, Jr., Kermit, Ethel, Archie, and Quentin, romping with a bear named Jonathan Edwards and a guinea pig named Father Grady (after a family friend), or sneaking the family pony into the White House to comfort an ailing sibling. Edith Roosevelt, handsome and statuesque, brought a new, more natural dignity to the White House; an archetypal First Lady, she was entirely at ease with elegance.

But it was T. R. himself, contagiously energetic, who held the White House spotlight. "I enjoy being President," he said in 1903, and America shared his joy through its

Sunday newspapers. Roosevelt made the Presidency come alive. He "belonged" to the people, representing at once what they were and what they wanted. The man on the street could identify with him: pillow fighting with his children after critical sessions of state, sparring with John L. Sullivan in the White House gym, getting away from it all to hunt panthers in Colorado. He was perennially young. Quipped one observer: "You must always remember that the President is about six."

Roosevelt was always at the center of action, and by design. "When Theodore attends a wedding," a relative sighed, "he wants to be the bride, and when he attends a funeral he wants to be the corpse." Critics found him pushy, but as novelist Owen Wister wrote, "A creature charged with such a voltage as his, became the central presence at once, whether he stepped on a platform or entered a room." T. R. read Tacitus and Milton or played tennis and medicine ball in free moments. In one White House jujitsu session, he had the pleasure of seeing Secretary of War William Howard Taft's three-hundred-pound hulk expertly floored by a diminutive Japanese.

The hero of American youth, Roosevelt arose at 6 A.M. for push-ups and boxed daily. He championed the fifty-mile hike, rode to hounds, and played football on the White House lawn. When he was not exercising or running the government, he headed a Boy Scout troop in Oyster Bay, Long Island, or wrote books, such as *Winning the West*.

Teddy Roosevelt was a President of "firsts." He was the first President to leave the shores of the United States while in office—in a 1908 visit to the Panama Canal site. He was the first Republican President from the East and the first Vice President who acceded to the Presidency to be elected to the office in his own right. He was the first President to fly (though not until 1910), and the purchase of a twenty-five-thousand-dollar plane from the Wright brothers during his Presidency gave birth to the U.S. Army Air Forces. He was the first President to invite a Negro—Booker T. Washington—

to dine at the White House. He established a White House press room, added two office wings to the Mansion to ensure greater family privacy, and originated such classic American expressions as "lunatic fringe" and "my hat is in the ring." An act of mercy while hunting—T. R.'s refusal to shoot a small bear—inspired a cherished American toy, the Teddy bear.

No tight-lipped conformity or discreet silence for T. R. He loved hard and hated hard and never hesitated to declare an opinion on any subject that caught his attention. To disagree with him, in his mind, was tantamount to moral subversion. "He killed mosquitoes," writes one biographer, "as if they were lions." T. R.'s anger, his valet recalled, "was a thing to behold. But it was extremely rare." It must often have been as transparent as it was rare, for many of his adversaries forgave T. R.'s bluster. As Irvin Cobb put it: "You had to hate the Colonel a whole lot to keep from loving him."

As his first term ended, Roosevelt could not look forward to the Republican nomination with unqualified certainty, for he had alienated large segments of the Republican party and many big-business men. But the election of 1904 was to prove that he could still muster the support of some of the nation's biggest money men. Aware, no doubt, of T. R.'s formidable value as a safety valve of reform, Morgan, Harriman, Rockefeller, Frick, and Gould cheerfully backed him. Running against the colorless Alton B. Parker, the Colonel galloped to victory, 7,628,461 votes to 5,084,223.

Escorted to the Capitol steps by cowboys, Indians, and the inevitable Rough Riders on March 4, 1905, Roosevelt delivered an Inaugural Address notable for its brevity and for its consciousness of America's new role in the world. "We have become a great nation, forced by the fact of its greatness into relations with the other nations of the earth, and we must behave as beseems a people with such responsibilities." Wearing a ring containing a lock of hair from Lincoln's brow, the President continued: "Our forefathers faced certain perils which we have

DRAWING THE LINE IN MISSISSIPPI

Copyright, 1906, by Edward Stern & Co., Inc.

"They spent some days in seeing the town:
Doing Fifth Avenue up and down."

T. R.'s refusal to shoot a bear cub became an instant legend, first inspiring cartoons and then a series of stories, The Adventures of the Roosevelt Bears. *Above right, the Teddy bears stroll down Fifth Avenue.*

outgrown. We now face other perils, the very existence of which it was impossible that they should foresee." The development of corporate capitalism, T. R. declared, had given America "marvelous material well-being," but had also imposed "the care and anxiety inseparable from the accumulation of great wealth in industrial centers." This crisis, Roosevelt warned, must be faced squarely and solved: "If we fail, the cause of free self-government throughout the world will rock to its foundations. . . ."

Now President in his own right, Theodore Roosevelt resumed his battle against the abuses of big business. In 1906 he signed the Pure Food and Drug Act, prohibiting the manufacture, sale, or interstate transportation of adulterated food, drugs, medicine, or liquor, and requiring honest labeling of ingredients. An act was passed ordering the regular inspection of stockyards and packing houses. The Hepburn Act gave the Interstate Commerce Commission the right to regulate the rates of railroads, express companies, and terminal facilities.

Roosevelt has been accused of using reform largely as an instrument of political power. It is pointed out that even in the famed Northern Securities case no criminal prosecutions were pursued. It is noted that

the conservative Taft instituted more than twice as many suits against the trusts as did T. R. It has been shown that despite his image as a popular crusader, T. R.'s major advisers were industrialists or bankers. It is lamented that in seizing leadership of the progressive movement from men such as La Follette and Bryan, Roosevelt in fact emasculated it. Even on the purely human level of race relations, it is argued, T. R.'s agreement with Booker T. Washington to appoint "just enough [Negroes] to make it evident that they were not being entirely proscribed" embodied unconscionable hypocrisy.

These criticisms cannot be denied. Roosevelt was unquestionably a pragmatic politician, a realist unwilling to risk personal position for pie in the sky. He worked with his party as closely as possible. "One must learn . . ." he said, "not to jeopardize one's power for doing the good that is possible by efforts to correct evils over which one has no control. . . ." Roosevelt was not a basic theorist, as Jefferson had been. He did not seek a fundamental change in the socioeconomic structure. Embodying and sustaining the central prejudices and interests of his class, he was concerned less with the sources than with the unsettling symptoms

ALTON B. PARKER

Teddy Roosevelt, fast becoming a popular legend in his own time, was opposed in 1904 by honest, straightforward, colorless Judge Alton B. Parker. Appealing to big business, the Democrats portrayed Parker as a staunch conservative; but as one newspaper said, industry preferred "the impulsive candidate of the party of conservatism to the conservative candidate of the party which business interests regard as permanently and dangerously impulsive." Parker was defeated, as one wag put it, "by acclamation." Had the Democrats given a truer picture of their candidate, the landslide might not have been so severe. Born and educated in upstate New York, Parker had been elected Ulster County surrogate in 1877. At every subsequent point in his judicial rise he showed himself to be a leading Democratic vote getter and a loyal supporter of his party's candidates. By 1897 he had been named chief justice of the state court of appeals. Parker's judicial record was generally liberal—decidedly so in labor cases. He did nothing to promote his own candidacy in 1904, fearing that he might discredit himself as a judge, and insisted on informing the convention that he advocated the gold standard. Nevertheless, he was nominated on the first ballot. But the handwriting was on the wall, and William Jennings Bryan, the nominee in the two previous elections, remarked, "As soon as the election is over I shall . . . organize for the campaign of 1908."

of social evil. Where radicals would sew a new fabric, he patched. But when all this is said, it remains incontestable that Roosevelt wrote a record of reform without precedent in America. He gave voice and dignity to the great cry for justice that Americans too long had dared not speak.

Always he stressed executive leadership and federal priority. Roosevelt personally coerced, for example, the San Francisco school authorities to act reasonably when that city's exclusion and segregation of Japanese school children critically strained relations between Washington and Tokyo. Through Roosevelt's efforts Japan agreed to sign the famed "Gentleman's Agreement" of 1908, which restricted the emigration of Japanese labor to the United States.

In foreign affairs T. R.'s second term was no less dramatic than the first. Alarmed by Japan's victories over Russia at Port Arthur and Mukden, T. R. personally prevailed on the Mikado and the Czar in 1905 to accept international arbitration of their lengthy war. Roosevelt's suggested terms of settlement were largely incorporated in the Russo-Japanese agreement signed aboard the presidential yacht, *Mayflower*, at Portsmouth, New Hampshire, on September 5. For his efforts Roosevelt won the Nobel Peace Prize.

President Roosevelt, at the request of the Kaiser, also persuaded France to attend a thirteen-nation peace conference in Algeciras in January, 1906, to settle its differences over territorial control of, and commercial access to, North Africa. In the Far East in 1908 the United States signed an Open Door pact with Japan—the Root-Takahira Agreement—guaranteeing the two countries "equal opportunity for commerce and industry" in China.

T. R. sustained his close vigil in Latin-American affairs. When an anarchic Cuba requested American aid in restoring order in 1906, Roosevelt intervened directly, dispatching Secretary of War William Howard Taft to head an occupation administration until an election could be held. Again T. R. had acted without consulting Capitol Hill.

"I should not dream of asking the permission of Congress . . . " he told Taft. "You know as well as I do that it is for the enormous interest of this government to strengthen and give independence to the executive in dealing with foreign powers. . . . Therefore the important thing to do is for a President who is willing to accept responsibility to establish precedents which successors may follow. . . ."

Easily the most decisive of Roosevelt's foreign policy moves in his second term was his dispatching of the Battle Fleet of the United States Navy—sixteen battleships and twelve thousand men—on a world cruise from late 1907 to February of 1909. The first ports of call were in Japan. Alarmed by reports of a Japanese military build-up aimed at the United States and concerned, said biographer James Bishop, lest the Japanese believe he had protected their interests in San Francisco out of fear, T. R. saw the fleet off on a "courtesy" cruise, which, he insisted, would have a "pacific effect." Japan greeted this first visit of a Western battle fleet to its home waters with enthusiasm and interest. As for Roosevelt, he hailed the cruise as "the most important service that I rendered to peace." In sending the fleet he had acted alone, as with Cuba. When the chairman of the Senate Committee on Naval Affairs had told T. R. that the fleet could not go because Congress would not vote the money, Roosevelt tartly replied that he had enough money to get the fleet to the Pacific. If Congress refused to finance its return, the fleet would have to stay there.

For critics of his interventionist and preparedness policies T. R. had few words. "This people of ours," he explained in 1908, "simply does not understand how things are outside our boundaries." Roosevelt thought he did. In any case, wrote biographer Hermann Hagedorn, T. R. "found the government of the United States in the position among world powers of a new boy in school; he left it firmly established in the first rank."

At home Roosevelt waged evangelical war on "the timid good," the pacifists, the effete. The White House, he decided, was a "bully

LIBRARY OF CONGRESS

CHARLES W. FAIRBANKS

Although their political views were not compatible, Charles Warren Fairbanks was selected as Theodore Roosevelt's running mate in 1904 to balance the Republican ticket. Born in a one-room log farmhouse in Ohio, Fairbanks moved to Indianapolis in the 1870's and became a markedly successful attorney for railroad companies. He rose to national prominence as keynote speaker at the Republican convention of 1896. The following year Fairbanks was elected to the United States Senate, where he was an influential spokesman for the McKinley administration. The cool, conservative legislator, who controlled the Indiana Republican machine, had presidential aspirations, and during the 1904 campaign he traveled more than twenty-five thousand miles, hoping that the party leaders and voters would nominate him four years later. But President Roosevelt, fearing with good reason that Fairbanks would try to thwart his Square Deal programs, largely ignored his Vice President in public and made fun of him in private. He openly discussed his potential successors in Fairbanks' presence. Fairbanks was chairman of the Platform Committee at the 1912 Republican convention and predictably preferred William Howard Taft rather than former President Roosevelt. An unsuccessful favorite-son candidate for the Republican presidential nomination four years later, Fairbanks died in 1918 at the age of sixty-six.

pulpit" from which to preach "the fundamental fight for morality." "Keep your eyes on the stars, but . . . your feet on the ground." Be like the soldier and hunter; help restore "the fighting edge" to American life.

Teddy Roosevelt left his pulpit on March 4, 1909. On the night of his election victory in 1904 he had renounced a third term. So, having helped elect Taft as his successor, he stepped down, no longer forced, he said, to "one long experiment of checking [his] impulses with an iron hand."

Nineteen days after leaving the White House, he was off on a Smithsonian-sponsored hunting expedition to Africa, where he bagged more than five hundred animals and birds. He emerged from the jungle to review the Kaiser's troops, lecture at Oxford and the Sorbonne, represent Taft at the funeral of Edward VII, and deliver a Nobel Peace Prize speech. "I felt that if I met another king I should bite him," Teddy said.

Greeted on his return by a Fifth Avenue parade unequaled until Charles A. Lindbergh's reception in 1927, Roosevelt retired to his beloved Sagamore Hill in Oyster Bay, New York, but not for long. Angered by William Taft's decision to be his own boss in the Presidency and itching for his old power, T. R. took to the hustings. On August 31, 1910, at Osawatomie, Kansas, he delivered the most radical speech of his life. By the Square Deal, he now said, "I mean not merely that I stand for fair play under the present rules of the game, but that I stand for having those rules changed so as to work for a more substantial equality of opportunity and of reward for equally good service." He had moved far to the left. To the anger of businessmen, he now insisted that "property shall be the servant and not the master. . . . The citizens of the United States must effectively control the mighty commercial forces which they have themselves called into being." He advocated the adoption of an inheritance tax, health insurance, and direct primaries, and called for more powerful labor unions subject to a more centralized federal government.

For the moment he had one obvious purpose: to destroy the ungrateful Taft. "My hat is in the ring," the Colonel declared, "the fight is on, and I am stripped to the buff." He raised his banner: "We stand at Armageddon, and we battle for the Lord." But the Republican convention of 1912 chose Taft, and T. R. bolted the party. Pronouncing himself fit as a bull moose, he accepted the presidential nomination of the Progressive party. Shot by a would-be assassin in Milwaukee on October 14, 1912, Roosevelt was saved only by a metal spectacle case and a folded speech in a breast pocket that covered his heart. Despite pain, he continued his speech, heroically delivering a fifty-minute address. It was a noble moment in a most vindictive campaign. Roosevelt was to beat Taft by 631,851 votes, but in the process he would split the Republican party and give the Presidency to Wilson.

After winning a lawsuit against an editor who had charged him with tippling, T. R. was off in 1914 for a crisis-filled expedition to an unknown tributary of the Amazon. He returned home with an injured thigh and gravely weakened by jungle fever. Still restless for action when war struck Europe, he urged Wilson to let him raise a regiment to fight the Kaiser. Denied this role by the President because of his age and "intolerance of discipline," T. R. raged against Wilson. In an awful act of personal vengeance he collaborated with Henry Cabot Lodge to destroy Wilson's League of Nations.

Roosevelt stumped vigorously in Liberty Bond drives to finance the war. But his spirit, darkened by his son Quentin's death behind German lines in July, 1918, was sinking daily. On Armistice Day, November 11, 1918, the Colonel, just past sixty, entered the hospital with inflammatory rheumatism. On January 6, 1919, while Republicans talked of his fitness for the Presidency in 1920, he died of a coronary occlusion.

"He wanted to put an end to all evil in the world between sunrise and sunset," Benjamin Harrison had said of T. R. In the daylight given to him, most would agree, the Colonel had not fared badly in this fight.

—WILSON SULLIVAN

Theodore Roosevelt

A PICTURE PORTFOLIO

J. DOYLE DEWITT COLLECTION

*The Toby above is just one indicator of the wide-
spread popularity T. R. enjoyed. Holding a gun
and a book, he wears his Rough Rider uniform.*

Moving clockwise from the photograph above, one can mark T. R.'s progress—mental and physical—from an apprehensive, thoughtful lad of five to a determined-looking young man ten years later and finally to a glowering collegiate boxer, in battle array. T. R. hoped to win the Harvard lightweight championship, but never did.

638

A FAST PACE

I rose like a rocket," recalled Roosevelt of his early years in the New York assembly. Friends of the socialite-reformer predicted that his political career would be brief, but admirers noted that he had "the distinction of having convictions and living up to them." When his wife died, T. R. fled to the Badlands, where he ranched and wrote, proclaiming himself "a literary feller, not a politician, nowadays." But soon his vitality reasserted itself. "Black care rarely sits behind the rider whose pace is fast enough," he remarked. Back home, he campaigned for Republican presidential candidate James G. Blaine in 1884; politics, Roosevelt discovered, could provide an even faster pace than ranching.

Roosevelt headed the New York delegation to the Republican National Convention in 1884, when the photograph at left was taken. The next year he posed (above) for a shot to promote his Hunting Trips of a Ranchman. *The cowboy outfit was authentic, but the picture was taken in a New York studio.*

In the cartoon above, T. R. is being readied to fight for the New York mayoralty in 1886—a contest he knew would be "perfectly hopeless." Soon afterward he followed Edith Carow to London and married her there.

"I AM FIGHTING
VILE CRIME"

The decade beginning in 1886 was one of the most active in Teddy Roosevelt's life. That fall he was beaten in a mayoralty contest about the outcome of which he had had no false hopes. He rewed despite Victorian misgivings ("I have no constancy! I have no constancy!"); the next September his gentle Edith presented him with Theodore Roosevelt, Jr., of whom the proud father boasted, "He exercises more vigorously than anyone I know." But time began to hang heavy at Sagamore Hill; Roosevelt needed a new outlet for his energy. Senator Henry Cabot Lodge, who more than once would help T. R. along his way, prodded President Benjamin Harrison into giving the New Yorker a thirty-five-hundred-dollar-a-year post on the Civil Service Commission. Soon Teddy initiated an across-the-board program of enforcement of the Civil Service Law, and one of his first targets was Postmaster General John Wanamaker, master spoilsman. He accused Wanamaker of "slanderous falsehoods . . . sly in-

tolerance, cruelty, and meanness that would be shocking to a barbarian." Republican politicos soon were screaming for Roosevelt's head, but the public was on his side and so was the responsible press. Even the New York *Sun*, champion of the spoils system, commented, "Poor Harrison! If he has erred he has been punished. The irrepressible, belligerent, and enthusiastic Roosevelt has made him suffer and has more suffering in store for him." But Roosevelt became restive and began looking for other dragons to slay. Returning to New York to try to straighten out its corrupt police force, Roosevelt's zeal was unbounded. "I am fighting vile crime and hideous vice," trumpeted the new commissioner. And he got results. Police misconduct trials were opened to the public and press, and blackmailing by policemen was sharply curbed. Yet Commissioner Roosevelt was sure he had "offended so many powerful interests and so many powerful politicians that no political preferment in future will be possible for me."

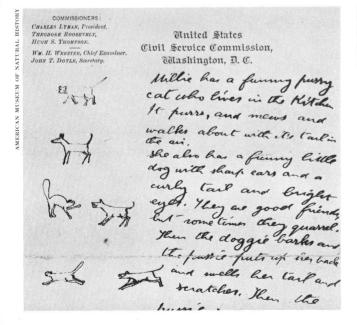

From Washington, Civil Service Commissioner Roosevelt wrote to son Ted, left, doodling some pictures in the margins. The cartoon above, whose caption begins, "He's all right when you know him . . ." reflects the animosity generated by Roosevelt's enforcement of the ban on Sunday drinking.

Before he left the Navy Department in favor of active combat, Roosevelt sent a message to Brooks Brothers, right, asking for a suitable uniform. (Brooks met its deadline.) Roosevelt and his Rough Riders chafed at having to drill—at San Antonio, Texas—and wait—at Tampa, Florida—but finally they were crammed aboard a transport bound for Cuba and glory. On July 1, T. R.'s men were in the vanguard at the storming of San Juan Hill (below), at whose summit Roosevelt found trenches "filled" with corpses of Spaniards.

Navy Department,

Washington, D. C. April 30, 1898 /89

Brooks Brothers,
    Twenty-second St.& Broadway, New York.
    Can you make me so I shall have it here by next Satur-
day a blue cravennet regular lieutenant-colonel's uniform
without yellow on collar, and with leggings? If so make it.

Theodore Roose

Charge Mr Roosevelt

"DASH AND DARING"

Senator Lodge promised President McKinley that Roosevelt would behave himself if named assistant secretary of the Navy. But after he was appointed, T. R. promptly told the Naval War College, "No triumph of peace is quite so great as the supreme triumphs of war." Long an advocate of a powerful fleet, he was in favor of building new ships of all types and advised Navy Secretary Long that torpedo-boat officers should operate their craft with "dash and daring" and that the boats should be "habitually used under circumstances which imply the risk of an accident." T. R. yearned to match his actions to his words. "Destiny assisted Roosevelt in certain instances," said author Julian Street, "but he himself usually assisted Destiny to assist him." Soon he and his Rough Riders— "the society page, financial column, and Wild West Show all wrapped up in one"— were giving Destiny a great big boost.

Charles Johnson Post, painter of both the pictures on these pages, shows Teddy Roosevelt, above, in a rumpled uniform—and in one of his favorite roles.

"Roosevelt's Idea of Reorganization," above, shows the governor keeping things stirred up, as always. McKinley and T. R. were seldom together in the 1900 campaign—except on songbooks like the one below.

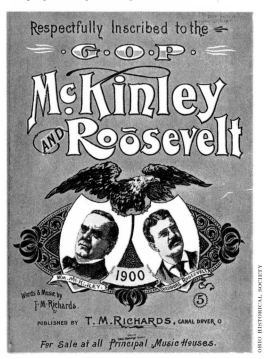

PUSHING AHEAD

How are you feeling, Colonel?" asked a reporter as T. R. returned from Cuba. "Disgracefully well!" bellowed Teddy, well aware of his soaring political stock. Much to the dismay of the reform Republicans, he soon was plotting his gubernatorial campaign with Republican boss Tom Platt. Roosevelt wanted to work within the party organization as much as possible; he told a college classmate that he planned "to be just as good . . . [a governor] as the politicians will let me be." But he could not govern without "the indispensable virtue of honesty," and in 1900 he wrote, "I have never done and shall never do one thing I ought not to do at the request of Senator Platt." Roosevelt was a monkey wrench in the New York political machine; he knew very well that Platt encouraged T. R.-for-Vice-President movements only "to get me out of the State" and was gloomy at the prospect of being "planted" for four years. When he was nominated and elected, he felt that his rise in politics was over: "I shall probably end my life as a professor in some small college." During the summer of 1901 Vice President Roosevelt divided his time between speaking engagements and taking his children and assorted cousins on long camping trips. ("My, but Uncle Ted is bully!" said a nephew. "He never asked me to wash once!") On Friday the thirteenth of September Roosevelt was looking forward to a posthike dinner at a mountain lodge when he heard that McKinley was near death. The carriage ride to the special train at North Creek was made over twisting, rainwashed roads. "Push ahead!" he urged his drivers. "If you are not afraid, I'm not. Push ahead!" The new President might have been speaking to the whole country.

The New

LARGEST REPUBLICAN CIRCULATION

VOL. XIV.—WHOLE NO. 5,036.   NEW YORK, SATURDAY MORNI...

DEATH TAKES THE
AFTER A GALI
A NATION

Roosevelt Found by Guide When Hunting on Mountain Top, Fifty-five Miles from Any Railroad.

CANNOT REACH BUFFALO UNTIL THIS AFTERNOON

Special to The Press.

ALBANY, Sept. 13.—Away on the top of Mount Marcy, attired in full hunting costume and with his gun slung over his shoulder, Theodore Roosevelt was found at 5 o'clock this evening and informed by a haggard, travel-stained guide that he was needed in Buffalo "immediately."

That word of command was sufficient to tell him what the weary messenger could not.

"Immediately," and the thoughts of the huntsman turned from the great gnarled oaks, the rippling streams, God's free air and the cool, shaded recesses where the sick room in Buffalo, with drawn blinds, gentle nurses, grave-faced surgeons and a stricken wife gathered about the broken form of the Executive.

FAR FROM ANY RAILROAD.

"Immediately," and he started on the long walk of ten miles to the upper Ta...

the train for a moment in all those hours. Full steam was kept up, and the engineer and fireman remained at their posts, not even leaving the engine cab for dinner or supper, so important was this errand of life and death.

When word was sent from the lower club house that Roosevelt had passed there all took a few hours' needed sleep, as their services would not be required until tomorrow morning.

Superintendent Hammond late to-night telegraphed from North Creek that he feared Roosevelt would not reach there until 6 o'clock to-morrow morning at the earliest. That means he will be here about 8 o'clock, and cannot reach Buffalo until to-morrow afternoon.

WHERE HE HEARD FIRST NEWS.

It was on Friday afternoon, September 6, while Vice President Roosevelt was enjoying the hospitality of the Vermont Fish and Game League at Isle La Motte, near Burlington, that the news of the great national calamity first reached him. Immediately after the shooting two telegrams were sent apprising him of the tragedy that had been enacted in the Temple of Music in Buffalo, and informing him that President...

MRS. M'KINLEY KNEW OF END

Was Told Early in the Day Her Husband Must Die.

WAS BRAVE THROUGH IT ALL

From a Staff Correspondent of The Press.

BUFFALO, Sept. 14.—In that unearthly light that surrounds a deathbed with all its unearthly halo a soft radiance was cast upon a woman who stood bravely by the President from the sound of the first pistol shot to the hour of gathering gloom.

It was her place, for she was his wife.

An invalid who not so long ago had been only a short distance removed from death's door; weak, and with a perfect trust that whatever Providence might have in store was for the best, yet she leaned heavily on her husband, the Chief Executive of this United States. He was not the President to her, only husband.

When the blow came early this morning she did not collapse or grow ill or cry out. She asked meekly to be permitted to see her husband—that was all. They had been together long, and could look back through it all without one faint shadow over bright memories.

ASKS TO SEE HIM.

"May I see him?" was all the wife and womanly woman asked.

With...

"GOD'S

M...
earth w...

He was
death in
conscious...

The subheads on the front page of the New York Press *of September 14, 1901, the day William McKinley died, focused on Vice President Roosevelt. Theodore Roosevelt was sworn in as President at Buffalo that night.*

The cartoon above, "Jack and the Wall Street Giants," shows an intrepid, if tiny, Roosevelt looking for action. But T. R. did not believe in the wholesale dissolution of big-business combinations. He saw the situation in terms of "good" and "bad" trusts—and while President, saw that the bad ones ran the Supreme Court gantlet.

T. R. BARES HIS TEETH

Where are our offices," T. R. had boomed when he became New York's police commissioner. "Where is the board room? Now, what do we do?" Such bustling exuberance would hardly do as he succeeded McKinley, but Henry Adams was soon ascribing to him "the quality that medieval theology assigned to God— *he was pure act.*" Yet T. R. moved with relative circumspection. As one observer said, "He stood close to the center and bared his teeth at the conservatives of the right and the liberals of the extreme left"—and used his executive authority deftly. He hounded the "malefactors of great wealth" by putting muscle into the Sherman Antitrust Act rather than by trying to ram through new legislation; the old guard could not complain and progressives were happy.

Roosevelt was not a President who kept his "talents undamaged in a napkin." During the coal strike he justified taking action by recalling the "old common law" precept that "a peasant could take wood that was not his if necessary for the preservation of life and health in winter weather." His Attorney General had never heard of the principle, but that neither surprised nor stopped T. R., who had made it up for the emergency. Above all else was the ever-present vitality. One newspaper marveled at "the scrapes he gets into, the scrapes he gets out of—the things he attempts . . . accomplishes . . . demolishes—his appointments and his disappointments . . . his assumptions, presumptions, omnisciences, and deficiencies." Said William Allen White: "If he was a freak, God and the times needed one."

President Roosevelt poses, above, with mine workers after the settlement of the coal strike of 1902. Although the laborers' demands for better hours had not been met and the owners had been soothed with a 10 per cent hike in coal prices, Roosevelt seemed to the public to be a new and fearless champion of the working class.

Edith Roosevelt, wrote presidential aide Archie Butt, spent "seven years in the White House without making a mistake," quite a tribute to a wife and mother who had to keep a vaudevillian household on an even keel and to function as First Lady to boot. Mrs. Roosevelt's habitual poise and equanimity, mirrored in the serene painting above by Theobald Chartran, usually saw her through. Edith oversaw the remodeling of the White House from, in President Roosevelt's words, "a shabby likeness of the ground floor of the Astor House into a simple and dignified dwelling for the head of a republic."

WHITE HOUSE CIRCUS

The populace, it was said, could no more ignore Roosevelt "than a small boy can turn his head away from a circus parade followed by a steam calliope." Watching the Executive Mansion became a national pastime. The young Roosevelts, along with cousins and pals, formed "the White House Gang," roller skating in the hallways, stilt walking in the high-ceilinged rooms, roaming at will from attic to cellar— usually accompanied by a member of the family menagerie. Precocious, vivacious "Princess Alice" startled dignitaries by sliding down banisters; she carried a live garter snake in her purse; she replied to invitations with a breezy "That'll be bully!" Alice was married in the White House and cut the cake with a borrowed military saber. Roosevelt, once asked if he could not control her, said: "I can be President of the United States or I can control Alice. I cannot possibly do both." T. R., of course, was the font of all this energy, and he showed no sign of letting up. He did his best to find recruits for his rigorous "obstacle walks" (jaunts that went through, over, and under things, but never around) and truly enjoyed seeing a congressman or ambassador panting in his wake. The President continued to box, but one day he took a blow that eventually blinded his left eye—a well-kept secret. Roosevelt's friends remained as varied as his interests. White House guests included Rudyard Kipling, George Trevelyan, Bat Masterson, and John Burroughs. With a bewildered Roosevelt niece between them, T. R. and Burroughs spent a large part of one luncheon arguing whether a certain bird's call was "twee twee" or "twee twee twee." The White House under Roosevelt was a multi-ringed circus, and the country loved it.

T. R., Jr., and his pet parrot, Eli, posed for the photograph above in 1902. Below, would-be knight-errant Quentin and a White House policeman size each other up. The Roosevelts, wrote Allen Churchill, might have been created by Booth Tarkington.

MEN OF ACHIEVEMENT

ALEXANDER GRAHAM BELL

By family tradition, Alexander Graham Bell was keenly interested in acoustics—specifically, in teaching the deaf to speak. Shortly after his emigration from Scotland in 1870 he was doing just that, at a special school in Boston, and training other teachers as well. An early interest in telegraphy led him to try to develop a "speaking" model; by June of 1875 his apparatus was transmitting varied pitches, and the following March an intelligible sentence was sent and received. Bell's device changed sound into electrical current and back into sound again. Voice waves made a disk vibrate, causing interruptions in the current of a wire connected to a second disk. These variances made the second disk vibrate precisely as the first—made it "talk." The commercial possibilities were obvious: the Bell Telephone Company had to fight more than six hundred lawsuits to protect its patents. At his Volta Laboratory, Bell invented the photophone for the transmission of speech by light, and the telephone probe for locating metal objects in human bodies. He patented improvements on Edison's phonograph and made important contributions to the stability of early aircraft. Among many other positions, Bell—who became an American citizen in 1882—was president of the National Geographic Society and a regent of the Smithsonian Institution. He died in Nova Scotia in 1922.

THOMAS EDISON

In 1870 Thomas Edison sold the rights to an improved stock ticker he had designed and used the money to begin staffing an "invention factory"; during the next decade he made his mark as one of America's great inventors. In 1874 he produced a multiplex telegraph capable of sending four messages simultaneously over a single wire; in 1876 he devised a carbon telephone transmitter; a year later the phonograph was born when Edison reproduced sound with a hand-cranked, foil-wrapped cylinder and a scoring needle. He was thirty-two in 1879, the year he developed a practicable carbon filament light bulb (earlier bulbs had been too expensive). Ever alert to the commercial possibilities of his efforts, Edison worked on auxiliary equipment—generators, conductors, cables —and soon established the Pearl Street power station in New York. He later invented the mimeograph and improved upon (among others) such items as the fluoroscope, the motion-picture projector, the electric dynamo, the storage battery, and railroad signaling devices; he was hailed as "America's most useful citizen." But more and more he concentrated on organizing companies to make and sell his products. He held a total of 1,093 patents, and his frequent battles to protect them led to his remark that a patent is "simply an invitation to a lawsuit." Thomas Edison died in 1931.

BROWN BROTHERS

COURTESY OF FORD MOTOR CO.

ORVILLE and WILBUR WRIGHT

"For some years I have been afflicted with the belief that flight is possible to man," wrote Wilbur Wright to a fellow aeronautics pioneer in 1900. Only the year before, Wilbur and his younger brother, Orville, partners in a bicycle-manufacturing firm in Dayton, Ohio, had constructed a kitelike biplane. In 1900 they built their first free-flying glider and conducted the first of their famous experiments at Kitty Hawk, North Carolina. With the pilot lying flat to reduce air resistance, the plane could be made to glide more than three hundred feet. After testing another glider with the help of a wind tunnel, the Wrights built their first powered plane, a four-cylinder machine of 750 pounds, which they launched at Kitty Hawk in 1903. The first powered flight in history lasted only twelve seconds, but it was the beginning of modern aviation. The brothers perfected their machine and two years later made a twenty-four-mile circuit flight over Huffman Field in Dayton. In 1909 the Wright brothers' patented machine was adopted by the United States Army, and in the same year the American Wright Company was organized to manufacture airplanes commercially. After Wilbur's death at forty-five in 1912, Orville Wright became president of their company; he lived until 1948, when the elder statesman of aviation died at the age of seventy-seven.

HENRY FORD

Even as a young boy Henry Ford had a passion for machinery. Abandoning the Michigan farm on which he was born, Ford moved to Detroit as a machine-shop apprentice at the age of sixteen, began experimenting with various types of engines, and in 1887 became chief engineer at the Edison power company. His most exciting work, however, was being done in a woodshed behind his house, where, in 1896, he completed his first motor vehicle, a crude contraption of two cylinders mounted on bicycle wheels. Five years later his more sophisticated "999" racing car broke all speed records and made him an international figure. In 1903 he organized the Ford Motor Company, and six years later the first "Model T" rolled off the assembly line. Ford had realized a lifelong dream. By perfecting the art of mass production he had revolutionized industry, bringing luxury items within reach of the average citizen. In 1914 he made headlines by instituting an unprecedented eight-hour day, by more than doubling the minimum daily wage to five dollars, and by organizing an employee profit-sharing plan. A dedicated pacifist, Ford sent a "Peace Ship" to Europe in 1915 in a valiant, if naïve, attempt to mediate World War I. Three years later he ran unsuccessfully for the Senate. With his son, Edsel, he established the Ford Foundation in 1936. He died in 1947.

651

MAN OF ACTION

"STAND PAT!"

The 1904 campaign button above repeats the "stand-pat" theme the Republicans had used successfully four years earlier. Roosevelt was worried about the election ("I know that after the crest is a hollow"), but his personal crest had not yet begun to break.

Now that he was in office in his own right and not "by act of God," T. R. began to press harder for reform legislation. At first he remained unwilling to alienate the conservatives and settled for less than total victory in railroad and meat-packing regulation. But soon the Senate's reactionary attitude began to chafe (he was barely able to set aside an additional seventeen million acres in federal land before a law was passed requiring congressional approval in creating future reserves). When business blamed him for the Panic of 1907, Roosevelt snapped, "If trouble comes from having the light turned on, remember that it is not really due to the light but to the misconduct which is exposed." As T. R. grew more openly liberal, he naturally fell from party grace; at the end of his term he rued that "the period of stagnation continued to rage with uninterrupted violence."

Greatly impressed by Upton Sinclair's The Jungle, *T. R. investigated the Chicago meat-packing industry, as the graphic cartoon above indicates. A law was passed calling for meat inspection at government expense, which to the progressives seemed less than the "drastic and thoroughgoing" legislation T. R. had demanded.*

Aside from the usual satisfaction he took at being at the center of things, Roosevelt must have been especially gratified in 1906 when, from the cab of a steam shovel (left), he oversaw the early progress of the Panama Canal. When Colombia had refused to ratify a canal treaty in 1903, T. R. had become firmly set against "those contemptible little creatures in Bogota" who would not give him his canal at his price. "You could no more make an agreement with the Colombian rulers," he snorted, "than you could nail currant jelly to a wall." It was much easier dealing with the new Republic of Panama—and Roosevelt got his big ditch.

Teddy's big stick went to sea in 1907 when the "White Fleet" made its "courtesy" cruise to impress world powers. Below, some American sailors try to impress the girls in Sydney, Australia.

Above, Roosevelt poses in 1909 with a testament to his prowess as a hunter. Young Kermit went along on the safari, which saw T. R. bag more than five hundred assorted birds and animals—including seventeen lions. Below, Germany's Kaiser Wilhelm II and the ex-President of America discuss world problems. T. R.'s bully European swing included "an elegant row" at the Vatican and the gift of a Teddy bear from Cambridge students.

BULL MOOSE

"All I want now is privacy," claimed Teddy, home in 1910 from adventures in Africa and Europe. "I want to close up like a native oyster." Just as he had done following his mayoralty defeat long before, he retreated to Sagamore Hill and became restless. But this time the goad to renewed activity was different. As Allen Churchill wrote, T. R. had become "a hater ... capable of man-sized fury. . . . Theodore, who always liked to say he felt strong as a bull moose, now began to resemble a wounded one." The old Rough Rider longed to sink his spurs into the flanks of the Republican wheel horse, President William Taft. Calling his former friend "hopeless," Roosevelt ignored advice to wait and make his move in 1916. He was dead set on reasserting—immediately—the primacy he assumed he had not lost. But a Roosevelt stampede never materialized at the party convention; repudiated, he cast his lot with the Progressives. Campaigning in Milwaukee, T. R. was shot at close range by a fanatic; the bullet passed through his glasses case and a manuscript of his speech and lodged within him. Displaying incredible composure, Roosevelt put his hand to his mouth and coughed. Seeing no blood, he knew that his lung was not punctured. He addressed the man who had tried to murder him as "You poor creature!" and went on to speak for nearly an hour to an understandably astounded and hypnotized audience. Later, the examining physicians marveled at T. R.'s physique and decided it was safe to leave the bullet where it was—four inches deep in his chest. Roosevelt himself thought that he "might be stiff next morning." The election went to New Jersey's governor, Woodrow Wilson, the beneficiary of the Republican schism. Disappointed, Roosevelt successfully sued a newspaper that called him a drunkard—and then went off to explore the Amazon River.

"Look up, not down—
Look out, not in—
Look forward, not backward—
And lend a hand."

Founders' Day
October 27, 1912

THE

Progressive Party

T. R.: RU OR RU NOT? *asked a headline in the New York* American *in 1911. The following year his hat was in the ring; he felt shortchanged by the Republican convention and ran as a "Bull Moose" Progressive. A third-party ribbon appears above.*

"NOTHING TO REGRET"

We have nothing to regret," said Roosevelt after his defeat in 1912, but defeat inevitably made him something of a political outcast. He and a friend went to a meeting of the Harvard Board of Overseers and found the atmosphere icy; they were, said T. R., "like a pair of Airedale pups in a convention of tomcats." The European war, however, provided a new outlet for Roosevelt's energy. He called the sinking of the *Lusitania* "murder on the high seas" and deplored all who would put "peace above righteousness"—and that included Woodrow Wilson. The President, stormed T. R., was using "elocution as a substitute for action." When America finally went to war, Roosevelt hoped to relive old times by leading men at the front. But Wilson refused his request, "actuated," said Roosevelt, "by the basest and most contemptible political reasons." T. R.'s sons were fighting in Europe, and humorist Finley Peter Dunne told him, "The first thing you know, your four sons will put the name Roosevelt on the map." But Quentin was killed in mid-1918, and, said family friend Hermann Hagedorn, "the boy in Theodore died." T. R. suffered from rheumatism, a middle-ear infection, and a thigh wound that refused to heal, yet he still wrote editorials and articles and still read voraciously. But in the early hours of January 6, 1919, the Rough Rider died. "Death had to take him sleeping," said Vice President Thomas R. Marshall, "for if Roosevelt had been awake, there would have been a fight."

Roosevelt poses above with one of his grandchildren. He once said, "I think a baby's hand is the most beautiful thing in the world." On the left is Sagamore Hill's North, or Trophy, Room, crammed with the tokens of an energetic life. With death nearly upon him, T. R. turned to Edith and said, "I wonder if you will ever know how I love Sagamore Hill." The rhinoceros-foot inkwell below was kept on the former President's desk.

657

FACTS IN SUMMARY: THEODORE ROOSEVELT

CHRONOLOGY

UNITED STATES		ROOSEVELT
	1858	*Born October 27*
Civil War begins	1861	
Lee surrenders	1865	
	1880	*Graduates from Harvard*
		Marries Alice Lee
		Enrolls in law school
Arthur becomes President	1881	*Elected to New York State assembly*
	1884	*Alice Roosevelt dies*
	1886	*Runs unsuccessfully for mayor of New York*
		Marries Edith Carow
Benjamin Harrison inaugurated	1889	*Appointed U.S. civil service commissioner*
	1895	*Appointed president of N.Y. Board of Police Commissioners*
McKinley elected President	1896	
	1897	*Appointed assistant secretary of the Navy*
Spanish-American War	1898	*Organizes "Rough Riders"*
Annexation of Hawaii		
Philippines, Puerto Rico, and Guam ceded to U.S.		*Commands forces at Kettle Hill*
		Elected governor of New York
McKinley re-elected	1900	*Elected Vice President*

UNITED STATES		ROOSEVELT
Platt Amendment adopted by Cuba	1901	*Becomes President*
		Signs Hay-Pauncefote Treaty
McKinley assassinated		
Philippine Government Act	1902	*Enforces antitrust laws*
		Forces arbitration of anthracite coal strike
U.S. recognizes Republic of Panama	1903	*Directs negotiations for Panama Canal Zone*
		Settles Alaska boundary dispute
U.S. intervenes in the Dominican Republic	1904	*Issues corollary to Monroe Doctrine*
		Elected President
	1905	*Mediates Russo-Japanese peace treaty*
Hepburn Act	1906	*Effects immigration compromise with Japan*
Pure Food and Drug Act		
Financial panic	1907	*Sends U.S. Navy on voyage around the world*
Taft elected President	1908	*Calls White House Conservation Conference*
	1909	*Ends presidential term*
		Embarks on safari
Wilson elected President	1912	*Runs for President on Progressive party ticket*
	1913	*Leaves for South America*
Wilson re-elected	1916	
U.S. enters World War I	1917	*Request to raise voluntary division refused*
	1919	*Dies January 6*

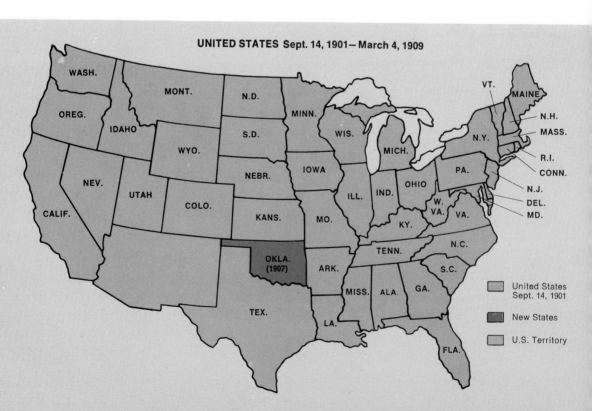

UNITED STATES Sept. 14, 1901—March 4, 1909

United States Sept. 14, 1901

New States

U.S. Territory

BIOGRAPHICAL FACTS

BIRTH: New York, N.Y., Oct. 27, 1858

ANCESTRY: Dutch, Scotch, English, Huguenot

FATHER: Theodore Roosevelt; b. New York, N.Y., Sept. 22, 1831; d. New York, N.Y., Feb. 9, 1878

FATHER'S OCCUPATIONS: Glass importer; merchant; banker

MOTHER: Martha Bulloch Roosevelt; b. Roswell, Ga., July 8, 1834; d. New York, N.Y., Feb. 14, 1884

BROTHER: Elliott (1860–1894)

SISTERS: Anna (1855–1931); Corinne (1861–1933)

FIRST WIFE: Alice Hathaway Lee; b. Chestnut Hill, Mass., July 29, 1861; d. New York, N.Y., Feb. 14, 1884

FIRST MARRIAGE: Brookline, Mass., Oct. 27, 1880

SECOND WIFE: Edith Kermit Carow; b. Norwich, Conn., Aug. 6, 1861; d. Oyster Bay, N.Y., Sept. 30, 1948

SECOND MARRIAGE: London, England, Dec. 2, 1886

CHILDREN: Alice Lee (1884–); Theodore (1887–1944); Kermit (1889–1943); Ethel Carow (1891–); Archibald Bulloch (1894–); Quentin (1897–1918)

EDUCATION: Private tutoring; B.A. from Harvard; studied law at Columbia

HOMES: 28 East 20th Street, New York, N.Y.; Sagamore Hill, Oyster Bay, N.Y.

RELIGIOUS AFFILIATION: Dutch Reformed

OCCUPATIONS BEFORE PRESIDENCY: Writer; historian; politician

MILITARY SERVICE: Lt. colonel, colonel, First U.S. Volunteer Cavalry Regiment ("Rough Riders"), 1898

PRE-PRESIDENTIAL OFFICES: New York State Assemblyman; U.S. Civil Service Commissioner; President of New York Board of Police Commissioners; Assistant Secretary of the Navy; Governor of New York; Vice President

POLITICAL PARTY: Republican; ran on Progressive ticket in 1912

AGE AT INAUGURATION: 42

OCCUPATIONS AFTER PRESIDENCY: Writer; politician

DEATH: Oyster Bay, N.Y., Jan. 6, 1919

PLACE OF BURIAL: Young's Memorial Cemetery, Oyster Bay, N.Y.

THE FIRST ADMINISTRATION

INAUGURATION: September 14, 1901; Buffalo, N.Y.

SECRETARY OF STATE: John Hay

SECRETARY OF THE TREASURY: Lyman J. Gage; Leslie M. Shaw (from Feb. 1, 1902)

SECRETARY OF WAR: Elihu Root; William H. Taft (from Feb. 1, 1904)

ATTORNEY GENERAL: Philander C. Knox; William H. Moody (from July 1, 1904)

POSTMASTER GENERAL: Charles E. Smith; Henry C. Payne (from Jan. 9, 1902); Robert J. Wynne (from Oct. 10, 1904)

SECRETARY OF THE NAVY: John D. Long; William H. Moody (from May 1, 1902); Paul Morton (from July 1, 1904)

SECRETARY OF THE INTERIOR: Ethan A. Hitchcock

SECRETARY OF AGRICULTURE: James Wilson

SECRETARY OF COMMERCE AND LABOR: George B. Cortelyou; Victor H. Metcalf (from July 1, 1904)

SUPREME COURT APPOINTMENTS: Oliver Wendell Holmes (1902); William R. Day (1903)

57th CONGRESS (March 4, 1901–March 4, 1903):
Senate: 55 Republicans; 31 Democrats; 4 Others
House: 197 Republicans; 151 Democrats; 9 Others

58th CONGRESS (March 4, 1903–March 4, 1905):
Senate: 57 Republicans; 33 Democrats
House: 208 Republicans; 178 Democrats

ELECTION OF 1904

CANDIDATES	ELECTORAL VOTE	POPULAR VOTE
Theodore Roosevelt Republican	336	7,628,461
Alton B. Parker Democratic	140	5,084,223
Eugene V. Debs Socialist	—	402,283
Silas C. Swallow Prohibition	—	258,536
Thomas E. Watson People's	—	117,183

THE SECOND ADMINISTRATION

INAUGURATION: March 4, 1905; the Capitol, Washington, D.C.

VICE PRESIDENT: Charles Warren Fairbanks

SECRETARY OF STATE: John Hay; Elihu Root (from July 19, 1905); Robert Bacon (from Jan. 27, 1909)

SECRETARY OF THE TREASURY: Leslie M. Shaw; George B. Cortelyou (from March 4, 1907)

SECRETARY OF WAR: William H. Taft; Luke E. Wright (from July 1, 1908)

ATTORNEY GENERAL: William H. Moody; Charles J. Bonaparte (from Dec. 17, 1906)

POSTMASTER GENERAL: George B. Cortelyou; George von L. Meyer (from March 4, 1907)

SECRETARY OF THE NAVY: Paul Morton; Charles J. Bonaparte (from July 1, 1905); Victor H. Metcalf (from Dec. 17, 1906); Truman H. Newberry (from Dec. 1, 1908)

SECRETARY OF THE INTERIOR: Ethan A. Hitchcock; James R. Garfield (from March 4, 1907)

SECRETARY OF AGRICULTURE: James Wilson

SECRETARY OF COMMERCE AND LABOR: Victor H. Metcalf; Oscar S. Straus (from Dec. 17, 1906)

SUPREME COURT APPOINTMENT: William H. Moody (1906)

59th CONGRESS (March 4, 1905–March 4, 1907):
Senate: 57 Republicans; 33 Democrats
House: 250 Republicans; 136 Democrats

60th CONGRESS (March 4, 1907–March 4, 1909):
Senate: 61 Republicans; 31 Democrats
House: 222 Republicans; 164 Democrats

STATE ADMITTED: Oklahoma (1907)

WILLIAM HOWARD TAFT

Villiam Howard Taft was mightily glad when he knew for certain that he would have to leave the White House at the end of a single term. During his Presidency he had lost his closest friend; many of his programs and policies had been defeated; his wife's health had failed; and he himself, engaging in political struggles for which he had neither the taste nor the temperament, had grown fatter than ever and very weary. He had run for a second term only to keep that former closest friend, Theodore Roosevelt, from becoming President again and destroying—or so Taft felt—constitutional government. He had few illusions left about himself as President. To Dr. John Wesley Hill—who suggested after the humiliating 1912 election that Taft might be renominated in 1916—he wrote that he doubted the Republicans would turn to him again. "I have proven," he said with typical objectivity, "to be a burdensome leader and not one that aroused the multitude. . . . I am entirely content to serve in the ranks." Taft was, however, underestimating himself. He could never be a member of the rank and file: neither character nor upbringing would allow it.

Taft's father, Alphonso, had been Secretary of War and Attorney General under Grant and minister to Austria-Hungary and then to Russia under Arthur. He was a remarkable man, determined, practical, single-minded. At the start of his career he had settled on Cincinnati as the city in which he would practice law because it had "very few men . . . of much talent . . . while there is an immense amount of business." Quite as pragmatically he had chosen two wives—Fanny, who died in 1852, then Louise, William's mother—and raised, with a deep, patriarchal love, six children, the conscious beginning of a dynasty. From his sons Alphonso Taft demanded "self-denial and enthusiastic hard work," first rank in class, careers in the law, and pre-eminence wherever

Joaquin Sorolla y Bastida painted this portrait of Taft in 1909.

they went. "I am not superstitious . . ." William Taft wrote to his wife as he attended his dying father in 1891, "but I have a kind of presentiment that Father has been a kind of guardian angel to me in that his wishes for my success have been so strong and intense as to bring it [success], and that as his life ebbs away and ends I shall cease to have the luck which has followed me thus far. . . . [and that] I shall settle down to humdrum commonplace practice in Cincinnati, managing to eke out only enough to support us."

It was a remarkable prophecy, coming as it did from the man who was then Solicitor General of the United States. It was, of course, not fulfilled. Taft continued to advance until he held the highest office in the United States, the Presidency, and finally the office he had wanted most, the Chief Justiceship of the Supreme Court.

The future President was born on September 15, 1857. "He has such a large waist," his mother told a relative, "that he cannot wear any of the dresses that are made with belts." Called Willie, Will, and Big Lub, Taft went to the Sixteenth District School and then to Woodward High, where he ranked second in his graduating class. (When he had ranked fifth after one school marking period, his father had commented, "Mediocrity will not do for Will.") In 1874 he entered Yale, where he became, according to a classmate, "the most admired and respected man not only in my class but in all Yale." Once again he was second in his class.

The summer after graduation he began reading law in his father's office and that fall entered Cincinnati Law School. Soon he was supplementing his education and earning an income through a job as court reporter for the Cincinnati *Commercial.* Even before he passed the state bar examination, he became, in 1880, a Republican politician, participating in his father's unsuccessful campaign for the governorship of Ohio. Later that year he supported the successful candidate for county prosecutor and was himself appointed assistant prosecutor. In 1882 Taft was named district collector of internal revenue by President Chester A. Arthur.

Mrs. Taft apparently had found a belted dress big enough for baby Will by the time this was taken.

He kept the job for only a year; he was not trained to handle its complexities, and, moreover, he found himself in an unsettling disagreement with Arthur. The President wanted to replace, for political reasons, some men in the district office whom Taft considered his best employees. Taft would not cooperate and finally resigned to enter private law practice. But he remained active in politics, and in 1887, when Taft was thirty, he was named to a vacancy on the bench of the state superior court. He soon won election to the judgeship in his own right.

In 1890 Taft went to Washington, at the behest of President Harrison, to assume the office of solicitor general—the federal government's attorney before the Supreme Court. By then he had married Helen Herron, a Cincinnati girl whose ambition for Taft matched that of Taft's father. At the age of seventeen she had decided she would marry a man she thought would some day be President. Before Alphonso Taft died, he had begun to believe his son could be President and had told him so. Helen—"Nellie"—took up where Alphonso left off.

Congress created appeals courts in the federal districts in 1891, and Will Taft coveted an appointment to a new judgeship on the sixth circuit—Ohio, Kentucky, Michigan,

Taft excelled as a student at Woodward High and was a fair baseball player, with a strong arm.

and Tennessee. But this meant leaving Washington, and Nellie tried to talk him out of it. It would, she warned, "put an end to all the opportunities . . . of being thrown with the bigwigs." But when the appointment was offered, he took it. In the interpretation of law he found the order, traditions, and relative quiet he craved. ("I love judges," he had once said, "and I love courts. They are my ideals, that typify on earth what we shall meet hereafter in heaven under a just God.")

In his new position Taft helped strengthen the virtually unused Sherman Antitrust Act. He was the first judge to state flatly and thoroughly that laborers had a right to strike. And he also sided with labor in cases involving injuries caused by employer negligence. By his peers he was considered a good judge, even an outstanding one, and soon he was in line for a Supreme Court seat.

Then, in January, 1900, his life took an unexpected turn. President McKinley called him to Washington and asked him to head a commission being formed to govern the recently annexed Philippine Islands. The Filipinos wanted independence, and there was considerable popular sentiment in the United States for providing it quickly. But although Taft had disapproved of the annexation, he now shared McKinley's view that the Filipinos would have to be taught self-government before independence could be granted.

He hesitated over taking the assignment because he hated to leave the bench. But when McKinley promised an eventual appointment to the Supreme Court, Taft decided to accept. In mid-April, 1900, accompanied by Nellie and his three children, he sailed for the Philippines. He expected to be away less than a year. As it turned out he became the first American civil governor of the islands in July, 1901, and remained in that post until the beginning of 1904. Sympathetic toward the restless, emotional Filipinos, he brought them quickly into their government. He built up educational facilities, revolutionized the corrupt courts, improved roads and harbors, and fought to open markets for Philippine products. Because land owned by the Catholic Church and rented out to Filipino farmers had for years been a source of native irritation, Taft negotiated with the Church, and even made a trip to Rome, to acquire the land for the islanders themselves.

Taft worked incessantly despite illness and despite the heat—which he hated. The new President, Theodore Roosevelt, twice offered Taft the long-awaited appointment to the Supreme Court. But Taft felt responsible for the Filipinos' welfare, and Roosevelt was able to get him back to Washington at last only by making him Secretary of War, a post that would allow Taft to continue to oversee the Philippines.

His friendship with Theodore Roosevelt, which had begun during Taft's tenure as solicitor general, blossomed into an extraordinary relationship. Roosevelt was tense, energetic, inclined to be carried away by his enthusiasms, and very conscious of himself as "the Leader." Taft was judicious and judicial, a highly competent administrator, and as faithful a follower as Roosevelt could wish. The two men encouraged, checked, and nourished each other. Taft quickly found that his role far exceeded that of an ordinary Secretary of War: he was an adviser, a roving ambassador, even a stand-in. Once Roosevelt went off on vacation, telling the press the government was in good hands. Taft was in Washington, he said, "sitting on the lid." Taft was sent to Panama to "make the dirt fly" on the Canal. He returned to the Philippines to smooth out some difficulties there and on the way stopped in Japan to discuss the Russo-Japanese War. In 1906 he went to Cuba, then in the throes of revolution, to negotiate peace.

Roosevelt had once described the qualities needed in a governor of the Philippines as being the ones that would make a good President and Chief Justice. Taft, he had said then, was the only American who filled the bill. Now, as the President looked ahead to 1908, he offered Taft a remarkable choice. They talked about it a good deal, and one night in the White House library Roosevelt broached the subject to the Tafts again. Sitting in a chair with his eyes shut, Roosevelt intoned: "I am the seventh son of a seventh daughter and I have clairvoyant powers. I see a man weighing three hundred and fifty pounds. There is something hanging over his head. I cannot make out what it is. . . . At one time it looks like the presidency, then again it looks like the chief justiceship." "Make it the presidency," said Nellie. "Make it the chief justiceship," said Taft.

The rebus on this campaign button reads, "You and I Ted," referring to Roosevelt's support of Taft.

It was an honest desire on Taft's part. Although he was in the race for the presidential nomination by the summer of 1905, he did not really want it. "If the Chief Justice would retire," he said, "how simple everything would become." But Chief Justice Melville W. Fuller did not retire, and there were strong forces pushing Taft toward the White House. Roosevelt encouraged him. So did Nellie and the rest of the Taft clan—except his mother, who thought he would be unhappy as President. When Roosevelt, unsure of what Taft wanted, offered to appoint him to a vacant associate justiceship in 1906 and promised to raise him to presiding officer of the Supreme Court if the opportunity arose, the family fought successfully to keep the Secretary of War on the political merry-go-round.

Roosevelt, by controlling the 1908 convention, gained the nomination for his chosen successor, and by casting his charismatic aura about Taft, also won the election for him. When Taft defeated William Jennings Bryan by more than a million votes, Roosevelt capsuled his attitude toward the victory in a letter to historian George O. Trevelyan: "Taft will carry on the work substantially as I have. . . . I have the profound satisfaction of knowing that he will do all in his power to further . . . the great causes for which I have fought and that he will persevere in every one of the great governmental policies in which I most firmly believe." Commented contemporary historian Mark Sullivan: "In short, Taft will be me!"

But Taft could not be Roosevelt, and he knew it. "The chief function of the next administration," he had said, "is to complete and perfect the machinery" needed to effect Roosevelt's progressive ideas. Clearly his term would be slower paced, more legalistic, and less exciting than his predecessor's. It would be disappointing to a public used to a show in Washington and disappointing, ultimately, to Roosevelt. Taft foresaw this. As his friend left for a post-presidential hunting trip in Africa, Taft wrote a fond farewell message in which he told Roosevelt that whenever he was addressed as Mr. President

PUCK

This 1909 cartoon pictures Taft as Saint Patrick, driving the evildoers out of American commerce.

he instinctively looked around to see where the President—Roosevelt—was. He said he wished he could have discussed some of his early problems as President with Roosevelt and then added: "I have no doubt that when you return you will find me very much under suspicion by our friends in the West [the progressive Republicans]. . . . I have not the prestige which you had. . . . I am not attempting quite as much as you did. . . . I have not the facility for educating the public as you had through talks with correspondents, and so I fear that a large part of the public will feel as if I had fallen away from your ideals; but you know me better and will understand that I am still working away on the same old plan. . . ."

The plan of which Taft spoke largely involved reform at home, demanded by the continuing industrial revolution. Business

was tremendously powerful and not well regulated. The exploitation of land and natural resources posed grave danger to the nation's supply of water, timber, minerals, and farm land. A growing population and migration from the farms to the industrialized cities were creating a new urban America, with attendant problems. Government, too, was growing—and needed reorganizing.

On the record, Taft did not do badly. He moved quickly to fulfill a campaign promise for a lower tariff schedule—a reform favored particularly by farmers and consumers alarmed at the rising cost of living. Big business, on the other hand, having forced tariffs upward over the past twenty years, did not want them lowered, and the President had to struggle to get even a nominally reduced tariff through Congress. Economist F. W. Taussig has commented that the Payne-Aldrich Tariff, while it contained "no downward revision of any serious consequence," nonetheless represented a turning away from protectionism. The businessmen had been checked. They were further checked by the Taft administration's enforcement of the Sherman Antitrust Act. The Roosevelt years had seen forty-four antitrust suits brought against allegedly monopolistic corporations. Taft's Attorney General, George W. Wickersham, with the President's enthusiastic support, instituted ninety such suits.

Taft also initiated a bill, which became the Mann-Elkins Act of 1910, giving the Interstate Commerce Commission jurisdiction over the communications industry and making it easier for the I.C.C. to regulate transportation rates. Another act, one of the last that Taft signed, further enhanced the I.C.C.'s powers by allowing it to base its judgments concerning increases in railroad rates on an investigation of the physical value of a railroad and its cost of operation. Taft, later labeled conservative, was thus invading the "private sector." He invaded it again by favoring the enactment of a 2 per cent tax on corporate income, which Taft believed would "give the federal government an opportunity to secure most valuable information in respect to the conduct of corporations, their actual financial condition."

In the area of conservation, Taft was again not the innovator but the legalizer. Roosevelt had, on his own authority, taken millions of acres of land out of the public domain to protect them; Taft doubted that the President had this right and got Congress to enact a law specifically giving the Executive such power. At the end of Roosevelt's administration large sections of land in the Northwest had, by executive action, been brought under federal protection as possible water-power sites; Taft quickly rescinded the order and initiated a study by the Geological Survey to determine just which acreage should be withdrawn. A twenty-million-dollar bond issue was also authorized to provide funds for irrigation projects.

Taft's governmental reforms were impressive. By keeping a close watch on administrative spending he saved millions of dollars. He set up the Commission on Efficiency and Economy to report on the financial operations of the federal government; although no action was taken on the recommendations of the commission during Taft's term, they led to the creation of the Bureau of the Budget under Harding. The Taft-sponsored Publicity Act opened to public scrutiny the lists of campaign contributions made in races for the House of Representatives. Taft issued an Executive Order bringing eight thousand assistant postmasters into the civil service. A constitutional amendment providing for the direct election of United States senators was sent to the states for ratification. And to help finance government, Taft advocated and Congress passed another amendment, which authorized federal income taxes.

All told, it was a productive administration domestically, but there were failures in domestic policy that were politically fatal to the President. The causes lay in schisms within the Republican party. Taft felt forced, by the nature of his first Congress, to depend upon the conservatives in his party, particularly the immensely powerful House Speaker, Joseph G. ("Uncle Joe") Cannon of Illinois. This meant he had to offer the *quid pro quo* of political support; and he laid himself open

to attack by the progressives, who desperately wished to replace the old leadership. When the Payne-Aldrich Tariff was passed—after Taft had skillfully won Cannon's support on the issue—the progressives were dissatisfied; some of them claimed that the law actually increased the tariff rates. This was not true, but clearly the new tariff was only a start at reform. During a thirteen-thousand-mile tour of the nation in 1909, Taft chose the heart of progressive country—Winona, Minnesota—as the place to make the unfortunate claim that the tariff bill was "the best bill that the Republican party ever passed."

His legalistic approach to conservation also got him in trouble with the progressives. Before six months of his administration had elapsed, he was locked in combat with the conservationists, particularly with the fanatic Rooseveltian Gifford Pinchot, whom Taft had retained as chief of the Forest Service. In November, 1909, Secretary of the Interior Richard A. Ballinger was charged with corruption for allowing private acquisition of vast coal lands in Alaska. Pinchot wrote a letter to a progressive senator in which he attacked both Ballinger and Taft, who was supporting his Secretary. For this insubordination the President fired Pinchot —reluctantly, knowing it might affect his friendship with Roosevelt. To his dismay, the uproar that followed eventually forced Ballinger's resignation, though the facts indicated that he had behaved impeccably.

Because of his fight with the progressives, and because he disliked using "patronage as a club," Taft never had effective control over Congress. And when, in 1910, the Republicans lost their majority in the House, Taft had an even more difficult time getting domestic legislation passed.

Nor was his record in foreign affairs impressive. He and his Secretary of State, Philander C. Knox, extended the Open Door policy to Latin America and created "Dollar Diplomacy," which they viewed as a logical extension of the Open Door demands for fair treatment in foreign trade. In the future, their policy implied, the American government's prestige—and its troops, if necessary —would be used to further American business interests abroad, while those interests themselves would be used to influence foreign governments. Because of this policy, which the United States chose to continue after Taft's term, America earned the lasting distrust of revolutionaries around the world.

Taft caused an uproar in foreign capitals when he stated that since the United States had built the Panama Canal, American shipping should be exempt from tolls when it opened. There was some justification for this point of view, but it was in conflict with the Hay-Pauncefote Treaty, in which the United States had agreed that all nations would be charged equal tolls. Taft was adamant, but Wilson later reversed the ruling.

Taft fought hard for a reciprocity treaty with Canada to lower the tariff barriers between the two nations. In July, 1911, he finally forced the treaty through Congress. But Canadians had become alarmed at the possibility that the treaty would be used by the United States as a wedge for the ultimate annexation of Canada, and in a Canadian election, reciprocity lost.

The administration did have some small diplomatic successes, but the balance sheet clearly had more debits than credits, particularly after the Senate defeated the measure Taft had hoped would be a bright achievement in foreign policy. Taft favored the creation of some system by which the nations of the world would be able to adjudicate disagreements that might lead to war. In 1910 he began sounding out other countries on the subject, but few were interested. The next year, however, treaties were worked out with Great Britain and France; the United States and each "partner" nation agreed to submit disputes to an authority, such as the International Court at The Hague. These treaties went further than earlier agreements in that they included, as potentially subject to arbitration, questions of national honor—in Taft's words, "the questions which . . . are likely to lead to war." Since there might be some doubt as to whether an issue was properly justiciable by the arbitration

JAMES S. SHERMAN

The delegates to the 1908 Republican convention, resentful that Roosevelt had chosen their presidential candidate, named the ultraconservative representative from New York, James S. Sherman, as Taft's running mate. Born in Utica in 1855, Sherman had been a banker and businessman and a member of Congress almost without interruption since 1887. He was considered an outstanding parliamentarian. For a while he and Taft got on well together; the President even played golf with Sherman—and though Taft was a confirmed duffer, "Sunny Jim" played a worse game. Sherman offered some useful political advice to his chief. He set up a committee to investigate the Ballinger affair in such a way that proadministration findings were assured. When Taft, caught in the middle of a New York State political battle between Sherman and Roosevelt, sided first with Sherman, then with T. R., and finally blamed the fight on Sherman, the Vice President dutifully kept quiet. Taft gave Sherman no favors in return and even dropped him as a golf partner. Despite the split, Sherman was renominated in 1912—the first Vice President to be so honored since John Calhoun. Taft had more than one reason to lament this fact: Sherman died on October 30, thus weakening an already losing cause. Less than a week later, three and a half million Americans voted for the Taft-Sherman ticket, one half of which was dead.

authority, each question was first to be studied by a joint high commission, composed of three representatives of each party to the dispute. This commission would then decide whether the dispute would be arbitrated. The Senate, led by Henry Cabot Lodge, encumbered the treaties with reservations and lopped off the section concerning the high commission; instead, it gave to itself and to the President the right to decide whether to present a question for arbitration. "To play the game of 'Heads I win, tails you lose,'" Taft said, "is to accomplish nothing . . . toward Christian civilization." He refused to sign the Senate's product.

One of Taft's major opponents in the arbitration-treaty argument had been Theodore Roosevelt, home from his African safari unscathed, refreshed, but decidedly at loose ends. Inevitably, he re-entered the political arena, and almost as inevitably he found himself on the side of the progressives, vis-à-vis his old friend. Taft, puzzled and sorrowful, refused for many months to respond publicly to Roosevelt's assaults. But when Roosevelt took radical, "socialistic" positions on public affairs, Taft decided to fight for re-election. Even after this open split, while Roosevelt continued to make accusations—often exaggerated and sometimes utterly untrue—Taft held back from answering. His political advisers finally convinced him that he had to answer, and he did so in a speech on April 25, 1912. A reporter, looking for Taft after the address, found him sitting alone, head in hands. "Roosevelt was my closest friend," he said, and then he burst into tears.

Fight back or not, Taft was doomed. "The only question now," Chauncey M. Depew said after Taft won the Republican nomination and the Roosevelt forces decided to run the Colonel on the Progressive ticket, "is which corpse gets the most flowers." Roosevelt won 600,000 more popular votes than Taft. But Woodrow Wilson, the Democratic candidate, won the election.

"The nearer I get to the inauguration of my successor the greater the relief I feel," wrote Taft a month after the election. And so in March of 1913, at the age of fifty-five,

he happily returned to private life. The problem of what to do with his time was solved by Yale University, which offered him the Kent Chair of Constitutional Law. He said that he could not accept a chair but that a sofa of law would be fine.

But he was not to remain a private citizen for long. President Wilson named him co-chairman of the National War Labor Board during World War I. He also continued to work for the creation of a world peace organization. And then in 1921 Harding gave Taft the assignment he had wanted for decades, the Chief Justiceship of the Supreme Court. As head of the Court for nine years, he won congressional support for reforms in the federal judiciary. A conference of senior circuit court judges, headed by the Chief Justice, was set up to coordinate the federal courts. The Supreme Court, faced with an impossibly cluttered docket, was given some choice in what cases it would hear so that it could concentrate more on cases involving interpretation of the Constitution.

Taft's role as Chief Justice was thus largely that of a consolidator, not unlike the role he had tried to play as President. This is not to say that he made no contributions of importance to the interpretation of law. He wrote, for example, the majority opinion in *Myers v. United States*, a decision that asserted the President's right to remove executive appointees without the advice and consent of the Senate. He was part of a majority that denied to Congress the right to use taxes as a weapon to restrict practices it disapproved of. He helped to limit the powers of individual states in the regulation of commerce and to enlarge federal powers in the same sphere.

His weight went down. Nellie, who suffered a stroke shortly after her husband became President, had recovered. He was happy. "The truth is that in my present life I don't remember that I ever was president," he wrote in 1925. And so he lived out his life, until a heart ailment forced him to retire from the Supreme Court in February, 1930. He died a month later.

—MICHAEL HARWOOD

A PICTURE PORTFOLIO

This postal card, made for the campaign of 1908, used yarn for Taft's tie, felt for his suit, and real brass buttons.

HEIR APPARENT

When Elihu Root told President Roosevelt in 1903 that he planned to resign as Secretary of War, Roosevelt begged his friend William Howard Taft to accept the post. Taft, then governor of the Philippines, loved his job and had already turned down a Supreme Court seat to stay in the Pacific. "If only there were three of you!" Roosevelt wrote in a letter that convinced Taft to come home. "Then I would have put one of you on the Supreme Court . . . one of you in Root's place . . . and [made] one of you permanently governor of the Philippines." His enthusiasm for Taft appeared boundless. In 1901 he had said that Taft would be an ideal Chief Justice and President, and after having picked Taft to succeed him in 1908, T.R. told him, "I have always said you would be the greatest president, bar only Washington and Lincoln. . . ."

From the confines of the law court Judge Taft (shown at top in an 1887 photograph) moved into the wide arena of world affairs in 1900. During the next eight years, as governor of the Philippines and Roosevelt's Secretary of War, he traveled some 100,000 miles. Above, he visits the Philippine Islands with Alice Roosevelt in 1905.

By 1906 Taft was thought to be Roosevelt's crown prince (above). They and Elihu Root (made Secretary of State in 1905) were close friends, referring to each other by nicknames taken from The Three Musketeers. *Taft tried to convince Roosevelt that Root should be the heir apparent, but T. R. did not think Root could win.*

671

The Taft-Sherman ashtray above, with the names of past Republican candidates for the Presidency on its rim, is a souvenir of the 1908 campaign.

Taft predicted that the months before Election Day would be "a kind of nightmare for me," for he hated stumping. Below, he speaks from his train.

JOYS AND SORROWS

Taft's victory in 1908 was a triumph for the whole Taft clan, which had been pushing him toward the Presidency for years. Brother Charles, for instance, had allowed Will to make the most of his promotion to Secretary of War—a post that demanded much entertaining—by giving him up to $10,000 a year. Charles also reportedly spent $800,000 to propel him into the White House. Now, as Will, his wife Nellie, and their three children took over the Mansion, their administration promised to be as happy and brilliant as Taft's famous smile. The salary of the President had just been increased to $75,000 a year, with a $25,000 travel allowance. Nellie dressed the servants in livery and brought in so many Philippine-style furnishings and so many greens and flowers that the White House became known as the Malacañan Palace—the name of the Philippine governor's home. As expected, their party-giving was spectacular; and their administration was marked by a number of pleasant "firsts." Taft was the original golfer-President. He was the first to throw out the baseball to open the American League season. Nellie planted the first of many cherry trees from Japan at the Tidal Basin in Washington. Taft was the first to have an official presidential automobile, and the White House stables were replaced by a garage. For the first time a biplane landed on the south lawn. There was also a "last": after Taft, no President kept a cow. But all told, the Taft family's term in the Executive Mansion was not very pleasant. Nellie had a stroke a few months after the inaugural festivities and turned most of her duties as hostess over to her sisters and her daughter, Helen. President Taft quickly became exhausted by his responsibilities as Chief Executive and chief of the divided Republican party. He grew fatter than ever and began falling asleep in public.

Helen—Nellie—Taft (left, in 1909) wanted to be First Lady more than her husband wanted to be President. Therefore, she did not believe he should go onto the Supreme Court, no matter how deeply he desired to; before 1908 she thought the subject "cropped up with . . . annoying frequency." Handsome and strong-minded—and occasionally a bit waspish—she was an able and beloved helpmate. When she suffered a stroke soon after her husband's inauguration, William Taft painstakingly taught her to talk again.

Taft's size was a subject of national humor. Once, when he was in the Philippines and there was concern about his health, he reassured Root that he had just ridden twenty-five miles into the hills and had "stood trip well." Cabled Root: "How is the horse?" Below, White House workmen pose in a tub made for Taft when he was President.

A BATTLE LOST

As his biographer Henry F. Pringle has pointed out, Taft inevitably uttered "at least one unfortunate phrase . . . in every major campaign" he fought as President. In one of Taft's most important battles—an attempt to secure a reciprocity agreement with Canada—there were two such mistakes. He viewed reciprocity arrangements, under which the signatories lowered or canceled duties on goods traded between them, as one method of reducing the nation's high tariff schedule. Although he had defended the Payne-Aldrich Tariff Act as the best bill the Republicans had ever passed, it fell far short of what he wanted. So in 1910 he began talks with the Canadian finance minister, and by the beginning of 1911 an agreement had been drawn up eliminating or lowering almost all duties on farm products and a number on manufactured goods that crossed the border. But in Canada, among other objections, there was a lingering fear that the United States wanted to annex its neighbor. Taft declared, as the debate went on, that Canada and Great Britain were "coming to a parting of the ways." He repeated this phrase even after Representative James Beauchamp "Champ" Clark of Missouri had stirred Canadian anger by telling the House he personally supported reciprocity as a step to annexation. Once the measure had been enacted by Congress, at some cost to Republican unity, Taft unwisely thanked the pro-annexation William Randolph Hearst for the support the Hearst papers had given. This emotionalized the issue further. When it came to the test at a national election in Canada in September of 1911 (Rudyard Kipling wrote a warning: "It is her own soul that Canada risks today"), reciprocity lost.

Taft is depicted, at right, performing the reciprocity marriage. He has made the minister's traditional request that anyone who has good reason for objecting to the ceremony speak out, and "Tariff-Protected Monopolies" are all furiously doing so.

674

ON THE HIGH COURT

JOHN MARSHALL HARLAN

"Let it be said," John Marshall Harlan once remarked, "that I am right rather than consistent." The inconsistency he showed during his thirty-four years on the Supreme Court resulted from a border-state heritage that made him a spokesman for both nation and individual. A conservative Kentuckian, he had fought for the North during the Civil War. After four years as state attorney general he joined the Radical Republican camp, and his support of Rutherford B. Hayes won him appointment to the High Court in 1877. Harlan was a vigorous dissenter. In 1895 his minority voice defended the nation's right to levy an income tax and urged broad construction of the Constitution's commerce clause. In 1883, while his peers invalidated the Civil Rights Act of 1875, Harlan used the personal inkwell of Roger Taney—author of the Dred Scott decision—to dissent. He believed in the sanctity of the police powers of the states. He could not abide legislation by the judiciary; in the Standard Oil case of 1911 he was angered when the Court decided the Sherman Antitrust Act prohibited only "unreasonable" restraints of trade. One friend remarked that Harlan, who died in 1911, slept "with one hand on the Constitution and the other on the Bible, safe and happy in a perfect faith in justice and righteousness."

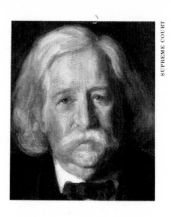

MELVILLE FULLER

Melville Fuller, named Chief Justice by Grover Cleveland in 1888, remained an old-guard Democrat throughout his twenty-one-year tenure on the Supreme Court. He believed in states' rights and personal liberty, holding that Congress derived its powers from specific grants, not from any implicit national sovereignty. After the war with Spain a series of insular cases determined the status of new American colonial acquisitions. Fuller felt that the Constitution should follow the flag and vigorously dissented when the Court upheld tariffs on territorial goods to protect mainland producers. A colony, he reasoned, should not be "a disembodied shade . . ." with its commerce "absolutely subject to the will of Congress, irrespective of constitutional provisions." Fuller had moved from Maine to Chicago in 1856, when he was twenty-three. His conscientiousness and his intelligence made him a successful lawyer in cases ranging from ecclesiastical disputes to municipal contracts. An active Democrat, his anti-Blaine campaigning in 1884 won Cleveland's gratitude. Fuller was noted for the dignity, tact, and good humor with which he ran his Court. He was also a regent of the Smithsonian Institution and a trustee of his alma mater, Bowdoin College. Chief Justice Fuller died on the Fourth of July, 1910.

EDWARD D. WHITE

The man whose "rule of reason" dictum in the Standard Oil case of 1911 so galled John Harlan was Supreme Court Chief Justice Edward D. White. In his twenty-seven years on the High Court, White left a puzzling, self-contradictory record. He dissented, for instance, in *Lochner v. New York*, which invalidated a New York law setting a ten-hour day for bakers; yet he also dissented in *Bunting v. Oregon*, which upheld a similar law. He concurred in upholding a New York workmen's compensation act, but dissented in a case sustaining a similar law in Washington. A native of Louisiana, White served in the Confederate army and then entered Louisiana politics. He was a state senator and a member of the state supreme court before his election to the United States Senate in 1890. Cleveland appointed him to the Supreme Court in 1894 for political reasons, and White's elevation to Chief Justice in 1910 probably resulted from President William Howard Taft's wish to dissolve some of the Democratic solidarity of the Solid South. White ran a dignified, kindly Court; his abiding patience made him especially popular with young, inexperienced attorneys. Regrettably, his opinions often showed a certain labored wordiness and his reasoning was not always clear. Chief Justice White was seventy-five when he died in 1921.

OLIVER WENDELL HOLMES, JR.

"The life of the law . . ." wrote Oliver Wendell Holmes, Jr., "has been experience. The felt necessities . . . have had a good deal more to do than the syllogism in determining the rules by which men should be governed." A Boston Brahmin and a veteran of the Civil War, Holmes became an attorney and a legal editor whose skepticism and refusal to accept all legal precedents and principles as automatically valid characterized his opinions during fifty years on the Massachusetts and United States supreme courts. He played no favorites; with a singularly detached intelligence firmly grounded in legal philosophy and psychology, he was generally liberal and usually on the dissenting side. He shocked Roosevelt, who had appointed him to the Supreme Court in 1902, by sharply criticizing the Sherman Antitrust Act in the Northern Securities case, but later introduced the "stream of commerce" concept that greatly tightened federal control over interstate trade. He established "clear and present danger" as the sole basis for limiting freedom of speech (but then saw the Court disavow his dictum). Holmes hated verbosity: "The 'point of contact' is the formula, the place where the boy got his finger pinched; the rest of the machinery doesn't matter." Justice Holmes retired in 1932 at the age of ninety and died three years later.

The Taft-Roosevelt split had become a bitter national joke (as the 1912 cartoon at right indicates), and the public wished it mended. At a meeting in 1911 the two men sat side by side. "Once," said an onlooker, "when they whispered together and got to laughing, it so pleased the people that they all broke into cheering and applause." Archie Butt, a friend to both Taft and Roosevelt, grew so distraught over the fight that he went to Europe for a rest. He started home on the Titanic, but was drowned when it sank.

The defeated President was happy to leave office. Below, accompanied by Senators Augustus O. Bacon of Georgia (far left) and Murray Crane of Massachusetts, he rides in the 1913 inaugural parade with President-elect Wilson.

UNDER ATTACK

When it was suggested to Taft in 1910 that his old friend Roosevelt would try to get the 1912 nomination away from him, Taft responded, "Theodore wouldn't do that." But T. R. was clearly disappointed in the man he had praised so highly less than two years before. "For a year after Taft took office . . . I would not let myself think ill of anything he did," he told Henry Cabot Lodge. "I finally had to . . . admit to myself that . . . I had all along known he was wrong on points to which I had tried to deceive myself by loudly pro-claiming . . . that he was right." When Roosevelt threw his hat in the ring for 1912, he loosed a barrage of attacks on Taft which were not to cease for years. Taft was seen as a "Buchanan president" who "meant well but meant well feebly," a "first-class lieutenant but no leader." The well-meaning, feeble leader had, however, sufficient power to win renomination, despite Roosevelt's strenuous opposition. Roosevelt ran anyway, on the Progressive ticket. In the election in November, Taft finished a poor third, and Democrat Woodrow Wilson won the Presidency.

In 1921 President Warren Harding appointed Taft Chief Justice of the Supreme Court, making him the only man to serve as both President and head of the High Court. Taft, in his judicial robes above, administered the presidential oath to two Republicans, Calvin Coolidge in 1925 and Herbert Hoover in 1929. The genial Chief Justice, who died in 1930, became one of the most beloved Americans.

FACTS IN SUMMARY: WILLIAM HOWARD TAFT

CHRONOLOGY

UNITED STATES		TAFT
Dred Scott decision	1857	*Born September 15*
Lincoln inaugurated	1861	
Civil War begins		
Battle of Gettysburg	1863	
Lincoln assassinated by Booth	1865	
Johnson impeached	1868	
Grant elected President		
	1870	*Enters Woodward High School*
Grant re-elected President	1872	
Hayes inaugurated	1877	
	1878	*Graduates from Yale University*
Garfield elected President	1880	*Graduates from Cincinnati Law School*
Arthur becomes President	1881	*Becomes assistant prosecutor of Hamilton County, Ohio*
	1882	*Appointed district collector of internal revenue*
Cleveland elected President	1884	
	1886	*Marries Helen Herron*
Interstate Commerce Act	1887	*Appointed to Ohio superior court*
Benjamin Harrison inaugurated	1889	
Sherman Antitrust Act	1890	*Becomes U.S. solicitor general*
Sherman Silver-Purchase Act		
Cleveland elected President	1892	*Appointed judge of U.S circuit court of appeals*
Repeal of Sherman Silver-Purchase Act	1893	
McKinley elected President	1896	*Becomes dean of Cincinnati Law School*
Spanish-American War	1898	
McKinley re-elected President	1900	*Becomes president of Philippine Commission*
Theodore Roosevelt becomes President	1901	*Appointed civil governor of the Philippines*
Department of Commerce and Labor established	1903	
Roosevelt elected President	1904	*Appointed Secretary of War*
Hepburn Act	1906	*Goes to Cuba to end revolution*
Pure Food and Drug Act		
Panic of 1907	1907	
White House Conservation Conference	1908	*Elected President*
Peary explores North Pole	1909	*Fights for reduced tariff rates*
Payne-Aldrich Tariff Act		*Proposes federal income tax amendment*
		Institutes "Dollar Diplomacy"

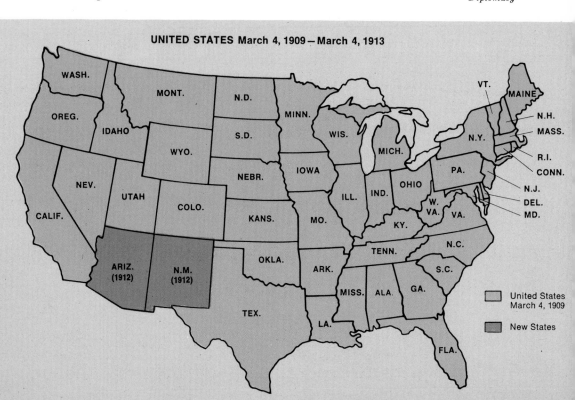

UNITED STATES March 4, 1909 — March 4, 1913

Republican insurgents gain strength	1910	*Supports Ballinger in conservation controversy*
Mann-Elkins Act		*Appoints Commission on Efficiency and Economy*
Postal Savings Act		*Strengthens Interstate Commerce Commission*
Democrats win control of House		*Advocates arbitration treaties with France and Great Britain*
National Progressive Republican League founded	1911	*Advocates reciprocity treaty with Canada*
		Breaks American Tobacco and Standard Oil trusts
Vice President Sherman dies	1912	*Loses Roosevelt's support*
Wilson elected President		*Loses presidential election*
Sixteenth and Seventeenth amendments ratified	1913	*Becomes Kent professor of constitutional law at Yale*
Federal Reserve Act		
Panama Canal opened	1914	
Wilson re-elected	1916	
U.S. enters World War I	1917	
World War I ends	1918	*Appointed joint chairman of National War Labor Board*
Harding inaugurated as President	1921	*Appointed Chief Justice of the Supreme Court*
Coolidge becomes President	1923	
Hoover elected President	1928	*Upholds President's removal powers*
	1930	*Dies March 8*

BIOGRAPHICAL FACTS

BIRTH: Cincinnati, Ohio, Sept. 15, 1857

ANCESTRY: English; Scotch-Irish

FATHER: Alphonso Taft; b. Townshend, Vt., Nov. 5, 1810; d. San Diego, Calif., May 21, 1891

FATHER'S OCCUPATIONS: Lawyer; Secretary of War; Attorney General; diplomat

MOTHER: Louise Torrey Taft; b. Boston, Mass., Sept. 1, 1827; d. Cincinnati, Ohio, Dec. 7, 1907

BROTHERS: Henry Waters (1859–1945); Horace Dutton (1861–1943)

SISTER: Frances (1865–1950)

HALF BROTHERS: Charles Phelps (1843–1929); Peter Rawson (1845–1889)

WIFE: Helen (Nellie) Herron; b. Cincinnati, Ohio, 1861; d. Washington, D.C., 1943

MARRIAGE: Cincinnati, Ohio, June 19, 1886

CHILDREN: Robert Alphonso (1889–1953); Helen (1891–   ); Charles Phelps II (1897–1917)

EDUCATION: Woodward High School, Cincinnati, Ohio; B.A. from Yale University; Cincinnati Law School

RELIGIOUS AFFILIATION: Unitarian

OCCUPATIONS BEFORE PRESIDENCY: Lawyer; judge

PRE-PRESIDENTIAL OFFICES: Assistant Prosecuting Attorney, Hamilton County, Ohio; Ohio Superior Court Judge; U.S. Solicitor General; Federal Circuit Court Judge; Civil Governor of Philippines; Secretary of War

AGE AT INAUGURATION: 51

OCCUPATIONS AFTER PRESIDENCY: Kent professor of constitutional law, Yale University; joint chairman of National War Labor Board; Chief Justice of U.S. Supreme Court

DEATH: Washington, D.C., March 8, 1930

PLACE OF BURIAL: Arlington National Cemetery, Washington, D.C.

ELECTION OF 1908

CANDIDATES	ELECTORAL VOTE	POPULAR VOTE
William H. Taft Republican	321	7,675,320
William J. Bryan Democratic	162	6,412,294
Eugene V. Debs Socialist	—	420,793
Eugene W. Chafin Prohibition	—	253,840
Thomas L. Hisgen Independence	—	82,872

THE TAFT ADMINISTRATION

INAUGURATION: March 4, 1909; House of Representatives, Washington, D.C.

VICE PRESIDENT: James S. Sherman

SECRETARY OF STATE: Philander C. Knox

SECRETARY OF THE TREASURY: Franklin MacVeagh

SECRETARY OF WAR: Jacob M. Dickinson; Henry L. Stimson (from May 22, 1911)

ATTORNEY GENERAL: George W. Wickersham

POSTMASTER GENERAL: Frank H. Hitchcock

SECRETARY OF THE NAVY: George von L. Meyer

SECRETARY OF THE INTERIOR: Richard A. Ballinger; Walter L. Fisher (from March 7, 1911)

SECRETARY OF AGRICULTURE: James Wilson

SECRETARY OF COMMERCE AND LABOR: Charles Nagel

SUPREME COURT APPOINTMENTS: Horace H. Lurton (1910); Charles E. Hughes (1910); Willis Van Devanter (1911); Joseph R. Lamar (1911); Edward D. White, Chief Justice (1910); Mahlon Pitney (1912)

61st CONGRESS (March 4, 1909–March 4, 1911):
Senate: 61 Republicans; 32 Democrats
House: 219 Republicans; 172 Democrats

62nd CONGRESS (March 4, 1911–March 4, 1913):
Senate: 51 Republicans; 41 Democrats
House: 228 Democrats; 161 Republicans; 1 Other

STATES ADMITTED: New Mexico (1912); Arizona (1912)

WOODROW WILSON

I
t was the early evening of September 15, 1910, and the scene was the Taylor Opera House in Trenton, New Jersey. A lean man with iron-gray hair and slate-blue eyes behind glittering, rimless glasses was being helped through a mass of admirers toward the stage door. "God! look at that jaw!" exclaimed an onlooker. He was getting his first glimpse of Thomas Woodrow Wilson, president of Princeton University and the man the Democrats of New Jersey had just nominated as their candidate for governor.

Not all the Democrats assembled in Trenton that evening were elated over the choice. Wilson was the candidate of Newark and Jersey City political bosses, and the progressives at the convention awaited his acceptance speech with sullen suspicion. The determined thrust of his jaw, which so startled the man at the stage door, should have been a warning to the bosses and progressives alike that Woodrow Wilson was not going to be the candidate of any faction. He was then, as ever after in his spectacular political career, his own man and his own man only. "I did not seek this nomination," Wilson said in his acceptance speech. "It has come to me absolutely unsolicited." If elected, he promised, he would be free to serve uncommitted by any prior pledges. This personal declaration of independence brought the progressives at the convention roaring to their feet. "Thank God, at last a leader has come!" one of them reportedly shouted.

It was a curious, twisting road that had led Woodrow Wilson to the New Jersey gubernatorial nomination in 1910. The candidate—and future President of the United States—had been born on December 28, 1856, in Staunton, Virginia. His father, Joseph Ruggles Wilson, was a native Ohioan of Scotch-Irish stock and had been a printer and a teacher before becoming minister of

Woodrow Wilson, portrayed by John Singer Sargent in 1917

In 1883, the year this picture was taken, Wilson enrolled at Johns Hopkins as a graduate student.

Staunton's First Presbyterian Church. Jessie Woodrow, his mother, was the daughter of another Presbyterian minister and had been born in England. A year after the birth of their first son, the Wilsons moved to Augusta, Georgia.

Woodrow Wilson later said that his first recollection was of hearing, when he was only four, that Abraham Lincoln had been elected President and that there would be war. The next few years were stamped with the bitter events of the Civil War and Reconstruction in Georgia and in South Carolina, to which his family moved in 1870. Three years later, Wilson enrolled at Davidson College, a small Presbyterian school in Piedmont, North Carolina. He was only sixteen, a frail and timid youth away from home for the first time. He left Davidson after only one year and spent the next fourteen months regaining his health.

In September, 1875, he entered the College of New Jersey, at Princeton. An intense and hard-working student, Wilson excelled at debate and oratory during his undergraduate years. Daydreaming of the political career to which these talents might lead, he wrote out on cards one day: "Thomas Woodrow Wilson, Senator from Virginia."

Upon his graduation from Princeton in 1879, Wilson entered the University of Virginia Law School. But frail health once more cut short his formal education, and he completed his law studies at home. In June, 1882, he started to practice law in Atlanta and the following October was admitted to the Georgia bar.

Young Wilson's path took an important turn when, in the fall of 1883, he entered graduate school at Baltimore's Johns Hopkins University. Less than two years later, in January, 1885, his first statement of political philosophy, *Congressional Government*, was published to unanimously enthusiastic reviews. The book submitted the constitutional system of checks and balances to a practical, political scrutiny and found it sorely lacking. It was Congress, wrote Wilson, that was dominant. The United States would be better served by its elected representatives, he suggested, if Congress reorganized itself along the British cabinet system, whereby the majority political party in the House of Commons provides a Prime Minister and cabinet members from among its own ranks. The President, he wrote, was nothing but an ineffective figurehead.

While still basking in the prominence that publication of his book had brought him, the graduate student was married in June, 1885. He had met his bride, Ellen Louise Axson, two years earlier in Rome, Georgia. The couple's first home was at Bryn Mawr College in Pennsylvania, where, that fall, Wilson took up the duties of associate professor of history. In June, 1886, he was awarded a Ph.D. from Johns Hopkins and for two more years continued to teach the fashionable young ladies at Bryn Mawr, a job he began to find tedious. His salary was only fifteen hundred dollars per year.

After two more years of teaching—at Wesleyan University in Middletown, Connecticut—Wilson was offered, and enthusiastically accepted, a full professorship of jurisprudence and political economy at his beloved alma mater, Princeton. Steadily he built a towering reputation in academic circles. In addition to his work at Princeton, he lectured at New York Law School, continued his studies at Johns Hopkins, and by 1902 had published nine scholarly volumes and thirty-five articles. Three times in these years he was offered the presidency of the University of Virginia and each time declined—as if waiting for another, more challenging opportunity. It came on June 9, 1902, when the board of trustees of Princeton unanimously elected him president.

Wilson's tenure at Princeton began with several notable triumphs. He was successful in reorganizing Princeton's course of studies and its departmental structure and in introducing the preceptoral system of education. Then in June, 1907, he launched an attack on Princeton's eating clubs, which he felt emphasized social rather than intellectual values. Wilson proposed to substitute a system of quadrangles, wherein the students could live and eat as well as study together. At first the trustees approved Wilson's plan. But when the school's alumni violently objected, the trustees backed down, and Wilson—in a preview of a later crusade to win people to his viewpoint—appealed over their heads. Traveling around the country, he undertook to explain his plan to members of various alumni clubs. He failed to rouse a following, however, and the next year the quadrangle plan was dropped. During the

Princeton Tiger

THE REAL PHANTOM SHIP

As the cartoon above illustrates, Wilson's tenure as president of Princeton had its stormy moments.

last two years of his presidency a more serious struggle developed over the location and control of a graduate school. The issue—a largely independent graduate school located off campus versus a subordinate institution on campus—seems trivial today. Yet at this time Wilson dramatically demonstrated the stubborn refusal to compromise that was to lead to his greatest defeat as President of the United States. He wanted the graduate school under his control, on campus; he saw the issue as a test of his power and prestige, and he was prepared to resign if he did not have his way. Wilson turned the dispute into a mortal contest between democracy and the forces of special privilege. The latter, in his somewhat curious viewpoint, would be served by a separate, aristocratic graduate school. The increasingly bitter fight raged on for two years and ended anticlimactically in June, 1910. A several-million-dollar bequest to Princeton rested on the establishment of an independent graduate school, off campus. Wilson, swallowing his pride, accepted the money and the battle was over. By that time, however, university affairs no longer held much interest for him, and the following October 20 he resigned. The philosopher and scholar had caught the political bug.

"It is immediately, as you know, the question of my nomination for the governorship of New Jersey," Woodrow Wilson wrote a friend the month of his defeat in the graduate-school controversy, "but that is the mere preliminary of a plan to nominate me in 1912 for the presidency."

The plan had been developing since 1906, when Colonel George Harvey, influential editor of *Harper's Weekly*, had boldly proposed the Princeton leader as the Democratic candidate for President—if not in 1908, then in 1912. In the fall of that year there was talk of Wilson running for United States senator from New Jersey in 1907, and Princeton's president cocked an attentive ear. The bosses of Newark and Jersey City thought they had found a perfect front man, but when progressive Democrats in the state announced that they would fight Wilson's nomination, he withdrew from the race rather than compete in what promised to be a sordid struggle.

In 1908 the Democrats nominated William Jennings Bryan for President for a third time. Although remaining a loyal Democrat, Wilson refused to share a speaker's platform with Bryan. "[He] is the most charming and lovable of men personally, but foolish and dangerous in his theoretical beliefs," Wilson told a reporter. Bryan's defeat by William Howard Taft that November removed the most powerful obstacle to a Wilson presidential candidacy in 1912. Clearly the Democrats would need a fresh face at the end of the next four years.

Curiously enough, Woodrow Wilson, regarded as generally conservative, was himself searching for a fresh identity. Along with Bryan's noisy campaigns, Theodore Roosevelt's Presidency had set the entire country to thinking about progressivism. But, in Wilson's opinion, neither Bryan nor Roosevelt was a successful reformer. "We must now stop preaching sermons," he told a St. Louis audience in March, 1909, "and come down to those applications which will actually correct the abuses of our national life, without any more fuss, and without any more rhetoric."

The following October, Wilson was elected president of the Short Ballot Association, a national group that believed that reduction of the number of elected city officials would lead to more efficient and responsive municipal government. Woodrow Wilson took up this cause as he did all his involvements—he made it a crusade. At Colonel Harvey's suggestion, Wilson next turned his attention to the Republicans' highly protective Payne-Aldrich Tariff. Soon thereafter he was swinging out against the trusts.

The New Jersey political bosses who had wanted Wilson as their candidate for United States senator in 1907 now urged him to run for governor in 1910. His speeches and arti-

cles were making him a widely known, popular figure. His political innocence would no doubt make him a cooperative partner, the bosses believed. His philosophy, as far as they were concerned, was of minor importance. An intermediary wrote to the Princeton president in June, 1910, offering him the gubernatorial nomination. The bosses had "not the slightest desire" that Wilson commit himself "in any way as to principles, measures or men," the man wrote. They only wanted a pledge that if elected governor, Wilson "would not set about fighting and breaking down the existing Democratic organization and replacing it with one of [his] own." Wilson, who apparently had only a vague notion of what party organizations were, easily gave the pledge. The nomination at Trenton's Taylor Opera House followed in due course.

"I never before appeared before an audience and asked for anything," he apologized in his first purely political address. But Wilson soon warmed up to campaigning. And on November 8 he won 34,000 more votes than the combined total of his Republican opponent and several minor candidates.

Wilson's governorship must be classed as one of the most successful in New Jersey or

A New Jersey newspaper cartoon (right) applauded the initiation of Governor Wilson's reform program with the caption "Good Lord! He Really Meant It!"

any state. Even before his inauguration on January 17, 1911, he moved to declare his independence from the bosses who had nominated him. One of them, James Smith, Jr., of Newark, decided to seek re-election to the Senate seat he had held without distinction in the 1890's. At the time, United States senators were still elected by state legislatures, but Wilson had advocated making the results of the recently instituted party primaries binding on the legislators. He exerted great pressure on Smith, who had not even entered the primary, to retire from the senatorial contest. When the Newark boss refused, the governor-elect moved with skill and speed to line up supporters in the legislature. By the end of December he had enough votes to defeat Smith, and when the legislature assembled the next month, James E. Martine, the primary victor, was quickly-elected. Thus, from the very outset of his political career, Wilson was indelibly marked as a progressive and an independent.

The new governor immediately drafted a program of reform on which he intended to base his entire administration. It consisted of four measures: direct primaries and election reform, legislation against corrupt practices, a workmen's compensation law, and regulation of public utilities. By April, bills pertaining to all four issues had been passed by the legislature, despite opposition by the bosses. But in the fall 1911 elections Wilson fought a two-front war and lost. Machine candidates defeated Wilson progressives in the Newark Democratic primary. And, on November 7, the Republicans surprisingly captured control of both houses of the New Jersey legislature.

Wilson's record with the 1912 session of the New Jersey legislature was nearly as dismal as his 1911 record was bright. He vetoed fifty-seven measures, revealing once again the tragic flaw in his character: an utter inability to compromise with opponents. "He had to hold the reins and do the driving alone," historian Arthur Stanley Link wrote in *Wilson: The Road to the White House;* "it was the only kind of leadership he knew."

Wilson's impressive electoral victory in 1910 and his record of accomplishment in the first year of his governorship had made him a leading contender for the 1912 Democratic presidential nomination. But despite his tireless pursuit of the endorsement in speaking tours that crisscrossed the continent in late 1911 and early 1912, the nomination was by no means Wilson's for the asking. In a series of primary victories James Beauchamp "Champ" Clark, the Speaker of the House, demonstrated that he had captured Bryan's agrarian following in the Midwest and Far West. A second candidate, Oscar W. Underwood of Alabama, chairman of the House Ways and Means Committee, was busily wrapping up state delegations in the South. By March, 1912, Wilson was writing gloomily to a political friend that Clark, Underwood, and Governor Judson Harmon of Ohio were conspiring to block his own nomination. On April 9 Clark defeated Wilson in the Illinois primary by a ratio of 3 to 1. "The back of the Wilson movement was broken yesterday in Illinois . . ." a Newark newspaper declared.

In November, 1911, Wilson had met "Colonel" Edward M. House, a wealthy Texas politician, who would develop an irrepressible yen to be a President maker. From the very first, the two found themselves in almost complete accord. Within a year their friendship ripened into an intellectual intimacy that has few if any equals in the history of American politics. Although House was never to hold elective or appointive office under Wilson, he in time became second only to the President in the Wilson administration. Feared and distrusted as the *eminence grise*, or power behind the throne, at the White House, House retained Wilson's full confidence almost till the end. "Mr. House is my second personality," Wilson once confessed. "He is my independent self. His thoughts and mine are one." But this communion of spirits was a thing of the future in 1912. Far from being President maker of that campaign, House was one of the first to look about for other candidates when the Wilson boom collapsed.

When the Democratic convention met at Baltimore on Tuesday, June 25, Champ Clark was the leading contender, with some 435 votes. A two-thirds majority—726 of the 1,088 delegates—was needed for the nomination. With only 248 votes pledged to his candidacy, the most Wilson could hope for was an alliance with Oscar M. Underwood or one of the other minor candidates that would give him the 363 votes necessary to block Clark.

The nominations got under way during the night of June 27. As predicted, Clark led the first ballot with 440½ votes; Wilson was second with 324; Harmon third with 148; Underwood fourth with 117½. Not until the tenth ballot, on the afternoon of June 28, was there any significant change in the voting. Then Tammany Hall delivered all 90 New York votes to Clark. But the expected band wagon failed to get rolling; Wilson and Underwood delegates stood fast, and the convention once more adjourned.

On the fourteenth ballot, on June 29, Bryan announced that he could no longer back Clark, who had been endorsed by Tammany, and was therefore shifting his support to Wilson. But again no landslide developed. The voting continued through Monday, July 1. On the thirtieth ballot Wilson passed Clark, but was still 266 votes short of the two-thirds majority.

The deadlock was finally broken on Tuesday, July 2, when Illinois switched to Wilson on the forty-third ballot. Several states, including Wilson's birthplace, Virginia, followed the Illinois lead, and on the forty-sixth ballot, Underwood released the delegates pledged to him. Harmon's men were also released, and Wilson, with 990 votes, was declared the Democratic nominee for President of the United States.

The Republicans, meeting two weeks earlier in Chicago, had renominated President William Howard Taft. That summer Theodore Roosevelt organized a third party, the Progressive or Bull Moose party, which nominated him in August. It would be the first real three-way contest for the Presidency since 1860. Yet, by mid-August, it was generally agreed that the contest was between Wilson and Roosevelt; Taft was on the side lines. The portly President sat on his front porch, but sedentary campaigning was not for the dynamic Roosevelt or, finally, for Wilson. At first disdaining long public-appearance trips as undignified, Wilson soon found himself drawn more and more into active campaigning. Moreover, he found that not only was he good at stumping but that he actually was enjoying it.

The climax of Wilson's campaign came on October 31 with an address to a nearly hysterical throng at New York's Madison Square Garden. "What the Democratic party proposes to do is to go into power and do the things that the Republican party has been talking about doing for sixteen years," he shouted. "There is a very simple way of doing it—to direct the provisions of your law against every specific process of monopoly which has by crushing competition built up the control of small numbers of men, and then direct the punishment against every individual who disobeys the law."

On November 5 Thomas Woodrow Wilson was elected the twenty-eighth President of the United States. The final tally was: Wilson, 6,296,547; Roosevelt, 4,118,571; Taft, 3,486,720. (Socialist Eugene V. Debs received nearly a million votes.) Taft won only 8 electoral votes, Roosevelt 88, and Wilson took the remaining 435.

Perhaps the most important event of the 1912 presidential campaign was a quiet meeting, on August 28, between Wilson and Louis D. Brandeis, who was to help shape what came to be known as the New Freedom. That day Wilson entertained Brandeis, one of the nation's most outstanding progressive lawyers; the two talked through lunch and for three hours thereafter.

Brandeis was the formulator of a philosophy of government regulation of competition as a curb against monopoly. He wanted to sweep away monopolies by eliminating all the measures of government that bestowed special privileges on special interests. He wanted to restore completely the freedom of competition that he felt was the basis of

America's greatness. Wilson's career, from the presidency of Princeton through the Presidency of the United States, is the story of a basically conservative man's slow but certain conversion to progressivism. The meeting with Brandeis was one of the most important factors in that conversion.

The New Freedom, as preached to Wilson by Brandeis and later articulated in the campaign by the candidate himself, took shape in a number of far-reaching and important reforms by the new Democratic administration after Wilson's inauguration on March 4, 1913. A downward revision of the tariff, the first major overhaul of the American protective system in sixty-five years, was the principal item of business. Throughout the nineteenth century high duties on European imports had been imposed by the federal government to protect America's fledgling manufacturers. But as American industry thrived, such duties, by keeping out lower-priced goods from abroad, had a tendency to raise the American cost of living to an unnaturally high level. This government-sponsored protection of industry came to be looked upon as a subsidy to business, paid out of the pocket of the consumer.

To underline the importance he attached to tariff reform, Wilson called Congress into special session on April 7 and the next day dramatically appeared in person to address a joint session—the first President since John Adams to do so. The purpose of Wilson's appearance on Capitol Hill, he said in the tariff address of April 8, was to demonstrate that the President "is a person, not a mere department of the Government hailing Congress from some isolated island of jealous power, sending messages, not speaking naturally and with his own voice—that he is a human being trying to cooperate with other human beings in a common service."

Exactly one month later, on May 8, the House passed the Wilson-supported Underwood tariff bill, and the measure went to the Senate. Not yet popularly elected, members of the Upper House were considered by many to be representatives of special interests rather than of the people. The Seventeenth

EUGENE V. DEBS

In 1912 Eugene V. Debs was the presidential candidate of the Socialist party for the fourth consecutive time. Long before his conversion to socialism in 1895, Debs had been an important force in the labor-union movement. A fireman on the Terre Haute and Indianapolis Railway, he helped to organize the Brotherhood of Locomotive Firemen in 1875, becoming a national officer five years later. As president of the American Railway Union, which he helped to found in 1893, he led its members in a sympathy strike against the Chicago Pullman Company in 1894. Arrested and sentenced to six months in prison, Debs became acquainted with the writings of Karl Marx and emerged from jail a socialist. In 1897 he founded the Social Democratic Party of America, which three years later became the Socialist Party of America. After Debs had urged opposition to the war with Germany and had publicly denounced the sedition policy of the government, he was sentenced to ten years imprisonment in 1918. In spite of his confinement he headed the Socialist ticket for the fifth time in 1920 and polled more than 900,000 votes. Pardoned by President Harding in 1921, Debs spent his last five years in the service of his party. He was an editor of two Socialist journals, *Appeal to Reason* and *American Appeal*, and author of a book on prison conditions, *Walls and Bars*, published posthumously in 1927.

Amendment to the Constitution, providing for direct election of United States senators, was in the process of being ratified by the state legislatures, but would not be adopted until May 31, 1913.

That summer the long and often heated debate on the Underwood bill droned on in the Senate despite the efforts of Wilson and his supporters to achieve quick enactment of the reform considered the keystone of the New Freedom. Finally, on September 9, the senators voted. But when they passed the bill, by a seven-vote margin, it not only lowered duties 4 per cent below the House version but it also included a progressive income tax. Earlier attempts by Congress to tax incomes had been declared unconstitutional by the Supreme Court. The Sixteenth Amendment, providing for a federal tax on incomes, had been passed by Congress in 1909, but had not been ratified by the states until February, 1913. Those who linked the income tax to tariff reform argued that any duties on imports whatsoever unfairly taxed the consumer. Revenue to support the government should be based on the accumulation of wealth and not on the consumption of goods. It was apparently a persuasive argument with senators about to face popular elections for the first time. In retrospect, the passage of this first income tax law is seen as the most enduring legacy of the 1913 tariff reform.

While the battle for tariff revision was still raging, Wilson undertook a second and even more important fight. "It is absolutely imperative," he announced to a joint session of Congress on June 23, 1913, "that we should give the business men of this country a banking and currency system by means of which they can make use of the freedom of enterprise and of individual initiative which we are about to bestow upon them [by tariff reform]. We are about to set them free; we must not leave them without the tools of action when they are free."

It is difficult for subsequent generations, accustomed to a sound and stable currency

A mass meeting of the Industrial Workers of the World was held in New York on May Day, 1914 (above). Organized in 1905, the I.W.W. wished to abolish wages and organize industrial unions as the basis of a workers' government. The group's influence was lessened by its refusal to support the war effort in 1917.

rigidly controlled by the federal government, to imagine the chaos that marked American banking and currency before Wilson. In 1913 the country's seven thousand banks were only loosely controlled by Washington, and they operated without any real coordination among themselves. Even worse, there was no uniform currency but rather a miscellaneous collection of gold and silver coins, certificates, greenbacks, and National Bank notes.

Champion of the conservative viewpoint was Representative Carter Glass of Virginia, chairman of the House Banking Committee. The day after Christmas, 1912, Glass had visited the President-elect at Princeton to present his proposal for a system of independent, privately controlled reserve banks. Such a decentralized system, Glass argued, would take banking control out of the hands of Wall Street interests. Wilson appeared to go along with Glass, suggesting only that the system of reserve banks be coordinated by a government board. The board, Wilson remarked, would be but a capstone to Glass's system and not by any means the central bank the Virginian opposed. In subsequent months Glass and his supporters worked out an elaborate banking structure that would have given control of both banking and currency to private bankers. The President meanwhile was coming under increasing pressure from Brandeis and other progressives to place control of the system firmly under the federal government.

For six months after his second address to Congress, Wilson was occupied almost exclusively with the struggle for banking and currency reform. "Now it is the currency I have tackled," he wrote to a friend that June. "Not an hour can I let it out of my mind." On December 23, 1913—almost a year to the day since he had first discussed the matter with Representative Glass—Woodrow Wilson signed into law the act creating the Federal Reserve System. Glass's plan for independent, regional federal reserve banks was preserved, but they were to be regulated by the Federal Reserve Board appointed by the President and not includ-

Wilson composed speeches on this typewriter, which could be adapted to type either Greek or English.

ing, as Glass had wanted, bankers. Through the long fight Wilson and his progressive supporters had conceded nothing vital.

Tariff and banking reforms, then, were the principal achievements of the New Freedom. In other areas Wilson indicated that his halting journey along the road to progressivism had not really taken him far from his conservative starting point. The President refused to endorse a federal child-labor law introduced in the House early in 1914 because he felt it was unconstitutional. Although he had seemed to favor woman suffrage during the 1912 campaign, he repeatedly held off delegations of suffragettes with the excuse that failure of the Democratic platform to endorse the vote for women prevented him from supporting the measure. With his approval, white and Negro workers were segregated in government offices. And in 1913 he backed down on appointing Brandeis to his Cabinet (either as Attorney General or Secretary of Commerce) in the face of outraged protests from conservatives and anti-Semites. In 1916, however, he appointed, and won the confirmation of, Brandeis as an associate justice of the Supreme Court.

Wilson enjoyed being President. He had the self-confidence and dedication of a man who felt himself not only uniquely endowed but perhaps divinely ordained to hold the highest office in the land. Such a bold egotism was to make possible his early triumphs in the Presidency; it was also to lead to his tragic failures later.

He once confessed, in an address to members of the National Press Club, that "my constant embarrassment is to restrain the emotions that are inside of me. You may not believe it, but I sometimes feel like a fire from a far from extinct volcano, and if the lava does not seem to spill over it is because you are not high enough to see into the basin and see the caldron boil." But few people were to see behind the austere façade Woodrow Wilson presented to the world. It has been his fate to be remembered by the American people as one of the least lovable of their Presidents.

In 1962, four decades after Wilson's death, the publication of his love letters to Ellen Axson during their engagement revealed a new, unexpectedly passionate side of the man's personality.

Twenty-six-year-old Woodrow Wilson had caught a first glimpse of the woman he was to marry during a church service in Rome, Georgia, in April, 1883. Within six months they were engaged to be married, and he wrote in a rush of emotion "how passionate love grew rapidly upon me; how all my thoughts used to center in plans to win you; what castles my hopes used to build and how I used to sicken at the prospect of hope deferred; and then how, much sooner than I had dared to hope, how by a seeming accident, we met and you gave your heart to me, it all seems so like a sweet dream that I am afraid to credit my memory."

To Ellen alone he revealed himself. In one memorable letter he related that he had awakened laughing from a joyous dream. "Can you love me in my every humour?" he asked, "or would you prefer to think of me as always dignified? I am afraid it would kill me to be always thoughtful and sensible, dignified and decorous."

"I would have you catch a glimpse of my purpose for the future," he wrote Ellen three days before their wedding on June 24, 1885, "and of the joy which that future

contains *for me*, of the gratitude I feel for *your* priceless gift of love, and of the infinite love and tenderness which is the gift of my whole heart to you. . . ." The touching message was to be his last letter to her, he believed, for after the wedding he would never allow her to be separated from him for a single day.

Woodrow, Ellen, and their three daughters—Margaret, Eleanor, and Jessie—made the White House a happy home. Two of the Wilson girls were married during their father's Presidency: Jessie on November 25, 1913, to Francis B. Sayre of Williams College; and Eleanor on May 7, 1914, to William G. McAdoo, Secretary of the Treasury in President Wilson's Cabinet.

Eleanor's wedding turned out to be one of the last public appearances the First Lady was to make. The preceding March she had fallen in her room and seemed to recover rather slowly from the accident. It was not until several months later, when it was too late to do anything, that her illness was diagnosed as tuberculosis of the kidneys and Bright's disease. At the end of May, 1914, she became bedridden, and on August 6—five days after World War I had erupted in Europe—she died. Gently releasing his wife's hand, which he had been holding in a bedside vigil, Wilson went to a window, stared out, and cried, "Oh my God, what am I to do?"

The man most deeply concerned by Wilson's seemingly incurable depression following Ellen's death was the White House physician, Dr. Cary T. Grayson. Wilson had inherited the Virginia doctor from Taft, and the two had quickly become intimate friends. It was Grayson who had urged the President to take up golf and who was his constant companion at regularly prescribed visits to the links.

In October, 1914, only two months after Ellen Wilson's death, Dr. Grayson introduced an attractive Washington widow, Edith Bolling Galt, to the President's cousin, Helen Woodrow Bones, then serving as White House hostess. In March, 1915, Miss Bones invited Mrs. Galt, by then a close friend, to tea at the White House. Wilson arrived unexpectedly with Grayson, and the two men joined the ladies for tea. A few days later, Wilson invited Mrs. Galt to dinner and shortly thereafter began taking long drives with her.

On May 4, he proposed marriage, but Mrs. Galt asked him to wait. Two weeks later she joined the official party aboard the presidential yacht, which was reviewing the Atlantic fleet in New York Harbor. "I feel like I [am] living in a story—and fear to move, lest I wake up and find it a dream . . ." she wrote. In September, she accepted Wilson's proposal.

"She seemed to come into our life here like a special gift from Heaven," Wilson wrote to a friend, "and I have won a sweet companion who will soon make me forget the intolerable loneliness and isolation of the weary months since this terrible war began." On December 18, 1915, the two were married quietly at Mrs. Galt's home in Washington, D.C.

"It would be the irony of fate if my administration had to deal chiefly with foreign affairs," Woodrow Wilson had said to a friend shortly before his inauguration. The 1912 campaign for the Presidency had been waged exclusively on domestic issues, and his mandate from the electorate was for progress and reform at home that would leave little time for matters beyond America's shores. Yet Wilson was to be faced with more immediate and far-reaching international problems than any of his predecessors. Almost from his inauguration in March, 1913, until his retirement eight years later in March, 1921, he was to be confronted with an unending series of foreign crises for which there were no precedents nor easy solutions.

In selecting his Cabinet, Wilson had no alternative to naming William Jennings Bryan Secretary of State. The long-time leader of the party, casting aside personal ambition and forgetting former slights, had loyally supported Wilson both in the convention and in the campaign; his considerable following of progressives was instru-

THOMAS R. MARSHALL

"Democrats, like poets, are born, not made," cracked Thomas R. Marshall, two-term Vice President of the United States. A loyal member of the Democratic party, Marshall was politically influential, but held no public office until 1908, when the fifty-four-year-old lawyer was elected governor of Indiana. During his four years in office he opposed rigid prohibition laws and pushed forward an important program of social and labor legislation. Presented as a favorite-son candidate at the Democratic convention of 1912, he was given the second spot on the ticket after the presidential nomination went to Woodrow Wilson. As Vice President, Marshall brought wit and humor to the routine task of presiding over the Senate. During one particularly wearisome debate, while a senator droned on about the needs of the country, Marshall turned to someone nearby and made his famous remark: "What this country needs is a really good five-cent cigar." The Vice President's role was complicated after 1918 by President Wilson's long illness. While the President lay incapacitated some members of the government felt that Marshall should assume Wilson's office; but the Constitution was not specific on the matter, and the Vice President was unwilling to appear to be a usurper. Thomas Marshall left office in 1921. In 1925, the year in which he died, he published his *Recollections*, a humorous account of his life.

mental in tipping the balance in Wilson's favor. Although the appointment of Bryan caused dismay among Wilson's more sophisticated and conservative supporters, the two dissimilar leaders got along quite well in the initial stages of the administration. Yet the President must have winced at the humorous uproar over Bryan's banishment of liquor from all diplomatic functions and the introduction of what the newspapers came to call "grape-juice diplomacy."

But Wilson had chiefly his own naïveté to blame for the long and ultimately unsuccessful imbroglio with Mexico. Applying his personal Calvinistic standards of right and wrong, he authorized American military intervention in the complex and largely misunderstood Mexican Revolution. By 1917, when United States troops were finally withdrawn, he had succeeded in doing little more than embittering United States-Mexican relations for decades to come.

But it was the outbreak of World War I in August, 1914, that was to lead to Wilson's most agonizing trials, his supreme triumphs, and—finally—his deepest tragedy.

Enduring the personal anguish of his first wife's illness and death, Woodrow Wilson was able to do nothing to mediate the international crisis. He did insist, however, on American neutrality. Setting this course for the United States, and keeping to it for the next two and one-half years, were to test all President Wilson's powers of leadership and perseverance.

At first the United States was probably as neutral as possible. Certain ties of history, language, and culture made most Americans favorably disposed toward Britain and France. On the other hand, large and vociferous minorities of Irish-Americans and German-Americans were either unrelentingly hostile to the British or openly sympathetic to Germany and Austria-Hungary. Throughout the period of uneasy American neutrality, there were a number of clashes with Britain but none that would have led to war. The introduction of unrestricted submarine warfare by Germany in early 1915 was the element that most sorely

Edith Bolling Galt, portrayed in a painting by Adolph Muller-Ury, was forty-three years old when she became the second Mrs. Woodrow Wilson.

tested, and eventually defeated, Wilson's efforts to keep America on the side lines.

The first major crisis resulted from the sinking, by a German U-boat on May 7, 1915, of the British Cunard liner *Lusitania*. Among the 1,198 who went down with the ship were 128 Americans. In one of the most unfortunate speeches of his career, three days later in Philadelphia, Wilson seemed to articulate a policy of peace at any price that was widely interpreted as cowardice. "There is such a thing as a man being too proud to fight," he said. "There is such a thing as a nation being so right that it does not need to convince others by force that it is right." Nevertheless, through successively stronger diplomatic protests to Germany, Wilson won his point. On September 1, 1915, Germany announced that it would not attack unarmed passenger liners.

In November, 1916, Wilson was narrowly re-elected to a second term on the campaign slogan "He kept us out of war."

He received 9,127,695 votes to the 8,533,507 of his Republican challenger, former Supreme Court Justice Charles Evans Hughes. The electoral vote was so close, however, that at first it appeared Hughes had taken California and thus the election.

Hughes, the story goes, went to bed on election night thinking he had been elected. When a reporter tried to reach him early the next morning with the news that he had lost California, an aide loftily said: "The President can't be disturbed." "Well," replied the reporter, "when he wakes up tell him he's no longer President." The closeness of the vote led the Republicans to hope for a recount that would reverse the outcome, and Hughes did not send a telegram conceding the election to Wilson for two weeks. Dryly commenting on the delay, Wilson said of the telegram: "It was a little moth-eaten when it got here but quite legible."

Despite its narrowness, Wilson interpreted his victory as a mandate from the people to act as international peacemaker. He started by asking the opponents to state their war aims. The Germans refused to do so, and the Allied response indicated a determination to fight to the finish. Thus rebuffed by the belligerents, Wilson went before the Senate on January 22, 1917, to deliver his clarion call for a "peace without victory." The Senate cheered Wilson's noble sentiments; Robert La Follette called the address "the greatest message of a century." But un-

known to the President, Germany was already taking steps that made America's involvement in the war inevitable.

Shortly after 4 P.M. on January 31, 1917, the German ambassador arrived at the State Department to keep an appointment with Secretary of State Robert Lansing, who had replaced Bryan. Tears welled in the German's eyes as he delivered the diplomatic note announcing that his country would resume unrestricted submarine warfare the following day. All the concessions President Wilson had wrung from Germany since the *Lusitania* was sunk in mid-1915 were at one stroke abrogated.

Four days later, on February 3, in another speech to Congress, Wilson announced that he was severing diplomatic relations with Germany. He made one last effort to stay out of the war. Hoping to avoid a confrontation with Germany, he asked Congress for permission to arm United States merchant ships against submarine attack. By a lopsided vote of 403 to 13, the House passed the armed ship bill on March 1. In the Senate, however, eleven members, led by La Follette of Wisconsin and George Norris of Nebraska, filibustered until the session's end

President Wilson, to the delight of his wife (who is seated at his right), smilingly carries on the tradition begun by William Howard Taft as he opens the 1916 American League season by throwing out the first baseball.

This painting of Marines in France was done by a Marine artist-historian, Captain John W. Thomason, Jr.

on March 4, the day before Wilson's second inauguration. Wilson raged at the action of what he called a "little group of willful men," but immediately got a ruling from the State Department that he had authority to arm merchant ships entering the war zone without the consent of Congress.

The same day the House was voting, the State Department released for publication an intercepted telegram from German Minister of Foreign Affairs Alfred Zimmermann to the German ambassador in Mexico. The inflammatory message had been decoded by experts in London. In the event of war between Germany and the United States, Zimmermann had signaled, Mexico was to be offered an alliance and given assistance in regaining from America lost territory in New Mexico, Texas, and Arizona. Mexico was to urge Japan to join her in the attack on the United States. As sensational as the Zimmermann telegram was, it took several more sinkings of merchant ships, with the loss of American lives, to drive Wilson over the brink.

On the evening of April 2 Wilson went before a special session of both houses of Congress to ask for a declaration of war against Germany. The President reviewed his efforts to maintain neutrality and commented bitterly on Germany's increasing disregard for

that neutrality. "There is one choice we cannot make, we are incapable of making," he said to those who might still hope to avoid hostilities, "we will not choose the path of submission. . . . We are glad now that we see the facts with no veil of false pretense about them," he continued, "to fight thus for the ultimate peace of the world and for the liberation of its peoples, the German peoples included: for the rights of nations great and small and the privilege of men everywhere to choose their way of life and of obedience. The world must be made safe for democracy." The Senate, by a vote of 82 to 6 on April 4, and the House, by 373 to 50 two days later, approved the declaration of war.

Woodrow Wilson, ironically, is not remembered for the war he won but rather for the peace he lost. He proved wise in his choice of the man to lead the American forces in France, General John J. "Black Jack" Pershing—and wise in his determination that Pershing's American Expeditionary Forces should fight as an independent unit alongside the Allies.

America was sadly unprepared for the vast undertaking of a foreign war, and more than a year passed before United States troops entered the fighting in division strength. Meanwhile, in the spring of 1918, Germany launched a series of initially successful offensives that nearly defeated the Allies. At Château-Thierry and Belleau Wood in June, however, the doughboys helped stop the Germans, and that summer Americans contributed substantially to the Allied counteroffensives that turned the tide.

Secret negotiations for peace were already under way when Wilson appealed to the voters on October 25, 1918, to elect Democrats in the forthcoming congressional elections as an endorsement of his wartime policies. But Americans were already tiring of Woodrow Wilson and his war; on November 5 the Republican party gained control of the House by 47 votes and of the Senate by 2 votes. Six days later World War I came to an end.

Just a week after the November 11 armistice, Wilson announced that he would lead the United States delegation to the peace conference in Europe. On frequent trips to Europe in the preceding four years, Colonel House had been perfecting a role he loved to play, that of Wilson's personal and confidential emissary—at first offering the President's mediation between belligerents and after April, 1917, representing him among the Allies. Hearing of Wilson's intention to attend the peace conference, House cabled him from Paris: "Americans here whose opinions are of value are practically unanimous in the belief that it would be unwise for you to sit in the Peace Conference. They fear that it would involve a loss of dignity. . . ." Such a trip would also be a startling break with tradition. No American President had ever traveled to Europe during his term in office. President Wilson was adamant. He would head the delegation to Paris. Since any treaty that came out of the peace conference would have to pass the United States Senate, Wilson was urged to include Republicans in the delegation. Inexplicably, he refused, announcing that the party would include, in addition to himself, only Colonel House, Secretary of State

The friendship between the capable, faithful "Colonel" Edward M. House (right) and Wilson became a casualty of the President's fatigue and ill health.

Lansing, General Tasker H. Bliss (United States representative on the Supreme War Council), and Henry White, a former diplomat, nominally a Republican but one with no political influence.

In a memorable address before Congress the preceding January 8, President Wilson had outlined fourteen points as the basis for peace. Eight of the famous Fourteen Points pertained to territorial adjustment after the war. Others called for open treaties and open negotiations of treaties, freedom of the seas, removal of economic barriers and equality of trade, reduction of armaments, and impartial adjustment of colonial claims. The fourteenth—and as far as the President was concerned the most important—related to a league of nations.

In his insistence on going to Europe, in all the negotiations at Paris, and in his subsequent fight to get the Treaty of Versailles through the Senate, President Wilson revealed that the League of Nations was of such intense importance to him that he was

willing to sacrifice everything to obtain it.

On December 4 the President and Mrs. Wilson sailed from New York on the liner *George Washington*. In France, in Britain, in Italy, Wilson received tumultuous receptions from war-weary populaces; they served to reinforce his growing conviction that he was the apostle of peace who represented the people of the world. It did not take him long after the formal opening of the peace conference in Paris on January 18, 1919, however, to realize that he would have to fight for that vision. Most of the work was conducted by the "Big Four"—Wilson, Lloyd George of Britain, Georges Clemenceau of France, and Vittorio Orlando of Italy. The other three were quietly contemptuous of the President: many of Wilson's points directly contradicted their secret treaties, and they were unwilling to surrender the territorial concessions contained in those agreements. The only thing the three seemed to agree on was a desire for vengeance on Germany.

In the subsequent months of negotiations Wilson time and time again conceded on matters of substance to maintain his one guiding principle: the League must be a part of the treaty.

In mid-February he returned to America to sign important measures before the adjournment of Congress. At an otherwise cordial dinner meeting with members of Congress, he failed to convince Republican opponents of the necessity for the League. Republican Senator Henry Cabot Lodge, a white-bearded patrician from Massachusetts, was emerging as the leader of the opposition. On March 2 he was among the thirty-nine Republican senators—enough to block Senate approval of ratification—who signed a round-robin resolution opposing the League as Wilson had outlined it and demanding that the League not be incorporated in the treaty.

Two days later, just before sailing again for Europe, Wilson spoke at a New York rally and hurled defiance at the senators. Upon his return with the completed treaty, Wilson predicted, the senators would not only find the Covenant of the League of Na-

In this drawing by Edouard Requin, the "Big Four" sign the Versailles Treaty; from left to right are Georges Clemenceau of France, Wilson, David Lloyd George of Great Britain, and Vittorio Emanuele Orlando of Italy.

tions included in it, they would find "so many threads of the treaty tied to the Covenant that you cannot dissect the Covenant from the treaty without destroying the whole vital structure."

Back in Paris, Wilson concentrated even harder on the League, to the exclusion of almost all other important items of business— including what to do with the upstart Bolsheviks who had seized power in Russia in November. In April, Wilson suffered an attack of influenza, which many later felt marked the beginning of a long decline in his mental and physical powers. He grew suspicious and resentful of House's role and even came to believe that his long-trusted adviser was betraying him.

The political wrangling at the conference grew worse, the meetings often verging on barroom brawls. At one point, the President had to step between Lloyd George and Clemenceau, who were about to exchange blows. Wilson threatened once to leave the conference, and Orlando actually did withdraw temporarily after the American President had appealed over his head to the Italian people. Wilson was scarcely on speaking terms with his French hosts by the conference's end.

Only two dejected, politically inconsequential Germans could be found to sign the treaty of vengeance on June 28, 1919. From a seat near Edith Wilson in Versailles's glittering Hall of Mirrors, Mrs. House jumped up to see her husband sign: "Please let me stand long enough to see my lamb sign." That was the last day on which Wilson was ever to see or speak to her "lamb"; the friendship was beyond repair.

Two days after his return to the United States on July 8, Wilson offered the Treaty of Versailles in an address to the Senate. "The stage is set, the destiny disclosed . . ." he concluded. "We can only go forward, with lifted eyes and freshened spirit, to follow the vision. . . . The light streams upon the path ahead, and nowhere else."

Most of the members of the Democratic minority in the Senate supported the treaty and the League of Nations, and they would

Poland awarded Wilson its White Cross medal (above) for his efforts to promote an enduring world peace.

follow faithfully Wilson's leadership in the subsequent fight over approval of ratification. The Republican opponents, however, were split into two factions: a moderate group led by Lodge, who wanted to ratify a peace treaty and worry about the League later; and the "irreconcilables," such as La Follette, Idaho's William E. Borah, and California's Hiram Johnson, who rejected the League out of hand.

In September, 1919, Wilson—realizing he lacked the votes in the Senate—appealed directly to the people. Traveling nearly ten thousand miles through the Midwest and West, he delivered some forty speeches in thirty cities between September 4 and 24. At Pueblo, Colorado, on September 25, he stumbled while stepping up to the speaker's platform. But he went on to deliver an emotional oration that brought tears to many eyes and that he concluded with tears streaming down his own face.

That night Wilson suffered what probably was a slight stroke. The months and years of his wartime Presidency, the six-month-long ordeal in Paris, the frustrations upon his return to Washington, the grueling tour —all had taken their toll. The remainder of the trip was canceled, and the presidential train rushed back to the Capital. There, on October 2, Wilson had a second, far more severe stroke that left him partially paralyzed.

For the next seven months the President was almost a recluse in the White House, cut off from most contacts with the outside world and attended principally by the faithful Dr. Grayson, his private secretary, Joseph Tumulty, and Mrs. Wilson.

Much has been written—mostly unfavorable—about Edith Wilson's role during the President's invalidism, and she has been called the nation's first Lady President. In her memoirs she confessed that she had acted, at the doctors' advice, as a screen around her husband, judging just what messages from congressmen and Cabinet members should be brought into the sickroom. When she emerged with verbal instructions or a document with an illegible scrawl that purported to be her husband's signature, no one was able to say just who was making the decisions.

Congress sent a delegation to determine whether Wilson was truly incapacitated. Vice President Thomas R. Marshall fretted about being asked to take over, and Secretary of State Lansing, after he convened and presided over a Cabinet meeting in Wilson's absence, was dismissed.

These same months witnessed the culmination of the fight for the treaty and the League in the Senate. On November 6 Lodge announced that he was for ratification but with—ironically—fourteen reservations. In a letter from the sickroom on November 18, Wilson directed his supporters to reject Lodge's reservations, and the Democrats joined the irreconcilables in voting against an amended treaty on November 19. Unconditional acceptance was then defeated by the moderate Republicans.

Subsequent attempts to revive the treaty in the early months of 1920 failed, and on May 20 Congress passed a joint resolution declaring the war at an end. Wilson vetoed the measure, which was not passed again until July 2, 1921. By that time Wilson was no longer President.

Wilson attempted to make the 1920 presidential election a "solemn referendum" for the League. There is even evidence that, ill as he was, he wanted a third-term nomination. But as the enfeebled Chief Executive sat on the side lines, the Democratic nominee, James M. Cox of Ohio, tirelessly thumped for the League—and went down to defeat at the hands of Warren G. Harding.

On March 4, 1921—Harding's Inauguration Day—police screened off photographers as Wilson was all but bodily lifted into the car that would take him and the President-elect to the Capitol. There, in the President's room, as the clock ticked away the last minutes of his term, he signed a few final bills. At last a committee from both houses of Congress arrived to ask permission to adjourn; its chairman was Henry Cabot Lodge. The two embittered opponents—Wilson throughout had blamed the Massachusetts Republican for singlehandedly defeating the League—addressed one another in frigid, formal phrases.

Former President and Mrs. Wilson did not stay for Harding's Inaugural Address, but left the Capitol by a side door and went immediately to the house on S Street in Washington's Northwest section that they had purchased for their retirement. Woodrow Wilson lived out the remaining three years of his life in semiseclusion. At first a guard had been hired, but there were no crowds of curious people to be restrained and he was dismissed.

In early 1924 word leaked out of the quiet house that Wilson was dying. Crowds once more gathered as famous people came to leave their cards. At 11:15 A.M. on February 3 Wilson died; his last word had been "Edith."

Calvin Coolidge—President since Harding's death the preceding summer—attended the small private funeral at the S Street house, but Senator Lodge, named to a committee to represent Congress, was excluded at Mrs. Wilson's request. Colonel House was not invited.

For the next four decades, Edith Wilson kept alive the memory of her husband, her increasingly infrequent appearances in public always eliciting the comment: "Is *she* still living?" She died in October, 1961, on the day she was scheduled to appear at the dedication of the Woodrow Wilson Bridge, which crosses the Potomac.

—JOSEPH L. GARDNER

Woodrow Wilson

A PICTURE PORTFOLIO

In 1919, after Wilson had sacrificed his health to crusade for peace and American participation in the League of Nations, he was awarded the Nobel Peace Prize.

Woodrow Wilson campaigned vigorously in the 1912 election, stumping the country from the rear platform of a train (above). His easy humor pleased the crowds, who gathered in railroad yards and on top of boxcars to hear him. "Fellow citizens and gentlemen in the pit, and ladies and gentlemen in the boxes," he began at one whistle-stop. The voters liked the candidate's lucid arguments for the New Freedom and his pledge of economic emancipation through tariff, trust, and banking reform.

A former college professor, Wilson (looking fragile and scholarly on the 1912 campaign button at right) had to overcome the stigma of the egghead. But his unaffected manner soon won the confidence of the voters. "Give it to 'em, Doc," yelled out one small-town farmer during one of Wilson's speeches, "you're all right."

WIN WITH WILSON

"PRESIDENT OF ALL
THE PEOPLE"

Woodrow Wilson led the Democrats to victory in 1912 as a new force in the progressive movement. Former president of Princeton University and governor of New Jersey, he was neither as conservative as his Republican opponent, William Howard Taft, nor as radical as the impulsive Theodore Roosevelt, candidate of the third-party Progressives. Rational and articulate, Wilson presented an intelligent, liberal program that he heralded as the New Freedom. His was, however, a somewhat limited progressivism, stressing economic rather than social reforms; Wilson did not approve of direct social legislation. He attacked former President Roosevelt's proposed minimum-wage program as paternalistic and dismissed the problem of woman suffrage as "not a question that is dealt with by the National Government at all." One of Wilson's concerns was winning the votes of immigrant groups. Ten years earlier he had published a conservative *History of the American People*, in which he had deplored the new wave of immigration. While he had since altered his position, Italian-, Hungarian-, and Polish-born voters could not easily forget a passage in the *History* referring to them as "the more sordid and hapless elements of their population. . . ." The Negroes were another minority group that posed a problem. Although the Democratic managers did not wish to alienate Negro voters in the North, they were determined to preserve the Solid South, even if it meant, as a party spokesman declared in an unfortunate editorial, "the subjection of the negro, politically. . . ." Yet there is little doubt that Wilson himself had profound concern for social justice. And the results of the election seemed to indicate that most Americans were convinced, as a Negro editor put it, that Wilson would be "President of all the people of every section, and of every race."

The 1912 campaign became a three-way race for the Presidency when Theodore Roosevelt, declaring himself "as strong as a bull moose," bolted the Republican party to head the new Progressive ticket. The Clifford Berryman cartoon above shows the three candidates, Wilson, Taft, and Roosevelt, starting off on the rough road that would lead one of them to the White House. Roosevelt's Bull Moose hampered the progress of the conservative Republican candidate, and Taft soon dropped behind. The race became a contest between Roosevelt and Wilson, whose progressive platforms seemed to be very similar. (Editor William Allen White likened the difference to "that fantastic imaginary gulf that always has existed between tweedle-dum and tweedle-dee.")

JOY AND SADNESS

After all the official ceremonies of Inauguration Day, 1913, the Wilson family was finally left alone with a few personal friends. Happily they set out to explore the Executive Mansion. "There was a continual running through the house from one room to another," an observer recalled, "a shrill voice screaming to someone else as a new place was discovered." The President, his wife, Ellen, and their three daughters were delighted with their new quarters. Mrs. Wilson converted the upstairs Oval Room into a family haven of books and paintings. But the harmony was shattered by Ellen's death the next summer. "I never understood before what a broken heart meant," the President told a friend.

The Wilson girls shared a love for music, dance, and theater. In a 1913 benefit performance of the Bird Masque, *vivacious Eleanor Wilson (above) danced the part of Ornis, the Bird Spirit. Her older sister Margaret provided the voice in the background.*

The First Lady serves tea to her three daughters, Margaret, Eleanor, and Jessie, in a 1913 oil by Robert Vonnah (right). Ellen Wilson was a creative woman with a talent for painting, but her easel was put aside while she worked tirelessly to help eliminate the squalid slums in the District of Columbia.

Wilson's two youngest daughters were married in the White House within six months of each other; Jessie (with wedding party above) to Francis B. Sayre and Eleanor to her father's Secretary of the Treasury, William G. McAdoo. The eldest daughter, Margaret (below with her "graphanola"), seemed to be content with a more contemplative life.

UPS AND DOWNS

Wilson's first term was a triumph for his economic program. Import duties were lowered by the Underwood Tariff (containing a provision for the new federal income tax), banking and currency control were centralized under the Federal Reserve System, and monopolies were further restricted by the Federal Trade Commission and Clayton Antitrust acts. The President's foreign policy, however, was less successful, involving the United States in the chaotic Mexican Revolution. Shortly before Wilson's inauguration, Mexico's democratic revolutionary leader had been assassinated and a reactionary dictatorship had been established under General Victoriano Huerta. Refusing to recognize the oppressive regime, Wilson began to exert pressure to remove Huerta. Although Wilson's actions undoubtedly grew out of a belief in the virtues of democracy and the evils of dictatorship, his interference angered not only Huerta but the Mexicans as well. When an incident involving the arrest of American citizens provided an excuse for armed United States intervention at Veracruz in 1914, the Mexicans united behind the dictator. The dispute was arbitrated, Huerta resigned, and the Americans withdrew—but seeds of resentment had been planted.

BROWN BROTHERS

Wilson sits with members of his first Cabinet, above. They are (left to right) Secretary of the Treasury William McAdoo, Attorney General James McReynolds, Secretary of the Navy Josephus Daniels, and Secretary of State William J. Bryan. Bryan resigned when American involvement in World War I seemed to be imminent.

Wilson's Latin-American policies were often moralistic and didactic. "I am going to teach the South American republics to elect good men!" he once told a British diplomat. In a 1913 cartoon from London's Punch magazine (left), Wilson wags his finger at Mexico in obvious disapproval of the course of the Mexican Revolution. America's interference in its neighbor's affairs created deep, lasting resentments in Mexico.

In the "Woodrow and the Bean-Stalk" cartoon below, Wilson chops the tangled roots of high protection and fells the giant representing monopoly. Wilson's downward revision of the tariff was part of a larger program of economic reform designed to check the power of the trusts, revitalize competition among smaller businesses, and bolster the United States economy in general.

CUNARD

EUROPE VIA LIVERPOOL

LUSITANIA

Fastest and Largest Steamer
now in Atlantic Service Sails
SATURDAY, MAY 1, 10 A. M.
Transylvania, Fri., May 7, 5 P.M.
Orduna, - - Tues., May 18, 10 A.M.
Tuscania, - - Fri., May 21, 5 P.M.
LUSITANIA, Sat., May 29, 10 A.M.
Transylvania, Fri., June 4, 5 P.M.

Gibraltar—Genoa—Naples—Piraeus
S.S. Carpathia, Thur., May 13, Noon

NOTICE!

TRAVELLERS intending to
embark on the Atlantic voyage
are reminded that a state of
war exists between Germany
and her allies and Great Britain
and her allies; that the zone of
war includes the waters adja-
cent to the British Isles; that,
in accordance with formal notice given by the Imperial German Government, vessels flying
the flag of Great Britain, or of
any of her allies, are liable to
destruction in those waters and
that travellers sailing in the
war zone on ships of Great
Britain or her allies do so at
their own risk.

IMPERIAL GERMAN EMBASSY

WASHINGTON, D. C., APRIL 22, 1915.

CULVER PICTURES

*Despite Germany's warning (above), Ameri-
cans were stunned by the* Lusitania *sinking.*

AVOIDING WAR

Wilson's problems
with Mexico were not over. In January,
1916, a Mexican chieftain called Pancho
Villa began a vindictive campaign that culminated in a bloody raid on Columbus,
New Mexico. Wilson ordered a punitive expedition against Villa, who lured the gringos
deep into Mexico. Alarmed by American
penetration, the Mexican government called
out its own forces, and all-out war was narrowly avoided when Wilson withdrew the
troops. Meanwhile, the United States was
trying to avoid becoming involved in a conflict of far greater proportion, the one then
raging in Europe. Issuing a neutrality proclamation, the President asked Americans to
be "impartial in thought as well as in action." But Germany's violations of neutral
rights and the *Lusitania* sinking strained
neutrality almost to the breaking point.

A punitive expedition against the bloodthirsty Mexican bandit Pancho Villa in 1916 gave the United States an opportunity to test combat planes like the Curtiss model above, later used in World War I.

As America headed toward war, pacifist delegations such as the one below stepped up their pleas for peace.

Gossips had a heyday as the President began courting Edith Galt. The couple slowed down wagging tongues by getting married in December, 1915. (Above is a newspaper illustration celebrating the match.) On one occasion Wilson had sent orchids to Mrs. Galt with this charming note: "You are the only woman I know who can wear an orchid. Generally it's the orchid that wears the woman."

The button (left) and truck (below) urged Wilson's re-election.

A SHORT-LIVED PEACE

As the threat of war increased, the nation was faced with the 1916 presidential election. Opposing Republican Charles Evans Hughes, Wilson and his Democratic managers based their campaign on the issues of progressivism and peace. Having recently signed reform measures implementing farm credit, federal workmen's compensation, restriction of child labor, and an eight-hour day for railroad workers, Wilson's record was stronger than ever. He had reversed his 1912 position on social-welfare legislation and had adopted a progressive platform that one independent supporter described as "national in scope, liberal in purpose, and effective in action." But Americans were less concerned with domestic issues than with the uncertainties of the war in Europe. Sensing the overwhelming desire of the average citizen to stay out of the conflict, the Democrats effectively pointed out that "our country is at peace in a world at war." Wilson's victory owed much to the fact that he had, somehow, managed to keep the country neutral. Knowing how easily that neutrality could be destroyed, the President made a last noble plea for peace in January, 1917. Calling for freedom of the seas, disarmament, and government by consent of the people, he appealed to the belligerents for "peace without victory." His plea fell on deaf ears; in February Germany resumed unrestricted submarine warfare. No longer able to resist "the irresistible logic of events," the United States, on April 6, 1917, declared war on Kaiser Wilhelm's Germany.

CHARLES EVANS HUGHES

Charles Evans Hughes was perhaps the only candidate capable of wooing the Progressives back into the Republican fold in 1916. An associate justice of the Supreme Court and a former governor of New York, he was remembered by Progressives for reforming state government, whereas Republicans liked his conservative record on the Court. A graduate of Brown University, Hughes received his law degree from Columbia in 1884. Practicing in New York City, he distinguished himself as counsel for the prosecution in a number of cases involving abuses by public utilities and life insurance companies. He served as New York's liberal governor from 1906 until 1910, when his Supreme Court appointment removed him from the political fray that split the Progressives from the regular Republicans two years later. Nominated by the Republicans in 1916, he was supported by the Progressives after Theodore Roosevelt refused their nomination; Roosevelt reluctantly endorsed the bewhiskered Hughes, whom he once dubbed the "bearded lady." Narrowly defeated by Wilson, Hughes returned to law. He served as Secretary of State from 1921 to 1926, became a member of the Permanent Court of Arbitration in 1926, and in 1930 was appointed a judge on the Permanent Court of International Justice. That same year he was named Chief Justice of the Supreme Court. He served in that post until 1941.

WAGING WAR

Amerca had to wage the war she had declared, and Wilson's gargantuan task was to overcome the nation's peacetime mentality and the unpreparedness of its industrial machine. Trench warfare soon stripped the fighting of its glamour, and it was not easy to make conscription palatable to Americans. The War Industries Board, headed by Bernard Baruch, had almost dictatorial control over the country's commerce, but did not abuse it; the wartime administration was free of corruption. Some programs—notably shipbuilding—never really got rolling, but the nation went along with "Wheatless Mondays" and "Meatless Tuesdays." Britain got her food, and France eventually got her men—more than two million of them. A barrage of Wilsonian propaganda pamphlets eroded German morale; even General Erich Ludendorff, still blind to other defeats, later admitted that "Germany failed in the fight of intellects."

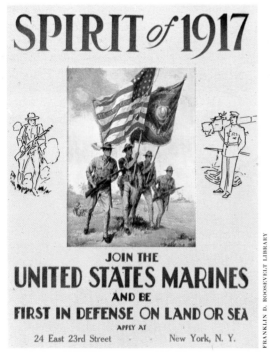

Posters such as the one above urged American men to rally to the defense of their country in 1917.

Etched against the stubble of once-wooded French terrain, Americans of the Second Division's 23rd Infantry (above) keep low to avoid German fire. Among the Americans stationed in Europe during World War I were Douglas MacArthur, George C. Marshall, George S. Patton, Fiorello La Guardia, and Harry S. Truman.

FIGHTING AMERICANS

ALVIN C. YORK

Alvin C. York, a thirty-year-old sergeant from Tennessee, displayed such great bravery in 1918 that his name became an international synonym for heroism. York was a member of the American First Army, which had been assigned the thankless task of ousting the Germans from the Argonne Forest just west of the Meuse River. The Yanks were fighting a canny enemy in rugged, dreary terrain; the going was slow and confusion reigned. On October 8 York led a detachment that suffered heavy losses while forcing the surrender of a group of Germans. When a sudden machine-gun burst killed most of York's companions, he dropped to one knee, wiped out the machine-gun nest with rifle fire, and then shot the Germans who charged him. In all, he killed twenty enemy soldiers. Coolly marching his prisoners ahead of him, Sergeant York captured a second machine-gun emplacement. He took a total of one hundred and thirty-two prisoners and captured thirty-five machine guns. Marshal Ferdinand Foch called it the greatest achievement by any noncommissioned officer in the war, and General Pershing officially cited York's valor. York, who was awarded the Congressional Medal of Honor and the French Croix de Guerre, was portrayed by Gary Cooper in the prize-winning 1941 motion picture *Sergeant York*.

WILLIAM L. MITCHELL

Billy Mitchell, thwarted in his attempts to convince officials of the future importance of aviation, was vindicated only after his death. Mitchell enlisted in the Army in 1898. He served in Cuba, the Philippines, and Alaska and in 1912, at thirty-two, became the youngest member of the General Staff. Aware of the airplane's great military potential, he helped form the American Expeditionary Forces Aviation Program in 1917. The following year Mitchell led 1,481 Allied aircraft in World War I's primary air effort, the assault on the Saint-Mihiel salient. As assistant chief of air service after the war, Mitchell advocated a separate air force, but was frustrated by conservative military leaders. He felt the airplane had made the battleship obsolete and proved his point by bombing target ships off the Virginia coast. The Navy and War departments remained obdurate, however, and after two naval air accidents in September of 1925, Mitchell accused them of "criminal negligence." He was court-martialed and suspended from duty in 1926. Mitchell continued to stress the need for air superiority and warned that American defenses were inadequate. The Army Air Corps was created in 1926, but he still lamented the tardiness of official action. He was awarded a posthumous Medal of Honor in 1946.

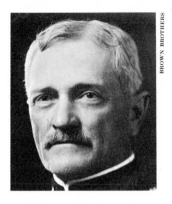

BROWN BROTHERS

CULVER PICTURES

JOHN J. PERSHING

"General Pershing is the stubbornest man I know," said Georges Clemenceau, "and I am saying that knowing Mr. Wilson. . . ." An obstinate man himself, Clemenceau knew whereof he spoke. When John J. Pershing led the American Expeditionary Forces to France in 1917, he insisted that it be an independent army (otherwise, he felt, American morale would suffer), and he resisted many of the repeated attempts to use his men as reinforcements. The A.E.F.'s first battle as the American First Army was at Saint-Mihiel in September of 1918, and Pershing's 1,200,000 doughboys followed that victory with the Meuse-Argonne campaign, which brought Germany to its knees. An 1886 graduate of West Point, Pershing fought Indians in the West and served in Cuba during the Spanish-American War and in the Philippines later. He was made a brigadier general in 1906. The deaths of his wife and three daughters in a fire in 1915, and the frustratingly futile pursuit of Pancho Villa in Mexico the following year, left their marks on Pershing: more than ever the stern disciplinarian deserved his sobriquet Black Jack. In 1919 Pershing was made general of the armies, a position previously held only by George Washington. His *My Experiences in the World War* won a Pulitzer Prize in 1932. General Pershing died in July, 1948.

EDWARD V. RICKENBACKER

Edward V. Rickenbacker, unable to apply for Army flying school because, at twenty-six, he was considered too old, went to France as a chauffeur on General Pershing's staff. There, in 1917, he convinced Billy Mitchell to approve him for aerial training, and he eventually became the top American pilot of World War I. Between early 1918 and the armistice, he shot down twenty-two German planes and four observation balloons; his total would undoubtedly have been higher had not an ear infection grounded him for two months. Captain Rickenbacker received the Croix de Guerre and the Congressional Medal of Honor. Always drawn to machines that combined speed and danger, Eddie Rickenbacker had been a professional racing driver from 1911 to 1917. An auto company of his own failed in 1925, and after a series of jobs in aviation he engineered the purchase of Eastern Air Lines in 1938. He was that company's president until 1953 and chairman of its board until he retired in 1963. During World War II Rickenbacker flew special noncombat missions that took him from Iceland to Australia. In October of 1942 his plane was forced down in the South Pacific; twenty-three days on a life raft inspired his book, *Seven Came Through*, published in 1943. His World War I experiences are recorded in his *Fighting the Flying Circus*.

DISAPPOINTMENT

"What I seem to see—
I hope I am wrong—is a tragedy of disappointment." The speaker was Woodrow
Wilson, on his way to the Paris peace conference, but it was an uncharacteristic remark. Despite recent off-year election embarrassments, Wilson still felt that he and
his Fourteen Points would make the world
"fit and safe to live in." His anxieties were
fleeting, for Europe welcomed him as a
messiah, convincing him that there was,
after all, hope for implementing his program. But, as historian John Garraty wrote,
Wilson's "combination of altruism, idealism
and power was his undoing, for it intensified
his tendency to be overbearing and undermined his judgment." Wilson did not understand the aims and bartering tactics of his
colleagues in Paris. Remarked Lloyd George
—who had just made political hay at home
on a "Make Germany pay" platform—"If
you want to succeed in politics, you must
keep your conscience well under control."
Caring only for France, Georges Clemenceau
said, "Mr. Wilson bores me with his Fourteen Points; why, God Almighty has only
ten!" The Allies, with their secret treaties
and their eye-for-an-eye attitude toward
Germany, tended to regard the points as a
ruse de guerre that had made the enemy
surrender but bound the victors no longer.
Wilson permitted a number of his points to
be modified, but insisted that any treaty provide for a league of nations—a league that
would compensate for the compromises he
was making along the way. The Allies, with
Wilson's concessions in hand, were willing;
but at home the President found that the
package deal was unpopular, and his own attitude ("The Senate must take its medicine")
only calcified the opposition. Weary in body
and mind, Wilson wanted to take his cause
to the people. "I know I am at the end of my
tether," he said, but "the trip is necessary
to save the Treaty. . . . No decent man can
count his own personal fortunes."

Between his arrival in Europe and the opening of the peace conference, Wilson visited Italy and England. In London he received the gold chest shown above, containing portraits of himself and King George. Wilson did not tour any former combat areas, and some Army personnel chafed at the thought of his ocean liner riding at anchor while they could not go stateside for lack of transportation. But the soldiers shown left, above, took jubilant exception to "Hindenburg Strasse" in a French town and renamed it for their President. Wilson was cheered everywhere he went in those hopeful, preconference days, and the extent of his influence was reflected in a standing joke among American newsmen working in Rome. Two Italian laborers, the story went, met on the street. One said that the Pope was ailing; the other replied, "Ah, that is too bad, I hope he doesn't die . . . for el Presidente Wilson might appoint a Protestant." The Big Four are shown at left during the peace talks. Lloyd George, far left, listens to Italy's Vittorio Orlando make a point; President Wilson stands with Georges Clemenceau of France, possessor of a magnificent walrus mustache.

Wilson is shown above in San Francisco in 1919, a few days before he was stricken. Senators Hiram Johnson, James Reed, and William Borah, opposed to the treaty, followed Wilson's itinerary and delivered anti-League speeches to the same audiences the President had addressed. The defeat of the League of Nations inspired innumerable cartoons, such as the one below, entitled "Grasping at Straws," from the San Francisco Chronicle.

"WE SHALL PREVAIL"

"Can you come to me, Edith?" called Woodrow Wilson from the next compartment, "I'm terribly sick." Aboard the presidential train in the early hours of September 26, 1919, the tour in defense of the League of Nations came to an abrupt halt. Wilson indeed was ill: this stroke was followed by another a week later, and White House physician Cary Grayson was convinced that there had been serious brain damage. For more than half a year the world knew little about the President of the United States. Edith, Grayson, and Joe Tumulty, Wilson's secretary, sheltered him with astonishing success, keeping the extent of his disability the strictest of secrets. Wilson remained adamant that the League be accepted without reservations ("Let Lodge compromise!") and eventually saw all hope for American participation in the League— and the treaty—evaporate. Wilson grew testy; at times he brooded; there were periodic lapses of memory and unpredictable crying spells; he doted on the movies that were shown at the White House two or three times a week. On April 13, 1920, he held his first Cabinet meeting in months. Secretary of Agriculture David Houston said the President "looked old, worn and haggard; it was enough to make one weep." When the Wilsons vacated the White House and moved to S Street in 1921, the former President's life became quiet and routine. He moved about with the help of an elevator and the ever-present cane; Grayson allowed him one visitor a day, for half an hour; Edith screened the mail, played Canfield with him, read him to sleep. Still, the fire smoldered. To an Armistice Day crowd, gathered in front of the house three months before he died, Woodrow Wilson said, in a firm voice, "I have seen fools resist Providence before and I have seen their destruction, and it will come upon these again, utter destruction and contempt; that we shall prevail is as sure as that God reigns."

HARRIS & EWING

Woodrow Wilson steadies himself, above, for what would be one of his last photographs. His strokes had paralyzed his left side. While recovering he took pains to show only his right profile in public and kept his useless left hand out of sight.

FACTS IN SUMMARY: WOODROW WILSON

CHRONOLOGY

UNITED STATES		WILSON
Buchanan elected President	1856	*Born December 28*
Lincoln elected President	1860	
Civil War begins	1861	
Battle of Gettysburg	1863	
Lee surrenders at Appomattox	1865	
Lincoln assassinated		
Andrew Johnson impeached	1868	
Grant elected President		
Bank panic	1873	*Enters Davidson College*
	1875	*Enters Princeton*
Hayes elected President	1877	
	1879	*Studies at University of Virginia Law School*
Garfield elected President	1880	
	1882	*Admitted to the bar*
Pendleton Act	1883	*Studies at Johns Hopkins University*
Cleveland elected President	1884	
	1885	*Publishes* Congressional Government
		Marries Ellen Axson
		Teaches at Bryn Mawr
	1886	*Receives Ph.D. from Johns Hopkins*
Harrison elected President	1888	*Teaches at Wesleyan*
Sherman Antitrust Act	1890	*Appointed professor at Princeton*
Cleveland re-elected President	1892	
McKinley elected President	1896	
Spanish-American War	1898	
Theodore Roosevelt becomes President	1901	
Northern Securities case	1902	*Named president of Princeton*
Taft elected President	1908	
Mann-Elkins Act	1910	*Elected governor of New Jersey*
	1912	*Elected President*
Sixteenth Amendment	1913	*Asks Congress to lower tariffs*
Seventeenth Amendment		*Proposes Federal Reserve Act*
Underwood Tariff		
Federal Reserve Act		
World War I begins	1914	*Orders troops to occupy Veracruz*
Federal Trade Commission Act		*Urges establishment of Federal Trade Commission*
Clayton Antitrust Act		
		Ellen Wilson dies
Lusitania sunk	1915	*Warns Germany against attacks on neutral ships*
		Marries Edith Galt
		Orders troops to intervene in Haitian revolt
National Defense Act	1916	*Sends troops to Mexican border*
Federal Farm Loan Act		*Re-elected President*
Denmark cedes Virgin Islands to U.S.		*Asks belligerents in Europe to state war aims*
Germany resumes unrestricted submarine warfare	1917	*Severs diplomatic relations with Germany*
War with Germany declared		*Asks Congress to declare war on Germany*
Liberty Loan Act		*Establishes War Industries Board*
Selective Service Act		*Places railroads under federal control*
Espionage Act		
Congress adopts prohibition amendment		
Sedition Act	1918	*Issues Fourteen Points*
Belleau Wood		*Appoints National War Labor Board*
Second Battle of the Marne		*Sails to France to attend peace conference*
Meuse-Argonne Offensive		
War ends November 11		
Eighteenth Amendment ratified	1919	*Helps draft Treaty of Versailles and League of Nations Covenant*
Senate rejects League of Nations		*Tours country on behalf of League of Nations*
		Incapacitated by stroke
		Awarded Nobel Peace Prize
Nineteenth Amendment ratified	1920	
Harding elected President		
	1921	*Retires to private life*
Coolidge becomes President	1923	
	1924	*Dies February 3*

BIOGRAPHICAL FACTS

BIRTH: Staunton, Va., Dec. 28, 1856
ANCESTRY: Scotch-Irish
FATHER: Joseph Ruggles Wilson; b. Steubenville, Ohio, Feb. 28, 1822; d. Princeton, N.J., Jan. 21, 1903

FATHER'S OCCUPATION: Presbyterian minister

MOTHER: Jessie Woodrow Wilson; b. Carlisle, England, 1836; d. Clarksville, Tenn., April 15, 1888

SISTERS: Marion (1850–1890); Annie Josephine (1854–1916)

BROTHER: Joseph (1866–?)

FIRST WIFE: Ellen Louise Axson; b. Rome, Ga., May 15, 1860; d. Washington, D.C., Aug. 6, 1914

FIRST MARRIAGE: Savannah, Ga., June 24, 1885

SECOND WIFE: Edith Bolling Galt; b. Wytheville, Va., Oct. 15, 1872; d. Dec. 28, 1961

SECOND MARRIAGE: Washington, D.C., Dec. 18, 1915

CHILDREN: Margaret Woodrow (1886–1944); Jessie Woodrow (1887–1932); Eleanor Randolph (1889–1967)

EDUCATION: Private tutors; Davidson College; Princeton University; University of Virginia Law School; Johns Hopkins University

RELIGIOUS AFFILIATION: Presbyterian

HOME: Woodrow Wilson House, 2340 S Street, N.W., Washington, D.C.

OCCUPATIONS BEFORE PRESIDENCY: Lawyer; teacher; college president

PRE-PRESIDENTIAL OFFICE: Governor of New Jersey

POLITICAL PARTY: Democratic

DEATH: Washington, D.C., Feb. 3, 1924

PLACE OF BURIAL: Washington Cathedral, Washington, D.C.

ELECTION OF 1912

CANDIDATES	ELECTORAL VOTE	POPULAR VOTE
Woodrow Wilson Democratic	435	6,296,547
Theodore Roosevelt Progressive	88	4,118,571
William H. Taft Republican	8	3,486,720
Eugene V. Debs Socialist	—	900,672
Eugene W. Chafin Prohibition	—	206,275

FIRST ADMINISTRATION

INAUGURATION: March 4, 1913; the Capitol, Washington, D.C.

VICE PRESIDENT: Thomas R. Marshall

SECRETARY OF STATE: William Jennings Bryan; Robert Lansing (from June 23, 1915)

SECRETARY OF THE TREASURY: William G. McAdoo

SECRETARY OF WAR: Lindley M. Garrison; Newton D. Baker (from March 9, 1916)

ATTORNEY GENERAL: James C. McReynolds; Thomas W. Gregory (from Sept. 3, 1914)

POSTMASTER GENERAL: Albert S. Burleson

SECRETARY OF THE NAVY: Josephus Daniels

SECRETARY OF THE INTERIOR: Franklin K. Lane

SECRETARY OF AGRICULTURE: David F. Houston

SECRETARY OF COMMERCE: William C. Redfield

SECRETARY OF LABOR: William B. Wilson

SUPREME COURT APPOINTMENTS: James C. McReynolds (1914); Louis D. Brandeis (1916); John H. Clarke (1916)

63rd CONGRESS (March 4, 1913–March 4, 1915):
Senate: 51 Democrats; 44 Republicans; 1 Other
House: 291 Democrats; 127 Republicans; 17 Others

64th CONGRESS (March 4, 1915–March 4, 1917):
Senate: 56 Democrats; 40 Republicans
House: 230 Democrats; 196 Republicans; 9 Others

END OF PRESIDENTIAL TERM: March 4, 1917

ELECTION OF 1916

CANDIDATES	ELECTORAL VOTE	POPULAR VOTE
Woodrow Wilson Democratic	277	9,127,695
Charles E. Hughes Republican	254	8,533,507
A. L. Benson Socialist	—	585,113
J. Frank Hanly Prohibition	—	220,506

SECOND ADMINISTRATION

INAUGURATION: March 5, 1917; the Capitol, Washington, D.C.

VICE PRESIDENT: Thomas R. Marshall

SECRETARY OF STATE: Robert Lansing; Bainbridge Colby (from March 23, 1920)

SECRETARY OF THE TREASURY: William G. McAdoo; Carter Glass (from Dec. 16, 1918); David F. Houston (from Feb. 2, 1920)

SECRETARY OF WAR: Newton D. Baker

ATTORNEY GENERAL: Thomas W. Gregory; A. Mitchell Palmer (from March 5, 1919)

POSTMASTER GENERAL: Albert S. Burleson

SECRETARY OF THE NAVY: Josephus Daniels

SECRETARY OF THE INTERIOR: Franklin K. Lane; John B. Payne (from March 13, 1920)

SECRETARY OF AGRICULTURE: David F. Houston; Edwin T. Meredith (from Feb. 2, 1920)

SECRETARY OF COMMERCE: William C. Redfield; Joshua W. Alexander (from Dec. 16, 1919)

SECRETARY OF LABOR: William B. Wilson

65th CONGRESS (March 4, 1917–March 4, 1919):
Senate: 53 Democrats; 42 Republicans
House: 216 Democrats; 210 Republicans; 6 Others

66th CONGRESS (March 4, 1919–March 4, 1921):
Senate: 49 Republicans; 47 Democrats
House: 240 Republicans; 190 Democrats; 3 Others

END OF PRESIDENTIAL TERM: March 4, 1921

WARREN GAMALIEL HARDING

Will Rogers called it the "great morality panic of 1924." Stirred by rumors of corruption in the Harding administration and further stirred, no doubt, by the fact that 1924 was an election year, Congress had decided to do some investigating. The resulting panic was a two-way affair: certainly the haste of the potential accused to find an inconspicuous niche somewhere was no madder than the dash of the opportunists anxious to act as accusers. The press and public, however, seemed to enjoy the investigations and to enjoy watching the politicians go at one another with lynch-mob vindictiveness.

The rumors were well-founded—truer, probably, than their mongers had known. First there was Secretary of the Interior Albert B. Fall, who had leased two government oil deposits—the Teapot Dome reserve in Wyoming and the Elk Hills fields in California—to private interests from which he had received at least one hundred and twenty-five thousand dollars in personal "loans." Then there were Harding's Veterans Bureau chief and alien property custodian, who were denounced (and eventually imprisoned, as was Fall) for defrauding the government by awarding—or, more accurately, selling—contracts to whoever gave them the largest kickback. And, to make matters worse, there was Attorney General Harry M. Daugherty, who, it was discovered, had known all about the corruption, but had not prosecuted the corrupt nor even tried to stop them. Indeed, he was too busy with his own very profitable business: collecting graft from prohibition violators. There were big men involved, and little men, oil millionaires and bureaucrats—all infecting the United States government with a malignancy not easily removed.

The Teapot Dome scandal was the most spectacular and notorious of all, for it revealed how thoroughly corruption had penetrated the Harding ad-

This portrait now hangs in the Harding Museum in Marion, Ohio.

ministration. The President had surrounded himself with his old political cronies. He had made them his government and he trusted them. As a result, the executive branch was a tightly assembled, smooth-running machine. Chief Executive, Cabinet members, department heads—all knew and liked each other, worked well together, and gladly approved whatever one of them wanted approved. In one instance Fall suggested that the oil reserves for which Navy Secretary Edwin Denby was responsible be transferred to the Department of the Interior. Harding and Denby had no objection; the President signed and Fall leased. Everything was properly signed and filed. Even after the scandal broke, it took the government three years to legally invalidate the Teapot Dome and Elk Hills leases.

Mercifully, Warren Gamaliel Harding did not have to endure the disgrace of his misplaced trust. He had died on August 2, 1923, a year before the scandals were made public. "Few deaths are unmingled tragedies," wrote biographer Samuel Hopkins Adams. "Harding's was not. He died in time." If he had lived, he would have been brokenhearted, but he probably would have stood by his friends; for Warren Harding, by near-unanimous agreement of historians a very poor President, was a very good friend.

Harding, the oldest of eight children, was born on November 2, 1865, in Blooming Grove, Ohio. His father was a farmer, horse trader, and casual speculator with a talent for veterinary work and an abiding interest in medicine. In fact, when Warren was eight years old, George Harding went off to medical school and returned home a physician.

But it was one of George Harding's speculative investments that had the greatest impact on his son. Two years earlier, the elder Harding had bought an interest in a regional newspaper, and the six-year-old Warren was allowed to be the printer's errand boy. Young as he was, he was significantly affected by his brief exposure to the newspaper business.

Later in his career, Warren Harding would reminisce fondly about his rural up-

Warren Harding was a sixteen-year-old schoolteacher when he posed for this photograph in 1882.

bringing. The truth was, however, that he did not like farm chores; Harding preferred the life in town. Although he was not much of a scholar, his mother hoped he might become a preacher and in 1879 sent him to Ohio Central College. He was not interested in the ministry and apparently was not sure what he wanted to do with his life, but he did enjoy the school. He was an althorn player in the band, an occasional debater, and editor of the yearbook. During vacations he took what employment he could find: he worked in a sawmill, as a broom-maker, and as a railroad construction laborer.

But manual labor was easy compared to teaching school, which he did after his graduation in 1882. "It was the hardest job I ever had," he recalled, and he resigned after one term, joining his family in the town of Marion, where his father had moved in search of a greener practice. There Harding studied law for a while, but did not like it and quit; he tried selling insurance, but did not like that either. He loved Marion, however, and made a reputation as a good leader and capable handler of money by successfully managing the finances of the local baseball team and of the Citizens' Cornet Band.

His big chance came in 1884. The *Star*, a town newspaper that was failing, was for sale for three hundred dollars and acceptance of its mortgage. Harding talked two friends into a partnership, arguing that Marion's potential growth ensured a sound future. The first several years were gloomy; his friends lost interest, and Harding bought them out. Soon Marion did in fact begin to grow. Although the *Star* did not exactly prosper, it held its own and survived.

"You can read the Marion *Star* for the thirty-odd years that Warren has owned it," George Harding later recalled, "without finding a vilification of anybody in any issue." Harding himself observed in retrospect that "the paper was always on a higher plane than getting even." In truth, Harding, like most small-town newspapermen, could match venom with the best of them and did so regularly. Once, when his chief competitor expressed in print doubt about the sincerity of the *Star*'s Republicanism, Editor Harding published the following comments: "This Crawford . . . foams at the mouth whenever his sordid mind grasps anything done without his counsel. . . . This sour, disgruntled, and disappointed old ass [is] an imbecile whose fits will make him a paralytic, then his way of spitting venom will end."

Crawford's charge that Harding was a "Republican for revenue only" was only partially true. In the *Star*'s early years the editor had tried to maintain an independent editorial policy, for although the town and state were Republican, Marion County was Democratic. Advertising space for official state notices, however, was purchased only in faithfully Republican newspapers, and Harding, anxious to acquire the additional income, finally announced that the *Star* would thenceforth speak for Republicanism. But revenue was not the whole story: Harding's partisanship had often been revealed in the pages of his paper.

After 1891 everything changed at the *Star*. The changes were effected by Florence Kling De Wolfe, the daughter of a rich Marion real-estate and banking magnate. In that year Harding was twenty-six years old; Florence, a widow with a son, was thirty-one. He was handsome, amicable, pleasant, and passive;

HARDING MEMORIAL LIBRARY

Above is the library of Harding's house in Marion, Ohio. Like the homes of many American Presidents, Harding's has been converted into a memorial library and a museum of the President's papers and personal belongings.

she was plain, lacking in charm, fiercely independent, and aggressive. None of Harding's more trustworthy biographers have found the slightest evidence that the two were in love; not one seems to know exactly why they married. But marry they did. Shortly thereafter, when Harding was feeling ill, his wife appeared at the *Star* office. "I went down there intending to help out for a few days," she remembered, "and remained fourteen years." She organized things. She hired and trained a force of delivery boys (whom she was not above spanking, if necessary). She gave very few raises. (Harding would occasionally give raises behind her back; it did not matter to him how much his employees earned because he usually won half the payroll back from them at poker anyway.) "It was her energy and business sense which made the *Star*," according to one of her newsboys. "Her husband was the front. . . . He was a fine small-town or city booster and wrote editorials telling how Marion, Ohio, had more miles of Berea sandstone sidewalks than any town of its size in the United States. Nay, he ventured to say, in the whole world. This was his best line." The recollecting newsboy was Norman Thomas, the Socialist, who always remained a welcome guest in the Harding home—even after that home was the White House.

In the last decade of the century Warren Harding began to take a more active part in Republican politics. The party was glad to have him: he was a prospering editor; an influential citizen active in church, civic, and business ventures (as the *Star* prospered and its editor's influence increased, he became a board member of several Marion corporations); a good speaker; and a willing campaigner. In 1892 he even agreed to be the Republican sacrificial lamb by running for county auditor, an election he was sure to lose. Defeat came very easily. But by 1898 he was taking politics a little more seriously and chose to run for an office he could, and did, win—state senator. "It was not long," wrote a reporter, "before Harding was the most popular man in the legislature. He had the inestimable gift of never forgetting a

man's face or name. He was a regular he-man . . . a great poker-player, and not at all averse to putting a foot on the brass rail." His genuine charm, friendliness, and enthusiasm made him an ideal conciliator for the faction-ridden Ohio Republican party.

Affability—the factor that made Harding and more than compensated for his lack of political expertise—had always eluded Harry M. Daugherty, a skillful, shrewd machine politician and lobbyist who knew everything about politics except how to win elections. Daugherty had first seen Harding at a Republican rally, and because Harding had looked so statesmanlike, had thought, "Gee, what a President he'd make!" The two men became well acquainted during Warren Harding's tenure in the state legislature, and Daugherty began applying his political skills to advance the career of his new friend. In 1902 he helped Harding win the lieutenant governorship. After one term Harding refused to run again. The Republican party in Ohio was engaged in bitter internal quarrels from which Harding, the conciliator, preferred to remain aloof—especially since the Democrats were enjoying a rare dominance in the state. In 1910 he ran for governor and lost. Two years later, however, President William Howard Taft chose Harding to nominate him for re-election at the Republican National Convention. That same year Harding lost a second bid for the Ohio governorship and was prepared to abandon politics, but his wife and Harry Daugherty pressed him into running for the United States Senate in 1914. Taking full charge of the campaign, Daugherty guided Harding to victory.

Harding, who looked like a President, looked even more like a senator; it was said that he could have worn a toga and gotten away with it. The prestige, the social life, and both the camaraderie and the sparring of the Senate were very precious to him, although he did not care much for the work. He preferred golf course to office, race track to committee room, ball park to Senate chamber, and poker table to almost anything.

Harding was reliably Republican and predictably conservative as a senator, vacillating

The presidential election of 1920 was the first in which women (such as the New Yorkers above) were permitted to vote. Warren Harding's handsomeness undoubtedly caused some ladies to vote for the Republican ticket.

only when the prescribed party posture was at odds with the feelings of his constituency. He voted for whatever was good for business, even supporting legislation allowing private interests to employ public resources. He opposed all regulation of industry, even when wartime security required it. And he distrusted labor: on such issues as the eight-hour day for railroad employees and child-labor restriction he chose not to vote at all.

Senator Harding opposed confirmation of Louis D. Brandeis' appointment to the Supreme Court. On the prohibition amendment, he voted "wet" on the first thirty roll calls, but when he saw that the prohibitionists were going to prevail, switched on the final ballot to "dry." And although he admitted that he thought the law unenforceable, he voted to override Wilson's veto of the Volstead Act. Despite his more or less isolationist posture (it was a party-dictated position; Harding himself was fuzzy on international affairs), he generally supported the President's conduct of the war, though not always his aims. He was, in sum, a United States senator of little distinction. And yet in one significant respect he was unique: Warren Harding was a gentleman, a decent and generous person. He was genuinely loved.

These were the happiest years of Harding's life. He won consistently at poker; he had many good friends; his matronly wife had even emerged as something of a socialite. Harding and his wife traveled a good deal

together, and the senator took occasional trips alone—especially to New York.

It was in New York that Warren Harding renewed his old acquaintance with Nan Britton. Eight years before, the twelve-year-old girl—precocious, pretty, and physically mature—had often stopped in the Marion *Star* office to deliver school news to the editor. She would linger as long as possible, for she thought herself infatuated with the forty-two-year-old Harding. In 1916, when she was twenty, her father died and she moved to New York. She wrote to Senator Harding: could he help her get a job in Washington? He called on her in New York and convinced her to remain in that city. He helped her secure a job there and visited her often. Their child was born on October 22, 1919. Like so many of Harding's relationships, his affair with Nan gave him pleasure, but did great damage to his name after his death.

After World War I America was a frustrated country. Its economy was suffering through a staggering postwar inflation (which would shortly slide into a recession); its statesmen were divided over the controversial League of Nations. Senator Harding, worried that he might not be re-elected, began to speak out, and his words voiced the sentiments of the frustrated nation. What had we fought the war for anyway? What had been made safe for democracy? Certainly not Europe, which was no less troubled than it had been before the war and which was threatened with engulfment by the Red plague from Russia. Now it was America that required our attention, and Harding defined the patriot's duty: "To safeguard America first. To stabilize America first. To prosper America first. To think of America first. To exalt America first. To live for and revere America first." Americans, he said, wanted a return to "normalcy."

While Harding was trying to remind his Ohio constituents that he was clever, patriotic, and soon to be a candidate for reelection to the Senate, the Republican party was looking for a presidential nominee. The national frustration being what it was under Wilson, the proper candidate would, the party leaders estimated, have little trouble winning. And yet the leaders knew they would have to be careful: a wrong candidate, another party split like the Bull Moose disaster in 1912, and their good prospects would dissipate. They wanted a probusiness conservative and an isolationist, but at the same time someone inoffensive to labor, to the progressive wing of the party, and to those voters who might not be anti-League. Most of all they wanted someone they could "depend on"—that is, control. The ring grew crowded with hats, but there was still some shopping to be done.

Republican power was centered in the Senate. One summer day in 1919 one of the most powerful party leaders, Senator Boies Penrose, sent for Harding. "Harding," he said, "how would you like to be President?"

Harding had been worrying about his chances of returning to the Senate, not of achieving the Presidency. He had no money, he protested, and he was not at all certain that he was fit for the job. "Am I a big enough man for the race?" the senator asked his mentor. "Don't make me laugh," answered Daugherty. And it was he who convinced Mrs. Harding, who was at first unreceptive to the idea, that her husband should run. Once convinced, she matched Daugherty in enthusiasm—enthusiasm that Harding never shared.

There was no Harding band wagon. The candidate did badly in primaries. He wanted to withdraw from the race, but Mrs. Harding would not let him. During discouraging times early in 1920, Harry Daugherty was quoted in *The New York Times*: "I don't expect Senator Harding to be nominated on the first, second, or third ballots, but I think we can afford to take chances that, about eleven minutes after two, Friday morning of the convention, when ten or twenty weary men are sitting around a table, someone will say, 'Who will we nominate?' At that decisive time the friends of Harding will suggest him and can well afford to abide by the result."

At the Chicago convention those men—there were actually fifteen—sent for Warren Harding and asked if there was anything in his past that might embarrass the party if he were to be its presidential candidate. There was Nan Britton, of course (who was in Chicago at that moment), and the baby, and the old Marion rumor, spread by the *Star*'s competitors, that the Hardings were part Negro; but Harding said No, Nothing. Shortly after two o'clock on Friday morning the door of the smoke-filled caucus room opened and the fifteen men emerged. Warren G. Harding would be nominated. Informed, the anointed candidate said, "Well, we drew to a pair of deuces and filled."

Boies Penrose was dying at home in Pennsylvania. He got up enough strength, however, to dispatch some advice to Republican leaders: "Keep Warren at home. Don't let him make any speeches. If he goes out on a tour somebody's sure to ask him questions, and Warren's just the sort of damned fool that will try to answer them." And home he was kept, running a front-porch campaign. In the election Harding defeated James M. Cox by seven million votes.

"Well, Warren Harding," his wife said, "I have got you the Presidency; what are you going to do with it?" Mrs. Harding was not the only person who thought herself responsible for Harding's election. Harry Daugherty thought himself responsible; Harding's Ohio cronies demanded plenty of spoils; Senator Fall of New Mexico had helped and wanted his due. Harding was not totally naïve. He knew that his mentors were not the most talented men in government, but he brought them into his administration. "God," he said, "I can't be an ingrate!"

Harding did make three outstanding appointments to his Cabinet: Charles Evans Hughes, Secretary of State; Andrew Mellon, Secretary of the Treasury; and Herbert Hoover, Secretary of Commerce. When Mellon's budget-reform program was passed in June, 1921, Harding appointed the able Charles G. Dawes director of the Budget Bureau. And he named former President Taft Chief Justice of the Supreme Court.

But for the most part, Warren Harding was baffled by the job. "I listen to one side and they seem right," he commented on one issue, "and then—God!—I talk to the other side and they seem just as right, and here I am where I started. I know somewhere there is a book that will give me the truth, but hell! I couldn't read the book." To a White House visitor he admitted: "I knew that this job would be too much for me."

While Daugherty was collecting graft, while Fall was leasing government oil to Harry Sinclair and Edward L. Doheny, while Charles Forbes of the Veterans Bureau and Thomas Miller, alien property custodian, were fattening their bank accounts at the government's expense, the President was trying to deal with the recession he had inherited. Although the deflation was checked somewhat during Harding's administration, the farmer's plight was not relieved. Harding tried unsuccessfully to produce solutions to the labor problems of 1921 and 1922, especially in the coal and railroad industries, but, to his credit, he did increase the responsibilities of the talented Herbert Hoover, whose recommendations he invariably approved. He seldom showed initiative, in part because he believed in all but unquestioning executive cooperation with Congress. He withdrew, for example, his advocacy of a department of public welfare when congressional leaders opposed it; he favored American membership in the World Court, but acquiesced to the congressional reservation that the United States should join only if

JAMES M. COX

The political background of James M. Cox, the Democratic presidential candidate in 1920, was not unlike that of his opponent, Warren G. Harding. Both men were Ohioans, both rose to prominence as journalists, and both were relatively unknown outside the Buckeye State. There the resemblance ended. In contrast to the handsome and conservative Harding, Cox was a stocky, bespectacled liberal of unimpressive appearance. A self-made millionaire, he began as a reporter and editor and eventually became the publisher of several Ohio newspapers. In 1908 he was elected to Congress, and in 1913 he began the first of two nonconsecutive terms as governor of Ohio. Cautiously progressive, he championed labor and reform without alienating conservatives, whose support proved crucial at the 1920 convention. Nominated on the forty-fourth ballot, he chose as his running mate Franklin D. Roosevelt, the young assistant secretary of the Navy. Cox's campaign lacked the dignity of his opponent's. The cocky liberal approached his audiences "a little like a frontier 'bad man' shooting up the meeting." Committed to Wilsonian progressivism and entry into the League of Nations, Cox was overwhelmingly defeated by Republican Warren G. Harding's "back to normalcy" campaign. Retiring from politics, Cox served as an American delegate to the World Monetary and Economic Conference in 1933.

the Court was totally divorced from the League of Nations; he proposed legislation that would have empowered the President to negotiate the settlement of war debts, but yielded to Congress' demands that it be the bargaining agent.

Such negotiations, however, and the signing of peace treaties with Germany, Austria, and Hungary did require some executive leadership, but this Harding left to Secretary of State Hughes. In May, 1921, Congress passed a naval appropriation bill with a rider urging the President to call an international conference to discuss naval disarmament. Hughes was placed in charge of the conference, which met in Washington on November 12. Nine different treaties were signed in all; they settled some old disagreements between the belligerents. The United States, Great Britain, France, Italy, and Japan agreed on a ten-year moratorium, during which no capital ships would be built; most of the major powers agreed to scrap some of their ships. The conference was probably the most successful venture of the Harding administration.

"God, what a job!" Harding said as his awareness of his responsibility increased. Occasionally he was guided by moral rather than political correctness. In his first year in office Harding ignored the advice of his friends and pardoned imprisoned Socialist Eugene V. Debs. "I was persuaded in my own mind that it was the right thing to do," Harding wrote in a letter to a friend. In the same letter he admitted "growing less a partisan than [he] once was." Did this mean that the President was going to rise up and do the job? For the moment, perhaps, but then he would be gripped by melancholy. One night Charles Forbes reported, "I went with the President to the rear lawn of the White House, and he cried."

Forbes, of course, was one of those then stabbing the President in the back. Late in 1922 the rumors began to circulate in government circles. Early the next year they were strong enough—and true enough—to foster two tragedies: Charles Cramer, a lawyer working with Forbes on the Veterans Bureau Frauds, shot himself to death, leaving a suicide note addressed to the President personally (Harding refused to open it); and Daugherty's Ohio associate of many years, Jesse Smith, either committed suicide or was murdered. Fall took this as a warning and resigned, thus heightening the rumors. The President began to feel the pressure: he sent Nan Britton to Europe and took a cross-country trip with Mrs. Harding. "In this job," he finally admitted as he left Washington, "I am not worried about my enemies. It is my friends that are keeping me awake nights."

Harding never returned to Washington. He died in San Francisco on August 2, 1923. A blood clot in the brain was probably the cause. (On the trip, he had suffered from heart and stomach trouble, pneumonia, and ptomaine poisoning, and he was utterly exhausted.) Mrs. Harding refused, however, to allow an autopsy. The rumors started: he had killed himself; Daugherty had killed him; Mrs. Harding had killed him. But the evidence for any death but a natural one is nonexistent. He died, one is tempted to conclude, because it was the best thing to do.

He was mourned first and then disgraced. Teapot Dome and related scandals lasted until 1927; when the investigations ended, Nan Britton published *The President's Daughter*, a plea for some of the estate for their child. (She received nothing.)

Warren Harding had been elected President because he had promised a "resumption of our onward, normal way." During his brief administration, however, a new norm emerged. Half of the American people lived in cities; cars were shrinking the country and radios were bringing America's regions still closer together. Prohibition was ignored, which reduced respect for all laws. Jazz flourished and so did the Ku Klux Klan. Babe Ruth, movie stars, and gangsters were national heroes. In this America of flappers and jelly beans, of artists who called their generation "lost," a return to normalcy was out of the question. Nothing could be returned to. Everything had changed.

—DAVID JACOBS

Warren G. Harding [signature]

A PICTURE PORTFOLIO

The Republican National Convention of 1920 issued this medal to commemorate its nomination of Senator Warren G. Harding of Ohio for the Presidency.

HARDING MEMORIAL LIBRARY

A highly skilled handshaker who genuinely loved people, Warren Harding got as big a kick out of his front-porch campaign for the Presidency as did the legions of callers who journeyed to Marion, Ohio. Above: the candidate, himself an althorn player, poses with a visiting tuba. Right: callers from a Pittsburgh Republican club. Below: Harding with the entertainers Blanche Ring and Al Jolson.

HARDING MEMORIAL LIBRARY

OHIO HISTORICAL SOCIETY

The Republicans stood for "normalcy" and "order."

THE AVAILABLE MAN

As the election year of 1920 approached, the Republican party scented victory, and Harry Daugherty—Warren Harding's mentor—foresaw a dogfight for the presidential nomination. Confident that the national convention would find itself unable to agree on a candidate, Daugherty wanted to make it known that his protégé was "available," so he painted a picture of a reluctant but dedicated public servant prepared to sacrifice for his party and country. "Senator Harding," he wrote in 1919 of the onetime newspaperman, "has practically been forced into every contest for high honors he has ever received." Once the name of Warren Gamaliel Harding did emerge from the room full of smoke and party leaders, the campaign was patterned after William McKinley's. It was a front-porch campaign; Harding sat at home while his managers raised money to bring the people to visit him. Bands came to play for him and glee clubs serenaded him; Al Jolson wrote a song, which he sang enthusiastically to Harding on the candidate's front porch:

> *We think the country's ready*
> *For another man like Teddy.*
> *We need another Lincoln*
> *To do the country's thinkin'.*
> (Chorus) *Mist-ter Hard-ding,*
>   *You're the man for us!* . . .

BABBITT IN
THE WHITE HOUSE

President Warren G. Harding was an easy target. For the Sinclair Lewises and Sherwood Andersons, his small-town mentality and talk of a return to an impossible "normalcy" were proof that he was Babbitt in the White House. His simplistic platitudes were grist to acerb H. L. Mencken's mill. And his performance in office inspired F. Scott Fitzgerald's play *The Vegetable*, in which Jerry Frost complains: "I never asked to be President. Why—why, I don't even know how in hell I ever *got* to be President!" Warren Harding's problem was America's problem: recently urbanized,

its technology creating a totally new society, the nation nevertheless still fancied itself an agrarian country and prized the old farm-and-village virtues. Harding was aware of the technological advances—he was, in fact, proud of them—but he did not understand their implications. Despite this lack of perspicacity and notwithstanding the wrath of the intellectuals, Warren Harding actually did more than any other President to preserve the Constitution of the United States. He removed that great document from the files of the State Department, where it was rotting, and put it in a protective glass case.

According to contemporaries, Mrs. Harding (above), who had urged her husband to try for the Presidency, was effusive and uncertain as the First Lady.

In 1921 Harding agreed to go on a camping trip designed to show how safe automobiles were. With him at right are Henry Ford, Thomas Edison, Harvey Firestone, and Bishop William Anderson.

RADIO PICTURE

Presented to
Warren G. Harding
First Radio Picture
(Transmitted 15 Miles)
1922
C. Francis Jenkins
Washington, D. C.

In 1922, when radio was still quite young, technology produced the radio picture. The first image to be transmitted was the face of Warren Harding (above).

Undoubtedly the most notable achievement of the Harding administration was the Washington conference on naval disarmament. At right are the delegates from Japan, England, the United States (Charles Evans Hughes), France, and Italy. Nine treaties were signed as the result of the conference, which proved that although the United States had refused to join the League of Nations, it was not completely isolationist.

George Bellows' lithograph below illustrates a phenomenon of the twenties, Billy Sunday. Thousands of people regularly looked forward to a soul-whipping by the big-league baseball player turned evangelist.

PARADOXES

The pictures on these two pages illustrate the paradoxes of American life during Warren Harding's administration. The people had endorsed Harding's campaign cry of "America first!"; yet as a powerful nation the United States could not ignore its responsibilities, and therefore a conference to limit the growth of naval armament and to discuss Far Eastern problems convened in Washington in 1921. Congress had joined the great moral crusade being waged from the nation's pulpits and had condemned Wickedness. But those who did not like prohibition went out and got drunk anyway. The President—depicted as the personification of small-town virtues—gambled, drank, and kept a mistress; but so did many other Americans. And some of those who did not wished that they did.

The accessible and ubiquitous speak-easy made prohibition tolerable, sometimes even enjoyable, for urban Americans. The painting above was one of many that Ben Shahn did on the subject of life in the twenties.

737

In 1923 Warren Harding was a sick man. He had stomach troubles, lung troubles, heart troubles, friend troubles. As the Washington rumor mill began to churn out stories of corruption in high places— places his cronies occupied—he decided to go on a trip. He journeyed across the country and then north from Tacoma to Alaska (right). But this "voyage of under- standing" provided no relief. Rather than go to bed and think about his troubles, he chose to play bridge through the night. He grew weaker, and on August 2, in San Francisco, he died. When his body was re- turned to the White House (below), he was mourned, but public sentiment changed because of the scandalous disclosures.

AN UNSAVORY LEGACY

Here was a man," eulogized Herbert Hoover, "whose soul was seared by a great disillusionment. . . . Warren Harding had a dim realization that he had been betrayed by a few of the men whom he had believed were his devoted friends. That was the tragedy of . . . [his] life. . . ." If the life was tragic, however, the death was merciful. In the second year of his administration, rumors of corruption had begun to spread, stimulating—and stimulated by—a resignation, a suicide, a mysterious death. The strain was too much for the already weak heart of the President, and he died, his own death adding fuel to the fire of rumors. When, six months later, the Walsh committee uncovered the Teapot Dome scandal and continued to find evidence of more corruption, the rumors were confirmed. Everybody told everybody else that he had told him so. Senator Henry Cabot Lodge captured the spirit of the affair in an original poem, which he read into the Congressional Record early in 1924:

Absolute knowledge have I none.
But my aunt's washerwoman's sister's son
Heard a policeman on his beat
Say to a laborer on the street
That he had a letter just last week—
A letter which he did not seek—
From a Chinese merchant in Timboctoo,
Who said that his brother in Cuba knew
Of an Indian chief in a Texas town,
Who got the dope from a circus clown,
That a man in Klondike had it straight
From a guy in a South American state,
That a wild man over in Borneo
Was told by a woman who claimed to know,
Of a well-known society rake,
Whose mother-in-law will undertake
To prove that her husband's sister's niece
Has stated plain in a printed piece
That she has a son who never comes home
Who knows all about the Teapot Dome.

When the Harding administration scandals began to be uncovered, a Memphis newspaper published the cartoon above, entitled "Assuming Definite Shape."

As the cartoon above indicates, the Republicans were in an embarrassing position in 1924; but in spite of the scandals, they kept the Presidency.

FACTS IN SUMMARY: WARREN G. HARDING

CHRONOLOGY

UNITED STATES		HARDING
Lee surrenders at Appomattox	1865	*Born November 2*
Lincoln assassinated		
Johnson impeached	1868	
Grant elected President		
Hayes elected President	1877	
Bland-Allison Act	1878	
	1879	*Enters Ohio Central College*
Garfield elected President	1880	
Garfield assassinated	1881	
Arthur becomes President		
	1882	*Moves to Marion, Ohio*
Pendleton Act	1883	
Cleveland elected President	1884	*Purchases Marion Star with help of friends*
Interstate Commerce Act	1887	
Harrison elected President	1888	
Sherman Antitrust Act	1890	
Sherman Silver-Purchase Act		
	1891	*Marries Florence Kling De Wolfe*
Cleveland re-elected President	1892	
McKinley elected President	1896	
Sinking of the U.S.S. *Maine*	1898	
War with Spain		
Annexation of Hawaii		
Treaty of Paris		
McKinley re-elected President	1900	
McKinley assassinated	1901	
Roosevelt becomes President		
Hay-Pauncefote Treaty		
	1902	*Elected lieutenant governor of Ohio*
Roosevelt elected President	1904	
Hepburn Act	1906	
Pure Food and Drug Act		
Taft elected President	1908	
	1910	*Loses bid for Ohio governorship*
Wilson elected President	1912	*Nominates Taft at Republican convention*
Income tax amendment adopted	1913	
Federal Reserve Act		
Federal Trade Commission Act	1914	*Elected to U.S. Senate*
Sinking of the *Lusitania*	1915	
Mexican Border Campaign	1916	*Votes against confirmation of Brandeis as Supreme Court justice*
Wilson re-elected President		*Gives keynote address at Republican convention*
War with Germany	1917	*Supports Espionage Act*
Selective Service Act		
Battle of Belleau Wood	1918	
Meuse-Argonne campaign		
World War I ends		
Eighteenth Amendment ratified	1919	
Senate refuses to ratify Treaty of Versailles	1920	*Speaks against U.S. membership in League of Nations*
Nineteenth Amendment ratified		*Elected President*
Budget and Accounting Act	1921	*Recommends emergency tariff act*
Washington Armament Conference		
Sheppard-Towner Act		
Capper-Volstead Act	1922	
Teapot Dome transactions		
Second Central American Conference		
Intermediate Credit Act	1923	*Dies August 2*

BIOGRAPHICAL FACTS

BIRTH: Blooming Grove, Ohio, Nov. 2, 1865
ANCESTRY: English and Scotch-Irish
FATHER: George Tryon Harding; b. Blooming Grove, Ohio; d. Santa Ana, Calif., Nov. 19, 1928
FATHER'S OCCUPATIONS: Farmer; physician
MOTHER: Phoebe Dickerson; b. Blooming Grove, Ohio, Dec. 21, 1843; d. May 20, 1910
BROTHERS: Charles Alexander (1874–1878); George Tryon (1878–1934)
SISTERS: Charity Malvina (1867–1951); Mary Clarissa (1868–1913); Eleanor Priscilla (1872–1878); Abigail Victoria (1875–1935); Phoebe Caroline (1879–1951)
WIFE: Florence Kling De Wolfe; b. Marion, Ohio, Aug. 15, 1860; d. Marion, Ohio, Nov. 21, 1924

MARRIAGE: Marion, Ohio, July 8, 1891

EDUCATION: Local schools; Ohio Central College

HOME: Harding Home and Museum, 380 Mt. Vernon Ave., Marion, Ohio

RELIGIOUS AFFILIATION: Baptist

OCCUPATION BEFORE PRESIDENCY: Newspaper editor

PRE-PRESIDENTIAL OFFICES: Member of Ohio Senate; Lieutenant Governor of Ohio; U.S. Senator

POLITICAL PARTY: Republican

AGE AT INAUGURATION: 55

DEATH: San Francisco, Calif., Aug. 2, 1923

PLACE OF BURIAL: Hillside Cemetery, Marion, Ohio

ELECTION OF 1920

CANDIDATES	ELECTORAL VOTE	POPULAR VOTE
Warren G. Harding Republican	404	16,143,407
James M. Cox Democratic	127	9,130,328
Eugene V. Debs Socialist	—	919,799
P. P. Christensen Farmer Labor	—	265,411
Aaron S. Watkins Prohibition	—	189,408

THE HARDING ADMINISTRATION

INAUGURATION: March 4, 1921; the Capitol, Washington, D.C.

VICE PRESIDENT: Calvin Coolidge

SECRETARY OF STATE: Charles Evans Hughes

SECRETARY OF THE TREASURY: Andrew W. Mellon

SECRETARY OF WAR: John W. Weeks

ATTORNEY GENERAL: Harry M. Daugherty

POSTMASTER GENERAL: Will H. Hays; Hubert Work (from March 4, 1922); Harry S. New (from March 5, 1923)

SECRETARY OF THE NAVY: Edwin Denby

SECRETARY OF THE INTERIOR: Albert B. Fall; Hubert Work (from March 5, 1923)

SECRETARY OF AGRICULTURE: Henry C. Wallace

SECRETARY OF COMMERCE: Herbert C. Hoover

SECRETARY OF LABOR: James J. Davis

SUPREME COURT APPOINTMENTS: William H. Taft, Chief Justice (1921); George Sutherland (1922); Pierce Butler (1922); Edward T. Sanford (1923)

67th CONGRESS (March 4, 1921–March 4, 1923): Senate: 59 Republicans; 37 Democrats House: 301 Republicans; 131 Democrats; 1 Other

68th CONGRESS (March 4, 1923–March 4, 1925): Senate: 51 Republicans; 43 Democrats; 2 Others House: 225 Republicans; 205 Democrats; 5 Others

END OF PRESIDENTIAL TERM: August 2, 1923

OHIO HISTORICAL SOCIETY

President Warren G. Harding poses on the golf course with a cigar and an unidentified child, above. Harding was a good golfer, usually shooting in the 90's, but the pressures of the Presidency weakened his game.

CALVIN COOLIDGE

As soon as Calvin Coolidge had been nominated for Vice President in a stiflingly hot hall in Chicago in 1920, commentator H. L. Mencken of the Baltimore *Sun* "retired to the catacombs under the auditorium to soak my head and get a drink. In one of the passages," he recalled, "I encountered a colleague from one of the Boston papers, surrounded by a group of politicians, policemen and reporters. He was making a kind of speech. . . . To my astonishment I found he was offering to bet all comers that Harding, if elected, would be assassinated before he had served half his term. Some one in the crowd remonstrated gently, saying that any talk of assassination was unwise and might be misunderstood. . . . But the Bostonian refused to shut down. 'I don't give a damn,' he bawled, 'what you say. I am simply telling you what I know. I know Cal Coolidge inside and out. He is the luckiest——in the whole world!' "

The Boston journalist was only one of many observers who could find no reason other than luck for Coolidge's steady advancement. The vice presidential nominee was not physically impressive; sandy-haired, pale, thin, and tight-lipped, he could not compete with Harding's florid handsomeness. "In appearance he was splendidly null," wrote a neighbor in Massachusetts, "apparently deficient in red corpuscles, with a peaked, wire-drawn expression. You felt that he was always about to turn up his coat collar against a chilling east wind." Painfully quiet and shy, Coolidge was no backslapper. His speaking voice has been likened by several of his major biographers to a quack. He was concerned more with thrift than show: Henry Cabot Lodge is said to have remarked that any man who lived in a two-family house—as Coolidge did— was out of the question as a presidential candidate. Yet Coolidge was consistently successful in politics, and there was more to it than incredibly good

President Coolidge, in a gentle portrait by Philip de László

luck. Throughout his life he was thorough, fair, and restrained. He was a rarity in politics—a philosopher of government and an honest man, dedicated to the welfare of the community. His limitation as a statesman— he was simplistic in a variegated world—was also his strength. The electorate trusted him and frequently expressed that trust in huge majorities at the polls.

He was born in Plymouth Notch, in southern Vermont, on July 4, 1872. Then, as now, the mountainous region retained some of the character of the frontier; the rocky soil resisted cultivation and the wilderness tenaciously encroached on the farms. Plymouth's inhabitants honored old Puritan values— hard labor, self-sufficiency, and community responsibility. Emotion was seldom shown. Wit was dry and understated.

The future President was originally named after his father, John Calvin Coolidge, a farmer, storekeeper, and holder of local and state offices. Calvin—the first name was

This photograph of Coolidge as a senior at Amherst College shows him carefully dressed à la mode.

soon dropped—lived a farm boy's life: there was firewood to be split, corn to be planted, maple sap to be collected. Coolidge went to the local school, where he showed no remarkable aptitude, but at the age of thirteen he passed the examination qualifying him to teach school. He then went on to study at Black River Academy, a private school in Ludlow, twelve miles from home. Before he was eighteen, Coolidge had lost his grandfather, his mother, and his red-haired younger sister, Abbie.

Coolidge planned to enter college in the fall of 1890, but he caught a bad cold on his way to Massachusetts for the Amherst College entrance examinations and failed them. He spent the following spring term at St. Johnsbury Academy in upstate Vermont and then was admitted to Amherst on the recommendation of the principal. At college he was an "Ouden," or nonfraternity man, for the first three years; he played no sports and was only a fair student. But by his senior year diligence in study and an ability to make people laugh had given him some status in his class and confidence in himself. This confidence was enhanced immeasurably by his exposure to Charles E. Garman, professor of philosophy, who taught that Christianity, in particular Congregationalist Christianity, was superior to all other philosophical systems in the world. Garman thus rationalized for a grateful Coolidge all the things the student had been raised to believe in: hard work; consecration to the welfare of one's neighbor; the performance of good works, all of which serve God's plan. Coolidge made a fraternity his senior year; in the spring he graduated *cum laude*.

That fall he was back in the vicinity— at Northampton, only a few miles from the college—to begin studying law in the office of John C. Hammond and Henry P. Field. Almost immediately he entered politics. Henry Field was the Republican candidate for mayor of Northampton in the fall of 1895, and Coolidge served as one of his campaign workers. Field won, and in the same election John Hammond was elected district attorney. So, said Coolidge laconically, "I saw something of the working of the city government and the administration of the criminal law." He did not take undue advantage of these fortunate connections, but entered the Republican organization at the bottom. By 1897 he was a party committeeman in his ward. That year he was admitted to the bar and shortly thereafter opened an office.

Coolidge's social life consisted mostly of visits to people who made him feel at home —those who ran or frequented the barbershop, the cobbler's, the druggist's. Otherwise he kept to himself, reading and thinking. He was looked upon as an "odd stick," tight with his words, his confidences, and his money, but he was also earning a reputation as an honest worker and a faithful friend.

Then, unexpectedly, he fell in love. His choice was Grace Goodhue, "a creature of spirit, fire, and dew," wrote Alfred Pearce Dennis, "given to blithe spontaneous laughter . . . as natural and unaffected as sunlight. . . ." She was a graduate of the University of Vermont and taught at a school for the deaf in Northampton. Recognizing the contrast between them, Coolidge remarked that "having taught the deaf to hear, Miss Goodhue might perhaps cause the mute to speak." This was typical Coolidge self-deprecation, but Grace did help him with the social side of politics, providing a buffer for his sharp edges and relief from the moodiness he often displayed in public. They were married in October, 1905. Their first son, John, was born the following fall and the second, Calvin, in 1908.

By then Coolidge had risen through the posts of county court clerk, city councilman, and city solicitor and had served two terms in the state house of representatives. He continued to rise rapidly: after two terms as mayor of Northampton he was elected in 1911 to the state senate, where, three years later, he was made presiding officer. Elected lieutenant governor in 1915, he was chosen governor in 1918.

Coolidge claimed in later years that each step upward, until he became president of the state senate, was taken because it would serve the public and make him a more successful lawyer, not because he wanted a career in politics; he also liked to please his father. His ambition was tempered by his shyness. "It's a hard thing for me to play this game," he told his friend Frank Stearns. "In politics, one must meet people. . . . When I was a little fellow . . . I would go into a panic if I heard strange voices in the kitchen. . . . and the hardest thing in the world was to have to go through the kitchen door and give them a greeting. . . . I'm all right with old friends, but every time I meet a stranger, I've got to go through the old kitchen door, back home, and it's not easy."

Still, having been chosen president of the senate, he decided to try for the governorship. And, having won that post, he did well, successfully encouraging the enactment of laws prohibiting unfair practices by landlords, raising workmen's compensation allowances, and limiting the work week for women and children to forty-eight hours. He mediated labor-management arguments fairly. And he urged increases in pay for factory workers, teachers, and the Boston police force, as well as better working conditions for the police.

Had he been successful in this last effort he might never have become President. But the city government, administered by a Democratic mayor, did little to improve the policemen's lot, and by the summer of 1919 Boston's police had decided to join the American Federation of Labor. "A police officer," said Police Commissioner Edwin U. Curtis, "cannot consistently belong to a union and perform his sworn duty." Curtis suspended nineteen members of the policemen's union. Coolidge might then have moved in to mediate the potentially dangerous situation. But jurisdictions were unclear: the police commissioner was appointed by the governor (Coolidge's predecessor had named Curtis) and was more or less a law unto himself, responsible to no one. This was not just a labor-management quarrel; Coolidge would have had to mediate between government agencies, and he refused to do it. Publicly he took the position that the demands of the police were reasonable, but that they should not unionize or go out on strike—which they did on September 9, the day after the suspensions. Coolidge still preferred to leave the initiative in the hands of the local officials, but they let the situation get out of control. The night of the walkout there was looting and rioting in Boston. By the time the mayor asked Coolidge to call out part of the state guard to restore order, a general strike—one that might spread beyond Boston—seemed possible. By not acting as commander in chief of the commonwealth Coolidge was jeopardizing the peace and risking the Republican hold on the governorship, since he was up for re-election that fall. Party leaders put pressure on him, and after a tense day and a second violent night he finally took charge. He activated the rest of the guard. Curtis had been virtually replaced by an act of the mayor; Coolidge restored his power. Then, in a proclamation, Coolidge asked for the support of the public and the police. The situation quieted, and as it did, Coolidge emerged a national hero. He was a defender of the faith against "the Reds." All that was needed to cap the event was a battle cry, and soon he supplied it: "There is no right to strike against the public safety by anybody, anywhere, any time." The spark had been struck that would make him President, and he was re-elected governor by a landslide.

Frank Stearns, a Boston merchant and Amherst alumnus, had been promoting the fortunes of Calvin Coolidge since 1915. He had a collection of Coolidge's speeches (*Have Faith in Massachusetts*) published, and in 1920—while Coolidge was blocking all formal attempts to make him an active presidential candidate—Stearns sent a copy of the book to every delegate chosen to attend the Republican National Convention. At the convention a second collection of Coolidge speeches was distributed. The senators who controlled the convention dictated the presidential candidate, however, and Coolidge did not have a chance. But then the delegates rebelled: instead of choosing the anointed candidate as Harding's running mate, they backed Coolidge.

When the presidential election was over, Warren Harding set a precedent by asking Coolidge to sit as an official member of the Cabinet. But Coolidge did not excel as Vice President. His contributions to Cabinet meetings were few. Once, when asked to use his power of recognition as the Senate's presiding officer to favor the administration, thus displeasing an important senator, he avoided the duty. At the critical moment he handed the gavel to a proadministration senator, left the chamber, and returned when the deed was done. His office required him to attend social functions, and he had other opportunities to cultivate high-level politicians. But for the most part he kept to himself, even in company. "Silent Cal," the Yankee loner, was still put off by the strangers in the kitchen.

There were indications that the party might not renominate him in 1924, but "Coolidge luck" intervened. On August 2, 1923, when the Vice President was on vacation in Plymouth, Harding died in San Francisco. A few hours later Calvin Coolidge was sworn in as the thirtieth President by his father, a notary public, in the lamplit sitting room of the Coolidge home in Vermont.

Coolidge, a throwback to old American attitudes, was the ideal man to carry on Harding's promotion of "normalcy." His mode of action was thoroughly conservative. "If you see ten troubles coming down the road," he would say, "you can be sure that nine will run into the ditch before they reach you and you have to battle with only one of them."

Though his administration exuded calm, Coolidge attacked his job with characteristic thoroughness and organization. Through his office in the first few months passed experts in many fields: the members of the Harding Cabinet, liberals and conservatives, enemies and friends. All had their brains picked. Most of the ordinary problems of administration he delegated to his staff and his department heads. It is said, for example, that he once refused to read a batch of papers sent to him by Secretary of Labor James J. Davis, who wanted the President's approval of a decision he had made. "You tell ol' man Davis I hired him as Secretary of Labor," he said, "and if he can't do the job I'll get a new Secretary of Labor." He handled his first major domestic crisis the same way. When a coal strike was threatened in Pennsylvania for September 1, 1923, he talked to Commerce Secretary Herbert Hoover, the members of the U.S. Coal Commission, the head of the Interstate Commerce Commission, and Pennsylvania Governor Gifford Pinchot and dumped the responsibility in their laps. It was Pinchot who worked out the settlement.

Similarly, when the Harding scandals began to break in January, 1924, Coolidge let events more or less take their own course in Congress, although he did appoint special counsel to investigate the questionable oil leases. When the Senate demanded that Secretary of Navy Edwin Denby be asked to resign, Coolidge declared, at the insistence of two leading senators, that he would not dismiss Denby without proof of guilt—but he accepted the Secretary's resignation when Denby offered it. Pressed by Senator William E. Borah and others to fire Attorney General Harry Daugherty, Coolidge called in Borah and confronted him with Daugherty. In a painful scene the two antagonists fought the matter out while Coolidge watched silently. After Daugherty had left the room in a rage, Coolidge told Borah, "I reckon you are right." But Daugherty did not resign and Coolidge did not act even though a Senate investigation was casting dark shadows on the Attorney General's reputation. Only when Daugherty refused to allow the Senate investigators into his department's files did Coolidge ask for his resignation.

The President's policy of watchful waiting, his delegation of responsibility, his caution, and his tolerance for people who disagreed with him sometimes led to conflicts of purpose within the administration. These habits were also responsible for his lamentable failure to act decisively when he

LIBRARY OF CONGRESS

JOHN W. DAVIS

John W. Davis, the presidential choice of the seventeen-day-long Democratic convention of 1924, was a man with exceptional ability and a straightforward manner; "the type," noted one political observer, "that street-railway conductors like to have for a superintendent—that is, 'a mighty fine man.'" A leading Wall Street corporation lawyer, Davis had formerly served as congressman from West Virginia, solicitor general of the United States for five years under President Wilson, and ambassador to Great Britain from 1918 to 1921. He was an adviser to Wilson at the peace conference at Versailles and a staunch supporter of the League of Nations. One of several favorite sons at the 1924 convention, Davis began to look attractive as a compromise candidate when the convention became hopelessly split on the issue of the Ku Klux Klan. While anti-Klan forces insisted upon New York liberal Alfred E. Smith, pro-Klan delegates continued to support William G. McAdoo. On the one hundred and third ballot Davis was nominated to break the deadlock. Running against Republican Calvin Coolidge and Progressive Robert M. La Follette, Davis was defeated in a landslide Republican victory. It was his last bid for public office. An eminently able lawyer, legislator, and diplomat, he was forgotten by his party and returned to private practice. He died in 1955, prior to his eighty-second birthday.

KEEP COOL WITH **COOLIDGE** FOR PRESIDENT

lick here

RED GARTER · CAMPAIGN HEADQUARTERS

The sticker above is from the campaign of 1924, which featured a song promising that "when old November says 'Howdy do,'" Americans would elect Coolidge and Dawes.

saw that the stock market was getting out of hand. But they helped to win him a nomination for President in his own right. One of his first acts as President had been to appoint a skilled Southern Republican politician, C. Bascom Slemp, White House secretary. Slemp was a former congressman, a veteran dispenser of patronage and raiser of funds, and his job—which he performed successfully—was to get Coolidge a four-year term. As the Harding scandals unfolded in Congress the Democrats tried to implicate Coolidge, but he actually benefited from their charges. He handled the situation with restraint, while the Democrats, attacking a man who was obviously the epitome of honorable government, appeared vindictive. The Republicans drew together in self-defense behind Coolidge; nomination of Harding's successor began to seem the best way of demonstrating to the electorate that the corruption of individuals, not of the whole Republican party, was responsible for the disgraceful oil leases. Herbert Hoover was dispatched to California to conduct the Coolidge campaign in the state primary, in which his most formidable competitor for the nomination, Senator Hiram Johnson, was also entered. After a victory there, Coolidge won the nomination easily. Charles G. Dawes was chosen as his running mate.

Elected by a plurality of some two and a half million popular votes over the combined total of his Democratic opponent, John W. Davis, and Progressive Robert M. La Fol-

lette, Coolidge could now turn his attention to the enactment of his legislative program —such as it was. He believed that the most important product of government was good community behavior on the part of the people it served. Peace and prosperity would foster good behavior. Prosperity was undeniably linked to business, which, as he said in one of the most famous of his pithy epigrams, was America's chief business. So he maintained high tariffs to protect American industries. Regulation of business was relaxed. Federal gift taxes were eliminated, and other taxes were lowered, while the national budget and debt were sharply reduced. The result was "Coolidge Prosperity."

Unfortunately, the prosperity stood on unsteady legs—the hyperactive stock market. And when those legs trembled, Coolidge and his Secretary of the Treasury, Andrew Mellon, steadied them by public reassurances, and stock sales continued to increase. Coolidge was warned by a number of experts of the sickness of the market, and there are indications that he believed the warnings. But as he saw it, regulation of the New York Stock Exchange was the responsibility of New York State, not of the federal government. He did allow the Federal Reserve Board to try to tighten money, but in general he felt he could only sustain public confidence and hope the proper people would act to cure the sickness.

Much of the speculation depended on brokers' loans to investors; when in 1928 those loans stood at about four billion dollars, there was considerable uneasiness in the economic community over the high figure.

Therefore, in January Coolidge issued a statement saying the loans were not too great: bank deposits were on the rise, too, as were the number of securities offered for sale. Almost immediately afterward, in conversation with H. Parker Willis, an important business editor, he remarked, "If I were to give my own personal opinion about it, I should say that any loan made for gambling in stocks was an 'excessive loan.' " Willis was astonished. "I wish very much, Mr. President," he said, "that you had been willing to say that instead of making the public statement you did." Coolidge explained that he regarded himself "as the representative of the government and not as an individual" and indicated that he had simply repeated what his economic advisers had said.

Save for greasing the wheels of business, Coolidge's administration produced little effective legislation. Farmers were suffering from overproduction and poor prices, and the President vetoed two versions of the McNary-Haugen bill, which would have made the government responsible for fixing prices and selling surplus crops. Farmers, he thought, should work out their own problems.

If he was laissez faire in domestic matters, he was an active diplomat—notwithstanding Elihu Root's remark that "he did not have an international hair in his head." Coolidge had the guidance of two excellent Secretaries of State, Charles Evans Hughes and Frank B. Kellogg. In addition he had good instincts of his own. A month after he came to office an earthquake and typhoon devastated Japan. The night he got the news, he ordered the Pacific fleet to Yokohama to help the Japanese. The good effects of this action were, however, undone by the disastrous Immigration Act of 1924, which, against Coolidge's strongly expressed wishes, included a provision banning Japanese from entry.

American relations south of the border were improved largely through Coolidge's appointment of excellent emissaries. He set a precedent when, at the invitation of the

LIBRARY OF CONGRESS

ROBERT M. LA FOLLETTE

Robert M. La Follette, a dynamic liberal from Wisconsin, entered the 1924 election at the head of a third party called the Progressives. An attorney, he had been elected to Congress in 1884, where he served as a Republican for six years. Breaking with the party bosses, he was elected governor of Wisconsin in 1900 and instituted a progressive form of government that during his three terms became known as the Wisconsin Idea. The program included tax reforms, regulation of public utilities, direct primaries, and employment of technical experts in government. Elected to the Senate in 1906, La Follette continued to push for liberal legislation. In 1911 he drafted the platform of the National Progressive Republican League and was bitterly disappointed the next year when he lost the Progressive nomination to Theodore Roosevelt. Opposing United States entry into World War I, he was one of the "little group of willful men" who opposed many of President Wilson's goals, including membership in the League of Nations and the World Court. During the Coolidge administration he played an important part in exposing the Teapot Dome oil scandal, and his liberal following grew. In 1924 he was drafted to run for President on a new Progressive ticket and received nearly one-sixth of the votes cast. With his death the following summer, La Follette's Progressive party collapsed.

President of Cuba, he went to Havana in January, 1928, to address the Sixth Inter-American Conference.

Aside from the ban on Japanese immigration, which helped lead to war in the Pacific less than twenty years later, American foreign policy that had the greatest repercussions involved Europe and the attempts to secure a permanent peace. Germany owed a reparations debt to the Allies. The Allies, in turn, owed debts to the United States. Partly due to the high tariff, Europe did not have a large surplus of dollars with which to meet its commitments to America, and Germany was unable to keep up her payments to the Allies. Although Coolidge was unwilling either to lower tariffs or cancel the Allies' debts, American financing did maintain the status quo for a while. As Coolidge's most recent biographer, Donald R. McCoy, has put it, the two and a half billion dollars lent to Germany under the Coolidge administration's Dawes Plan for supporting the German economy "corresponded to the amounts that that country paid in reparations, which in turn corresponded to the war debt payments that the United States . . . received from its wartime allies."

Like Harding, Coolidge had to face the questions of participation in the League of Nations and improvement of the diplomatic machinery for keeping the world out of war. American membership in the League was still politically impossible, but under Coolidge the country took part in numerous League-sponsored conferences. Entry of the United States into the Permanent Court of International Justice, which President Coolidge endorsed, was prevented by the "reservationism" that had kept the United States out of the League. In 1927 Coolidge asked for a conference of the great naval powers, hoping to limit the growth of navies, but the conference was a failure. A treaty to outlaw war, worked out by Kellogg and Aristide Briand of France in 1928, was signed by sixty-two nations, but it included no provisions for enforcement.

"Coolidge's chief feat," wrote H. L. Mencken, with typical exaggeration, "was to sleep more than any other President. . . .

The itch to run things did not afflict him; he was content to let them run themselves." Yet Mencken summed him up in sympathetic tones: "His failings are forgotten; the country remembers only . . . that he let it alone. Well, there are worse epitaphs for a statesman."

The country owed something else to Coolidge: at a moment when the Presidency was in danger of losing a great deal of prestige due to the Harding scandals, he reaffirmed its dignity by the honesty of his public actions. The White House, said Alice Longworth after her first post-Harding visit, had changed. "The atmosphere was as different as a New England front parlor is from a back room in a speakeasy."

The office was exhausting to him. His health and stamina were poor. And just after he had gained the signal triumph of nomination for his own term, his younger son, Calvin, died of blood poisoning. "When he went the power and the glory of the Presidency went with him," wrote Coolidge. Shortly afterward he told his father he would never again stand for public office. On August 2, 1927, the fourth anniversary of his succession, he announced, "I do not choose to run for President in 1928." Ten years, he told Senator Arthur Capper, "is longer than any other man has had it—too long!" There were other reasons, too. "Poppa says there's a depression coming," remarked Grace Coolidge, speaking of her husband. Coolidge himself said that he thought the time was near for government to become more aggressive and constructive. "I do not want to undertake it," he said.

And so he retired to Northampton and the two-family house. But his privacy was continually invaded there, and in 1930 he and Grace moved to a twelve-room home on nine acres, where he could sit in a rocker on the porch without attracting the curious. Coolidge wrote a newspaper column for a year and an autobiography. And he watched, with increasing bewilderment, the crash and the Depression. He died on January 5, 1933, of a coronary thrombosis.

—MICHAEL HARWOOD

A PICTURE PORTFOLIO

*The button above, from the campaign of 1924, pro-
moted a President of whom a Northampton acquaintance once said, "I had confidence in him as a shrewd
man who could not be taken in by politicians."*

A POPULAR CHOICE

A hero as a result of the police strike in Boston, Coolidge was boomed for President in 1920 by many Massachusetts Republicans. He was an also-ran in the contest for the presidential nomination, but then unexpectedly became Harding's running mate. The senatorial junta that dominated the convention intended to put Senator Irvine H. Lenroot of Wisconsin on the ticket with Harding. But as Lenroot's name was being placed in nomination, many bitter delegates began to leave the hall and there were shouts of "Coolidge!" from the floor. An Oregon delegate stood on a chair and called for recognition. The chairman let him speak. Most of what he said was lost in the clatter and murmur, until the closing words: "For the exalted office of Vice President Governor Calvin Coolidge of Massachusetts!" The cheering rebels could not be halted, and Coolidge was nominated on the first ballot. The news reached him by phone. His wife, knowing how disappointed he had been at his poor showing earlier, said, "You're not going to take it, are you?" "I suppose I'll have to," Governor Coolidge answered.

Above, Massachusetts state guards remove a mob from Boston Common during the police strike in 1919. Governor Coolidge's actions to resolve the crisis, though often criticized as belated, made him a national figure.

Vice President Coolidge, with Harding above, dutifully praised the President in speeches "from Maine to California, from the Twin Cities to Charleston."

On the morning of August 3, 1923, Coolidge was sworn into the Presidency by his father. (Above is a depiction of the event by Arthur I. Keller.) He said later that although in 1920 he was not sure that he could fill the office, in 1923 he "felt at once that power had been given me to administer it."

BEHIND THE MASK

A few days after Calvin Coolidge entered the White House, he wrote a brief note to Jim Lucey, the Northampton cobbler in whose shop he had passed long hours and who had advised Coolidge on many matters, from romance to politics. "... I want you to know," he said, "that if it were not for you I should not be here and I want to tell you how much I love you." The personality of the new President, though superficially dull, was actually complex. Coolidge had deep, suppressed emotions, a flair for wit and poetry, and a strong need to control his environment. In his home he was absolute lord; he closely supervised White House guest lists and menus and would not even let his wife in on the plans for social functions. When she protested one morning at breakfast and asked that she be given a regular list of what was scheduled, he moved his newspaper to one side just long enough to say, "Grace, we don't give out that information promiscuously." He often hid his love for her behind teasing and silence, but whenever they were separated he missed her terribly and fretted for her safety. Once, when she was late coming back from a hike, he had the Secret Service man who had accompanied her transferred and would not talk to her for days. Occasionally Coolidge revealed a distinctly poetic streak. Speaking extemporaneously at Bennington in his native state in the fall of 1928 he said, "Vermont is a state I love. I could not look upon the peaks of Ascutney, Killington, Mansfield, and Equinox, without being moved in a way that no other scene could move me. It was here that I first saw the light of day; here I received my bride, here my dead lie, pillowed on the loving breast of our everlasting hills."

Howard Chandler Christy painted the handsome portrait, at left, of Mrs. Coolidge with her white collie, Rob Roy; it still hangs in the White House.

President Coolidge is shown, left, at the White House lily pond with, from left, his elder son, John, Mrs. Coolidge, and young Calvin. The second son died of blood poisoning soon after Coolidge was nominated for his own full term. President Coolidge wrote sorrowfully: "I do not know why such a price was exacted for occupying the White House."

John Coolidge, below with Plymouth neighbors, listens to his son's acceptance speech in 1924. The President was not an exciting public speaker, and he was glad he "came in with the radio. . . . I have a good radio voice," he said, "and now I can get my message across . . . without acquainting [people] with my lack of oratorical ability. . . ."

Anarchists Bartolomeo Vanzetti and Nicola Sacco (above, in a painting by Ben Shahn) were sentenced to death for a 1920 robbery-murder in Massachusetts. Despite a six-year court fight and appeals to Coolidge by many American liberals who believed the convictions reflected antialien prejudices, Sacco and Vanzetti were executed in 1927. Below, Coolidge signs the sixty-two-nation Kellogg-Briand Pact outlawing war. The United States, carrying out new and unsettling responsibilities as a world leader, had helped to initiate the treaty.

A NEW ORDER

America in the mid-twenties was caught up in a many-pronged revolution. War had ended in disillusionment. Wilson's dream of an ordered world was dead. So was American isolation. The returning servicemen, filled with cynicism and despair as a result of the brutality of battle, infused their generation with a defensive "to-hell-with-it" spirit. Sciences such as psychiatry and anthropology contributed by attacking cherished beliefs about love, the human spirit, God. Prohibition—a counter-revolution expressing a hope of man's perfectibility—was not obeyed and in the end helped overturn the old order. The Red Scare, another form of violent reaction to unusual ideas, had died down, but still smoldered, threatening ostracism of the nonconformist; its place at stage center was taken by the Ku Klux Klan, whose membership rose from practically zero in 1920 to nearly four and a half million in 1924. That same year the Democrats denied Al Smith the presidential nomination largely because he was a Catholic. Mass communication media, especially the wire services and radio, made America more of a unit than ever before; the upheaval in morals, social concepts, and religion was particularly disturbing to the country because the new communication devices allowed millions to simultaneously experience and react to it. Coolidge's response to the uneasiness was largely to ignore its symptoms while promoting, by personal example, such virtues as law and order, calmness, civic responsibility. A prewar, small-town Yankee attitude toward government, it had no chance of long-term success, but it displayed Calvin Coolidge at his best.

CHARLES G. DAWES

President Coolidge's colorful, outspoken Vice President, Charles G. "Hell and Maria" Dawes, was one of the most able statesmen of his time. Born in Ohio in 1865, he practiced law in Lincoln, Nebraska; moved to Evanston, Illinois, in 1894; and became a leading businessman, banker, and financier. Entering politics in 1896, he managed William McKinley's campaign in Illinois and was subsequently appointed comptroller of the currency. Chief procurement officer and a brigadier general during World War I, he was called upon by a postwar congressional committee to testify on military spending. Enraged at the petty nature of the investigation, he exploded in one of his famous outbursts: "*Hell and Maria*, we weren't trying to keep a set of books, we were trying to win the war!" In 1921 Dawes became the country's first director of the Bureau of the Budget. In 1924, while he served as chairman of a commission to settle the complex problems of German reparations, his Dawes Plan won him the Nobel Peace Prize. That year he was elected Vice President on the Republican ticket. Clashing head on with the Senate on the matter of rules, he gradually tempered his aggressive approach and won the respect of that body. Declining to run for re-election, he served as ambassador to Great Britain and head of the Reconstruction Finance Corporation under President Herbert Hoover. Dawes died in 1951.

NEWSMAKERS

NATIONAL ARCHIVES

BROWN BROTHERS

RICHARD E. BYRD

During Richard E. Byrd's distinguished career as an explorer—begun in the twenties and spanning thirty years—he not only opened up millions of square miles of thitherto uncharted polar lands, but also proved the airplane to be a versatile instrument of exploration and scientific research. Byrd graduated from the U.S. Naval Academy in 1912 and commanded two American naval air bases in Canada during World War I. On May 9, 1926, he and his copilot, Floyd Bennett, became the first men to fly over the North Pole, for which both received the Congressional Medal of Honor. The following year Byrd headed the crew that delivered the first transatlantic mail; poor visibility forced them down in the surf off Ver-sur-Mer, but the mail got through. In September of 1928 Byrd embarked on the first of five Antarctic expeditions. He flew over the South Pole in 1929 and was made a rear admiral for this accomplishment. During a solitary encampment at an Antarctic weather station in 1934, Byrd nearly died of carbon monoxide poisoning because of a defective stove. He conducted further Antarctic explorations in 1939 and 1946, between which he performed reconnaissance in the Pacific and in Europe. Byrd's Antarctic expedition in 1955 helped United States preparations for the International Geophysical Year.

ROBERT H. GODDARD

BELIEVES ROCKET CAN REACH MOON! scoffed *The New York Times* in 1920 while reporting on an essay by Robert Hutchings Goddard, professor of physics at Clark University in Massachusetts. An early experimenter with solid-fuel rocketry, Goddard, who was a graduate of Worcester Polytechnic Institute, soon began to explore liquid propellants. On a raw day in March of 1926 he set up a steel framework to house an apparatus comprising some tubing and a few cylinders. The world's first liquid-fuel rocket rose forty feet, leveled off, and crashed less than two hundred feet away. The test did not create much of a stir, but supported by the Guggenheim Fund for the Promotion of Aeronautics, Goddard persevered. By 1928 one of his rockets soared two thousand feet into the air, and in 1935 one reached an altitude of almost a mile and a half. His work was not lost on the Germans, who patterned the V-1 rocket on Goddard's prototypes; German rocket expert Wernher von Braun later acknowledged that "Dr. Goddard was ahead of us all." During World War II Goddard directed research on naval jet aircraft and on the bazooka and made rockets that traveled seven hundred miles per hour. Goddard died in 1945 at the age of sixty-two. Fifteen years later the government paid one million dollars for the use of his patents.

CHARLES A. LINDBERGH

Charles Lindbergh, said Will Rogers, proved that "a person can still get the entire front page without murdering anybody." This quiet flyer was just the hero that an age jaded by corruption and violence needed. Raised in Minnesota, Lindbergh studied engineering and went to flying school; by 1925 he was a pilot in the Army's Air Mail Service. He decided to try for the twenty-five-thousand-dollar prize being offered for a nonstop flight to Paris and prepared by setting a transcontinental record in his monoplane, *The Spirit of St. Louis*. He took off from New York on the morning of May 20, 1927, and landed at Le Bourget Airfield in Paris thirty-three and a half hours later. At twenty-five, Lindbergh was an international idol. A parade in New York (eighteen hundred tons of shredded paper were thrown from windows in his honor) was followed by a number of successful good-will tours. After the Lindberghs' son was kidnapped and murdered in 1932, they moved to Europe. Returning in 1939, Lindbergh was rebuked by President Roosevelt for his isolationist stand, and he resigned from the Air Corps. After Pearl Harbor, however, Lindbergh supported the war effort. In 1954 he was recommissioned a brigadier general in the Air Force Reserve. His autobiography, *The Spirit of St. Louis*, won a 1954 Pulitzer Prize.

CLARENCE DARROW

"Civilization is on trial," said defense attorney Clarence Darrow during the John Scopes evolution case of 1925. And although Scopes was convicted of violating a law prohibiting the teaching of the Darwinian theory in Tennessee schools, Darrow's trenchant cross-examination of William Jennings Bryan—one of the state's lawyers—made Fundamentalism, the literal interpretation of the Bible, seem ludicrous. Darrow began his law career in Ohio and nine years later moved to Chicago, where he was active in Democratic politics and where he won wide repute as a labor counselor. He defended Eugene Debs after the Pullman strike of 1894, and in 1902 he was chief counsel for the miners on Roosevelt's arbitration commission during the Pennsylvania coal strike. After he was falsely charged (and cleared) on two counts of attempting to incite perjury, Darrow made a spectacular name for himself in criminal law. His use of psychiatric evidence averted the death penalty for child-murderers Leopold and Loeb in 1924, and his work in the notorious Massie murder case of 1932 resulted in light sentences for the four defendants. Darrow believed that even the most reprehensible criminals were entitled to counsel. He defended more than fifty persons charged with first-degree murder, but only one of Darrow's clients was executed.

WHITE HOUSE HUMOR

Calvin Coolidge, said Will Rogers, never told jokes, but "had more subtle humor than almost any public man I ever met." Rogers once invited Coolidge to a show, describing it as two or three hours of Rogers talking, plus a vocal quartet. "Yes," said Coolidge, straight-faced, "I like singing." His humor often had a bite to it, a touch of the put-down. His wife's first apple pie was less than a success, but Coolidge earnestly touted it to some of her friends, and after they had choked it down and complimented their embarrassed hostess, he asked, "Don't you think the road commissioner would be willing to pay my wife something for her recipe for pie crust?" In the White House he liked to press buzzers and set the staff running while he disappeared. But the President, too, was used as an object of fun. At the theater one night comedian Groucho Marx stared out at the presidential box and said to the Chief Executive, who was famous for retiring at an early hour, "Isn't it past your bedtime, Calvin?"

Vanity Fair's idea of an "Impossible Interview" linked Coolidge with the reticent actress Greta Garbo.

The President allowed himself to be photographed in all sorts of situations that, considering his sphinxlike and shy demeanor, made him appear a bit ridiculous. Above he is shown with a group of bewigged and costumed ladies from the Jefferson Memorial Commission. At right he wears a cowboy outfit (with his nickname on the chaps), while below, in an Indian war bonnet, he bears more than a faint resemblance to W. C. Fields. A friend declared that Coolidge hated being photographed, but he was probably one of the most frequently snapped men of his era. He was once asked how he got his exercise. "Having my picture taken," he said. When some of his friends objected to the picture of him as a cowboy because it was making people laugh, the President responded, "Well, it's good for people to laugh."

FACTS IN SUMMARY: CALVIN COOLIDGE

CHRONOLOGY

UNITED STATES		COOLIDGE
Grant re-elected President	1872	Born July 4
Hayes elected President	1877	
Garfield elected President	1880	
Garfield assassinated	1881	
Arthur becomes President		
Cleveland elected President	1884	
Presidential Succession Act	1886	Enters Black River Academy
Harrison elected President	1888	
	1891	Enters Amherst College
Cleveland re-elected President	1892	
	1895	Graduates cum laude from Amherst
McKinley elected President	1896	
	1897	Admitted to the bar
War with Spain	1898	Becomes member of Northampton city council
Treaty of Paris		
	1899	Elected Northampton city solicitor
McKinley re-elected	1900	
McKinley assassinated	1901	
Theodore Roosevelt becomes President		
Theodore Roosevelt elected President	1904	
	1905	Marries Grace Goodhue
Pure Food and Drug Act	1906	Elected to Massachusetts house of representatives
Taft elected President	1908	
Mann-Elkins Act	1910	Elected mayor of Northampton
	1911	Elected state senator
Wilson elected President	1912	
Federal Reserve Act	1913	
Clayton Antitrust Act	1914	Becomes president of Massachusetts senate
Lusitania sunk	1915	Elected lieutenant governor of Massachusetts
Wilson re-elected President	1916	
War with Germany	1917	
Belleau Wood	1918	Elected governor of Massachusetts
Meuse-Argonne Offensive		
War ends November 11		

UNITED STATES		COOLIDGE
Prohibition amendment ratified	1919	Settles Boston police strike
Senate rejects League of Nations		
Nineteenth Amendment ratified	1920	Elected Vice President
Harding elected President		
Business recession	1921	
Washington Armament Conference		
Harding dies	1923	Becomes President
		Sends fleet to aid victims of Japanese earthquake
Bonus bill passed over presidential veto by Congress	1924	Wins Republican primary in California
Teapot Dome scandal		Elected President
Dawes Plan		Vetoes bonus bill
Scopes trial	1925	
Billy Mitchell trial		
Revenue Act	1926	
Geneva Conference on Naval Disarmament	1927	Refuses to run for re-election
Sacco and Vanzetti executed		Vetoes McNary-Haugen bill
Merchant Marine Act	1928	Issues statement saying brokers' loans were not excessive
Hoover elected President		Attends Sixth Inter-American Conference in Havana
Agricultural Marketing Act	1929	Publishes autobiography
Stock market crash		
	1930	Writes occasional newspaper column
		Elected president of American Antiquarian Society
Franklin Delano Roosevelt elected President	1932	
	1933	Dies January 5

BIOGRAPHICAL FACTS

BIRTH: Plymouth Notch, Vt., July 4, 1872
ANCESTRY: English
FATHER: John Calvin Coolidge; b. Plymouth, Vt., March 31, 1845; d. Plymouth Notch, Vt., March 18, 1926
FATHER'S OCCUPATIONS: Storekeeper; farmer
MOTHER: Victoria Josephine Moor Coolidge; b. Plymouth, Vt., March 14, 1846; d. Plymouth Notch, Vt., March 14, 1885
SISTER: Abigail (1875–1890)

WIFE: Grace Anna Goodhue; b. Burlington, Vt., Jan. 3, 1879; d. Northampton, Mass., July 8, 1957

MARRIAGE: Burlington, Vt., Oct. 4, 1905

CHILDREN: John (1906–); Calvin (1908–1924)

EDUCATION: Plymouth district school; Black River Academy; St. Johnsbury Academy; Amherst College

HOME: Coolidge Homestead, Plymouth Notch, Vt.

RELIGIOUS AFFILIATION: Congregationalist

OCCUPATION BEFORE PRESIDENCY: Lawyer

PRE-PRESIDENTIAL OFFICES: Member Massachusetts House of Representatives; Mayor of Northampton, Mass.; Member and President of Mass. Senate; Lt. Gov. of Mass.; Governor of Mass.; Vice President

POLITICAL PARTY: Republican

AGE AT INAUGURATION: 51

OCCUPATION AFTER PRESIDENCY: Writer

DEATH: Northampton, Mass., Jan. 5, 1933

PLACE OF BURIAL: Hillside Cemetery, Plymouth, Vt.

FIRST ADMINISTRATION

INAUGURATION: August 3, 1923; Plymouth Notch, Vt.

SECRETARY OF STATE: Charles Evans Hughes

SECRETARY OF THE TREASURY: Andrew W. Mellon

SECRETARY OF WAR: John W. Weeks

ATTORNEY GENERAL: Harry M. Daugherty; Harlan F. Stone (from April 9, 1924)

POSTMASTER GENERAL: Harry S. New

SECRETARY OF THE NAVY: Edwin Denby; Curtis D. Wilbur (from March 18, 1924)

SECRETARY OF THE INTERIOR: Hubert Work

SECRETARY OF AGRICULTURE: Henry C. Wallace; Howard M. Gore (from Nov. 22, 1924)

SECRETARY OF COMMERCE: Herbert C. Hoover

SECRETARY OF LABOR: James J. Davis

68th CONGRESS (March 4, 1923–March 4, 1925):
Senate: 51 Republicans; 43 Democrats; 2 Others
House: 225 Republicans; 205 Democrats; 5 Others

END OF PRESIDENTIAL TERM: March 4, 1925

ELECTION OF 1924

CANDIDATES	ELECTORAL VOTE	POPULAR VOTE
Calvin Coolidge Republican	382	15,718,211
John W. Davis Democratic	136	8,385,283
Robert M. La Follette Progressive	13	4,831,289

SECOND ADMINISTRATION

INAUGURATION: March 4, 1925; the Capitol, Washington, D.C.

VICE PRESIDENT: Charles G. Dawes

SECRETARY OF STATE: Frank B. Kellogg

SECRETARY OF THE TREASURY: Andrew W. Mellon

SECRETARY OF WAR: John W. Weeks; Dwight F. Davis (from Oct. 14, 1925)

ATTORNEY GENERAL: John G. Sargent

POSTMASTER GENERAL: Harry S. New

SECRETARY OF THE NAVY: Curtis D. Wilbur

SECRETARY OF THE INTERIOR: Hubert Work; Roy O. West (from Jan. 21, 1929)

SECRETARY OF AGRICULTURE: William M. Jardine

SECRETARY OF COMMERCE: Herbert C. Hoover; William F. Whiting (from Dec. 11, 1928)

SECRETARY OF LABOR: James J. Davis

SUPREME COURT APPOINTMENT: Harlan Fiske Stone (1925)

69th CONGRESS (March 4, 1925–March 4, 1927):
Senate: 56 Republicans; 39 Democrats; 1 Other
House: 247 Republicans; 183 Democrats; 4 Others

70th CONGRESS (March 4, 1927–March 4, 1929):
Senate: 49 Republicans; 46 Democrats; 1 Other
House: 237 Republicans; 195 Democrats; 3 Others

END OF PRESIDENTIAL TERM: March 4, 1929

© 1928 Life

"Mr. Coolidge refuses point-blank to leave the White House until his other rubber is found," said this cartoon by Gluyas Williams in Life *magazine in 1928.*

HERBERT CLARK HOOVER

When Herbert Hoover was campaigning for the Presidency in 1928, he told the generally prosperous nation that he envisioned the imminent end of poverty in the United States—provided, of course, that he was elected. He did win the Presidency, but the vision turned out to be a hallucination. Instead of seeing well-fed Americans driving to good jobs in new cars, he saw them standing in bread lines or selling apples on street corners. Instead of watching people purchase gleaming consumer goods from stores, he saw them improvising to stay alive. The improvised products, however, did have brand names. Newspapers wrapped around the body for warmth were "Hoover blankets." Cars that had broken down and had to be pulled by mule teams were "Hoover wagons." The ubiquitous empty pocket turned inside out was a "Hoover flag," and unappetizing jack rabbits were called Hoover hogs. Spotting the nation from coast to coast were compounds of ramshackle shanties, made of packing crates and scrap tin or tar paper, built by destitute Americans with nowhere to go. These little towns were called Hoovervilles.

One of the largest Hoovervilles sprang up across the Anacostia River from Washington, D.C., in May, 1932. Its residents were veterans who had come to the Capital to lobby for passage of a bill that would have moved up the payment date of their service bonus from 1945 to 1932. When the bill failed, the veterans, who called themselves the Bonus Expeditionary Force, remained. The President refused to see them. "It is one of the most profound and important of exact psychological truths," he had written a decade before, "that man in the mass does not think but only feels. . . . Popular desires are no criteria to the real need; they can be determined only by deliberate consideration, by education, by constructive leadership." Constructive leadership,

Herbert Hoover, painted by Henry R. Rittenberg

however, was not within Herbert Hoover's capability during this crisis. The tempers of the bonus marchers boiled as the temperature rose during a July heat wave. The President received athletes and essay winners at the White House, but he would not see the marchers.

Toward the end of the month, the veterans sought relief from the heat by camping by day in the cool, stone government buildings and by sleeping at night on the Capitol mall. When the police tried to move them out of the buildings, some resisted; two were shot and killed. Hoover called in the Army. Under the leadership of General Douglas MacArthur, resplendent in his shiny riding boots, tanks rolled up Pennsylvania Avenue to disperse the loiterers on the Capitol grounds. Troops drove the veterans and their families from the Anacostia camp with bayonets and tear gas and then set the shacks aflame. Scores were hurt, among them women and children. "Thank God," Hoover said during his bid for re-election later that year, "we still have a government . . . that knows how to deal with a mob."

Herbert Clark Hoover, the second son of Jesse Clark and Hulda Minthorn Hoover, was born at West Branch, Iowa, on August 10, 1874. His father, a blacksmith by trade, died from typhoid at the age of thirty-four. Two years later, when Herbert was only eight, his mother died of pneumonia.

The uncles and aunts who raised him were, like his parents, devout Quakers. Hoover's reserved and impersonal manner was often attributed to his ascetic upbringing, which also encouraged his boundless energy and industry and nurtured the concept of service that was an animating force throughout his life.

In the fall of 1891 Hoover enrolled at the new free university founded by Senator Leland Stanford in California. There, according to fellow undergraduate Will Irwin, Hoover won a sort of eminence, if not affection. " 'Popularity' is not exactly the word for his reaction and influence on his fellows," wrote Irwin. "A better word probably would be 'standing.' " Hoover supported himself

while at college, and there met his future wife, Lou Henry, the daughter of a Monterey banker. Hoover was not a brilliant student, and he was never quite able to get the hang of writing English without using stuffy phrases and occasionally impenetrable sentences. But his devotion to engineering—his major field of study—was unstinting, romantic, and idealistic. "To feel great works grow under one's feet and to have more men constantly getting good jobs is to be the master of contentment," he wrote later.

Following his graduation in 1895, Hoover went to the gold-mining district of Nevada City and there got a menial job "pushing a car in the lower levels of the Reward mine for $2 a day, on a ten-hour night shift and a seven-day week." Tall, sturdy, and energetic, with broad shoulders, hazel eyes, a round face, and straight grayish-brown hair, Hoover was an optimist and was confident that he would prosper. But after only a few months the work slackened and Hoover found himself out of a job. "I then learned what the bottom levels of real human despair are paved with," he recalled. "That is the ceaseless tramping and ceaseless refusal at the employment office day by day."

Despite these humble beginnings and early hard times, Hoover was to accumulate, by 1914, a personal estate that was estimated to be worth four million dollars. Starting with an engineering job in Australia, followed by another in China and then by a partnership in the London firm of Bewick, Moreing and Company, Hoover rose to pre-eminence in his field. A leading international engineer and businessman, he traveled the globe many times over.

The future President was always to look back nostalgically on this pre-World War I period as a good time when "the Government offered but small interference with the economic life of the citizen."

With the advent of the Great War, Hoover—who now had two sons, Herbert, Jr., and Allan, both born in London—became involved in humanitarian work on a vast scale as the head of an organization that developed into the Commission for Relief in

President Harding (left) watches Hoover speak to a crowd during a trip to Alaska in 1923. En route, Harding asked what Hoover would do about scandal in the administration. "Blow it out at once," said Hoover.

Belgium. This charitable work enraged some American isolationists, notably Senator Henry Cabot Lodge of Massachusetts, who wanted Hoover prosecuted for dealing independently with a foreign government. During the war years, the commission spent nearly one and a half billion dollars and fed as many as ten million persons at one time.

With the entry of the United States into the war, Hoover returned home to serve as food administrator, another challenging assignment that he handled with great skill. To "Hooverize," in those days, meant to save food. At the war's end, he returned to Europe to help alleviate starvation in Austria and Germany and, later, in Russia. Said John Maynard Keynes of Hoover's relief activities, "Never was a nobler work of disinterested good will carried through with more tenacity and sincerity and skill. . . ."

Hoover's entrance into politics in the twenties was inevitable, since, as Keynes pointed out, "Mr. Hoover was the only man who emerged from the ordeal of [the] Paris [peace conference] with an enhanced reputation." Franklin Delano Roosevelt said of him at this time, "He is certainly a wonder, and I wish we could make him President of the United States." Hoover's nonpartisan-

ship jelled into a moderate Republicanism, and according to historian Frederick Lewis Allen, he "was conducting a highly amateur campaign for the nomination; the politicians dismissed him with a sour laugh." The 1920 Republican presidential nomination went instead to Warren G. Harding, and Hoover was later named Secretary of Commerce.

The extent to which he revitalized a moribund Commerce Department was remarkable. A predecessor had told him that he would have to work only two hours a day, "putting the fish to bed at night and turning on the lights around the coast. . . ." Instead, Hoover made the department as important as any in the big-business-oriented administrations of Harding and Coolidge. Hoover, who believed passionately in thrift, hard work, and self-reliance, encouraged those values both in his department and in the nation. He saved a great deal of money for the country by eliminating bureaucratic inefficiencies. In his attacks on waste, he instituted an impressive—some said endless—sequence of meetings and conferences. (His own estimate was more than three thousand.)

On the issue of who should control hydroelectric power—government or industry—Hoover said, "It is my own view that Fed-

*Lou Henry Hoover, above in a Richard Brown paint-
ing, was a gracious First Lady who did a great deal
of entertaining during her husband's administration.*

eral Government should not go into the
business of either generating or distributing
electrical power." The Secretary of Commerce's words were printed in pamphlets
that were widely distributed by the privately owned public-utility interests.

When Calvin Coolidge announced that
he did not choose to run for re-election
in 1928, Hoover nevertheless asked the
President if he meant to file in the Ohio
primary. "No," said Coolidge. Would he
mind if Hoover filed? "Why not?" said Coolidge. Some months later, when Hoover offered him his four hundred convention delegates, Coolidge replied, "If you have four
hundred delegates, you better keep them."

The campaign of 1928 pitted Hoover
against Governor Alfred E. Smith of New
York, a Catholic, a "wet" in regard to
prohibition, and a big-city politician with
ties to Tammany Hall. Hoover later noted
that he was sure he would win "if we made
no mistakes. General Prosperity was on my
side." Except for farmers, everybody was
doing just fine: wages and profits were high,

and the stock market was soaring. "We in
America today," said Herbert Hoover on
August 11, 1928, "are nearer to the final
triumph over poverty than ever before in
the history of any land. The poorhouse is
vanishing from among us. We have not yet
reached the goal, but given a chance to go
forward with the policies of the last eight
years, we shall soon with the help of God be
in sight of the day when poverty will be
banished from this nation." It was a noble
and apparently attainable vision to which
the electorate responded warmly. Hoover
received 444 electoral votes to Smith's 87.

Hoover's inauguration took place on a
cold and rainy day, but all the portents were
otherwise auspicious. "We have reached a
higher degree of comfort and security than
ever existed before in the history of the
world," he said. From Coolidge, Hoover received the following advice on how to deal
with White House visitors: "Nine-tenths of
them want something they ought not to
have. If you keep dead still they will run
down in three or four minutes. If you even
cough or smile they will start up all over
again."

As President, Hoover was energetic and
hard-working. Up by seven each morning,
he was soon out on the lawn tossing a medicine ball with old friends, Cabinet members,
and White House regulars. Then he went in
to begin work.

Just seven months after Hoover's inauguration, the bottom fell out of Republican
prosperity. The security turned out to be
illusory and the comfort transient. The first
awful Wall Street lurch occurred on Thursday, October 24, otherwise known as Black
Thursday. On that day, wrote John Kenneth Galbraith, "12,894,650 shares changed
hands, many of them at prices which shattered the dreams and the hopes of those who
had owned them." The next day, following a
dramatic noontime meeting of several important bankers, at which millions of dollars
reputedly were pledged to support the market, Wall Street rallied. That weekend
President Hoover was quoted as having said
that "the fundamental business of the coun-

try, that is production and distribution of commodities, is on a sound and prosperous basis." But the following Tuesday, October 29, was, according to Galbraith, "the most devastating day in the history of the New York stock market, and it may have been the most devastating day in the history of markets."

In the White House the President acted swiftly by announcing a tax cut meant to increase purchasing power and expand business investment. But taxes were already low and Hoover's cut accomplished little. The President held conferences with business leaders, asking them to maintain wages and production levels. These sessions were often followed by confident forecasts of the future. John Galbraith called them "no-business meetings," from which "no positive action resulted. At the same time they gave a sense of truly impressive action. . . . Some device for simulating action, when action is impossible, is indispensable in a sound and functioning democracy. Mr. Hoover in 1929 was a pioneer in this field of public administration." By March of 1930, Hoover looked for the worst of the crisis to be over within sixty days. Before the Chamber of Commerce in May, Hoover said, "I am convinced that we have now passed the worst and with continued unity of effort we shall rapidly recover."

At first Hoover tried to encourage expansion of public and private construction—the "greatest tool which our economic system affords for the establishment of stability." He urged larger expenditures by industry and state governments; Washington, he said, would do its best "within its own province." But private industry was feeling the pinch, and state and federal building projects were too modest to prevent a sizable decline in total construction.

Ultimately public works as an aid to recovery were doomed because of the President's preoccupation with a balanced budget. Hoover loathed the idea of deficit; "the primary duty of the Government," he said, was "... to hold expenditures within our income." In December of 1930 he denied that public

The mid-term cartoon above shows Hoover trying to soothe a set of noisy triplets while the opposition donkey provides a braying counterpoint. The President has no way of escaping from the wrath of the American people in the Depression cartoon below.

769

works were the answer: "Prosperity cannot be restored," he said, "by raids upon the public Treasury."

In summer, 1930, the Republican Congress had passed, with Hoover's approval, the Hawley-Smoot Tariff, which served to aggravate conditions. Its high tariff wall outraged many nations with which the United States traded, and resulted in a drastically reduced foreign market. It was, wrote Richard Hofstadter, "a virtual declaration of economic war on the rest of the world."

The rest of the world was not doing so well either. The collapse of the Kreditanstalt, Austria's largest bank, caused the same sort of depression in Western Europe in 1931 that the stock market crash had caused in the United States. On June 20, realizing that the payment of war debts and reparations was not possible, Hoover advocated a one-year moratorium on all international debt payments. French opposition delayed acceptance of the moratorium, with the result that all German banks failed. The proposal was passed on July 6, but the German collapse had already started a chain reaction that worsened the depression in Europe.

In the Far East, a crisis erupted in Manchuria in September, 1931, when an alleged act of Chinese sabotage induced Japan to seize Mukden and eventually to overrun all of Manchuria and turn it into the puppet state Manchukuo. Secretary of State Henry L. Stimson suggested that America respond with force or threat of force and possibly (in conjunction with the League of Nations) with economic sanctions. But Hoover rejected any posture that would disturb America's isolationist position. He would employ moral condemnation and no more.

Hoover's diplomatic high-mindedness was presaged by an earlier moral response to the question of recognition of the Soviet government in Russia: "I often likened the problem to having a wicked and disgraceful neighbor. We did not attack him, but we did not give him a certificate of character by inviting him into our homes."

But if not invited into American homes during the thirties, communism and its rash

of spokesmen could hardly help but find some sympathetic ears in the United States. Factories were shutting down, businesses failing, banks closing; unemployment hit twelve million in 1932, and that year nearly two million hoboes were roaming the countryside. Farm Belt towns were deserted; in cities, girls worked fifty-five-hour weeks in sweatshops for less than a dollar; formerly self-reliant men stood in bread lines waiting for soup. Yet in the Depression's third winter (1931–32) there was little sign of organized revolt; the country was numb and dispirited and was waiting for something to be done.

In the fall of 1931 Hoover had said with disarming candor that "the sole function of government is to bring about a condition of affairs favorable to the beneficial development of private enterprise." At another time he had said, "I am opposed to any direct or indirect government dole" for the unemployed. He had therefore vetoed the Norris bill, which Congress had passed on March 3, 1931. Once before, Senator Norris of Nebraska had won passage of a bill for a government-operated Tennessee Valley project at Muscle Shoals, only to see it suffer a presidential veto (by Calvin Coolidge). The project would not have been a "government dole." It would have provided work for thousands of American people. But President Hoover said, "I am firmly opposed to the Government entering into any business the major purpose of which is competition with our citizens."

The dole—direct federal relief to individuals—was anathema to Hoover for several reasons. He felt the Constitution did not permit it. He thought that a dole could only serve to feed the panic he continued to minimize. Relief was a matter of state and local responsibility; to tamper with that principle would "have struck at the roots of self-government." And the dole ran counter to his thesis of "rugged individualism"; a dole would have "injured the spiritual responses of the American people." Federal aid was the last bastion, the final alternative to starvation, and Hoover said he had "faith in the American people that such a day shall not come."

But the resources of public and state relief organizations dwindled as the demands upon them rose (some state constitutions prohibited the use of funds for direct aid). The President set up the Organization on Unemployment Relief to coordinate local efforts; its primary achievement was an advertising campaign exhorting Americans to support private charity.

Although there was some response to the emergency (in many areas bartering organizations sprang up: tradesmen and artisans swapped their wares for staples), local efforts fell far short of what was needed. The head of the Wisconsin Farmers' Union told a congressional committee about his members' discontent: "I almost hate to express it, but I honestly believe that if some of them could buy airplanes, they would come down here to Washington to blow you fellows all up."

Hoover had no fear of injuring the spiritual responses of America's financial and industrial leaders, for whom he created the Reconstruction Finance Corporation with a credit pool of five hundred million dollars. Hoover felt that the RFC was salutary because it required firm collateral—it was businesslike; it lent, it did not give away. The theory behind it, Will Rogers said, was that "the money was all appropriated for the top in the hopes it would trickle down to the needy." But it did not trickle down. There was favoritism in loan disbursement (two RFC board members authorized sizable loans to banks of which they were directors), which, combined with publicized tax abatements extended to some giants of industry, reinforced the public's view that the federal government was interested in helping only big business.

Through it all, Hoover's dedication to principle remained firm; as Arthur Schlesinger, Jr., has said, circumstance "helped confirm his intellectual rigidities." Experimentation was out of the question; his conservative theory of government left no room for it. He called for voluntary cooperation:

CHARLES CURTIS

A liberal editor, Oswald Garrison Villard, called him "the apotheosis of mediocrity," but the voters of Kansas were more appreciative of Charles Curtis; he served them in Congress for thirty-four years. Son of an abolitionist father and a Kaw Indian mother (the latter was the reason for his nickname Indian), Curtis was born in Topeka in 1860, attended mission and public schools, and became a lawyer in 1881. He was sent to the House of Representatives in 1893 and was elevated to the Senate in 1907. There he remained, except for a two-year hiatus, until 1929, becoming the Republican Whip and, in 1924, the Majority Leader. He was olive-skinned, short, and stout, with a voice, someone said, that suggested "the quick bark of the prairie dog. . . ." Though not noted for imagination, he was praised by Senator William Borah as a "great reconciler, a walking political encyclopedia, and one of the best political poker players in America." Having lost the 1928 presidential nomination to Hoover, Curtis accepted the second spot. He served without distinction as Vice President. He began wearing a top hat and snapped at a hostess who had addressed him informally, "Where do you get that 'Charley' stuff? Don't you know I am Vice President now?" After he and Hoover had failed to eliminate each other from the ticket in 1932, both were renominated and beaten. Curtis died in Washington in 1936.

he asked farmers not to "deliberately over-plant" and told business that self-regulation was "the truest form of self-government." He continued to veto bills that might constitute raids on the Treasury. And in the summer of 1932 the bonus marchers sang:

—*Mellon pulled the whistle,*
Hoover rang the bell,
Wall Street gave the signal
—*And the country went to Hell!*

The President was not ignorant of the suffering going on about him. As his political philosophy and humanitarian instincts clashed, he grew gloomy and grumpy; his press relations worsened; one Cabinet member said a session with the President was "like sitting in a bath of ink."

Hoover believed that his re-election in 1932 was crucially important to the nation; he campaigned furiously against F. D. R., who he said proposed "changes and so-called new deals which would destroy the very foundations of our American system." Hoover was convinced that he had done everything in the government's power "to save community values and protect every family and fireside, so far as it was humanly possible, from deterioration. . . ." He stood squarely on his record. At Madison Square Garden on October 31 he said, "This thirty years of incomparable improvement in the scale of living . . . did not arise without right principles animating the American system which produced them. Shall that system be discarded because vote-seeking men appeal to distress and say that the machinery is all wrong and that it must be abandoned or tampered with?" He thought not, but the voters disagreed. Roosevelt received 472 electoral votes to Hoover's 59.

Hoover was the first Chief Executive, said Arthur Krock, "for whose nomination, election and repudiation after one term the American people, not the party leaders, were wholly responsible." He was, Krock thought, plagued by "his inability to convey to the people the humanitarian qualities and understanding of their plight which were essential in the desperate circumstances." It is certainly true that few, if any, Presidents left the White House under a darker cloud.

In the post-presidential years, Hoover resided in Palo Alto, California, where he and Mrs. Hoover occupied themselves with the activities of the Hoover Institute on War, Revolution and Peace at Stanford University. Hoover opposed American entry into World War II. "To align American ideals alongside Stalin will be as great a violation of everything American as to align ourselves with Hitler," he said in June, 1941.

Following the death of Mrs. Hoover in 1944, the former President thrice returned to public service. After the war in Europe ended, President Truman asked him to help organize the food-distribution programs for Europe's thousands of displaced persons. In 1947 Truman authorized a Hoover Commission to consider reorganization of the executive branch of the government. The commission functioned as a sort of efficiency expert, making recommendations intended to eliminate administrative waste. President Eisenhower authorized another Hoover Commission in 1953.

Between Coolidge's death and Truman's departure from office, Hoover was the only living ex-President, and until Eisenhower's term ended, the only living Republican ex-President. As such he became a much-exalted permanent fixture at Republican conventions, where he was invariably welcomed with "spontaneous" demonstrations. The convention of 1964 was the first one he missed, being too ill to attend.

Active to the end of his days—he employed six secretaries to handle his correspondence—Hoover died at the age of ninety on October 20, 1964. Only one other President, John Adams, had lived as long.

Hoover had been brilliantly successful as an engineer and as a humanitarian, but historians have not been kind in their appraisals of his four-year Presidency. As Arthur Schlesinger, Jr., has written, Herbert Hoover's tragedy was that "of a man of high ideals whose intelligence froze into inflexibility and whose dedication was smitten by self-righteousness."

—SAUL BRAUN

A PICTURE PORTFOLIO

In this caricature from Liberty *magazine Herbert Hoover is shown with symbols of the two primary concerns of his life—engineering and government.*

Hoover complained that Grant Wood's painting (above) made his birthplace seem too elaborate.

The picture at left was taken in 1898, when the twenty-four-year-old Hoover was in Australia representing a London mining firm, Bewick, Moreing and Company. One of his first acts was to recommend the investment of half a million dollars in a prospective gold field that other agents had passed up. The firm gambled—and the Gwalia mines, as they were known, began a long succession of annual yields averaging more than a million dollars. In 1900 Hoover and his bride were caught in Tientsin, China, during the Boxer Rebellion. Under siege for over two weeks, Hoover felt he had been advised "by way of artillery" that the Chinese Bureau of Mines no longer required his services as an engineer.

"LOCAL RESPONSIBILITY"

Well," said Herbert Hoover in 1914, "let fortune go to hell." He had made plenty of money, and as one of the world's leading engineers, was in line to make a great deal more. Perhaps it was a Quaker reaction to his good fortune, perhaps it was the knowledge that his family would never be in want; at any rate, he agreed to head the Belgian relief program —on two conditions: he demanded full command and refused any pay. "By his brilliantly successful administration of relief organizations," wrote Samuel Morison and Henry Commager of Hoover's pre-presidential years, he ". . . earned the reputation of a great humanitarian; by his active and progressive administration of the Commerce Department he . . . won the confidence of business." Under Presidents Harding and Coolidge, Hoover was, said banker S. Parker Gilbert, "Secretary of Commerce and Under-Secretary of all other departments," even though he was not especially friendly with either Chief Executive. (On Harding's Alaskan trip in 1923 Hoover was among those obliged to play bridge from breakfast to midnight; he resolved never to play the game again.) Hoover's wealth was not a political liability; he was seen as a shining example of "rugged individualism." In 1927, when the Mississippi River burst its banks, Secretary Hoover oversaw the relief operation, riding the flood to even greater esteem. A drought in the same area in 1930 hit the already depressed Farm Belt hard. Although there were limited federal loans and money from the Red Cross, Hoover, then President, was criticized for not authorizing direct federal aid to individuals. Such relief, he said, was a matter of "local responsibility."

Director of postwar American relief in Europe, Hoover met in Poland in 1919 with Monsignor Ratti (above), who became Pope Pius XI in 1922. Between them is Ignace Paderewski, pianist and Polish Prime Minister.

ALFRED E. SMITH

"He has," said Franklin Roosevelt of Alfred Emanuel Smith, "a marvelous faculty for cutting the Gordian knots of argument . . . with the sharp sword of common sense." Unhappily for "the Happy Warrior," his common sense, combined with a flair for politics and a long record of useful public service in the state of New York, was not enough to win him the Presidency, for Smith was a Catholic. Born in 1873 on New York City's Lower East Side, he was a newsboy and a fish-market employee in his teens. He entered politics as a Tammany Hall supporter and was sent to Albany as an assemblyman in 1904, beginning a career that led to the governorship in 1919. Except for one two-year interval, he remained in that office through 1928. He was honest and progressive, a plain talker who knew his business and kept his promises. Three times an aspirant to the Democratic presidential nomination, he won it once, in 1928. His fire and charm notwithstanding, he was an embarrassing candidate. He called for repeal of prohibition, which took courage. He consciously clung to the Lower East Side pronunciation of words, such as "raddio." But each time he lost a battle in national politics, whether in convention or against Hoover, the basic reason was that capsuled by H. L. Mencken: "Those who fear the Pope outnumber those who are tired of the Anti-Saloon League." Smith, who became a bitter maverick, died in New York in 1944.

PROSPERITY
DEPARTS

If Smith had been Protestant, dry, and born in a log cabin of good yeoman stock," wrote William Leuchtenburg of the 1928 presidential campaign, "he still would have been defeated. . . . In the atmosphere of the 1920's, the Republican party was almost unbeatable." Observed Will Rogers at the time: "You can't lick this Prosperity thing; even the fellow that hasn't got any is all excited over the idea." When Herbert Hoover defeated Smith and moved into the White House, he did not know that time bombs left by his G.O.P. predecessors soon would explode. A "fever of speculation," as he himself had put it in 1926, had too long been raging through the nation's economy while the federal machinery to arrest it had lain idle. But Hoover scarcely treated the symptoms, much less the disease itself; he had become, in the words of historian John Hicks, "the . . . chief theologian of conservative Republicanism, a sort of St. Thomas Aquinas who reconciled the party's principles and stated them admirably." He remained a thrall to a code of ideas that permitted, at best, strictly limited federal intervention in the crisis. Hoover was not deaf to the cries of his countrymen: he tried to persuade business leaders to maintain wages, and the Federal Farm Board, set up in 1929, was empowered to buy up some surplus produce. But businessmen cut wages, and farmers produced faster than the F.F.B. could buy; farm prices tumbled and discontent rose accordingly. Nothing the self-manacled government tried seemed to work; unemployment rose and Herbert Hoover's popularity waned. Urged to inspire the American people to take positive action, a gloomy President Hoover said, with cryptic candor, "I have no Wilsonian qualities."

OUR NEXT PRESIDENT

HERBERT C. HOOVER

The 1928 campaign poster (left) reflects the calm confidence of presidential candidate Herbert Hoover. In the cartoon below, he and Democrat Al Smith dash off to stump for the Presidency in areas they both hoped to sweep. Republicans piously asked, "Shall Dry America elect a 'cocktail President'?" But the campaign was basically city versus country. (Hoover described himself as "a boy from a country village, without inheritance or influential friends . . ." whereas Smith was a resident of New York City.) Though badly beaten, Smith carried the twelve biggest cities in the nation, presaging the urban-based Democratic party of the Franklin Delano Roosevelt era.

777

President Hoover strolls on the White House lawn with his wife, right, during one of the many social functions held during his administration. A sharply contrasting social stratum in the Capital in 1932 was the ragtag army of jobless veterans who demanded advance payment of their World War I bonus. "They had marched on Washington," wrote John Weaver, "not with the clenched fists of revolt, but with the slumped shoulders of helpless acquiescence. They were the kind of men to be found in bread lines, not at barricades." Hoover would not see them. After refusing to leave the city, the marchers were confronted by United States Army regulars (led by General Douglas MacArthur), who put their pitiful hovels to the torch (below).

STOCK PRICES SLUMP $14,000,000,000 IN NATION-WIDE STAMPEDE TO UNLOAD; BANKERS TO SUPPORT MARKET TODAY

Sixteen Leading Issues Down $2,893,520,108; Tel. & Tel. and Steel Among Heaviest Losers

PREMIER ISSUES HARD HIT

The New York Times *headline of October 29, 1929, above, starkly revealed the state of American finance. That day the bottom fell out of the market: more than sixteen million shares were sold and many leading stocks dropped forty to sixty points in value. The roar of the twenties had been reduced to a whimper.*

NO FEDERAL DOLE

As Hoover's administration—and the Depression—continued, the President still felt constitutionally constrained from authorizing federal relief to individuals. Of a proposed two-billion-dollar public-works program he said, "This is not unemployment relief. It is the most gigantic pork-barrel ever perpetrated by the American Congress." He approved the Reconstruction Finance Corporation, which lent money to railroads, banks, and agricultural agencies, because firm collateral was demanded; this was businesslike and sensible, he felt, whereas a federal dole was not. In 1931 Hoover wisely tried to ease the economic strain in Europe by proposing a one-year moratorium on the payment of war debts. But at home bread lines lengthened because local agencies and private charities were overburdened. Hoover's stock fell as low as the securities on the New York Exchange, yet some supporters maintained that the political tide was turning in his favor. Calvin Coolidge knew better. In his syndicated column in 1931 he wrote: "The country is not in good condition." The next year the nation elected a man who offered help.

FACES ON CAPITOL HILL

BOTH: WIDE WORLD

WILLIAM E. BORAH

"If the Savior of man would revisit the earth and declare for a League of Nations," cried Senator William E. Borah of Idaho in 1919, "I would be opposed to it." That year he stumped against democracy's hopeful savior, Woodrow Wilson, his treaty, and his League. But despite Borah's bitter isolationist attitude, he harbored a strong desire for world peace. He introduced a resolution that led to the Washington Armament Conference of 1921, which established a 5-5-3 ratio of naval tonnage for the United States, Britain, and Japan, respectively. As chairman of the Senate Foreign Relations Committee after 1924, he worked to improve inter-American relations and to establish international monetary conventions; he supported the Kellogg-Briand Pact of 1928, which outlawed war as a tool of national policy. Borah had risen to prominence as a lawyer in Boise, Idaho, in the 1890's; he was elected to the Senate in 1907, and as a moderate Republican he advocated the creation of a department of labor and the direct election of senators. His political independence worked against him in 1936 when he vainly sought the G.O.P. presidential nomination. Borah criticized many New Deal programs on constitutional grounds, and he advocated strict neutrality when war broke out in Europe. The senator died in 1940.

GEORGE W. NORRIS

"We want the House to be representative of the people," declared George W. Norris in 1910, "and each individual member to have his ideas presented and passed on." Norris, in the fourth of five consecutive terms as a representative from Nebraska, was successful in his crusade to strip the Speaker of the House of his dictatorial power; after 1910, committee appointments were determined by the membership as a whole. In 1912 Norris, who had served for seven years as a district judge in Nebraska, was elected to the first of five terms in the Senate. Officially a Republican, he strove to be "independent of all parties" and characterized a group of Harding-Coolidge appointments as "the nullification of federal law by a process of boring from within." A liberal, he supported Theodore Roosevelt in 1912, but opposed American entry into World War I and into the League of Nations. For years he envisioned a federal program to turn the vast energy of the powerful, flood-prone Tennessee River into a great power source for the whole region, but his farsighted legislation was vetoed by Presidents Coolidge and Hoover. The Tennessee Valley Authority was finally established in 1933, and Norris Dam was named after him. Defeated in a three-way Senate race in 1942, Norris died two years later at the age of eighty-three.

FIORELLO LA GUARDIA

"I stand for the Republicanism of Abraham Lincoln," said Fiorello La Guardia in 1922, "and let me tell you that the average Republican leader east of the Mississippi doesn't know anything more about Abraham Lincoln than Henry Ford knows about the Talmud." Statements like that, characteristic of "the Little Flower" during his thirty-year political career, made most Republicans—his nominal colleagues—cringe. The son of an Italian immigrant, La Guardia was a national congressman from 1916 to 1932 (except for two years when he was president of the Board of Aldermen in his native New York City). A staunch progressive, he crowned his federal career with the Norris-La Guardia Act of 1932, which restricted the courts in issuing injunctions to break strikes. In 1933 La Guardia succeeded in his second attempt at winning the mayoralty of New York. Re-elected twice, his coalition administrations—fusing New Dealers, disillusioned Tammany Democrats, and reformers of every stripe—bettered New York in virtually every area of municipal government. A shrewd politician, La Guardia also radiated an energy and a charm that endeared him to his city. He directed the Office of Civil Defense in 1941 and the United Nations Relief and Rehabilitation Administration in 1946. He died the next year at sixty-four.

HUEY LONG

"Most of the people would rather laugh than weep," reasoned Huey Long, and for the last seven of his forty-two years he used laughter —among other tools—to rule Louisiana like a czar. Shrewdly, unrestrainedly, he appealed to the poor; elected to the state Railroad Commission in 1918, he waged popular battles with "the interests," the big-business men that he felt controlled the state. After Long became governor in 1928, he issued free school textbooks, built new roads, eliminated the poll tax. A colorful, flamboyant demagogue, Long won a Senate seat in 1930, but did not take it until he had hand-picked his gubernatorial successor. On the Senate floor he read recipes for fried oysters and tried to pass a law on how to play the jew's-harp. Nursing presidential aspirations of his own, he defied the New Deal (N.R.A., he said, stood for "Nuts Running America") and proposed his own "Share Our Wealth" plan for a guaranteed annual income. In 1935 Long, who maintained a personal army not unlike Hitler's brown shirts, was shot and killed by a man who felt that Long had slurred his family's honor. Long founded a political dynasty that continues today. A Southern politician once called him "the smartest lunatic I ever saw." Of himself, Huey Long remarked on one occasion, "Just say I'm *sui generis*, and let it go at that."

During a trip to Europe in 1938, Herbert Hoover met with Adolf Hitler in Berlin (above) on March 8. He found the Führer *"highly intelligent,"* but with *"trigger spots in his mind which . . . set him off like a man in furious anger."* Hoover did not know that Hitler planned to devour Austria a few days later.

As coordinator of Food Supply for World Famine, Hoover (above in Poland in 1946) again directed postwar relief. At right, he addresses the 1956 G.O.P. National Convention.

CRITIC AND
STATESMAN

It is the more abundant life—without bacon," said ex-President Hoover of the New Deal's planned scarcity program for agriculture. Hoover was an outspoken critic of Roosevelt's, deploring "the gigantic growth of personal power of the President" and claiming that Congress had "been reduced to a rubber stamp for the Executive." He maintained that only the advent of World War II solved the unemployment problem and noted that the national debt more than doubled in the eight years after he left office. (He spoke of the decimal point as "wandering around among the regimented ciphers trying to find some of the old places it used to know.") In response, the administration launched investigations of Hoover's term (turning up no scandal) and changed the name of Hoover Dam to Boulder Dam (in 1947 Harry Truman changed it back). To millions Hoover was a symbol of hard times and not until after World War II—and after his re-emergence as an international humanitarian—was there substantial mellowing of that attitude. Under Truman and Eisenhower, Hoover headed commissions to streamline the executive branch; 70 per cent of their suggestions were enacted. But many still remembered him, as one writer put it, for the "most serious error of his amazing career": running for President—and winning.

REPUBLICAN
NATIONAL
CONVENTION

FACTS IN SUMMARY: HERBERT CLARK HOOVER

CHRONOLOGY

UNITED STATES		HOOVER
	1874	Born August 10
Hayes elected President	1877	
Garfield elected President	1880	
Arthur becomes President	1881	
Cleveland elected President	1884	Moves to Newberg, Oregon
Harrison elected President	1888	
	1891	Enters Stanford University
Cleveland re-elected	1892	
	1895	Graduates from Stanford
McKinley elected President	1896	
	1897	Works as mining engineer in Australia
Spanish-American War	1898	
Treaty of Paris		
	1899	Marries Lou Henry
McKinley re-elected	1900	Helps defend Tientsin during the Boxer Rebellion
McKinley assassinated	1901	Becomes junior partner in mining firm
Roosevelt becomes President		
Roosevelt elected President	1904	
Taft elected President	1908	
Wilson elected President	1912	Becomes trustee of Stanford University
World War I begins in Europe	1914	Serves as chairman of American Relief Committee in London
Lusitania sunk	1915	Serves as chairman of Belgian Relief Commission
Wilson re-elected	1916	
War with Germany	1917	Appointed U.S. food administrator
Battle of Belleau Wood	1918	
Meuse-Argonne campaign		
Eighteenth Amendment ratified	1919	Establishes Supreme Economic Council
Paris peace negotiations		
Harding elected President	1920	Becomes president of the American Engineering Council
Washington Armament Conference	1921	Appointed Secretary of Commerce
Harding dies	1923	
Coolidge becomes President		

UNITED STATES		HOOVER
Coolidge elected President	1924	
Merchant Marine Act	1928	Elected President
Agricultural Marketing Act	1929	Announces tax cut
Stock market crash		
Naval disarmament conference in London	1930	Proposes decentralized work programs for unemployed
		Opposes federal relief
Bonus bill	1931	Submits Wickersham Report on prohibition to Congress
		Opposes repeal of Eighteenth Amendment
		Proposes one-year moratorium on payment of foreign debts
		Recommends Federal Home Loan Bank Act to Congress
Reconstruction Finance Corporation	1932	Vetoes Wagner-Garner bill
Glass-Steagall Act		Calls out Army to disperse bonus marchers
Bonus march		
Patman bonus bill		Opposes economic boycott of Japan
League of Nations adopts Stimson Doctrine		Loses presidential election
Bonus marchers routed		
Roosevelt elected President		
Twentieth Amendment ratified	1933	Retires to Palo Alto, California
New Deal measures		
Social Security Act	1935	
Roosevelt re-elected	1936	Becomes chairman of Boys Clubs of America
U.S. enters World War II	1941	
Normandy invasion	1944	Lou Hoover dies
Roosevelt re-elected		
Roosevelt dies	1945	
Truman becomes President		
World War II ends		
	1946	Serves as coordinator of Food Supply for World Famine
	1947	Serves as chairman of Commission on Organization of the Executive Branch of the Governmen
Truman elected President	1948	
Korean War	1950	
	1951	Publishes Memoirs

Eisenhower elected President	1952	*Advocates U.S. withdrawal from Europe*
Korean armistice	1953	*Heads second Hoover Commission*
Eisenhower re-elected	1956	
	1958	*Publishes* The Ordeal of Woodrow Wilson
Kennedy elected President	1960	
Johnson becomes President	1963	
	1964	*Dies October 20*

WIDE WORLD

Former President Herbert Hoover chatted with John F. Kennedy shortly after the young Democrat from Massachusetts had been elected Chief Executive. Hoover was eighty-six years old at the time of the meeting.

BIOGRAPHICAL FACTS

BIRTH: West Branch, Iowa, Aug. 10, 1874
ANCESTRY: Swiss-German
FATHER: Jesse Clark Hoover; b. Miami County, Ohio, Sept. 2, 1846; d. West Branch, Iowa, Dec. 14, 1880
FATHER'S OCCUPATION: Blacksmith
MOTHER: Hulda Randall Minthorn Hoover; b. Norwich, Oxford County, Canada, May 4, 1849; d. West Branch, Iowa, Feb. 22, 1883
BROTHER: Theodore Jesse Hoover (1871–1955)
SISTER: Mary "May" Hoover (1876–1950)
WIFE: Lou Henry; b. Waterloo, Iowa, March 29, 1875; d. New York, N.Y., Jan. 7, 1944
MARRIAGE: Monterey, Cal., Feb. 10, 1899
CHILDREN: Herbert Clark (1903–   ); Allan Henry (1907–   )
EDUCATION: Local schools; Newberg Academy; graduated from Stanford University (1895)
HOME: Herbert Hoover Birthplace, West Branch, Iowa
RELIGIOUS AFFILIATION: Quaker
OCCUPATION BEFORE PRESIDENCY: Engineer
PRE-PRESIDENTIAL OFFICES: Chairman of Commission for Relief in Belgium; U.S. Food Administrator; Chairman of Supreme Economic Council; Secretary of Commerce
POLITICAL PARTY: Republican
AGE AT INAUGURATION: 54
OCCUPATIONS AFTER PRESIDENCY: Chairman of Commission for Polish Relief; chairman of Finnish Relief Fund; coordinator of Food Supply for World Famine; chairman of Commissions on Organization of the Executive Branch of the Government (Hoover Commissions); writer
DEATH: New York, N.Y., Oct. 20, 1964
PLACE OF BURIAL: Hoover Presidential Library, West Branch, Iowa

ELECTION OF 1928

CANDIDATES	ELECTORAL VOTE	POPULAR VOTE
Herbert C. Hoover Republican	444	21,391,993
Alfred E. Smith Democratic	87	15,016,169
Norman Thomas Socialist	—	267,835

THE HOOVER ADMINISTRATION

INAUGURATION: March 4, 1929; the Capitol, Washington, D.C.
VICE PRESIDENT: Charles Curtis
SECRETARY OF STATE: Henry L. Stimson
SECRETARY OF THE TREASURY: Andrew W. Mellon; Ogden L. Mills (from Feb. 13, 1932)
SECRETARY OF WAR: James W. Good; Patrick J. Hurley (from Dec. 9, 1929)
ATTORNEY GENERAL: James DeWitt Mitchell
POSTMASTER GENERAL: Walter F. Brown
SECRETARY OF THE NAVY: Charles F. Adams
SECRETARY OF THE INTERIOR: Ray L. Wilbur
SECRETARY OF AGRICULTURE: Arthur M. Hyde
SECRETARY OF COMMERCE: Robert P. Lamont; Roy D. Chapin (from Dec. 14, 1932)
SECRETARY OF LABOR: James J. Davis; William N. Doak (from Dec. 9, 1930)
SUPREME COURT APPOINTMENTS: Charles Evans Hughes, Chief Justice (1930); Owen J. Roberts (1930); Benjamin N. Cardozo (1932)
71st CONGRESS (March 4, 1929–March 4, 1931):
Senate: 56 Republicans; 39 Democrats; 1 Other
House: 267 Republicans; 167 Democrats; 1 Other
72nd CONGRESS (March 4, 1931–March 4, 1933):
Senate: 48 Republicans; 47 Democrats; 1 Other
House: 220 Democrats; 214 Republicans; 1 Other
END OF PRESIDENTIAL TERM: March 4, 1933

FRANKLIN DELANO ROOSEVELT

It seems to be a quality of the Roosevelt character," said Secretary of the Interior Harold L. Ickes, "either to inspire a mad devotion that can see no flaw or to kindle a hatred of an intensity that will admit of no virtue." And, indeed, in the twelve years and forty days of his Presidency, Franklin Delano Roosevelt aroused a loyalty and an opposition unequaled in American history.

To his enemies, Roosevelt was a dictator, a charlatan, a grinning poseur—"that Red in the White House." Crowning his domestic treason, they cried later, Roosevelt had personally plunged America into war with Germany and Japan only to sell out to Stalin. To those who admired F. D. R.—a decisive majority of Americans in four presidential elections—he was the friend of the poor, the champion of minorities, the defender of labor, the patrician savior of capitalism from a menacing American communism in the nation's worst economic depression, the inspiring architect of the Allied victory over the Axis powers, and the prophet of a new world order under the United Nations.

But no American, F. D. R. friend or foe, could deny the vast drama and impact of Roosevelt's turbulent reign in the White House, the bloodless revolution he wrought in the economy and society of the nation through legal means, the sheer weight of his will on the form and scope of the presidential office, or the force of his personal diplomacy in the shaping of modern history. When he died, wrote William S. White, it seemed as if "history itself had died," so central and vibrant a part of American life had F. D. R. been. And to a generation who had known no other President, it seemed, too, as if the Presidency had died, as if the United States could not go on.

There was virtually nothing in Franklin Delano Roosevelt's early background to augur the momentous role he would play as President. He was born

Franklin D. Roosevelt, photographed in 1939 at the wheel of his hand-controlled Ford

on January 30, 1882, in upstate New York's Dutchess County. A fifth cousin of President Theodore Roosevelt, F. D. R. was the indulged only son of James and Sara Delano Roosevelt and the quintessence of social privilege and wealth.

"All the good that is in me," F. D. R. would recall, "goes back to the Hudson"— to the quietly elegant Roosevelt estate at Hyde Park and to his formidable parents. "Poughkeepsie Jimmy" Roosevelt, mutton-chop whiskered and tweedy, was a wealthy gentleman farmer of Dutch descent with substantial interests in coal, shipping, and railroads. A registered Democrat—to the dismay of his Oyster Bay, Long Island, kin —he bolted his party temporarily in 1904 to vote for T. R., "because," he explained, "he's a Roosevelt." Sara, of Flemish descent, half the age of her husband and independently wealthy, was the dominant influence on young Franklin. "Imperious, lovable, well-meaning, [and] overgenerous," in the words of F. D. R.'s son James, Sara smothered her child with a dictatorial love.

F. D. R. dismissed his youth as "a little rowing, much outdoor life, quite some study, and then I went to Harvard." It was much more than that—an idyl of aristocracy. "He was brought up," said an aunt, "in a beautiful frame," a portrait of wealth's special perquisites: governesses, private tutors, dancing school, hunting and riding, his own pony. His mind, Sara explained, was kept "on nice things, at a high level."

Roosevelt's youth, however, was not wholly frivolous. He read a great deal (Mark Twain was a favorite) and acquired early his mother's and his "Uncle" Theodore's love for the sea. He was exposed in his private education to wider, more liberal dimensions of social thought and conscience, principally through the good offices of a Swiss governess, Mlle Jeanne Sandoz, to whom Roosevelt, as President, would write: "I have often thought that it was you, more than anyone else, who laid the foundation for my education."

Sara liberated Franklin when he was fourteen, allowing him to enter Massachusetts'

The portrait above of the squire of Hyde Park, James Roosevelt, was painted by Felix Moscheles.

elite Groton School. Under the tutelage of Dr. Endicott Peabody, students received moral instruction in the responsibility of the wealthy to aid and lead the less fortunate. Old for a Groton novice, F. D. R. was excluded from the school's already well-established cliques. And though he won prizes for punctuality and for prowess in Latin, acted in a school show, and served as manager of the baseball team, Roosevelt failed to achieve the social acceptance through success in competitive sports that he deeply craved. "He was nice," said a classmate, "but colorless." At Groton, however, F. D. R. learned to get on with boys his own age. And if not distinguished as a scholar, he appears to have moved closer to a social consciousness, defending independence for the Boers and the Filipinos in a senior-class debate and working in a camp for underprivileged boys.

In the fall of 1900 F. D. R. entered Harvard, where his rooms were chosen and decorated by the ubiquitous Sara, and his circle of friends was scrupulously limited to the Groton and prep-school coterie. Franklin again went all out to make the football team, but was turned down when he weighed in at a brittle one hundred and

*Sara Roosevelt (above in a portrait by Pierre Trou-
betzkoy) said that her son took after the Delanos.*

forty-six pounds. He became, instead, a
cheerleader. Already a handsome and lithe
six-foot-one, he was possessed of a charm
that would become, in biographer Allen
Churchill's words, "almost tangible."

Majoring in political history and government, F. D. R. appeared more troubled by
failing to make Harvard's top social club
(Porcellian) than by failing to better his
leisurely C average. His somewhat casual
scholarship notwithstanding, he won his
B.A. degree in three years. As president of
Harvard's undergraduate newspaper, *The
Crimson*, the Hyde Park patrician rarely
ventured beyond convention and trivia, en-
listing his readers in support of causes no
more crucial than "constant support" of
the football team. He deplored President
Roosevelt's vigorous settlement of the coal
strike for its elevation of the Executive over
Congress, organized a student committee to
aid the Boers, and appealed to Southern
colleges to embrace Harvard's policy of
admitting Negroes.

The death of James Roosevelt during
Franklin's study at Harvard, combined with
Sara's sustained generosity, made F. D. R.
an independently wealthy young man. Appointed sole guardian of her son, Sara

promptly took rooms near Harvard to supervise his life and development more
closely. But despite his privileges and
Sara's stultifying pampering, Franklin was
not totally oblivious to the responsibilities
of his class. Of the Roosevelts he proudly
observed: "They have never felt that because they were born in a good position they
could put their hands in their pockets and
succeed." On the contrary, he said, they
have felt that there was "no excuse for them
if they do not do their duty by the community. . . ." At Harvard F. D. R. won
his first election: he was chosen chairman of
his class committee.

Franklin also found romance in Cambridge. As a Harvard junior, F. D. R. invited his distant cousin, Eleanor Roosevelt,
to a party to help, he explained, "fill out
chinks." Soon thereafter Eleanor accepted
Roosevelt's prompt proposal of marriage,
and despite Sara's intense opposition, the
cousins were married on March 17, 1905.
Theodore Roosevelt gave the bride away.

Eleanor would bear Franklin Roosevelt
six children: a boy who lived only seven
months; Anna, the naughty and clever
"Sis," who would accompany her father to
Yalta; James, Roosevelt's devoted and intimate White House aide, later a liberal California congressman; Elliott, rebel and
rancher, who would ignore family precedent
and eschew Harvard; F. D. R., Jr., who
would serve as lawyer and congressman and
run unsuccessfully for the New York governorship; and John, who would defy Roosevelt traditions by becoming a Wall Street
Republican. The Roosevelt brood was not
always a comfort to its parents, particularly in the White House, earning more than
its share of notoriety—through divorces,
scandals, financial misfortune or caprice,
public fist fights, and political controversy. But Franklin and Eleanor chose to take
these contretemps in stride, maintaining a
highly permissive attitude.

In marriage Eleanor was to grow in self-
confidence and stature. As a youth she had
been wracked by acute shyness and a sense
of her own ungainliness and relative lack of

beauty. She entered life with Franklin hindered by her fear of coping with new domestic and social duties and with the imperious Sara. Through her financial control of Franklin, Sara literally assumed command of Eleanor's household and built adjoining town houses for herself and Franklin's ménage on New York's fashionable East 65th Street. Eleanor would never really win the battle with Sara, who would remain convinced that Eleanor had stolen her boy from her too soon.

But Eleanor Roosevelt would win, and win handsomely, her battle with life. With every new challenge she seemed to grow taller. The once ugly duckling—by immersing herself in social reform and by subordinating her fears to concern for the fears and needs of others less fortunate than she— would become, in Harry Truman's words, "First Lady of the World." Her influence in expanding F. D. R.'s somewhat parochial social consciousness was conclusive. It was she who, during her service as a settlement worker, introduced a debonair F. D. R. to "the other half" in a tour of a cold-water tenement in New York. "He was absolutely

shaken," Eleanor would recall, ". . . and kept saying he simply could not believe human beings lived that way."

Shortly before his marriage Roosevelt had enrolled at Columbia University Law School. He continued his studies there until 1907, when he passed his bar exam. He then enjoyed the predictable life of the well-heeled urban lawyer, commuting weekends to Hyde Park and holidays to the Roosevelts' massive "cottage" on Campobello Island off the coast of Maine.

The pattern of F. D. R.'s life changed in 1910 when he accepted an offer from upstate Democratic chieftains to run in his district for the New York State senate. Notwithstanding the fact that only one Democrat had been elected to this post in fifty-four years, F. D. R. took to the hustings. "Call me Franklin," he cried to farmers, promising a renewed Democratic party and a standardized apple barrel. Roosevelt won the election by 1,140 votes.

"His seat in the Senate wasn't warm," lamented an Albany veteran, "before he became a bolter." The Hyde Park neophyte promptly led insurgents opposed to the

Roosevelt, newly appointed to the Navy Department, took part in Flag Day ceremonies in 1913. He is at far right in the photograph above; at the left are William J. Bryan, Josephus Daniels, and Woodrow Wilson.

party's election of a Tammany drone for the United States Senate—and he won. "There is nothing I love as much as a good fight," Roosevelt said. Reported *The New York Times*: "With his handsome face and his form of supple strength, he could make a fortune on the stage and set the matinee girl's heart throbbing with subtle and happy emotion."

A New York *Herald* correspondent named Louis McHenry Howe—who would become F. D. R.'s lifelong confidant and political aide—found him, at first, "a spoiled, silk-pants sort of guy." But F. D. R. profited from his tenure as state senator. He learned how to campaign, how to meet people, how to lobby for desired goals. When he stood for re-election in 1912, aided by Howe, who was by then devoted to him, he increased his margin of victory to 1,631 votes.

Albany did not hold F. D. R. for long. When the Democratic presidential convention was called to order in Baltimore in 1912, the dashing young Roosevelt was on the scene, plumping hard for candidate Woodrow Wilson. For Josephus Daniels "it was a case of love at first sight," so struck was the Southerner by Roosevelt's good looks and zeal. Wilson proclaimed Franklin "the handsomest young giant I have ever seen." Instrumental in swinging the pivotal New York delegation to Wilson on the forty-sixth ballot, thus assuring him the nomination, F. D. R. wired Eleanor: "WILSON NOMINATED THIS AFTERNOON. ALL PLANS VAGUE. SPLENDID TRIUMPH."

Josephus Daniels' plans were not vague. Appointed Secretary of the Navy by President Wilson, he urged F. D. R. to join him as assistant secretary. His offer was almost rapturously accepted by the sea-loving Roosevelt. "It is interesting to see," wrote Cousin Theodore, "that you are in another place which I myself once held." F. D. R. soon grew contemptuous of Daniels. "I am *running* the real work here," he assured Eleanor, adding that Daniels was "bewildered by it all but very sweet and sad" and hopelessly limited by "his faith in human nature and civilization and similar idealistic nonsense. . . ." Roosevelt's arrogance was modified by the fact that he proved, indeed, to be an efficient administrator and ultimately acknowledged his debt to Daniels. The Navy post was his baptism of fire in the use of political strategy and persuasion in an executive position. But more than that, he did much to prepare the United States Fleet for World War I and himself gained priceless experience for a greater conflict. And if the Dollar Diplomacy landing of Marines to crush Haitian revolutions—F. D. R. hoped "for all time to come"—exacerbated already bitter relations between North and South America, F. D. R.'s famed North Sea Mine Barrage—a 240-mile-long curtain of mines to block German submarine attacks on Allied shipping—won him justified esteem, for the barrage encouraged a German naval revolt that was to prove a decisive factor in bringing about the armistice.

As assistant secretary, Roosevelt took time out in 1914 to run unsuccessfully for the nomination for United States senator from New York, but his heart remained with the Navy. He toured the war zone in 1918 and even offered to fight in the war, but failed to win Wilson's consent. F. D. R. represented the Navy Department as an observer at the Versailles Peace Conference. Roosevelt was not averse to spending hundreds of millions of dollars without congressional approval and had no evident qualms about borrowing a destroyer for a private visit to Campobello. But when he resigned his post on August 6, 1920, he wrote humbly to Daniels: "You have taught me so wisely and kept my feet on the ground when I was about to skyrocket. . . ."

F. D. R.'s star shone still more brightly at the Democratic convention of 1920, where he rose to second the presidential nomination of Alfred E. Smith. The Democrats, however, preferred the less controversial James M. Cox of Ohio, who chose thirty-eight-year-old Franklin Roosevelt as his running mate. "He met the geographical requirement," explained Cox, who was no doubt also impressed by Roosevelt's magic name and his popularity in the wartime Navy Department. Roosevelt campaigned

Roosevelt loved to sail with his children. The picture above shows him with sons James and Elliott.

vigorously, pushing hard for the League of Nations. Of a swing through forty-two states F. D. R. said, "I got to know the country as only a candidate for national office or a traveling salesman can get to know it." Women swarmed around him as he pleaded for a continuation of Wilson's policies. "If things go through on November second," he promised, "I am going to make an effort to put the job of Vice President on the map for the first time in history." He never got a chance because Cox lost to Warren G. Harding.

Trounced but unbowed, Roosevelt joined a law firm as a working partner. Shuttling between New York City and Hyde Park, he embraced the cloistered life of the well-to-do: visiting much-indulged sons at Groton; serving as a Harvard overseer; golfing, hunting, and sailing off Campobello. All told, his son James recalled, Roosevelt was "the handsomest, strongest, most glamorous, vigorous, physical father in the world."

In August, 1921, the privileged and insulated world of Franklin D. Roosevelt collapsed. Yachting off Campobello, Roosevelt fell into the frigid waters of the Bay of Fundy, sustaining severe body shock. The next day, again sailing, he beached his boat on an island near Campobello to fight a forest fire, after which he plunged for refreshment first into an island lake and then into the icy waters of the bay. Returning home, still in his wet bathing suit, he sat reading in the chilling air. Overcome by a sudden stab of pain and a chill, he went to bed. He awoke the next day in fever and pain, his knees failing when he tried to get up. The following morning the heir to Hyde Park lay paralyzed from the chest down.

A local doctor diagnosed Roosevelt's condition as a deep cold. Another, announcing that a blood clot had lodged in the spinal cord inducing temporary paralysis, prescribed massage. Ten days later, on Eleanor's initiative, a specialist was called in, and he confirmed her fear: Franklin Delano Roosevelt, aged thirty-nine, had been struck down by infantile paralysis. F. D. R. lay in pain so great that his immobile legs could not bear even the weight of his bed sheet. When his legs jackknifed, they had to be encased in a cast to keep them straight. His back and arms, even his eyesight, seemed threatened. And only by mid-September would his doctor permit his arduous journey to New York for more effective treatment. "He has such courage, such ambition, and yet . . . such an extraordinarily sensitive emotional mechanism," said his doctor, George Draper, "that it will take all the skill which we can muster to lead him successfully to a recognition of what he really faces without crushing him."

It seemed probable that F. D. R. would never walk again, never stand again, never sit on or rise from a chair again, unaided. He would be forced to crawl from room to room, to pull the dead weight of his lower limbs up flights of stairs, to submit to being carried about like a child, and to carry papers and books in his teeth. In the prime of his gifted and beautiful life, he was suddenly a cripple, dependent on help to fulfill his smallest need.

But, said his old running mate, James M. Cox, "never a note of despair came from him. He was always brave and hopeful." And Roosevelt found new cause for hope as life and strength flowed once more into his arms, his chest, and his back. Then he could sit up again. By late December, 1921, F. D. R. was judged well enough to be taken home to East 65th Street. In the spring he donned painful braces, which were strapped around his waist, attached to the heels of his shoes, and jointed and clamped at the knees. In his home he moved about in a small armless wheel chair. And through faithful exercise with special equipment he built up his chest, neck, and arm muscles to prodigious strength. "Maybe my legs aren't so good," he joked, "but look at those shoulders. Jack Dempsey would be green with envy."

Roosevelt confronted and conquered his tragedy in what writer John Gunther has called "a triumph of pure grit, the conquest of flesh by will and spirit." He defied his mother in her attempt, as James Roosevelt has said, to commit him to "a hole in the good Roosevelt earth at Hyde Park into which he could crawl and hide. . . ." Instead, he accepted the challenge of Eleanor and Howe, who was still heroically loyal, to achieve a victory of the mind that was independent of physical well-being. On his back now, he still wrestled with the children. He contrived a manually operated automobile in which he rode through the Hyde Park countryside. And by the autumn of 1924 he had discovered a joyous new therapy: the 88-degree waters of Warm Springs, Georgia, where he vowed to swim his legs back to life.

Throughout this ordeal, F. D. R. never succumbed to self-pity. "No sob stuff," he would say to those who presumed to pity him. And, far from breaking him, close observers agreed, illness lifted Roosevelt to a new, more noble stature. He utterly conquered personal fear. He gained new perspective, new depth, new compassion. "If you have spent two years in bed trying to wiggle your big toe," he once said, "everything else seems easy." In illness, Louis Howe said, "his thoughts expanded, his horizon widened. . . . He thought of others who were ill and afflicted and in want. . . . Lying there, he grew bigger, day by day."

The years following F. D. R.'s polio attack were politically undistinguished. He resumed his legal career, tended his stamp collection, worked on a movie script on the history of "Old Ironsides"—which was turned down—and squandered money on such speculative ventures as an intercity dirigible freight line. The year 1924, however, marked Roosevelt's dramatic, if brief, return to national politics when he agreed to head Alfred E. Smith's presidential campaign in New York State. Smith, governor of New York, would lose the Democratic nomination to John W. Davis. But Roosevelt's appearance at Madison Square Garden on June 26 to nominate "the Happy Warrior" remains a signal event in American political history. After weeks of practice

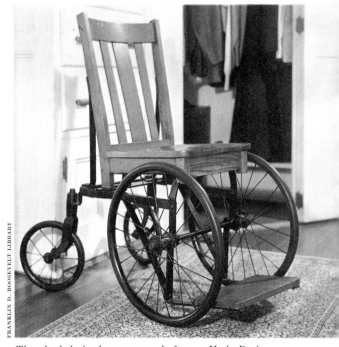

The wheel chair above was made from a Hyde Park kitchen chair. Its lack of arms made getting on and off it easier for the crippled Franklin D. Roosevelt.

Roosevelt was able to take ten painful steps alone to the rostrum to address the convention. "As he propelled himself," wrote biographer Allen Churchill, "Franklin looked pale and drawn. But on reaching the lectern his face broke into a wide, flashing grin and his head tossed back in the proud old gesture that once annoyed people but now seemed full of gallantry and courage." Less than three years after his nearly fatal attack, Roosevelt—and the Smith nomination—received an ovation lasting one hour and thirteen minutes. "Adversity," said the New York *World*, "has lifted him above the bickering, the religious bigotry, conflicting personal ambitions, and petty sectional prejudices. . . . It has made him the one leader commanding the respect and admiration of delegations from all sections of the land."

Of Roosevelt's great political appeal Smith had no doubt. Finally nominated for the Presidency to run against Herbert Hoover in 1928, Smith virtually begged Roosevelt to run for governor of New York, principally to help him carry the state and to assure continuation of his progressive policies in Albany. Roosevelt flatly refused. He remained hopeful that if he continued his hydrotherapy at Warm Springs he could discard his braces. Nevertheless, he was nominated for governor by acclamation at the New York State convention. To Republican protestations that Roosevelt's crippled legs disqualified him for the office, Smith replied gruffly: "We do not elect [a governor] for his ability to do a double back flip or a handspring."

Roosevelt entered the fray with high spirits and vast energy. Mocking Republican whispers about his "unfortunate" condition, he stormed through the state, covering as many as one hundred and ninety miles a day. Notwithstanding his vigorous campaign and his magical effect on crowds, Roosevelt won the governorship by only a shaky 25,564 votes, while Smith lost his home state by some 103,000 votes.

F. D. R.'s primary task was to continue Smith's progressive program. But he also pursued bold new policies. In the field of agriculture he advocated not merely improved marketing facilities and more equitable farm taxes but a more productive use of land. With no great success, F. D. R. also fought for the electrification of farm homes at reasonable rates, through closely regulated and publicly owned agencies.

Governor Roosevelt was harassed on two political fronts. He was opposed by Smith and his lieutenants, who were embittered both by Roosevelt's electoral showing in 1928 and by his defiance of Smith in matters of patronage. F. D. R. was also opposed by the Republican-controlled legislature. Already he was condemned for executive "avarice, usurpation and presumption." The people of New York State did not agree. During the widespread Depression resulting from the stock market crash of October, 1929, it was clear that new answers, new alternatives to Albany's pattern of rural politics, were needed, and needed desperately. And Roosevelt made it plain in his 1930 campaign for re-election that he had some answers. The results of the election were unprecedented. Roosevelt took forty-one of the fifty-seven counties outside New York City, and swept the state by 725,001 votes. Overnight he became an outstanding candidate for the 1932 presidential nomination.

Advised by a brain trust that included Judge Samuel I. Rosenman, Frances Perkins, Henry Morgenthau, Jr., and political trouble shooter James A. Farley, Roosevelt acted to lift New York out of the Depression. On August 28, 1931, he set forth a credo of government and economy that was the harbinger of the New Deal: "What is the State?" he asked. "It is the duly constituted representative of an organized society of human beings, created by them for their mutual protection and well-being." To New York—and to the nation—he announced: "The duty of the State toward the citizens is the duty of the servant to its master." One of the government's central duties, Governor Roosevelt declared, was "caring for those of its citizens who find themselves the victims of such adverse circumstance as makes them unable to obtain even the necessities for mere existence without the aid of others."

Roosevelt is sworn in for his second term as governor by Judge Irving Lehman, brother of the then lieutenant governor, Herbert H. Lehman (at left, with his wife). At right are the governor's wife and his mother.

Roosevelt sponsored legislation—in a still Republican legislature—for improvement of labor conditions, for old-age pensions, judicial reform, farm relief, unemployment relief, reforestation, a 50 per cent rise in the state income tax aimed at a more equitable tax burden, and public works to employ the hungry and the poor. He crowned his anti-Depression program by establishing the epochal Temporary Emergency Relief Administration, which was given an initial thirty million dollars to assist the jobless and needy. New York thus became the first state to grant the unemployment relief the nation so desperately needed.

In his second term Roosevelt moved reluctantly against Tammany Hall, in the person of New York City's debonair Irish mayor, James Walker. F. D. R. needed Tammany to carry New York City. But with his eye already on the Presidency, he needed political purity even more. In a series of public hearings, conducted only after prolonged vacillation, Roosevelt solemnly interrogated the wayward mayor, revealing scandal after scandal. When Walker broke under the continuing pressure, Roosevelt allowed him to resign, thus pleasing the public and escaping the wrath of Tammany Hall regulars, who could not blame Roosevelt directly for dismissing their chieftain.

Unemployment relief and Jimmy Walker aside, Roosevelt was preoccupied in his second Albany term with running for the Presidency. With Farley computing political arithmetic around the country, with Howe still at F. D. R.'s side as his eyes and ears and legs, and with an expanded council of advisers that included Columbia Professors Raymond Moley, Adolf A. Berle, Jr., and Rexford G. Tugwell, who were all writing speeches and germinating ideas, Roosevelt waged an aggressive campaign to line up delegates. He entered the convention in June, 1932, with 666¼ of the 770 votes needed for nomination.

Facing a four-cornered Democratic opposition—Al Smith, Newton D. Baker, John Nance Garner, and Maryland's Governor Albert Ritchie—Roosevelt maintained a studied posture of political ambivalence and accommodation. To gain William Randolph Hearst's vital support, for example, he renounced the League of Nations in its 1932 form. He derided Smith's program of public works as a superficial, stopgap solution to the Depression. "A real economic cure," he pronounced in April, 1932, "must go to the killing of the bacteria in the system rather than to the treatment of external symptoms." The federal government, he repeated, could no longer safely stand by in sanctimonious

The bumper plate above showed the voters how F. D. R. liked his name to be pronounced.

neutrality while people starved. Denounced by Smith for "setting class against class," Roosevelt remained unmoved. Urging long-range economic planning and expanded buying power as solutions to the Depression, F. D. R. declared: "The country needs and, unless I mistake its temper, the country demands bold, persistent experimentation. . . . Above all, try something."

It was a radical appeal for strong, new techniques, one that frankly worried conservative and temporizing elements in the Democratic party. So F. D. R. and the party hacks locked horns at the convention, and in every way the battle within the Democratic party at Chicago was the real political conflict of 1932. Hoover had already been beaten by events.

On the convention's first ballot, F. D. R. polled his committed 666¼. Counting heads, the redoubtable "Field Marshal" Farley pleaded with Chicago's Mayor Anton Cermak to switch Illinois to Roosevelt, confident that Indiana would follow suit. Cermak declined. ("Had he jumped to our band wagon then," Farley later recalled, "he would not have been in Miami a few months later seeking political favors only to stop an assassin's wild bullet aimed at Roosevelt.") Roosevelt's tally edged up to 677¾ on the second ballot and to 683 on the third.

The Roosevelt forces caucused, and Farley's word went out: "Texas is our only chance." His strategy: call Congressman Sam Rayburn and have "Mister Sam" offer the Vice Presidency to Garner in exchange

for his support of F. D. R. Rayburn succeeded, first winning California's pledge to switch to Roosevelt, then getting Garner's approval to release the Texas delegation. The band wagon rolled. On the fourth ballot Roosevelt was nominated for the Presidency, receiving 945 votes to Smith's 190¼.

Breaking all precedent and defying those who advised a confident front-porch campaign, Roosevelt flew to Chicago to accept the nomination in person and to address an anxious nation: "I pledge you, I pledge myself," he declared, "to a new deal for the American people. . . . This is more than a political campaign; it is a call to arms. Give me your help, not to win votes alone, but to win in this crusade to restore America to its own people."

Everyone had underestimated Roosevelt's energy. In a coast-to-coast campaign, the indefatigable F. D. R. covered twenty-seven thousand miles, carrying his message of hope and promise of action to all but seven states. He promised unemployment relief, the repeal of prohibition, lower tariffs, and—of all things—a cut in government spending. But his seesawing campaign pronouncements indicated at this time no clear concept of the New Deal. They also revealed basic contradictions in his thinking. Roosevelt attacked, for example, President Hoover's excessive deficit spending, but promised to use government funds to aid the needy; he simultaneously advocated a lowered tariff and continued protection of United States industries.

In one campaign speech, however, delivered on September 23, 1932, F. D. R. spelled out the fundamental tenets of New Deal philosophy. Deploring the collapse of "equality of opportunity" and lamenting the fact that "some six-hundred-odd corporations . . . controlled two-thirds of American industry," F. D. R. called for retrenchment, for "administering resources and plants already in hand," for "meeting the problem of underconsumption," for "distributing wealth and products more equitably," for "adapting existing economic organizations to the service of the people." The age of the robber baron, in short, was over. "I do not believe," Roosevelt said, "that in the name of that sacred word, individualism, a few powerful interests should be permitted to make industrial cannon fodder of the lives of half the population of the United States."

For the nation's fourteen million unemployed, Roosevelt's sharp attack on irresponsible corporate interests constituted a promise of a thrilling new political leadership. For Herbert Hoover, however, the speech spelled virtual treason. A Roosevelt victory, he predicted, would mean that "grass will grow in the streets of a hundred cities." Worse than that, Hoover charged Roosevelt with embracing a "philosophy of government which has poisoned all Europe," suggesting, in short, that Roosevelt was prescribing communism for the United States. Though stung by Hoover's irrational charges, Roosevelt summoned enough coolness to say simply: "I . . . will not let Hoover question my Americanism."

The predominantly conservative Republican press joined the G.O.P. campaign attack on Roosevelt, portraying him as an agent of revolution. Rumors were peddled in the yellow press that polio would ultimately reach Roosevelt's brain, rendering him incoherent or insane. But Roosevelt knew, Raymond Moley said, that the "standpatters'" opposition was strategically necessary "if the campaign [was] to seem to the rank and file . . . something other than the usual campaign futilitarianism." The election results proved that Roosevelt had judged America's mood with precision. He swept the election by a popular vote of 22,809,638 to Hoover's 15,758,901 and carried all but six states.

In the four-month interregnum before Roosevelt took office, the Depression deepened: unemployment rose precipitately to fifteen million, more banks failed, bread lines lengthened. In an obvious move to embarrass Roosevelt politically, Hoover urged the President-elect to join him in a public declaration of opposition to public projects and in an embrace of Republican nostrums.

Roosevelt was unimpressed by Hoover's transparent political tactics and maintained a facade of affable neutrality. As he waited to assume national power, his calm was broken only momentarily by an unemployed bricklayer named Giuseppe Zangara. On February 14, 1933, after addressing a reception at Bay Front Park, Florida, the President-elect became the target of a spray of bullets aimed at him by Zangara, who harbored a pathological hatred for "all officials and everybody who is rich." Five in the Roosevelt entourage were wounded, Mayor Anton Cermak of Chicago fatally. Throughout the ordeal F. D. R. remained incredibly calm. And the nation's shock gave way to undiluted admiration for this new demonstration of Roosevelt's courage.

Inauguration Day, March 4, 1933, dawned sunny. On the Capitol steps Franklin Delano Roosevelt took the oath of office as the thirty-second President of the United States. Then he addressed a stricken nation:

"This is preeminently the time," President Roosevelt declared, "to speak the truth, the whole truth, frankly and boldly. This great Nation will endure as it has endured, will revive and will prosper. So, first of all, let me assert my firm belief that the only thing we have to fear is fear itself—nameless, unreasoning, unjustified terror which paralyzes needed efforts to convert retreat into advance. In every dark hour of our national life," Roosevelt assured the people, "a leadership of frankness and vigor has met with that understanding and support of the people themselves which is essential to victory." Asking for this support, he pledged action to employ the hungry, to restore the people's buying power and the value of their property, and to rake up "the withered leaves of industrial enterprise. . . ." The country, he continued, "asks for action, and action now. Our greatest primary task is to put people to work." And the government, he said, acting as it would in war, would itself recruit workers directly in "greatly needed projects to stimulate and reorganize the use of our natural resources." The President promised aid to farmers in more productive use of their land and in price subsidies. He promised to assist small-home owners in battling mortgage foreclosures. He promised regulation of price-fixing public utilities. He called for "a strict supervision of all banking and credits and investments. . . ."

Pledging himself to "a leadership which aims at a larger good," the new President declared: "I assume unhesitatingly the leadership of this great army of our people dedicated to a disciplined attack upon our common problems." In leading this attack, Roosevelt said, he would seek to maintain "the normal balance of executive and legislative authority. . . ." But if this constitutional balance proved unequal to meeting the national emergency, he warned, he would ask Congress for emergency powers "as great as the power that would be given to me if we were in fact invaded by a foreign foe." The people, he said, had chosen him to implement their wish for national "discipline and direction. . . . In the spirit of the gift I take it."

Then Roosevelt acted. After closing all banks for four days and placing an embargo on the export of gold, silver, and currency to protect United States reserves, the President summoned the Seventy-third Congress into special session on March 9. From that historic moment until June 16—one hundred days later—when Congress adjourned, President and lawmakers, responding to the national crisis with incredible unity, forged the bloodless American revolution of 1933 that is called the New Deal.

On March 9 the Emergency Banking Relief Act, passed and signed within eight hours, authorized a regulated reopening of the banks; gave the President power to control transactions in credit, currency, and foreign exchange; empowered the Treasury to call in gold and gold certificates and to issue more currency; and authorized the comptroller of the currency to administer insolvent banks. By March 13 the banks, no longer afraid, reopened their doors.

On March 20 the Economy Act cut by 15 per cent the salaries of all appointed federal personnel, reduced veterans' pensions, and reorganized certain government agencies to make them more efficient. Two days later the Beer-Wine Revenue Act legalized those beverages, thus adding to the nation's tax revenues. On March 31 the Civilian Conservation Corps was founded to employ young men in work projects designed to plant new forests, build dams, fight soil erosion, and construct federal and state parks.

In another major New Deal action the United States, by joint resolution of Congress, went off the gold standard on April 19. Though opposed by some conservatives as "the end of Western civilization," Roosevelt's bold action was praised by no less prestigious an institution than the House of Morgan for having "saved the country from complete collapse" by freeing the currency from crippling restrictions. The gold repeal made debts payable in legal tender, with the salutary result that prices and stocks rose, giving new life and volume to the economy, foreign trade was expanded, the gold drain to Europe was cut back, and domestic price levels and attempts to expand consumer buying power were freed from the dictates of a stifling world market.

The Federal Emergency Relief Act, providing direct relief to states and municipalities, was passed on May 12. An immediate grant of five hundred million dollars in emergency relief was authorized, to be administered by the Federal Emergency Relief Administration; the grant was later increased to five billion dollars.

Also on May 12 the Agricultural Adjustment Administration was founded to subsidize farmers by compensations for crop curtailment, thus reducing price-deflating overproduction. This program was to be implemented by establishing parity prices for farm products and by imposing limitations on the breeding of pigs and beef cattle. Some indication of the inventiveness of the Roosevelt program is the fact that piglets slaughtered in this breeding cutback were frozen and distributed free to families on relief. Farmers were given another badly needed boost on May 12 with the passage of the Emergency Farm Mortgage Act, which stopped foreclosures and authorized federal refunding of mortgages.

On May 18 the New Deal embraced a far-reaching economic plan that would command the attention of the world: the Tennessee Valley Authority Act. This historic measure called for the rehabilitation of the entire forty-thousand-square-mile Tennessee Valley basin through the institution of public power, cheap electricity, soil conservation, navigational improvements, flood control, land-use reform, afforestation, and massive industrial development.

A closer check on investments and investment manipulations was assured on May 27 by the Truth-in-Securities Act, which required the filing with the Federal Trade Commission of sworn information regarding securities sold in interstate commerce or publicly offered to prospective investors. Homeowners were buoyed on June 13 by the passage of an act creating the Home Owners Loan Corporation, which was authorized to refinance mortgages at more reasonable rates for nonfarm homeowners who could no longer carry old mortgage terms and to lend money for home taxes and repairs.

June 16, the last of the Hundred Days, witnessed the birth of three major New Deal reforms. Bank deposits were insured by the Glass-Steagall Banking Act, which created the Federal Deposit Insurance Corporation, separated investment from commercial banking, restricted the use of bank credit for speculation, and extended the regulatory authority of the Federal Reserve Board. The Farm Credit Administration provided for the refinancing of mortgages, set up local ad-

LIBRARY OF CONGRESS

JOHN NANCE GARNER

"Cactus Jack" Garner was a plain-spoken man. Serving as Franklin Roosevelt's Vice President for two terms, he characterized that office as "not worth a pitcher of warm spit" because "the Vice President is just a waiting boy, waiting just in case something happens to the President." There was some truth in what he said; in any case he had reason to be bitter. Born near Detroit, Texas, in 1868, he had won his first election in 1893, when he became a county judge, and after creating a congressional district for himself while a member of the Texas legislature, he had been elected to the House in 1902. He had served there thirty years, rising to the Speakership, a job he considered second only to the Presidency. He gave up the post, and a chance to win the presidential nomination, to avoid a disastrous convention deadlock in 1932; he handed his Texas and California votes to Roosevelt and agreed to be the ticket balancer. Though an exceptionally helpful assistant to F. D. R. in the early days of the New Deal, Garner watched in growing alarm as the President advocated greater executive power. Garner felt that it was his turn to be President in 1940, but Roosevelt ran for a third term. The "Texas Bearcat" quit politics and returned home, where, on each birthday, he repeated to visiting reporters his views on the Vice Presidency, the "unnecessary office." He died in 1967, just before his ninety-ninth birthday.

justment committees, and centralized the processes of providing farm credit.

The passage of the National Industrial Recovery Act, which created the National Recovery Administration, crowned the work of the Hundred Days. Its objective was to devise codes of fair competition and fair practices for industry and to guarantee labor's right to organize and to bargain collectively. The act also created the Public Works Administration to make jobs in construction projects for the unemployed.

Thus, within three months of his accession to the Presidency, Roosevelt had redeemed his pledge to act for the plain people. "Before the adjournment of the Special Session," Roosevelt told the lawmakers, "I want to convey to you . . . an expression of my thanks for making possible, on the broad average, a more sincere and whole-hearted cooperation between the legislative and executive branches of the United States Government than has been witnessed by the American people in many a long year." This cooperation, he said, "has proven that our form of government can rise to an emergency and can carry through a broad program in record time."

It had been, indeed, a splendid performance. Right-wingers condemned "the New Dole." An enraged judge complained that "King Franklin" was "playing tiddledy winks with the entire universe." But the people rejoiced at Roosevelt's bold action.

Nor was F. D. R. restricted by dogma. "It is common sense," he had said, "to take a method and try it. If it fails, admit it frankly and try another." And this is precisely how F. D. R. proceeded. The New Deal was less a carefully formulated stage-by-stage plan to renew the economy than a makeshift series of experiments, some brilliantly effective, some impractical, some discriminatory and punitive if noble in vision, but all aimed directly at real conditions of want. Roosevelt's program, wrote historian Samuel Eliot Morison, was "a new deal of old cards, no longer stacked against the common man. Opponents called it near-fascism or near-communism, but it was American as a bale of hay—an opportunist, rule-of-thumb method of curing deep-seated ills. Probably it saved

Not everyone admired the professors ("Brain Trust," sneered Louis Howe) whose ideas F. D. R. drew upon for the many imaginative programs that were the hallmark of the New Deal. This 1934 Vanity Fair cover shows a cap-and-gowned Dr. Braintrust tattooing on Uncle Sam the initials of New Deal programs.

800

the capitalist system in the United States. . . ."

Impervious to attacks by the very business interests he had saved, Roosevelt pushed forward with the New Deal. In August, 1933, the National Labor Board was organized to back labor's right to collective bargaining. The NLB was empowered to investigate and mediate labor disputes arising under the NIRA.

In November the Civil Works Administration, designed to employ four million Americans on federal, state, and local projects, was established. It was an emergency measure that was supplanted within a year by FERA and PWA activities.

On December 5 prohibition, a major source of violence, crime, and political corruption, was repealed. The Gold Reserve Act of January 30, 1934, authorized the President to revalue the dollar at 50 to 60 per cent of its gold content, permitting much greater flexibility in currency management.

The Securities Exchange Act, which had immense repercussions, was passed on June 6, 1934. It created the Securities and Exchange Commission to curb malpractices in the stock market. Under the law, stock exchanges had to be licensed and all securities had to be registered, while the Federal Reserve Board was authorized to limit the extension of credit for speculation.

Passed on June 19, 1934, the Communications Act created the Federal Communications Commission to regulate interstate and foreign communications. On June 28 the Federal Housing Administration was established under the National Housing Act.

The year 1935 saw no diminution of the New Deal tempo. On April 8 the Works Progress Administration was authorized to grant loans for nonfederal projects, placing five billion dollars in the President's hands for industrial pump priming. On July 5 the Wagner-Connery National Labor Relations Act committed the government, once again, to support the right of labor to organize and to bargain collectively. Under the act a new National Labor Relations Board was created. The Motor Carrier Act of August 9 put interstate bus and truck lines under the regulation of the I.C.C. The Wheeler-Rayburn Act of August 26 gave the Federal Power Commission authority to regulate electric-power holding companies in all phases of interstate commerce and empowered the Federal Trade Commission to regulate the gas industry.

Still the New Deal pushed on. On August 30 the Guffey-Snyder Bituminous Coal Stabilization Act gave the federal government power to establish an industrial code, to fix prices, and to oblige employers to accept unions and negotiate with their elected representatives. The act imposed on the selling price or market value of soft coal a 15 per cent tax, nine-tenths of which was to be remitted to producers who filed acceptance of the industrial code. Also passed in 1935 was the Wealth Tax Act. It increased surtaxes on individual incomes of fifty thousand dollars or more and on estates valued at more than forty thousand dollars.

Roosevelt's supreme domestic achievement in his first term, however, was the passage of the Social Security Act on August 14, 1935. This law provided for a system of old-age retirement payments, financed through a payroll tax on employers and employees, and for financial compensation to the unemployed during fixed periods. The act also provided aid to the needy, aged, and blind, and to dependent mothers and neglected children. It called for public-health-service agencies. Despite administrative flaws and uneven benefit standards, Arthur Schlesinger, Jr., observed, this law "still meant a tremendous break with the inhibitions of the past. The federal government was at last charged with the obligation to provide its citizens a measure of protection from the hazards and vicissitudes of life."

"In the field of world policy," Roosevelt had said in his Inaugural Address, "I would dedicate this Nation to the policy of the good neighbor—the neighbor who resolutely respects himself and, because he does so, respects the rights of others. . . ."

In July, 1933, Roosevelt refused to support the efforts of the London International Monetary and Economic Conference to sta-

Among the talented men assisting the President were, from left, Henry Morgenthau, Jr., farm adviser and Secretary of the Treasury; James Farley, politico par excellence; and Columbia Professor Adolf A. Berle, Jr.

bilize international exchange and to set a currency standard. In a clear contest between gold-standard countries, such as France, and countries off gold, such as Britain, Roosevelt adopted a unilateral policy of nationally managed currency and exchange, thus assuring American fiscal independence and freedom from arbitrary limitations imposed by European banks. He would not be pressured, F. D. R. said, into treaty-bound stabilization by world bankers. "A sufficient interval should be allowed the United States," Roosevelt wired to London, "to permit . . . a demonstration of the value of price lifting efforts which we have well in hand." F. D. R. denounced the "old fetishes of so-called international bankers," refusing, he said, to sacrifice the American effort to increase consumers' purchasing power through a stronger, more valuable dollar. Conservatives howled, but economist John Maynard Keynes hailed the President's defiance of Europe as "magnificently right."

Roosevelt approached other problems with less obvious nationalism. On November 16, 1933, he faced up to the persistent, if painful, reality of the Soviet Union's sixteen-year-old government by according Moscow diplomatic recognition. A factor in this action was the rise of Germany and Japan. The Japanese had invaded Manchuria in 1931; Hitler had achieved full dictatorial power in Germany by the end of March, 1933, had renounced the Versailles Treaty,

and had begun a massive military build-up. But America was preoccupied with domestic recovery and overwhelmingly opposed involvement in Europe's affairs.

At an Inter-American Conference held at Montevideo in December, 1933, Washington made an unprecedented pledge of non-intervention in South American affairs. The Tydings-McDuffie Act of March 24, 1934, provided for Philippine independence in 1946. A treaty with Cuba in May, 1934, repealed the hated Platt Amendment, which had permitted United States intervention in Cuban affairs. On June 12 of the same year, the President was authorized to raise or lower tariff rates up to 50 per cent in reciprocal agreements with other nations. And in December, 1936, arrangements for hemispherical consultation and united action in matters of common defense were concluded at the Buenos Aires conference.

Roosevelt's success in the Presidency was the result of his utter mastery of the art of politics. At the core of his administration's strength was his unassailable optimism and fearlessness. Historian Richard Hofstadter cited "Roosevelt's confidence that even when he was operating in unfamiliar territory he could do no wrong, commit no serious mistakes." From the start, F. D. R. employed two techniques of public communication that helped make his administration successful. First, he met the press, usually twice a week, in a sporting, free give-

Cordell Hull, above left, was Secretary of State from 1933 to 1944; Louis Howe, center, devoted twenty years to making F. D. R. President; Rexford G. Tugwell was another Columbia professor serving as an adviser.

and-take that put his achievements and his plans in the headlines. More important, he addressed the American people periodically by radio in his famed "fireside chats," explaining his programs and purposes with elegant simplicity. Roosevelt's voice, patrician and resonant, inspired confidence.

But Roosevelt was more than a first-class showman. As a politician he was as ruthless as Jefferson in matters of party loyalty and as skillful as Washington in gaining bipartisan support. Raymond Moley expressed concern over Roosevelt's "frightening . . . receptivity" to advice, but he also noted that "when [Roosevelt] wants something a lot he can be formidable—when crossed he is hard, stubborn, resourceful, relentless."

The basis of Roosevelt's political success, particularly with the Seventy-third Congress, was his appeal to reasonable men of both parties to join hands in a battle that transcended political lines. The President's success was nowhere more evident than in the words of the House Republican Whip, Bertrand Snell, as he accepted F. D. R.'s Emergency Banking Act: "The house is burning down," Snell explained, "and the President of the United States says this is the way to put out the fire." Republican opposition to Roosevelt would grow, but F. D. R.'s political base would remain the moderate wings of both parties.

Roosevelt was first and last a Democrat, however. He loved his party and lifted it from the disorder and bickering that had afflicted it as a minority party since Wilson, shaping it into a broad-based majority coalition. In Roosevelt's White House, thitherto unrepresented racial and national minorities found a political home, as did grateful farmers, laborers, progressives, intellectuals, women, small-business men, and the needy and dispossessed. F. D. R. himself could say "my old friend" in eleven languages, and preached that without hard precinct-pounding all the idealism in the world was useless.

As administrator of an eccentric, if gifted, Cabinet, Roosevelt pursued an almost overt policy of divide-and-conquer, pitting one of his trusted lieutenants against another, thus assuring himself of ultimate control in addition to more objective counsel and data. It was a pastiche Cabinet that consisted of irascible Harold L. Ickes, Secretary of the Interior; solemn Henry Morgenthau, Jr., Secretary of the Treasury from 1934 to 1945; visionary Henry A. Wallace, Secretary of Agriculture until he became Vice President in 1940; sensitive Cordell Hull, Secretary of State; and no-nonsense Frances Perkins, Secretary of Labor, the first woman to serve in a presidential Cabinet.

As a presidential theorist F. D. R. was less prolific than his cousin Theodore, but his concept of the nation's highest office emerged in his published words. He was, first of all, acutely conscious of the fact that only the

The cartoon above was the cover illustration for a pamphlet containing anti-New Deal doggerel, published during the presidential campaign of 1936.

President and Vice President were elected by the entire electorate and were, therefore, pre-eminent. He viewed the Presidency as the last court of national conciliation, where the Chief Executive defended the interests of all groups. In implementing the vaulting programs of the New Deal, for which there was little precedent, he assured Congress that he was not seeking "more power" per se, but rather "the tools of management and the authority to distribute the work" that would enable him to discharge his duties as specifically outlined in the Constitution. "To carry out any twentieth-century program," he told the people in a fireside chat, "we must give the executive branch of the government twentieth-century machinery to work with. I recognize that democratic processes are necessarily and rightly slower than dictatorial processes. But I refuse to believe that democratic processes need be dangerously slow."

"The function of Congress," he said, was "to decide what has to be done and to select the appropriate agency to carry out its will"; it was also empowered to "fix the amount of expenditure, the means by which it is to be raised and the general principles under which the expenditures are to be made." The rest of government, he said, was up to the President. He alone recommended objectives; the Congress adopted methods. His general approach to the Presidency, Roosevelt said, was to combine "Wilson's appeal to the fundamental" and T. R.'s success in "stirring people to enthusiasm over specific individual events. . . ." As for the burdens of the Presidency itself, F. D. R. said simply: "It's a terrible job. But somebody has to do it." In fact, Roosevelt seemed to enjoy the office immensely. His White House was filled with vivacity and gaiety, sustained by a parade of intellectuals, precinct politicians, scientists, Hollywood stars—all enriched and invigorated, said John Gunther, by F. D. R.'s "luminous expansiveness."

Though utterly dependent on his braces and wheel chair, Roosevelt did not once, until his post-Yalta appearance before Congress in 1945, project the image of a cripple. The responsible press made no reference to his illness. "Photographers," Margaret Bassett recalled, "were on their honor not to photograph him in his wheelchair." So adroit was the President in moving about, Secret Service man Michael Reilly said, that "literally thousands who had seen him at ball games, rallies, and inaugurations never suspected his condition." Indeed, far from appearing physically restricted, Roosevelt stood ten feet tall in the mind of the nation, the epitome of strength and leadership.

Renominated by acclamation in 1936, Roosevelt faced the amiable Alfred M. Landon, Republican governor of Kansas, in an election distinguished chiefly by its result: the greatest presidential election victory in American history. Roosevelt took every state except Maine and Vermont, rolled up a popular vote of 27,752,869 to Landon's 16,674,665, and carried into power a Congress in which Democrats reigned 331 to 89 in the House and 76 to 16 in the Senate.

Inaugurated on January 20, 1937—the first Chief Executive inaugurated on that date under the Twentieth Amendment—

President Roosevelt reviewed his victorious first four years. A strong government, he declared, had met the crisis and solved it. "Our progress out of the depression," he said, "is obvious." But the country was far from recovery. "I see one-third of a nation ill-housed, ill-clad, ill-nourished. . . . I assume the solemn obligation of leading the American people forward along the road over which they have chosen to advance."

But despite Roosevelt's overwhelming electoral mandate, the honeymoon of recovery was over. If F. D. R. believed that the Constitution was "so simple and practical that it is possible always to meet extraordinary needs . . . without loss of essential form," the Supreme Court did not. On May 27, 1935, the Court had voted 9 to 0 to declare the NIRA unconstitutional, saying that the federal government's regulation of businesses was an illegal intervention in intrastate affairs and a case of "delegation running riot." The decision had dire implications for the rest of the New Deal program because of the Court's narrow interpretation of the interstate commerce clause—the constitutional basis of federal reform. The Court cut down other vital New Deal legislation, declaring unconstitutional the AAA, the Railroad Pension Act, and the Guffey-Snyder Coal Act. Roosevelt was angered by the "nine old men" of the Court, who presumed, he said, to defy the will of the people. He saw the contest with the Court in simple terms: "whether the kind of government which the people of the United States had voted for in 1932, 1934, and 1936 was to be permitted by the Supreme Court to function" and whether the Court, functioning as a superlegislature, could torture the Constitution to conform to its "outmoded economic beliefs."

Roosevelt struck back. Without even consulting Democratic party leaders, he proposed his notorious "Court-packing" plan to Congress. Aimed at unseating Supreme Court justices who had ruled against the New Deal and at engineering a Court majority favorable to his program, this plan would have given the President the right to ap-

ALFRED M. LANDON

"I'm an oilman who never made his million," Alf Landon told interviewer Thomas Morgan in 1962. "A lawyer who never had a case. And a politician who only carried Maine and Vermont." Landon was born in Pennsylvania in 1887, moved to Kansas with his parents, and earned a law degree from the University of Kansas in 1908. After four years as a banker, he began drilling for oil, and though he "never made his million," he fared well. A Bull Moose Republican in 1912, he was leader of the liberal Republicans in Kansas by the mid-1920's. In 1928 he became the state party's Central Committee chairman. Elected to two terms as governor of Kansas (1933–1937), Landon wrote a creditable record marked by fiscal caution and reduced taxes. His supporters called him the Kansas Coolidge when he was boomed for President in 1936. Landon won the nomination on the first ballot, but lost the election to Roosevelt overwhelmingly. During the presidential campaign, Landon had abandoned his own moderate views and had adopted the conservative attitudes of the national party. In later years, however, he supported a nuclear test ban and urged American participation in the European Common Market. Landon was never a candidate for public office after the 1936 debacle. He remained active in politics, but spent most of his time managing his oil business and his three radio stations.

point one new justice (up to a total of fifteen) for each justice who refused to retire six months after reaching the age of seventy.

F. D. R.'s plan was ill-conceived and clumsily advanced. The President unwittingly played into the hands of reactionaries, who liked to picture him as a conniving despot, and he gravely disappointed the liberal community. After five and a half months of wrangling, the Senate Judiciary Committee defeated the bill 10 to 8.

Ironically the Court reversed its position in favor of the New Deal, approving, for example, the Wagner and Social Security acts in 5 to 4 decisions. With resignations and new appointments, the Court was soon favorable to the administration. But the Court-packing scheme hurt F. D. R. He no longer seemed invincible or above the fray.

Compounding this setback, Roosevelt personally entered the lists in the congressional elections of 1938. Determined to punish Democrats who had opposed his Court-packing plan and other New Deal measures, F. D. R. traveled across the nation in a highly personal campaign to unseat such political perennials as Maryland's Senator Millard Tydings and Georgia's Walter George. Only one man on F. D. R.'s purge list failed to win re-election, while the Republicans gained seventy-five seats in the House and seven in the Senate.

"I should like to have it said of my first administration," Roosevelt said, "that in it the forces of selfishness and lust for power met their match. I should like to have it said of my second administration that these forces have met their master." Relations between Roosevelt and these forces, however, were more like a stalemate. And in fact the New Deal had practically spent itself. True, the second Agricultural Adjustment Act, passed on February 16, 1938, authorized parity payments to farmers who limited crops and storage of surplus crops, conservation payments to farmers observing acreage allotments, and commodity loans. The Fair Labor Standards Act of June 25, 1938, established maximum hours and minimum wages and banned child labor in the production of goods shipped in interstate commerce. And in April, 1938, Roosevelt responded to—and resolved—an economic recession (7,500,000 workers were still unemployed) with massive government spending and launched an investigation into monopolies whose "cluster of private collectivisms," he charged, had destroyed private enterprise. But on January 4, 1939, even Roosevelt acknowledged that the liberal hour had ended. "Our full energies," he said, "may now be released to invigorate the processes of recovery in order to preserve our reforms."

The New Deal gave way not only to economic retrenchment but also to America's increasing involvement in world affairs. Isolationists raged against American participation in Europe's sordid affairs, urging an antiseptic Fortress Americana. United States officials abroad had warned as early as 1933 of Hitler's maniacal plans for a Third Reich through rearmament and blitzkrieg, of Japan's intent to vastly expand its Pacific empire, and of Mussolini's dream of African conquest. Diplomats had also warned that these powers were perilously close to forming an unholy alliance.

When the German occupation of the Rhineland in March, 1936, failed to stir Britain and France to action, Roosevelt was silent. Neither the formal alliance between Germany and Italy in the fall of 1936 nor Germany's alliance with Japan shortly thereafter seems to have moved the West. There is persuasive evidence that Roosevelt sensed the dimensions of the Axis threat to republican interests more acutely— and much earlier—than did London, Paris, or Moscow. On October 5, 1937, F. D. R. told a Chicago audience that America could no longer remain safe and apathetic before the Axis military build-up: "Let no one imagine," the President warned the nation, "that America will escape" the impending holocaust or that it "will continue tranquilly and peacefully to carry on the ethics and arts of civilization" through illusory programs of "isolation and neutrality."

In March, 1938, Hitler annexed Austria

Because of nationwide opposition to a third presidential term, F. D. R's popular plurality in 1940 was some six million votes smaller than in 1936.

without opposition. In September Hitler, Neville Chamberlain of England, Édouard Daladier of France, and Mussolini agreed at Munich that Germany might take Czechoslovakia's Sudetenland if Berlin promised to make no more territorial claims. Even Roosevelt joined the chorus of delight over "peace in our time."

On October 26, 1938, however, Roosevelt declared that "peace by fear has no higher or more enduring quality than peace by the sword." And in his annual message to Congress in 1939 he added: "There comes a time in the affairs of men, when they must prepare to defend not their homes alone but the tenets of faith and humanity on which their churches, their governments, and their very civilization are founded. . . . This generation," he said, repeating the words of his 1936 convention acceptance speech, "has a rendezvous with destiny. That prophecy comes true. To us much is given; more is expected. This generation will nobly save or meanly lose the last best hope of earth." On January 12 F. D. R. moved from rhetoric to reality by asking Congress for five hundred and twenty-five million dollars to strengthen naval and air defenses.

Two months later Hitler annexed Czechoslovakia. On Good Friday, Mussolini took Albania. And both defied Roosevelt's appeal of April 15 to end their aggression and join in negotiations to reduce arms and increase world trade. When in August Germany and Russia signed a nonaggression pact, Allied shock gave way to panic. Hitler's invasion of Poland on September 1 roused Britain and France from their slumber of hope to an open declaration of war.

Fighting a Congress impressed by reactionary isolationists, such as Gerald P. Nye and William Borah, Roosevelt vainly sought to repeal the arms embargo provisions of the Neutrality Act of 1937 to permit the sale of arms to the Allies, arguing that the act gave gratuitous aid to the Axis. But Congress was adamant. In the fall of 1939 it again proclaimed neutrality by requiring belligerents buying United States goods to pay cash and carry them to their home ports.

The American people, despite Roosevelt's appeals, remained 77 per cent opposed to involvement in the war, even, a poll taken early in 1940 revealed, if Britain and France were defeated. But a break in the United States official neutrality occurred on September 3, 1940, when F. D. R. authorized the exchange of fifty overage United States destroyers for ninety-nine-year leases on air and naval bases in the British West Indies.

After Hitler moved against Norway, the Netherlands, and Belgium in the spring of 1940, F. D. R. appealed for a vast increase in American plane production. With the fall of France in July, he warned that America could no longer remain "a lone island . . . in a world dominated by the philosophy of force." To the enemies of aggression the President declared that the United States would extend "the material resources of this nation" and build an American arms stockpile and training program "equal to the task of any emergency and every defense." On September 16, 1940, the nation's first peacetime draft was authorized.

Meanwhile, Roosevelt faced another presidential election, one that would represent his sharpest break with tradition. Roosevelt's own camp was split over his desire to seek a third term. But Roosevelt ran anyway —against the dynamic and popular Wendell L. Willkie. Republican placards urged that Roosevelt be called "Out stealing third," but the Democrats countered by pointing to his record as a leader, crying, "Better a 3rd termer than a 3rd rater!" Roosevelt won

In this 1944 caricature of world figures, Roosevelt, Churchill, and Stalin seem to be very confident of winning their game of dominoes against the despairing Axis triumvirate—Hirohito, Hitler, and Mussolini.

easily, 449 electoral votes to 82. But he had won by promising the American people that "your boys are not going to be sent into any foreign wars."

Events would soon show how empty that promise had been. In the teeth of Hitler's massive air assault on Britain, America's chances of staying out of the war became slimmer every day. In a fireside chat on December 29, 1940, the President declared that for its own survival America must aid the defenders of freedom abroad by becoming the "arsenal of democracy." And, in fact, the President had already ordered a top-to-bottom updating of the War and Navy departments, called for a two-ocean Navy, and established a defense board to prepare for war and speed arms production.

On January 6, 1941, F. D. R. addressed Congress: "Today," he said, "thinking of our children and their children, we oppose enforced isolation for ourselves or for any part of the Americas." A proper world order, he said, must be founded on "four essential freedoms": freedom of speech, freedom of worship, freedom from want, and freedom from fear. Roosevelt also urged passage of a lend-lease act that would empower him to sell, lease, or transfer matériel, food, and raw materials to nations fighting the Axis.

In April, with Denmark's permission,

Roosevelt established military and naval bases on Greenland. In May he ordered construction of a strategic bomber fleet and established the Office of Civilian Defense. When a United States destroyer was sunk by a Nazi submarine, Roosevelt announced a national emergency, closed German consulates, froze Axis credits in the United States, seized Axis ships in United States ports, and tightened the embargo on Japan. When Germany attacked the Soviet Union in June, lend-lease was extended to Stalin. In July, the Philippine army was accepted into the United States armed forces. That same month United States troops relieved British forces at bases in Iceland.

On August 14, 1941, in a symbolic meeting that left no further doubt of American intentions, Roosevelt met with Prime Minister Winston Churchill aboard ship in Argentia Bay off Newfoundland. In addition to its dramatic affirmation of Anglo-American solidarity, this historic meeting proclaimed the Atlantic Charter, which reaffirmed the four freedoms and espoused "the establishment of a wider and permanent system of general security." The charter would become the fundament of the United Nations.

Meanwhile, the shadow of Japan on world affairs loomed ever darker. The militarists of Tokyo had announced a protectorate over

French Indochina in July and were already advancing toward the East Indies and Malaya. Roosevelt had told Churchill at the Atlantic Charter meeting that he thought he could "baby the Japs along for another three months," and in fact both sides participating in American-Japanese negotiations were patently stalling for time to build up their arms.

On Sunday morning, December 7, 1941, this diplomatic charade was abruptly concluded when Japanese carrier-based bombers struck without warning at the American naval base at Pearl Harbor in the Hawaiian Islands. On the same day Japan bombed United States Army Air Forces units near Manila, moving soon after against Malaya, Hong Kong, the Philippines, Wake Island, Guam, and Midway.

On December 8 the President, aided by his son James, walked slowly into the House of Representatives to address an emergency

SAVE FREEDOM OF WORSHIP

EACH ACCORDING TO THE DICTATES OF HIS OWN CONSCIENCE

NORMAN ROCKWELL

BUY WAR BONDS

Norman Rockwell's "Four Freedoms" posters —Freedom of Worship (above) and of Speech, Freedom from Want and from Fear—helped bond sales.

session of Congress. He was greeted, said his press secretary, Alden Hatch, with "an elemental outburst" of cheering. The nation had been attacked, and it was afraid. As Roosevelt faced the Congress, Hatch reported, "there was a quality of hysterical relief . . . as though the sight of him had brought release from fear."

Roosevelt's voice—ringing, confident, defiant—spoke a whole nation's anger and resolution: December 7, he declared, was "a date that will live in infamy. . . . Always will we remember the character of the attack against us." But now, the President said solemnly, "hostilities exist. There is no blinking at the fact that our people, our territory and our interests are in grave danger." He urged that the Congress declare that a state of war existed between the United States and the Japanese Empire. "With confidence in our armed forces—with the unbounded determination of our people—we will gain the inevitable triumph—so help us God," the President said. With only one dissenting vote, war was declared on Japan, and soon thereafter the nation was also at war with Germany and Italy. A total of 16,353,659 Americans would serve; 405,399 of them would be killed and 670,846 wounded or maimed. But the Axis, representing the greatest assault on free institutions in the history of mankind, would be crushed, and out of the ashes of Wilson's League of Nations would rise Roosevelt's United Nations.

F. D. R.'s contributions to the Allied war effort and ultimate victory are incalculable. Any list of them, however, must include, above all, the continuing magic of his inspiring personal courage and the magnetism of a leadership that seemed to grow with each new crisis. Among his specific contributions were his brilliant mobilization of the American military and industrial war machine, his vigorous person-to-person strategic diplomacy, and his labor for the United Nations.

Though Roosevelt appears to have made some major military decisions, such as the one to invade Germany first through a second front in France, and though by June, 1940, he had already given the order that work on the atomic bomb should proceed, he was not directly involved in the general field conduct of the war. The excellent team of strategists to whom he delegated responsibility for the military execution of the war—Admiral William Leahy, General George C. Marshall, Admiral Ernest J. King, and General H. H. Arnold—worked with extraordinary efficiency and harmony. In mobilizing United States industry, F. D. R. also delegated vast authority to such captains of industry as Donald Nelson and William S. Knudsen, who headed a war effort that broke all records for productivity.

Roosevelt's almost magical personal diplomacy was conspicuously brilliant at three major wartime conferences. At Casablanca in January, 1943, he and Churchill met with their combined chiefs of staff to integrate Anglo-American invasion strategy, combining Churchill's plan to strike at the Axis' "soft underbelly" in the Mediterranean with the American proposal to strike directly against Germany through France. It was a momentous conference, held at a moment when Allied prospects had taken a favorable and decisive turn. The Russians had won at Stalingrad in a heroic reversal. Egypt had been saved from the Axis. It was, in Churchill's words, "the end of the beginning." The Casablanca Conference made clear to the Axis the Allied resolve to profit from the diplomatic errors of World War I peace negotiations; Stalin was assured that there would be no secret peace "deals" in the West. F. D. R. and Churchill announced that nothing less than "unconditional surrender" would be acceptable.

In November, 1943, in another historic encounter, Roosevelt met Joseph Stalin for the first time, at Teheran. Roosevelt and Churchill promised the Soviet Premier that they would provide his long-sought second front—in an Anglo-American invasion of Germany through France—in exchange for Stalin's promise to establish his own second front against Japan as soon as Germany's defeat was assured.

In February, 1945, F. D. R. again met with Stalin and Churchill, at Yalta in the Crimea, to fix the time of Russia's entry into the war with Japan and to agree on a plan for the postwar occupation of enemy territory. In exchange for the Soviet Union's agreement to fight Japan and join the United Nations, the Allies ceded to Stalin the southern part of Sakhalin Island, which was occupied by Japan, and recognized Russia's pre-eminent interests in Manchuria. Eastern Poland was also placed under Stalin's protection when the dictator promised to include democratic officials in its government. It was also agreed that until free elections could be held, interim coalition governments representing Communists and non-Communists would be set up in Austria, Hungary, Czechoslovakia, Bulgaria, and Rumania.

Few events of Franklin Roosevelt's administration have stirred such bitter controversy as the Yalta accords. Stalin, of course, had no intention of honoring these agreements, and after the war, imposed an iron Communist dictatorship throughout Eastern Europe. The Allies appear to have been less than astute in accepting Stalin's word, given the long record of published Communist canon. In fairness to the Allies, however, there were sound military reasons for yielding to Stalin's demands. The atomic bomb had not yet been perfected, and the Allies, in their efforts against Germany and Japan, still had to rely on conventional weapons. Russia had borne the brunt of the German military onslaught, having confronted up to two hundred German divisions. The Allies were also convinced that even after the conquest of the Japanese home islands by American and British troops, a strong Russian military presence would be required in Manchuria to defeat the Japanese war machine there. In short, Churchill and Roosevelt still needed Stalin and felt that a continuation of the alliance was worth his price. They were not, evidence suggests, under any illusion and were aware, certainly by mid-March, 1945, as their correspondence attests, that the conclusion of the hot war with the Axis powers would witness the advent of a cold war with the Kremlin.

Aside from the unfortunate concordat at Yalta, the conference represented a major victory for world order, for the realization of Roosevelt's dream—the United Nations. The dream was as old as late December, 1941, when F. D. R. had persuaded the Allies to accept the Declaration of the United Nations, which was based on the Atlantic Charter. Roosevelt himself had given the United Nations its name, convinced that it would represent his life's crowning achievement. And on August 21, 1944, the Allies had met at Dumbarton Oaks to design the preliminary structure of the organization.

At Yalta it was agreed, in an eloquent statement signed by Roosevelt, Churchill, and Stalin, that a "Conference of United Nations should be called to meet at San Francisco . . . on April 25, 1945." The United Nations would be "a general international organization to maintain peace and security. . . . To prevent aggression and to remove the political, economic and social causes of war through the close and continuing collaboration of all peace-loving peoples."

Not even the prosecution of world war or the pursuit of a lasting world peace, however, could stay the hand of domestic politics. Roosevelt faced a bitter campaign in his bid for a fourth term as President in 1944. Led by New York's Governor Thomas E. Dewey, Republicans waged a highly personal campaign against the President. They condemned the "Roosevelt War," whispered about the President's failing health, proclaimed the presence in the White House of pro-Communist influences, and charged F. D. R. with capitulation to the CIO in major domestic matters.

But Roosevelt was prosecuting a war and needed the moderate Republican supporters of Willkie, who was himself campaigning for an American consciousness of its crucial role in "one world." "There are enlightened, liberal elements in the Republican party," Roosevelt declared in a candid bid for their votes, "and they have fought hard and honorably to bring the party up to date. . . . Millions of Republicans all over the nation

THOMAS E. DEWEY

"How," asked Alice Longworth, "can you vote for a man who looks like the bridegroom on a wedding cake?" Thomas Dewey's cold and polished appearance, seldom offset by indications of good-fellowship or of a sense of humor, negated much that was in his favor. It was a major reason for his failure to defeat Willkie at the Republican convention of 1940 and for his losses to Roosevelt and Truman in two presidential elections. Born in Michigan in 1902, Dewey graduated from the University of Michigan in 1923 and from Columbia University Law School in 1925. He was named chief assistant United States attorney in New York's Southern District before his twenty-ninth birthday. Hard-working, hardheaded, and efficient, he became a United States attorney, a special prosecutor for the state against crime, and then a district attorney of New York County, writing a spectacular record of successful prosecutions. Though in 1938 he lost his first race for governor, he came so close to victory that he immediately became a powerful figure in the Republican party. His career for the next ten years was pointed toward the White House; he was elected governor in 1942 and re-elected in 1946, and in 1944 and 1948 he was the Republican presidential nominee. He fully expected to win in 1948, but was upset by Harry S. Truman. Elected to a third term as governor of New York, Dewey later practiced law in New York City.

are with us . . . in our unshakable determination to build the solid structure of peace." It was a moving appeal for national unity on issues that transcended party lines.

In perhaps the most historic speech of his final campaign for President, F. D. R. declared that America's power imposed upon it a responsibility to lead the battle for reason in world affairs. "Peace, like war," he insisted, "can succeed only where there is a will to enforce it and where there is available power to enforce it. The Council of the United Nations must have the power to act quickly and decisively to keep the peace by force, if necessary." It would not be another League of Nations—an assemblage of hand-wringing debaters. "A policeman," he continued, "would not be a very effective policeman if, when he saw a felon break into a house, he had to go to the town hall and call a town meeting to issue a warrant before the felon could be arrested."

Roosevelt and his running mate, Harry S. Truman, defeated Dewey by a popular vote of 25,606,585 to 22,014,745 and an electoral vote of 432 to 99. On a bitter cold January 20, 1945, Franklin D. Roosevelt, for the fourth time, took the oath of office as President of the United States. It was a solemn and simple ceremony, consciously austere, befitting the leader of a nation at war. "We have learned," the tired President said in his brief Inaugural Address, "that we cannot live alone, at peace; that our own well-being is dependent on the well-being of other nations far away. . . . We can gain no lasting peace," he warned, "if we approach it with suspicion and mistrust or with fear. We can gain it only if we proceed with the understanding, the confidence, and the courage which flow from conviction."

In this spirit of confidence and trust, the ailing President, his body weakened by the campaign, went to meet Stalin and Churchill at Yalta. Early in 1944 he had ignored his doctors' advice that he take a rest. During the campaign, angered by Dewey and by whispers that he was not well, he had shown his old mettle by greeting three million New Yorkers, for example, in an open car in a blinding rain. On his way to a reception immediately following his fourth Inaugural Address he had collapsed in Jimmy Roosevelt's arms. "I knew," said Jimmy of that moment, "that his days were numbered." At Yalta, Churchill noted that F. D. R. "seemed placid and frail. I felt that he had a slender contact with life." When he addressed the Congress after the Yalta Conference, the President, for the first time, remained seated, referring to the weight of his braces and to the arduous trip he had just completed.

In early April, following a medical checkup and an order to rest, President Roosevelt left Washington for Warm Springs. On his agenda was the preparation of his opening address to the United Nations on April 25.

On April 12, 1945, F. D. R. donned his Harvard crimson tie and black Navy cape to sit for a portrait by artist Elizabeth Shoumatoff in his Warm Springs cottage. At 1:15 P.M. he put his hand to his head, complained of a violent headache, and slumped back in his chair. Carried to his bed, he lay in a coma and cold sweat until, at 3:35 P.M., he died. The cause of death was a massive cerebral hemorrhage.

Millions, to whom Roosevelt was the Presidency itself, mourned the fallen Commander in Chief as if they had lost their own father, as if the nation could not go on. As F. D. R.'s cortege moved from Warm Springs slowly northward by train, the nation wept. Secret Service man Michael Reilly, who had guarded and aided and lifted "The Boss," spoke for a nation to whom Roosevelt's smiling courage had seemed almost immortal: "I never believed he'd die."

On July 11, 1944, at sixty-two, Roosevelt had permitted himself a nostalgic lament as he led a nation at war and worked toward the peace to follow. "All that is within me," he had said, "cries out to go back to my home on the Hudson River." Now his wish was granted. As the Allied armies moved closer to Berlin and as American troops moved, island by island, closer to Japan, winning the victory he had forged, Franklin Delano Roosevelt was buried at Hyde Park.

—WILSON SULLIVAN

A PICTURE PORTFOLIO

This glass decanter, made during the 1936 presidential campaign, celebrated the creation of TVA.

The Hyde Park house, encircled by woods and fields, is shown, top, as it was during F. D. R.'s childhood.

The portrait above was made by Charles S. Forbes in 1895, the year before Roosevelt left for Groton.

As editor and president of The Crimson—*the high point of his three years in Cambridge—Roosevelt (seated to the left in the photograph at right) urged support of the football team and asked that board-walks be placed on the campus during the winter.*

814

TRANQUIL SEAS

The 'River families,'" wrote Arthur Schlesinger, Jr., about the Hyde Park Roosevelts and their set, "were born to [a] spacious sense of tradition and of leisure. Their world opened up before them, a solid and pleasant place, in which their task was to carry on and fortify standards they inherited from their fathers." Thus, two years after he was born, Franklin Roosevelt was enrolled in the exclusive Groton School. Until he actually entered Groton, at fourteen, he was educated genteelly by tutors and his horizons were broadened by travels in Europe. He learned the outdoorsman's arts, and in his own twenty-one-foot sailboat, became a capable seaman. Though Groton removed him from the insulation of family, it maintained the insulation of class. *Noblesse oblige* was stressed; so were cold baths, athletics, chapel, and the gentlemanly hobby of ornithology, in which Franklin was already proficient. He slid through the academic program with middling grades. Having been discouraged from applying to the Naval Academy by his father, who favored a law career, he entered Harvard, where he kept a car and a trotter, maintained an unexceptional academic average, joined the Hasty Pudding Club, and lived in one of the fanciest dormitories; he did, however, become managing editor and president of the college daily, *The Crimson*, and was elected class chairman. During his last year at Harvard he chose his bride, his fifth cousin, Eleanor Roosevelt. Franklin's hovering "mummie," Sara, thought he was too young to be married and tried to avert the nuptials by taking him on a trip. But on Saint Patrick's Day, 1905, Franklin and Eleanor were wed, and launched on a sea that promised to be calm and sparkling—and not dangerously deep.

Eleanor thought herself ugly, but she was a pretty bride; the photograph at right, taken by F. D. R. in Venice during their honeymoon, was his favorite.

FRANKLIN D. ROOSEVELT LIBRARY

ADVERSITY STRIKES

Adversity is wont to reveal genius, prosperity to hide it," said the satirist Horace. Admitted to the bar in 1907, Franklin Roosevelt won election to the state senate as a Democrat from a Republican district; his famous surname was largely responsible for that victory, but he won re-election two years later. He went to Washington at the age of thirty-one as the youngest assistant secretary of the Navy in history and made enough of an impression to be chosen in 1920 as the running mate of presidential nominee James Cox. But Roosevelt was thought by many to be an arrogant lightweight. The battle with infantile paralysis that began in 1921 changed all that: arrogance, tempered by adversity, became indomitable courage, and Franklin Delano Roosevelt's love of action found a new outlet in meaningful words and deeds.

In the nation's Capital in 1919, Franklin and Eleanor Roosevelt and their five attractive children sat for the winsome family portrait above. From left to right are Anna, Franklin, Jr., James, John, and Elliott.

As assistant secretary of the Navy, Roosevelt (left) reviews sailors in France in 1918. Two years later he became a candidate for the Vice Presidency (above).

Roosevelt (below with John W. Davis, center, and Al Smith) was drafted to run for governor in 1928 to help Smith win New York in the presidential contest. Smith said the job would not require F. D. R. to cut back on therapy for his polio-crippled legs. "Don't hand me that baloney," Roosevelt replied, but he accepted and won.

NORMAN M. THOMAS

Because he was a Socialist, Norman Mattoon Thomas was never able to win an election. Yet he ran for mayor of New York twice, for governor two times, and for President of the United States six times. Despite his inevitable defeats, he remained a force in American life, always—as *The New York Times* put it—"jumping in wherever he thinks human beings are abused or human rights ignored, and doing something about it." Born in Marion, Ohio, in 1884, Thomas, who worked as a newsboy for Warren Gamaliel Harding's newspaper, the Marion *Star*, attended Princeton University, and after graduating from Union Theological Seminary in 1911, followed his father into the Presbyterian ministry. His inability to believe that a benevolent God would permit war was one of the reasons for his ceasing to be an active minister in 1918. (He left the ministry officially in 1931.) During World War I Thomas became a pacifist and joined the Socialist party. Writer, labor organizer, editor of Socialist periodicals, and a founder of the American Civil Liberties Union, he ran for the New York governorship in 1924, for mayor of New York City the following year, and made the first of his six tries for the Presidency in 1928. In 1932, in the depths of the Depression, Thomas polled almost a million votes, the greatest number he would ever receive. He remained an active champion of peace and of the rights of man.

"ALL YOU HAVE GOT TO DO IS STAY ALIVE"

In the 1932 presidential primaries, Governor Roosevelt lost Massachusetts to Al Smith and California to John Nance Garner. Even so, he held a big edge by the time the convention began. At the end of the third roll call he led Smith by nearly 500 votes and Garner by nearly 600, but he needed about 90 more votes for the two-thirds majority demanded by convention rules. The Texas delegation began to think that he could be stopped and that in the ensuing scramble Garner might win. Then the Roosevelt people offered the second spot on the ticket to Garner. "Texas is our only chance," Jim Farley admitted. Speaker Garner made a crucial move; he saw that if F. D. R. did not get Texas and California on the next ballot, there would be a deadlock. California would support Roosevelt if released but Texas would not unless Garner was the running mate. Though Garner did not want the office, he did want to prevent the kind of bitter stalemate that had wrecked the party in 1924. He ordered Sam Rayburn to give the Texas and California votes to Roosevelt. Frantic, angry, even weeping, the Texas delegates nearly rebelled; they ratified Garner's wish by only 3 votes. Appropriately, the fourth-ballot break was revealed to the convention by William McAdoo, a loser in the 1924 deadlock. "All you have got to do," Garner told F. D. R., "is stay alive until election day."

Repeal of prohibition was a Democratic pledge in 1932, as the bumper plate above shows.

Because of an attempt on F. D. R.'s life, the Inauguration Day cover below was not used.

A NEW DEAL

Fifteen million Americans had no jobs in 1933. The currency and the banks were unstable, farm prices were low, and many people were about to lose their homes and their farms. For much of the population, living conditions were desperate. To the nation Franklin Roosevelt offered, in his first Inaugural Address, freedom from fear and a promise of a new deal. "The money changers," he said, "have fled from their high seats in the temple of our civilization. We may now restore that temple to the ancient truths. The measure of that restoration lies in the extent to which we apply social values more noble than mere monetary profit." Idealism generated ideas, and the confident activity in Washington, the willingness to experiment that was evident in F. D. R.'s first hundred days and later, buoyed the country's spirits and kept the unfortunate from turning to radical, violent solutions. Nevertheless, for years "Brother, Can You Spare a Dime?" expressed conditions in the United States more accurately than the Democratic party's favorite campaign song, "Happy Days Are Here Again."

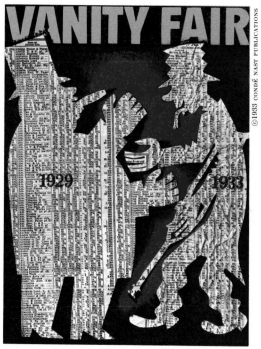

© 1933 CONDÉ NAST PUBLICATIONS

In 1933 Vanity Fair *noted the fourth anniversary of the crash with the cover illustration above; it features a plutocrat cut out of a pre-Depression stock page and a beggar made from a current list.*

The two scenes at right—an impoverished mother and child and a jobless man slumping against an empty store—were typical of the hard times. But with an assurance that was uniquely American, poet Carl Sandburg promised: "The people will live on./ . . . The people so peculiar in renewal and comeback,/ You can't laugh off their capacity to take it."

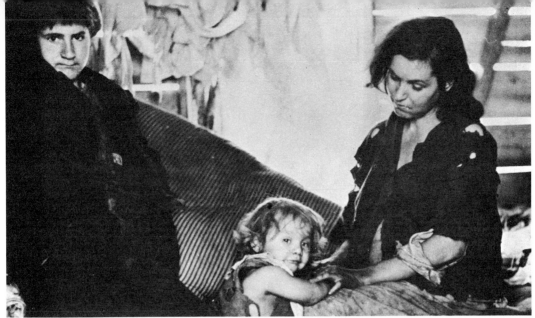

NEW DEALERS

HAROLD L. ICKES

"Combative, shrewd, belligerent" Harold Ickes "was never a bore," said F. D. R.'s Attorney General, Francis Biddle. Ickes was the administration's "Old Curmudgeon"—a sharp-tongued and egocentric figure who served as Secretary of the Interior throughout the New Deal and into the Fair Deal before one of his many angry resignations was finally accepted. He had been born in Pennsylvania, had attended college and law school at the University of Chicago, and had been admitted to the Illinois bar in 1907. A liberal reformer in politics, and a Republican, Ickes supported Teddy Roosevelt in the Bull Moose campaign of 1912. When T. R.'s cousin Franklin ran for President in 1932, Ickes backed the Democrats. He was director of the Public Works Administration from 1933 to 1939 while serving very capably as head of the Interior Department; during World War II he was also administrator of petroleum, solid fuels, coal mines, and fisheries. Constantly suspicious that others were undermining him, he blew up from time to time and sent letters of resignation to F. D. R., who shrugged off each one as impossible to consider—apparently the kind of reassurance the Secretary wanted. After resigning from the Truman administration in 1946, Harold Ickes practiced law and wrote political commentary. He died in 1952.

HARRY L. HOPKINS

"Quick, alert, shrewd, bold, and carrying it off with a bright Hell's bells air, Hopkins is in all respects the inevitable Roosevelt favorite," noted an astute political observer in 1938. A native Iowan who had been a social worker in New Orleans and New York, Harry L. Hopkins joined the New Deal in 1933 as head of the Federal Emergency Relief Administration. From then until 1941 he occupied successively the posts of WPA administrator, Secretary of Commerce, and lend-lease administrator. Meanwhile, he had become Roosevelt's most trusted friend and adviser, and in 1940—after nearly dying from an illness that continued to plague him throughout his life—he was moved into the White House as a permanent guest. As adviser in residence to the President during most of World War II, Hopkins occupied a position of enormous power and prestige. He attended most of the international conferences (Atlantic Charter, Casablanca, Cairo, Teheran, and Yalta) and acted as the President's emissary on important missions to London and Moscow. His ability to cut through to the heart of complex issues (Winston Churchill once dubbed him "Lord Root of the Matter") won his chief's unbounded confidence. After serving as special adviser to President Truman, Hopkins resigned in July, 1945, and died six months later.

CULVER PICTURES

WIDE WORLD

FRANCES PERKINS

Secretary of Labor Frances Perkins was the first woman to hold a Cabinet post. When a reporter asked her if being a woman was a handicap, she replied in her cultured Bostonian accent, "Only in climbing trees." She was, wrote Arthur Schlesinger, Jr., "brisk and articulate . . . a Brahmin reformer . . . [with] a compulsion to instruct. . . ." Born in 1882 and educated at Mount Holyoke College, the University of Pennsylvania, and Columbia University (where she earned a master's degree in 1910), she was a young social worker when she witnessed the Triangle Shirtwaist Factory fire in New York in 1911. She was employed by the state's Factory Investigating Commission, which was established because of the fire, and later became executive secretary of the New York Committee on Safety. Subsequently she held several important state posts concerned with industry and labor. She had been Governor Roosevelt's industrial commissioner for four years when he, newly elected to the Presidency, appointed her to his Cabinet. Persuasive, energetic, a New Dealer to the core, she helped bring about numerous reforms and innovations, including Social Security. After leaving office in 1945, Madame Perkins —as she was called—remained active in public affairs. She gave many lectures—the last one two weeks before she died in 1965.

SIDNEY HILLMAN

During Roosevelt's search for a vice presidential candidate in 1944, he settled briefly on James Byrnes, but warned convention managers to "clear it with Sidney." Columnist Westbrook Pegler wanted to know how Sidney Hillman—"this nontoiling sedentary conspirator"—had attained so much power. Born in Lithuania in 1887 and imprisoned in Russia for political activities when he was still in his teens, Hillman emigrated to America in 1907. While working as a clothing cutter in Chicago he became an influential union leader. His Amalgamated Clothing Workers of America eventually enrolled three hundred and fifty thousand members. Hillman served F. D. R. in a number of government posts and as a labor adviser. In 1943 he was head of the CIO's Political Action Committee, a group that supported prolabor candidates. After he blackballed the conservative Byrnes and approved Truman instead in 1944, Hillman worked hard for the Democratic ticket. "Clear everything with Sidney," the Republicans chanted during the campaign, urging the voters to "DEFEAT THE HILLMAN-BROWDER AXIS." (Earl Browder was the Communist party candidate for President in 1936 and 1940.) Republican efforts to link Hillman— and thereby the President—to Communism failed. The labor leader died in 1945.

"ALPHABET SOUP"

Breaking political tradition, Roosevelt's party gained seats in the mid-term congressional elections of 1934. As the cartoon above indicates, the voting proved that the people liked F. D. R.'s program.

We have had so many Presidents who were obvious numskulls," H. L. Mencken wrote in 1934, "that it pleases everyone to contemplate one with an active cortex. . . ." The cortex of the New Deal was indeed active. It produced a multitude of programs, which quickly came to be known by their initials, such as CCC, TVA, AAA. The "alphabet soup" proved heartening to the nation. The economy was steadied, agricultural production and prices were brought under regulation, mortgages were eased for homes and farms, and labor's right to organize and bargain won government sanction. People were put to work—building roads, dams, and schools, planting forests, and even painting murals, producing plays, and writing state histories. Still, Roosevelt—re-elected in a landslide in 1936—saw that there was much more to do. America was not yet, he said in his second Inaugural Address, "the promised land."

Roosevelt (above, in 1938) used the radio effectively to take his case to the nation from time to time; millions listened to his speeches, which were known as his fireside chats. Said John Gunther, "He gave the impression . . . of speaking to every listener personally. . . . [One] could practically feel him physically in the room."

The murals at right (TVA Worker and Family, left, and Surveying New Lands) were done by Henry Varnum Poor for the Justice Department building under the Works Progress Administration's art program.

U.S. DEPT. OF JUSTICE

IMPEDIMENTS
TO PROGRESS

By the time the New Deal passed the precedent-breaking Social Security Act in August, 1935, it had already begun to lose momentum. The Supreme Court had declared the National Industrial Recovery Act unconstitutional that May. Soon more programs were invalidated. After his landslide re-election, F. D. R. tried unsuccessfully to legislate a change in the Court's conservative make-up, but other forces rose to oppose further change. Vice President Garner spoke for an increasingly recalcitrant Congress when he urged President Roosevelt to slow down, warning, "You know you've got to let the cattle graze."

With the Senate having defeated his plan for packing the Supreme Court (above), and the new Congress elected in 1938 promising to be conservative and independent (right), the bloom was definitely off the F. D. R. rose by the middle of his second term. His early popularity had encouraged a personal rather than a party-regular approach to government, which had led to trouble as the Depression had eased. F. D. R. had not conferred with or even told Democratic leaders about the Supreme Court bill before he had sent it to Congress—a bad error. His cause had not been helped by his interference in the Senate's choice of a Majority Leader during the debate. Then he had taken to the stump during the election campaign of 1938 in an effort to defeat the conservative Democratic legislators who had been trying to slow the pace of reform. He had been rebuffed: all but one of his targets had been re-elected. The American public, like many legislators, had been offended by the highhandedness of President Roosevelt.

"MOTHER, WILFRED WROTE A BAD WORD!"

Many of the more affluent members of American society regarded Roosevelt as "That Man" and cursed him as a traitor to his class. The cartoon above (published in 1938) reflected their antipathy.

ON THE COURT

HUGO L. BLACK

Justice Hugo L. Black, President Roosevelt's first appointee to the Supreme Court, has been described as "an evangelical progressive." A dynamic, liberal Alabama lawyer, Black was elected to the Senate in 1927, where his championship of important progressive legislation brought him to prominence during the New Deal. His appointment as associate justice in 1937 (representing the first break in the conservatives' long monopoly of the Court) was greeted with initial criticism because Black had been affiliated briefly with the Ku Klux Klan. But criticism waned as the justice began to assert his liberal views in a number of important dissenting opinions. In 1938 Black was the first to argue that corporations are not "persons" and are, therefore, not protected by the Fourteenth Amendment. A staunch defender of personal liberties, he argued in a brilliant 1947 dissent that under the same amendment the Court must "extend to all the people of the nation the complete protection of the Bill of Rights." He attacked the requiring of non-Communist oaths in 1950 and the Smith Act in 1951 as violations of freedoms granted by the First Amendment. In the 1960's Justice Black was the senior associate of the Court (he became eighty years old in 1966), and continued to be a leading defender of civil liberties.

HARLAN FISKE STONE

"The only check upon our own exercise of power is our own sense of self-restraint," cautioned dissenting Justice Harlan Fiske Stone as the Supreme Court launched its attack on New Deal legislation in 1935. Six years later, in 1941, President Roosevelt elevated his liberal ally to Chief Justice. A graduate of Columbia Law School, Stone began his career as professor and dean of his alma mater, where he served for twenty-four years. In 1924 he was appointed Attorney General of the United States, and the following year, at the age of fifty-three, he was made an associate justice of the Supreme Court. One of a small liberal minority, Stone agreed with Brandeis and Cardozo that the Court should exercise restraint in invalidating social and economic reform legislation. "Courts are not the only agencies of government that must be assumed to have capacity to govern," he declared in a minority opinion upholding the constitutionality of the New Deal's Agricultural Adjustment Act. Defending "freedom of mind and spirit," he was the only justice in 1940 to oppose state legislation requiring compulsory salute of the flag. In 1943, however, he upheld executive authority to restrict civil liberties during the wartime emergencies of World War II. Chief Justice Stone died of a stroke in 1946, when he was seventy-three years old.

LOUIS D. BRANDEIS

"In the last century, our democracy has deepened," noted Louis D. Brandeis shortly before his appointment to the Supreme Court in 1916. "Coincidentally," he continued, "there has been a shifting of our longing from legal justice to social justice." Known as the people's attorney, Brandeis—a graduate of Harvard Law School (1878) and a prominent Boston lawyer—was deeply committed to public justice and to the cause of the workingman. In 1907 he was responsible for a Massachusetts bill providing laborers with their own organizations to supply low-cost life insurance; and in 1908, in *Muller v. Oregon*, he presented a historic brief opposing hard labor for women on "non-legal" medical and sociological grounds. An advocate of "regulated competition" to curb monopoly, he acted as an adviser to President Wilson on antitrust, banking, and labor legislation. As associate justice of the Supreme Court from 1916 to 1939, Brandeis was important for his dissenting opinions. He aligned with liberal Justices Holmes, Stone, and Cardozo; during Franklin D. Roosevelt's administration, he defended many of the New Deal measures against the conservative majority of the Court. Upon his retirement the eighty-three-year-old jurist turned his energies to the Zionist movement. Justice Brandeis died in Washington, D.C., in 1941.

FELIX FRANKFURTER

Felix Frankfurter's appointment to the Supreme Court in 1939 was warmly applauded by liberals. A professor of law at Harvard University, the Vienna-born scholar had won liberal support during his defense of the anarchists Sacco and Vanzetti in 1927. Later, as adviser to President Roosevelt, Frankfurter was regarded by many as the "Academic Eminence" of the New Deal. Once on the bench, however, his opinions on cases dealing with civil liberties put Frankfurter on the far right of the New Deal Court. His view that the freedoms of the First Amendment could not be construed as absolute led him to sustain a number of laws that restricted those freedoms, even when he found them personally repugnant. "The Court is not saved from being oligarchic because it professes to act in the service of humane ends," he once wrote. Thus in 1940 he upheld a compulsory flag salute law; in 1941 he approved limitations on the freedom to picket when it engendered force and violence; and in 1951 he upheld the Smith Act, prohibiting the advocacy of forceful overthrow of the government. Though he was called the Supreme Court's Emily Post, many critics admired Justice Frankfurter's strict adherence to legal propriety and to the tenet of judicial self-restraint. He retired from the Court in 1962, when he was eighty.

A RELUCTANT ARSENAL

Isolationism was not exclusively an American philosophy during the 1930's; the world-wide depression created enough problems to fully occupy most governments. The internationally minded nations, it seemed, were the totalitarian ones, and the democracies looked away as Japan overran Manchuria; as Mussolini invaded Ethiopia; as Spanish democracy was overthrown by fascist rebels under Franco with German and Italian help; as Hitler discarded the Versailles Treaty and rearmed and occupied the "demilitarized" Rhineland. If President Roosevelt had misgivings about isolationism, he could hardly overlook the will of the people—and a 1937 Gallup Poll revealed that 94 per cent favored a policy aimed at staying out of foreign wars over a policy aimed at trying to prevent war's outbreak. Nevertheless, the President began to increase the anti-Nazi content of his messages to Congress and of his fireside chats. When Hitler seized Czechoslovakia in 1939, Roosevelt asked for a repeal of the 1937 Neutrality Act. Congress refused; thus, if war were to break out, the United States would still be forbidden to sell munitions to France and England. But Hitler, in a brutal way, gave F. D. R. assistance: he invaded Poland and thereby convinced the American people that he was a danger even to them and had to be stopped. The Neutrality Act was loosened up a bit. Finally, in 1941, with almost all Europe in the grip of the Third Reich, Congress approved Roosevelt's request for seven billion dollars for "lend-lease," which authorized the supplying of matériel to any nation whose defense was vital to America—the new "arsenal of democracy."

In June, 1939, Queen Elizabeth and King George of England (to F. D. R.'s right, above) and Canadian Prime Minister McKenzie King (at far right) called on the Roosevelts (Franklin, James, Sara, and Eleanor) at Hyde Park. On September 1, German troops removed a Polish border barricade (right) and invaded their neighbor, beginning World War II.

NEW YORK *Daily News*

CAF, WARSAW

WENDELL L. WILLKIE

"Wendell Willkie is just a simple barefoot Wall Street lawyer," cracked Harold Ickes. The highly capable Hoosier was, indeed, a man of contradictions. He was both boyishly rumpled and sophisticated. Scrupulously honest in one instance, he would adopt a no-holds-barred approach the next. A Democrat, he ran at the head of a national Republican ticket. Willkie, who was born in 1892, graduated in 1913 from the University of Indiana and earned a law degree in 1916. After World War I he became an expert counsel for utility companies and in 1933 was made president of a utility with interests in the territory soon to be covered by the New Deal's TVA project. A consequent battle with the government over private versus public control of utilities brought him to national attention. "We want Willkie!" cried the Republican rank and file in 1940, despite the protests of party managers. Nominated, he was hamstrung by the fact that he agreed with much of Roosevelt's program, but after a dignified, low-keyed start, he began attacking the New Deal's economic policies. Losing to F. D. R. by almost five million votes, he then supported the administration's aid to the Allies, served F. D. R. on missions abroad, and wrote a book, *One World*, which advocated postwar international cooperation. But his attempt to win the 1944 Republican presidential nomination failed, and Willkie died that same year.

"I WANT TO WRITE HISTORY"

At first Franklin D. Roosevelt refused to consider running for an unprecedented third term. He suffered from a sinus condition and was exhausted by the pressures of office. "I want to go home to Hyde Park," he said. "I want to take care of my trees. . . . I want to make the farm pay. I want to finish my little house on the hill. I want to write history." But the threat of war helped change his mind. So did his desire to see a liberal Democrat succeed him: the leading contenders for the nomination were conservatives—James Farley, John Nance Garner, James Byrnes. F. D. R. agreed to run, but insisted that the delegates pledged to him be told they were "free to vote for any candidate." (Chicago bosses made a mockery of this statement immediately after it was read to the convention by staging a fifty-three-minute demonstration for Roosevelt.) No one could beat F. D. R. after he announced he would serve again, although Farley and Garner tried. Once more Roosevelt had defied political tradition, thereby angering the party regulars; bad feeling ran high, and in order to gain the vice presidential nomination for his choice—Henry Wallace—F. D. R. had to threaten to refuse to run himself. In the subsequent campaign against Willkie he promised the voters that American troops would not be sent to "any foreign wars." He knew, however, how close to home the war was coming and was frustrated by the political necessity of not saying so. To a suggestion that the words "except in case of attack" be added to the platform pledge of neutrality, the President answered bitterly, "If someone attacks us, then it isn't a foreign war, is it? Or do they want me to guarantee that our troops will be sent into battle only in the event of another Civil War?"

Roosevelt and Secretary of Agriculture Henry Wallace (above) beat the Republican ticket of Willkie and Senator Charles McNary handily. Recalling a campaign speech by F. D. R. in Cleveland, Robert E. Sherwood wrote: "Roosevelt said that, when the next four years are over, 'there will be another President'. . . ." There were shouts of "No!" from the crowd. "[He] thrust his mouth close to the microphone and went right on talking so that the shouts which suggested that he might be elected permanently should not be heard over the radio." At right and below is an assortment of anti-Roosevelt campaign buttons.

I'M AGAINST THE 3rd TERM

WASHINGTON WOULDN'T

GRANT COULDN'T

ROOSEVELT SHOULDN'T

NO CROWN FOR FRANKLIN

NO 3RD TERM

TWO TIMES IS ENOUGH FOR ANY MAN

NO MAN IS GOOD THREE TIMES

Japan's attack on Pearl Harbor (above) on December 7, 1941, all but eliminated America's Pacific defense apparatus, and a tense West Coast half expected an invasion. Although it never came, Japanese-Americans had to stay in "relocation" centers, such as Camp Salinas, California (below), for the duration of the war.

DR. WIN-THE-WAR'S
HOME REMEDIES

Old "Dr. New Deal," explained President Roosevelt, had done his job in helping to cure the nation's economic illness. But after America had been plunged into war, F. D. R. continued, a different specialist had been needed, and "Dr. Win-the-War" had been called in. With the patient crying "Remember Pearl Harbor!" the doctor was perhaps overzealous in his prescription of preventive medicine: fearing an invasion of the West Coast, the War Department urged the President to move more than a hundred thousand Japanese-Americans—most of them in California—to concentration camps. Since nothing was done about Americans of German or Italian origin, it would appear that racism—bolstered by pressure from California businessmen who had found the Japanese-Americans to be outstanding and highly competent competitors—was an important factor in the unconstitutional internment. For the most part, however, remembering Pearl Harbor was the best medicine for forgetting the Depression—and curing it. Suddenly there were too many jobs instead of a job shortage. When young men went to war, or to shipyards and munitions plants, ladies put on pants and learned how to solder and rivet. Volunteers rolled bandages, carried messages around town, and crated refreshments and magazines for shipment overseas. Housewives bought food and clothing with ration stamps and trimmed the fat from meats and saved it in the tin cans that were collected for re-use. Older men were air raid wardens, checking the lights during frequent drills. Movies said "The End —Buy War Bonds," books were printed on cheap paper because of the war and said so, and the trusty brands of bubble gum were available—in very limited quantity—only once a week. The home front was strong, and Americans were thankful that it was a home front and not a battleground. The war was all around, but the fighting was "over there."

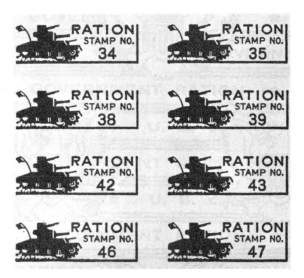

There were good jobs to be had during the war; but to purchase food, gasoline, shoes, clothing, and other items, ration stamps (above) were required in addition to money.

The new war bred fewer slogans, sadder songs, and a quieter patriotism than had World War I. But Americans were determined to roll up their sleeves, dig in, and get it over with—and the "weaker sex" was not excepted.

Although the Allies seemed confident of victory, they had difficulty early in the war reversing their defensive role and going on the offensive. Far Eastern Commander General Douglas MacArthur decided to turn the Pacific tide at New Guinea, the world's second largest island. After the initiative had seesawed from the Japanese to the Australians and Americans throughout 1942, MacArthur sent General Robert Eichelberger to take Buna on the Papua Peninsula—or else not to come back alive. Within a month, Buna was secure, but at terrible cost to the troops (right), who suffered from disease and hunger as well as from battle injuries. The invasion of Europe did not come until June 6, 1944. Under General Dwight D. Eisenhower, the largest expeditionary force in history (below) landed in Normandy—the beginning of Hitler's end.

U.S. ARMY

U.S. COAST GUARD

GLOBAL CONFLICT

The war, in a sinister way, created "one world." It stained the snow of the Ukraine, the sand of North Africa, the swamps of Australia and New Guinea. It was waged in the sky and on the waters of the Atlantic and the Pacific and the Mediterranean. It was a horrendous spectacle, a case for pacifism and yet a case against it, for it was fought to kill a malignant evil. It had its share of noble adversaries, such as England's Bernard Montgomery and Germany's Erwin Rommel, of unlikely heroes, such as Haile Selassie of Ethiopia, of tyrants turned buffoons, such as Benito Mussolini, of fanatic kamikazes and storm troops; and it had more than its share of dead—white, yellow, black, soldiers, old people, children—from every continent on the bloodied earth.

A Persian artist commemorated the Teheran Conference with the depiction above of Churchill, Stalin, Roosevelt (all wearing turbans), and the soon-to-be-defeated Axis leaders.

WARTIME WASHINGTONIANS

WILLIAM D. LEAHY

After forty-six years in the Navy (twenty-two of them spent at sea), Admiral William D. Leahy retired in 1939, only to be called back three years later to serve as President Roosevelt's military chief of staff. After graduating from Annapolis in 1897, Leahy had served in the Spanish-American War, in the Philippine insurrection, and in China during the Boxer Rebellion. He was chief of staff during the United States occupations of Nicaragua in 1912 and Haiti in 1916 and a commander during World War I. He held several important posts, including chief of naval operations, prior to his retirement in 1939. President Roosevelt appointed Leahy governor of Puerto Rico that year and in 1940 named him ambassador to Vichy France. "Bill," F. D. R. once told Leahy casually, "there is going to be a war, and I am going to need you." Leahy became chief of staff to the Commander in Chief in 1942, serving with General George C. Marshall, Admiral Ernest J. King, and General Henry H. Arnold as the joint chiefs of staff. He accompanied Roosevelt to many wartime conferences, including Yalta in 1945. A few months later he attended the Potsdam Conference with Truman, under whom he served as chief of staff until 1949. Leahy, who was made a five-star admiral in 1944, told his wartime experiences in a book, *I Was There*.

HENRY STIMSON

Henry Stimson was a member of the Cabinets of four Presidents. He ended his thirty-four-year national career in 1945 when he retired as Secretary of War shortly after Japan's surrender. During the wearying days of World War II Stimson was, as Attorney General Francis Biddle said, "a heroic figure of sincerity and strength," and President Truman awarded him the Distinguished Service Medal. Stimson had been Secretary of War before—for a Republican (Taft) in peacetime (1911 to 1913). He had been United States district attorney for southern New York from 1906 until 1910, when he had run unsuccessfully for the governorship of New York. He had served as a colonel in the artillery in World War I. In 1927 President Coolidge sent Stimson to arbitrate an election in Nicaragua; he then served as governor general of the Philippines and as Herbert Hoover's Secretary of State. Stimson led the American delegations at the London Naval Conference of 1930 and at the Geneva Disarmament Conference two years later. The Japanese invasion of Manchuria prompted the Stimson Doctrine of 1932, advocating nonrecognition of territories and agreements gained by aggression. Stimson supported President Roosevelt's foreign policy and was appointed to the Cabinet in 1940; he died in New York ten years later.

FRANK KNOX

Secretary of the Navy Frank Knox had had
a long and colorful career before he entered
President Roosevelt's Cabinet in 1940. The
son of a grocery-store owner, Knox (who was
christened William Franklin) was raised in
Michigan, graduated from a small college in
1898, and that same year joined Teddy Roosevelt's Rough Riders in the Spanish-American War. Returning to the Middle West, he
took a job as a reporter and eventually became the editor and publisher of several influential newspapers, including the Chicago
Daily News, which he published until his
death. Entering World War I as a private,
Knox was a major when the conflict ended.
He returned to journalism and resumed his
interest in politics. A staunch Republican,
he was a leading opponent of the New Deal,
and in 1936 he ran for Vice President on the
Republican ticket, which was headed by Alfred Landon. Four years later Knox was
tapped by Franklin D. Roosevelt, who
wanted to form a bipartisan Cabinet and
felt that Knox's military experience would
be valuable. It was Secretary of the Navy
Knox who informed Roosevelt of the tragic
event of 1941 ("Mr. President, it looks as if
the Japanese have attacked Pearl Harbor!").
Thereafter Knox helped build the most
powerful two-ocean Navy in history. He
died at the age of seventy, on April 28, 1944.

EDWARD R. STETTINIUS, JR.

Edward R. Stettinius, Jr., was Secretary of
State during the last years of World War II.
A former industrialist and financier, he had
begun working for the Roosevelt administration while still serving as board chairman
of United States Steel. After heading the
War Resources Board in 1939, he resigned
from private business the next year to devote all his energies to government service.
Following a year on the Council of National
Defense and two years as lend-lease administrator, he was appointed under secretary of
state in 1943 and succeeded Cordell Hull as
Secretary in 1944. As President Roosevelt's
chief adviser during the critical prelude to
peace, he attended the Yalta Conference in
1945. (Four years later his account of the
Big Three power conflicts, *Roosevelt and the
Russians: The Yalta Conference*, was published.) Perhaps his greatest contribution to
peace, however, was his role in the formation of the United Nations. Having helped
lay the groundwork for the organization at
Dumbarton Oaks in 1944, he attended the
United Nations Charter conference at San
Francisco in April, 1945, and two months
later left his post as Secretary of State to
become the first United States delegate to
the United Nations. Resigning from that
position in 1946, Edward R. Stettinius died
three years later, at the age of forty-nine.

ALLIANCES

At this moment, the worst in her history," wrote Charles de Gaulle of his fallen homeland, "it was for me to assume the burden of France." The same thoughts evidently ran through the mind of General Henri Honoré Giraud, an escapee from a Nazi prison. In Casablanca in 1943 Roosevelt and Churchill made the rivals shake hands, but it did not work: the Free French had to struggle among themselves before uniting to liberate France. Later that year, at Cairo, the Prime Minister and the President met again—this time with Chiang Kai-shek. It was difficult to determine whether Chiang regarded the Japanese or the Chinese Communists as his foremost enemy. At Teheran, in November and December, Roosevelt and Churchill met with Stalin for the first time. Then, and during all subsequent Big Three conferences, F. D. R. had to sit between the old Bolshevik and the British conservative: they could not bear each other. Even Roosevelt and Churchill, who were tremendously fond of one another, had their disagreements; the President, for instance, continually pressed for the British to relinquish their colonies, much to Churchill's annoyance. The field commanders were not operating in perfect harmony, either. Montgomery and Eisenhower seldom agreed, and General MacArthur frequently found himself at odds with Admirals King, Nimitz, and Halsey. But with the Allies there was at least a common determination to fight and win. Hitler's partners, on the other hand, were rapidly losing both strength and determination. Hitler never could get Francisco Franco of Spain to fight; and Mussolini got himself in so much trouble that Hitler had to send precious troops to defend Italy as the *Duce*'s power crumbled. And when the *Führer* asked Japan to assist him by attacking the Soviet Union, Tojo refused.

F. D. R. met Churchill and Stalin for the last time at Yalta. Behind are Anthony Eden, Edward Stettinius, Vyacheslav Molotov, and W. Averell Harriman.

The simplest but perhaps the most appropriate Roosevelt obituary was the inclusion of his name atop the war casualty list (right) printed in the nation's newspapers. F. D. R.'s coffin was loaded aboard a train in Warm Springs, where Chief Petty Officer Graham Jackson (below) played a requiem on his accordion. The train moved on to Washington, D. C., and the body lay in a shut coffin in the White House before continuing its slow, sad journey. Then the funeral train headed north; all along the way people watched it pass and said good-by to the only President many of them could remember. At Hyde Park a minister said a prayer, an airplane circled, West Point guns fired a salute, and the coffin bearing President Roosevelt was lowered into the ground.

Today's Army-Navy Casualty List

Washington, Apr. 13.—Following are the latest casualties in the military services, including next-of-kin.

ARMY-NAVY DEAD

ROOSEVELT, Franklin, D., Commonder-in-Chief, wife, Mrs. Anna Eleanor Roosevelt, the White House.

Navy Dead

DECKER, Carlos Anthony, Fireman 1c. Sister, Mrs. Elizabeth Decker Metz, 16 Concord Pl., Concord, S. I.

ED CLARK, *Life* MAGAZINE © TIME, INC.

"IMMORTAL FAME"

When Roosevelt returned from Yalta in 1945, he addressed Congress and the nation from his chair. "I hope," he said, "that you will pardon me for the unusual posture of sitting down. . . . It makes it a lot easier for me not having to carry about ten pounds of steel around on the bottom of my legs." The President had seldom before remained seated during a speech and had never referred to his braces. That he did both at this time suggests that he had indeed become an old, ill man, and that he knew it. He spent as much time as possible at Warm Springs, Georgia, where the therapeutic waters had done so much for him so many times before. On April 12, early in the afternoon, he was sitting for a lady portraitist when he said, "I have a terrific headache." He lost consciousness—a consciousness that had been concerned for twelve years with Depression and War, with facts and figures and recoveries and setbacks, with old judges and young Communists, with freedoms and defenses and strategies and personalities and Republicans, with the rise of Germany and the fall of Germany, and already with trouble brewing in the Middle East—and he died. The word went out. A young soldier on a troop ship bound for Cherbourg said, "But the war's almost over. . . ." Stalin, clearly moved by grief, permitted Moscow's newspapers to print the President's picture and news of his death on the front page (foreign news was usually published on the back page). Churchill said that he felt as though he had been "struck a physical blow." He gave the news to the House of Commons, and his voice broke as he spoke of the "loss of the famous President . . . whose friendship for the cause of freedom and for the cause of the weak and poor have won him immortal fame." And all over the world people said that the President had died, and nobody asked which President, or President of what, because to them Franklin Delano Roosevelt had been The President.

Roosevelt was mourned and then memorialized all over the world. The stamps shown here are just three of the many that were issued in honor of F. D. R., himself an ardent philatelist. Disagreements over design delayed the erection of a Roosevelt monument in Washington, D.C.

ALL: BRUCE LEISH COLLECTION

ELEANOR

The young GI could scarcely believe it. It was true, though. There indeed was Eleanor Roosevelt, right on Guadalcanal in the middle of a war. Everyone knew that she was apt to appear anywhere; but it still took some getting used to—the First Lady doling out soup on a Depression bread line, or visiting a WPA project, or lunching with the union of railroad porters, or reading to kids in the desolate Dust Bowl, or tending the sick in city slums. She had been taught, like all young ladies of breeding, that she, as one of the privileged, was obliged to do something for the less fortunate; but the lesson took far more strongly than her teachers had intended. She got the idea that the elevation of the human condition was more than an afternoon-a-week affair: it was a reason for being. She had gone to the right schools without mastering the right "style." She was clumsy instead of poised, shy instead of coy, a wallflower instead of a belle. She was the homely daughter of a pretty mother who called her Granny and of a father who loved her, but drank too much and died young. Her engagement to her fifth cousin, Franklin, was regarded as incredible: he was handsome and playful, a prince with a future in politics. She was plain

(or so she thought) and, at the time, a volunteer inspector of women's lavatories in garment factories. But they did get married, and they lived how and mostly where his mother, Sara, told them to. She had to fight Sara in 1921 when Franklin came down with paralytic polio. His mother wanted him to retire to Hyde Park, but Eleanor won, and by 1924 Roosevelt had a future in politics again. He became governor of New York, and she worked in the slums. He was a presidential candidate, and she ate with the bonus marchers. He was President, and she went everywhere. Columnist Westbrook Pegler hated her, as did isolationist Father Coughlin and the Daughters of the American Revolution.

"I can always say," the President told a worried adviser, "I can't do a thing with my wife." When he died, reporters who asked her plans were told, "The story is over." It was not. She wrote columns for newspapers, was a delegate to the United Nations, worked with emotionally disturbed children, supported reform Democrats in New York, and met the world's statesmen, including Nikita Khrushchev of Russia (below). When Eleanor died in 1962, many editors remembered an old *New Yorker* cartoon and reprinted it as a eulogy: deep in a mine a soot-covered worker with a lantern on his head stops his coal shoveling and says to another miner, "For gosh sakes, here comes Mrs. Roosevelt."

FACTS IN SUMMARY: FRANKLIN DELANO ROOSEVELT

CHRONOLOGY

UNITED STATES		ROOSEVELT
	1882	*Born January 30*
Cleveland elected President	1884	
McKinley elected President	1896	*Enters Groton School*
War with Spain	1898	
McKinley re-elected	1900	*Enters Harvard*
McKinley assassinated	1901	
Theodore Roosevelt becomes President		
	1903	*Receives B.A. from Harvard*
Roosevelt elected President	1904	*Enters Columbia Law School*
	1905	*Marries Anna Eleanor Roosevelt*
Financial panic	1907	*Admitted to the bar*
Taft elected President	1908	
	1910	*Elected to New York State senate*
Wilson elected President	1912	*Supports Wilson for Presidency*
		Re-elected state senator
Sixteenth Amendment ratified	1913	*Becomes assistant secretary of the Navy*
Seventeenth Amendment ratified		
Federal Reserve Act		
War in Europe	1914	*Tries unsuccessfully for nomination for U.S. senator*
U.S. enters World War I	1917	
Battle of Belleau Wood	1918	*Sent to Europe on inspection tour*
Second Battle of the Marne		
World War I ends		
Eighteenth Amendment ratified	1919	*Attends peace conference at Versailles*
Senate refuses to join League of Nations		
Harding elected President	1920	*Nominated for Vice President*
Washington Armament Conference	1921	*Stricken with polio*
Harding dies	1923	
Coolidge becomes President		
Coolidge elected President	1924	*Nominates Al Smith at Democratic convention*
Hoover elected President	1928	*Elected governor of New York*
Stock market crash	1929	

UNITED STATES		ROOSEVELT
Reconstruction Finance Corporation created	1930	*Re-elected governor of New York*
	1931	*Establishes New York Temporary Emergency Relief Administration*
	1932	*Wins Democratic presidential nomination*
		Elected President
Twentieth Amendment ratified	1933	*Escapes assassin's bullet in Miami*
Emergency Banking Relief Act		*Inaugurated as President*
Economy Act		*Declares four-day bank holiday*
Civilian Conservation Corps created		*Calls Congress into special session and asks for New Deal legislation*
Federal Emergency Relief Act		
Agricultural Adjustment Act		*Begins fireside chats*
Tennessee Valley Authority Act		*Abandons gold standard*
Federal Securities Act		*Forms Farm Credit Administration*
Home Owners Loan Corporation established		*Establishes National Labor Board*
Federal Bank Deposit Insurance Corporation created		*Recognizes Soviet Russia*
National Industrial Recovery Act creates National Recovery Administration and Public Works Administration		
Civil Works Administration established		
Twenty-first Amendment ratified		
Gold Reserve Act	1934	*Establishes Export-Import Bank*
Federal Farm Mortgage Corporation established		*Vetoes independent offices appropriations bill increasing government salaries and veterans' pensions*
Independent Offices Appropriations Act passed over veto		
Johnson Debt Default Act		
Home Owners Loan Act		
Securities and Exchange Commission created		
Federal Communications Commission established		
National Labor Relations Board created		
Federal Housing Authority created		

Domestic	Year	President
Works Progress Administration established	1935	*Outlines social reforms of second New Deal*
NIRA declared unconstitutional by Supreme Court		*Establishes Resettlement Administration*
National Labor Relations Act creates new NLRB		*Establishes Rural Electrification Administration*
Social Security Act		*Vetoes Patman bonus bill*
Banking Act		*Establishes National Resources Committee*
Public Utility Holding Company Act		*Establishes National Youth Administration*
Revenue Act revises tax structure		
Neutrality Act of 1935		
Adjusted Compensation Act passed over President's veto	1936	*Vetoes Adjusted Compensation Act*
Neutrality Act of 1936		*Re-elected President*
Soil Conservation and Domestic Allotment Act		*Attends Inter-American Conference in Buenos Aires*
Merchant Marine Act		
AAA declared unconstitutional by Supreme Court		
Neutrality Act of 1937	1937	*Unsuccessfully tries to expand Supreme Court*
Farm Security Administration established		*Urges quarantine of aggressor nations*
Business recession		*Calls Congress into special session*
National Housing Act creates U.S. Housing Authority		
Conservatives block passage of legislation by special session of Congress		
Agricultural Adjustment Act	1938	*Asks Congress for increased armament appropriations*
Naval Expansion Act		*Campaigns unsuccessfully against conservative Democratic congressmen*
House Un-American Activities Committee established		
Temporary National Economic Committee recommends ways to curb monopolies		
Fair Labor Standards Act		
Administration Reorganization Act	1939	*Asks Congress for funds for emergency program for national defense*
Cutback in relief expenditures		*Proclaims U.S. neutrality*
Hatch Act		*Told by Albert Einstein that atomic bomb is possible*
World War II begins		*Recommends "cash and carry" export of arms to belligerents*
Neutrality Act of 1939		

War Events	Year	President
France falls to Germans	1940	*Sends Sumner Welles to determine war aims of belligerents*
Alien Registration Act		*Agrees to establish Permanent Joint Board on Defense with Canada*
Act of Havana		*Sends destroyers to Britain in exchange for naval bases*
Selective Training and Service Act		*Re-elected President*
Japan joins Axis		*Sets up Office of Production Management to send aid to Allies*
Lend-Lease Act	1941	*Enunciates Four Freedoms*
Germans invade Russia		*Proclaims national emergency*
Pearl Harbor attacked		*Promises U.S. aid to U.S.S.R.*
U.S. declares war on Japan		*Confers with Churchill and announces Atlantic Charter*
Germany and Italy declare war on U.S.		
Battle of Bataan	1942	*Signs United Nations Declaration*
Battle of Java Sea		*Establishes War Production Board*
Doolittle's raid on Tokyo		*Sets up Office of Price Administration*
Battle of Coral Sea		*Orders relocation of Japanese-Americans*
Battle of Midway		*Confers with Molotov on lend-lease*
U.S. Marines land on Guadalcanal		*Confers with Churchill on war strategy*
Operation TORCH in North Africa		
Naval Battle of Guadalcanal		
Enrico Fermi achieves first nuclear chain reaction		
Battle of Kasserine Pass	1943	*Meets with Churchill at Casablanca*
U.S. South Pacific Offensive		*Meets with Churchill in Washington*
Invasion of Sicily		*Attends First Quebec Conference*
Invasion of Italy		*Meets Churchill and Chiang Kai-shek in Cairo*
U.S. Central Pacific Offensive		*Attends Teheran Conference with Stalin and Churchill*
		Orders Army to take over railroads to prevent strikes
U.S. takes Marshall and Mariana islands	1944	*Confers with De Gaulle in Washington*
Allies land in France		*Meets MacArthur and Nimitz at Pearl Harbor*
Philippines Campaign		*Attends Second Quebec Conference*
Dumbarton Oaks Conference on U.N. Charter		*Re-elected President*
U.S. forces enter Germany		
Battle of Leyte Gulf		
Battle of the Bulge		

U.S. troops
capture Manila

Battle of Iwo Jima

Allies take Cologne
and Düsseldorf

Allies cross Rhine

Battle of Okinawa

U.S. Ninth Army
reaches the Elbe

1945 *Confers with Churchill
on Malta*

*Meets Stalin and
Churchill at Yalta*

Dies April 12

BIOGRAPHICAL FACTS

BIRTH: Hyde Park, N.Y., Jan. 30, 1882
ANCESTRY: Dutch
FATHER: James Roosevelt; b. Hyde Park, N.Y., July 16, 1828; d. New York, N.Y., Dec. 8, 1900
FATHER'S OCCUPATIONS: Lawyer; financier; railroad vice president
MOTHER: Sara Delano Roosevelt; b. Newburgh, N.Y., Sept. 21, 1854; d. Hyde Park, N.Y., Sept. 7, 1941
HALF BROTHER: James Roosevelt (1854–1927)
WIFE: Anna Eleanor Roosevelt; b. New York, N.Y., Oct. 11, 1884; d. New York, N.Y., Nov. 7, 1962
MARRIAGE: New York, N.Y., March 17, 1905
CHILDREN: Anna Eleanor (1906–   ); James (1907–   ); Elliott (1910–   ); Franklin Delano, Jr. (1914–   ); John Aspinwall (1916–   )
EDUCATION: Private tutor; Groton School; B.A. from Harvard University (1903); studied law at Columbia University
HOME: Hyde Park, N.Y.
RELIGIOUS AFFILIATION: Episcopalian
OCCUPATIONS BEFORE PRESIDENCY: Lawyer; politician
PRE-PRESIDENTIAL OFFICES: Member New York State Senate; Assistant Secretary of the Navy; Governor of New York
POLITICAL PARTY: Democratic
AGE AT INAUGURATION: 51
DEATH: Warm Springs, Ga., April 12, 1945
PLACE OF BURIAL: Hyde Park, N.Y.

ELECTION OF 1932

CANDIDATES	ELECTORAL VOTE	POPULAR VOTE
Franklin D. Roosevelt Democratic	472	22,809,638
Herbert C. Hoover Republican	59	15,758,901
Norman Thomas Socialist	—	881,951
William Z. Foster Communist	—	102,785
William D. Upshaw Prohibition	—	81,869

THE FIRST ADMINISTRATION

INAUGURATION: March 4, 1933; the Capitol, Washington, D.C.
VICE PRESIDENT: John N. Garner
SECRETARY OF STATE: Cordell Hull
SECRETARY OF THE TREASURY: William H. Woodin; Henry Morgenthau, Jr. (from Jan. 8, 1934)
SECRETARY OF WAR: George H. Dern
ATTORNEY GENERAL: Homer S. Cummings
POSTMASTER GENERAL: James A. Farley
SECRETARY OF THE NAVY: Claude A. Swanson
SECRETARY OF THE INTERIOR: Harold L. Ickes
SECRETARY OF AGRICULTURE: Henry A. Wallace
SECRETARY OF COMMERCE: Daniel C. Roper
SECRETARY OF LABOR: Frances Perkins
73rd CONGRESS (March 4, 1933–January 3, 1935):
Senate: 60 Democrats; 35 Republicans; 1 Other
House: 310 Democrats; 117 Republicans; 5 Others
74th CONGRESS (January 3, 1935–January 3, 1937):
Senate: 69 Democrats; 25 Republicans; 2 Others
House: 319 Democrats; 103 Republicans; 10 Others
END OF PRESIDENTIAL TERM: January 20, 1937

ELECTION OF 1936

CANDIDATES	ELECTORAL VOTE	POPULAR VOTE
Franklin D. Roosevelt Democratic	523	27,752,869
Alfred M. Landon Republican	8	16,674,665
William Lemke Union	—	882,479
Norman Thomas Socialist	—	187,720
Earl Browder Communist	—	80,159

THE SECOND ADMINISTRATION

INAUGURATION: January 20, 1937; the Capitol, Washington, D.C.
VICE PRESIDENT: John N. Garner
SECRETARY OF STATE: Cordell Hull
SECRETARY OF THE TREASURY: Henry Morgenthau, Jr.
SECRETARY OF WAR: Harry H. Woodring; Henry L. Stimson (from July 10, 1940)
ATTORNEY GENERAL: Homer S. Cummings; Frank Murphy (from Jan. 17, 1939); Robert H. Jackson (from Jan. 18, 1940)
POSTMASTER GENERAL: James A. Farley; Frank C. Walker (from Sept. 10, 1940)
SECRETARY OF THE NAVY: Claude A. Swanson; Frank Knox (from July 10, 1940)

SECRETARY OF THE INTERIOR: Harold L. Ickes
SECRETARY OF AGRICULTURE: Henry A. Wallace;
Claude R. Wickard (from Sept. 5, 1940)
SECRETARY OF COMMERCE: Daniel C. Roper; Harry
L. Hopkins (from Jan. 23, 1939); Jesse H. Jones (from
Sept. 19, 1940)
SECRETARY OF LABOR: Frances Perkins
SUPREME COURT APPOINTMENTS: Hugo L. Black
(1937); Stanley F. Reed (1938); Felix Frankfurter (1939);
William O. Douglas (1939); Frank Murphy (1940)
75th CONGRESS (January 3, 1937–January 3, 1939):
Senate: 76 Democrats; 16 Republicans; 4 Others
House: 331 Democrats; 89 Republicans; 13 Others
76th CONGRESS (January 3, 1939–January 3, 1941):
Senate: 69 Democrats; 23 Republicans; 4 Others
House: 261 Democrats; 164 Republicans; 4 Others
END OF PRESIDENTIAL TERM: January 20, 1941

One of several popular songs praising F. D. R.

ELECTION OF 1940

CANDIDATES	ELECTORAL VOTE	POPULAR VOTE
Franklin D. Roosevelt Democratic	449	27,307,819
Wendell L. Willkie Republican	82	22,321,018
Norman Thomas Socialist	—	99,557

THE THIRD ADMINISTRATION

INAUGURATION: January 20, 1941; the Capitol, Washington, D.C.
VICE PRESIDENT: Henry A. Wallace
SECRETARY OF STATE: Cordell Hull; Edward R.
Stettinius (from Dec. 1, 1944)
SECRETARY OF THE TREASURY: Henry Morgenthau, Jr.
SECRETARY OF WAR: Henry L. Stimson
ATTORNEY GENERAL: Robert H. Jackson; Francis
Biddle (from Sept. 5, 1941)
POSTMASTER GENERAL: Frank C. Walker
SECRETARY OF THE NAVY: Frank Knox; James V.
Forrestal (from May 18, 1944)
SECRETARY OF THE INTERIOR: Harold L. Ickes
SECRETARY OF AGRICULTURE: Claude R. Wickard
SECRETARY OF COMMERCE: Jesse H. Jones
SECRETARY OF LABOR: Frances Perkins
SUPREME COURT APPOINTMENTS: Harlan Fiske
Stone, Chief Justice (1941); James F. Byrnes (1941);
Robert H. Jackson (1941); Wiley B. Rutledge (1943)
77th CONGRESS (January 3, 1941–January 3, 1943):
Senate: 66 Democrats; 28 Republicans; 2 Others
House: 268 Democrats; 162 Republicans; 5 Others
78th CONGRESS (January 3, 1943–January 3, 1945):
Senate: 58 Democrats; 37 Republicans; 1 Other
House: 218 Democrats; 208 Republicans; 4 Others
END OF PRESIDENTIAL TERM: January 20, 1945

ELECTION OF 1944

CANDIDATES	ELECTORAL VOTE	POPULAR VOTE
Franklin D. Roosevelt Democratic	432	25,606,585
Thomas E. Dewey Republican	99	22,014,745
Norman Thomas Socialist	—	80,518

THE FOURTH ADMINISTRATION

INAUGURATION: January 20, 1945; the White House,
Washington, D.C.
VICE PRESIDENT: Harry S. Truman
SECRETARY OF STATE: Edward R. Stettinius
SECRETARY OF THE TREASURY: Henry Morgenthau, Jr.
SECRETARY OF WAR: Henry L. Stimson
ATTORNEY GENERAL: Francis Biddle
POSTMASTER GENERAL: Frank C. Walker
SECRETARY OF THE NAVY: James V. Forrestal
SECRETARY OF THE INTERIOR: Harold L. Ickes
SECRETARY OF AGRICULTURE: Claude R. Wickard
SECRETARY OF COMMERCE: Jesse H. Jones; Henry
A. Wallace (from March 2, 1945)
SECRETARY OF LABOR: Frances Perkins
79th CONGRESS (January 3, 1945–January 3, 1947):
Senate: 56 Democrats; 38 Republicans; 1 Other
House: 242 Democrats; 190 Republicans; 2 Others
END OF PRESIDENTIAL TERM: April 12, 1945

HARRY S. TRUMAN

The 1951 baseball season got under way with all attendant ritual. It began, as usual, in the nation's Capital, in archaic Griffith Stadium, which was decked out for the occasion in the customary festive bunting. The traditionally large Opening Day crowd was on hand; so was the President to throw out the first ball.

On that same April Friday, in New York, another ritual was being performed: the ticker-tape parade. Seven and a half million people turned out under a seven-hundred-ton downpour of colorful debris and cheered themselves hoarse for four hours. The hero for whom this demonstration, the most spectacular in the city's history, was staged was General Douglas MacArthur, who had been relieved of his command in Korea by the President.

As MacArthur's motorcade inched its way along Broadway, President Harry S. Truman stood up in Washington to throw the baseball. There was a second's hush; then some paper cups flew in his direction and a chorus of boos rose from the crowd. Like the echo of thunder in a deep canyon the booing rolled around the old wooden stands; it continued as the President threw the ball; it followed him as he turned, lowered his head, and climbed the steps toward the exit ramp. Not until he had left the ball park did the commotion die down and the baseball game begin.

When the "average-man" President ordered the bigger-than-life hero to leave Korea and come home, he knew what he was letting himself in for; the nationwide veneration expressed for MacArthur and the vilification heaped on Truman came as no surprise. But when it was later suggested that the dismissal had been the most courageous act of his Presidency, Truman disagreed. "Courage didn't have anything to do with it," he said. "General MacArthur was insubordinate and I fired him. That's all there was to it."

Harry S. Truman, photographed by Fritz Henle

"That's all there was to it" was one of Harry Truman's pet phrases. It made the decisions of his administration sound like simple choices between black and white. But the facts indicate otherwise. His Presidency began with the explosion of the atomic bomb and ended with a war in Korea. He was a war President, a postwar President, and a cold-war President. The future of mankind—indeed, whether there would be a future at all—often depended on the course he chose to take. And few of the issues he faced were black or white; most were a cold and subtle gray.

Just as the decisions he made were more complex than he admitted, Truman the man was much more prismatic than he appeared. When Franklin Roosevelt's death made him President, Truman seemed to be an ordinary man suddenly catapulted into a position of awesome power. "Boys," he said to the White House reporters, "if you ever pray, pray for me now." When they called him Mr. President, he said, "I wish you didn't have to call me that." So strong was the average-man image that even those who admired him said that he "rose" to the occasion, that the office made the man.

Two incidents, however, suggest that Truman was not so average after all. He had been President for less than two full days when he phoned an administrative official to inform him of a presidential appointment. The official wanted to know if the President had made that appointment before he died. "No," Truman snapped. "He made it just now." The new Chief Executive had only ten days to prime himself for his first meeting with Russian diplomats. The ambassador to Moscow, Averell Harriman, was understandably distressed: America's growing disagreements with the Soviet Union were subtle and complex, even for the well informed. Two days before the meeting, Harriman called on the President in an effort to prepare him. "I had talked with Mr. Truman for only a few minutes," Harriman recalled, "when I began to realize that the man had a real grasp of the situation. What a surprise and a relief this was! . . . He

knew the facts and sequence of events, and he had a keen understanding of what they meant." So, while the mourning American people saw a bewildered man as their new President, Truman was actually taking over with firmness and perspicacity.

Born on May 8, 1884, in Lamar, Missouri, Truman was afflicted from boyhood with poor eyesight. Bright and sociable, he had many friends, but tired of being a spectator at their games; he could not play because he was afraid of breaking the thick-lensed eyeglasses he had to wear after 1892. By the time he was thirteen or fourteen, he had read every book in the public library at Independence, Missouri, where his family had moved. His favorite subject was history, which he continued to read for the rest of his life. Again and again his debt to history was mentioned in his writings and reflected in his presidential decisions.

His father's financial difficulties around the turn of the century made it impossible for Truman to enter college, and his poor eyesight prevented his admittance to West Point. Until the outbreak of World War I, he worked first at a series of clerical jobs—most of them in Kansas City—and then returned to his parents' farm outside Independence. In August, 1917, the National Guard unit to which he belonged was mobilized, and he served in France as an artillery officer. He was discharged as a captain in May, 1919.

Seven weeks later he married Elizabeth Wallace. He and Bess had been sweethearts since they had been in the same fifth-grade class. Because Truman had had no definite future, he had been reluctant to marry, although they had had an "understanding." When he returned home from the war, he was thirty-five years old and Bess was a year younger. Future or no future, they married. They had one child, Margaret.

Truman and an Army friend, Eddie Jacobson, raised some money and opened a haberdashery in Kansas City. At first they did very well, but their customers—mostly farmers and laborers—were hard hit by the recession of 1921. The shop had to be closed

Harry Truman wore strong eyeglasses from the age of eight. In baseball games, he recalled, "I umpired because I couldn't see well enough to bat."

in 1922, but Truman continued to pay his debts and avoided bankruptcy.

At about the time that the haberdashery was failing, Mike Pendergast, an Army buddy of Truman's and the brother of Kansas City political boss Tom Pendergast, talked Truman into running for district judge (in Missouri an administrative, not a judicial, position). He won and served capably for two years, but suffered his only political defeat in 1924, when he lost his bid for re-election. In 1926, however, "Big Tom" himself guided Truman to victory in a race for chief judge of Jackson County.

Tom was not anxious to have the incorruptible Truman in the United States Senate, but when several faithful Pendergast men refused to run, the boss turned to the judge. Truman won his Senate seat in 1934, and even the anti-Pendergast Kansas City *Star* had to admit that with Truman, "a man of unimpeachable character and integrity," in the Senate, "Missouri [could] expect that its interests [would] be safeguarded and advanced from a national standpoint."

Pendergast was anti-Roosevelt, but Truman voted consistently for New Deal measures. Nevertheless, Truman was regarded in Washington as "the Senator from Pendergast." He found it difficult to establish a rapport with the administration, especially after Pendergast was jailed for income tax evasion in 1939. Frustrated and finding it difficult to make ends meet in Washington, Truman considered not standing for re-election in 1940. But then Missouri Governor Lloyd Stark, once a Pendergast man, publicly repudiated the boss and decided to run for Truman's Senate seat. President Roosevelt preferred Stark and offered Truman an appointment to the Interstate Commerce Commission. Truman's proud mind was made up for him: he *had* to make the race.

But the Pendergast machine was now impotent and could offer him little help. Truman had no money for rallies or radio broadcasts, so he drove around the state in his own car and met the people where they lived or worked. A few Senate colleagues came into Missouri to campaign for Truman. Labor began to support the candidate, and contributions started to trickle in. He narrowly defeated Stark in the primary and won a comfortable plurality in the election.

During the campaign Truman had been struck by the waste and inefficiency he had seen at some of the munitions plants and Army bases he had visited; afterward, he quietly drove through twelve Southern states to see how widespread the problem was. In the next session of Congress he spoke at length about the shoddiness and wastefulness of the defense program. The Senate yawningly established the Special Committee to Investigate the National Defense Program with Truman as chairman. Its purpose was to make certain that the taxpayer was getting matériel that was worth the price he was paying. After Pearl Harbor, the Truman committee became much more important. Without seeking headlines, it made them by exposing corporations that were growing rich on the war by making bad equipment in overstaffed plants. It was estimated that by 1944 the committee had saved the taxpayers approximately fifteen billion dollars. The administration, of course, was no longer dissociating itself from Truman: he had become one of the most respected men in the Senate.

As the Democratic National Convention of 1944 approached, President Roosevelt's candidacy for a fourth term was a foregone conclusion. But there was a powerful drive among many party leaders to drop Vice President Wallace from the ticket. His evangelistic liberalism and his affection for Russia had made many enemies. Plenty of volunteers for the Vice Presidency were available, but none were acceptable to National Chairman Robert Hannegan. He preferred either William O. Douglas, the Supreme Court justice, or Senator Harry S. Truman. Neither wanted the nomination.

On the eve of the vice presidential balloting, Hannegan summoned Truman to his

BOB, FILL ME IN ON WHAT HAPPENED AFTER THEY NOMINATED ME. I HAVEN'T KEPT UP WITH POLITICS. WHAT BECAME OF HENRY WALLACE? HOW DID THEY HAPPEN TO PICK TRUMAN?

HANNEGAN

LIBRARY OF CONGRESS

As this exaggerated cartoon implies, F. D. R.'s mind was not on a running mate in 1944. Busy with the war, he let Democratic National Chairman Bob Hannegan survey the field, and Truman was selected.

suite. The chairman picked up the phone and held it away from his ear. "Bob," boomed the big, unmistakable voice of Franklin Roosevelt, which was clearly audible to Truman, "have you got that fellow lined up yet?" "No," said Hannegan. "He is the contrariest Missouri mule I've ever dealt with." "Well, you tell him," said the President, "that if he wants to break up the Democratic party in the middle of a war, that's his responsibility." Without waiting for a reply, Roosevelt hung up.

"Why the hell didn't he tell me in the first place?" Truman said. Despite the spirited supporters of Henry Wallace, Truman was nominated on the second ballot.

Roosevelt won his fourth term, and Truman moved from his desk in the Senate to the podium. Just after he adjourned that body on April 12, 1945, he was called to the White House. When he arrived he was escorted to Eleanor Roosevelt's study. The First Lady approached him and put her arm around him. "Harry," she said, "the President is dead." It took him a moment to find his voice; then he asked if there was anything he could do for her. "Is there anything *we* can do for *you?*" she responded. "For you are the one in trouble now."

He was indeed. Within months the atomic bomb would blast in the atomic age, the war would end, and the cold war would begin; labor would revolt, Congress would revolt, some Cabinet members would revolt, and Truman would write, "Charlie Ross said I'd shown I'd rather be right than President, and I told him I'd rather be anything than President."

As the defeat of Germany became imminent, the Allied powers found it increasingly difficult to get along with one another. At Yalta, several months before his death, Roosevelt had met with Stalin and Churchill to determine the postwar alignment of Europe. The liberated nations were to be reconstructed as soon as possible, and free elections were to be held to determine the nature of their governments. The United States and Great Britain had fulfilled this agreement in the Low Countries; but in Po-

President Harry Truman looks delighted as U.S. Ambassador Edward R. Stettinius signs the United Nations Charter in 1945. Standing behind Stettinius is Republican Harold E. Stassen, who had helped draft the charter.

land, liberated by the Red army, the democratic leaders in exile were not permitted to return, and a Soviet puppet government was established.

In San Francisco the anti-Fascist nations of the world were converging to write the charter of the United Nations. Russia wanted Poland to be seated. The Western Allies refused, however, because democratic elections had not been held there. The chiefs of staff and a number of Roosevelt's advisers told Truman that if Poland were not seated, Russia would walk out of the San Francisco Conference and the United Nations would be doomed. Ambassador Harriman, however, recommended otherwise. On April 23 he brought Soviet Foreign Minister Vyacheslav Molotov and Ambassador Andrei Gromyko to the White House to meet the new President, who proceeded to issue a tongue-lashing regarding the observance of agreements. "I have never been talked to in my life like this," Molotov said. Truman replied, "Carry out your agreements and you won't get talked to like this."

The Russians gave in a little; so did the United States. A few exiled Poles were taken into the Polish government, and Poland was seated. The United Nations Charter was signed on June 26. Secretary of State Edward R. Stettinius was appointed ambassador to the United Nations, and James

Byrnes, who had hoped for the 1944 vice presidential nomination that Truman had received, was appointed Secretary of State.

Meanwhile, on May 7, the war in Europe ended; and in July President Truman traveled to Potsdam, Germany, to meet with Churchill and Stalin. The principal achievements of this conference were the establishment of territorial lines in Europe and the renewal of the Yalta agreement that the Soviet Union would enter the war against Japan. On such matters as the reconstruction of Poland, the rights of the Western powers to their prewar property in Rumania and Bulgaria, and the presence of American troops in the Mediterranean and the Near East, there was no decision. From such issues sprang the cold war.

At Potsdam President Truman was informed that the first test of an actual atomic bomb had been successful; it was up to him to formalize the unofficial decision to employ it. Truman had learned about the atomic bomb for the first time after becoming President, and he had promptly established a committee of distinguished citizens to study the military and moral issues that the emergence of atomic power would raise. The committee agreed that the bomb should be used against Japan, but could not agree on whether or not the United States atomic secrets should be shared with other nations.

As justifiably complicated as the moral issue of using the bomb has become through the years, at the time whether to use it was the less difficult of the two questions. Available information indicated that although the Allies were closing in on the Japanese islands, the invasion itself would probably take as much as a year at a possible cost of a million Allied casualties. Moreover, the drive toward Japan had been slowed by Japanese suicide pilots. The kamikazes could not have turned the tide of the war, but the tactic was terrifying. Under these circumstances the decision to use the bomb was made. Hiroshima was all but obliterated on August 6; Nagasaki, three days later. The Japanese agreed to surrender on August 14.

But with his advisory committee unable to advise, the question of multilateral or unilateral control of atomic energy was left in Truman's hands. In November, in a message to the United Nations, Truman said, "We are prepared to share, on a reciprocal basis, with other members of the United Nations detailed information concerning the practical industrial application of atomic energy." But to the surprise of everyone, the Soviet Union voted *Nyet*. "It was," said Truman, "an astonishing thing. All the representatives of the other countries in the world sat in stunned silence. . . . They all expected that the Russians would agree, and so did I. And it left the situation in such a way that everybody lost." The fact was, though nobody knew it then, that the Russians were already learning about atomic energy.

As the shooting war abroad ended, Truman's war with Congress at home began. The nation's wartime economy had to be adapted to peace. To make the conversion and retain stability the President issued, on August 18, a "hold-the-line order," which extended wartime controls on production, wages, and prices. Truman knew his history: wars were invariably followed by inflation, then by bust. The only way to avoid another recession was to calculate the conversion and make it a gradual one.

On September 6 he sent his recommendations to Congress and included suggestions for federal aid to education, an increase in the minimum wage, a medical insurance plan, and civil rights legislation. The uproar in Congress was immediate. "This is the kickoff," said Republican Charles Halleck. "This begins the campaign of 1946."

The principal problem, as Truman saw it, was price control. Although there was plenty of money around, consumer goods were scarce; people willingly paid outrageous prices for a pair of nylon stockings or a coffee pot. To make matters worse, business was hoarding the goods it was producing, waiting for the end of controls. If controls were suddenly dropped, prices would rise even higher; so would the cost of living; so would wage demands. That was the normal inflationary pattern that Truman wanted to avoid. The "compromise" control bill that Congress grudgingly passed was so full of

© 1946 HERBLOCK IN THE WASHINGTON *Post*

"Are You Sure You Didn't Miss Anything?" Truman asks after his rocky first year in the Presidency.

loopholes that it was unenforceable. Truman vetoed it, but a stronger bill was not enacted, and the Office of Price Administration went out of business in June, 1946. Predictably, prices soared. By August there were consumer strikes and a public uproar so great that Congress hastily produced a new law calling for a gradual phasing-out of price regulation. It was—and Congress knew it—too late. The administrative machinery of the OPA had been disassembled.

A higher cost of living requires higher wages. No longer hampered by the no-strike laws of wartime and anxious to test the strong right-to-strike legislation passed in the 1930's, organized labor emerged from the war with muscles flexing. By the end of 1945 nine hundred thousand workers were on strike from several industries, and early in 1946 another million joined them.

The most serious threats came from the United Mine Workers and the various railroad unions. John L. Lewis had closed the soft-coal mines in March, 1946, and with factories inoperative and the lights of cities dimming because of fuel shortages, the people would not put up with a shutdown of transportation, too. In April Truman discovered that eighteen of the railmen's twenty major leaders were willing to settle for the contract the government had helped negotiate. The two dissenters were the President's old friends Alvanley Johnston (Brotherhood of Locomotive Engineers) and A. F. Whitney (Brotherhood of Railroad Trainmen). He called them to the White House in early May and erupted: "If you think I'm going to sit here and let you tie up this whole country, you're crazy as hell."

On May 21 Truman seized the coal mines and sent Secretary of the Interior Julius A. Krug to settle with Lewis. The settlement infuriated the mine operators, but they had no choice in the matter, and the miners went back to work.

The railroad strike, meanwhile, was scheduled to begin on May 25. The day before, the President told his Cabinet that he intended to draft the striking employees into the Army and thus compel them to run

Labor leader John L. Lewis, above in an Esquire *cartoon, was a perpetual thorn in Truman's side.*

the trains. On the afternoon of the twenty-fifth, Truman addressed a special session of Congress to ask for the induction bill. Just as he came to that part of the speech, a note was handed to him: "Agreement signed, strike over." Truman asked for the anti-strike legislation anyway, but the Senate defeated the measure.

In October, John L. Lewis acted up again. Engaged in a power struggle with other union leaders, Lewis decided to demonstrate his strength in a battle with the government. Using a minor point in the contract as an excuse, he demanded that negotiations be reopened. When Secretary Krug refused, Lewis said the mine workers would consider the contract void as of November 20. Bristling with anger, the President asked for an injunction, and on November 18 the court ordered the miners not to strike. They struck anyway, and on December 3 the union was fined three and a half million dollars, and Lewis personally, ten thousand.

Truman said that his wife Bess (left) was "the Boss" but that daughter Margaret "bosses her."

Still the strike went on, and the President announced that he would make a radio appeal to the miners. Lewis must have feared that his men were no longer with him, for he ordered the miners back to work.

The public had so soured on organized labor throughout 1946 that Truman's firmness might have stopped or reversed the fast decline in his popularity; but he neutralized the effect by vetoing the antilabor Case bill of 1946. The Eightieth Congress, which was seated in 1947, was, however, a much more conservative legislature and was able to override Truman's veto of the somewhat milder labor-restricting Taft-Hartley Act.

The elections of 1946, which produced the first Republican-controlled Congress since 1930, were a serious repudiation of Truman's administration. Senator J. William Fulbright, then a freshman Democrat, suggested that Truman ought to resign, for the people were obviously against the President. There were many reasons for his unpopularity: labor did not like his toughness, and business did not like his position on controls; the South had no use for his civil

rights proposals, and the North did not like his "style."

Secretary of State Byrnes, who felt that he and not Truman should be President, thought he could make foreign policy unilaterally. Once, when Truman asked him for a report on the Moscow conferences Byrnes had been attending, the Secretary replied that he intended to make a radio broadcast about the talks; Truman could listen to it. On the other hand, Henry Wallace acted as if he were Secretary of State, when in fact he was Secretary of Commerce. While Byrnes was standing firm in discussions with the Soviet diplomats, Wallace was criticizing that firmness. When Wallace attributed his own "neither pro-British . . . nor pro-Russian" attitude to the President, Truman had to fire him, although he "hated to do it."

Byrnes's resignation—which Truman probably requested—came in April, 1946, but did not become effective until his replacement, General George C. Marshall, returned from China in January, 1947. Marshall's frustrating China mission reflected the worldwide situation after the war. In the Orient as in Europe, the Axis had been defeated by uncomfortable alliances of potential antagonists. After the war had ended, the old lines had been redrawn. General Marshall, anxious to pledge American dollars to a peaceful China, was unable to effect a coalition between Chiang Kai-shek's Nationalists and the Communists. One by one the formerly Nazi occupied nations of Eastern Europe had become little more than Soviet colonies. In Iran, where the Allies had maintained several bases, the Russians refused to evacuate according to agreement. In Greece the opposing forces—one Communist, one royalist—were at each other's throats as soon as the British withdrew.

In August, 1946, Russia made a new move in the Middle East. Soviet troops massed along the Turkish border to "protect" Turkey's Black Sea coast. In a note handed to the Soviet ambassador, the policy that would become the Truman Doctrine was foreshadowed: "It is the firm opinion of this government [the United States] that Turkey should continue to be primarily responsible for the defense of the Straits [the Bosporus and the Dardanelles]. Should the Straits become the object of attack or threat of attack by an aggressor, the resulting situation would constitute a threat to international security . . . ." An American naval task force was sent on "routine training maneuvers" off the Turkish coast. And early in 1947 Truman asked Congress for huge sums for aid to Greece and Turkey. That, essentially, was the Truman Doctrine. Its ideological premise was "containment." It told the Soviet Union that it could expand no farther. It was a strong statement, but it placed the initiative for starting a war squarely in Russian hands.

The Truman Doctrine was not universally applicable. In many places, including Italy, France, the Low Countries, and Scandinavia, the Communists were well organized

TRUMAN LIBRARY

The ancient vase above was a gift from the Greek people in appreciation of the Truman Doctrine.

and operated legally. So long as these nations remained impoverished, the possibility of Communist dominance was great.

On June 5, 1947, Secretary of State Marshall said in a speech at Harvard University that the policy of the United States was not directed against a country or an idea, but "against hunger, poverty, desperation, and chaos. Its purpose should be the revival of a working economy in the world. . . ." The United States would offer all the funds necessary to nations that wanted to reconstruct their economies. By implication, this American economic aid was also to be made available to the countries of Eastern Europe; but Russia denounced the Marshall Plan as an "imperial" plot to enslave Europe.

The British historian Arnold Toynbee has written that the most significant achievement of the modern era was not the discovery of atomic power but the attention lavished on the world's poorer nations by the more privileged ones. The Marshall Plan distributed more than twelve billion American dollars to the people of Europe for reconstruction. There were, certainly, some strings attached, but they did not limit the development of freedom and prosperity.

Truman's efforts to avoid war were challenged in June, 1948, when the Russians closed off the autobahn through the Soviet occupation zone in Germany, blocking Allied access to Berlin. Although it was obviously a hostile move, the blockade was a clever diplomatic ploy, for it placed in American hands the responsibility of making the first military move. Truman quickly turned the dare around: he began sending airplanes—carrying supplies—over the Soviet zone and into West Berlin. This put it to the Soviets to fire the first shot, and they did not.

Despite his successes and imaginativeness in foreign policy, Truman was still not getting along with the Eightieth Congress. It had defeated or ignored most of his Fair Deal proposals; it had, against Truman's wishes, cut the budget and passed tax reductions. And Congress was only one of Truman's troubles as his first term approached its end. As Arthur Krock wrote in *The New*

York Times in April, 1948: "A President whose defeat at the next poll is generally prophesied faces difficulties in performing his office that conceivably bring disaster. . . . At this writing, the President's influence is weaker than any President's has been in modern history."

Truman had decided to seek a four-year term of his own, and the decision prompted a variety of responses. Radicals were appalled, reactionaries shocked, regular Democrats gloomy, and regular Republicans joyful. The left, led by Henry Wallace, organized a third party to fight for the Presidency. The South, dismayed by Truman's strong civil rights proposals, defected and ran South Carolina Governor Strom Thurmond as the Dixiecrat (States' Rights) candidate. The remaining Democrats, having been unable to convince General Dwight D. Eisenhower to become their candidate, had no choice but to accept Truman and look forward to inevitable defeat. The Republicans nominated Thomas Dewey, governor of New York. By selecting a moderate, the G.O.P. did not have to campaign against the New Deal—which meant that it did not have to run against the memory of Franklin Roosevelt. Indeed, the Republican platform called for such New Dealish measures as a national health plan, civil rights legislation, a federal housing bill, and extensions of Social Security coverage.

The President appeared before his battered party to accept its nomination. No one had mentioned the word "win" with any conviction. But Harry Truman said: "Senator [Alben] Barkley and I will win this election and make these Republicans like it—don't you forget that."

Next Truman announced his strategy: "On the 26th day of July, which out in Missouri we call 'Turnip Day,' I am going to call Congress back and ask them to pass laws to halt rising prices, to meet the housing crisis—which they are saying they are for in their platform. . . . Now my friends, if there is any reality behind that Republican platform, we ought to get some action from a short session of the Eightieth Congress.

They can do this job in fifteen days, if they want to do it. They will still have time to go out and run for office." There was no way for Congress to avoid Truman's trap. If the legislators passed his proposals, they would increase the President's strength; if they ignored them, they would remain the "do-nothing Eightieth Congress." They chose to do nothing, and Truman made the Congress itself a principal election issue.

After the July "turnip session," Truman assumed an optimism shared by almost no one. Although he was the incumbent, he was the underdog, and regular Democratic contributors saw no sense in throwing good money after bad. To reach as many people as he could, as cheaply as he could, the President set out on two major, and several short, whistle-stop train trips, stopping wherever enough people had gathered to hear him. While Tom Dewey was eloquently stating idealistic abstractions, Truman folksily ranted and raved—not so much against his opponent, not even so much against the Eightieth Congress, as against the people themselves. "If," he harangued, "you stay at home, as you did in 1946, and keep these reactionaries in power, you will deserve every blow you get. . . ." In Albuquerque, New Mexico, he later recalled, he was making such a speech when "some big voice way up in the corner of that 7,000 people auditorium said, 'Give 'em hell, Harry!' Well, I never gave anybody hell—I just told the truth on these fellows and they thought it was hell!" But the polls still forecast a landslide for Dewey.

Of election night, Truman later said, "At six o'clock I was defeated. At ten o'clock I was defeated. Twelve o'clock I was defeated. Four o'clock I had won the election. And the next morning . . . in St. Louis, I was handed this paper which said, 'DEWEY DEFEATS TRUMAN!' Of course, he wished he had, but he didn't and that's all there was to it!" There was something else to it: Congress was Democratic once again.

Foreign policy continued to occupy most of Truman's attention in his second term. World War III never came, but times were tense. The tension produced a major domestic issue in the United States: "loyalty." The result was one of the most appalling periods in the nation's history.

A democracy has the right—the obligation—to protect itself from those who would subvert it. But the "loyalty" crusade of the late 1940's and early 1950's was undemocratic. Investigators who appointed themselves to protect the Constitution thought the way to do it was to ignore that document.

In the years that followed the war, hundreds of government employees were fired on the basis of often anonymous reports alleging that they were or had been Communists, or had associated with Communists. They were deprived of their right to confront their accusers. They were not even told who their accusers were.

In 1948 the House Un-American Activities Committee, which Truman called the most "un-American activity in the whole government," sought and won the imprisonment of ten Hollywood screen writers for contempt of Congress. The writers were so cited because they had employed their constitutional rights: they had insisted on confronting their accusers; they had declined to testify against themselves; they had pointed out that under the American judicial system there was no such thing as "guilt by association." Whether any of the writers were Communists was not established—it was not illegal to be a Communist anyway. If they were in contempt of Congress, Congress was in contempt of the Constitution.

There had been a threat of internal subversion, and there can be little doubt that the espionage of the British spy Klaus Fuchs and of the Americans Ethel and Julius Rosenberg facilitated the Soviet mastery of atomic energy; but the security of the nation was not aided by the purges. A peak of absurdity was reached in 1950 when Senator Joseph McCarthy of Wisconsin, who had been voted "worst" United States senator by the Washington press corps just a few years before, found himself facing sure defeat in his bid for re-election. Looking for an issue to make his constituents forget his

ALBEN W. BARKLEY

Nominated by acclamation as President Truman's running mate in 1948, Alben Barkley of Kentucky told the cheering delegates, "I did not come here as a candidate; I did not become one after I got here, and I was not one." He left unsaid what many knew: as a liberal member of Congress since 1913 and Democratic leader in the Senate for more than a decade, he had been a vice presidential possibility for twenty years. He had wanted the office, and others had wanted him to have it. Some Democrats had even tried to get him to run against Truman in 1948, but he had resisted all attempts to become any sort of a candidate without the blessing of the President. Truman wanted Justice William Douglas to be the vice presidential nominee. He thought Barkley, at seventy, was too old. But when Justice Douglas refused the President's offer, Truman agreed to Barkley, who thus became the oldest Vice President of the United States, and one of the most popular. His grandson called him the Veep, and the nickname stuck—to the office as well as to Barkley. A widower, he was the only Vice President to marry in office. He and Truman set a high standard of working relations between a Chief Executive and a Vice President, but in 1952, when a new presidential candidate had to be found, Truman still felt that Barkley's age made him ineligible, and other Democrats agreed. Barkley was re-elected to the Senate and died in 1956.

dismal performance in Washington, he seized on the internal-security threat. As a result of his totally groundless accusations, scores of men lost their jobs, were degraded before their families and neighbors, had to change their names and cities of residence. But not one Communist or fellow traveler was found, not one spy convicted, not one person even indicted for a crime.

"Ask almost any school child," McCarthy advised, "who the architect of our Far Eastern policy is, and he will say 'Owen Lattimore.'" Lattimore, a Johns Hopkins professor and frequent missionary for the State Department, was, according to McCarthy, "the top Russian espionage agent" in the State Department. When Senator Millard Tydings of Maryland produced an FBI report showing that Lattimore could not have been a Communist at any time, McCarthy turned his attention to Tydings, who was running for re-election. McCarthy

had a fake photograph made showing the senator engaged in friendly conversation with Communist Earl Browder. Tydings' defense of Lattimore, McCarthy said, was only a diversionary trick to cloud his own Communist activities. That sort of logic infected Maryland no less than the rest of the country; Tydings was defeated.

The hysteria was translated into legislation in the McCarran act of 1950. Essentially, the bill required all Communists to register with the Justice Department (this, according to Truman, was like passing a law to make thieves report to the sheriff); provided for the deportation of any alien who had ever been a Communist; and prohibited employment of Communists or their dupes in positions relating to national defense. "It was," as Cabell Phillips has written, "a dragnet such as any dictator might envy." Truman vetoed the McCarran Internal Security Act, declaring that most

Private citizen Harry Truman returned periodically to his favorite presidential retreat, the Florida Keys. Above, with grandsons, Clifton and William Daniel, he dedicates the Truman Bridge at Duck Key in 1964; at right he relaxes at Key West.

of its provisions were unconstitutional. Congress passed it over his veto. (In 1965, the Supreme Court ruled the major part of the McCarran act—the registration provision—unconstitutional.)

McCarthy's power, meanwhile, seemed to be without limits. After the outbreak of the Korean War, the senator declared that General George C. Marshall, who had just resigned as Secretary of State, was the leading Communist in the United States. A resolution condemning McCarthy for the absolutely groundless accusation never got out of the Senate Rules Committee, and the senator who had introduced it, Democrat William Benton of Connecticut, was defeated when he ran for re-election.

Normally the nation unites behind its President in times of international tension. But the Red Scare of the late 1940's had split America in two. When the troops of North Korea invaded democratic South Korea in 1950, half the country blamed the "infiltrated" Truman administration for the circumstances that had allowed the attack to happen. Most of the other part doubted that American involvement in Korea was necessary.

After World War II, the United States and Russia, according to the agreements made at Potsdam, had jointly liberated and occupied Japanese-held Korea. The dividing line was the thirty-eighth parallel. South Korea had had its elections; North Korea had not. China, meanwhile, had been fighting a civil war with the result that in 1949 Chiang Kai-shek was forced to evacuate the mainland and retreat to Formosa. When the North Koreans crossed the border into the South, Truman's containment doctrine was put to the test in the Far East.

Truman sent American planes and ships to Korea on June 24, just hours after the invasion had taken place. That day the Security Council of the United Nations examined the events and declared that the invasion constituted an act of armed aggression. The council was in a position to convert Truman's unilateral decision into a United Nations action because the Soviet Union (which could have vetoed the resolution) was at the time boycotting sessions.

General Douglas MacArthur, then ranking officer in the Far East and military governor of Japan, was placed in command of the Korean operation, and from early in the conflict he disagreed with United Nations strategy, which was containment, not destruction, of the aggressor.

Truman's containment policy had worked well in Europe. The Marshall Plan and its extension, Point Four, were rebuilding the Western democracies. The Berlin Airlift had successfully called Russia's bluff, and the blockade of the autobahn had been removed in May, 1949. That same spring the North Atlantic Treaty Organization had been formed by the United States, Great Britain, France, Canada, Belgium, the Netherlands, Luxembourg, Italy, Denmark, Norway, Iceland, and Portugal. The treaty stated that an attack on one would be considered an attack on all and integrated the European defenses of all members.

But in Korea the problem was more complicated. The Russians were not actively involved; neither were the Chinese. But the chance of their intervention was great, and this possibility controlled United Nations strategy.

MacArthur insisted that the Chinese were not going to intervene and that thus there was no reason to limit Allied military action to the South. But as the United Nations forces neared the Yalu River, which separated North Korea from Manchuria, China did intervene; its troops poured across the border and pushed the Allies south of the thirty-eighth parallel.

United Nations orders maintained that all fighting was to be done in or over Korea; the war was not to be introduced into Chinese Manchuria. This presented MacArthur with the frustration of having planes from Chinese bases assault United Nations depots, supply lines, and troops and then retreat to their sanctuary north of the Yalu. By openly criticizing this state of affairs, MacArthur was not only publicly rebuking the Commander in Chief, the joint chiefs of staff, and the United Nations, he was informing the enemy of what was *not* going to be done. As the general began making public statements that were critical of his superiors and writing to the joint chiefs of staff complaining about official policy, Truman responded that he was sympathetic, but that he was losing patience with MacArthur.

On March 20, 1951, the United Nations drafted a proposal for a negotiated settlement of the war, and a copy was sent to MacArthur. In an extraordinary gesture, the general made in a public statement his own offer to negotiate. His plan completely disregarded the official statement made by the President and the United Nations.

Truman considered firing MacArthur then, but hesitated. A few days later, however, on April 5, House Minority Leader Joe Martin read a letter to the House from MacArthur, in which the commander again attacked the official policy of the United Nations. MacArthur had been ordered by the joint chiefs not to make any policy statements without clearance. Twice within ten days he disobeyed that order. On April 10, Truman ordered him to come home.

MacArthur had challenged the constitutional premise that military power is subject to civilian rule in the United States. Despite the hero's welcome that he received, MacArthur was not exonerated. The calls for impeachment of the President died out when Senate hearings revealed that Truman had been on firm constitutional grounds. MacArthur did not receive the presidential nomination he probably wanted, and Truman withstood the ball park boos and another year in the office he had had enough of.

Long-time Speaker of the House Sam Rayburn once said that as President, his friend Harry Truman had been "right on all the big things, wrong on all the little ones." Frankly corny and at times crude, Truman conducted what was probably the most liberal administration in the nation's history, but he surrounded himself with political hacks who were corrupt and inept, and he stood by them when they were denounced. One day he could be playing "Missouri Waltz" on the piano for foreign dignitaries; the next he could be proposing legislation so visionary that it would not be enacted until the 1960's (the Civil Rights Act of 1964 and Medicare of 1965). When a Washington music critic was harsh in a review of Margaret Truman's singing, the President threatened to punch him in the nose. Yet that same Harry Truman was, according to Arthur Krock of *The New York Times*, the only President from Woodrow Wilson through Lyndon Johnson who never took a journalist's criticism personally and never held a grudge.

In the final year of the Truman administration, Winston Churchill visited the United States. He had an admission for Truman: "The last time you and I sat across a conference table was at Potsdam. I must confess, sir, I held you in very low regard. I loathed your taking the place of Franklin Roosevelt. I misjudged you badly. Since that time, you more than any other man, saved Western civilization."

Truman was snubbed by Eisenhower at the latter's inauguration; forgotten, apparently, was Truman's offer to step down in favor of the general in 1948. He went home to Independence to start a library and to re-fight all his battles in his memoirs. Senator McCarthy implied that he was a traitor and subpoenaed him to appear at a congressional investigation. Truman refused. The Korean War was settled, the MacArthur furor died down, McCarthy was censured; in foreign policy Eisenhower repudiated little that Truman had done. His reputation began to rise as the "big things" lasted and the "little things" passed into insignificance.

On a 1964 television program based on his Presidency, Truman recalled: "The day I left Washington, I wrote my daughter Margaret a letter. . . . And it said this: 'There is an epitaph in Boot Hill cemetery in Arizona which reads, "Here lies Jack Williams. He done his damnedest! What more can a person do?"' Well, that's all I could do. I did my damnedest, and that's all there was to it!"

—DAVID JACOBS

A PICTURE PORTFOLIO

*On this 1948 campaign button President Truman
wears an uncharacteristically blank expression.*

JUST PLAIN "S."

Harry S. Truman was introduced early to the political arts of compromise and persuasion. When he was born in 1884, his mother's family wanted his middle name to be Solomon, but the Trumans insisted on Shippe. His parents avoided choosing between the two old family names by making it "S.," pure and simple. As he grew up, Truman—by his own admission—made a habit of studying his teachers to see what pleased them and often became their pet. He watched everyone closely and "usually was able to get what [he] wanted." He learned, by reading history, that "a leader is a man who has the ability to get other people to do what they don't want to do, and like it." He had no idea how important that lesson would become.

Truman joined a Kansas City unit of the Missouri National Guard in 1905. When his unit was nationalized in World War I, he and a friend, Eddie Jacobson, were placed in charge of the regiment's canteen, which under their direction actually made a profit. Truman was shipped to France as an artillery officer (above), but after the war he and Jacobson got together again and went into business.

Childhood sweethearts, Harry Truman and Bess Wallace were in their thirties before they were finally married (above) in 1919. That fall Truman and Jacobson opened their ill-fated haberdashery in Kansas City. (Co-owner Truman is at far left in the photograph at left.) Truman could see only one reason for the shop's failure: "In 1921 . . . the Republicans took over. . . ." The store closed in 1922, when Truman was a candidate for district judge. (Below is one of his campaign buttons.) In 1935 he was sent to Washington as a senator.

HARRY S. TRUMAN
FOR JUDGE
EASTERN DISTRICT

Above, vice presidential candidate Truman confers with F. D. R. at the White House before the election of 1944. Below, the new Vice President, who loved to play the piano, performs for actress Lauren Bacall.

"YOU'D BE PRESIDENT"

During his first six years in the Senate, Truman's relationship with the notorious Kansas City political boss Tom Pendergast kept him out of the Roosevelt administration's inner circle. In his second term, however, his work as chairman of the Special Committee to Investigate the National Defense Program catapulted him to a position of respectability. As the national convention of 1944 approached, he was often mentioned as a possible vice presidential candidate. Told that F. D. R. would endorse him for the nomination, Truman replied, "Tell him to go to hell. I'm for Jimmy Byrnes." But the pressure was increased, and finally Truman gave in, ac-

cepted the challenge, and defeated Henry Wallace in the convention balloting. He had, however, made one mistake; he had forgotten to clear it with "the Boss"—Mrs. Truman. As they made their way from the convention floor to their car, she asked, "Are we going to have to go through this all the rest of our lives?" Truman said nothing. "What would happen," she demanded, "if he should die? You'd be President." If Truman answered at all, the reply was lost as their car sped away. Three months after the inauguration, F. D. R. did die. "I felt," Truman said, "like the moon, the stars, and all the planets had fallen on me. I've got the most terribly responsible job a man ever had."

UNITED PRESS INTERNATIONAL

At about 5 P.M. on April 12, 1945, a bored Harry S. Truman, presiding over the Senate, dashed off a letter to his mother and sister: "I am trying to write you . . . while a windy Senator . . . is making a speech on a subject with which he is in no way familiar. . . . Turn on your radio tomorrow night . . . you'll hear Harry make a Jefferson Day address to the nation. . . . It will be followed by the President, whom I'll introduce." He did not know it then, but Roosevelt had died. Truman took the oath of office (above) two hours later.

"A NEW WEAPON"

After he was sworn in, President Truman held a brief meeting with the grief-stricken Roosevelt Cabinet and asked its members to remain at their jobs. They agreed and solemnly departed, except for Secretary of War Henry L. Stimson. When he and Truman were alone, the Secretary told him that the United States had an atomic bomb; it was the first Truman heard of it. Originally intended for use against Germany, the bomb was not ready for testing until after V-E Day; and when the test was successfully concluded on the New Mexico desert in July, 1945, Truman was at Potsdam near Berlin, conferring with Winston Churchill and Joseph Stalin. The President and Prime Minister discussed the best way to tell Stalin about the bomb. Finally, Truman decided to mention casually that the United States now had "a new weapon of unusual destructive force." Stalin, according to Truman, replied that he was "glad to hear it and hoped we would make 'good use of it against the Japanese.'" Stalin was a good actor: his spy network had already informed him about the bomb.

The new Big Three at Potsdam (above) radiated good fellowship, harmony, and confidence. Actually, though Truman liked Stalin, Churchill disliked Truman, and Stalin distrusted both. Churchill was defeated in a British election before the conference at Potsdam ended and was replaced by Clement R. Attlee. At right is the mushroom cloud over Nagasaki, Japan, after an atomic bomb was dropped there on August 9, 1945.

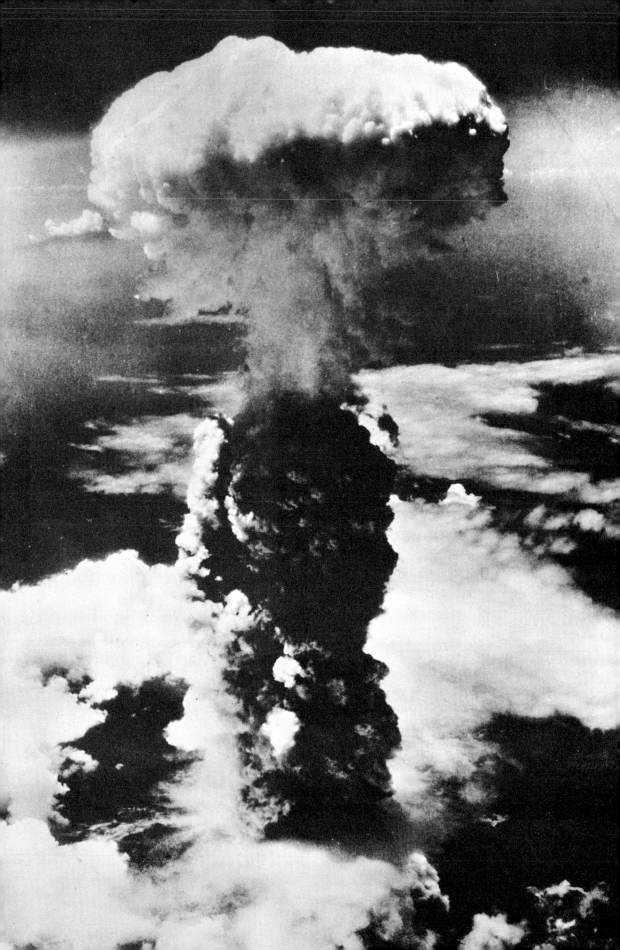

THE SCIENTISTS

ALBERT EINSTEIN

On August 2, 1939, the world-famous scientist Albert Einstein, alarmed at the progress of Nazi scientists in atomic research, wrote to President Roosevelt urging United States development of atomic weapons. His plea led to the creation of the atomic bomb six years later. Born in Ulm, Germany, in 1879, Einstein came to the world's attention in 1905 with his revolutionary theory that motion is not absolute but is relative to some fixed point of reference. In developing this special theory of relativity, he established the equivalence of mass and energy. It was his famous equation $E = MC^2$—a formula for the conversion of mass into energy—that made the atomic bomb possible. In subsequent research, Einstein expanded this concept in his general theory of relativity and opened new doors in the fields of gravitation, quantum theory, and the photoelectric effect of light. With the rise of Hitler in Germany, Einstein left Berlin and emigrated to America. Accepting a post at Princeton's Institute for Advanced Study in 1933, he remained there until his death in 1955, devoting his research to the formulation of a unified field theory. A gentle man with a penetrating sense of humor, Einstein—who won the Nobel Prize in 1921—once summed up his philosophy of life with this remark: "God is subtle, but he is not malicious."

ENRICO FERMI

In December, 1942, the beginning of the atomic age was announced by a coded telegram sent to Washington from the Chicago headquarters of the American atomic energy program: "The Italian navigator has entered the new world." The navigator referred to was Italian-born physicist Enrico Fermi, who had, in a nuclear reactor at the University of Chicago, just produced the first self-sustaining nuclear chain reaction in history. Fermi began experimenting with neutron bombardment in 1934, when he was a professor of physics at the University of Rome. While he narrowly missed discovering the secret of atomic fission himself, his work in the field led directly to that breakthrough and won him the Nobel Prize for physics in 1938. Leaving Fascist Italy, Fermi came to the United States in 1939 and became a professor at Columbia University. After the dramatic success of his nuclear reactor in 1942, he was transferred directly to the atomic bomb laboratory at Los Alamos. In 1946 he became a professor at the Institute of Nuclear Studies at Chicago, later renamed the Enrico Fermi Institute. Among his many contributions to physics were the Fermi-Dirac statistics of electron behavior, the theory of radioactive beta-ray disintegration, and the discovery of neptunium. He received the Special Award of the Atomic Energy Commission in 1954.

ERNEST ORLANDO LAWRENCE

The invention of the cyclotron by Ernest Orlando Lawrence was a giant step in the advancement of nuclear physics. Great strides had been made in the field of atomic research in the 1920's, but science had yet to produce a satisfactory device to penetrate the heart of the atom. In 1932 Lawrence, a professor of physics at the University of California, constructed the first such atom-smashing device—a circular, drum-shaped machine called a cyclotron. Within this device, atomic particles could be accelerated by repeated electrical charges to the extremely high velocities necessary to penetrate the nucleus of the atom, thereby causing atomic transmutation. After perfecting his cyclotron further, Lawrence proceeded with the systematic transmutation of all the atomic elements, and in 1936 he succeeded in the alchemist's dream of changing platinum into the next higher element, gold. That same year Lawrence was made director of the University of California Radiation Laboratory, and in 1939 he was awarded the Nobel Prize for his cyclotron. Using his invention to separate the highly fissionable uranium-235 from natural uranium, he was instrumental in the development of the atomic bomb during World War II. In 1957, the year before his death, Lawrence was the recipient of the Fermi Award of the Atomic Energy Commission.

JAMES B. CONANT

After the holocaust of World War II and the awesome demonstration of the atom's power to destroy, men of learning began to take a new look at the relationship of science to society. Scientist and educator James B. Conant, who had himself been instrumental in the production of the atomic bomb, was among those who later warned that "science alone, untempered by other knowledge, can lead not to freedom but to slavery." A graduate of Harvard, where he received a Ph.D. in 1916, Conant remained there as a chemistry professor, conducting important research in the field of organic chemistry. Appointed president of the university in 1933, he served in that position for twenty years. Chairman of the National Defense Research Committee from 1941 to 1946, Conant was a leading adviser in the government's atomic energy program, and after the war he helped to establish the National Science Foundation. Resigning from Harvard in 1953, he spent the next four years in West Germany as United States high commissioner and later as ambassador. Having recognized the need for "the interconnection of our new scientific knowledge and our older humanistic studies," Conant resumed his work in education under a Carnegie Foundation grant in 1957 and subsequently wrote a number of important books on education.

TRIALS AND
A NEW CRISIS

When President Truman said that he favored international trials for war criminals, he was severely criticized, and the Nuremberg Trials that resulted from his pressure are criticized to this day. What is forgotten, however, is that right after the war, critics of the plan did not oppose punishment—just trials. England, France, and Russia favored immediate executions without trials. But Truman, whose knowledge of history was extensive, was afraid that the horrible stories of Nazi concentration camps and of genocide would be regarded by later generations as "just a lot of propaganda." He wanted the films shown, the testimony recorded, and the Nazi directives read into a permanent document. He did not want Hitler to be remembered as a latter-day Napoleon. He wanted to set a precedent, to establish individual responsibility and punish guilty civilians along with the military. "Is it just . . ." he asked, "that the soldier who pulls the trigger or shovels the people into ovens shall be tried for murder . . . [while] the head of the government under whose activities and directives [he acts] shall be immune? . . . Now . . . nobody can say that it never happened, because the thing is on the record. Never again can men say, 'I was following orders.' And never again can men in power give such orders." The Nuremberg Trials were held, and their revelations shocked the world. Less than two years after they ended, Germany again became the focal point of world attention. Russia blocked off the autobahn to West Berlin in June, 1948, and a hot war was averted by the 321-day Berlin Airlift. Suddenly it became essential to have the support of the German people: the Russians, whose homeland had been ravaged by the Nazis, demanded East German support; the less-victimized, more-forgiving Americans simply wooed the West Germans and began the process of wiping the smeared slate clean.

Berlin, situated deep in the Soviet-occupied section of Germany, was divided into four sectors, each of which was controlled by one Allied power. But in 1948 the Russians closed the road that led through East Germany to Berlin. It was not the first hostile act of the cold war, but it was probably the one that firmly established the belligerence of the United States and the Soviet Union toward each other. President Truman responded by ordering supplies flown over East Germany to Berlin, daring the Russians to fire. At left, German workers unload fresh milk from an American plane. Below, children watch the arrival of a United States aircraft. The blockade, lifted in 1949, was a blunder: it made the Germans objects of sympathy. Inadvertently, the Russians had boosted West Germany onto the road to postwar recovery.

At left and right are two souvenirs of the greatest upset in presidential election history, a Truman pen
and a premature newspaper. Below, Truman speaks
at a whistle-stop in Idaho—the kind of gathering
that forged the unexpected victory in 1948. It was
probably in the Farm Belt that his "give-'em-hell"
tactics worked best. Congress had not provided ade-
quate storage bins for the abundant crops. "When
you have to sell your grain below the support price
because you have no place to store it," Truman
harangued, "you can thank this same Republican
Congress." The farmers, who were enjoying their
greatest prosperity in thirty years, played safe and
stuck with President Truman and the Democrats.

Friend of the People
HARRY S. TRUMAN
J. DOYLE DEWITT COLLECTION

"WHAT A LIFE!"

Had dinner by myself tonight . . ." Truman noted in 1949. "Barnett in tails and white tie pulls out my chair, pushes me up to the table. John in tails and white tie brings me a fruit cup, Barnett takes the empty cup. John brings me a plate, Barnett brings me a tenderloin. John brings me asparagus, Barnett brings me carrots and beets. . . . Barnett takes the plate and butter plates. John comes in with a napkin and silver crumb tray—there are no crumbs but John has to brush them off the table anyway. . . . Barnett brings me some chocolate custard. John brings me a demitasse (at home a little cup of coffee—about two good gulps) and my dinner is over. I take a hand bath in the finger bowl and go back to work. What a life!" Whatever Truman might have felt about the formality of presidential dining, he had fought the fight of his life to retain his job. No one—except himself—had thought he would remain in the White House. He had, a year before, run for reelection against a confident Thomas E. Dewey, and he had run with his own party divided, its left and right wings having bolted. But, on that 1949 evening, it was Harry Truman who responded when the butler said, "Mr. President, dinner is served."

MEN OF INFLUENCE

ARTHUR H. VANDENBERG

Senator Arthur H. Vandenberg's "long day's journey into our times" (in Dean Acheson's words) began in the heartland of isolationism. An influential Republican newspaper editor in his native Michigan, Vandenberg was appointed to fill a vacant Senate seat in 1928 and was subsequently elected to four full terms. He opposed lend-lease but altered his stance after the attack on Pearl Harbor, a day that "ended isolationism for any realist." His conversion to internationalism was gradual, however, and his support of Roosevelt's and of Truman's foreign policies was not unqualified—especially regarding some aspects of America's postwar involvement abroad. Acheson noted a certain "ritual of statesmanship" in Vandenberg's position on such projects as the United Nations Relief and Rehabilitation Administration and the Marshall Plan—first "opposition," then "gestation," and finally a demand for political concessions before giving his full and weighty stamp of approval. A delegate to the United Nations in 1945 and an adviser at the Paris conference of foreign ministers in 1946, Vandenberg became chairman of the Senate Committee on Foreign Affairs. He introduced a resolution stating America's "determination . . . to exercise the right of individual *or collective* self-defense," the basis for United States participation in NATO. Vandenberg died in office in 1951.

SAM RAYBURN

"They don't make them like that any more," was John F. Kennedy's apt remark as he left the bedside of a moribund Sam Rayburn in the fall of 1961. "Mr. Sam" was elected to the first of a record twenty-five consecutive congressional terms in 1912; he was Speaker of the House for seventeen years, more than doubling Henry Clay's tenure. Tennessee-born and Texas-raised, Rayburn knew poverty firsthand. His father told him, "Character is all I have to give you. Be a man." Rayburn worked his way through college and prepared for service on Capitol Hill with six years in the state legislature. Though a staunch Democrat, he was justly noted for his skill at persuasion and constructive compromise. In 1941 Congress was ready to kill the draft; Rayburn marshaled all his resources and saved it—by one vote—four months before Pearl Harbor. He led the postwar fight against isolationism, which could only "break the hearts of the world." Permanent chairman of three Democratic National Conventions, he was one of the most powerful men in government (he did some of his best politicking at informal "Rayburn Board of Education" sessions in his office). Once he was asked how he could remember all the promises he had made—or had refused to make. "If you tell the truth the first time," answered the Speaker of the House, "you don't have to remember."

ALL: WIDE WORLD

DEAN ACHESON

In 1945 Under Secretary of State Dean Acheson said he had "no objective reason to suppose" that the vital interests of the United States and Russia would ever conflict. By 1949, just after he became head of the Department of State, he (along with millions of Americans) had changed his stance. He then saw communism as "economically fatal to free society and to human rights and fundamental freedoms." Over the next four years Acheson confirmed his commitment to this stiffer view. He helped create NATO and engineered the 1951 peace treaty with Japan; he supported the European Defense Community and implemented President Truman's policies in Korea. Acheson, who had attended Groton, Yale, and Harvard Law School, had been appointed under secretary of the treasury in 1933; opposed to F. D. R.'s gold-purchase plan, he was back in private practice inside of a year. In 1941, however, he became assistant secretary of state. He soon helped secure congressional passage of the lend-lease bill and, later, of the Bretton Woods Monetary Agreement. In 1946 he headed the committee that produced the Acheson-Lilienthal report, on which Bernard Baruch based his proposal for international control of atomic energy. Acheson returned to private practice in 1953; during the fifties he wrote a number of books on statecraft.

BERNARD M. BARUCH

"Most Presidents have received more advice than they can possibly use," wrote Harry S. Truman in his *Memoirs*. "But Baruch is the only man to my knowledge who has built a reputation on a self-assumed unofficial status as 'adviser.'" A millionaire at the age of thirty, financier Bernard M. Baruch left Wall Street in 1916 to advise President Wilson on national defense. He was chairman of the War Industries Board during World War I and later participated in the peace negotiations at Versailles. Between the world wars he helped to formulate policy on agriculture, neutrality, and defense, and in 1943 he was made special adviser to the Office of War Mobilization. In 1946 President Truman appointed him United States representative to the United Nations Atomic Energy Commission, in which capacity he presented the American plan for an international ban on atomic weapons. "We must elect World Peace or World Destruction," he warned in his opening statement. Russia's rejection of the plan was one of Baruch's greatest disappointments. "It took four years to win the war," wrote the aging statesman in 1960, "but in the fifteen years since, we have not yet been able to win the peace." Resigning from the commission in 1947, Baruch continued to serve the government in his capacity as an unofficial adviser. He died at ninety-five in June, 1965.

RENOVATIONS

White House social life under the close-knit Trumans was lively and informal and, thanks to Margaret's policy of being "at home" to all her school friends, youth oriented. In 1947, however, the Mansion's various creaks and tremblings and sagging second floor began to worry Truman, and when some beams gave way under the weight of Margaret's piano, he secured a congressional appropriation to thoroughly renovate the whole place. The President had an impressive knowledge of architecture and kept a close watch on all the reconstruction. While the work was being done the Trumans moved across the street to Blair House, where, in 1950, two Puerto Rican national-

ists tried to kill the President. Truman was unhurt, but one Secret Service man and one would-be assassin were killed. The surviving gunner was sentenced to execution, but Truman commuted the sentence to life imprisonment. When the White House was ready for occupancy again, Margaret was around less; she had begun to try to build a career as a concert singer. When Truman was widely criticized for writing a blunt, bitter letter to a critic who had reviewed one of his daughter's performances harshly, the President wrote in his diary: "I'm accused of putting my baby who is the apple of my eye in a bad position. I don't think that is so. She doesn't either—thank the Almighty."

Blair House (above) was home for the Trumans for more than three years. From there the President took his famous morning strolls at a pace so quick that younger aides and reporters found it difficult to keep up.

With the White House being gutted and rebuilt (left), Mrs. Truman entertained guests in the Blair House sitting room (above).

Seated above is Alger Hiss, a State Department official who was convicted of perjury for denying old Communist ties. At right, Dean Acheson, with Truman and Alben Barkley, signs the NATO pact. Far right: victorious Chinese Communists in 1949.

SAUVONS LES ROSENBERG

MAGNUM/HENRI CARTIER BRESSON

WIDE WORLD

CONTAINMENT
AND HYSTERIA

World War II had been won because the Allies had subordinated their special interests to create unity. Capitalist and Communist, Chiang Kai-shek and Mao Tse-tung, Winston Churchill and Joseph Stalin, Greek monarchist and Greek rebel—all had fought together to break the back of the German, Italian, and Japanese aggressors. But postwar misunderstandings, naïveté, and distrust destroyed the inspiring unity quickly. As the Soviet sphere enlarged, as Mao and Chiang refused to cooperate and warred again, and as United States-Soviet Union relations deteriorated, the American people fidgeted. President Truman developed an effective containment policy, restricting Russian expansion and dealing with the Berlin blockade effectively, but the tension grew. Some voices in Congress began blaming the administration for all the tension—in effect, for all the world's troubles. Communist expansion, they said—wherever it occurred—was the result of "disloyalty" in American government. One of the nation's periodic witch hunts began. When Russia exploded an atomic bomb—its development had been facilitated by the treason of Klaus Fuchs in Britain and the Rosenbergs in the United States—and the Communists drove Chiang Kai-shek from the Chinese mainland, the hysteria at home worsened. It was, as one thing led to another and McCarthyism emerged, almost farcical: somebody knew someone who said so-and-so had married the sister of a French Communist, and soon so-and-so lost his job. Truman implored his countrymen not to "play it safe," not to hesitate to speak out on controversial issues. But playing it safe became the rule for many Americans for almost a decade.

At left, Parisians demonstrate vainly to save Ethel and Julius Rosenberg, convicted in 1951 of having given atomic secrets to Russia. They were the only American traitors ever executed in peacetime.

"THE GREATEST
LIVING AMERICAN"

I have no feelings," George Catlett Marshall told Dean Acheson in 1947, "except a few which I reserve for Mrs. Marshall." Joseph McCarthy agreed. Charging in 1951 that the general was a Communist-dominated traitor, the senator from Wisconsin asserted that Marshall "would sell his grandmother for any advantage." The charge, of course, was ridiculous. Despite his poor health, Marshall had been quietly serving his country for years while yearning for a retirement that America could not afford to let him have.

McCarthy's "man steeped in falsehood" had been promoted over thirty-four senior officers to the post of Army chief of staff by President Franklin D. Roosevelt, and he had been the principal military strategist for all Allied operations in Europe and the Pacific during World War II. The man who McCarthy said was party to "a conspiracy so immense and an infamy so black as to dwarf any previous venture in the history of man" was, after the war, immediately pressed into service by President Truman, who asked him to tackle the frustrating and hopeless job of trying to make peace between the warring Nationalist and Communist forces in China. The hard-working soldier turned statesman —whose activities as Truman's Secretary of State from 1947 to 1949, McCarthy held, were "invariably serving the world policy of the Kremlin"—helped the President to formulate the containment policy that halted Russian expansion and the Marshall Plan that revitalized Europe. As Secretary of Defense in 1950 and 1951, Marshall rebuilt the armed forces, equipping them to deal with Communist aggression during the Korean conflict.

Actually, both Marshall and McCarthy had lied. While Secretary of State, Marshall told Acheson, his major associate, that he had no feelings so that Acheson would not hesitate to criticize the State Department. McCarthy lied, political commentator Richard H. Rovere has written, to demonstrate that not even the most "unassailable" American was immune to his inquisition. He succeeded in muddying the chaste reputation of the man who Truman said was "the greatest living American."

Born in Uniontown, Pennsylvania, in 1880, Marshall began his Army career in 1901, after graduating from the Virginia Military Institute. Serving in the Philippines from 1913 to 1916, he was called by his commanding officer "the greatest military genius since Stonewall Jackson." During World War I he was instrumental in plotting the successful strategy of the St. Mihiel and Meuse-Argonne offensives. His administrative skills were bolstered by an extraordinary ability to recognize talent—one of the reasons why Roosevelt elevated him to the number one military position during World War II. It was General Marshall who recommended that Dwight D. Eisenhower be appointed— over three hundred and sixty-six senior officers—to command the United States forces in Europe.

In 1952, however, when Ike was running for the Presidency, he gave Marshall what was probably his most stinging slap in the face: Eisenhower refused to condemn McCarthy's assault on his old mentor. The retirement that Marshall had so long sought was finally his after Eisenhower's election. But both Eisenhower and the American people who had put up with the vilification of one of their greatest men were reminded of George Catlett Marshall's achievements when he was awarded the Nobel Prize for Peace in 1953, five years before his death.

George C. Marshall, painted by Thomas E. Stephens

MISCALCULATIONS

Early in 1950, when Secretary of State Dean Acheson defined the United States "defense perimeter" in the Far East, he excluded the Republic of South Korea. Korea, strategists had decided, was not worth defending. But in June, when troops from Communist North Korea crossed the thirty-eighth parallel and invaded the South, the strategists realized that they had miscalculated. It was probable that the North Koreans had been goaded by Red China, which was anxious to flex its international muscles. If Truman's containment policy was to mean anything, it would have to apply to Asia as well as to Europe. With the sanction of the United Nations, Truman appointed General Douglas MacArthur to command the United Nations troops (sixteen nations sent men, but 90 per cent of the soldiers were American). When the Chinese swarmed across the Yalu River in November —despite the general's repeated assurances that China would not enter the war—MacArthur diverted attention from his miscalculation by demanding permission to bomb China. Leaders of both the United States and the United Nations were certain that that would lead to World War III and refused. But MacArthur also miscalculated the nature of his chief, Harry Truman. The general continued to issue public statements and to write to sympathetic Republican congressmen. Ordered to refrain, he persisted, and Truman fired him. He came home to a hero's welcome and made a stirring speech to Congress. But the Constitution supported the President, and so did most military men. As General Omar Bradley testified, to attack China would have involved "us in the wrong war, at the wrong place, at the wrong time and with the wrong enemy."

Officially, the conflict in Korea was not a war; it was a "police action" by United Nations forces. At right, American soldiers cautiously search enemy huts for North Korean or Chinese guerrillas.

At their Wake Island meeting (above) in October, 1950, General Douglas MacArthur assured President Truman that Red China was not going to intervene in Korea. But on November 26, hordes of Chinese crossed the Yalu and swarmed over United Nations lines. Although the safe-conduct passes (below) dropped among enemy troops caused some defections, they had little effect on what MacArthur called the "bottomless well of Chinese manpower."

SAFE CONDUCT PASS

SOLDIERS OF THE UN FORCES:
This certificate guarantees good treatment to any enemy soldier desiring to cease fighting. Take this man to your nearest officer and treat him as an honorable prisoner of war.

Douglas M. Arthur
DOUGLAS MacARTHUR
General of the Army
Commander-in-Chief

대한민국 병사에게
이것은 적의 군인으
로서 누구나 항복하기를
원하는 자에게 인도되며
이 사람들을 가까이
오를 봉하는 증명이다
이 사람을 먼저
스로좀 폴로 대우하시오
백아더장군
명령

TRUMAN'S ADVERSARIES

UNITED PRESS INTERNATIONAL

LIBRARY OF CONGRESS

JOHN L. LEWIS

"He who tooteth not his own horn," said John Llewellyn Lewis, "the same shall not be tooted." And tooting his own horn—to a score that was often at great variance with the one being read by the conductor of the national orchestra—the labor leader with a flair for drama was a famous public figure during and after the New Deal. Born in Lucas, Iowa, in 1880, he became, at the age of seventeen, a coal miner, like his Welsh father. Lewis was a talented organizer and speaker; before he was thirty he was president of a United Mine Workers local in Illinois, and by 1920 he was head of the four-hundred-thousand-member national union. His leadership was at first conservative; he was a Republican, and the twenties were years of normalcy. The United Mine Workers shrank to about a quarter of its former size. But Lewis revitalized the union during the New Deal, and he and it became increasingly influential forces in national affairs. He tormented Presidents Roosevelt and Truman with defiance, sarcasm, and strike after strike, especially during World War II, which he seemed to view mainly as a chance to build union power. "Well, you have to admit," said F. D. R. (whose election Lewis had supported only once—in 1936), "Lewis has done a lot for the miners." Lewis, whose heavy eyebrows made him a favorite of cartoonists, retired in 1960.

HENRY WALLACE

During his twenty years in national politics Henry Wallace underwent a drastic ideological metamorphosis—and, finally, a dramatic reversal. Born in Iowa, he was a Republican and editor of the influential *Wallaces' Farmer* from 1924 until 1933, when F. D. R., whom he had supported, named him Secretary of Agriculture. Wallace supervised the controversial Agricultural Adjustment Administration, which hiked farm prices by a systematic destruction of produce. Conservative Democrats protested when F. D. R. chose him as the vice presidential candidate in 1940 ("Just because the Republicans have nominated an apostate Democrat," said one, "let us not for God's sake nominate an apostate Republican"), but Wallace was nominated and elected. In addition to making a number of wartime good-will tours, he headed two important economic bodies, but he had little influence with the Senate. He openly sympathized with Russia and was dropped from the ticket in 1944. Wallace then served as Secretary of Commerce but was dismissed for criticizing President Truman's "get tough" policy toward the U.S.S.R. Joining the Progressives, Wallace ran for the Presidency in 1948; four years later he published "Why I Was Wrong," an explanation of his new enmity toward Stalin's Soviet Union. An eminent plant geneticist, Wallace retired and turned to farming; he died in 1965.

J. STROM THURMOND

Senator J. Strom Thurmond of South Carolina was described by *Time* magazine as "one of the Senate's deepest-dyed conservatives and most colorful characters." A former lawyer, state legislator, and circuit judge, Thurmond was elected governor of South Carolina on the Democratic ticket in 1946, and two years later ran for the Presidency as the candidate of the States' Rights party. The governor's Southern followers, popularly known as the Dixiecrats, had bolted the Democratic party when its candidate, Harry S. Truman, had come out for a strong civil rights platform. Unabashedly opposing any program of "social equality by Federal fiat," Thurmond captured four Southern states and received a popular vote of 1,169,063. Entering the United States Senate as a Democrat in 1955, he set a filibuster record two years later in a one-man battle against civil rights legislation. In 1962 he set off a congressional investigation with charges that the State Department was "muzzling" the military, which alone had a real "understanding of the Communist threat." Having gone about as far right as possible within the Democratic party, Senator Thurmond supported Barry Goldwater for the Presidency in 1964. Firmly ensconced in the Republican right wing, he remained, as the *New Republic* commented in 1965, "a determined defender of lost causes. . . ."

DOUGLAS MacARTHUR

When Douglas MacArthur promised to return to the Philippines after the Japanese had forced him to retreat in 1942, he was displaying both the dedicated courage that made him an effective general and the egocentricity that his critics decried. The top scholar in the West Point class of 1903, MacArthur had served first in the Far East and had then participated valiantly in the Meuse-Argonne campaign of World War I. After three years as superintendent at West Point and further service in the Far East, he became a full general. In 1930 he was named Army chief of staff. MacArthur retired in 1937 but was recalled in 1941 to head the Far East command. In May, 1942, his forces began the long drive to retake the Philippines—and in October, 1944, the general, true to his word, waded ashore at Leyte. Awarded a fifth star in 1944, he received Japan's surrender on September 2, 1945. He then oversaw the occupation of Japan and in 1950 took command of the United Nations forces in Korea. Because MacArthur publicly criticized American and United Nations policies in Korea, Truman relieved him of command in 1951. Accorded a hero's welcome by the American people, he was considered a presidential prospect, but the Republicans chose Eisenhower. MacArthur became chairman of Remington Rand, Incorporated, and died in 1964.

RESPONSIBILITIES

In retirement, Harry Truman often acted the curmudgeon—perhaps to conceal the fact that he was becoming a mellow old gentleman who genuinely liked people. Journalist Eric Sevareid discovered in 1964 that there was a side to Truman that was seldom noticed. "We were aware," he wrote, "of his sensitivity about the institution of the presidency . . . [and] lack of sensitivity to criticism of himself.

Back home in Independence, Truman (above) set up a library, wrote his memoirs, answered mail, and dismissed suggestions that he had been a great President. In 1961 he visited Washington and played the piano for John F. Kennedy and his guests (right).

MAGNUM/ELLIOTT ERWITT

What we were not aware of . . . was his sensitivity about the feelings of other people." Once, Sevareid elaborated, Truman, who was speaking to a college audience, had admonished a student for referring to the governor of the state as a "local yokel." Instantly Truman "realized how a public scolding by a former President could mark and mar the boy's inner life and his standing in the community." So he sought out the boy, re- assured him, and followed, as a friend, his scholastic progress and later career. Truman's kindness gave Sevareid "an insight to the responsibilities of a President that I did not have, and it has immeasurably added to my own residue of memories about the man from Missouri. . . . He may live to be 100— his is strong stock—but this, I know, is the specific memory that will return to me when his time does come."

FACTS IN SUMMARY: HARRY S. TRUMAN

CHRONOLOGY

UNITED STATES		TRUMAN
Cleveland elected President	1884	Born May 8
Sherman Antitrust Act	1890	Moves to Independence
Cleveland re-elected	1892	Enters elementary school
War with Spain	1898	
McKinley assassinated / Theodore Roosevelt becomes President	1901	Graduates from high school / Works as timekeeper for railroad
	1902	Works for Kansas City Star
Elkins Act	1903	Becomes bank clerk in Kansas City
	1905	Joins Missouri National Guard
Pure Food and Drug Act	1906	Works on father's farm
Wilson elected President	1912	
War with Germany	1917	Elected first lieutenant in National Guard regiment
Battle of Belleau Wood / Second Battle of the Marne / World War I ends	1918	Commands Battery D, 129th Field Artillery, with rank of captain / Fights at St. Mihiel, Meuse-Argonne, Sommedieu
Eighteenth Amendment ratified	1919	Marries Bess Wallace / Opens haberdashery
Capper-Volstead Act	1922	Elected judge of county court for Eastern District, Jackson County, Mo.
	1924	Loses bid for re-election
	1926	Elected presiding judge of county court, Jackson County, Mo.
Hoover elected President	1928	
Stock market crash	1929	
Roosevelt elected President	1932	
New Deal measures	1933	
National Labor Relations Board created	1934	Elected to U.S. Senate
Works Progress Administration created / Social Security established	1935	
Roosevelt re-elected	1936	
Roosevelt attempts to increase Supreme Court membership	1937	
World War II begins in Europe	1939	
Roosevelt re-elected	1940	Re-elected to Senate
Pearl Harbor bombed / U.S. declares war on Japan	1941	Appointed chairman of Senate Committee to Investigate the National Defense Program
Battle of Midway	1942	
Allies invade Italy	1943	
Allied invasion of Normandy / Roosevelt re-elected	1944	Elected Vice President
Roosevelt dies / Germany surrenders / United Nations Charter signed / Atomic bombs dropped on Hiroshima and Nagasaki / Japan surrenders	1945	Becomes President / Attends Potsdam Conference / Orders A-bombs dropped on Japan / Appoints Nuremberg Trials justices
Atomic Energy Commission established / Paris Peace Conference	1946	Recommends statehood for Alaska and Hawaii / Seizes railroads and coal mines / Proclaims Philippine independence
Taft-Hartley Act passed over presidential veto	1947	Issues Truman Doctrine / Establishes Marshall Plan
Berlin Airlift	1948	Elected President
NATO pact signed	1949	Formulates Point Four program
Korean War begins / U.N. sanctions U.S. action in Korea / Internal Security Act passed over veto	1950	Sends U.S. troops to Korea to repel Communist invasion / Vetoes Internal Security Act
Japanese Peace Treaty signed	1951	Relieves MacArthur of Far East command
Eisenhower elected President / Supreme Court declares seizure of steel mills illegal / Bricker amendment	1952	Seizes steel mills to prevent strike / Warns against danger of McCarthyism
Eisenhower inaugurated / Korean War armistice	1953	Retires to Independence
Eisenhower re-elected	1956	Publishes memoirs
Federal troops sent to Little Rock, Ark.	1957	Presents Truman Library to National Archives
Kennedy elected President	1960	Supports Stuart Symington for presidential nomination
Kennedy assassinated / Johnson becomes President	1963	
Intensification of war in Vietnam	1966	

BIOGRAPHICAL FACTS

BIRTH: Lamar, Mo., May 8, 1884

ANCESTRY: Scotch-English

FATHER: John Anderson Truman; b. Jackson County, Mo., Dec. 5, 1851; d. Grandview, Mo., Nov. 3, 1914

FATHER'S OCCUPATION: Farmer

MOTHER: Martha Ellen Young Truman; b. Jackson County, Mo., Nov. 25, 1852; d. Grandview, Mo., July 26, 1947

BROTHER: Vivian (1886–1965)

SISTER: Mary Jane (1889–   )

WIFE: Elizabeth Virginia Wallace; b. Independence, Mo., Feb. 13, 1885

MARRIAGE: Independence, Mo., June 28, 1919

CHILD: Margaret (1924–   )

EDUCATION: Graduated from public high school

RELIGIOUS AFFILIATION: Baptist

OCCUPATIONS BEFORE PRESIDENCY: Railroad timekeeper; bank clerk; farmer; haberdasher

MILITARY SERVICE: Missouri National Guard; captain in 129th Field Artillery (1918–1919)

PRE-PRESIDENTIAL OFFICES: County Judge for Eastern District of Jackson County, Mo.; Presiding Judge, County Court, Jackson County, Mo.; United States Senator; Vice President

AGE AT INAUGURATION: 60

OCCUPATION AFTER PRESIDENCY: Writer

FIRST ADMINISTRATION

INAUGURATION: April 12, 1945; the White House, Washington, D.C.

SECRETARY OF STATE: Edward R. Stettinius; James F. Byrnes (from July 3, 1945); George C. Marshall (from Jan. 21, 1947)

SECRETARY OF THE TREASURY: Henry Morgenthau, Jr.; Fred M. Vinson (from July 23, 1945); John W. Snyder (from June 25, 1946).

SECRETARY OF DEFENSE (Department created in September, 1947): James V. Forrestal

SECRETARY OF WAR: Henry L. Stimson; Robert P. Patterson (from Sept. 27, 1945); Kenneth C. Royall (from July 25, 1947—Department disbanded in September, 1947)

ATTORNEY GENERAL: Francis Biddle; Thomas C. Clark (from July 1, 1945)

POSTMASTER GENERAL: Frank C. Walker; Robert E. Hannegan (from July 1, 1945); Jesse M. Donaldson (from Dec. 16, 1947)

SECRETARY OF THE NAVY: James V. Forrestal (Department disbanded in September, 1947)

SECRETARY OF THE INTERIOR: Harold L. Ickes; Julius A. Krug (from March 18, 1946)

SECRETARY OF AGRICULTURE: Claude R. Wickard; Clinton P. Anderson (from June 30, 1945); Charles F. Brannan (from June 2, 1948)

SECRETARY OF COMMERCE: Henry A. Wallace; W. Averell Harriman (from Jan. 28, 1947); Charles Sawyer (from May 6, 1948)

SECRETARY OF LABOR: Frances Perkins; Lewis B. Schwellenbach (from July 1, 1945); Maurice J. Tobin (from Aug. 13, 1948)

SUPREME COURT APPOINTMENTS: Harold H. Burton (1945); Fred M. Vinson, Chief Justice (1946)

79th CONGRESS (January 3, 1945–January 3, 1947):
Senate: 56 Democrats; 38 Republicans; 1 Other
House: 242 Democrats; 190 Republicans; 2 Others
80th CONGRESS (January 3, 1947–January 3, 1949):
Senate: 51 Republicans; 45 Democrats
House: 245 Republicans; 188 Democrats; 1 Other

ELECTION OF 1948

CANDIDATES	ELECTORAL VOTE	POPULAR VOTE
Harry S. Truman Democratic	303	24,105,812
Thomas E. Dewey Republican	189	21,970,065
Strom Thurmond States' Rights	39	1,169,063
Henry Wallace Progressive	—	1,157,172
Norman Thomas Socialist	—	139,414
Claude A. Watson Prohibition	—	103,224

SECOND ADMINISTRATION

INAUGURATION: January 20, 1949; the Capitol, Washington, D.C.

VICE PRESIDENT: Alben W. Barkley

SECRETARY OF STATE: Dean G. Acheson

SECRETARY OF THE TREASURY: John W. Snyder

SECRETARY OF DEFENSE: James V. Forrestal; Louis A. Johnson (from March 28, 1949); George C. Marshall (from Sept. 21, 1950); Robert A. Lovett (from Sept. 17, 1951)

ATTORNEY GENERAL: Thomas C. Clark; J. Howard McGrath (from Aug. 24, 1949); James P. McGranery (from May 27, 1952)

POSTMASTER GENERAL: Jesse M. Donaldson

SECRETARY OF THE INTERIOR: Julius A. Krug; Oscar L. Chapman (from Jan. 19, 1950)

SECRETARY OF AGRICULTURE: Charles F. Brannan

SECRETARY OF COMMERCE: Charles Sawyer

SECRETARY OF LABOR: Maurice J. Tobin

SUPREME COURT APPOINTMENTS: Thomas C. Clark (1949); Sherman Minton (1949)

81st CONGRESS (January 3, 1949–January 3, 1951):
Senate: 54 Democrats; 42 Republicans
House: 263 Democrats; 171 Republicans; 1 Other
82nd CONGRESS (January 3, 1951–January 3, 1953):
Senate: 49 Democrats; 47 Republicans
House: 234 Democrats; 199 Republicans; 1 Other

DWIGHT DAVID EISENHOWER

On June 23, 1942, a little-known fifty-one-year-old major general boarded a London-bound plane in Washington, D.C. He had recently been appointed to command the European Theater of Operations—ETO, the new military organization that formally signaled America's entry into the fight against Nazi Germany. Newspapermen who had done their homework had learned only that the officer was generally regarded as a technical expert, that he was genial and was well liked by his colleagues, and that his friends called him Ike.

So limited was the reputation of Dwight David Eisenhower in 1942 that he might well have been considered a secret weapon. But Great Britain, unimpressed by Ike's appointment, was given no reason to hold such a romantic hope. Except for the British Isles, Russia, and several neutral, or nominally neutral, nations, all Europe belonged to Hitler's Third Reich. To the east, the Russians had stopped the Germans before they reached Moscow, but the winter was over and the Germans were still deep in Soviet territory. To the south, on the sands of North Africa, English troops reeled under successive defeats administered by General Erwin Rommel; two days after Eisenhower arrived in London, Rommel crossed the border into Egypt. It could hardly escape the attention of the British that the man America had sent to reverse the course of the war was one whose military career was known only through the official mimeographed biography handed out by the United States War Department.

Eisenhower had graduated from West Point (at the bottom edge of the top third of his class) in 1915. During World War I he had commanded a tank-training school at Camp Colt, near Gettysburg, Pennsylvania. By the time he had turned twenty-seven, he had had some six thousand men under his

President Eisenhower in 1956

Dwight, extreme left, was about ten when the family sat for this portrait. Between David and Ida Eisenhower is Milton—with curls; Earl and Roy are to Ike's left in the second row; at top are Edgar and Arthur.

command and had become noted for his administrative ability.

From 1922 to 1924 he had served in the Panama Canal Zone as an executive officer for Brigadier General Fox Connor, who had compared Eisenhower favorably with a young major named George C. Marshall and had inspired Ike to continue studying strategy and the history of warfare. (Eisenhower had always been interested in those subjects. He had read about Hannibal during his high-school years, had analyzed the mistakes of the British as he had wandered over Revolutionary War battle sites near West Point while a student there, and had digested the lessons of the Battle of Gettysburg when he had been at Camp Colt.)

In 1925 Eisenhower entered the Command and General Staff School. Although he had previously been an average student, he graduated first in a class of two hundred and seventy-five, having been able to cope with the competitive pressures that drove other Command students to exhaustion, retirement, and even nervous breakdowns and suicide. In 1927 Ike was assigned to write a guide to the European battlefields of

World War I. It remains one of the best works on the war and is—in view of Eisenhower's syntax as President—remarkably articulate. From 1929 to 1932 he served as an assistant executive to the assistant secretary of war, and was then assigned to the staff of General Douglas MacArthur, the Army chief of staff, in Washington. From 1935 until Hitler attacked Poland in 1939, he was General MacArthur's assistant in the Philippines. Subsequently Eisenhower was assigned to various posts within the United States.

In September of 1941, in order to test the new Army the United States was training for the impending war, a mock battle was staged in Louisiana. Eisenhower was named chief of staff for the Third Army, which fought and won two battles against the Second Army. He had learned about tanks during World War I, he had learned to fly a plane in the Philippines, and he had always believed that mastery of these two weapons would determine the victor in any future war. It was the precise coordination between tanks and planes that won the battles in Louisiana. Two days after the victory,

Ike once figured out that the house in Abilene had 818 square feet (including this parlor); there were eight in the family, and his mother "not only managed to fit us all in, she used the space beautifully."

Eisenhower was promoted to the temporary rank of brigadier general.

Shortly after the attack on Pearl Harbor, Eisenhower was called to Washington to serve as an assistant chief of staff to George C. Marshall. He helped draft a global strategy for the war, followed this up with an outline for a cross-Channel invasion of the Continent, designed the ETO command that would carry out the strategies, and then boarded the plane to London.

His career seemed to have been respectable but not especially brilliant. Looking for some factor that might have accounted for Ike's appointment to the monumental ETO job, the journalists turned to his private life. Eisenhower, one of six sons of David and Ida Elizabeth Stover Eisenhower, had been born in Denison, Texas, on October 14, 1890. (A seventh son had died in early childhood.) When he was still an infant, his family moved to Abilene, Kansas, where he lived until he went to West Point. Ike's father, a mechanic in an Abilene creamery, held weekly Bible reading sessions; his mother was a Fundamentalist—and a pacifist. Although the sons were never religious, they

did absorb a profound belief in honesty and justice.

At the time of Eisenhower's birth, Abilene was only beginning to transform itself from a frontier cow town into a modern city of paved streets, sewers, streetcars, and telephones. The railroad tracks separated the well-to-do and the poor sections of town; Eisenhower lived on the wrong side of the tracks. There was a traditional rivalry between the boys who lived in the two sections, and every year a representative from each side met in a fist fight. When Eisenhower was fifteen, he engaged a boy named Wes Merrifield in such a contest. Merrifield was bigger and quicker, and the town's boys believed that Eisenhower would be knocked out in no time at all. After two full hours of fighting, however, Merrifield announced that he could not beat Eisenhower. Refusing to say that he could not beat Merrifield, Eisenhower reportedly admitted, "Well, Wes, I *haven't* licked you."

A few months after his fight with Merrifield, Eisenhower fell and skinned a knee. Blood poisoning developed and spread through his entire leg, and the doctor insisted

897

that amputation was necessary. According to a biographer, Kenneth S. Davis, Eisenhower told his brother Edgar to stand guard at his bed to prevent the doctor from operating: "You got to promise me you won't let 'em do it," he sobbed. "You got to promise. I won't be a cripple. I'd rather die." For two days and nights, Edgar stood by as the doctor warned David and Ida Eisenhower that Ike might die. When the infection subsided, the lesson was not lost on Eisenhower: sheer will was a strong weapon.

Although the sport most commonly associated with Eisenhower is golf, football was his favorite. At first he played in the line and then switched to left half at West Point. While tackling Jim Thorpe, he wrenched a knee and a week later broke the knee in another game. He never played again. (His friends at West Point would say later that they thought his inability to play football

was the greatest disappointment of his life.) Football is a sport of exacting teamwork—and "teamwork" and "cooperation" are two words that occur very often in Dwight Eisenhower's speeches and writings as general and President.

All the Eisenhower boys were expected to help support the family. As youngsters, they took the produce grown in their garden, put it in a wagon, and sold it on the north side of town. Later Eisenhower worked in the Abilene creamery, where he met Everett "Swede" Hazlett, Jr., a young man who had managed to earn an appointment to the United States Naval Academy. Swede suggested that it would be fun if Eisenhower joined him at Annapolis. Eisenhower agreed, and took the examinations for both Annapolis and West Point. It was, of course, West Point to which he was appointed.

Reporters who wrote about Eisenhower in June, 1942, were able to add that in the autumn of 1915, two weeks after he was posted to Fort Sam Houston in San Antonio, Texas, he met and courted Mamie Doud, a strikingly pretty brunette socialite from Denver. Four months later they became engaged, and on July 1, 1916, they were married. Their first son, born in 1917, died in 1921; a second boy, John, was born in 1922.

That first impressions count is attested to by Eisenhower's career. In 1942 the journalists created an image that has not changed materially. They found him to be likable, modest, kindly, and a good administrator—brilliant, if at all, only in tactical matters. Failing to discover anything about him that portended greatness, they portrayed him as a good man.

Of Eisenhower's command in World War II, little needs to be said. He led the invasions of North Africa, Sicily, and the Italian mainland, the cross-Channel invasion of France, and the defeat of the German armies beyond the Rhine. It has often been remarked that he was not a general but an

U.S. ARMY

In April of 1945, Generals Bradley, Patton, and Eisenhower, left to right, inspected art treasures stolen by the Nazis and cached in German salt mines.

In 1948 Secretary of Defense Forrestal sought the military views of the head of Columbia University.

administrator, not a strategist but a super-executive, not a great commander but a public relations expert who put over the biggest campaign of them all. But Eisenhower's role should not be underestimated. Although he was not a dashing, colorful general like Douglas MacArthur, it seems highly unlikely that a MacArthur, with all his bravura, could have welded together, as Eisenhower did, the Allied forces into a smooth, efficient war machine.

Eisenhower emerged from the war as the famous Ike, the military hero with the infectious grin who had led the troops to victory, and the personification of the good American who had overcome evil.

In Berlin in 1945, Eisenhower later wrote in *Mandate for Change*, "President Truman, riding with General Bradley and me . . . abruptly said that he would help me get anything I might want, including the Presidency in 1948." Eisenhower laughed and continued to laugh at such propositions for several years. After the war, he served as chief of staff, overseeing the demobilization of the American forces, a task he found "frankly distasteful."

As suggestions that he run for President became more persistent, Eisenhower noted that his "sense of humor was beginning to show signs of wear and tear." In 1948, just before the primaries, he wrote his famous letter to a newspaper publisher in New Hampshire, in which he stated that "the necessary and wise subordination of the military to civil power will be best sustained . . . when lifelong professional soldiers, in the absence of some obvious and overriding reasons, abstain from seeking high political office." Politics, he said, "is a profession; a serious, complicated, and, in its true sense, a noble one. . . . nothing in the international or domestic situation especially qualifies for the most important office in the world a man whose adult years have been spent in the country's military forces." It was a remarkable statement of principle from a military man—and, of course, it only made him more desirable to the electorate.

Also in 1948, Eisenhower's war memoirs, *Crusade in Europe*, were published, and they added to his fame and popularity. He served for two years as president of Columbia University in New York City, and was recalled to the Army in 1950 by President Truman to head the creation of military forces for the North Atlantic Treaty Organization, a job he completed with dispatch.

It may well have been the Korean War that placed Eisenhower in the Presidency. He deeply felt, as he had said and written, that the freedom won in World War II should be preserved and a better world created. His feelings coincided with those of most Americans. When in the fall of 1950 Chinese troops entered the Korean War and pushed the forces of the United Nations south of the thirty-eighth parallel, it seemed that all the gains won in the bloody years of World War II were to be lost. "At best," as Eisenhower wrote, "the prospects in Korea appeared to be for an eventual stalemate; at worst they boded . . . the beginning of World War III." Americans turned to the man who embodied the triumph of the last war; simply to place him in America's highest office seemed to reaffirm the permanence of its hard-fought-for values. In retrospect, political writers have tended to denigrate the voters' wish for a "father image," the need for "security." But the need was profound, and it was one to which Eisenhower—whether he possessed ambitions or not—could not fail to respond.

Once he had committed himself to the Presidency, his campaign was less a contest than a prolonged triumphal parade. He had repeatedly said that he had never been a political animal. There was, in fact, some question as to whether Eisenhower was a Republican or a Democrat. He permitted Senator Henry Cabot Lodge to announce that he was a Republican and promptly took the Republican nomination from Senator Robert A. Taft on the first ballot at the 1952 convention. The campaign was disappointing. Eisenhower remained genial but aloof, declining to engage in telling debate with his opponent, the witty and urbane Adlai Stevenson. Eisenhower spoke of the evil of Communist infiltration in the government, of corruption in Washington, and of the need to end the Korean War. He confined himself to lofty ideals: freedom in America and in the world; individualism and self-reliance; compassion for the weaker and less fortunate.

The most embarrassing moment in the campaign occurred when his running mate, Richard Nixon, had the charge of corruption turned against him. He was accused of having accepted a substantial sum of money from businessmen to finance his career. The episode was doubly embarrassing not because the accusation was true but because Nixon chose to tearfully defend himself, flanked by his wife, and his dog, Checkers, on nationwide television.

Eisenhower remained aloof from the controversy surrounding Senator Joseph R. McCarthy and from McCarthy's charge that Eisenhower's old friend and mentor, General Marshall, had been a pawn of the Communists. When Eisenhower declined to give McCarthy a roasting for the attack, and when he publicly embraced Senator William Jenner of Indiana, who had called Marshall "a living lie," he was severely criticized. He chose to wait, he told his friends, until McCarthy destroyed himself, insisting that it was McCarthyism, not McCarthy, that needed destroying—and that only McCarthy himself could destroy McCarthyism. It was a neat explanation, but Eisenhower always tried to shun difficult, emotion-charged situations. During the war, he had insisted that his officers argue out their differences of opinion among themselves rather than bring them to him.

His most successful campaign maneuver was his promise to go to Korea and end the war there if elected. The promise clinched what was probably already a certain victory. He carried all but nine states, trouncing Stevenson with a plurality of more than six million votes.

In his book *The Effective Executive*, Peter F. Drucker remarked that a perfectly efficient executive nearly always ends up by creating a tedious organization. Eisenhower, "the Great Delegator," came close to being a tedious administrator—and would have been, had not several of his aides turned out to be unpredictable.

He made his political liaison man, former New Hampshire Governor Sherman Adams, assistant to the President and gave him Cabinet rank. Eisenhower's critics have maintained that he surrendered too much of his power to Adams; Eisenhower, however, clearly felt that domestic politics required a Cabinet official in the same way that foreign affairs required a Secretary of State. His mistake was openly delegating great power to Adams. There was little grief when the latter finally tendered his resignation after it was discovered that he had accepted favors (including the famous vicuna coat) from a New England industrialist.

The most diverting man in Eisenhower's Cabinet was Charles E. Wilson, the Secretary of Defense. As the president of General Motors Corporation, he had accumulated several millions of dollars worth of General Motors stock and expected to receive cash and stock bonuses for four more years. In reviewing his appointment to the Cabinet, the Senate wondered aloud whether Wilson might be inclined to favor General Motors in government contracts because of his conflict of interest. "For years," Wilson replied, "I thought what was good for the country was good for General Motors and vice versa." Though Wilson was finally persuaded to divest himself of his stock, political pundits mocked him for years thereafter. In the hands of cartoonist Al Capp, his statement became a belligerent, self-satisfied "What's good for General Bullmoose is good for the country." With the help of Admiral Arthur W. Radford, chairman of the joint chiefs of staff, Wilson did a creditable job, unifying the armed forces and making them into a defense establishment capable of effecting the much-criticized policy of massive retaliation. He managed, too, to call the members of the National Guard a bunch of "draft dodgers" and to characterize the Suez Crisis as a mere "ripple." Although he may have been right, Wilson was an embarrassment to the administration and finally resigned at the beginning of President Eisenhower's second term.

The globe-trotting and moralistic John Foster Dulles, Eisenhower's Secretary of State, stated the most chilling of all cold-war policies in a *Life* magazine article in 1956: "The ability to get to the verge [of war] without getting into the war is the necessary art. . . . If you are scared to go to the brink, you are lost. We've had to look it square in the face—on the question of enlarging the Korean war, on the question of getting into the Indochina war, on the question of Formosa. We walked to the brink and we looked it in the face."

This was brinkmanship. It was in this context of "thinking about the unthinkable" that Herman Kahn was led to write *On Thermonuclear War*, which embraced the notion that one day Russia and the United States could trade the annihilation of Moscow for that of New York in a war lasting several minutes. It is some measure of the impact brinkmanship had on many Americans that some critics could greet Kahn as a moderate.

On July 26, 1953, a few months after Eisenhower took office, the Korean War was ended by armistice. It cannot be said that

Mamie's 1953 inaugural-ball gown was embroidered with over two thousand stones—all sewed on by hand.

Eisenhower ended the war, as he had promised in his campaign. The North Koreans and Chinese had already decided to stop fighting. It can be said, however, that Eisenhower resisted any temptation to move into North Korea, as South Korea's President Syngman Rhee was so anxious to do. In April, after the Communists had offered to resume peace talks, Rhee had written Eisenhower that South Korea would continue to fight. When Eisenhower scotched that idea, the Communists and the United Nations forces agreed on voluntary repatriation of prisoners of war—the greatest stumbling block in negotiations to that point—and began to discuss a cease-fire line. Then Rhee permitted twenty-five thousand anti-Communist North Korean prisoners to escape, and Eisenhower found it necessary in a press conference to remind a reporter: "The enemy is still in *North* Korea." A scorching letter to Rhee and the visit of a State Department aide finally brought forth Rhee's public promise to abide by an armistice—and the war was ended.

In *The Cold War As History*, Louis J. Halle called Dulles a "hard" and Eisenhower a "soft" in the Russian-American contest. Whereas Eisenhower worked tirelessly to reduce tensions between the two nations, Dulles, in his public utterances and diplomatic maneuvers, tended to draw the line separating the two nations more sharply. Ultimately, Eisenhower's attitudes can be said to have won out, but not before the fight against what was identified as a monolithic communism was carried into Asia. American money financed in large part the French struggle against Communists in Vietnam, and it was with great reluctance that Eisenhower declined to send troops to aid the French at Dienbienphu. Shortly after the French forces were defeated in 1954, the Southeast Asia Treaty Organization (SEATO) was established. The United States pledged that any armed attack against a member nation in Southeast Asia (including South Vietnam) "would endanger its own peace and safety." The treaty was one more extension of America's commitment to keep the peace;

by the time Eisenhower left office in 1961, that commitment had been extended to cover most of the earth.

On April 22, 1954, after many years of wrangling over false charges of subversion in the military forces, Joseph McCarthy was taken to task by his strongest opponent, the United States Army. Charles Wilson characterized McCarthy's attacks on the Army as "just damn tommyrot." Senator Ralph Flanders of Vermont remarked on the Senate floor: "He dons his war paint. He goes into his war dance. He emits his war whoops. He goes forth to battle and proudly returns with the scalp of a pink Army dentist. We may assume that this represents the depth of the seriousness of Communist penetration at this time."

The Army seized upon its own notion of a serious charge—that McCarthy's aide Roy M. Cohn had demanded special treatment for his former associate Private G. David Schine, under the threat that Cohn would "wreck the Army" if not satisfied. For a period of more than fifty days, the Army proceeded to wreck McCarthy in televised hearings in which doctored photographs were revealed, points of order were made, and, finally, as Eisenhower wrote, "a near fist fight [broke out] between Roy Cohn and the counsel for Democratic members of the subcom-

WIDE WORLD

The public was kept well informed of Eisenhower's progress during the medical crises of his two terms. Here the Walter Reed Hospital commandant, General Leonard Heaton, explains Ike's ileitis operation of 1956.

mittee." Eisenhower himself remained aloof from the proceedings, arguing (he was considerably more justified this time than he had been in his explanation for avoiding condemnation of McCarthy during the campaign) that the President should not wage war on a member of the legislature. McCarthy was condemned by the Senate on December 2 and died a broken and pathetic man three years later.

On May 17, 1954, the Supreme Court handed down its epochal decision that racial segregation in public schools was unconstitutional. It was with that decision that students began to march, picket, and riot for civil rights. Eisenhower had always been committed to "equality before the law of all citizens. . . ." To civil rights leaders, however, his response to the Supreme Court decision seemed minimal. Not until Governor Orval Faubus of Arkansas called out National Guard troops to prevent Negro students from entering Central High School in Little Rock in September, 1957, did Eisenhower act firmly. On only thirteen previous occasions had a President dispatched federal troops into a state to enforce federal law. But after rioting broke out in Little Rock, Eisenhower sent in one thousand paratroopers and federalized more than ten thousand National Guardsmen. Nothing of consequence was accomplished in Little Rock itself. But four days before Governor Faubus called out the National Guard, the first civil rights bill to pass Congress since 1875 had been approved, with President Eisenhower's blessing, authorizing a Civil Rights Commission. Civil rights, the most painful domestic problem, was brought into the open.

Although much of his foreign policy during his first four years solidified the hostility between America and Russia, Eisenhower nonetheless worked at reducing the tension. In one of his first speeches as President (to the American Society of Newspaper Editors on April 16, 1953), Eisenhower had said: "Every gun that is made, every warship launched, every rocket fired signifies, in the final sense, a theft from those who hunger and are not fed, those who are cold and are

Herblock's cartoon "With the Greatest of Ease" summed up the 1956 election. Ike's grip on the voters was firm, but his coattails could not carry other Republican aspirants. For the first time in over a century a re-elected President did not carry in majorities in both houses of the Congress.

© 1956, CARTOON FROM *Herblock's Special for Today*, SIMON & SCHUSTER, 1958

not clothed. . . . The cost of one modern heavy bomber is this: a modern brick school in more than thirty cities. . . . We pay for a single fighter plane with a half-million bushels of wheat. We pay for a single destroyer with new homes that could have housed more than eight thousand people." Humanity, he had said, hung from a "cross of iron." He had proposed universal disarmament.

During the presidential campaign, Eisenhower had pledged "peace and prosperity." As he left civil rights largely to the Supreme Court and to local authorities, and McCarthy to the Army, he left the engineering of prosperity to Secretary of the Treasury George Humphrey. In spite of Eisenhower's often-stated dislike for the welfare state, New Deal policies were continued. Ten million people were added to the Social Security rolls during his two terms; student loans were made available through the National Defense Education Act of 1958; and the Department of Health, Education, and Welfare was created.

The President himself concentrated on his search for peace, maneuvering around the "brinks" and over the "summits" of international diplomacy. It was the one area in which he took sufficient pains to create a novel proposal and to follow it up with his

BOTH: WIDE WORLD

Castro (above) took over Cuba early in 1959; that autumn the Khrushchevs (below) came to America.

Francis Gary Powers' trial as a U-2 spy in 1960 (below) dashed hopes for a thaw in the cold war.

SOVFOTO

own specific suggestions. "The United States pledges before you," he said in an address to the United Nations in December of 1953, "...its determination to help solve the fearful atomic dilemma—to devote its entire heart and mind to find the way by which the miraculous inventiveness of man shall not be dedicated to his death, but consecrated to his life." He proposed a stockpile of atomic materials for peaceful purposes. That proposal, along with his attempts to effect a disarmament treaty, died a-borning. His failure to make headway in what he considered his preeminent task resulted in the most subdued passage in Eisenhower's memoirs: "In the end our accomplishments were meager, almost negligible. . . . the most significant, possibly the only, achievement of the entire effort was the wider education of all civilized peoples in the growing need for disarmament. . . ." In this "bleak" defeat, Eisenhower admitted candidly, "I suffered my greatest disappointment."

Several months after the first of the Geneva Summit Conferences convened in 1955 and failed to produce any easing of cold-war tension, Eisenhower was struck with a coronary occlusion. He was hospitalized early on the morning of September 24, 1955, emerged a month later in bright red pajamas bearing the legend "Much Better, Thanks," and finally returned to the White House on November 11. His attack and temporary disability raised the question of how the business of the President was to be handled when he could not perform his duties, a question that would be resolved by a new constitutional amendment passed in 1967. It also raised the question of whether or not he would seek re-election in 1956. On February 29, 1956, he announced that "my answer will be positive, that is, affirmative." Then on June 7, he suffered an attack of ileitis that required an emergency operation. His two illnesses only enhanced the love the electorate bore him, and—after weathering a "dump Nixon" movement—the Eisenhower team was returned to office with a plurality over Adlai Stevenson, the Democratic candidate, of more than nine and a half million votes.

At the end of Eisenhower's first term the world witnessed one of the most pointless and tragic consequences of the misunderstandings of the cold war. On January 27, 1953, John Foster Dulles had announced by radio to the people of Eastern Europe that they could count on the United States for support in throwing off Soviet domination. A bill was introduced in Congress (it became known as the Captive Peoples Resolution) deploring "the forcible absorption of free peoples into an aggressive despotism." When Stalin died in March of that year, the resolution was shelved, but in April Eisenhower again called for "full independence of the East European nations." In June, however, when East Germans rioted, Eisenhower refused to intervene. Then the new Soviet leaders began to relax their hold on Eastern Europe, hoping that by easing the pressure on their captive nations they could avoid an explosion. In 1956 Khrushchev denounced Stalin and Stalinism at the Twentieth Party Congress and called, as Louis J. Halle has said, "for greater individual liberty." In April, 1956, the Cominform was dissolved, and in October Poland declared itself a neutral state. The Poles attested to their friendship with Russia—but gained some measure of dignity in their stand. In Hungary, meanwhile, all the signals from America and Russia were read incorrectly, and the Hungarians declared their own independence from Russia in November, 1956. The Red army (200,000 troops with 2,500 tanks and armored cars) moved into Budapest in the early morning of November 4 and did not leave until 32,000 people had been killed, more than 195,000 had fled their homeland, and Hungary had been returned to despotism. The two great powers, ever suspicious of each other and increasingly moralistic in their criticisms of each other, were laboring toward a *détente*. As they did so, they misled Hungary into a suicidal position—and drew back once again to their mutually hostile postures.

More than any other single event, the launching of Sputnik I on October 4, 1957, epitomized for many of the President's crit-ics a sense of drift in his second administration. It was not until 1954 that Eisenhower had had his "first intimation that the orbiting of an earth satellite was either feasible or desirable." Eisenhower could argue with some justification that America's lag in space exploration had begun with Truman. Yet the National Aeronautics and Space Administration was not set up until July of 1958—eight months after the Russians had launched two satellites.

Criticism intensified after the launching of Sputnik. America, it seemed, was on the defensive. Its foreign policy was a reaction to Russian initiative. Its domestic programs were responses to pressures from such groups as civil rights organizations. Its program for national defense lagged behind that of the Russians, allegedly producing a "missile gap." And its sense of adventure, represented by the exploration of space, was inert. Peace and freedom, it seemed, were slowly being eroded. Prosperity was shaky at best. (An "adjustment," or recession, began in late 1957.) The launching of Sputnik was taken to illustrate the inferiority of American education. Perhaps the most serious blow of all was psychological: it was the first time most Americans could remember that the United States was second best at something. It was a rude realization.

In November of 1957, Eisenhower suffered his third illness, a slight stroke. "Gradually," he wrote in 1960, "memory of words returned; the doctors pronounced me 95 per cent recovered and said that before long I should be completely cured. In this prediction they were not wholly accurate. From that time onward I have frequently experienced difficulty in prompt utterance of the word I seek. Even today, occasionally, I reverse syllables in a long word and at times am compelled to speak slowly and cautiously if I am to enunciate correctly. This is not, I am told, particularly noticeable to anyone else but it certainly is to me." It certainly was to others, too. Yet, Eisenhower's choice of words in speech (his writing had always been perfectly clear and had showed considerably more wit than his speeches) had never been distinguished. In the 1915 yearbook for West Point he had written a parody of his own manner of speaking: "Now, fellers, it's just like this. I've been asked to say a few words this evening about this business. Now, me and Walter Camp, we think. . . ."

In 1957, after the British, French, and Israelis had attacked Egypt because of President Nasser's seizure of the Suez Canal—and had been criticized by the United Nations and the United States—Eisenhower feared that the Middle East was open to a Communist take-over. To discourage such a power move, he promulgated what came to be known as the Eisenhower Doctrine, which stated that America would aid, financially and militarily, any country in the Middle East threatened by any other country "controlled by international communism." Thus in July, 1958, President Chamoun of Lebanon requested American forces to fend off an armed rebellion that he said had been instigated by Nasser. Ike sent the Sixth Fleet and more than fourteen thousand soldiers and Marines to Lebanon, and the crisis abated. In October, American troops were withdrawn, having proved, Ike said, "in a truly practical way that the United States was capable of supporting its friends."

Ike approached another small brink in the late summer of 1958 over Quemoy and Matsu, the offshore islands that the Communist Chinese had bombarded in 1954 and chose to shell again that August. The Nationalist Chinese had been building up forces on the islands, and it is likely that the Communists wished only to test American determination in the area. They eventually lost interest and ceased shelling the islands, "except upon unusual or ceremonial occasions," as Eisenhower wrote. They permitted, in this "Gilbert and Sullivan war," the Chinese Nationalists to resupply the islands by convoy on the odd-numbered days of the month.

Eisenhower's final attempt at a Summit Conference was set for May 16, 1960. "From the autumn of 1959 to the spring of 1960," Eisenhower wrote in *Waging Peace*, "most people of the Western world felt that a slight but discernible thaw was developing in the icy tensions . . . between the West and the Soviet Union. This impression resulted partially from Mr. Khrushchev's agreement at Camp David to remove his threat to end the presence of Allied forces in West Berlin." On May 1 a high-flying U-2 reconnaissance plane was shot down over Russia. Five days later Premier Khrushchev informed the Supreme Soviet that crucial parts of the plane were in Soviet hands, that the equipment clearly indicated the U-2 was an espionage plane, and that the pilot, Francis Gary Powers, also captured, had admitted as much. Eventually Ike acknowledged the truth but did not express regrets. The Summit collapsed, and Eisenhower gradually drew back into his role of elder statesman as Vice President Nixon carried the Republican standard into battle against John F. Kennedy.

Before he retired to Gettysburg with his wife, Eisenhower took upon himself one more important duty, that of warning the nation of the "conjunction of an immense military establishment and a large arms industry," which, he said, was "new in the American experience." "We recognize the imperative need for this development," he said in his Farewell Address. "Yet we must not fail to comprehend its grave implications. Our toil, resources, and livelihood are all involved; so is the very structure of our society. In the councils of government we must guard against the acquisition of unwarranted influence, whether sought or unsought, by the military-industrial complex. The potential for the disastrous rise of misplaced power exists and will persist. We must never let the weight of this combination endanger our liberties or democratic processes. We should take nothing for granted."

If to many historians the Eisenhower years seem years of drift and indifference, it can be said as well that Eisenhower took a nation utterly fatigued from depression and two wars, frightened of nuclear holocaust, and riven with doubt about its heritage and destiny, and kept it safe and alive until it was ready to deal with life with a new-found, youthful vigor.

—CHARLES L. MEE, JR.

Dwight D. Eisenhower

A PICTURE PORTFOLIO

*One of the most familiar—and straightfor-
ward—slogans in American campaign history*

Young Dwight (foreground above) and pals often went on fishing trips; below, he is seen as a cadet in 1915. In 1932 he was an aide to General Douglas MacArthur (right). "I studied dramatics under him for five years in Washington and four in the Philippines," remarked Eisenhower.

A SMALL-TOWN BOY

During Dwight Eisenhower's youth, Abilene, Kansas, was the quintessence of a rural American town. Situated near the precise geographical center of the country, it was placid, law-abiding, churchgoing. "Self-sufficiency, personal initiative, and responsibility were prized," recalled Ike's brother Milton; "radicalism was unheard of." Dwight's boyhood was a normal blend of ups and downs, of pleasure and pain. He learned the value of a dollar through the hard work it took to get one. He fought with boys from the other side of town—but they all jammed into Cecil Brooks's telegraph office to get inning-by-inning reports on World Series games. In the spring of 1903, Ike and some friends took a piece of sidewalk planking and floated down Buckeye Street, which was filled with flood waters. They were well on their way to the rampaging Smoky Hill River when they were rescued, and Ike found that initial parental relief soon gave way to punishment. In school Ike hated algebra, liked spelling and arithmetic, and struggled with penmanship. His studies stood him in good stead when he applied to West Point. (Her son safely on the Academy-bound train, pacifist Ida Eisenhower cried for the first time in Milton's memory.) On Valentine's Day of 1916 Ike proposed to Mamie Doud, and on their wedding day a few months later he was promoted to first lieutenant. Ike had a stateside assignment during World War I; thereafter, despite such high points as being cited for "unusual intelligence and constant devotion to duty" by General Pershing, he often was in the doldrums as a peacetime officer. But he stuck with it, and during his tour of the Philippines with General MacArthur in the thirties he noted Japan's military build-up. Late in 1939 colleagues tagged him Alarmist Ike as he warned of inevitable American involvement in World War II. The Louisiana war-games exercises of 1941 first put Eisenhower in the public eye; he was to remain there for two decades.

Mamie Doud, eighteen when the photograph above was taken in 1915, was the belle of San Antonio. Once Ike had to make a date with her a month ahead.

"I HATE WAR"

WIDE WORLD

Above, the SHAEF command plans the Normandy invasion early in 1944. Field Marshal Sir Bernard Montgomery is seated at Ike's left; he is also standing behind him in the picture below, in which the commander talks to the troops before OVERLORD.

FRANK SCHERSCHEL, © TIME, INC.

I am glad it suits you," said General George C. Marshall to Eisenhower, referring to a directive on the role of the commander—whoever it would be—of the new European Theater of Operations, "because these are the orders you're going to operate under." It was mid-1942, and in London (and later at various fronts) ETO Commander Eisenhower's greatest task would be fostering a spirit of Allied unity. Over the next few years his conscientiousness, tactfulness, and ability to inspire creative compromise kept the Allied gears well oiled and well meshed. War-battered Britons liked his "breezy charm" (he had said his luxury suite at Claridge's was like "living in sin" and had moved to more modest quarters); the press called him a happy blend of an "intelligent Oxford don" and a "Rotarian speaker." But Eisenhower was also a forceful general. In late 1942 he flew to Gibraltar to oversee the start of Operation TORCH, which, by the following May, drove the Nazis out of North Africa. During the subsequent Italian campaign, Ike was given command of Supreme Headquarters of the Allied Expeditionary Forces. OVERLORD, the cross-Channel assault on Hitler's Fortress Europe, was Eisenhower's concern. He increased OVERLORD's forces to five divisions (an earlier plan—"fatally weak," he said—had called for three) and had to sweat out last-minute weather changes before beachheads were established on June 6, 1944. Early in the following year the Allies thwarted Adolph Hitler's final offensive, and in May Germany surrendered. General Eisenhower was the incarnation of the Allied triumph, but he said honestly, "I hate war as only a soldier who has lived it can, only as one who has seen its brutality, its futility, its *stupidity*."

As spring came to war-weary Europe in 1945, German cities were captured at the rate of nearly one a day. By mid-April, Seventh Army troops, right, were patrolling the streets of devastated Waldenburg.

After the war Eisenhower received Russia's Order of Victory (above left); it was the first time a foreigner had won the medal. The Commander in Chief adds an oak-leaf cluster to Ike's Distinguished Service Medal, above right. Below, in Kansas City, Missouri, a victorious Ike responds to the cheers of a nation.

"HERO AND SAVIOR"

A Roper Poll in mid-1948 showed Dwight Eisenhower to be the favorite of both parties in that year's presidential race. Ike had returned to an adoring America. He had survived a stint as chief of staff, with its vexing problems of demobilization and of the consolidation of all branches of the military under a single Department of Defense. In October, 1948, he became president of Columbia University, having stopped the draft-Ike movements with a firm statement that he would not accept nomination. When, in 1951, President Truman sent Ike to Europe to head the NATO forces, the stage was set for the repetition of what Marquis Childs referred to as "the Toynbeean withdrawal and return of the hero and savior, a rhythm of the first importance in Eisenhower's career." In January, 1952, Ike confirmed Senator Henry Cabot Lodge's summary of his "political convictions" by agreeing to accept the Republican presidential nomination if it was offered to him. A Herblock cartoon that year showed Eisenhower standing on the European shore and pondering an American coastline studded with microphones as a companion asked him, "All Ready for D-Day?"

Above, the university's president and its coach, Lou Little, watch Columbia's 1948 varsity. Early in his Army career, Ike had coached a football team.

Happy candidates Dwight Eisenhower and Richard Nixon pose with their wives on the G.O.P. convention platform on July 12, 1952. The previous day Minnesota had switched its votes from Harold Stassen to Ike, initiating a first-ballot stampede.

A FINE IMPRESSION

In 1909 a reviewer for an Abilene newspaper said that in the senior-class play Dwight Eisenhower "gave an impression that many professionals fail to reach." The critic might have repeated those words in 1952 when Eisenhower, indisputably an amateur in politics, left an impression that few pros could have bettered. The G.O.P. had been out of office for two decades, and lacked appealing candidates; Senator Robert Taft, "Mr. Republican," was unable to prevent Ike's first-ballot nomination. Commented The Washington *Post*, "It is no exaggeration to say that his nomination reflects the dominant mood of the country." Aroused by Senator Joseph McCarthy's spectacular investigations, dismayed by the mink-coat and deep-freeze scandals and the exposure of "influence peddlers" in Washington, frustrated by the Korean War and the Communist take-over in China, the nation's voters wanted a change. It was not, however, all smooth sailing for Eisenhower, an inexperienced campaigner. He was sometimes nervous before TV cameras, and he did not always field nettlesome questions deftly; the Scripps-Howard newspaper chain said, "Ike is running like a dry creek." But he learned fast and realized that he had to create party unity. He handled the corruption charge made against his running mate, Richard Nixon, with kid gloves and endorsed the re-election bids of Senator Joe McCarthy and Senator William Jenner of Indiana, another superpatriot. Some saw these stances as a lowering of the Eisenhower integrity, but most Republicans stayed with him because of his personal magnetism and the victory it promised them. In the November election, the nation embraced its hero, a man it hoped could lead as well in peace as he had in war.

At right, some of 1952's bumper crop of campaign items: Ike buttons in Spanish and Hebrew, a G.O.P. stocking, and a simulated diamond and ruby pin.

TAFT

"MR. REPUBLICAN"

I don't know what I'll do without him," lamented President Eisenhower upon the death of Senator Robert A. Taft in 1953. A year earlier the two men had been rivals for the Republican presidential nomination, and Taft had been bitterly disappointed by his defeat. Only after Eisenhower's endorsement of a number of Taft's policies did the senator offer his support. Once an agreement had been reached, however, Taft devoted his full energies to pushing the Eisenhower program through the Senate. "No twentieth-century President," wrote historian Stephen Hess, "has had a more effective legislative leader."

Taft came by his leadership abilities naturally. His grandfather, Alphonso Taft, had been President Grant's Attorney General and later minister to Austria and Russia; his father, William Howard Taft, had been President of the United States and Chief Justice of the Supreme Court. Like those distinguished statesmen, Robert Taft began his career as a lawyer. After studying at Yale and Harvard, he established a practice in Cincinnati, Ohio, and in 1921 he was elected to the state legislature. In 1938 he entered the United States Senate, where his best-known piece of legislation was the Taft-Hartley Act of 1947, designed to check the power of unions. Although Taft was a conservative Republican, his Senate career was not without its inconsistencies. As a laissez-faire economist he was vehemently opposed to the national recovery and relief programs of the New Deal; yet he supported federal aid for housing and education. An isolationist, he opposed lend-lease, selective service, and major foreign aid programs; but though he criticized the Truman Doctrine, which extended aid for the containment of communism abroad, he was tolerant of the McCarthy investigations at home. Perhaps the greatest paradox of all, however, was summed up in an observation by John F. Kennedy: "The late Senator Robert A. Taft of Ohio was never President of the United States. Therein lies his personal tragedy. And therein lies his national greatness." For although Taft was an astute politician, he had a sense of integrity and statesmanship that came before any political consideration. He stated his views in bold, blunt terms no matter how unpopular they might have been. "It is not honest to be tactful," he once said. So although he was revered in the Senate as a man of honor, logic, and impeccable honesty, "Mr. Republican," as he came to be known, was three times defeated for his party's presidential nomination—in 1940 by Wendell Willkie, in 1948 by Thomas Dewey, and in 1952 by Dwight D. Eisenhower. "It kills me to have to do this to him," groaned one Taft delegate as he switched his vote to Eisenhower. But the Republicans wanted a winner, and Ike's argument, "Taft can't win," was effective.

Taft spent the last year of his life in the service of the new President. As Senate floor leader, he was of inestimable value to Eisenhower. And in spite of some basic differences on budget and foreign policy, Eisenhower accepted the senator's conservative counsel on many important issues. Then in April, 1953, Taft felt the first pain of fatal cancer in his hip; three months later he was dead. Few senators have been mourned as Taft was. His colleagues named him the most outstanding senator of all time, and a massive Robert A. Taft monument was erected on the Capitol grounds. "The American people have lost a truly great citizen," eulogized Eisenhower, "and I have lost a wise counselor and valued friend. . . ."

Deane Keller's fresco of Taft is in the United States Capitol.

Eisenhower had promised that he would go to Korea, and in December of 1952 the President-elect did just that; the picture on the right shows him there. Negotiations to end the Korean conflict were already in progress.

The new President's Cabinet and other advisers sat for the picture below in May of 1953. Clockwise from Henry Cabot Lodge II, lower left, they are Douglas McKay, George M. Humphrey, Richard Nixon, Herbert Brownell, Sinclair Weeks, Oveta Culp Hobby, Sherman Adams, Joseph M. Dodge, Arthur S. Flemming, Martin P. Durkin, Arthur Summerfield, John Foster Dulles, President Eisenhower, Charles E. Wilson, Ezra Taft Benson, and Harold E. Stassen.

ROCKY ROADS

The new President saw himself as a symbol of national unity, but his hopes for ushering in a new Era of Good Feelings were soon dashed. He was criticized for selecting a Cabinet filled with businessmen ("eight millionaires and a plumber," said one newspaper—the plumber being Martin Durkin, ex-president of the Journeymen Plumbers and Steamfitters Union, who resigned as Secretary of Labor in less than a year). Defense Secretary Charles Wilson's controversial views, expressed with energetic candor, prompted the joke that at General Motors he had invented the automatic transmission so that he would have one foot free to put in his mouth. Joseph McCarthy, far from showing gratitude for Ike's campaign endorsement, stepped up his witch hunt, to the enduring discomfort of the President and to the detriment of morale wherever the senator struck. Democrats laughed up their sleeves when the Republican "soil bank" program looked more like a New Deal measure than a product of the administration's much-touted "dynamic conservatism." There were loud cries of "Give-away Program" as Eisenhower's conservation and power-source policies tended to favor private enterprise. So it went for Ike in civilian boot camp. But if the road to domestic tranquillity was rocky, it was not nearly so tortuous as the path to international peace.

Aide Roy Cohn (above, right) whispers to Senator Joseph McCarthy during the televised Army hearings of 1954. President Eisenhower refused to censure McCarthy openly because, as he told friends, he did not care to "get in the gutter" with him.

919

WIDE WORLD

At the Summit in 1955 were, above from the left, Anthony Eden of England, Edgar Faure of France, President Dwight D. Eisenhower, and Nikolai Bulganin of Russia. The good will of Geneva was short-lived: in 1956 Britain and France were bearing arms, right, in Suez.

EASTFOTO, CHINA

After the division of Indochina in 1954, the People's Army had no trouble (above) taking over North Vietnam.

MAGNUM/DAVID SEYMOUR

THEORY AND PRACTICE

Almost from the start, demands were heard for the ouster of John Foster Dulles, Eisenhower's trusted shaper of foreign policy. "Hard" on communism, Dulles was unwilling to negotiate with the Red bloc, which, in his moralistic view, was an evil that surely would crumble under America's potential for "massive retaliation." (Russia's development of the same potential did not alter the Dulles line.) He spoke of recapturing the "crusading spirit of the early days of the Republic," but in only a few cases did the administration boldly implement its stated policy of brinkmanship. The gap between theory and practice shook the free world's faith in American leadership. Uneasy peaces left Korea and Indochina breeding grounds for further flare-ups of hot warfare; in 1956 Hungary found it could not count on the United States when the fat was in the fire; that year, too, the United States call for a cease-fire in Suez—however just—antagonized Britain and France, her two firmest allies. But if Dulles was having his problems, the view from the Summit was hardly any clearer. At Geneva in 1955 Eisenhower concluded, "It is not always necessary that people should think alike and believe alike before they can work together"; this flimsy "spirit of Geneva" would afford little protection against the continuing chill of the long cold war.

Russian tanks roll through Budapest, above, putting down the Hungarian uprising of 1956. The United Nations issued a protest, and President Eisenhower said, "The heart of America goes out to the people of Hungary."

"THE VIRUS OF
MORALITY"

A funny thing happened to me on the way to the White House!" said Adlai Stevenson after the presidential election of 1952. "I was happy to hear that I had even placed second."

Stevenson had not wanted the Democratic nomination in the first place. He had hoped to be re-elected governor of Illinois; he had been uncertain of his ability to serve as President; he had been reluctant to oppose the probable Republican candidate, General Dwight Eisenhower, the popular war hero who was, according to Stevenson, as familiar as "the catchup bottle on the kitchen table." Despite his reluctance, Stevenson had been drafted by the Democrats and, as expected, had been badly beaten.

But curiously, when President Eisenhower, more popular than ever, stood for re-election four years later, Adlai Ewing Stevenson actively sought his party's nomination, won it, and leaped into a campaign that offered him virtually no chance of victory. Against the wishes of his advisers, the former Chicago lawyer and diplomat aimed his attacks not only at the administration in general but at the popular Ike in particular; and he raised the important but avoidable issue of nuclear fallout. Eisenhower called Stevenson's request for an end to atmospheric testing of nuclear bombs a "moratorium on common sense." (Two years later, Ike would make the same proposal.) Typical of the odds against which Stevenson was running was a series of crises in the Middle East—just two weeks before Election Day—which, although largely the result of administration blunders, served to further solidify the American people behind President Eisenhower. Stevenson carried only seven states in the November election.

Theodore H. White once suggested that Stevenson placed "the virus of morality in the bloodstream of both parties." While the urbane Stevenson, namesake of a grandfather who had been Grover Cleveland's second Vice President, was himself too genuinely humble to admit that that was his aim, it was probably the reason why he sought a hopeless candidacy. Condemning the use of "soft soap, slogans, gimmicks, bandwagons and all the other infernal machines of modern high-pressure politics" as "contempt for people's intelligence, common sense and dignity," he introduced a wit, an eloquence, and a moral tone to campaigning that had not before been present. And because he respected the people whose support he sought, he became not the postelection recluse and public joke that two-time losers so often become, but, as Walter Lippmann put it, "a living specimen of the kind of American that Americans themselves, and the great mass of mankind, would like to think that Americans are."

In 1961 Stevenson wanted to be Secretary of State, but President John Kennedy appointed him ambassador to the United Nations. During the Cuban Missile Crisis the next year, when Soviet Ambassador Valerian Zorin hedged on Stevenson's query regarding the presence of Russian missiles in Cuba, the American ambassador cried, "I am prepared to wait for my answer until hell freezes over!" But as his role in policy making declined even more under President Johnson, the United Nations job increasingly frustrated and exhausted Stevenson. In 1965 in London, a few days before his fatal heart attack, he privately announced his intention to resign soon. "Ah, well," Stevenson sighed, "for a while, I'd really just like to sit in the shade with a glass of wine in my hand and watch the people dance."

Adlai E. Stevenson in 1952

REACTING

As his second term progressed, President Eisenhower resembled more and more the Dutch boy with his finger in the dike. While the country's problems continued to develop, the administration—marked by conservatism and an urge to decentralize—created few new federal responsibilities. Toward the end of the term, for example, the President vetoed a bill aimed at making the federal government responsible for coping with the pollution of rivers. In his veto message Eisenhower declared: "Because water pollution is a uniquely local blight, primary responsibility . . . must be assumed . . . by State and local governments . . . and industry." The trouble was that many local officials and businessmen refused to accept the burden, and water pollutants continued to pour into the nation's rivers. Clearly, if the situation were left as it was, it would eventually deteriorate until the federal government would *have* to take charge. Thus instead of appearing dynamic by thrusting duty on the states and cities, the administration was criticized for trapping itself into acting defensively. Similarly, Eisenhower did little, through moral persuasion or otherwise, to bring about desegregation of schools in the South until—three years after the Supreme Court decision ordering integration—Governor Orval Faubus of Arkansas called out the National Guard to defy a federal court order, thereby compelling Eisenhower to send federal troops to Little Rock and to federalize the National Guard there. And it took the launching of the Russian Sputniks to spur the Eisenhower administration into two of its most important accomplishments: the creation of the National Aeronautics and Space Administration and the strengthening of American education, particularly in the sciences.

At left, an American satellite is launched in 1958. Right, the Arkansas National Guard, federalized by President Eisenhower, keeps the peace at Central High School in Little Rock in September, 1957.

When Dulles resigned in April, 1959, Ike named Christian Herter Secretary of State, but became at the same time his own chief diplomat. Above, he is in Rome (with son John and daughter-in-law Barbara, center) to see Pope John; at right, in Manila and in Buenos Aires.

A HARRIED LEADER

Eisenhower, despite his uncertain health, had to lead in a world that expected a great deal from the United States. International confidence was shaken in November, 1957, by the President's third serious illness—a mild stroke; it occurred less than three weeks before a scheduled meeting of the NATO heads of state. (Told by doctors that he could not go to a state dinner the night of the stroke, he fumed, "If I cannot attend to my duties, I am simply going to give up this job.") He recovered rapidly and he helped make the NATO conference a success. But the "missile gap" and Russia's lead in the space race were constantly troubling. And not long after the stroke, Richard Nixon's trip to South America revealed strong anti-American sentiment there. Late in the summer of 1958 the mainland Chinese began heavy shelling of the islands of Quemoy and Matsu; the Seventh Fleet was posted to shepherd anti-invasion troops from Taiwan to the offshore islands. There was no invasion, but there was considerable criticism abroad of American actions. Khrushchev's threat to turn over to East Germany the access routes to Berlin was withdrawn at Camp David in September, 1959, but the thaw ended when an American spy plane was shot down over Russia in 1960. A poll that year showed American prestige overseas in marked decline. Perhaps Eisenhower could have prevented some of the prestige loss. Still, his difficulties demonstrated what Pakistan's President Ayub Khan referred to as America's unique role. Because it was powerful *and* democratic, the United States was "placed in the unenviable position of returning hostility with consideration, coldness with warmth, indifference with attention, and friendship, of course, with friendship."

In India in 1959, Ike (being introduced at the University of New Delhi, left) was met by what Jawaharlal Nehru (seated) called India's greatest demonstration since its independence day in 1950.

927

WASHINGTON FACES

UNITED PRESS INTERNATIONAL

WIDE WORLD

OMAR N. BRADLEY

Musing over the contention that successful battle strategy is best conceived at a distance from the heart-wrenching realities of death and injury in the field, Omar Nelson Bradley once remarked that war is fought by men and is "as much a conflict of passion as it is of force. . . . Far from being a handicap to command, compassion is the measure of it." Combat reporter Ernie Pyle met the tenor-voiced Missourian during World War II and wrote: "I don't believe I have ever known a person so unanimously loved and respected by the men around and under him." Born in 1893, Bradley was a member of the same West Point class as Dwight Eisenhower. He rose slowly in the peacetime Army until, in February, 1941, he was made commandant of the Infantry School at Fort Benning, Georgia, and became the first member of the class of 1915 to be promoted to star rank. World War II saw Bradley rise from command of a division to command of the Twelfth Army Group—four armies that drove northward across Europe into Germany. A four-star general by V-E Day (he was awarded a fifth in 1950), he served successively as administrator of veterans' affairs, as Army chief of staff, and, from 1949 to 1953, as the first chairman of the joint chiefs of staff. Bradley retired in 1953 and subsequently became a business executive.

J. EDGAR HOOVER

"The Federal Bureau of Investigation, the G-men and Mr. J. Edgar Hoover," said British writer Cyril Connolly, "form one of the most important elements of the American myth—symbols of perfection in detective methods, wholesome anticommunism, ruthless pursuit of gangsters and spies, and of a dedicated, puritanical but unselfseeking chief above and outside politics. . . ." John Edgar Hoover's home, from the day of his birth, January 1, 1895, was Washington, D.C. He attended public school there and worked his way through George Washington University, receiving his master of laws degree in 1917. A special assistant to Attorney General A. Mitchell Palmer during the Red Scare of the Wilson administration, he was made head of the FBI in 1924, at the age of twenty-nine. The bureau came to bear his stamp in everything: its special training courses and advanced methods of detective work, its thoroughness, the high level of honesty on the part of its agents, and its conservatism in politics. Through its successes against crime and its carefully handled public relations Hoover grew to have considerable influence in Congress and a large measure of autonomy in the government. He had a marked ability to survive in office despite criticism of his attitudes and power by civil libertarians.

JOHN FOSTER DULLES

"Foster has been studying to be Secretary of State since he was five years old," President Eisenhower once said of John Foster Dulles. Actually, Dulles began his diplomatic career at the age of nineteen when he attended the Hague Conference in 1907 as secretary to the Chinese delegation. He served in World War I and was one of Wilson's advisers on the Versailles Treaty. Thereafter he became a leading international lawyer. He served as a delegate to the United Nations from 1946 to 1950, and in 1951 he negotiated the Japanese Peace Treaty. Appointed Secretary of State in 1953, Dulles was given unprecedented authority in shaping American foreign policy during the Eisenhower administration. "I think he is the wisest, most dedicated man that I know," avowed the President. Although few took issue with his dedication, many critics questioned the wisdom of Dulles' doctrine of massive retaliation as a deterrent to Communist aggression—particularly in view of the Soviet Union's nuclear power and Dulles' willingness to go to the "brink of war" if necessary. During his six-year tenure, Dulles was instrumental in holding back Chinese Communist aggression at Quemoy and Matsu and in halting the Anglo-French seizure of the Suez Canal. Dulles died in May, 1959, after treatment for a malignant tumor.

EARL WARREN

The appointment of Governor Earl Warren as Chief Justice of the Supreme Court put the capstone on a career devoted to politics and public service. Warren, the son of Scandinavian immigrants, was born in 1891 in Los Angeles. Educated in public schools and at the University of California, he was awarded his law degree in 1914. In 1925 he became district attorney of Alameda County, serving in that position until he won election as California attorney general in 1938. He was elected governor in 1942, 1946, and 1950. Warren was the state's favorite son at the Republican National Conventions of 1944 and 1948 and was Thomas Dewey's running mate in the 1948 campaign. After Chief Justice Fred Vinson died, President Eisenhower, in September, 1953, appointed Warren to replace him. The next May Warren read the Court's unanimous decision nullifying the legitimacy of "separate but equal" (segregated) public education. This and other liberal decisions by the Court brought demands by ultraconservatives for Warren's impeachment. But perhaps the most trying assignment of Warren's life was the chairmanship of the commission investigating President Kennedy's assassination; the commission failed to lay to rest national doubts about the sad event, and was the subject of a heated controversy.

Golfer Eisenhower is shown above in 1964—playing in a benefit match for the Heart Fund. Painter Eisenhower made the portrait of Lincoln below from an 1863 photograph.

"YOU DO NOT LEAD BY HITTING PEOPLE"

Dwight Eisenhower was indebted to the military, for it had given him a career that had led to the Presidency; he was also, to a great extent, sympathetic to private enterprise. Yet as he left the White House in 1961, he warned the nation of the dangers inherent in a society dominated by a "military-industrial complex." He was not turning against those who had made him a public figure or sustained him in public office; he was reasserting his primary allegiance—to the best interests, as he saw them, of the nation as a whole. This enduring attitude helps to explain Eisenhower's attempts to remain above partisan politics, to embody a unified America rather than a single political party. He had a textbook concept of the division of power in federal government and seldom tried to force measures through the national legislature. ("You do not lead by hitting people over the head," he often said, although once he admitted that dealing with a Democratic Congress was "no bed of roses.") Nevertheless, his two administrations were not without accomplishments. Social Security was expanded; the minimum wage was raised to a dollar an hour; two civil rights bills were passed; an Air Force Academy and the Department of Health, Education, and Welfare were created; the St. Lawrence seaway project was authorized and completed. Eisenhower's foreign policy record and his failure to act at home when action seemed to many to be desperately needed have often been criticized. But postwar America had wanted a President in whom the average citizen could place absolute confidence. Eisenhower had filled the bill and had done his best to continue the nation's progress toward "the great destiny for which she was created."

Presidents Kennedy and Johnson periodically sought Eisenhower's views; the former Chief Executive walks with John Kennedy, right, at Camp David during the Cuban Missile Crisis of 1962.

FACTS IN SUMMARY: DWIGHT D. EISENHOWER

CHRONOLOGY

UNITED STATES		EISENHOWER
Sherman Antitrust Act	1890	*Born October 14*
	1911	*Enters U.S. Military Academy*
Lusitania sunk	1915	*Commissioned 2nd lt.*
Wilson re-elected	1916	*Marries Mamie Doud*
Second Battle of the Marne	1918	*Commands tank-training center*
	1922	*Assigned to Panama*
	1925	*Attends Command and General Staff School*
Hoover elected President	1928	*Writes guide to French battlefields*
Stock market crash	1929	*Works in office of asst. secretary of war*
Franklin Roosevelt elected President	1932	*Attached to staff of Gen. Douglas MacArthur*
Social Security Act	1935	*Assigned to Philippines*
World War II begins	1939	*Returns to U.S.*
Roosevelt re-elected	1940	*Named chief of staff of Third Division*
War with Japan and Germany	1941	*Wins mock battle in Louisiana*
Battle of Bataan Operation TORCH	1942	*Named assistant chief of staff to Gen. Marshall*
Battle of Guadalcanal		*Assumes command of ETO*
		Directs invasion of North Africa
Battle of Tarawa Italian Campaign	1943	*Directs invasions of Sicily and Italy*
D-Day Battle of Leyte Gulf Battle of the Bulge	1944	*Named supreme commander of A.E.F.* *Directs Normandy invasion*
Truman becomes President	1945	*Accepts surrender of Germany*
A-bombs dropped on Japan		*Becomes chief of staff, U.S. Army*

UNITED STATES		EISENHOWER
Truman elected	1948	*Named president of Columbia University*
Korean War begins	1950	
	1951	*Commands SHAPE*
	1952	*Elected President*
		Visits Korea
Armistice signed in Korea	1953	*Names Earl Warren Chief Justice*
Supreme Court orders school desegregation	1954	*Refuses to condemn Senator McCarthy*
Army-McCarthy hearings		*Gives air support to French in Indochina*
SEATO pact signed		
	1955	*Attends Summit Conference at Geneva*
		Suffers heart attack
Hungarian Revolt	1956	*Re-elected President*
Suez Crisis		*Undergoes operation for ileitis*
Civil Rights Commission established	1957	*Announces Eisenhower Doctrine*
Soviets launch Sputnik I		*Sends troops to Little Rock, Ark.*
Business recession		*Proposes nuclear test ban*
		Suffers stroke
Explorer I launched	1958	*Sends U.S. troops to Lebanon*
NASA created		
Red Chinese shell Quemoy and Matsu		
Alaska and Hawaii admitted to Union	1959	*Meets Khrushchev at Camp David*
U-2 incident	1960	*Visits South America*
Kennedy elected President		
Bay of Pigs	1961	*Retires to Gettysburg*
Johnson becomes President	1963	
Vietnam War intensified	1966	*Undergoes gall bladder operation*

Alaska and Hawaii, the forty-ninth and fiftieth states, were admitted to the Union in Eisenhower's second term.

BIOGRAPHICAL FACTS

BIRTH: Denison, Texas, Oct. 14, 1890

ANCESTRY: Swiss-German

FATHER: David Jacob Eisenhower; b. Elizabethville, Pa., Sept. 23, 1863; d. Abilene, Kan., March 10, 1942

FATHER'S OCCUPATION: Mechanic

MOTHER: Ida Elizabeth Stover Eisenhower; b. Mount Sidney, Va., May 1, 1862; d. Abilene, Kan., Sept. 11, 1946

BROTHERS: Arthur (1886–1958); Edgar (1889–   ); Roy (1892–1942); Earl (1898–   ); Milton (1899–   )

WIFE: Mamie Geneva Doud: b. Boone, Iowa, Nov. 14, 1896

MARRIAGE: Denver, Colo., July 1, 1916

CHILDREN: Doud Dwight (1917–1921); John Sheldon (1922–   )

EDUCATION: Public schools; U.S. Military Academy, West Point, N.Y. (graduated 1915)

RELIGIOUS AFFILIATION: Presbyterian

MILITARY SERVICE: Commissioned 2nd lt. in U.S. Army (1915); served in various posts in United States, Panama, and Philippines (1915–1942); named commander of European Theater of Operations (1942); named supreme commander of Allied Expeditionary Force in Western Europe (1943); promoted to general of the Army (1944); named Army chief of staff (1945); appointed supreme commander of Allied powers in Europe (1951)

AGE AT INAUGURATION: 62

OCCUPATION AFTER PRESIDENCY: Writer

ELECTION OF 1952

CANDIDATES	ELECTORAL VOTE	POPULAR VOTE
Dwight D. Eisenhower Republican	442	33,936,234
Adlai E. Stevenson Democratic	89	27,314,992
Vincent Hallinan Progressive	—	140,023

FIRST ADMINISTRATION

INAUGURATION: January 20, 1953; the Capitol, Washington, D.C.

VICE PRESIDENT: Richard M. Nixon

SECRETARY OF STATE: John Foster Dulles

SECRETARY OF THE TREASURY: George M. Humphrey

SECRETARY OF DEFENSE: Charles E. Wilson

ATTORNEY GENERAL: Herbert Brownell, Jr.

POSTMASTER GENERAL: Arthur E. Summerfield

SECRETARY OF THE INTERIOR: Douglas McKay; Frederick A. Seaton (from June 8, 1956)

SECRETARY OF AGRICULTURE: Ezra Taft Benson

SECRETARY OF COMMERCE: Sinclair Weeks

SECRETARY OF LABOR: Martin Durkin; James P. Mitchell (from Jan. 19, 1954)

SECRETARY OF HEALTH, EDUCATION, AND WELFARE (Department created April 1, 1953): Oveta Culp Hobby; Marion B. Folsom (from Aug. 1, 1955)

SUPREME COURT APPOINTMENTS: Earl Warren, Chief Justice (1953); John M. Harlan (1955); William J. Brennan, Jr. (1956)

83rd CONGRESS (January 3, 1953–January 3, 1955):
Senate: 48 Republicans; 47 Democrats; 1 Other
House: 221 Republicans; 211 Democrats; 1 Other

84th CONGRESS (January 3, 1955–January 3, 1957):
Senate: 48 Democrats; 47 Republicans; 1 Other
House: 232 Democrats; 203 Republicans

ELECTION OF 1956

CANDIDATES	ELECTORAL VOTE	POPULAR VOTE
Dwight D. Eisenhower Republican	457	35,590,472
Adlai E. Stevenson Democratic	73	26,022,752
T. Coleman Andrews States' Rights	—	107,929

SECOND ADMINISTRATION

INAUGURATION: January 20, 1957; the Capitol, Washington, D.C.

VICE PRESIDENT: Richard M. Nixon

SECRETARY OF STATE: John Foster Dulles; Christian A. Herter (from April 22, 1959)

SECRETARY OF THE TREASURY: George M. Humphrey; Robert B. Anderson (from July 29, 1957)

SECRETARY OF DEFENSE: Charles E. Wilson; Neil H. McElroy (from Oct. 9, 1957); Thomas S. Gates, Jr. (from Jan. 26, 1960)

ATTORNEY GENERAL: Herbert Brownell, Jr.; William P. Rogers (from Jan. 27, 1958)

POSTMASTER GENERAL: Arthur E. Summerfield

SECRETARY OF THE INTERIOR: Frederick A. Seaton

SECRETARY OF AGRICULTURE: Ezra Taft Benson

SECRETARY OF COMMERCE: Sinclair Weeks; Frederick H. Mueller (from Aug. 6, 1959)

SECRETARY OF LABOR: James P. Mitchell

SECRETARY OF HEALTH, EDUCATION, AND WELFARE: Marion B. Folsom; Arthur S. Flemming (from Aug. 1, 1958)

SUPREME COURT APPOINTMENTS: Charles E. Whittaker (1957); Potter Stewart (1958)

85th CONGRESS (January 3, 1957–January 3, 1959):
Senate: 49 Democrats; 47 Republicans
House: 233 Democrats; 200 Republicans

86th CONGRESS (January 3, 1959–January 3, 1961):
Senate: 64 Democrats; 34 Republicans
House: 283 Democrats; 153 Republicans

STATES ADMITTED: Alaska (1959); Hawaii (1959)

JOHN FITZGERALD KENNEDY

Just after sunset on the evening of August 1, 1943, fifteen PT boats moved out of Rendova Harbor in the South Pacific's Solomon Islands. Word had come that the Japanese would be moving in large force that night toward neighboring Kolombangara Island, and every available American boat had been ordered out into Blackett Strait on patrol duty.

To the men on board the departing PT boats, the Southern Cross was briefly visible amidst the early evening stars. Then the cloud bank that had been wrapped around Rendova Peak spread into a dark overcast and drifted out over Ferguson Passage, the waterway leading to Blackett Strait. The hours of patrol passed slowly, and on one of the PT boats a seaman was asking his skipper about his personal recollections of Winston Churchill. The boat's commander, twenty-six-year-old Lieutenant (junior grade) John Fitzgerald Kennedy, could easily oblige the man's curiosity, for he was the son of a former American ambassador to Great Britain's Court of St. James's and had moved easily in international diplomatic and political circles.

A 1940 graduate of Harvard University, Kennedy had been named an ensign in the United States Naval Reserve in October, 1941, and had been ordered to duty in the Pentagon. When Japan attacked Pearl Harbor on December 7, he had immediately requested sea duty. Not until the following year, however, was he sent to the PT boat-training school that led to his South Pacific assignment in April, 1943.

Not long after midnight, on August 2, Lieutenant Kennedy maneuvered *PT-109* near two other boats and suggested that they reverse their direction and make another sweep of Blackett Strait. There was no sign of the enemy in the inky blackness. Some minutes later, a man on board Kennedy's boat sud-

John F. Kennedy

denly shouted, "Ship at two o'clock!" The young officer had only a moment to glance up at the huge, looming prow cutting through a phosphorescent wave. In less than a minute it had sliced through *PT-109*. The stern, just behind Kennedy, went down in an instant, carrying two of the thirteen men on board to their death. Gasoline tanks burst into fire, and the survivors struggled against the suction of the passing ship only to surface into curtains of flame.

The Japanese destroyer *Amagiri* disappeared into the night. The other PT boats, having failed in attempts to destroy the enemy ship, raced for their home base. Kennedy had been hurled backward against the rear wall of the cockpit by the impact of the collision. Ensign George "Barney" Ross, a friend of Kennedy's who had merely come along for the ride that night, awoke from a faint to find himself in the water. In the engine room, Patrick McMahon—at thirty-seven the "old man" of *PT-109*—had been severely burned. The other eight men seemed not to have been seriously injured.

In the blackness of the night, Kennedy helped round up the survivors until all were either on or clinging to the floating hulk of *PT-109*'s forward section. Through the early morning hours of Monday, August 2, the men idly discussed whether they would fight or surrender if the Japanese appeared. When the hulk gave signs of sinking, Kennedy ordered his men to swim to a nearby island. Holding on to a plank so they would not become separated, nine of the men began kicking off toward shore. McMahon was too badly burned to swim, and so Kennedy clamped his teeth on the man's life preserver strap and set out to tow him to shore. It took them four hours to swim to a tiny islet.

That night Kennedy walked out on a coral reef as far as he could go and then swam to the middle of Ferguson Passage, where he waited for several hours in the forlorn hope that another PT boat patrol would spot him. The following night Barney Ross made a similar attempt to get help, but those two nights the PT boats were on a sweep elsewhere. On Wednesday, August 4, Kennedy

moved his pathetic party some two miles across an inlet to a larger island, where they hoped to find food. Again Kennedy used his teeth to tow McMahon.

Still desperate for food, Kennedy and Ross swam to a third island on Thursday. They found a wrecked Japanese vessel with a case of hard candy, which Kennedy took back to the second island. His men, the surprised lieutenant discovered, had visitors—natives working for the Allied forces. Carrying a message scratched on a coconut shell, the natives informed Allied agents in the area of the survivors. Other natives took Kennedy to the island of Gomu, and soon his party was rescued.

A brief eighteen years later, the hero of *PT-109* would stand on a platform outside the Capitol in Washington and on a bitterly cold but brilliantly clear January day proclaim: "Let the word go forth from this time and place, to friend and foe alike, that the torch has been passed to a new generation of Americans—born in this century, tempered by war, disciplined by a hard and bitter peace, proud of our ancient heritage. . . ."

The thirty-fifth President was born into an aristocracy—that of the Boston Irish. The 1914 marriage of his parents, Joseph Patrick Kennedy and Rose Fitzgerald, had been solemnized by William Cardinal O'Connell, for it united two of the city's most politically prominent families. Rose's father, the affable John F. "Honey Fitz" Fitzgerald, had been mayor of Boston. Joseph's father, Patrick J. Kennedy, was a former state representative and one of Boston's most powerful ward bosses.

Joseph P. Kennedy bypassed politics as a means of gaining power and took a more direct route—high finance. When he had been out of Harvard University for less than two years, he borrowed enough money to win control of a small East Boston bank; at twenty-five he was hailed as the nation's youngest bank president. The home in which Rose and Joseph P. Kennedy started their marriage was a gray frame dwelling in middle-class Brookline, Massachusetts. It was in this house that their first two sons were born:

Joseph P., Jr., in 1915, and, on May 29, 1917, John Fitzgerald Kennedy.

During World War I Joseph Kennedy served as assistant general manager of Bethlehem Steel Company's Quincy, Massachusetts, shipyard, where he had some rather strained dealings with the dynamic but highhanded assistant secretary of the Navy, Franklin D. Roosevelt. When the war ended, Kennedy entered the investment house of Hayden, Stone and Company and started to build his first million. By the end of the 1920's, the shrewd and ambitious young Irish-American had made his mark in securities, real estate, and the new movie industry. In 1925 he established the first of three trust funds that would make each of his children a multimillionaire.

The following year Joseph Kennedy moved his business operations—and his growing family—to New York. But after 1928 a rambling summer house at Hyannis Port on Massachusetts' Cape Cod was the clan's real home. By that time, in addition to Joseph, Jr., and John, there were Rosemary, Kathleen, Eunice, Patricia, Robert, and Jean. With eight children, the proud parents

named a sailboat they had acquired the *Tenovus*. The arrival of their ninth and last child, Edward ("Teddy"), in February, 1932, coincided with the purchase of a new boat, appropriately called *Onemore*.

In later years much would be made of the influence John F. Kennedy's father and older brother had exerted on him. A certain amount of the father's often ruthless drive was transmitted to the entire family. Even in family sports, such as swimming, sailboat racing, and touch football games on the lawn at Hyannis Port, each Kennedy was taught to play to win.

In his early years, John Kennedy too often found himself in the shadow of Joe, Jr. At Choate, an exclusive preparatory school in Wallingford, Connecticut, Joe won the Harvard Trophy for his combined success in sports and scholarship. Young Jack, a "gentleman C scholar," finished sixty-fourth in a class of one hundred and twelve. Partly to avoid further competition with his brother, Jack decided not to follow Joe to Harvard, but enrolled instead at Princeton. However, during a summer visit to England, where he studied briefly at the London School of Eco-

The picture above shows Lieutenant (j.g.) John F. Kennedy arriving at Gomu Island in the Solomons after his rescue by natives during World War II. Kennedy and his PT boat crew had been marooned on another island.

Ambassador to Great Britain Joseph P. Kennedy took his two oldest sons to England in 1938. John, left, and Joseph, Jr., right, who had engaged in fierce fist fights as children, had become friendly rivals.

nomics, he contracted jaundice. His illness forced Jack to start late at Princeton, and a recurrence of the ailment caused him to drop out of college during the Christmas recess. In the fall of 1936 he entered Harvard. In his first two years he was again a C student.

Meanwhile, Joseph P. Kennedy had seen his old adversary from the Quincy shipyard days, Franklin D. Roosevelt, elected President in 1932. Two years later Kennedy was appointed to the Securities and Exchange Commission, one of Roosevelt's New Deal reforms, and served as its first chairman, from July, 1934, to September, 1935. During the 1936 presidential campaign Joseph Kennedy published a book, *I'm for Roosevelt*, which endeared him to F. D. R. His reward for this campaign support was appointment, in December, 1937, as ambassador to the Court of St. James's.

His father's new position gave Jack access to many of Europe's most influential men. Taking off the second semester of his junior year at Harvard, he traveled across Europe, including Russia, as the storm clouds of World War II were gathering. Back in London on September 1, 1939, when Hitler's invasion of Poland finally triggered the war in Europe, Jack Kennedy caught his first glimpse of conflict when he went to Scotland to help American survivors of a torpedoed British ship, the *Athenia*.

Sobered by his experiences in Europe, young Kennedy returned to Harvard and in his senior year became a candidate for a degree with honors in political science. His undergraduate thesis, a study of Allied appeasement of Hitler, was later published under the title *Why England Slept* and became a best seller.

During the winter of 1939–40 Joseph Kennedy grew increasingly pessimistic about Britain's chances of survival, and after the fall of France in June, 1940, he began to think of Hitler's triumph as inevitable. In December he resigned his ambassadorship to return to the United States to champion nonintervention. After Pearl Harbor, Kennedy volunteered for service with F. D. R.'s wartime administration but was never given another government assignment. Thus, as his oldest sons donned uniforms, his influence in government receded.

Four months after Lieutenant John F. Kennedy's dramatic rescue in the Solomon Islands, he was rotated back to the States. He had contracted malaria, and the fall he had taken at the time of the collision with the *Amagiri* had aggravated a back injury sustained a few years earlier during a football game at college. A disc operation was performed on his back at the Chelsea Naval Hospital near Boston. It was while he was a patient there that Jack learned that his older brother, Joe, Jr., had been killed during an air mission over Europe.

Early in 1945 Jack was separated from the service. Through his father, he got a job as a writer with Hearst's International News Service and covered the founding of the United Nations in San Francisco. A journalist's career was not likely to satisfy either Jack or his father, however. Kennedy had confided to a close friend, Paul B. "Red" Fay, that he would soon be "trying to parlay a lost PT boat and a bad back into a political advantage."

A persistent legend about the Kennedy family is that Joseph P. Kennedy had slated his eldest son for the White House and that when Joe, Jr., was killed, Jack was drafted for the job. Whatever the validity of such a tale, early in 1946 John F. Kennedy announced his candidacy for United States representative from Massachusetts' Eleventh Congressional District in East Boston.

After an absence of twenty years, the Kennedys returned to Boston—to campaign for Jack. Honey Fitz, a spry octogenarian, was dusted off to sing "Sweet Adeline" for sentimental old-timers, but in all other respects the campaign was a modern blitz. Old friends from Choate and Harvard were enlisted in the crusade, and Navy buddies flocked in from across the country to call attention to the candidate's war record. The attractive Kennedy ladies, mother and sisters, fanned out across the district to attend campaign tea parties and to hand out literature. Twenty-year-old brother Bobby, also just home from the Navy, took over the campaign in one particularly difficult area. There was a heavy advertising budget, and a reprint of a *Reader's Digest* article about *PT-109* was widely distributed.

Overcoming charges of carpetbagging and vote buying on his father's part, Jack Kennedy won the Democratic primary by a 2 to 1 plurality over his nearest opponent.

In East Boston, the Democratic nomination was as good as election, and he won easily in November. Two years later, in 1948, he had no Republican rival at all; and in 1950 he was elected to a third term in the House of Representatives by a ratio of 5 to 1.

Only twenty-nine years old when he first took his seat in Congress in January, 1947, Jack Kennedy was occasionally mistaken for an elevator operator. He was one of a minority opposing the conservative Taft-Hartley labor bill and he unsuccessfully supported federal aid to housing. In foreign affairs Congressman Kennedy was a maverick. He blamed President Truman and Secretary of State Marshall for the loss of China to the Communists in 1949 and criticized the administration's defense-spending policies. Yet he did not strongly endorse Truman's intervention in Korea and voted to trim economic aid abroad.

After his re-election in 1948 Kennedy began to think of higher office—either governor or United States senator from Massachusetts. He began spending four-day weekends in Massachusetts, ranging far from his district to make political speeches. In April, 1952, he announced that he would oppose the re-election of Senator Henry Cabot Lodge II. The contest, in a sense, was a rerun of the 1916 senatorial election in which Lodge's grandfather, Henry Cabot Lodge, Sr., had defeated Honey Fitz. But Jack was running as an entirely different kind of candidate from his grandfather. He was, said a fellow politician, "the first Irish Brahmin."

The familiar Kennedy barrage of billboards, tea parties, and reprints of the *Reader's Digest* article was loosed. And on Election Day in November, 1952, Kennedy defeated Lodge by more than 70,000 votes, while Eisenhower carried the state for the Republicans by more than 200,000 votes.

Two of the most notable accomplishments of his Senate years had nothing to do with politics. On September 12, 1953, he married the talented and beautiful Jacqueline Bouvier at a glittering Newport, Rhode Island, ceremony. And in 1955 Kennedy wrote *Profiles in Courage*, the best-selling book that would win him a Pulitzer Prize for biography. The writing of the book was the outgrowth of another major occurrence of his early senatorial years, one that nearly brought a tragic end to his career.

Through his years in Congress, Kennedy continued to be plagued with a bad back, and by the summer of 1954 he could get about only on crutches. Told that a spinal-fusion operation involved serious risk, he slapped his crutches and said bitterly: "I'd rather die than spend the rest of my life on these things." Twice following an operation that October, Kennedy was close to death, and he survived only to learn that the surgery had not been fully successful. A second operation was performed in February, 1955. Kennedy's

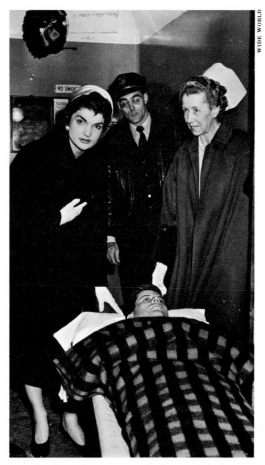

Above, Senator and Mrs. John Kennedy leave the hospital after his October, 1954, spinal operation. In February he returned for additional surgery.

back condition was never completely cured. At a 1961 tree-planting ceremony in Canada he once more injured his back, and thereafter he reportedly never had a day without pain.

Kennedy spent the early months of 1955 recuperating at his father's Palm Beach, Florida, home. He used this period of forced inactivity to research and write *Profiles in Courage*, biographical sketches of senators who had put principles ahead of politics.

During Kennedy's illness, in December, 1954, the Senate had voted to condemn Wisconsin's Senator Joseph McCarthy for his irresponsible crusade against Communists in government. Kennedy's failure to pair or to announce his position on this issue was later the basis for attacks on his own political courage. McCarthy, like Kennedy a Roman Catholic, had a large and vociferous following, including many Boston Irish, outside Wisconsin.

Friends later speculated that Kennedy's decision to seek the Presidency was made during his months of convalescence in Florida. The following year, 1956, was a presidential election year, but the unsuccessful Democratic standard-bearer of 1952, Adlai E. Stevenson, was clearly going to be given a second try at the office. Following his expected renomination, Stevenson dramatically left open to the convention the selection of a vice presidential candidate. As millions watched on television, Kennedy ran neck and neck with Senator Estes Kefauver of Tennessee for two ballots, only to lose to him on the third.

Jack Kennedy's tireless campaigning for the Stevenson-Kefauver ticket won the admiration of his fellow politicians. In 1958 he was re-elected to the Senate by a majority of 874,608 votes. Backed by this impressive endorsement, he became the favorite for the 1960 vice presidential nomination. "I'm not running for Vice-President any more," Kennedy told one Democrat, however. "I'm now running for President."

The Kennedy candidacy, according to Theodore H. White, was launched at a meeting held by sixteen people in Robert Ken-

While convalescing from his 1955 back operation, Jack Kennedy painted this Mediterranean scene.

nedy's house at Hyannis Port on October 28, 1959. The senator and his associates, who included his father and two brothers, were to make a President, White has written, "with greater precision, against greater odds, across more contrary traditions, than had been shown by any group of amateur President makers since Abraham Lincoln's backers, a century before, had changed the structure of nineteenth-century politics."

With the lamentable exception of Warren G. Harding, no man had gone directly from the United States Senate to the Presidency. Curiously, three of Kennedy's rivals for the 1960 Democratic nomination were fellow senators—Hubert H. Humphrey of Minnesota, Stuart Symington of Missouri, and Lyndon B. Johnson of Texas. In the background, waiting for the lightning strike of a third nomination, was Adlai E. Stevenson of Illinois.

To prove false the political axiom that no Roman Catholic could be elected President, Kennedy decided he would have to fight for the nomination in the primaries. When he announced his candidacy on January 2, 1960, he declared his intention of facing the electorate in the New Hampshire primary, the earliest in the nation, the following March. To no one's surprise he rolled up an impressive vote from his fellow New Englanders. The major tests, however, would be in Wis-

consin and West Virginia, in both of which he would be facing the redoubtable Hubert Humphrey. Symington and Stevenson remained inactive candidates, each hoping for a deadlocked convention. Lyndon Johnson said that he was too busy as Senate Majority Leader to campaign.

The blitz technique, developed in the earlier Kennedy campaigns in Massachusetts, was transferred full scale to Wisconsin in April, 1960. An important addition was the Kennedy family airplane, a converted Convair named for the senator's daughter, Caroline, born in 1957. Running against the Kennedys, Humphrey complained, was "like an independent retailer competing with a chain." (Kennedy brushed aside complaints that family money was buying the election by reading at a dinner in New York City an imaginary wire from his father: "Dear Jack: Don't buy one vote more than necessary. I'll be damned if I'll pay for a landslide.") On April 5 Kennedy captured 56 per cent of the vote in the Wisconsin primary. But the result was not decisive; he would have to meet Humphrey once again on May 10 in West Virginia.

Kennedy had selected the West Virginia battleground with care. The predominantly Protestant state—only 5 per cent of its population was Catholic—was also one of the poorest in the Union. If a Catholic and a rich man's son could win there, Kennedy reasoned, he could win anywhere. And so it proved. Jack Kennedy carried the primary with 61 per cent of the vote, and Humphrey was forced to withdraw as a candidate.

Led by Bobby Kennedy, the senator's campaign staff had been quietly and inexorably rounding up delegates in states without primaries. Before the July 11 opening of the convention in Los Angeles, Kennedy had 600 of the 761 votes needed to win the nomination. There was still opposition, however. In a withering attack, former President Harry S. Truman questioned the senator's maturity. If elected at the age of forty-three, Kennedy would be the second youngest man to serve in the White House. (Theodore Roosevelt, who became President when he was forty-two, was the youngest.) In a brilliant rebuttal, Kennedy pointed out that his fourteen years in Congress gave him more government experience than all but a few Presidents—not including Truman—had had at the time of their accession to the office. A further challenge was posed by the venerable Mrs. Eleanor Roosevelt, who urged Stevenson's renomination.

Despite these obstacles, Kennedy's nomination came, almost anticlimactically, on the first ballot. His closest rival, Lyndon B. Johnson, was promptly offered, and accepted, the vice presidential nomination. According to some reports, Kennedy had not really expected the proud and sensitive Johnson to take the second spot, but the choice of the Texan was a shrewd one. It healed party wounds and gave geographical and religious balance to the ticket.

In one of the early addresses of his campaign, Kennedy moved to eliminate his religion as a political issue. The platform he chose was a daring one, a meeting of the Greater Houston Ministerial Association in Texas. There, to a largely hostile audience, he pledged that his Catholicism would in no way hamper the exercise of his presidential duties. He believed, as firmly as they did, he said, in the separation of church and state.

Many political observers felt that the election was won by Kennedy in the series of four television debates held in September and October with his Republican opponent, Richard M. Nixon. Before audiences estimated at sixty-five to seventy million Americans, a relaxed and self-confident John F. Kennedy traded words with an often tired and uncertain Nixon.

On Election Day, November 8, 1960, John F. Kennedy was elected President by the narrowest popular margin in the twentieth century. Only 113,057 votes out of nearly 69,000,000 cast separated Kennedy and Nixon. "So now my wife and I prepare for a new administration, and a new baby," he said in acknowledging Nixon's concession. Sixteen days later, John, Jr., was born.

In accepting the Democratic nomination the preceding July, Kennedy had enunciated his doctrine of the New Frontier and had said that it "sums up not what I intend to *offer* the American people, but what I intend to *ask* of them." The New Frontier was defined as "uncharted areas of science and space, unsolved problems of peace and war, unconquered pockets of ignorance and prejudice, unanswered questions of poverty and surplus." The American people, Kennedy insisted, were at a turning point "between the public interest and private comfort, between national greatness and national decline, between the fresh air of progress and the stale, dank atmosphere of 'normalcy.'"

On January 20, 1961, John F. Kennedy, in one of history's most stirring Inaugural Addresses, pledged himself to get the country moving again. "Now the trumpet summons us again—not as a call to bear arms, though arms we need—not as a call to battle, though embattled we are—but a call to bear the burden of a long twilight struggle year in and year out, 'rejoicing in hope, patient in tribulation'—a struggle against the common enemies of man: tyranny, poverty, disease and war itself. . . . And so, my fellow Americans: ask not what your country can do for you—ask what you can do for your country."

As Kennedy announced his choices for the Cabinet and for an expanded White House staff, comparisons began to be made between F. D. R.'s New Deal Brain Trust and J. F. K.'s New Frontiersmen. Harvard and MIT, it was said, would soon lose all their professors to Washington.

Because of the Kennedy style and Kennedy wit his live press conferences were among television's most entertaining shows. On the New Frontier the men seemed more brilliant and efficient, the women more charming and attractive, the social gatherings gayer.

Along more serious lines, the Food for Peace program, initiated during Eisenhower's administration, was taken over by the Kennedy administration in an effort to solve the problem of agricultural surpluses at home while winning friends abroad. Borrowing an idea from Senators Hubert Humphrey and Richard Neuberger, the President announced on March 1, 1961, the formation of the Peace Corps, which would send volunteer workers to underdeveloped countries. At an impressive White House gathering of Latin-American diplomats on March 13, he launched the Alliance for Progress, an ambitious program for economic cooperation and social development.

Political commentators made new comparisons between F. D. R. and Kennedy, writing of a second Hundred Days that would duplicate or even surpass the accomplishments of Roosevelt's first three months in office. Then came the Bay of Pigs.

During the closing months of the Eisenhower administration, the Central Intelligence Agency had begun training a force of anti-Castro Cubans in a Guatemalan jungle camp. Between his election and inauguration, John F. Kennedy learned of the plans to land this force in Cuba in an attempt to overthrow the Cuban dictator, who had taken his island into the Communist camp. New to his office, Kennedy let the professional intelligence and military men talk him into endorsing the invasion. Early in April, the force was put ashore at Cuba's Bay of Pigs—and was easily repelled by Castro. The debacle cost Kennedy the support of liberals at home and resulted in a great loss of prestige abroad.

A second international crisis loomed in Southeast Asia, where the United States moved close to intervention in Laos but settled for an international conference that established a neutral country.

Curious to meet the adversary who could cause him so much trouble in far corners of the globe, Kennedy arranged a rendezvous in Vienna in June with Russia's Nikita Khrushchev. The two days of talks were grim and unproductive, serving only to demonstrate the resolution and inflexibility that separated East and West. Khrushchev threatened to isolate the Western enclave in Berlin by signing a separate peace treaty with East Germany the following December. "It will be a cold winter," President Kennedy warned. That August the East Germans sealed off West Berlin by building their notorious wall.

RICHARD M. NIXON

Because of his youth, experience, oratorical ability, and California residence, Richard Milhous Nixon was an ideal running mate for Dwight D. Eisenhower in 1952. And so, just after his fortieth birthday, Nixon became the second-highest official in the federal government. Born in Yorba Linda, California, in 1913, he had graduated from Whittier College in 1934 and from Duke University Law School in 1937. After serving in the Navy during World War II, he entered California politics and was elected to the House of Representatives in 1946. He gained prominence as a member of the Committee on Un-American Activities and was elevated to the Senate in 1950. Opponents criticized Nixon's tactics, and Adlai Stevenson described him as "the kind of politician who would cut down a redwood tree, then mount the stump and make a speech for conservation." But Ike called Nixon "a courageous and honest man," and because of Eisenhower's several illnesses, the Californian became the most active Vice President up to that time. Nixon was the Republican presidential nominee in 1960, but John F. Kennedy outshone him in their televised debates and narrowly defeated him in the election. Two years later, Nixon lost a gubernatorial contest in California. A candidate for the presidential nomination in 1968, Nixon was regarded as the front-runner by most Republican leaders.

President Kennedy, above with President Adolfo Lopez Mateos of Mexico, was greeted with enthusiasm in Mexico City during his 1962 visit. Latin-American attitudes toward the United States were improving rapidly.

The 1961 visit to Europe also included stops in London and in Paris, where Jacqueline Kennedy dazzled even the austere General de Gaulle. Noting the press coverage given his wife, Kennedy introduced himself at a Paris luncheon as "the man who accompanied Jacqueline Kennedy to Paris. . . ."

Despite setbacks abroad, John F. Kennedy continued to push for progress at home. In 1961 and 1962 he announced plans for a national program to combat mental retardation, vigorously backed a trade expansion act, forced the steel industry to back down on a price increase, and pledged a reduction in taxes to boost the economy.

Sensitive to the narrowness of his own victory two years earlier, Kennedy campaigned exhaustively in the 1962 congressional elections. And the Democrats made the best mid-term showing since 1934 for a party in power, winning four Senate seats and losing only two in the House. Happily for Kennedy, the election followed his finest moment in office, the October, 1962, Cuban Missile Crisis.

During the early autumn, it had become evident to American intelligence that Fidel Castro was strengthening his ties to the Soviet Union. Aerial photos taken by a U-2 reconnaissance plane on Sunday, October 14, revealed that the Russians were installing offensive missiles on the island, only ninety miles off the Florida coast. There were two extreme choices open to the President: an aerial strike that would eliminate the missile threat but would risk nuclear war with Russia, or passive acceptance of the Russian challenge. Kennedy declined to consider either.

In a series of agonizing conferences over the next ten days, Kennedy and his associates reached a brilliant compromise: a naval quarantine of the island that would prevent further Soviet supplies from reaching Cuba, and a pledge that the United States would not invade if the Russians promised to dismantle and remove the missiles already there. A formula was found to allow the overextended Khrushchev to save face, and the crisis was resolved in America's favor. John F. Kennedy had demonstrated to his nation and the world the maturity and strength of the New Frontier.

In the aftermath of Cuba, Kennedy moved rapidly for a new understanding with the Soviet Union. In July, 1963, a nuclear

es caro — Charles!

As the French cartoon (left) suggests, De Gaulle was quite taken with Mrs. Kennedy during her 1961 trip. The next year the First Lady and her sister, Princess Lee Radziwill, went to India and rode an elephant (right).

test ban treaty was concluded with Russia and Great Britain. The hot line, providing instant communication with the Kremlin, was installed in the White House during that summer, and in October Kennedy authorized the sale of United States surplus wheat to the Russians.

The most persistent and nettlesome domestic problem facing Kennedy during his three years in office was that of civil rights. Not strongly committed to the issue during his congressional days, Kennedy, as President, saw the demand of Negroes for equal rights as only one of his many domestic concerns. He made a conscious effort to appoint qualified Negroes to federal jobs at high levels. But he did not press for creation of a federal Department of Housing and Urban Development after it became known that Southerners would oppose the appointment of Robert C. Weaver, a Negro, as the new department's Secretary. Courting Negro votes during the 1960 campaign, Kennedy had said that it would take only the "stroke of a pen" to issue an Executive Order against racial discrimination in federal housing; in office, it took him twenty-two months to make that pen stroke. Feeling that uni-

versal suffrage was the key to Negro progress, he urged Attorney General Robert Kennedy, his brother, to intervene throughout the South in voting cases.

In September, 1962, Kennedy was compelled to send federal marshals to enforce a court order admitting James Meredith to the University of Mississippi. When violence erupted on the campus, the President federalized the National Guard and moved regular troops into the state. Negro demonstrations in 1963 further forced Kennedy's hand. In April local authorities in Birmingham, Alabama, used fire hoses and police dogs to break up civil rights marches, and the President again sent in federal troops. In the following months he helped achieve the peaceful integration of the University of Alabama, endorsed the impressive March on Washington by two hundred and fifty thousand civil rights advocates, and pressed for passage of the most comprehensive civil rights law in the nation's history (up to that time). In November, 1963, the bill passed its first important hurdle when the House Judiciary Committee reported it favorably.

That same month, far across the globe in South Vietnam, the assassination of Pres-

945

ident Ngo Dinh Diem revealed to Kennedy once more the unending complexities of America's foreign relations. Only the preceding spring Secretary of Defense Robert McNamara had announced that the United States had "turned the corner" in its efforts to bolster the South Vietnamese regime against communism, but it now appeared that the war was entering a dangerous phase.

As 1963 drew to a close, Kennedy was faced with many problems, not the least of which was the need to build his political strength before the presidential election of November, 1964. In September he had made a highly successful "nonpolitical" tour to eleven Western states; by early November he had carried the message of his administration's accomplishments and aspirations to Massachusetts, Maine, New York, Pennsylvania, and Florida. There was special need for him to repair political fences in Texas, and he scheduled for late November a trip that would take him to San Antonio, Houston, Austin, Fort Worth, and Dallas.

In August, Mrs. Kennedy had given birth to a boy who had died of respiratory ailments thirty-nine hours later, and since then she had been convalescing. But she decided to accompany her husband to Texas.

A brash, rapidly expanding city, Dallas had a reputation for violence and extremism. The right-wing political groups in the city openly expressed their hatred of President Kennedy and his liberal policies. In 1960 Lyndon Johnson and his wife had been spat upon during a campaign appearance in the city; in October, 1963, United Nations Ambassador Adlai Stevenson, after having been vilified by demonstrators and hit with a sign in Dallas, had warned that the President might not be safe there. During Stevenson's visit Kennedy's picture had appeared on posters marked "Wanted for Treason." On November 21, the day before John F. Kennedy's arrival, a columnist for the Dallas *Morning News* wrote ominously, if flippantly, about the possibility of someone's letting go "with a broadside of grape shot in the presidential rigging if he spoke about Cuba, civil rights, taxes, or Vietnam."

On Thursday, November 21, the Kennedys received warm welcomes at San Antonio, Houston, and, late that night, Fort Worth. At noon the following day they stepped out of the presidential airplane, *Air Force One*, into warm sunshine at Dallas' Love Field. In an open limousine, the Kennedys rode with Governor and Mrs. John B. Connally. "You certainly can't say that the people of Dallas haven't given you a nice welcome," Mrs. Connally turned to say to the Kennedys. Moments later, at approximately 12:30 P.M., the car passed by the Texas School Book Depository, where—Dallas police later said—Lee Harvey Oswald waited with a rifle at a sixth-floor window.

A first bullet pierced the President's neck; a second shattered his brain. Rushed to Parkland Hospital, Kennedy was declared dead shortly after 1 P.M.

For most of the next horrifying four days, millions around the globe sat, stunned and saddened, by their radios and television sets to listen to and watch the final scenes of the meaningless tragedy. Oswald was apprehended, and on Sunday, November 24, in front of millions watching on television, was killed by Dallas night-club owner Jack Ruby.

World leaders and royalty came to Washington for the somber state funeral on Monday. But the most commanding presence that day was the black-shrouded widow, who conducted herself with unflinching dignity during the harrowing hours of the procession from the White House, the funeral mass, the burial on a hillside at Arlington National Cemetery, the lighting of the eternal flame over her husband's grave, and the reception later for the visiting dignitaries.

"I don't think there's any point in being Irish if you don't know that the world is going to break your heart eventually," Assistant Secretary of Labor Daniel P. Moynihan remarked at the time of the assassination. "I guess that we thought we had a little more time. . . . Mary McGrory said to me that we'll never laugh again. And I said, 'Heavens, Mary. We'll laugh again. It's just that we'll never be young again.' "

—JOSEPH L. GARDNER

A PICTURE PORTFOLIO

This 1960 campaign button reflects the enormous popularity of John F. Kennedy among young Americans.

COMPETITIVENESS
AND AMBITION

Second best," Joseph Patrick Kennedy frequently reminded his family, "is a loser." The spirited competitiveness that he instilled in each of his four sons would, Joe Kennedy hoped, be applied to politics, that most competitive of activities. His own father, and his wife's, had been major figures in the Irish clique that ran Boston; he had earned a fortune great enough to make all his nine children independently wealthy, and his sons would therefore be able to rise to much greater heights than their grandfathers had. Joe, Jr., seemed the most likely to transform his father's dreams into reality. He was a top scholar, a splendid athlete, and—when Mr. Kennedy was away—the totalitarian leader of the clan. Smaller, not as strong or good-looking but just as hardheaded, John Kennedy resented having to match his brother's achievements and often did not try. As he followed Joe through private schools on the inevitable road to Choate and Harvard, he was an indifferent student and sportsman. He even attended Princeton University briefly before he finally entered Harvard. When the United States entered World War II, Joe, Jr., became a flyer and was killed; Jack went to sea and became a hero and the new focal point of the Kennedys' ambitions.

In the 1921 photograph above, Mrs. Rose Kennedy (daughter of politician John "Honey Fitz" Fitzgerald, once the mayor of Boston) poses outdoors with her family. Eunice, Kathleen, and Rosemary are by their mother; four-year-old John Fitzgerald Kennedy is sitting on the kiddy car and Joe, Jr., stands beside him.

At the age of ten, John Kennedy (above) was a good, but not outstanding, football player for the Dexter School.

The picture below was taken at an American Embassy party in London when Joseph P. Kennedy was United States ambassador. Jack was then twenty-one years old.

Navy Lieutenant (j.g.) Kennedy, above, used his father's political influence uniquely— to get him away from a desk and into action.

949

Afternoon teas, hostessed by Kennedy's sisters and mother, began when J. F. K. was a candidate for Congress (above) and were a part of all his later campaigns. Elected to the Senate in 1952, Kennedy was one of Washington's most eligible bachelors until September 12, 1953, when he married Jacqueline Bouvier (below).

ON THE RISE

Candidate for Congress John F. Kennedy had looks, brains, money, a well-known name, and—most necessary of all in 1946—a heroic war record. (As commander of an ill-fated PT boat in the Pacific, he had saved the lives of several of his men.) Running on that record he won handsomely. After six years in the House of Representatives, he set his sights on a higher prize—the Senate seat of Henry Cabot Lodge II. In addition to his own family name, which was more famous in Massachusetts than Kennedy's, Lodge had Dwight Eisenhower's immense popularity working for him, for he was Ike's campaign manager. Nevertheless Kennedy won; and four years, one marriage, two back operations, and one prize-winning book later, he sought the 1956 Democratic vice presidential nomination. He failed to get it, but set his sights on 1960.

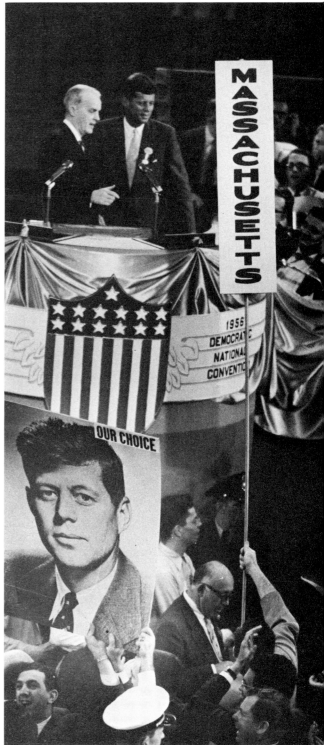

"A PROFILE IN COURAGE"

ELECT U. S. SENATOR
JOHN F. KENNEDY
VICE PRESIDENT

Adlai Stevenson, the 1956 Democratic presidential nominee, left the selection of a running mate to the convention delegates. On the third ballot, Senator Estes Kefauver defeated John Kennedy. That Kennedy (at right with Chairman Paul Butler) did so well was remarkable, for he would not have balanced the ticket. Even his campaign button (above), which recalled the title of his book, was a reminder of his similarities to the urbane, articulate Stevenson. Estes Kefauver, who was Southern and folksy, seemed likely to draw more votes for the Democrats.

RUNNING HARD

The barriers blocking John Kennedy's way to the 1960 Democratic nomination and to the Presidency itself were formidable. His wealth undoubtedly helped him overcome them, but it was also held against him. If his father had influence, he also had enemies. Kennedy was young, and a Roman Catholic, and he lacked the backing of the party leaders. But evasiveness was never a Kennedy characteristic, and the candidate faced the roadblocks as they came. He reduced fears that a Catholic could not be elected President by winning the primary in West Virginia, where his religion, wealth, and Boston accent were considered serious detriments. Just before the convention, he replied to charges that he was too young by pointing out that he was older than Thomas Jefferson had been when he wrote the Declaration of Independence, than George Washington had been when he commanded the Continental Army, than Columbus had been when he discovered America. After winning the nomination, Kennedy placed religious bigots on the defensive, complimented the voters with a high-level, gimmick-free campaign, and dispelled the myth of his immaturity in a series of televised debates with his opponent, Vice President Richard M. Nixon. When Nixon criticized Harry Truman's use of profanity in a campaign speech, Kennedy added his own censure. "I have sent him," Kennedy said, "the following wire. 'Dear Mr. President: I have noted with interest your suggestion as to where those who vote for my opponent should go. While I understand and sympathize with your deep motivation, I think it is important that our side try to refrain from raising the religious issue.'"

Top: during the presidential campaign of 1960, enthusiastic Kennedy supporters (some too young to vote) press forward, hoping to touch the candidate. Kennedy's impressive performance in the televised debates with Nixon (right) won him votes, but he was elected President by a very narrow margin.

MEN OF THE NEW FRONTIER

ROBERT F. KENNEDY

Thirty-six-year-old Robert F. Kennedy, brother of the President-elect, seemed to many Americans a poor choice for Attorney General; even Bobby thought the appointment ill-advised, but he gave in to the urgings of his brother and father. "I see nothing wrong," quipped J. F. K., amidst the storm of protest, "with giving Robert some legal experience as Attorney General before he goes out to practice law." Educated at Harvard and the University of Virginia Law School, Robert Kennedy worked as a lawyer in government after completing his education, taking time out to supervise his brother's campaigns. He had been a counsel for the McCarthy committee in 1953, but had resigned in protest against its excesses and had become counsel for the committee's Democratic minority. He had been counsel for the Senate Rackets Committee and in that capacity had begun a long fight with Teamster's Union boss James Hoffa. Kennedy proved to be an able head of the Justice Department and was his brother's most trusted adviser. After J. F. K.'s assassination, Robert served in Johnson's Cabinet until 1964, when he left to run successfully for the Senate from New York. Kennedy, an outspoken critic of L. B. J.'s Vietnam policy, announced in March, 1968, that he was a candidate for the Presidency.

W. AVERELL HARRIMAN

Would not naming elder statesman Averell Harriman to a post in the Kennedy administration, Robert Kennedy wanted to know, "be just an act of sentiment?" Sentimental or not, the appointment paid dividends: Harriman served first as an effective roving ambassador, then as assistant secretary of state for Far Eastern affairs and as under secretary for political affairs. In 1965 Lyndon Johnson reappointed him ambassador at large, employing Harriman's diplomatic skills wherever they were needed. Born in 1891, Harriman was educated at Groton and Yale, and inherited millions of dollars from his father, a Republican, at the age of seventeen. In 1928 he became a Democrat and subsequently held a number of important posts. Developing into a top-flight diplomat during the Roosevelt and Truman administrations, Harriman unsuccessfully sought the Democratic presidential nomination in 1952 and 1956. He was governor of New York for one term, but was defeated for re-election by Nelson Rockefeller in 1958. Although he was almost seventy and hard of hearing, his greatest service to his country was still ahead of him: in 1963 he was sent to Russia to work out a nuclear test ban treaty. "As soon as I heard that Harriman was going," one Russian diplomat said, "I knew you [Americans] were serious."

ARTHUR J. GOLDBERG

ROBERT S. McNAMARA

In less than five years, the energetic and highly respected Arthur J. Goldberg held three of the nation's most important offices. John F. Kennedy appointed him Secretary of Labor, then associate justice of the Supreme Court; under Lyndon Johnson, Goldberg was named to succeed Adlai Stevenson as United States ambassador to the United Nations. Raised on Chicago's West Side, the youngest of eight children of Russian immigrant parents, he went to work as a delivery boy in a shoe factory when he was twelve years old. He studied at public schools and at a junior college in Chicago, then worked his way through Northwestern University, which awarded him his doctorate of jurisprudence in 1930. By the late 1930's he had begun handling law cases for labor unions, and after serving during World War II in the Office of Strategic Services, he became a leading labor lawyer. Through his work on labor legislation Goldberg met John F. Kennedy, then the junior senator from Massachusetts, and later served as a Kennedy adviser during the 1960 presidential campaign. As Secretary of Labor, Goldberg mediated a number of important labor disputes before he was appointed to the High Court in 1962. His liberal record and his reputation as a skilled bargainer led to his United Nations assignment three years later.

Robert Strange McNamara has been called the first truly effective Secretary of Defense. Applying to his job new techniques of management, he brought his department under strict civilian control. He led in the diversification of American weapons and military techniques, which resulted in the abandonment of dependence on nuclear weapons and gave Presidents new alternatives to draw upon in times of crisis. Born in 1916, McNamara graduated from the University of California and Harvard Business School, taught at Harvard, served as a statistician for the Air Force in World War II, and became a Ford Motor Company "Whiz Kid" in 1946. Fifteen years later, having been president of Ford for one month, McNamara was asked to take charge of the Defense Department for President John F. Kennedy. On the New Frontier, and later in the Great Society, his hardheadedness and abilities were much admired. The praise was not, however, universal. Some hawkish critics felt that McNamara had opposed rapid escalation of the war in Vietnam, while some doves held the Secretary responsible for the continuance of the fighting there. President Lyndon Johnson, however, said, "I thank God every night for Bob McNamara." Late in 1967, it was announced that he would become head of the World Bank in 1968.

Years of turmoil had made Laos a tinderbox, but in Vienna in 1961 Kennedy and Nikita Khrushchev (above) agreed to support its neutralization. Below, Kennedy explains the details at a press conference.

A BEGINNING

As he confessed in his Inaugural Address, President Kennedy did not expect to achieve the real and lasting peace that had eluded the world for so long. He did, however, mean to begin. The ill-fated Bay of Pigs invasion was a disastrous start, but afterward people abroad began to notice that American foreign policy was indeed changing. The old cold-war clichés were disappearing. The support that used to go to any Latin-American government that called itself anti-Communist—no matter how totalitarian—could no longer be expected, as Kennedy led the hemisphere into an Alliance for Progress, an effort to strengthen democracy in the Americas. The President could be tough, but he was willing to work with Nikita Khrushchev and did, seeking new formulas for peace and hoping to bring about a nuclear test ban treaty. When internal conflicts in Southeast Asia threatened to erupt into a major war, Kennedy rejected the assumption that neutral nations were anti-American and reversed the trend in Cambodia and in Laos. Times were still tense, but foreign skeptics, who were convinced that the United States did nothing selflessly, were confounded by the Peace Corps, which added helping hands to helping dollars, exemplified the new American attitude, and carried the spirit of the new young leader of the United States everywhere.

President Kennedy often spoke of the idealism of a "new generation of Americans." The Peace Corps put that idealism to work. Originally suggested by Senators Hubert Humphrey and Richard Neuberger in the 1950's, the corps was established by Kennedy, who became closely associated with its purpose. The young volunteer above, serving in Chimbote, Peru, built the school in which he taught.

In 1962 Mrs. Kennedy (above in the East Room) conducted a televised tour of the White House and explained her redecorating. The Bellangé chair (above right) is one of the Monroe administration pieces that the First Lady found and returned to the Mansion. She was especially proud of the redecorated Red Room (below).

THE KENNEDY STYLE

Whatever their politics, most Americans enjoyed having a stylish First Family. The Kennedys were unique: he was the youngest man ever elected to the Presidency and she was the youngest and prettiest and most elegant First Lady in modern times; their two children—Caroline and "John-John"—were unabashed scene stealers. As the average age of Americans dipped lower and lower—soon a majority would be under twenty-five years old—the nation enjoyed watching a President who had wanted the job, who had worked to get it, and who loved having it. Kennedy was not the reluctant Dwight D. Eisenhower, nor the shocked Harry S. Truman. (Roosevelt, like J. F. K., had sought the office in 1932, but that was too far back for most Americans to remember.) The whole tone—the "style"—of the White House was sharper and livelier than it had been in years. Mrs. Kennedy dug into

White House history, searched the Mansion's storerooms, and redecorated the presidential home beautifully. Far from ignoring the demonstrators who appeared in front of the White House periodically, President Kennedy sent them coffee. One such demonstrator, a nuclear scientist with a "Ban the bomb" placard, was later invited to the Kennedys' dinner for American Nobel Prize winners. Robert Frost read one of his poems at the inauguration and W. H. Auden, Robert Lowell, and John Steinbeck sat on the rostrum. On another occasion, Pablo Casals played at a White House concert. There were cynics and critics, but Thornton Wilder said that Kennedy was creating "a whole new world of surprised self-respect" in the arts. "It is a good thing," Ernest Hemingway wrote, "to have a brave man as our President in times as tough as these are. . . ." Said Steinbeck, "What a joy that literacy is no longer prima-facie evidence of treason."

CECIL STOUGHTON

Above: President and Mrs. Kennedy congratulate virtuoso cellist Pablo Casals after a White House concert.

If Castro was, as the cartoon above implies, the creator of the 1962 Missile Crisis, he was also its main casualty. Clearly, Kennedy could not tolerate Soviet missiles in Cuba, and Khrushchev was not going to risk war to give Castro the "protection" he claimed American intentions warranted.

The huge crowd that welcomed J. F. K. to Berlin (top right) in 1963 became hysterical when he said, "All free men . . . are citizens of Berlin." In contrast, the civil rights marchers who converged on Washington (right) were quite restrained. But the whole country was impressed.

960

MAGNUM/CHARLES HARBUTT

COMMITMENT

In terms of tangible accomplishments, the first twenty months of the Kennedy administration had been unexceptional. In a subtler way, however, the period had been remarkable: the relationship between the people and the government had been re-established. Prodded by the President, the young and not so young became involved with issues; *commitment* was their watchword. This was important groundwork for Kennedy, who hoped to make 1963 a year of calculable achievement. It began, however, in the shadow of the Cuban Missile Crisis. In October, 1962, the President had insisted that Russia remove the missiles it had installed in Cuba and had ordered a blockade of the island. Kennedy was firm and the Russians complied, but because the President had also been restrained, the talks that led to the nuclear test ban treaty of 1963 were able to continue. That Kennedy had emerged as an international leader became apparent during his European trip as he was welcomed warmly in city after city. At home, responding to the brutality with which the American Negro's demand for equality was resisted, Kennedy said that civil rights was "a moral issue" and asked Congress to pass the strongest civil rights bill in history.

His reaction to crowds revealed much about the President. When a quarter of a million black and white Americans marched peacefully on Washington in August, 1963, he was proud—although the participants were by no means uniformly pro-Kennedy. When three-fifths of Berlin's people welcomed him with unrestrained enthusiasm, he was disturbed: he felt the crowd was hysterical, irrational. Best of all John F. Kennedy liked the reception he received in Ireland, where he recited an old Irish song: "Come back around to the land of thy birth./Come with the shamrock in the springtime. . . ." "This is not," he confessed, "the land of my birth, but . . . I certainly will come back in the springtime."

The President was killed and Texas Governor John Connally (above left in the car with the Kennedys) was wounded when an assassin fired at their motorcade in Dallas. In the blurred picture above—one frame of an amateur's movie film—Mrs. Kennedy climbs on the trunk of the car to help a Secret Service man aboard just after the shots. Right: the Kennedy family and the Johnsons after a service at the Capitol in Washington.

DAYS OF MOURNING

He died of exposure," wrote E. B. White just after President Kennedy was killed in Dallas, "but in a way that he would have settled for—in the line of duty, and with his friends and enemies all around, supporting him and shooting at him." Grief settled in places that would have surprised even Kennedy. Bells rang in London, dirges were played on Russian radios, and Charles de Gaulle was "stunned" that his people were weeping, "as though he were a Frenchman, a member of their own family." A native in Africa walked ten miles through the bush to tell the American consul, "I have lost a friend and I am so sorry." Americans were numb, disbelieving, and angry—not just at Lee Harvey Oswald, who had been arrested for the assassination, but even at the dead President. "He did not fear the weather . . ." White wrote, "but instead challenged the wind itself," and although the people admired that in him, they did not see why he had felt compelled to challenge the Dallas winds. "Nut country" the President had called it, but he went anyway and was killed.

He was buried three days later, and the traditional riderless horse that followed the coffin to the grave might have been created for this one awful day. He side-stepped and tossed his handsome head back and snorted and pulled, reluctant to go, his very determination and independence symbolizing the spirit of the fallen leader.

In the months that followed, John Kennedy was idolized and minimized. His place in history was argued about because making a country young again—giving it vigor—is a hard thing to measure. "For a time," writer Norman Mailer said, "we felt the country was ours. Now it's theirs again."

On November 25, the four dark days that began with the shooting of the President came to a close. At left, the funeral procession moves toward Arlington Cemetery, where John F. Kennedy was interred.

JACQUELINE

In the year of her husband's election to the Presidency, Jacqueline Kennedy admitted that she had been "born and reared a Republican." Then she added: "But you have to be a Republican to realize how nice it is to be a Democrat."

For a long while Mrs. Kennedy had not found anything "nice" about politics of any kind: she regarded it, early in her marriage to Senator John F. Kennedy of Massachusetts, as "sort of my enemy as far as seeing Jack was concerned." She had been an inquiring photographer for a newspaper when, in 1951, a married couple "who had been shamelessly matchmaking for a year" invited her and the senator to their home for dinner. In 1952, when Jacqueline was in Paris—virtually her second home—she ran into the American art critic Bernard Berenson, who told her, "American girls should marry American boys. They wear better." Heeding his advice, she headed home and on September 12, 1953, married Kennedy.

They were a fairy-tale couple—both good-looking, bright, rich, polished, and well traveled; but there were more differences between them than just party affiliation. Jack Kennedy, a product of Irish Boston and the grandson of two politicians, belonged to a tight-knit family that had been wealthy for only two generations. Jacqueline Bouvier of Newport, Rhode Island, belonged to international aristocracy, and her parents were divorced. If she was more comfortable in riding habit or on water skis, she was nevertheless a good sport when it came to touch football games on the lawn of the Kennedys' home. "Just tell me one thing," she said during her maiden encounter with the sport, "when I get the ball, which way do I run?"

As First Lady, Mrs. Kennedy did not merely have admirers, she had *fans.* She un-willingly vied with Elizabeth Taylor for the covers of movie magazines. Her hairdos set trends, her clothing was copied, advertisers sought models who looked like her. Powerless to stop the exploitation, she tried to divert attention from herself to her efforts at redecorating the White House.

The First Lady did not often campaign with her husband. In 1956, while he was seeking the Democratic vice presidential nomination at the convention, she was recovering from having given birth to a stillborn child. In 1958, when he sought re-election to the Senate, she had just given birth to Caroline. In 1960 she was pregnant with John, Jr. But after she recovered from the death of her newborn infant, Patrick, in 1963, she decided to accompany the President on a political trip to Texas. As usual she was a magnet for crowds and permitted Kennedy to make quips about her popularity as compared with his. (In Paris the President had introduced himself as the man who had accompanied Jacqueline Kennedy to Europe.)

She was there when he was shot in Dallas and she held his shattered head as he died; she even entered the hospital room while the doctors did everything they could think of to save a life that was already gone. Her incredible bravery during the four days that followed provided Americans with a noble model; like her, they took hold of themselves and controlled their grief.

While insistently maintaining her family's privacy after leaving Washington, Mrs. Kennedy was dedicated to preserving the memory of her husband. She supervised plans for a memorial library and sought to block publication of books that she regarded as sensational or that contained intimate details of her life with the late President.

Mrs. John F. Kennedy, photographed during her 1962 visit to Pakistan

FACTS IN SUMMARY: JOHN F. KENNEDY

CHRONOLOGY

UNITED STATES		KENNEDY		UNITED STATES		KENNEDY
U.S. enters World War I	1917	Born May 29		NATO pact signed	1949	Fights for federal aid to housing
Stock market crash	1929			Russia explodes atomic bomb		Criticizes Truman's China policy
Franklin D. Roosevelt elected President	1932			Nationalist Chinese evacuate mainland		
WPA created	1935	Graduates from the Choate School		Korean War begins	1950	Re-elected to House of Representatives
Social Security established		Studies at London School of Economics		First U.S. H-bomb test	1952	Defeats Henry Cabot Lodge in race for Senate
		Attends Princeton briefly		Eisenhower elected President		
	1936	Enters Harvard		Stalin dies	1953	Marries Jacqueline Bouvier
Roosevelt attempts to pack Supreme Court	1937			Armistice in Korea		
				Russia explodes H-bomb		
	1938	Serves in London as secretary to his father		Supreme Court desegregation order	1954	Undergoes spinal-fusion operation
France falls to Germans	1940	Graduates from Harvard		Army-McCarthy hearings		Fails to pair on McCarthy censure
		Publishes Why England Slept			1955	Undergoes second back operation
Pearl Harbor attacked	1941	Appointed ensign in Naval Reserve		Hungarian Revolt	1956	Publishes Profiles in Courage
Germany and Italy declare war on U.S.				Eisenhower re-elected President		Almost nominated for Vice President
Battle of Bataan	1942	Assigned to Motor Torpedo Boat Squadron				Campaigns for Stevenson
Battle of Midway				Civil Rights Act	1957	Supports Civil Rights Act
Sicily and Italy invaded	1943	Sent to South Pacific		Little Rock school integration crisis		Profiles in Courage wins Pulitzer Prize
U.S. offensive in Central Pacific		PT-109 sunk by Japanese destroyer		Russians orbit Sputnik I		
		Returns to U.S. because of back injury and malaria		First U.S. satellite orbited	1958	Re-elected to Senate
U.S. takes Marshall and Mariana islands	1944	Undergoes disc operation		Fidel Castro comes to power in Cuba	1959	Begins campaign for Presidency
Allies land in France		Joseph Kennedy, Jr., killed in action		U-2 shot down in Russia	1960	Wins primaries in New Hampshire, Wisconsin, and West Virginia
Philippines Campaign begins						Elected President
Battle of the Bulge						
Yalta Conference	1945	Employed by International News Service		Eisenhower breaks off diplomatic relations with Cuba	1961	Inaugurated as President
Roosevelt dies		Covers U.N. conference				Acts to brake recession and outflow of gold
Truman becomes President		Covers Potsdam Conference		Russian cosmonaut Gagarin becomes first man to enter space		Announces formation of Peace Corps
V-E Day				Invasion of Cuba by U.S.-supported exiles fails		Announces Alliance for Progress in Latin America
U.N. organized						
Potsdam Conference				Astronauts Shepard and Grissom make sub-orbital space flights		Accepts blame for Bay of Pigs debacle
First atomic bomb dropped on Hiroshima						Moves to neutralize Laos
V-J Day				Berlin Wall built		Confers with De Gaulle, Khrushchev, and Macmillan in Europe
War crimes trials held at Nuremberg	1946	Elected to House of Representatives				Suggests "peace race" in U.N. speech
Truman Doctrine	1947	Votes against Taft-Hartley Act				Declares continued U.S. support for Vietnam independence
Marshall Plan						
Taft-Hartley Act						
Berlin Airlift begins	1948	Re-elected to House of Representatives				
Truman elected President						

Lt. Col. Glenn in first U.S. orbital space flight	1962	*Asks for U.S.-Russian cooperation in space exploration*
Steel prices raised, then lowered		*Orders resumption of U.S. nuclear tests*
Geneva Conference ensures neutral Laos		*Forces steel companies to retract price increase*
Riots on University of Mississippi campus over admission of Negro		*Sends federal troops to University of Mississippi*
Soviet missile build-up in Cuba		*Campaigns in mid-term congressional elections*
Trade Expansion Act		*Meets Russian missile threat in Cuba with quarantine*
Democrats gain four Senate seats, lose two House seats in mid-term elections		*Orders end to racial discrimination in federal housing*
Major Cooper orbits earth twenty-two times	1963	*Sends federal troops to quiet Birmingham race riots*
Limited nuclear test ban treaty signed by U.S., U.S.S.R., and Great Britain		*Aids peaceful integration of University of Alabama*
March on Washington, D.C., by civil rights supporters		*Suggests combining of U.S. and Soviet efforts for moon exploration*
Stevenson abused during visit to Dallas		*Approves sale of wheat to Russia*
Armed forces coup in South Vietnam		*Assassinated in Dallas, November 22*

JACQUES LOWE

Kennedy and his family, during the campaign of 1960

ELECTION OF 1960

CANDIDATES	ELECTORAL VOTE	POPULAR VOTE
John F. Kennedy Democratic	303	34,226,731
Richard M. Nixon Republican	219	34,108,157

THE KENNEDY ADMINISTRATION

INAUGURATION: January 20, 1961; the Capitol, Washington, D.C.

VICE PRESIDENT: Lyndon B. Johnson

SECRETARY OF STATE: Dean Rusk

SECRETARY OF THE TREASURY: C. Douglas Dillon

SECRETARY OF DEFENSE: Robert S. McNamara

ATTORNEY GENERAL: Robert F. Kennedy

POSTMASTER GENERAL: J. Edward Day

SECRETARY OF THE INTERIOR: Stewart L. Udall

SECRETARY OF AGRICULTURE: Orville L. Freeman

SECRETARY OF COMMERCE: Luther H. Hodges

SECRETARY OF LABOR: Arthur J. Goldberg; W. Willard Wirtz (from Sept. 25, 1962)

SECRETARY OF HEALTH, EDUCATION, AND WELFARE: Abraham A. Ribicoff; Anthony J. Celebrezze (from July 31, 1962)

AMBASSADOR TO UNITED NATIONS: Adlai E. Stevenson

SUPREME COURT APPOINTMENTS: Byron R. White (1962); Arthur J. Goldberg (1962)

87th **CONGRESS** (January 3, 1961–January 3, 1963):
Senate: 65 Democrats; 35 Republicans
House: 263 Democrats; 174 Republicans

88th **CONGRESS** (January 3, 1963–January 3, 1965):
Senate: 67 Democrats; 33 Republicans
House: 258 Democrats; 177 Republicans

BIOGRAPHICAL FACTS

BIRTH: Brookline, Mass., May 29, 1917

ANCESTRY: Irish

FATHER: Joseph Patrick Kennedy; b. East Boston, Mass., Sept. 6, 1888

FATHER'S OCCUPATIONS: Financier; diplomat

MOTHER: Rose Fitzgerald Kennedy; b. Boston, Mass., 1891

BROTHERS: Joseph Patrick (1915–1944); Robert Francis (1925–   ); Edward Moore (1932–   )

SISTERS: Rosemary (1919–   ); Kathleen (1920–1948); Eunice Mary (1921–   ); Patricia (1924–   ); Jean Ann (1928–   )

WIFE: Jacqueline Lee Bouvier; b. Southampton, N.Y., July 28, 1929

MARRIAGE: Newport, R.I., Sept. 12, 1953

CHILDREN: Caroline Bouvier (1957–   ); John Fitzgerald (1960–   ); Patrick Bouvier (1963)

EDUCATION: Attended the Choate School; London School of Economics; Princeton University; graduated from Harvard University (1940); Stanford University

RELIGIOUS AFFILIATION: Roman Catholic

OCCUPATIONS BEFORE PRESIDENCY: Author; politician

MILITARY SERVICE: Ensign, lieutenant (j.g.), lieutenant, U.S. Naval Reserve (active duty 1941–1945)

PRE-PRESIDENTIAL OFFICES: Member U.S. House of Representatives; Member U.S. Senate

AGE AT INAUGURATION: 43

DEATH: Dallas, Texas, Nov. 22, 1963

PLACE OF BURIAL: Arlington National Cemetery, Arlington, Va.

LYNDON BAINES JOHNSON

Casting a lengthening shadow over American history for more than a generation, Lyndon Baines Johnson has stood, as journalists Rowland Evans and Robert Novak have pointed out, "near or at the center of power in Washington for all the great political events of our epoch. . . . No man in American history became President with a greater relish for power or with more experience. . . ."

Few Presidents have been as controversial as L. B. J. Eastern critics have lampooned him as petulant, impetuous, and unsophisticated, as a county chairman writ large, a cloakroom Machiavelli out of his depth in the Presidency, or a covert Dixiecrat. He has been booed in Dallas as a pawn of the Yankees and accused of preaching socialism on the Texas stump. To his admirers, however, Lyndon Johnson ranks with Franklin D. Roosevelt in vision and achievement. Democratic chieftain James A. Farley says flatly that "we never had a finer leader. . . ." Johnson, writes historian A. A. Berle of Harvard, "is not a romantic image. The brilliant court and flashing pennons of Camelot are not his. . . . Rather . . . the small-farmer's son become President has plotted out in his Great Society the contours and trace-lines of the next major social development in America."

On one point Johnson's detractors and loyalists agree unconditionally: L. B. J. has brought to the White House a political genius, a technique of persuasion and direction perhaps without parallel in American history. Richard Nixon concedes that he is "one of the ablest political craftsmen of our times." Adlai Stevenson hailed Johnson's "extraordinary managerial skill" and called him "a master of the art of the possible in politics."

Of L. B. J.'s political destiny his grandfather Sam had had no doubt. When Lyndon was born to Sam, Jr., and Rebekah Baines Johnson near Stonewall,

Lyndon B. Johnson in 1964

Texas, on August 27, 1908, Sam, Sr., spread the word to all who would listen: "A United States Senator was born this morning. . . ." Politics ran on both sides of the Johnson family line. L. B. J.'s ancestors had helped settle the South, one of them having served as governor of Kentucky. His paternal grandfather, a Confederate veteran, had settled and given his name to Johnson City, Texas. Rebekah Johnson's father had served in the Texas legislature and as Texas secretary of state, and Lyndon's father was also a member of the Texas legislature.

Lyndon Johnson emerged not from the Texas of oil barons or cowboys, but from the mean, stony, drought-cursed soil of the southwest hill country. The Johnsons were not poor, but they knew hard times and scrambled for what they earned. Sam was an occasional schoolteacher and a farmer who was hard hit by the agricultural depression of the twenties. "I know that as a farm boy I did not feel secure," President Johnson recalled, "and when I was 14 years I decided I was not going to be the victim of a system which would allow the price of a commodity like cotton to drop from 40 cents to 6 cents and destroy the homes of people like my own family."

"Thin as a willow fishing pole," Lyndon at fifteen already stood more than six feet tall. For pocket money, he worked at odd jobs: picking cotton, shining shoes at the Johnson City barbershop, passing out handbills. After graduating from high school, he went west. "Up and down the coast I tramped, washing dishes, waiting on tables, doing farmwork," he recalled, ". . . and always growing thinner and more homesick." Back home, he joined a road gang and, harnessed to mules, worked a buck scraper.

Agreeing with his mother that such a life honored neither him nor his eminent forebears, Johnson entered Southwest Texas State Teachers College in San Marcos in February, 1927. He majored in history, headed the debating team, and bulldozed his way to political primacy on campus. To finance his way through college—in an accelerated course—he worked as a school jan-

Lyndon Johnson, when he was eighteen months old

COURTESY OF LYNDON B. JOHNSON

itor, a secretary in the college president's office, and a teacher of Mexican-Americans. He graduated with a B.S. degree in 1930.

Immediately after college, Johnson taught public speaking at Houston's Sam Houston High School. In 1931 he campaigned hard for the election to the House of Representatives of a wealthy conservative, Richard M. Kleberg. When Kleberg won, Johnson accompanied him to Washington, where he served for four years as his secretary. Already enjoying the kindly paternal eye of his father's friend, Congressman Sam Rayburn, Johnson rapidly gained a reputation for political acuity, serving as the *de facto* leader of the Little Congress, an informal group of House secretaries.

On November 17, 1934, L. B. J., who had bought a ring for two dollars and fifty cents at Sears Roebuck, married Claudia Alta Taylor (nicknamed Lady Bird by a family cook), the daughter of a well-to-do eastern Texas landowner. She would bear him two daughters, Lynda Bird and Luci Baines.

In the spring of 1935 Johnson returned to Texas, where he served for eighteen months as state director of F. D. R.'s National Youth Administration. Under Johnson's efficient leadership, the NYA lent money to, or secured part-time employment in the construction of state parks, schools, and libraries for, an estimated seventy-five to one hundred thousand students, who were thus enabled to continue in college.

Lyndon Johnson's tenure as NYA director widened his political base in the Texas precincts. When the congressional seat in Johnson's Tenth District fell vacant early in 1937, L. B. J. threw his hat in the ring. Lumping his several conservative opponents together as an unholy alliance of "trembling, fear and reaction," Johnson equated a vote for himself with a vote for Roosevelt, espousing even F. D. R.'s ill-advised Supreme Court-packing plan. His strategy worked. On April 10 L. B. J., aged twenty-eight, was elected to Congress. The next day he met Roosevelt at Galveston and accepted F. D. R.'s invitation to accompany him across Texas. From that excursion Johnson emerged as an overt protégé of Roosevelt's. F. D. R. was responsible for Johnson's prompt appointment to the House Naval Affairs Committee. Johnson, a friend recalled, was "a real pusher . . . maybe a little too cocky . . . but he did get things done."

Johnson worked hard for his home district. He obtained millions of federal dollars for local projects and pressed successfully for rural electrification by public, rather than private, power companies. He was instrumental, too, in locating a naval air-training base in Corpus Christi and shipyards in Houston and Orange, all outside his district.

Vice President John Nance Garner's open defiance of F. D. R.'s bid for a third term in 1940 provided Johnson with another opportunity to stand up as a Roosevelt loyalist. He not only supported the President but he headed the House Democratic Congressional Campaign Committee, which was credited with averting Republican gains.

In April, 1941, L. B. J. made his first bid for a seat in the United States Senate. Announcing, from the steps of the White House, his decision to run, Johnson entered the fray against three opponents. During the campaign he strongly supported Roosevelt's program of military preparedness and his appeal for an end to isolationism. Ridiculed as a yes man, Johnson agreed: "I am a yes man," he declared, "for everything that is American." And if war should come, he pledged, and "my vote must be cast to send your boy to war, that day Lyndon Johnson will leave his seat in Congress to go with him." Johnson lost to Governor W. Lee O'Daniel by 1,311 votes. After this defeat he consciously moved to the right to consolidate his political power base in a more urban, ambitious Texas, which was dominated by conservative oil interests.

His defeat notwithstanding, Lyndon made good his pledge to leave his seat in Congress and go on active duty in the Navy. Assigned first to a post in San Francisco, he appealed to Roosevelt for a more active job. In May, 1942, Lieutenant Commander Johnson landed on New Caledonia, an island off the east coast of Australia, on a special presidential mission to assess American morale and military strength in the Pacific combat zone. In June, Johnson boarded a B-26 bomber en route from Port Moresby to a mission over the Japanese air base at Lae, near Salamaua. As the B-26 approached the target, one of its engines failed. The aircraft fell back from the bomber group, becoming an easy prey for attacking Japanese fighters. Though hit several times, Johnson's plane ducked out of range and, badly damaged, limped back to Port Moresby. For showing "marked coolness in spite of the hazard involved," L. B. J. was awarded the Silver Star Medal.

When Roosevelt ordered all congressmen serving in the armed forces to return home, Johnson assumed the chairmanship of a subcommittee of the Naval Affairs Committee; the subcommittee was charged with investigating Navy procurement procedures in order to eliminate waste. Congressman Johnson drafted the "work or fight" bill, which "froze" workers in key war positions and called for the drafting of those who would not work in war plants. He also supported the Smith-Connally antistrike act.

After V-J Day Johnson, a member of the Postwar Military Policy Committee, decried what he described as America's precipitate dismantling of its war machine and helped draft security legislation. He was also named to the Joint Committee on Atomic Energy. He approved of the controversial Taft-Hartley Act and voted to override President Truman's veto of that legislation.

In 1948 Johnson again sought a Senate seat, facing a conservative former Texas governor, Coke Stevenson, in the decisive Democratic primary. It was a virulent campaign. L. B. J. ran on a platform of preparedness, peace, and progress, urging stronger armed forces, a viable United Nations, and federal aid to Texas for soil conservation and rural electrification. Johnson also charged that the "big labor racketeers, the labor dictatorship" opposed him because he had voted for "the anti-Communist Taft-Hartley bill." Johnson—taking a position he would change in later years—attacked Truman's civil rights program as "a farce and a sham—an effort to set up a police state in the guise of liberty." He argued that his House vote against repealing the poll tax had been a defense of states' rights and said of his vote against appropriations for the Fair Employment Practices Commission: "If a man can tell you whom you must hire, he can tell you whom you can't hire."

The result of the first primary was inconclusive: Stevenson won 477,077 votes to Johnson's 405,617, while nine other candidates shared 320,000 votes. In a runoff election Johnson edged past Stevenson by a mere 87 votes. After torrid confrontations in court that are still shrouded in allegation and controversy, Johnson was certified as the Democratic candidate. He was then elected to the United States Senate by a ratio of 2 to 1.

Johnson was promptly named to the Senate Armed Services Committee, on which he pursued his central theme of military preparedness, joined Senator Stuart Symington in the latter's cold-war fight for a strengthened Air Force, and warned, in February, 1950, that the United States could no longer rely on the "security of an atomic monopoly." Johnson supported the Korean War effort, though he attacked Tru-

man's conduct of the war. He headed the Senate Preparedness Investigating Subcommittee, which fought military inefficiency and waste. He branded Truman's seizure of the steel mills "dictatorship" and voted to negate the President's veto of the McCarran-Walter Immigration Act. Conscious of his narrow victory in 1948, he mended his fences with Oil Texas and sided with the coalition of conservative Democrats and Republicans.

In the 1952 presidential campaign, Johnson supported Adlai Stevenson unenthusiastically but insisted that "the Democratic Party is best for Texas and the South and the nation." After Dwight Eisenhower's victory he said, "We have a new leader. I won't discuss the wisdom of the choice, but he is our leader. Some people have gone off into the corner to pout. Others want to tear down, but any jackass can kick down a barn. It takes a good carpenter to build a barn. We aim to build."

Most certainly Eisenhower's victory helped build Lyndon Johnson. In January, 1953, forty-four-year-old L. B. J. was elected Minority Leader of the Senate. Democrats, he announced, would not oppose for the sake of opposition. "All of us," he explained, "are Americans before we are members of any political organization." There was one major exception to his cooperation with Eisenhower. When the latter considered sending American planes to aid the beleaguered French forces at Dienbienphu in Indochina, Johnson declared that such action would place the United States "in clear danger of being left naked and alone in a hostile world. . . ." He demanded that the consent of the British be obtained before any intervention occurred. When the British turned down the proposal, the idea was abandoned.

The election of 1954, in which Johnson himself was easily re-elected, gave control of Congress to the Democrats and catapulted L. B. J. into a national prominence second only to Eisenhower's. At forty-six, Johnson was named Majority Leader of the Senate.

"I do not think it is an exaggeration to say," Walter Lippmann observed, "that Mr. Eisenhower's success as President began when the Republicans lost control of Congress and the standing committees." At no point in his career had Johnson pursued more effectively his political approach of good will: "Come now and let us reason together." He drummed up votes on both sides of the aisle for Eisenhower's Formosa Resolution, which warned Peking not to move against Taiwan; for Eisenhower's minimum-wage reform bill, topping the President's proposed ninety-cent minimum by ten cents; and for Eisenhower's Mutual Security Act and Reciprocal Trade Agreement extensions. Presidential historian Louis W. Koenig called L. B. J. "one of the most illustrious floor leaders in Senate history," a master architect of political accommodation who commanded "a relentless, overpowering persuasiveness. . . ."

Johnson's career as Majority Leader was interrupted on July 2, 1955, when he suffered a heart attack that was diagnosed as a "myocardial infarction of a moderately severe character." (L. B. J. later described the attack as being "about as bad as you can have and live.") He recovered quickly and was back in the Senate six months later.

In 1957 Johnson personally shepherded through the Senate the first civil rights bill in eighty-two years, and in 1960 guided the passage of the second, which provided new voting registration guarantees for Negroes. "More than any other politician since the Civil War," said James Reston in *The New York Times*, Johnson "has, on the race problem, been the most effective mediator between the North and the South."

When the Soviet Union rocked the United States out of its complacency by launching Sputnik I in 1957, Johnson initiated a Senate Preparedness Subcommittee investigation to find out why the Soviets had forged ahead in the space race, and again appealed for a strengthened strategic Air Force and for acceleration of America's space and missile effort. He also chaired the Senate Committee on Aeronautical and Space Sciences and helped establish NASA and the National Aeronautics and Space Council.

In June, 1957, Johnson called for "an open curtain for full discussion" between the United States and the Soviet Union. "Let the people know!" he declared. ". . . And when the people know, they will insist that

Vice President-elect Lyndon Johnson relaxes at his ranch in mid-November of 1960. L. B. J. had campaigned effectively in the South, an area of concern to Kennedy; the Republicans won only three Southern states.

Lady Bird Johnson, the energetic First Lady, visits an old Pueblo settlement at San Ildefonso, New Mexico.

the arms race, the nuclear explosions, the intercontinental missiles all be banished." In a dramatic demonstration of political unity, Johnson also appeared before the United Nations in 1958 as Eisenhower's personal envoy to plead for international cooperation in the use of outer space.

That Johnson was built of presidential timber his boosters never doubted. L. B. J. himself made behind-the-scenes soundings and permitted extensive politicking on his behalf, but he stayed out of the 1960 primaries, insisting that somebody had to "tend the store" in Washington.

At the convention Johnson had considerable delegate support. But John F. Kennedy could not be stopped despite an eleventh-hour confrontation with Johnson, in which the latter tried to ridicule Kennedy's lack of experience. On the first ballot Johnson polled 409 votes to Kennedy's winning 806.

Then, in one of the great political surprises of American history, Johnson was offered, and accepted, the vice presidential nomination. Political analysts agree that Johnson's appearance on the Democratic ticket spelled the difference between defeat and victory for John F. Kennedy, who indisputably needed Johnson to carry the South.

Vice President Johnson served as a presidential emissary abroad, making several celebrated trips. At home L. B. J. attended Cabinet sessions, served on the National Security Council, maintained a degree of liaison between the White House and Capitol Hill, and headed the National Aeronautics and Space Council, the Peace Corps Advisory Council, and the President's Committee on Equal Employment Opportunity.

The Vice Presidency was patently not compatible with Johnson's uninhibited ego, his ambition, or his phenomenal energy. Within a heartbeat of ultimate power, he exercised almost none. But on November 22, 1963, the tragedy in Dallas placed Lyndon Johnson at the summit of world power. Two hours after the assassination of John F. Kennedy, Johnson stood solemnly aboard the presidential plane, *Air Force One*, still on the ground at Dallas' Love Field, and took the oath of office as the thirty-sixth President. His oath taken and the transfer of executive power swiftly achieved, Johnson left little doubt of his determination to demonstrate that "our institutions cannot be disrupted by an assassin's bullet."

The new President spoke before a joint session of Congress on November 27. "All I have," he said, "I would have given gladly not to be standing here today." But John Kennedy's dream, he declared, would not die. Kennedy, Johnson recalled, had said, "'Let us begin.' Today in this moment of new resolve," Johnson told Congress, "I would say to all my fellow Americans, let us continue." Then Lyndon Baines Johnson, son of the South, appealed to Congress: "No memorial oration or eulogy," he declared,

An intent President Johnson watches the flight of a Saturn rocket launched at Cape Kennedy early in 1964.

"could more eloquently honor President Kennedy's memory than the earliest possible passage of the civil rights bill for which he fought so long."

In his first State of the Union message, delivered in January, 1964, President Johnson pressed the point home: "Let this session of Congress," he said, "be known as the session which did more for civil rights than the last hundred sessions combined. . . ." And in another historic departure, after renewing his appeals for medical care for the elderly and a tax cut, the President announced: "This administration today here and now declares unconditional war on poverty in America."

Johnson's skill as a legislative leader was then brought to bear upon Congress. In a rare display of bipartisan unity, the historic Eighty-eighth Congress passed the Civil Rights Act of 1964—including the public accommodations and the fair employment practices sections.

If the Civil Rights Act was the most dramatic, it was by no means the sole achievement of Johnson's first year in the White House. "Johnson had scarcely settled in office," wrote Michael Davie, "before bills were coming out of Congress like candy bars from a slot machine. . . ." Johnson asked for and got laws authorizing the tax cut requested by Kennedy; federal aid to mass transit facilities; a huge antipoverty program; and wheat and cotton price support,

including a food-stamp plan for providing food to the needy in urban areas. The Job Corps, designed to train young Americans and employ them in public projects, was also established.

Johnson's mastery of Congress and his clearly sincere determination to avoid identification with any single section or interest won him allegiance from both the business and the labor communities. When the railroad unions called a national strike for April 10, 1964, President Johnson summoned both labor and management to the White House. If both sides could not agree to a settlement that would be in the national interest, he announced, he would appeal to his overwhelmingly Democratic Congress to require compulsory arbitration of the dispute. An agreement was reached and the strike was averted. The railroad settlement epitomized the strength of the "Johnson treatment." As columnist Mary McGrory wrote, "The full treatment is an incredibly potent mixture of persuasion, badgering, flattery, threats, reminders of past favors and future advantages."

From the moment of his accession to the Presidency, Johnson labored under a great handicap. He governed in a climate of national grief and political polarities and in the shadow of a handsome young President who had enjoyed immense popularity. Johnson labored, too, under the bitter fact that Kennedy had been killed in Texas during an

975

Newlyweds Luci Johnson and Pat Nugent leave the Shrine of the Immaculate Conception on August 6, 1966. Lynda Bird (behind Luci) was maid of honor.

attempt to bridge a Democratic schism there. As White House cultural affairs gave way to the Johnsons' barbecues on the banks of the Pedernales River, critics concerned more with style than with achievement belittled the President. On at least one occasion, L. B. J. audibly bridled at his critics' reverence for J. F. K. "They say Jack Kennedy had style," he said, "but I'm the one who got the bills passed."

In his conduct of foreign policy, too, Johnson suffered by comparison with Kennedy's graceful image. In an effort to win the confidence of the world's leaders, Johnson addressed the United Nations less than a month after his accession to the Presidency.

"I have come here today to make it unmistakably clear that the assassin's bullet which took [Kennedy's] life did not alter his nation's purpose," he told the world body. Johnson urged a war on hunger, poverty, and disease. "The United States wants to see the cold war end . . ." he added; "the United States wants to press on with arms control and reduction. . . ."

In the first months of his Presidency, Johnson faced new challenges in the Caribbean. When Fidel Castro demanded the return to Cuba of the United States naval base at Guantanamo and shut off the installation's water, Johnson calmly ordered the base to devise its own water supply. He also threatened to dismiss Cubans who worked on the base unless they spent their wages there. When Cuban fishing boats appeared in United States waters, they were seized. Castro turned the water back on.

Johnson acted with similar restraint when President Roberto Chiari of Panama—spurred by nationalist rioting in the Canal Zone—demanded renegotiation of the Panama Canal treaty and severed diplomatic relations with Washington. After initial pique on both sides had cooled, Johnson announced that a new treaty would be negotiated, thereby restoring United States-Panamanian relations to their traditional balance.

The one issue that overshadowed Lyndon Johnson's Presidency from the start was the war for control of South Vietnam. Indisputably, Johnson inherited the situation from at least three previous administrations. In 1950 President Truman had pledged American "economic and military equipment to the Associated States of Indochina and to France in order to assist them in restoring stability and permitting these states to pursue their peaceful and democratic development." In 1954, after rebels had defeated the French at Dienbienphu, a nineteen-nation conference at Geneva divided French Indochina into Cambodia, Laos, South Vietnam, and Communist-controlled North Vietnam. The Eisenhower administration, while not officially a signatory of the Geneva Accords, issued a unilateral statement supporting them, thus endorsing the conference's call for the eventual unification of Vietnam through free elections and an interdict on foreign military intervention there. Eisenhower made a more specific commitment to South Vietnam's Premier Ngo Dinh Diem in a 1954 letter pledging to "assist the government of [South] Vietnam in developing and maintaining a strong viable state, capable of resisting attempted subversion, or aggression through military means," adding the condition that Saigon make every effort to instigate "needed reforms." When Eisenhower left the Presidency, fewer than one thousand American advisers were present in South Vietnam aiding in the fight against Vietcong guerrillas.

Under the Kennedy administration, the United States commitment to South Vietnam in military advisers and personnel rose to twenty-five thousand. This increase induced a counterescalation of opposition forces and of the activities of the National Liberation Front—the Vietcong's political arm—which had been founded in 1960. By September 3, 1963, Kennedy had concluded that Diem was "out of touch with the people" and warned: "In the final analysis, it is their war. We can help them, we can give them equipment, we can send our men out there as advisers but they have to win it."

Facing extreme demands from both left and right in the initial months of his own administration, President Johnson maintained, as late as February, 1964, that the Vietnam War was "first and foremost a contest to be won by the government and the people of that country for themselves." In August, 1964, however, when North Vietnamese torpedo boats twice fired on United States destroyers cruising eleven miles offshore in the Gulf of Tonkin, Johnson ordered retaliatory strikes on North Vietnamese installations. On August 5 he sought and received from Congress a resolution authorizing the President "to take all necessary measures to repel any armed attack against the forces of the United States and to prevent further aggression." The Congress stipulated, however, that all action in this connection must

WIDE WORLD

HUBERT H. HUMPHREY

Lyndon Johnson, according to Senator Russell Long, once called Hubert Horatio Humphrey "the greatest coordinator of mind and tongue in the world, being able to prepare a speech in the time it took to draw a deep breath." Humphrey had other, more practical talents as well, and they resulted in his election to the Vice Presidency in 1964. Johnson, as a senator, had found Humphrey not "like the other liberals. He wanted to get the job done." Politics, to both men, involved hard bargaining and compromise. Born in South Dakota in 1911, Humphrey, a druggist's son, had studied at the University of Minnesota and had then attended the Denver School of Pharmacy so that he could help his family during the Depression. He returned to the university to graduate and then earned his master's degree at Louisiana State in 1940. After working in government and as a teacher, he was elected mayor of Minneapolis in 1945 and senator in 1948, 1954, and 1960. He and Johnson, both of whom were former teachers, New Dealers, and eventually presidential aspirants, became close friends and allies in the Senate. Although Johnson turned the picking of a 1964 running mate into a suspenseful drama, Humphrey was the logical choice. As Vice President he served his chief loyally, lending public support where needed, going on diplomatic and political missions, and managing the administration's legislative efforts.

be consonant with the Constitution of the United States, the Charter of the United Nations, and the SEATO Treaty.

In the presidential campaign of 1964, President Johnson rejected escalation of the war. Facing Arizona's conservative Barry Goldwater, who had been embraced by America's radical right, he said that Goldwater's inflexibility and belief in simplistic military solutions would plunge the nation into nuclear holocaust and that his domestic program would abolish such commonly accepted benefits as Social Security. In city after city, Johnson deplored Goldwater's candid intention to escalate the war in Vietnam toward all-out victory. Repeatedly Johnson assured Americans: "We don't want our American boys to do the fighting for Asian boys. We don't want to get involved in a nation [China] with 700,000,000 people and get tied down in a land war in Asia." Johnson and his liberal running mate, Hubert Humphrey, won the election by the largest popular margin in American history, 43,129,484 votes to 27,178,188.

In accepting the Democratic nomination, Johnson had said: "This nation, this generation, in this hour has man's first chance to build a great society, a place where the meaning of man's life matches the marvel of man's labor." In January, 1965, he pledged new aid to education and to urban renewal, a war on disease and on air and water pollution, aid to depressed areas, and an end to voting restrictions based on color.

Again Johnson's leadership of Congress was phenomenal. Outstanding among his administration's achievements were laws authorizing unprecedented, massive federal aid to elementary and secondary schools; Medicare, which provided medical aid to those over sixty-five through the Social Security system; federal aid to the deprived Appalachian states; liberalized immigration; housing; and the creation of a Department of Housing and Urban Development. Under Johnson, too, America recovered its position in the space race, matching, in the summer of 1965, Russia's famed walk in space. And under Johnson the states ratified the Twenty-fifth Amendment, which provided for an orderly transfer of presidential power in the event of presidential incapacitation, resignation, or removal from office, and granted the President the power to name— with the approval of Congress—a new Vice President in the event of a vacancy.

The President's supreme achievement was the passage of the Voting Rights Act of 1965. In a dramatic nighttime personal appearance before Congress, Johnson urged passage of a law authorizing federal voting registrars to assure electoral justice to Negroes in areas where they were denied the vote. The Negroes' cause, he declared, "must be our cause too. Because it's not just Negroes, but really it's all of us who must overcome the crippling legacy of bigotry and injustice." Then Johnson gave presidential voice to the hymn of civil rights marchers: "And," said the President, "we shall overcome."

Another Caribbean crisis erupted in April, 1965, when a revolt broke out in the Dominican Republic. The President sent some

In this 1967 cartoon, the Democratic donkey watches in consternation as President Johnson tries to keep astride the widening "Credibility Gap."

Johnson conferred in August, 1966, with General William Westmoreland, commander in Vietnam.

twenty thousand troops to restore order. He subsequently justified this extreme action by insisting that "we don't propose to sit here in our rocking chair with our hands folded and let the Communists set up any government in the Western Hemisphere." But Communist involvement was questionable, and Johnson's response to the uprising badly damaged United States prestige.

In other major areas, however, Johnson's approach was marked by admirable restraint. Consistently nettled by France's Charles de Gaulle, who ordered NATO out of France in early 1967, Johnson maintained a dignified silence. Denounced by Peking, he refused to return invective. With the Soviet Union he continued to maintain *détente*, sustaining cultural exchange, urging the cooperative exploration of outer space, and signing in 1967 a historic treaty increasing the number of consulates in both nations.

The war in Vietnam, however, continued to escalate. On February 7, 1965, when Vietcong terrorists attacked an American military installation at Pleiku, Johnson ordered air strikes on North Vietnam that, as time passed, increased in intensity. On April 7, 1965, speaking in Baltimore, the President made United States policy explicit: "The central lesson of our time," he declared, "is that the appetite of aggression is never satisfied. . . . We must say in Southeast Asia, as we did in Europe, in the words of the Bible: 'Hitherto shalt thou come; but no further.' . . . Our objective is the independence of South Vietnam and its freedom from attack. . . . We will not withdraw, either openly or under the cloak of a meaningless agreement."

By November, 1965, the United States had committed 165,700 troops to Vietnam. Whereas 146 Americans were killed in battle in 1964, 1,104 died in 1965. In 1966, 5,008 Americans were killed and 30,093 wounded. Early in 1967, American artillery fired over the demilitarized zone into North Vietnam, the United States Navy bombarded the North Vietnamese shore, and the United States Air Force dropped mines into North Vietnamese rivers.

In March, Johnson met at Guam with South Vietnam's Premier, Nguyen Cao Ky (Ngo Dinh Diem had been overthrown in 1963), and with General William C. Westmoreland, commander of United States troops in Vietnam, in talks widely believed to foreshadow further escalation of the war. The President announced his determination "to resist aggression, and to make possible the sacred work of peace among men." By late April, United States planes had bombed Haiphong Harbor, Haiphong itself, and MIG fighter plane bases in the North. On April 26, United States jets struck at Hanoi's bridged rail link with China.

The bombing of the MIG airfields evoked new protests from prominent critics of the war. And when General Westmoreland, summoned to the United States by Johnson, declared that peace protests were encouraging Hanoi to continue its aggression, the administration was accused of attempting to stifle dissent and criticism at home.

Democrat George McGovern rose in the Senate to condemn the bombings as bringing the nation "one step closer to World War III involving the limitless legions of China backed by the enormous firepower of Soviet Russia. So I do not intend to remain silent in the face of what I regard as a policy of madness. . . ." Joined by Senators Robert Kennedy, J. William Fulbright, Frank Church, and Ernest Gruening, he charged that the Johnson administration was "confessing the weakness of its own case by trying to silence its critics. . . ." Quoting the Roman general Tacitus, Kennedy added: "We made a desert and we called it peace."

The liberal senators, sixteen of whom later issued a statement saying that although they urged negotiations, they did not advocate unilateral withdrawal of American troops, were not alone in their criticism of the administration's conduct of the war and its commitment of some 460,000 American troops by May 1, 1967. Many distinguished clergymen, professors, lawyers, and intellectual leaders joined the swelling ranks of unimpeachably loyal Americans who marched in protest against the war.

"The nation," Walter Lippmann warned, "is being governed without the support of, against the feeling of, great segments of its spiritual and intellectual leadership." Republican Senator Charles Percy declared that the administration's insistence that negotiations exclude the Vietcong was "unrealistic." Percy said, "We must answer whether we are prepared to allow our men to die at the rate of 150 to 250 a month, for an interminable number of years, in search of a total victory which cannot, in my judgment, really be achieved." Mississippi's Senator John Stennis, on the other hand, wanted to "remove the arbitrary restrictions and widen and expand the air war so as to strike all militarily significant targets. . . ." Others complained that the administration had not gone far enough and urged the bombing of Hanoi or war with China itself.

On May 19, American planes bombarded downtown Hanoi for the first time. Later that month, a new record for one week's American casualties was set: 2,929. And by July 2, the total number of United States troops killed in Vietnam stood at 11,323, with 68,341 wounded and 674 missing.

With the eruption of war in the Mideast in June, 1967, the administration faced a new challenge. Egyptian President Nasser's blockade of the Gulf of Aqaba (site of the strategic Israeli port of Elath) and the build-up of Arab forces along Israel's borders culminated in a massive Israeli offensive. Within six days, Israeli forces had thrust through the Sinai Peninsula to Suez, cleared the gulf, and seized Old Jerusalem and parts of Jordan and Syria. Israel's stunning victory was challenged by the Soviet Union, major supplier of arms to the Arabs. Premier Aleksei Kosygin himself flew to New York to demand—without success—that the United Nations condemn Israel.

Johnson maintained a studied neutrality in the crisis. Refusing to intervene in the fighting, L. B. J. declined to participate in the acrimonious debates at the United Nations, where Ambassador Arthur Goldberg urged direct Arab-Israeli negotiations with the aid of a third party. From Washington, Johnson called on the belligerents to honor "the recognized right of national life" and urged "justice for refugees . . . innocent maritime passage . . . limits on the . . . arms race . . . [and] political independence and territorial integrity for all." A historic Summit Conference, held by Johnson and Kosygin in Glassboro, New Jersey, produced no substantive results, both sides remaining adamant in their positions on Vietnam and the Mideast. But Johnson emerged from the talks with renewed stature, with an image of statesmanlike restraint. Most Americans agreed with the President that although amiable conversation does not in itself produce peace, "it does help a lot to sit down and look at a man right in the eye and try to reason with him. . . ."

Civil rights advocates were delighted in June by Johnson's appointment of Thurgood Marshall, a Negro, to the Supreme Court. Optimism gave way to despair in July, however, when massive Negro rioting in major American cities led to intervention by federal troops. "Looting, and arson, and plunder, and pillage," Johnson declared, "are not part of a civil rights protest. . . . And crime must be dealt with forcefully, and certainly, under law." Johnson's critics, however, charged that the President

Senator Eugene McCarthy announces that he will enter several presidential primaries in 1968.

himself had to share much of the blame for the riots, since the huge cost of the Vietnam War had forced drastic cutbacks in programs to relieve the urban poor and to fight racial bias in housing and employment.

In this climate of protest the United States was more sharply divided than at any time since the closing months of the Truman administration. By early autumn, 1967, L. B. J.'s government by "consensus" had split at the seams. In late September fifty-two House members cited a "growing uneasiness in Congress" over the "Americanization" of the Vietnam War despite Congress' limitation (in the Tonkin Resolution) of the American role to one of assistance. Senator Clifford Case of New Jersey, a moderate Republican, decried a "crisis of confidence" provoked by Johnson's alleged misuse of the resolution. Republican Senator Thruston Morton of Kentucky admitted that he had been wrong in supporting Johnson on Vietnam, and charged that the President had been brainwashed by the "military-industrial complex" into pushing for total victory. Democratic Senators Wayne Morse and J. William Fulbright, who maintained incessant fire on their party chief, were joined

more vigorously by Robert F. Kennedy, who charged that Johnson had "switched" from J. F. K.'s moderate Vietnam policy, thereby gravely weakening the nation's moral position.

The most startling Democratic challenge to Johnson occurred on November 30, when liberal Senator Eugene McCarthy of Minnesota announced that he would enter the 1968 presidential primaries, and would campaign chiefly on the issue of Vietnam. "My decision to challenge the President's position," McCarthy said, "has been strengthened by recent announcements from the Administration of plans for continued escalation and intensification of the war in Vietnam and, on the other hand, by the absence of any positive indications or suggestions for a compromise or negotiated political settlement. I am concerned that the Administration seems to have set no limits on the price that it will pay for military victory."

In Congress Johnson suffered major setbacks. Republican senators generally backed his programs, but recalcitrant House Republicans and Dixiecrats slashed the administration's antipoverty, open housing, crime control, model cities, and foreign aid programs. A 10 per cent surtax on income—which Johnson regarded as imperative—was not even reported out of committee.

It was L. B. J.'s darkest hour in the White House. Even his staunch Republican ally, Senate Minority Leader Everett Dirksen, spoke out against him at the end of the year. "As our casualties mount daily . . ." Dirksen said, "the unpopularity of the war among our people intensifies hourly and there is little evident reason to hope for victory in the foreseeable future. For there is no prospect of peace, no promise of stability, no hope for the better in the policies of this Administration." Nor could Johnson take comfort from a massive peace march to the Pentagon in late October, during which potential violence was checked only by the presence of armed federal troops and marshals. Campus demonstrations, picketing of draft induction centers, and ritual burning of draft cards occurred in various parts of the nation. Several prominent retired military leaders attacked the war as militarily and morally unsound. And the news from the front was grim: 9,353 Americans died in Vietnam in 1967—more than half the total of 15,997 killed in the war up to that time, and nearly twice the number killed in 1966.

Politically, Johnson appeared to be in trouble. As the election year neared, pollster George Gallup said that the 1968 presidential contest might be the hardest to predict since 1948.

Republicans greeted Johnson's reported decline in popularity with delight. The polls indicated that Richard M. Nixon was the first choice of a majority of Republicans and that Nelson Rockefeller of New York was his closest rival. Republican leaders believed, according to a fifty-state *New York Times* poll published on January 1, 1968, that if the election were held immediately, Johnson would defeat Nixon by a narrow margin. But Rockefeller, they felt, would trounce Johnson, especially if white supremacist George C. Wallace of Alabama ran on a third-party ticket.

If some Johnson loyalists were alarmed by these portents of defeat, L. B. J. did not seem to be. He had a poll of his own to cite: Gallup's year-end finding that in spite of all Johnson's reverses, 46 per cent of America's adults approved his handling of the Presidency, as opposed to 38 per cent the previous October. And if his situation was not precisely like Harry Truman's in 1948, his "give-'em-hell" style was. Addressing the AFL-CIO convention in Florida in early December, Johnson came out fighting, blasting the G.O.P. congressmen who had crippled his Great Society reforms: "In vote after vote," he declared, House Republicans had "lined up like wooden soldiers of the status quo," voting to kill Medicare, antipoverty funds, housing and rent supplements, and the minimum wage bill. "But they are not fooling anybody," Johnson cried, "are they? The people know that the old Republican buggy can go only one way —and that's backwards, downhill. . . ." Having triumphantly signed the new Whole-

some Meat and Flammable Fabrics acts— which extended federal supervision of those industries—the President enplaned on a 27,600-mile Christmas tour. In Melbourne he attended memorial services for Australian Prime Minister Harold Holt. At Camranh Bay in Vietnam, he assured servicemen that North Vietnam could not win. Home again, L. B. J. signed a law granting at least a 13 per cent increase in Social Security payments to twenty-four million Americans.

Late in January, 1968, the Vietcong attacked six major South Vietnamese cities with unprecedented force, assaulting even the American embassy in Saigon. In twelve days of fighting, 973 Americans, 2,119 South Vietnamese, and an estimated 30,795 enemy soldiers were killed. The administration was assailed for underestimating enemy strength and will and for overestimating the prospects for an Allied victory. Nor did the seizure of the American intelligence ship *Pueblo* by North Korea bolster American pride or Johnson's prestige. In March, Senator McCarthy won a stunning 42.4 per cent of the vote and twenty of the twenty-four delegates in New Hampshire's Democratic primary. McCarthy's showing prompted Senator Robert F. Kennedy to challenge L. B. J. for the nomination. Kennedy swiftly took to the campaign trail, condemning the President's war policy as "bankrupt."

But L. B. J. had a surprise of his own. On March 31, in one of the most dramatic political moves in American history, Johnson shocked the world by announcing that he would neither seek nor accept his party's nomination in 1968. ". . . I have concluded," he said, "that I should not permit the Presidency to become involved in the partisan divisions. . . ." He also announced the suspension of bombing over 76 per cent of North Vietnam and again invited Hanoi to the peace table. Some hailed the President for selfless courage and patriotism; others questioned his political motives. But on one point all Americans were agreed: L. B. J. remained one of the least predictable men ever to occupy the White House.

—WILSON SULLIVAN

A PICTURE PORTFOLIO

The Western background of Lyndon Baines Johnson was emphasized by the 1964 campaign item above. This ten-gallon hat was reproduced to be worn on Democratic lapels.

"LYNDON IS
UNRELENTING, TOO"

Lyndon and Lady Bird Johnson, who were married on November 17, 1934, were photographed near Mexico City during their honeymoon trip (above).

It was a hard land from which Lyndon B. Johnson came. His wife called it "unrelenting country," adding, "Lyndon is unrelenting, too." From the day in 1932 when—just out of teachers college and a job in a Houston high school—he came to Washington as secretary to Representative Richard M. Kleberg, he demonstrated his drive. By 1937 he had been elected to the House of Representatives; in 1948 he was chosen senator. Johnson understood power, and understanding it, was drawn to it. Power begins at home in politics. Thus he followed President Roosevelt's New Deal in response to the needs and wishes of his home district but later shifted to the right to accommodate the larger constituency of his home state as a whole—particularly the petroleum interests whose money was becoming a key to Texas elections. Power in Washington depends less on what a man believes than on how he goes about his business. As representative and senator, Johnson carefully cultivated his peers and superiors, particularly Roosevelt, congressional old hands such as Sam Rayburn and Georgia's Senator Richard Russell, and influential New Dealers—the people who made things tick in the Capital. His love of politics—he talked about it all the time—and his avoidance of doctrinaire attitudes on issues endeared him to the professionals. Most important, although Johnson remained sufficiently conservative to satisfy Texas and the powers that were in Congress, he tried to walk a path near the middle of American political philosophy; national power depended on his enlarging his constituency to national size—something no major Southern figure since Andrew Jackson, "the People's President," had been able to do. Lyndon Baines Johnson's reward was his election in 1953—when he was only forty-four years old—to the important post of Senate Minority Leader.

Above, Johnson meets President Roosevelt at Galveston, Texas, in 1937 after winning, on a strongly pro-New Deal platform, a special election for a seat in Congress. Below, the young Texan campaigns for the Senate in 1941, a race he barely lost. Behind him are his wife, left, and his mother, Rebekah Baines Johnson.

Above, Lyndon Johnson, the Senate Majority Leader, attends a 1958 Memorial Day ceremony at Franklin Roosevelt's grave. Mrs. Roosevelt, left, supported Stevenson rather than Johnson or Kennedy in 1960.

After losing the Democratic convention battle to Kennedy, Johnson surprised everyone, including J. F. K., by accepting second place on the 1960 ticket. Above, with his wife beside him, he salutes the cheering delegates.

CZAR OF THE SENATE

If the Senate leadership could be concentrated instead of broken up into sectional groups, Lyndon Johnson realized, the Upper House could wield much more power in the federal government. As Minority Leader during the first two years of the Eisenhower administration and Majority Leader from 1955 to 1960, Johnson was not only leader of the Senate Democrats in voting and in debate; because of the many friendships and alliances he had built and because his position made him chairman of three major Democratic caucus committees, he was master of the machinery that could make him a virtual czar of the Senate. With the acquiescence of the long-time *de facto* boss of the conservative Senate Democrats, Richard Russell—with whom Johnson had a good, carefully nurtured working relationship—he broke the traditional seniority rule for committee appointments. He could therefore name newer senators to important committees, which brought double dividends: the senators who had been placed in prestigious posts were grateful and repaid him in votes; and by spreading around the major assignments he cut the power of the seniority-heavy conservatives and increased his own power correspondingly. Such weapons as the handing out of Senate campaign funds and of choice office space were also used to build a united Johnsonian Senate. The results were often spectacular. "Lyndon's passed bills in a few days that I thought would take weeks," said the Senate parliamentarian, Charles Watkins. Among those bills were the first two civil rights acts in nearly a century. He was Majority Leader in a larger than usual sense: he acted as the chief embodiment of the national pro-Eisenhower consensus and helped pass Ike's legislation—sometimes in the face of Republican opposition. He thus became widely known and respected, a strong presidential possibility, and, in 1961, John Fitzgerald Kennedy's Vice President.

After years of great power and prominence, Johnson settled uneasily into the relative limbo of the Vice Presidency (above). "Lyndon's job," the President said, "is the hardest one he could ever have—and he is performing it like a man, M-A-N."

In the cabin of the presidential airplane, Air Force One, *ninety-eight minutes after John Kennedy was declared dead, Lyndon Johnson was sworn in as President (above) by United States District Judge Sarah Hughes. He is flanked by Lady Bird Johnson and Mrs. John F. Kennedy.*

Two days after the assassination, the alleged killer, Lee Harvey Oswald, was himself murdered (below) by Dallas night-club operator Jack Ruby while police stood by helplessly and millions of Americans watched on television. This, among other weird aspects of the assassination and its aftermath, raised fears that Oswald, if he was indeed the murderer, had acted as part of a conspiracy.

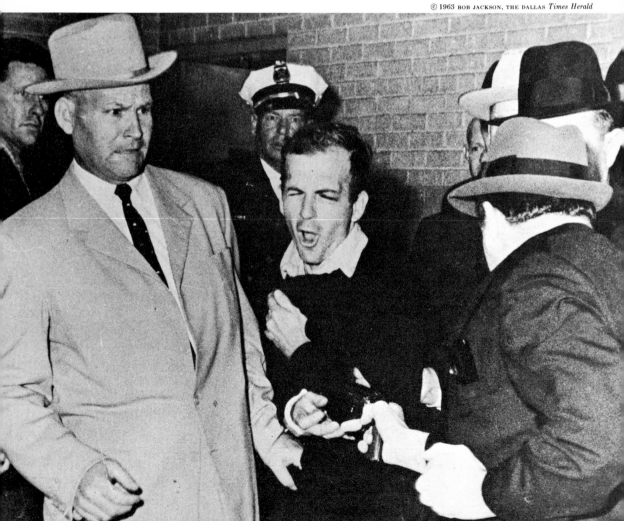

TRANSITION

Lyndon Johnson, a man with an intense need to act forcefully, had been dutifully hobbling himself for a thousand days, and could look forward to two thousand more of the same. Suddenly, because of an incredible tragedy, action was demanded of him. For the eighth time in one hundred and seventy-four years, a Vice President acceded to the powers of a deceased Chief Executive. Ominously, the assassination had taken place in Johnson's state, during a fence-mending visit demanded by a local party feud between liberals and conservatives for which Johnson had been partly responsible and for which he had been unable to provide a remedy. For the first time since the threatening cold war began, an emergency transition of power

had to be effected; the dead President had been better loved around the world than any predecessor, except possibly Franklin Roosevelt, and his place was to be taken by a man believed to be more a politician than a statesman, a man who was not so beloved nor so well-known. In the midst of national sorrow, Johnson took charge quickly. He set up a commission to investigate the assassination; he smoothed the transition and proved his faithfulness to the Kennedy tradition by asking Congress for—and getting—quick action on New Frontier legislation. Some of those closest to Kennedy could not forgive Johnson for taking over the Presidency with such sureness. But most Americans were grateful that John F. Kennedy had chosen so well at Los Angeles in 1960.

As the photograph above illustrates, the official report on the assassination, issued by the special commission headed by Chief Justice Earl Warren, did not end public questioning about the dismaying events in Dallas.

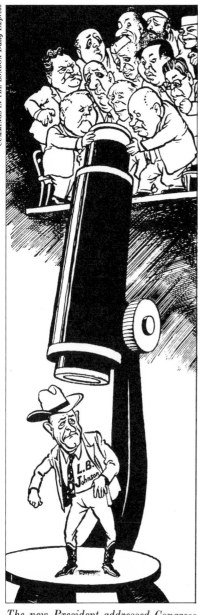

CUMMINGS IN THE LONDON *Daily Express*

The new President addressed Congress on November 27, 1963 (top right). World leaders looked on anxiously—as the London Daily Express *cartoon above indicates. Johnson was identified with Texas, which was considered by foreigners to be strange country even before John Kennedy was killed there.*

"AN ELEMENTAL FORCE"

Because the Eastern liberals distrusted Lyndon Johnson the Texas politician (in much the same way that rural Protestants had distrusted Kennedy the Catholic), it was often said that only through the Vice Presidency and succession by death could he have reached the White House. Being a sensitive man who was proud of his contribution to government, Johnson resented that deeply. Therefore it was inevitable that he would attempt to demonstrate that he deserved to be Chief Executive every bit as much as his predecessor had. In the process he created his own version of the Presidency. Kennedy had been rather gentle with Congress; Johnson brought it to heel as he forced it to approve the sale of wheat to Russia and to pass a strong civil rights act, federal aid to mass transportation and to education, and the antipoverty bill—all within nine months of the assassination. He used the telephone frequently to urge individual congressmen to back legislation. He made it clear that *he* was to make important decisions, not his advisers—among whom he labored to produce consensus support for whatever he wanted to do. In foreign affairs, as at home, he tried to operate on an intense face-to-face basis. When the republic of Panama cut diplomatic ties with the United States in January, 1964, he broke all the rules and placed a long-distance call to the Panamanian president. "LBJ has been hurling himself about Washington like an elemental force," commented *The New Republic*. "To be plain about it, he has won our admiration. . . ."

At left, in Panama, National Guardsmen break up one of the anti-American demonstrations over the Canal Zone that disrupted relations between the two nations for much of 1964. The central issue was renegotiation of the Canal treaty. Domestic politics made the presidents of each of the involved countries leery of seeming to give in to the other, but by that April a review of the old treaty had commenced.

BARRY M. GOLDWATER

"In your heart you know he's right," said
Barry Goldwater's supporters during the
election of 1964. The opinion of most Americans, however, was summed up in a pun:
Goldwater was too *far* right. A native of
Phoenix, Arizona, Goldwater had attended
military schools and the University of Arizona, and then had taken a job in the family
business, a department store. A member of
the Arizona National Guard, he was assigned to the Air Force in 1941 and served as
a pilot and instructor during World War II.
Named to the Phoenix city council in 1949,
when he was forty years old, Goldwater was
elected to the United States Senate three
years later. There he displayed the stern
conservatism and anti-Communist militancy
that made him the hero of the American
right. The conservatives, believing that the
Republican party should offer the electorate
"a choice, not an echo," gained control of
crucial state organizations and thus of the
1964 national convention and nominated
Goldwater for President. But most voters
were appalled by his alleged readiness to use
nuclear weapons freely in war, by the extremism of some of his partisans, and by his
seemingly outdated view of the role of government. They were not swayed by his personal attractiveness and gave him only
fifty-two electoral votes. He retired to private life following his defeat, but Goldwater's admirers urged him to run for the
United States Senate again in 1968.

A SMASHING
VICTORY

Since the Civil War,
no candidate from a state that had joined
the Confederacy had been elected President.
But in 1964 that tradition was broken—appropriately enough, by Johnson, master of
domestic consensus and moderation. Because he had committed himself to a New
Deal type of program—the Great Society—
he had become attractive to the urban centers of the Northeast, where he had only
recently been believed to be weakest. So,
even before the conservative Republicans
nominated Senator Goldwater and deliberately alienated the moderates in their party,
it appeared that Johnson would win the election. Goldwater's nomination gave the President an opportunity not just to win but to
win big, which he longed to do in order to
move out from under the shadow of his
succession by death. Yet despite the sense of
triumph that surrounded him through the
autumn, it was reported that this complicated man sometimes brooded over the ines-
capable fact that many pro-Johnson votes
would stem not from admiration for him,
but from antipathy to Goldwater. Nevertheless, his campaign consciously encouraged
such "anti" votes. It was clear when the returns were in that Johnson had left behind
much of the Deep South in his move toward
the middle: the electoral votes of five Southern states went to Goldwater. But President
Johnson won a record share of the nationwide popular vote: 61 per cent.

RURAL
JOHNSON
HUMPHREY
AMERICANS

Lyndon Johnson and Hubert H. Humphrey—two farm-land populists, long-time allies, and, by L. B. J.'s 1964 decision, running mates—confer aboard the presidential jet (above) en route to the Democratic convention in Atlantic City, New Jersey. Johnson is watching his own nomination on television.

Johnson's campaign caught fire in New England late in September. From then on his crowds were huge and enthusiastic, his momentum was uncheck-able. Below, he is greeted in Tennessee two weeks before the voting.

CONSENSUS AND
THE GREAT SOCIETY

On February 1, 1965, five months after Congress set up the Job Corps to train underprivileged youngsters, the first center was opened in Oregon. Above, Johnson visits a center in Texas later that year.

The Great Society was no mirage, no political ploy to be used in a campaign and then allowed to dwindle away. The legislative achievements of Johnson's first three months in office after his 1965 inauguration amply justified his claim of "a record of major accomplishments without equal or close parallel in the present era." They included passage of a plan for medical care for the aged (within the Social Security system), federal aid to elementary and secondary education, and aid to the impoverished areas in the Appalachians. "Indeed," wrote journalists Rowland Evans and Robert Novak, "Johnson kept one eye on the calendar in his frantic exhortations to the congressional leaders to pass as many bills as possible during *his* Hundred Days . . . ." L. B. J. did not slow down after his triumphs: later in 1965, Congress was prodded into passing a voting rights act to ensure political rights of Negroes; it also loosened immigration restrictions, created the Department of Housing and Urban Development, and set up the Economic Development Administration. "Toscanini was a great conductor, right?" one Johnson aide said. "He knew what the second violin could do, what the brass could do, what the whole orchestra could do. That's like Lyndon. . . . He's a political artist of genius." But columnist Max Lerner lamented "the smell of power that pervades L. B. J. and everything associated with him," and James Reston of *The New York Times* noted that Johnson "would like to call all the signals, carry the ball on every play and run his own interference." A member of Johnson's staff said, "He's liable to wake up in the morning and think everything's got loose in the night." And when, as was bound to happen, the national consensus that Johnson was so proud of began to crack, he responded to opposition as if it were a personal affront.

Above, retired workers demanding passage of Medicare picket a meeting of the American Medical Association.

Below is a rural North Carolina family—living in the kind of poverty that Johnson hoped to eliminate.

REBELLIONS

Johnson's legislative record was among the most remarkable in United States history; and astronaut Edward White's walk in space, the progress of the war on poverty, and the national beautification program (in which the President's competent wife took an active interest) filled him with pride of accomplishment. But in 1965, as the Great Society was propelled thunderously onward, the President had his troubles. Despite his continuing efforts for civil rights, Negroes were more and more impatient: there were marches, riots, and demonstrations. And the liberals, who had been backing him because of his domestic program, began sniping at his foreign policy in April, when the President, fearing that a civil war in the Dominican Republic would lead to a Communist take-over there, ordered United States Marines into the Caribbean republic. Johnson was upset by the attacks and tried desperately to win back liberal support. But many of his critics were implacable. In his book *Lyndon B. Johnson and the World*, Philip Geyelin wrote that Johnson's "irrelevant rationalizations and often inaccurate reconstruction of events [had changed] an essentially unmanageable and, in some ways, unavoidable crisis . . . into a crisis of confidence in [him]."

"It's fun. I'm not coming in," said an exhilarated Edward White as ground control tried to get him to end his walk in space (top, left)—highlight of a record-setting two-man mission in 1965.

Above, American paratroopers watch over Santo Domingo during the Dominican Republic crisis.

Thirty-five people died, and hundreds were hurt, in a race riot (left) in the Watts area of Los Angeles.

NAMES IN THE NEWS

DEAN RUSK

While noting Dean Rusk's "exceptional intelligence, lucidity and control" and his "talent for concise and dispassionate exposition," Arthur Schlesinger, Jr., described the Secretary of State as "irrevocably conventional." But if John Kennedy, who appointed Rusk to his Cabinet in 1961, found him exasperating at times (he "never gives me anything to chew on. . . . You never know what he is thinking"), Lyndon Johnson regarded him as a "wise counselor." "He is Number One in the Cabinet and he is Number One with me," Johnson said. Rusk once wrote that he agreed with Harry Truman's dictum "The President makes foreign policy." He served Johnson as a loyal chief of staff and administration spokesman, especially for Johnson's policies in Vietnam. The son of a tenant farmer, the Georgia-born Rusk had attended Davidson College and had been a Rhodes scholar at Oxford; later he was dean of faculty at Mills College in California. He served in Asia during World War II, after which he held several posts in the State Department. In 1951 he was named president of the Rockefeller Foundation. A firm, patient negotiator, he became a seemingly imperturbable Secretary of State. "We're eyeball to eyeball," he said during the Cuban Missile Crisis, "and I think the other fellow just blinked."

MARTIN LUTHER KING, JR.

"He has an indescribable capacity for empathy that is the touchstone of leadership," wrote *Time* magazine of the Reverend Dr. Martin Luther King, Jr. A Baptist clergyman and a doctor of theology, King emerged as a leader in the civil rights movement in 1955 while he was serving as a pastor in Montgomery, Alabama. Spurred into action by a bus segregation incident, he accepted the leadership of the Montgomery Improvement Association and directed a yearlong Negro boycott of city buses. His first major civil rights victory occurred in 1956 when the Supreme Court declared the Alabama bus segregation laws unconstitutional. An advocate of nonviolent resistance, Dr. King led subsequent protests throughout the United States, using civil disobedience as a weapon against discriminatory laws. "From my Christian background I gained my ideals," he once said, "and from Gandhi my operational technique." In 1963 King helped to organize a massive march on Washington, D.C., by citizens—whites as well as Negroes —who demanded the passage of a civil rights bill; the following year he was awarded the Nobel Peace Prize. In 1967 he urged immediate de-escalation of the Vietnam War. Dr. King was assassinated on April 4, 1968, in Memphis, Tennessee, where he had gone to support striking sanitation workers.

J. WILLIAM FULBRIGHT

"The most striking characteristic of a great nation," said Senator J. William Fulbright in 1965, "is . . . the wisdom and restraint . . . with which power is exercised." Chairman of the Committee on Foreign Relations since 1959, Senator Fulbright stated that the United States had, in Southeast Asia, revealed an "arrogance of power"; he also felt that the nation tended, as in the case of President Johnson's intervention in the Dominican Republic, to make "exaggerated estimates of Communist influence." These views made Fulbright a leader of those opposed to administration policy in Vietnam. He maintained that the cost of a complete military victory there would far exceed "the requirements of our interest and our honor," and urged a "negotiated settlement involving major concessions by both sides." Fulbright, a 1925 graduate of the University of Arkansas, was later a Rhodes scholar at Oxford and a law student at George Washington University. He then taught law and became president of the University of Arkansas in 1939. Elected to the House of Representatives on the Democratic ticket in 1942, he was sent to the Senate in 1944. Author of a resolution that led to the organization of the United Nations, Senator Fulbright sponsored a 1946 act establishing scholarships for American and foreign exchange students.

THURGOOD MARSHALL

Thurgood Marshall built a remarkable legal career on his conviction that all forms of racial segregation were unconstitutional. Born in Baltimore in 1908, he was educated in segregated schools. After his graduation from Howard University Law School in 1933, he established a practice and specialized in civil rights cases. In his capacity as special counsel to the National Association for the Advancement of Colored People, Marshall led the assault on state segregation laws, especially in the field of education. He argued thirty-two cases before the United States Supreme Court and won all but three of them. As a result of his efforts, Virginia's law ordering segregated seating in buses was declared to be unconstitutional when interstate travel was involved, and Texas Negroes were guaranteed the right to vote in primaries and serve on juries. His most dramatic success occurred in 1954, when the Court ruled that separate educational facilities were inherently unequal, and that segregated schools were therefore unconstitutional. In 1961 Marshall was appointed by President John F. Kennedy to the United States Court of Appeals. He was named Solicitor General five years later, and served in that post until 1967, when Lyndon B. Johnson selected Marshall to become the first Negro justice of the Supreme Court.

PROGRESS AND CRISIS

Johnson hoped to make a Great Society not only of the United States but also of the world. He tried to improve the *détente* between America and the Communist bloc, urged more trade between East and West, and asked for better weapons control. It was hinted that the United States was ready to re-evaluate its stance on Red China and to concede a "non-Western" Asia if China did not control it; to that end, an Asian Development Bank had already been started with American help. The President committed the United States indefinitely to the Alliance for Progress and tried to get Latin America to do more for itself in return for foreign aid; he encouraged self-help in all countries receiving aid, and withheld funds from those who took aid with one hand and thumbed their noses at American foreign-policy aims with the other. At home

In the photograph at left, residents of Hanoi wait in bomb shelters for the all-clear siren. At center, antiwar demonstrators gather in New York's Central Park before a "peace march" to the United Nations in 1967.

he continued to bombard Congress with legislative proposals, and he did win, among other laws, a strong auto and road safety act and a truth-in-packaging act to protect the consumer. But Congress, which had never knuckled under to a President for very long, ceased to be malleable. In the Senate particularly, the consensus was badly damaged by the war in Vietnam, which became the center of national attention and of bitter controversy. Johnson's policy was two-pronged: he selectively increased the military pressure on the North Vietnamese while at the same time hunting for diplomatic solutions. But as the death toll of American soldiers in Vietnam rose steadily, and as escalation increased fears of Red Chinese intervention, President Johnson was caught in a cross fire from his critics, some of whom wanted more fighting, and some, less.

American soldiers of the 1st Cavalry Division climb up to a hovering helicopter in South Vietnam, above. Troops from Australia, New Zealand, and South Korea also aided the South Vietnamese in their fight.

"RESTLESSNESS"

As the presidential election of 1968 approached, Lyndon Johnson—who, it was assumed, would be a candidate for re-election—was under attack from many quarters, domestic and foreign. Much of the support that his earlier social welfare programs had gained him at home had been lost by his Vietnam policies, which had also alienated many of the nation's European allies. Johnson was beset by economic problems, too. Inflation soared at home; the international demand for gold in exchange for American currency began to drain the gold reserve; and the devaluation of the British pound increased threats to the stability of the dollar.

In his 1968 State of the Union message, Johnson observed that there was "in the land a certain restlessness, a questioning." It seemed to political observers that the 1968 election would indicate to what degree Americans held Johnson responsible for their disquiet. The substantial vote accorded Senator Eugene McCarthy in the New Hampshire primary early in March, and the subsequent support for Senator Robert Kennedy's candidacy, indicated dramatically how divided the country was over Johnson's policies. Then, on March 31, the President appeared on television to announce both a pause in the bombing of most of North Vietnam and his decision not to seek re-election. "But let men everywhere know, however," Johnson concluded firmly, "that a strong and a confident and a vigilant America stands ready tonight to seek an honorable peace; and stands ready tonight to defend an honorable cause, whatever the price, whatever the burden, whatever the sacrifice that duty may require."

At right, President Johnson addresses American troops at Camranh Bay, South Vietnam, in December, 1967. During his five-day trip, he also attended memorial services for Australian Prime Minister Harold Holt and visited Pope Paul in Rome.

FACTS IN SUMMARY: LYNDON BAINES JOHNSON

CHRONOLOGY

UNITED STATES		JOHNSON
Taft elected President	1908	*Born August 27*
Coolidge elected President	1924	*Graduates from high school*
	1927	*Graduates from Southwest Texas State Teachers College*
Stock market crash	1929	
	1930	*Begins teaching in Houston*
	1931	*Campaigns for election of Richard Kleberg to Congress*
Roosevelt elected President	1932	*Goes to Washington as Kleberg's secretary*
New Deal legislation	1933	
NLRB created	1934	*Marries Claudia Taylor*
Social Security Act	1935	*Named director of National Youth Administration in Texas*
	1937	*Elected to Congress*
	1938	*Re-elected to Congress*
Roosevelt re-elected	1940	*Serves as chairman of Democratic Congressional Campaign Committee*
		Re-elected to Congress
Pearl Harbor bombed	1941	*Loses special U.S. Senate election*
U.S. enters World War II		*Goes on active duty in Navy*
Battle of Midway	1942	*Sent to Pacific as President's representative*
Battle of Guadalcanal		*Awarded Silver Star Medal*
Invasion of North Africa		*Re-elected to Congress*
U.S. offensives in Pacific and Italy	1943	
Allies land in France	1944	*Serves on Committee on Postwar Military Policy*
Philippines Campaign begins		
Truman becomes President	1945	
Atomic bomb dropped on Hiroshima		
Paris Peace Conference	1946	*Re-elected to Congress*
Truman Doctrine	1947	*Serves on House Armed Services Committee*
Marshall Plan		*Votes for Taft-Hartley Act*
Berlin Airlift	1948	*Serves on Joint Committee on Atomic Energy*
Truman elected President		*Elected to Senate*
NATO pact signed	1949	*Serves on Senate Armed Services Committee*
Russia explodes atomic bomb		

UNITED STATES		JOHNSON
Korean War begins	1950	*Heads Senate Preparedness Investigating Subcommittee*
	1951	*Elected Democratic Whip in Senate*
Eisenhower elected President	1952	
Armistice in Korea	1953	*Chosen Senate Minority Leader*
Supreme Court desegregation order	1954	*Re-elected to Senate*
Army-McCarthy hearings		*Elected Senate Majority Leader*
	1955	*Suffers heart attack*
School integration crisis in Little Rock	1957	*Manages passage of Civil Rights Act*
First U.S. satellite orbited	1958	*Serves as chairman of Special Space and Astronautics Committee*
Fidel Castro comes to power in Cuba	1959	*Named chairman of Aeronautical and Space Sciences Committee*
U-2 shot down in Russia	1960	*Loses presidential nomination to Kennedy*
Kennedy elected President		*Accepts vice presidential nomination*
		Elected Vice President
Eisenhower breaks off diplomatic relations with Cuba	1961	*Named head of the National Aeronautics and Space Council*
Peace Corps created		*Appointed chairman of President's Committee on Equal Employment Opportunity*
Invasion of Cuba by exiles fails		
Berlin Wall built		*Sent to Asia and Berlin by President*
Lt. Col. Glenn orbits earth	1962	*Makes Middle Eastern trip for Kennedy*
Cuban Missile Crisis		*Meets OAS ambassadors at LBJ ranch*
Limited nuclear test ban treaty signed	1963	*Becomes President*
Civil rights supporters march on Washington		*Appoints Warren Commission to investigate Kennedy assassination*
Kennedy assassinated in Dallas		*Urges passage of Civil Rights Act*
Riots in Panama Canal Zone	1964	*Acts to settle controversy with Panama*
Twenty-fourth Amendment ratified		*Announces war on poverty*
Civil Rights Act passed		*Forces settlement of railroad strike*
North Vietnamese torpedo boats attack U.S. destroyers		*Signs Civil Rights Act*
		Orders retaliatory bombing of North Vietnam
Congress gives President emergency powers for Vietnam conflict		*Signs Economic Opportunity Act*
		Elected President

Vietcong attack U.S. installation at Pleiku	1965	*Orders resumption of bombing of North Vietnam*
Dominican Republic crisis		*Sends U.S. troops to end Dominican uprising*
U.S. astronaut walks in space		*Signs Medicare Act and Voting Rights Act*
Race riots in Los Angeles		*Suspends bombing of North Vietnam in peace effort*
First U.S. "soft" lunar landing	1966	*Meets with Premier Ky in Honolulu*
U.S. bombs Hanoi		*Attends Manila Conference on Vietnam*
Escalation of U.S. bombing of North Vietnam	1967	*Meets with Premier Kosygin at Glassboro*
		Names Thurgood Marshall to Supreme Court
Peace marches in U.S.		
War in Middle East		*Flies to Australia, Vietnam, and Rome*
Riots in U.S. cities		
North Korea seizes U.S. ship	1968	*Announces pause in bombing of North Vietnam and states that he will not seek re-election*

BIOGRAPHICAL FACTS

BIRTH: Near Stonewall, Tex., Aug. 27, 1908

ANCESTRY: English

FATHER: Samuel Ealy Johnson, Jr.; b. Buda, Tex., Oct. 11, 1877; d. Austin, Tex., Oct. 11, 1937

FATHER'S OCCUPATIONS: Schoolteacher; farmer; state legislator

MOTHER: Rebekah Baines Johnson; b. McKinney, Tex., June 26, 1881; d. Austin, Tex., Sept. 12, 1958

BROTHER: Sam Houston (1914–   )

SISTERS: Rebekah Luruth (1910–   ); Josefa Hermine (1912–1961); Lucia Huffman (1916–   )

WIFE: Claudia Alta Taylor; b. Karnack, Tex., Dec. 22, 1912

MARRIAGE: San Antonio, Tex., Nov. 17, 1934

CHILDREN: Lynda Bird (1944–   ); Luci Baines (1947–   )

EDUCATION: Johnson City High School; Southwest Texas State Teachers College (B.S., 1930); attended Georgetown University Law School

RELIGIOUS AFFILIATION: Disciples of Christ

OCCUPATIONS BEFORE PRESIDENCY: Rancher; politician

PRE-PRESIDENTIAL OFFICES: National Youth Administration Director in Texas; Member U.S. House of Representatives; Member U.S. Senate; Vice President

MILITARY SERVICE: Lt. commander, commander, U.S. Naval Reserve (active duty 1941–1942)

AGE AT INAUGURATION: 55

FIRST ADMINISTRATION

INAUGURATION: November 22, 1963; aboard *Air Force One*, Dallas, Tex.

SECRETARY OF STATE: Dean Rusk

SECRETARY OF THE TREASURY: C. Douglas Dillon

SECRETARY OF DEFENSE: Robert S. McNamara

ATTORNEY GENERAL: Robert F. Kennedy

POSTMASTER GENERAL: John A. Gronouski

SECRETARY OF THE INTERIOR: Stewart L. Udall

SECRETARY OF AGRICULTURE: Orville L. Freeman

SECRETARY OF COMMERCE: Luther H. Hodges

SECRETARY OF LABOR: W. Willard Wirtz

SECRETARY OF HEALTH, EDUCATION, AND WELFARE: Anthony J. Celebrezze

AMBASSADOR TO THE UNITED NATIONS: Adlai E. Stevenson

88th CONGRESS (January 3, 1963–January 3, 1965):
Senate: 67 Democrats; 33 Republicans
House: 258 Democrats; 177 Republicans

ELECTION OF 1964

CANDIDATES	ELECTORAL VOTE	POPULAR VOTE
Lyndon B. Johnson Democratic	486	43,129,484
Barry M. Goldwater Republican	52	27,178,188

SECOND ADMINISTRATION

INAUGURATION: January 20, 1965; the Capitol, Washington, D.C.

VICE PRESIDENT: Hubert H. Humphrey

SECRETARY OF STATE: Dean Rusk

SECRETARY OF THE TREASURY: C. Douglas Dillon; Henry H. Fowler (from April 1, 1965)

SECRETARY OF DEFENSE: Robert S. McNamara; Clark M. Clifford (from March 1, 1968)

ATTORNEY GENERAL: Nicholas Katzenbach; W. Ramsey Clark (from March 10, 1967)

POSTMASTER GENERAL: John A. Gronouski; Lawrence O'Brien (from Nov. 3, 1965)

SECRETARY OF THE INTERIOR: Stewart L. Udall

SECRETARY OF AGRICULTURE: Orville L. Freeman

SECRETARY OF COMMERCE: John T. Connor; Alexander B. Trowbridge; C. R. Smith (from March 1, 1968)

SECRETARY OF LABOR: W. Willard Wirtz

SECRETARY OF HEALTH, EDUCATION, AND WELFARE: Anthony J. Celebrezze; John W. Gardner; Wilbur J. Cohen (from March 1, 1968)

SECRETARY OF HOUSING AND URBAN DEVELOPMENT (Department created Sept. 9, 1965): Robert C. Weaver

SECRETARY OF TRANSPORTATION (Department created Oct. 15, 1966): Alan S. Boyd

AMBASSADOR TO THE UNITED NATIONS: Adlai E. Stevenson; Arthur J. Goldberg (from July 26, 1965)

SUPREME COURT APPOINTMENTS: Abe Fortas (1965); Thurgood Marshall (1967)

89th CONGRESS (January 3, 1965–January 3, 1967):
Senate: 68 Democrats; 32 Republicans
House: 295 Democrats; 140 Republicans

90th CONGRESS (January 3, 1967–January 3, 1969):
Senate: 64 Democrats; 36 Republicans
House: 248 Democrats; 187 Republicans

INDEX

Roman numerals refer to the volume in which the
entry appears. Arabic numbers designate the page.

930, 945, 961, 972, 975, 978, 980, 987, 998
Civil Rights Act of 1866, I, 434, 435
Civil Rights Act of 1964, II, 864, 975
Civil Rights Commission, II, 903
Civil service, II, 528, 536, 537, 538, 541, 542, 557, 558, 568, 581, 583, 592, 666
Civil Service Commission, I, 476; II, 542, 641
Civil War, I, 246, 392–97 passim, 407, 408–20 passim, 435, 458–59, 470, 471, 474
   See also Ulysses S. Grant, Abraham Lincoln, and individual battles and generals
Civil War pensions, II, 558
   See also Dependent Pension Act
Civil Works Administration, II, 801
Civilian Conservation Corps, II, 798, 824
Clark, George Rogers, I, 41, 115
Clark, James Beauchamp, II, 674, 687, 688
Clark, William, I, 41, 115
   See also Lewis and Clark expedition
Clay, Henry, I, 131, 158, 159, 168, 169, 178, 179, 180, 186–87, 188, 189, 198, 206, 207, 218, 227, 228, 229, 231, 253, 262, 274, 275, 276, 281, 284, 293–94, 295, 300, 301, 317–18, 324–29, 402; II, 878
Clayton Antitrust Act, II, 706
Clayton-Bulwer Treaty, I, 318, 350, 366
Clemenceau, Georges, II, 698, 699, 715, 716, 717
Clemens, Samuel L., I, 461, 466; II, 548
Cleveland, Frances Folsom, II, 558, 566–67
Cleveland, Grover, II, 553–75 passim, 677
   appraisal of, II, 558, 562, 573
   birth and early life, II, 553, 554
   and cancer operation, II, 560
   and civil service reform, II, 557, 568
   death of, II, 562
   and 1884 election, II, 548, 553, 556, 557, 559, 564, 565
   and 1888 election, II, 557, 558, 568, 581, 586
   and 1892 election, II, 559, 560, 584
   and 1896 election, II, 562
   Facts in Summary, II, 574–75
   and gold standard, II, 558, 560, 561, 562, 573
   and Hawaii annexation dispute, II, 561, 562, 573, 584
   and Interstate Commerce Act, II, 557, 568
   and labor disputes, II, 562, 572, 573
   marriage of, II, 558, 566, 567
   and "Mugwumps" in 1884 election, II, 556, 557
   and patronage, II, 557–58, 560, 568

prepresidential politics and offices, II, 548, 554–56, 565
as President
   first term, II, 557–58, 566–68
   second term, II, 559–62 passim, 572–73
and repeal of Sherman Silver-Purchase Act, II, 560–61, 572
and "silver letter" of 1891, II, 559
and Tammany Hall, II, 555–58 passim, 565, 577
and tariff reduction, II, 558, 562, 568, 581
and Treasury surplus, II, 570–71
and Venezuelan-British border dispute, II, 561, 562, 573
and veto, II, 557, 568
Clinton, DeWitt, I, 132, 141, 240, 248
Clinton, George, I, 102, 132, 140
Clinton, Sir Henry, I, 20
Coal industry, II, 729, 857–58
   See also Labor and labor unions
Cohn, Roy M., II, 902, 919
Cold war, II, 810, 854, 855, 859, 874, 875, 899–906 passim, 921, 957
Colfax, Schuyler, I, 460, 464, 480
Colombia, II, 630, 653
Commission on Efficiency and Economy, II, 666
Communications Act, II, 801
Communism, II, 770, 861, 862, 915, 927, 976–80 passim
Compromise of 1850, I, 169, 306, 313, 317, 318, 325, 329–30, 332, 339, 345, 353, 366
   See also Fugitive Slave Law
Conant, James B., II, 873
Confederate States of America, I, 368, 389, 391, 407, 410, 415, 433, 459
   See also Civil War
Confederation, Articles of. See Articles of Confederation
CIO Political Action Committee, II, 823
Conkling, Roscoe, I, 461, 495–96, 498, 508, 509; II, 523, 524, 536–42 passim, 544, 545, 557, 587
Connally, John B., II, 946, 962
Conservation, II, 628–30 passim, 665, 666
Constitutional amendments, I, 158, 169; II, 666
   See also individual amendments
Constitutional Convention, I, 22, 44, 48, 50, 51, 129–30, 136, 137, 345
Continental Army, I, 14, 17–21 passim, 34, 37, 43, 53, 67
   See also Revolutionary War, George Washington
Continental Congress, First, I, 17, 40, 67, 74, 94, 154
   Second, I, 17, 18, 20, 34, 41, 51, 67, 94, 95, 129
Convention of 1818, I, 158, 291, 295
Cooke, Jay, I, 465
Coolidge, Calvin, II, 679, 700, 743–63 passim, 767–72 passim, 775, 779

accession to Presidency, II, 746, 753
birth and early life, II, 744
and Boston police strike, II, 745–46, 752
and coal strike, II, 747
death of, II, 750
domestic program, II, 748
Facts in Summary, II, 762–63
and foreign affairs, II, 749–50
and Harding scandals, II, 748, 750
honesty of, II, 744, 745, 748, 750
and Japanese, II, 749
marriage of, II, 745
and Massachusetts politics, II, 744–46
and 1920 election, II, 743, 746, 752
and 1924 election, II, 746, 748–49, 751, 755
and 1928 election, II, 750, 768
personality of, II, 743, 745, 746, 754, 761
prepresidential politics and offices, II, 743–46, 752–53
as President, II, 746–50 passim, 754–59 passim
and stock market, II, 748
and veto, II, 749, 780
as Vice President, II, 746, 753
Coolidge, Calvin (1908–1924), II, 745, 750, 755
Coolidge, Grace Anna Goodhue, II, 745, 750, 752, 754, 755, 760
Coolidge, John, II, 745, 755
Coolidge, John Calvin (1845–1926), II, 744, 745, 746, 750, 753, 755
Cooper, Peter, I, 507; II, 528
Copperheads, I, 425, 435
Corbin, Mr. and Mrs. Abel, I, 462
Cornell, Alonzo B., I, 495, 496, 508–9; II, 537, 548
Cornwallis, Lord Charles, I, 18–19, 20, 43
Corruption, government, I, 462–65 passim, 476, 477, 478, 480, 484, 489, 492; II, 522, 536, 553, 555, 626, 749, 795
   See also Ulysses S. Grant, Warren G. Harding
Cowpens, Battle of, I, 40
Cox, James M., II, 700, 728, 729, 791, 793, 816
"Coxey's Army," II, 562, 572, 573
Crawford, William, I, 165, 180, 188, 189, 204, 241
Crédit Mobilier, I, 464–65, 480; II, 523–24
Creek Indians, I, 181, 200, 201–2, 224–25
Crittenden, John J., I, 316, 332
Crittenden Resolution, I, 363, 389
Cromwell, William, II, 630
Cuba, I, 333, 338, 339, 349; II, 601–3, 604, 611, 612, 634, 664, 802, 943
Cuban Missile Crisis, I, 160, 171; II, 922, 930, 944, 960, 961
Currency, I, 26, 96, 208, 227, 231, 463; II, 690–91
   See also Gold, Silver, "Specie Circular"

as President, II, 723–24, 729–30, 734–37, 738–39
Harlan, John Marshall, II, 676, 677
Harmon, Judson, II, 687, 688
Harpers Ferry, Va., I, 365, 372, 394
Harriman, W. Averell, II, 840, 852, 855, 954
Harrison, Anna Symmes, I, 260, 261, 269
Harrison, Benjamin (1726–1791), I, 259; II, 578
Harrison, Benjamin, I, 261; II, 577–95 passim, 636, 641
    appraisal of, II, 578
    birth and early life, II, 578
    Cabinet of, II, 583
    and Chilean dispute, II, 584
    and civil service reform, II, 581, 583, 592
    in Civil War, II, 579, 580
    death of, II, 584
    and 1888 election, II, 558, 568, 577, 581, 586
    and 1892 election, II, 559, 584, 586, 592
    Facts in Summary, II, 594–95
    and Hawaii annexation dispute, II, 584
    and Italian government, II, 584
    and McKinley Tariff, II, 583
    marriage of, II, 578, 584
    and party politics, II, 578, 579, 580, 587, 592
    prepresidential politics and offices, II, 578–81 passim
    as President, II, 577–78, 581–84 passim, 587–89 passim, 592
    and social problems of industrial growth, II, 577–78, 582–83
    and U.S. Treasury, II, 570–71
    and Venezuelan-British border dispute, II, 584
Harrison, Caroline Scott, II, 578, 584, 586, 588
Harrison, Elizabeth Irwin, II, 578
Harrison, John Scott, II, 578, 579
Harrison, William Henry, I, 259–71 passim; II, 577, 578, 586, 662
    birth and early life, I, 259–60
    death of, I, 262, 268, 269, 273
    and 1836 election, I, 243, 249, 262, 267, 274
    and 1840 election, I, 241, 246, 259–69 passim
    Facts in Summary, I, 270–71
    inauguration of, I, 268, 269
    and Indians, I, 131–32, 260, 261, 265
    prepresidential offices, I, 131–32, 260, 262, 265
    as President, I, 262, 268–69
    and slavery, I, 260, 262
    and Tippecanoe, Battle of, I, 131–32, 261, 262, 265
    and War of 1812, I, 133, 261–62, 265
Hartford Convention, I, 149
Harvard University, I, 18, 64, 93, 176, 178, 182; II, 590, 624, 638, 656, 788, 789, 814, 815, 829, 859, 879, 935–39 passim, 942, 948, 954, 955

Harvey, George, II, 685
Harvie, Colonel John, I, 92
Havana Harbor, II, 602, 611
Hawaii, I, 333; II, 582, 584, 603, 612, 932
Hawley-Smoot Tariff, II, 770
Hawthorne, Nathaniel, I, 12, 346, 347, 350
Hay, Eliza Monroe, I, 166
Hay, John M., I, 381; II, 604, 615
Hay-Hernan Convention, II, 630
Hay-Pauncefote Treaty, II, 615, 667
    second Hay-Pauncefote Treaty, II, 630
Hayes, Fanny, I, 505
Hayes, Fanny Arabella, I, 490
Hayes, Lucy Ware Webb, I, 490, 491, 498, 500, 504, 505
Hayes, Rutherford, I, 489
Hayes, Rutherford Birchard, I, 489–511 passim; II, 519, 529, 598
    appraisal of, I, 489, 498
    and assertion of presidential authority, I, 496
    birth and early life, I, 489–90
    Cabinet of, I, 495, 506
    and Chinese immigration, I, 497–98, 511
    and civil service reform, I, 492, 495, 496, 498, 508; II, 537
    death of, I, 498
    and 1876 election, I, 491–92, 493, 494, 498, 500, 502–3
    Facts in Summary, I, 510–11
    inauguration of, I, 494
    marriage of, I, 490, 500
    and N.Y. Custom House, I, 495–96, 508–9; II, 537
    prepresidential politics, I, 491, 500
    as President, I, 489, 494–98 passim, 504–9 passim
    and railroad strike, I, 496, 497
    and Reconstruction, I, 489, 495, 498
    and reform in government, I, 492, 495–96, 498, 503, 504
    in Union army, I, 491, 500; II, 598
    and U.S. monetary problems, I, 496
    and veto, I, 496, 497–98, 511
Hayes, Scott, I, 505
Hayes, Sophia Birchard, I, 489–90
Hearst, William Randolph, II, 608, 674, 795
Heaton, Leonard, II, 903
Henderson, John B., I, 437, 451
Hendricks, Thomas A., II, 559
Henry, Patrick, I, 96, 154
Hermitage, The, I, 210, 212, 217, 218, 234, 235
Herndon, William H., I, 381, 400
Herold, David, I, 423
Herter, Christian, II, 926
Hillman, Sidney, II, 823
Hirohito, Emperor, II, 808
Hiroshima, II, 856
Hiss, Alger, II, 882
Hitler, Adolf, I, 171; II, 782, 802, 806–8 passim, 830, 836, 840, 874

Hoban, James, I, 86
Hobart, Garret A., II, 600, 601, 607
Hobby, Oveta Culp, II, 918
Hoffa, James, II, 954
Holmes, Oliver Wendell, Jr., II, 677, 834
Homestead Act, I, 389, 430, 431, 461
Hood, John Bell, I, 397, 410
Hooker, Joseph, I, 394; II, 580
Hoover, Allan Henry, II, 766
Hoover, Herbert Clark, II, 679, 739, 748, 765–85 passim, 796, 797
    appraisal of, II, 772
    birth and early life, II, 766, 772–75 passim
    and bonus marchers, II, 765–66, 778
    conservatism of, II, 767–72 passim, 775, 776
    death of, II, 772
    and Depression, I, 245; II, 765, 768–72, 776, 779
    and European relief in World War I and World War II, II, 766, 767, 772, 775, 782
    Facts in Summary, II, 784–85
    and federal dole, II, 770–71, 775, 779
    and foreign affairs, II, 770, 779
    and 1928 election, II, 765, 768, 777
    and 1932 election, II, 771, 772
    postpresidential offices, II, 772, 782
    prepresidential offices, II, 691, 749, 767, 775
    as President, II, 765–66, 768–72 passim, 775–79 passim
    as Secretary of Commerce, II, 767–68, 775
    and Soviet Union, II, 770
    and veto, II, 770, 772, 780
Hoover, Herbert Clark, Jr., II, 766
Hoover, J. Edgar, II, 928
Hoover, Lou Henry, II, 766, 768, 772, 774, 778
Hopkins, Harry L., II, 822
House, Edward M. ("Colonel"), II, 687, 697, 699, 700
House Un-American Activities Committee, II, 861
Houston, David F., II, 719
Houston, Samuel, I, 209, 234, 245, 278, 307
Howe, Louis M., II, 791, 793, 795, 800, 803
Howe, Richard, I, 18
Howe, William, I, 18, 19, 20, 37
Huerta, Victoriano, II, 706
Hughes, Charles Evans, II, 694–95, 711, 729, 730, 736, 749
Hull, Cordell, II, 803, 839
Hull, William, I, 133, 240
Humphrey, George M., II, 903, 918
Humphrey, Hubert H., II, 941, 942, 957, 977, 978, 993
Hungarian Revolt of 1956, II, 905, 921
Hutchinson, Thomas, I, 65, 67
Hyde Park, II, 788, 793, 814, 830

I

Ickes, Harold L., II, 803, 822
Illinois, I, 41, 384, 401
Immigration, I, 497–98; II, 582, 634, 703, 749, 750
Immigration Act of 1924, II, 749
Impeachment, I, 436
See also Andrew Johnson
Income tax, federal, II, 665–66, 690, 706, 801
Independence Day, I, 58, 72, 104, 160, 318
Independent Treasury, I, 245, 246, 250
Independent Treasury Act, I, 245, 250–51, 298
Indian Removal Act, I, 224
Indian Territory, I, 131
Indiana, I, 260; II, 539, 577, 580, 581, 587
Indians and Indian affairs, I, 14, 15, 27, 30, 40, 41, 96, 115, 127–28, 131, 135, 146, 164, 181, 224–25, 241, 366
See also individual chiefs and tribes
Indochina. *See* Vietnam
Industrial Workers of the World, II, 690
Inter-American Conferences, II, 564, 725, 802
Internal improvements, I, 158, 160, 169, 181, 182, 189, 190, 208
International Court, II, 667
Interstate Commerce Act of 1887, I, 481; II, 557, 588
Interstate Commerce Commission, II, 557, 629, 633, 665, 801
Intolerable Acts, I, 67
Irving, Washington, I, 241, 307
Isolationism, II, 597, 736, 757, 802, 806–8 *passim*, 830, 832, 878, 938
Israel, II, 906, 980
Italy, II, 584, 736, 806, 807, 808, 809, 830, 837, 840, 858, 863

J

Jackson, Andrew, I, 182, 197–237 *passim*, 239, 241, 242, 245, 259, 278, 292, 320, 322, 365, 374
appraisal of, I, 210
birth and early life, I, 199
and the common man, I, 197–99 *passim*, 210, 298
death of, I, 210, 234, 235
and Eaton affair, I, 205, 220–21, 242
and 1824 election, I, 180, 188, 189, 204, 218
and 1828 election, I, 175, 198, 204, 218, 219, 230, 241, 248
and 1832 election, I, 208, 228, 242
Facts in Summary, I, 236–37
inauguration of, I, 197–98
and Indians, I, 181, 200, 201–3 *passim*, 210, 224–25

influence on Presidency, I, 199, 206, 210
"Kitchen Cabinet" of, I, 206, 228, 230, 241
marriage of, I, 200, 212
military activities and career, I, 134, 144, 149, 159, 179, 199–202 *passim*, 206, 210, 214, 217
and National Bank, I, 206–7, 208, 227, 228–29, 231
and nullification, I, 207–8, 222
prepresidential offices, I, 199, 200, 203, 212, 217, 227
as President, I, 205–10 *passim*, 220–31 *passim*, 239, 242
Senate censure of, I, 274
and spoils system, I, 205
and Texas, I, 209, 234
Jackson, Andrew, Jr., I, 210
Jackson, Elizabeth Hutchinson, I, 199
Jackson, Rachel Donelson Robards, I, 197, 200, 201, 203, 204, 217, 218, 235, 242
Jackson, Robert, I, 199
Jackson, Thomas J. ("Stonewall"), I, 394, 395, 474
Jacksonian democracy, I, 189, 205, 239
Jacksonians, I, 180, 181, 182, 198
Jacobson, Eddie, II, 862, 866, 867
James, Thomas L., II, 524, 539, 540
Japan, I, 333, 350, 354; II, 634, 635, 696, 730, 736, 749, 750, 770, 802, 806, 808–9, 830, 840, 856, 863, 889
and atomic bomb, II, 855, 856, 869
Jay, John, I, 27, 48, 50, 68, 77, 130, 156, 176
Jay's Treaty, I, 25, 26, 27, 50, 70, 98, 156, 176
Jefferson, Jane Randolph, I, 92, 94
Jefferson, Maria ("Polly"), I, 93
Jefferson, Martha ("Patsy"), I, 93, 97
Jefferson, Martha Wayles, I, 93, 94, 96
Jefferson, Thomas, I, 17, 26, 27, 28, 69–70, 72, 80, 81, 86, 91–125 *passim*, 127, 128, 130, 137–41 *passim*, 153, 154–60 *passim*, 176, 177, 188, 205, 207, 210, 239, 241, 242, 260; II, 633
birth and early life, I, 92–93, 97
criticism of, I, 91, 99, 103
death of, I, 104
and Declaration of Independence, I, 94–95, 107, 108–9
and 1800 election, I, 99–100
and 1804 election, I, 102
and embargo, I, 102–3, 116
Facts in Summary, I, 124–25
in France, I, 99, 110, 111
as governor of Virginia, I, 96
inventions of, I, 120, 121, 123
and Lewis and Clark expedition, I, 102, 112
and Louisiana Purchase, I, 101–2, 112
marriage of, I, 93
and Napoleonic Wars, I, 116, 117

philosophy of, I, 97–98, 104
prepresidential politics and offices, I, 24, 51, 69, 81, 82, 91–98 *passim*, 205
as President, I, 100–103 *passim*, 112–19 *passim*, 205
range of interests and skills, I, 91–92, 97, 120, 121
and Republican party, I, 99, 163
and Revolution, I, 93–97, 107
as Secretary of State, I, 24, 26, 98
and states' rights, I, 99, 104
and Supreme Court, I, 104
and University of Virginia, I, 103–4, 120, 121, 134
as Vice President, I, 69–70, 98
and war with Tripoli, I, 101
writings by, I, 94, 98, 103, 107, 120
See also Monticello
Jenner, William, II, 915
Job Corps, II, 994
Johnson, Andrew, I, 429–53 *passim*; II, 536
abuse by press, I, 434, 442, 444
accession of, I, 432, 442
and Army Appropriations Act, I, 435
birth and early life, I, 430, 441
and Cabinet, I, 433, 438, 446, 506
and Congress, I, 429–38 *passim*, 442, 444
and the Constitution, I, 429, 434, 437, 438
death of, I, 438
and 1860 election, I, 431
and 1864 election, I, 396, 432, 442
and 1866 congressional elections, I, 434–35
Facts in Summary, I, 452–53
impeachment of, I, 375, 429, 435, 436–37, 446–49 *passim*, 461, 506
and Lee's surrender, I, 460
and Lincoln assassination plot, I, 423, 442
marriage of, I, 430, 441
and Mexico, I, 438, 445
prepresidential politics and offices, I, 430–32, 438–42 *passim*, 451
as President, I, 429, 432–38 *passim*, 442–51 *passim*
and press interviews, I, 448–49
and purchase of Alaska, I, 438, 444, 447
and Reconstruction, I, 429, 432–33, 442
and secession, I, 431–32
and slavery, I, 431, 434
and the Union, I, 430, 431, 432
and veto, I, 280, 430, 434, 435, 438, 444
as Vice President, I, 432, 442
vindication of, I, 438, 451
Johnson, Claudia Alta Taylor ("Lady Bird"), II, 970, 974, 984, 985, 986, 988, 996
Johnson, Eliza McCardle, I, 430, 431, 432, 440, 441, 450, 451
Johnson, Hiram, II, 699, 718, 748

and Civil War, I, 392, 393, 394,
407–20 *passim*, 432, 455, 458,
459
and 1860 election, I, 350, 367,
377, 387, 389, 401, 404, 405
and 1864 election, I, 395–99 *passim*, 411, 418, 442
and Emancipation Proclamation, I, 393, 394, 416, 417
Facts in Summary, I, 426–27
funeral of, I, 334, 398, 425
Gettysburg Address, I, 394–95
inaugurations, I, 390–91, 405,
432, 439
marriage of, I, 384
and Mexican War, I, 385
prepresidential politics and offices, I, 316, 383–89 *passim*,
401
as President, I, 391–98 *passim*,
405–25 *passim*
and Reconstruction, I, 397–98
and slavery, I, 330, 383–96 *passim*, 402, 405, 416, 417
speeches by, I, 386–87, 388, 390–
91, 397, 420
and the Union, I, 386, 391–96
passim, 415, 420, 442
Lincoln, Edward Baker, I, 385,
401
Lincoln, Mary Todd, I, 384, 389,
392–93, 398, 400, 401, 419
Lincoln, Nancy Hanks, I, 382
Lincoln, Robert Todd, I, 384–85,
398, 401, 419; II, 547
Lincoln, Sarah Bush Johnston, I,
382
Lincoln, Thomas, I, 382, 383
Lincoln, Thomas ("Tad"), I, 385,
391, 401, 419
Lincoln, William Wallace, I, 385,
392, 401
Lincoln-Douglas debates, I, 387,
402
Lindbergh, Charles A., II, 636, 759
Livingston, Edward, I, 203, 230
Livingston, Robert R., I, 23, 94,
101, 109, 114, 157, 162
Lloyd George, David, II, 698, 699,
716, 717
Locke, John, I, 98, 128
Lockwood, Belva Ann, II, 564
Lodge, Henry Cabot, II, 556, 636,
641, 643, 668, 698, 699, 700, 739,
743, 767, 939
Lodge, Henry Cabot II, II, 900,
918, 939, 951
London International Monetary
and Economic Conference, II,
801–2
Long, Huey, II, 781
Long, John, II, 625, 626, 643
Long Island, Battle of, I, 18
Longstreet, James, I, 474
Louis Napoleon, I, 333, 438, 445
Louis XVI, I, 110, 111, 156
Louis Philippe, I, 206
Louisiana, I, 41, 101, 162, 367,
368, 397–98, 417, 492–93, 494,
495, 503
Louisiana Purchase, I, 101–2, 112,
113, 131, 159, 177
Lusitania, II, 656, 694, 695, 708
Lyon, Matthew, I, 82, 83

M

McAdoo, William G., II, 692, 705,
706, 747, 818
MacArthur, Douglas, II, 713, 766,
778, 836, 840, 851, 863–64, 886,
887, 889, 899, 908, 909
McCarran Internal Security Act,
II, 862–63
McCarthy, Eugene, II, 981
McCarthy, Joseph, II, 861–62,
863, 864, 883, 885, 900, 902–3,
915, 919, 940
McClellan, George B., I, 334, 392,
394, 395, 396, 418, 458, 474
McDonald, John, I, 465
Macdonough, Thomas, I, 147
McGovern, George, II, 979–80
McHenry, James, I, 28
McKay, Douglas, II, 918
McKinley, Ida Saxton, II, 598,
599, 604
McKinley, William, II, 597–621
passim, 623, 625
assassination of, II, 604, 618–19,
645
birth and early life, II, 597–98
and Boxer Rebellion, II, 604, 612
in Civil War, II, 598
and 1896 election, II, 599, 600,
606, 607
and expansion, II, 603, 612
Facts in Summary, II, 620–21
and gold standard, II, 600, 604,
606
and labor disputes, II, 598–99
marriage of, II, 598
and 1900 election, II, 604, 612,
618, 627, 644
and Philippine annexation, II,
603–4, 613
prepresidential politics and offices, II, 598, 599–600
as President, II, 601–4 *passim*,
611–19 *passim*
and Spanish-American War, II,
601–3, 610, 612
and tariff, II, 583, 598–99, 601,
606
McKinley Tariff Act, II, 558, 585,
599, 601
Maclay, William, I, 46, 68, 69
McMahon, Patrick, II, 936
McNairy, John, I, 199
McNamara, Robert S., II, 946,
955
McNary, Charles, II, 833
McNary-Haugen bill, II, 749
Macon's Bill No. 2, I, 131, 132
McReynolds, James C., II, 706
Madison, Dolley, I, 130, 133, 134,
139, 144, 158, 252, 309
Madison, James (1723–1801), I,
127, 128, 129
Madison, James, I, 26, 48, 80, 97,
99, 103, 127–51 *passim*, 154, 155,
188, 190
birth and early life, I, 127–28
on checks and balances, I, 129,
137
death of, I, 134
and Democratic-Republican

party, I, 127, 130
domestic policies, I, 134, 140
and 1808 election, I, 130, 137,
141
and 1812 election, I, 130, 141
and European wars, I, 130–31
Facts in Summary, I, 150–51
as Father of the Constitution,
I, 127, 129–30, 136–37
and *The Federalist*, I, 130
marriage of, I, 130
postpresidential offices, I, 134
prepresidential politics and offices, I, 119, 127, 129, 130,
136–37, 163
as President, I, 130–34 *passim*,
138–52 *passim*
as Secretary of State, I, 130
and slavery, I, 130
and War of 1812, I, 132, 133,
134, 142, 144
Mahan, Alfred T., II, 625
Maine, I, 51, 159, 245, 277, 284,
353
Maine, II, 602, 610, 611
Manchuria, II, 770, 802, 810, 830,
838
Manila Bay, Battle of, II, 603, 613
Mann-Elkins Act, II, 665
Mao Tse-tung, II, 883
Marcy, William L., I, 205, 346,
349, 354–55, 357, 476, 503
Marshall, George C., II, 713, 810,
838, 858, 859, 863, 885, 896, 897,
900, 910
Marshall, John, I, 72, 100, 103,
119, 154, 197, 231, 374
Marshall, Thomas R., II, 693
Marshall, Thurgood, II, 980, 999
Marshall Plan, II, 859, 863, 881
Martin, Joseph, II, 864
Mason, George, I, 129
Massachusetts, I, 17, 64, 66, 67,
140, 165
Massachusetts General Court, I,
65–66, 74
Mateos, Adolfo Lopez, II, 944
Maximilian, Archduke, I, 438, 445
Maysville Road bill, I, 206, 242
Mazzei, Philip, I, 99
Meade, George, I, 394, 433, 474
Medical insurance plan, II, 856
Medicare, II, 864, 978, 995
Mellon, Andrew W., II, 729, 748
Mencken, H. L., II, 734, 743, 750,
824
Meredith, James, II, 945
Merrimac, I, 393
Meuse-Argonne Offensive, II, 715
Mexican War, I, 182, 286, 296,
302–4 *passim*, 306, 314, 353
Mexico, I, 209, 295, 314, 333, 366,
438, 445, 497; II, 694, 696, 706,
707, 708, 944
Miami Indians, I, 261, 265
Midway Islands, I, 438
Miller, Thomas, II, 723, 729
Minimum wage, I, 856; II, 930
Missouri, I, 158, 159, 348
See also Dred Scott decision
Missouri Compromise, I, 159–60,
169, 316, 348, 356, 363, 386, 402
Mitchell, William L., II, 714
Moley, Raymond, II, 795

1015

Molotov, Vyacheslav, II, 840, 855
Monetary system, I, 98, 227, 244, 245, 496
See also Gold, Silver, "Specie Circular"
Monitor, I, 393
Monmouth, Battle of, I, 20, 37, 38
Monopolies, II, 583, 674, 688
See also Trusts
Monroe, Elizabeth Kortright, I, 158, 160, 166, 167, 205, 309
Monroe, James, I, 101, 103, 114, 149, 153–73 *passim*, 179, 188, 190, 278, 353
  birth and early life, I, 154–55
  death of, I, 160
  as diplomat, I, 156, 157, 162–63
  and domestic affairs, I, 158–60 *passim*
  and 1816 election, I, 158, 165
  and 1820 election, I, 159
  Era of Good Feelings, I, 149, 153, 159, 164, 165
  Facts in Summary, I, 172–73
  foreign policy, I, 158, 160, 170
  and Latin-American policy, I, 160
  and Missouri Compromise, I, 158, 159–60, 169
  popularity of, I, 153, 165
  prepresidential politics and offices, I, 155–57, 160, 163, 165
  as President, I, 153–54, 158–60 *passim*, 164–70 *passim*
  in Revolution, I, 154–55
  as Secretary of War, I, 157–58
  and slavery, I, 158, 159
Monroe Doctrine, I, 159, 160, 161, 170, 171, 188, 333, 438, 497; II, 561, 631
Monroe-Pinckney Treaty, I, 157
Monterrey, Battle of, I, 297, 314, 315, 319
Montesquieu, Baron de La Brède et de, I, 128
Montgomery, Bernard, II, 836, 840, 910
Monticello, I, 91, 93, 95, 96, 97, 102, 103, 122, 123
Montpelier, Va., I, 127, 134, 139
Morgan, Daniel, I, 40
Morgan, John Pierpont, I, 461, 466; II, 561, 562, 588, 628, 629, 632
Morgenthau, Henry, Jr., II, 794, 802, 803
Mormons, I, 306, 366
Morris, Gouverneur, I, 136, 156
Morse, Samuel F. B., I, 230, 280, 331
Morse, Wayne, II, 981
Morton, Levi P., II, 538, 539, 581, 587
Morton, Oliver P., I, 451, 579, 580
Morton, Thruston, II, 981
Mosquito Coast, I, 350
Mount Vernon, I, 13, 15, 16, 22, 33, 44, 45, 46, 55, 57, 235
Mugwumps. *See* Republican party
Muller v. Oregon, II, 828
Murphy, Thomas, I, 462; II, 537
Mussolini, Benito, I, 171; II, 806–7, 808, 836, 840
Mutual Security Act, II, 973

N

Nagasaki, II, 856, 870
Napoleon, I, 101, 112, 114, 117, 130, 132, 133, 178, 179, 185
Napoleonic Wars, I, 116, 117, 131, 242
Nashville, Battle of, I, 397, 410, 432
Nasser, Gamal Abdel, II, 906, 980
National Aeronautics and Space Administration, II, 905, 924, 973
National Constitution Union party, I, 389
National debt, I, 114, 463; II, 748, 783
National Defense Education Act of 1958, II, 903
National Equal Rights party, II, 564
National health plan, II, 860
National Housing Act, II, 801
National Industrial Recovery Act, II, 800, 805, 806, 826
National Labor Relations Board, II, 801
National Progressive Republican League, II, 749
National Recovery Administration, II, 800
National Republican party, I, 169, 181
National Union party, I, 432, 434–35, 442
National Youth Administration, II, 970–71
Naturalization Act, I, 70, 71
Nebraska, I, 348, 402
Negroes, I, 479, 493; II, 536, 537, 633, 703
  See also Civil Rights, Slavery, Desegregation
Nelson, Thomas, Jr., I, 96
Neuberger, Richard, II, 942, 957
Neutrality Act of 1937, II, 807, 830
New Deal, II, 783, 794–806 *passim*, 820, 822, 824, 826, 828, 829, 860
New England, I, 67, 132, 153, 180, 208, 348
New Freedmen's Bureau bill, I, 434
New Freedom, II, 688–91 *passim*
New Hampshire, I, 22, 186
New Jersey, I, 18, 19, 20, 34, 37; II, 683, 685–87 *passim*
New Mexico, I, 296, 297, 298, 317, 318, 332
New Orleans, I, 27, 101, 113, 202, 203, 214, 411
New Orleans, Battle of, I, 134, 149, 179, 202, 214–15, 230
New York City, I, 17, 18, 19, 22, 34, 46, 51, 79, 141, 154–55, 208, 244, 425, 507; II, 555–56, 623, 625, 640, 641
New York Custom House, I, 462, 495; II, 537, 625
New York State, I, 20, 130, 157, 165, 240, 294, 301, 316, 322, 476;
II, 537, 539, 548, 794, 795
  and political machines, II, 536–42 *passim*, 556, 577, 644
New York State Temporary Emergency Relief Administration, II, 795
New York Stock Exchange, II, 748, 768, 801
  and 1929 crash, II, 768, 769, 779, 820
Nicaragua, I, 333, 350, 366
Nicola, Lewis, I, 21
Nicolay, John, II, 615
Nimitz, Chester, II, 840
Nixon, Richard M., II, 900, 906, 914, 915, 918, 927, 942, 943, 952, 982
Nonimportation Act, I, 116
Nonintercourse Act, I, 131, 132
Norris, George W., II, 695–96, 770, 780
Norris-La Guardia Act, II, 781
Norstad, Lauris, II, 982
North, the, I, 158, 316, 330, 332, 339, 363, 365, 433, 463
  See also Civil War, Slavery
North Atlantic Treaty Organization, II, 863, 882, 899, 913, 927, 979, 1002
Northern Securities Company, II, 628–29, 633
Northwest Ordinance, I, 388
Northwest Territory, I, 260–61
Nuclear test ban, II, 944, 961
Nullification, I, 100–101, 207, 222
  See also South Carolina
Nuremberg Trials, II, 874
Nye, Gerald, II, 807

O

Ochs, Adolph S., II, 609
Octagon House, I, 133
O'Daniel, W. Lee, II, 971
Office of Price Administration, II, 857
Ogle, Charles, I, 246
Olney, Richard, II, 562, 572
Omnibus bill of 1889, II, 583
Onís, Luis de, I, 159, 179
Open Door policy, II, 604, 612, 634, 666
Order of the Star-Spangled Banner, I, 334, 340
Ordinance of 1787, I, 96
Oregon State and Territory, I, 158, 160, 227, 277, 291, 294, 295–96, 302, 303, 316, 368, 493, 494, 503
Organization on Unemployment Relief, II, 771
Ostend Manifesto, I, 349, 355
Oswald, Lee Harvey, II, 946, 963, 988
Otis, James, I, 64, 66

P

Paderewski, Ignace, II, 775
Paine, Lewis, I, 423
Paine, Thomas, I, 69, 156

Reconstruction, I, 397–98, 429, 433, 446, 464, 478–79; II, 608
Reconstruction Act of 1867, I, 434, 435
Reconstruction Finance Corporation, II, 757, 771, 779
Reed, James, II, 718
Reed, Thomas B., II, 583, 588
Reform movement, I, 503, 506; II, 555
See also individual Presidents and reformers
Reid, John, I, 492
Republican party, I, 99, 334, 340, 349, 362, 364, 367, 370, 371, 389, 391, 396, 417, 432, 433, 480, 492, 500; II, 522–23, 528, 538–42 passim, 556, 568, 577, 581, 587, 588, 600, 635, 636, 647, 652, 655, 656, 666, 687, 697, 698, 699, 700, 728, 731, 733, 739, 746–47, 748, 772, 776, 811, 860, 915, 943, 964, 973, 978, 982, 992
formation of, I, 386
Half-Breeds, II, 522–23, 524, 528, 539
and Johnson impeachment, I, 429–38 passim
Mugwumps, II, 556
Stalwarts, II, 522–39 passim, 545
See also National Union party, Radical Republicans
Resaca de la Palma, Battle of, I, 314, 319
Resumption Act, I, 465
Revere, Paul, I, 64
Revolutionary War, I, 18–21, 33–43 passim, 51, 56
See also individual battles and generals, George Washington
Rhode Island, I, 280
Richmond, I, 97, 278, 392, 396
Rickenbacker, Edward V., II, 715
Robards, Lewis, I, 200, 217
Robertson, William H., II, 524, 539–40, 542
Rochambeau, Comte de, I, 20, 43
Rockefeller, John D., I, 498; II, 632
Rockefeller, Nelson, II, 982
Rommel, Erwin, II, 836, 895
Roosevelt, Alice Hathaway Lee, II, 624, 625, 639
Roosevelt, Alice Lee, II, 625, 631, 649, 670, 750
Roosevelt, Archibald Bulloch, II, 631, 656
Roosevelt, Cornelius Van Schaak, II, 623
Roosevelt, Edith Kermit Carow, II, 625, 631, 640, 641, 648, 657
Roosevelt, Eleanor, II, 789–90, 792, 793, 815, 816, 826, 844–45, 854, 986
Roosevelt, Elliott, II, 789, 792, 816
Roosevelt, Franklin Delano, I, 72; II, 608, 759, 767, 777, 779, 787–849 passim, 853, 854, 860, 868, 869, 937, 938, 942, 943, 959, 970, 971, 984, 985
as assistant secretary of the Navy, II, 791–92, 816, 817

and Atlantic Charter, II, 808
attempted assassination of, II, 796, 797, 819
birth and early life, II, 787–89, 790, 814, 815
and Casablanca Conference, II, 810, 840
death of, II, 812, 842, 843, 854, 869
and Depression, II, 794, 795–96, 797, 820
Facts in Summary, II, 846–49
and fireside chats, II, 803, 808, 824, 830
first Cabinet, II, 803
first hundred days, II, 798–800, 820
and Good Neighbor Policy, I, 171; II, 801
as governor of New York, II, 794–96
and Hyde Park, II, 792, 793, 812, 815, 826, 842
and industry, II, 796, 797, 800, 801, 810
and infantile paralysis, II, 792–93, 794, 816, 817, 843, 844
and international diplomacy, II, 801–2, 806–12 passim
and labor, II, 801, 806
and lend-lease, II, 807, 808, 830
marriage of, II, 789, 815
and New Deal, II, 794–806 passim, 826
and 1932 election, II, 772, 794–99 passim, 818, 819
and 1934 congressional elections, II, 824
and 1936 election, II, 804–5, 824, 826
and 1938 congressional elections, II, 806, 826
and 1940 election, II, 799, 807–8, 832, 833, 888
and 1944 election, II, 811, 812, 854, 868
and Pearl Harbor, II, 809
and preparations for World War II, II, 806–8
and prepresidential elections, II, 729, 791–94 passim, 816
prepresidential politics and offices, II, 790–91, 793, 794–95, 816, 817
as President, II, 787, 802, 804
first term, II, 797–805 passim, 820–26 passim
second term, II, 805–8 passim, 824–32 passim
third term, II, 808–12 passim, 835–40 passim
fourth term, II, 810–12 passim, 840–43 passim
and Social Security, II, 801, 806
speeches and Inaugural Addresses, II, 793, 797, 801, 805, 807, 808, 812, 820, 824
and Supreme Court, II, 805–6, 826
and Teheran Conference, II, 810, 837
and third-term controversy, II, 799, 807, 832
and United Nations, II, 808,

809, 811, 812
as vice presidential nominee, II, 791–92, 816
and World War II, II, 808–12 passim, 833
and Yalta Conference, II, 810–12 passim, 840, 843
Roosevelt, Franklin Delano, Jr., II, 789, 816, 826
Roosevelt, James (1828–1900), II, 788, 789
Roosevelt, James (1907–   ), II, 788, 789, 792, 809, 812, 816, 826
Roosevelt, Kermit, II, 631, 654, 656
Roosevelt, Martha Bulloch, II, 623, 625
Roosevelt, Quentin, II, 631, 636, 649, 656
Roosevelt, Sara Delano, II, 788–89, 790, 793, 815, 826, 844
Roosevelt, Theodore (1831–1878), 623, 624
Roosevelt, Theodore, II, 591, 623–59 passim, 664, 667, 668, 677, 686, 789
accession to Presidency, II, 627, 644, 645, 647
attempted assassination of, II, 636, 655
and Battle Fleet world cruise, II, 635, 653
"big stick" policy, II, 626, 630, 653
birth and early life, II, 623–25 passim
and coal strike, II, 629, 647
and conservation, II, 628–30 passim, 652, 666
death of, II, 636, 656, 657
Facts in Summary, II, 658–59
foreign trips of, II, 636, 654, 655
Inaugural Address, II, 632–33
interests and activities, II, 624–25, 632, 638, 644, 649, 656
and Latin-American affairs, II, 630, 634
marriages of, II, 624, 625, 640, 641
and naval supremacy, II, 625–26, 630
and 1900 election, II, 627, 644
and 1904 election, II, 632, 634, 635, 652
and 1912 election, II, 635, 636, 655, 656, 668, 679, 688, 703
and 1916 election, II, 711
and Panama Canal, II, 630–31, 632, 650, 653
popularity of, II, 627, 629, 637, 649
prepresidential politics and offices, II, 555, 588, 625–26, 627, 639–47 passim
as President, II, 627–36 passim, 647–49, 652–53
and reform, II, 625–35 passim, 641, 647, 652, 703
and Rough Riders, II, 611, 626, 637, 642, 643
and Russo-Japanese agreement, II, 634
at Sagamore Hill, II, 636, 641, 655, 657

677, 690, 805–6, 826, 828, 829, 862, 863, 903, 929, 955, 980, 999
See also Facts in Summary for each President, individual cases, Thomas Jefferson
Surratt, Mary, I, 423
Symington, Stuart, II, 941, 972

T

Taft, Alphonso, II, 661–62, 917
Taft, Helen, II, 672
Taft, Helen Herron, II, 662, 663, 664, 668, 672, 673
Taft, Louise Torrey, II, 661, 662, 664
Taft, Robert A., II, 900, 915, 917
Taft, William Howard, II, 553, 617, 632, 634, 636, 661–81 *passim*, 917
  birth and early life, II, 662, 663
  as Chief Justice, II, 662, 668, 679, 729
  and conservation, II, 666
  death of, II, 668
  and domestic legislation, II, 666
  Facts in Summary, II, 680–81
  and foreign affairs, II, 666–68, 674
  as governor of Philippines, II, 663
  marriage of, II, 662
  and 1908 election, II, 636, 664, 669, 672, 685
  and 1912 election, II, 635, 636, 668, 679, 688, 703, 726, 731
  and 1916 election, II, 661
  prepresidential politics and offices, II, 604, 662–64, 670, 671, 672
  as President, II, 661, 664–68, 672–75, 678–79
  and reform, II, 665–66
  as Secretary of War, II, 663–64, 670
  and tariff, II, 665, 666, 674
  and Theodore Roosevelt, II, 661, 663–65, 668, 670–71, 678–79
  and trusts, II, 633, 665
Taft-Hartley Act, II, 858, 917, 939, 972
Talleyrand, I, 70, 140, 162, 243
Tammany Hall, I, 240, 278, 476; II, 553, 555, 556, 558, 565, 577, 688, 795
Taney, Roger B., I, 208, 231, 374, 386, 388, 391
Tanner, James, II, 571, 581–82, 588
Tariff, I, 26, 169, 181–82, 190, 207, 208, 218, 222, 298, 389; II, 541, 558, 568, 599, 665, 666, 667, 674, 676, 689–91 *passim*, 748, 750, 796, 802
  See also Nullification, South Carolina, Trade, and individual tariffs
Taxes and taxation, I, 26, 48, 52, 65, 67, 72, 74, 75, 94, 101, 102;

II, 558, 748, 769, 801
  See also Income tax, Stamp Act, Whisky Rebellion
Taylor, Margaret Mackall Smith, I, 314, 322
Taylor, Richard, I, 313, 314
Taylor, Sarah Dabney Strother, I, 313, 314
Taylor, Zachary, I, 313–27 *passim*
  appraisal of, I, 313, 318, 324
  as Army officer, I, 314, 319, 320–21
  birth and early life, I, 313–14
  and Cabinet scandal, I, 318
  and Clayton-Bulwer Treaty, I, 318
  and Compromise of 1850, I, 313, 318, 325, 329, 332, 339
  death of, I, 318, 325
  and domestic affairs, I, 313–18 *passim*, 324–25, 329, 332
  and 1848 election, I, 246, 316, 322, 331, 385
  Facts in Summary, I, 326–27
  and Mexican War, I, 296, 297, 314, 315–16, 320–23 *passim*, 415
  and national politics, I, 314–16, 322, 323
  as President, I, 316–18, 324–25
Teapot Dome scandal, II, 723–24, 730, 739
Tecumseh, Chief, I, 131, 241, 260–61, 265
Tennessee, I, 180, 200, 212, 213, 392, 432
Tennessee Valley Authority, II, 770, 780, 799, 813
Tenskwatawa, I, 260, 261
Tenure of Office Act, I, 435, 436, 446, 448
Texas, I, 209, 277–78, 294, 295, 296, 307, 317, 318, 332, 368, 433; II, 942, 946, 962, 963, 964, 970–71, 972, 974, 984, 989, 994
Texas and Pacific Railroad bill, I, 494
Thames, Battle of the, I, 133, 241, 261–62, 265
Thirteenth Amendment, I, 396, 416, 420
Thomas, George H., I, 410
Thomas, Lorenzo, I, 436
Thomas, Norman M., II, 726, 818
Thurmond, J. Strom, II, 860, 889
Tilden, Samuel J., I, 246, 492–94, 502–3; II, 559
Tillman, Benjamin R., II, 562
Timberlake, John B., I, 205
Tippecanoe, Battle of, I, 131–32, 261, 265
Tompkins, Daniel, I, 157
Townshend Acts, I, 67
Tracy, Benjamin F., II, 582
Trade, I, 27, 94, 117, 130, 132, 171, 185, 207, 241, 244, 298, 333, 350, 354
  See also Open Door policy, Tariff
Treaty of Fort Wayne, I, 261
Treaty of Ghent, I, 134, 146, 147, 149, 178, 185, 186–87, 234
Treaty of Guadalupe Hidalgo, I, 297–98, 302, 317

Treaty of Morfontaine, I, 70, 84, 85
Treaty of Paris, I, 41, 50, 68, 77, 114
Treaty of Paris (1898), II, 603–4
Treaty of San Ildefonso, I, 101
Treaty of Versailles, II, 697–700 *passim*
Treaty of Washington, I, 481
Trent Incident, I, 375
Trenton, Battle of, I, 19, 34, 51, 155
Tripoli, I, 101, 102, 116, 146
Trist, Nicholas P., I, 297
Truman, Elizabeth Wallace ("Bess"), II, 852, 858, 867, 869, 881
Truman, Harry S., II, 713, 783, 790, 812, 851–93 *passim*, 899, 905, 913, 915, 941, 959, 972, 977
  accession of, II, 852, 869, 870
  appraisal of II, 852, 864
  and atomic bomb, II, 855, 856
  attempted assassination of, II, 880
  birth and early life, II, 852, 853, 866
  and Cabinet, II, 854
  and civil rights, II, 860, 889
  and Congress, II, 854, 856–60 *passim*, 883
  and containment, II, 858, 863, 885, 886
  Facts in Summary, II, 892–93
  haberdashery of, II, 852–53, 867
  and Japan, II, 855
  and Korean War, II, 863, 864
  and labor, II, 857–58
  library and memoirs of, II, 864, 890
  and MacArthur firing, II, 851, 864, 886
  marriage of, II, 852, 867
  and 1944 election, II, 823, 854, 868, 869
  and 1946 congressional elections, II, 858
  and 1948 election, II, 860, 861, 865, 894
  prepresidential politics and offices, II, 853, 854, 867, 868, 869
  as President, II, 854–64 *passim*, 870–87 *passim*, 905–6
  and price control, II, 856–57
  as senator, II, 853–54, 869
  as Vice President, II, 854, 868–69
  and World War I, II, 852, 866
  and World War II, II, 851, 854, 855
Truman, Margaret, II, 852, 858, 864, 880
Truman Doctrine, II, 858–59
Trumbull, Lyman, I, 437, 451
Trusts, II, 555, 583, 597, 628
Truth-in-Securities Act, II, 799
Truxton, Thomas, I, 83
Tugwell, Rexford G., II, 795, 803
Tumulty, Joseph, II, 700, 719
Tunis, I, 146
Turkey, I, 241; II, 858, 859
Tweed, William M., I, 461
Tweed Ring, I, 503

ACKNOWLEDGMENTS

The Bernard De Voto quotation on page 294 reprinted by permission of Houghton Mifflin Company, from *The Year of Decision 1846*, Copyright 1942, 1943 by Bernard De Voto.

The H. L. Mencken quotation on page 743 reprinted by permission of The Johns Hopkins Press, from *H. L. Mencken on Politics*, © Copyright 1956 by The Johns Hopkins Press.

The Truman quotation on page 877 reprinted by permission of Trident Press/ A Division of Simon & Schuster, Inc., from *Presidential Wit*, © Copyright 1966 by Bill Adler.

The Eric Sevareid quotation on pages 890–91 reprinted by permission of The Hall Syndicate, Inc. All Rights Reserved.

The Editors are grateful to these individuals and organizations for their invaluable assistance in the picture research for this project:

Adams National Historic Site: Wilhelmina Harris
Charles Baptie
Bowdoin College: Joseph D. Kamin
Buffalo & Erie County Historical Society: Paul F. Redding
Chicago Historical Society: Mary Frances Rhymer
Cincinnati Historical Society: Lee Jordan; Eleanor Wirmel
Colonial Williamsburg: Hugh DeSamper; Marguerite Gignilliat
John Coolidge
J. Doyle DeWitt
Eastman House: Beaumont Newhall
General Dwight D. Eisenhower
Grouseland: Mrs. Charles A. Hamke
The Hermitage: Stephen S. Lawrence
Harding Memorial Association: Warren C. Sawyer
Benjamin Harrison Home: Ruth Woodworth
Rutherford B. Hayes Library: Watt P. Marchman
Independence Hall: James R. Sullivan

Indiana Historical Society: Caroline Dunn
Andrew Johnson Home: Margaret Johnson Patterson Bartlett
Lyndon B. Johnson
Mrs. Joseph P. Kennedy
Stanley King
Paulus Leeser
Library of Congress: Virginia Daiker; Renata Shaw
Sidney Mayer
Metropolitan Museum of Art: Margaret Nolan
Mount Vernon: Christine Meadows
James Monroe Memorial Library: Laurence Gouverneur Hoes
National Gallery of Art: Ruth Dundas
National Archives: Josephine Cobb
National Broadcasting Company: Dan Jones
National Portrait Gallery: Robert G. Stewart
New-York Historical Society: Carolyn Scoon; Wilson G. Duprey
New York Public Library: Romana Javitz
Ohio Historical Society: Elizabeth R. Martin
James K. Polk Home: Sibyl A. Whelchel
Presidential Libraries: Herman Kahn
Franklin D. Roosevelt Library: Elizabeth B. Drewry; Joseph Marshall; William Stickle
Theodore Roosevelt Association: Helen MacLachlan
Richard Rudisill
Sagamore Hill National Historic Site: Mrs. Harold Kraft
Smithsonian Institution: Meredith Johnson
Tennessee State Library & Archives: Harriet C. Owsley
Time-Life, Inc.: Valerie Vondermuhl
Harry S. Truman Library: Philip C. Brooks; Cecil Smith
United States Defense Department: Colonel Robert A. Webb
United States Military Academy: J. Thomas Russell; Kenneth W. Rapp
United States Supreme Court: T. Perry Lippitt
Virginia State Library: Katherine M. Smith
Wheatland: Claire Parker
The White House: James R. Ketchum
Woodrow Wilson Home: Ruth L. Dillon